PROUD PATRIOT

A New York State Study

Philip Schuyler, 1733–1804. Miniature by John Trumbull, 1792.
© Yale University Art Gallery. Reprinted by permission.

Proud Patriot

PHILIP SCHUYLER
and the War of Independence,
1775–1783

DON R. GERLACH

Syracuse University Press

First Edition
92 91 90 89 88 87   5 4 3 2 1

Publication of *Proud Patriot* was assisted by funds received from the Buchtel College of Arts and Sciences of the University of Akron. Additional support was provided by a grant from the John Ben Snow Foundation.

Winner of the 1986 John Ben Snow Manuscript Prize.

The paper used in this publication meets the minimum requirements of American National Standard for Information Sciences—Permanence of Paper for Printed Library Materials, ANSI Z39.48—1984. ∞™

Library of Congress Cataloging-in-Publication Data

Gerlach, Don R., 1932–
    Proud Patriot.

    (A New York State study)
    Bibliography: p.
    Includes index.
    1. Schuyler, Philip John, 1733-1804. 2. Generals—
United States—Biography. 3. United States.
Army—Biography. 4. United States—History—Revolution,
1775–1783—Campaigns. 5. New York (State)—History—
Revolution, 1775–1783—Campaigns. I. Title. II. Series.
E207.S3G423 1987   973.3'3'0924   86-23167
ISBN 0-8156-2373-9 (alk. paper)

For the Memory of My Father and Mother
Ralph R. Gerlach, 1904–1967
Evelyn Bishoff Gerlach, 1906–1936

Contents

Illustrations

Acknowledgments

$\mathcal{I}$n addition to the acknowledgments tendered in my first book, *Philip Schuyler and the American Revolution in New York, 1733–1777,* I am compelled to mention the considerable assistance afforded in the preparation of this one by several other individuals and institutions. The personal courtesies and professional services of Mrs. Mildred Ledden of the New York State Library and Peter Christoph of the library's Manuscripts and Special Collections Division, together with those of James Corsaro and Lee Stanton, are particularly appreciated. Similarly, Kristin Gibbons and Paul Stambach, associated with the Schuyler Mansion at Albany, generously offered leads on several pieces of Schuylerana; and James E. Cyphers was especially helpful in supplying copies of material from the Rockefeller Archive Center. Eugene F. Kramer, former Senior Historian in the Office of New York State History, assisted me repeatedly in my successive summers of research in the collection made there of copies of practically all known Schuyler papers.

Grants supportive of my research and writing were graciously supplied by the University of Akron Faculty Research Committee (1963–72), the American Philosophical Society (1968–69), and the American Association for State and Local History (1963). A sabbatical leave for half a year from the University of Akron in 1980 enabled me finally to complete a draft of the work that had been otherwise so long delayed by a variety of academic duties and other scholarly efforts.

Not least of my gratitude is owed to Mrs. Garnette L. Dorsey, secretary extraordinary, who courageously and expertly translated my crabbed handwriting into clean typescript, thus saving considerable time and effort that otherwise would have been expended on making an appropriately clear copy for a typist. Her unfailing courtesy and her enthusiasm for expediting the work could not be exceeded by even the most sympathetic or helpful of colleagues. Similarly, Mrs. Inez Bachman worked heroically to complete the typing of the revised manuscript. And for their corrections, suggestions, and encouragement I am much obliged to June K. Burton, Elizabeth Coccio, Barbara Graymont, Aubrey C. Land, and James Kirby Martin.

The documentary citations will of course reveal to whom I am also indebted for a vast array of historical data and interpretation. I do, however, accept the responsibility for any errors that might have slipped into what I have written. Like the Venerable Bede, "I humbly beseech all who ... read this history ... that they will not forget frequently to ask for God's mercy upon my weaknesses." And because "I have diligently sought to put on record ... those events which I believe to be worthy of remembrance ... , let me reap among them all, the harvest of their charitable intercessions."

Introduction

We must confess the faults of our favourite, to gain credit to our praise
of his excellencies.

—Samuel Johnson

*T*he lack of fame is not an accurate measure of Philip Schuyler's
rank in the pantheon of the American revolutionary era and the
history of the early republic. The failure of historians and biographers to
make his name properly known is understandable, however, in view of
the fact that the difficulties in pursuing his story are sizable. Aside from
the usual task of grappling with the complexities of my subject's character,
I have confronted a wide variety of Schuyler's activities, ranging from
state and local politics and military and Indian affairs to business and
land management, the promotion of education and humanitarian reforms,
and the projection of inland lock and navigation improvements. The latter
subject alone, for example, is worthy of a separate monograph. Although
the sources are partly voluminous, there are also numerous gaps; the
record is fragmentary and scattered or incomplete; and the task of piecing
together letters, legislative journals, account books, and business papers
demands both talent and perseverance, which are qualities that few writers have yet demonstrated a willingness to apply.

Once citing the need for a full-length biography of his illustrious kinsman, the late Professor Robert Livingston Schuyler noted that the work
must account for a broad range of details and a multitude of varying
interests: a story of family economy, provincial politics, wartime activities
and Indian relations, government weaknesses, personal jealousies and in-
trigues, the ill will between Yankee and Yorker, military insubordination
and bungling, and self-seeking and disregard for the public welfare. Here,

too, must be included the tensions of revolutionary ardor, idealism, and pragmatic decision making.[1] I have endeavored to tell just such a story, weaving the personal details of a life into the larger tapestry of the politics of the revolutionary war. Here is the wartime career of a proud patriot who grappled with petty factionalism, personal animosities, and momentous public issues, the largest of which were how to win British recognition of colonial rights and liberties, and then how amateurs without many necessary institutional arrangements already in existence might win independence.

No one has yet fully rescued Schuyler from the neglect to which time and circumstance have consigned him. Since first delving into his life more than two decades ago, I have come more and more to realize the truth of Victor Paltsits's comment about the difficulties of portraying it. Chief of the American History Division of the New York Public Library, Paltsits once said that it would take ten years to write Schuyler's life, if one had nothing else to do.[2] The demands of the classroom and other academic activities have largely delayed my endeavors to offer this sequel to *Philip Schuyler and the American Revolution in New York, 1733–1777,* which was published in 1964. Having dealt principally with the Yorker's prewar career in the first volume, I have focused my attention upon his wartime activities as a discrete segment of his life, convinced that nowhere else can one find such a thorough account of it and that readers will find it a tale worth the telling. God willing, and a publisher permitting, there will be another volume to add to the series.

Although the long search through libraries and archives has been as time-consuming as it has been exciting, the flight of years has enabled me to benefit from the labors of many other authors and editors whose contributions are revealed in the notes and bibliography of this book. I have also, I hope, profited from a long association with my subject, and from the growth of an intimate acquaintance with his home ground and much of the terrain over which he moved.

Sir Lewis Namier once said that "a great historian is he after whom no one can write history without taking him into account; ... to be counted great, [he] must change the whole way of scholarship."[3] That judgment is applicable both to biographers and their subjects, and against it Philip Schuyler's stature may also be measured. Indeed, this man commands the attention of anyone who wishes to know eighteenth-century American history. George Dangerfield aptly likened him to "a kind of guidepost looming up upon the last great crossroad of New York provincial history." But Dangerfield also issued a challenge that has been uppermost in my mind since 1965. Like guideposts, he thought, Schuyler

PROUD PATRIOT

was "irretrievably wooden. His human side has vanished into limbo; no amount of biographical art could make anything out of . . . this formidable bore."[4]

That Schuyler is a formidable character I do not deny; but boring, no. I have tried to rescue him from the limbo to which he has been so long consigned and to portray him as the living figure with whom I have been happily acquainted. Whether I have succeeded in revealing his human side and how he reflected his own times and influenced the course of events then is for others to judge. For my failings I apologize not only to the reader but to the subject himself. The man merits the best arts of the biographer's or historian's craft. He also deserves to be rescued from the unfair strictures of harsh but careless critics. To do this one must be as painstakingly thorough in examining his activities as he was in the performance of them. While I admit my partiality, I am convinced that in order to understand a man one must be his friend. True friends of course are not hero-worshippers with blinders on, and I have tried to avoid the dangers of uncritical partisanship. Moreover, I am fully cognizant of the truth of Erik Erikson's admission that "any man projects on the men and times he studies some unlived portions and often the unrealized selves of his own life."[5] However, I have striven to tell Schuyler's story honestly and to answer the central question of all biography: How did they manage? Following Dr. Johnson's advice I have tried not to dwell on "those performances and incidents which produce vulgar greatness" but to "lead the thoughts into domestic privacies and to display the minute details of private life." And heeding John Jay's counsel as to how Schuyler might effectually exonerate himself from charges of military mismanagement and ineptitude, the reader should remember that historians have seldom given the Yorker his due. "Evidence of the Propriety of your Conduct," Jay wrote, "may be transmitted to Posterity as may contradict the many Lies which will be told them by writers under Impressions and under an Influence unfriendly to your Reputation."[6]

There will probably be those who may wish that a method and style other than the narrative had been employed, but history and biography are primarily a story. However else this tale may be told, I make no apologies for attempting to convey a sense of Schuyler's movement through the labyrinth of his age. For this I have relied upon much of his own language and that of his contemporaries, upon incidents and description that may seem tedious to some who are impatient for analysis. With John Brooke I also agree that "no fact however trivial is without value in reconstructing the life" of one's subject. On the other hand, it may be conceded that there is no surer proof of a crazy understanding than making too large a catalogue of things necessary. But like another historian explaining the style and structure of his book, I am hopeful that there are many "who believe as I do that presenting the texture of history is as important as drawing conclusions,"[7] and I only regret that economic restraints of publication have forced the elimination of rich detail.

Without attempting to evade all responsibility for explaining the causes and effects of Schuyler's activities, I am convinced that it is the deeds themselves that are more engaging. Even if all causes and effects were discoverable with accuracy, they would not be the most interesting part of human affairs; the value of history and biography is not utilitarian, nor is it scientific, but aesthetic and humanistic. The biographer, like the historian, may more precisely ascertain deeds than their causes and effects, and his task of character portrayal may be more successfully accomplished if it is modestly limited to the confines of what is possible to narrate. The reader, therefore, will be largely left with the freedom to speculate about Schuyler's motivation and the importance of his influence. I have endeavored to make only occasional generalizations and guesses, but I have not forgotten that biography is not divorced from moral exemplum. The struggles of a man are as important to delineate as their results, but the latter are not always as evident as the former. "It is the tale of the thing done, even more than its causes and effects, which trains the political judgment by widening the range of sympathy and deepening the approval and disapproval of conscience; that stimulates by example youth to aspire and age to endure; that enables us by the light of what men once have been, to see the thing we are, and dimly to descry the form of what we should be."[8]

The Pride and Pomp of War

1

Art thou officer? Or art thou base, common, and popular?
—*Henry V*, 4. 1. 37–38

Determined to press Britain to recognize American rights and liberties by employing military force, the Second Continental Congress began its struggle in June 1775 with a flourish of committee assignments. One was appointed to propose ways and means of supplying ammunition and military stores, another to establish rules for an army, and a third to estimate funds needed for the intercolonial effort. Delegates' thoughts also turned to the proper appointees to lead the armed forces. Both George Washington of Virginia and Philip Schuyler of New York were named to the committee to draft rules for the army on 14 June, and on the following day the Virginian was chosen commander in chief. On 16 June Congress further delineated an army organization to include two major generals; five brigadiers; and adjutant, commissary, and paymaster generals; but three days later, finding that these were insufficient to be spread among the various colonies, they increased the number of major generals to four and that of the brigadiers to eight. New England obtained the lion's share of the appointments; New York was given one of each in the top two ranks: Philip Schuyler as major general and Richard Montgomery as brigadier general.[1]

Geographic balance was not the only determinant in Schuyler's election. Congress sought to apportion general officers among the colonies in proportion to initial troop quotas, but it also selected leaders of "consequence" who were deemed fit to command Continental troops in the various provinces. The New York Provincial Congress recommended Schuyler and Montgomery as men of proper qualities: "Courage, Prudence, Readiness in expedients, Nice perception, sound Judgment and great attention . . . ," men of fortune who would give luster to their office rather than obtain it. Schuyler was to be a hostage "that his country, in his property, his kindred and connections, may have sure pledges that he will faithfully perform the duties of his high office, and readily lay down his power when the general weal shall require it."[2] And he did not lose his congressional status by virtue of his military commission. Elected a delegate by the New York Provincial Convention on 21 April, 1775, Schuyler retained his congressional seat until 13 May, 1777 when he, James Duane, and Philip Livingston were again elected delegates from New York. This was a remarkable fact indeed; no revolutionary ideology or rules were applied against plural office holding or the combination of military and civilian offices.

The day before Congress approved the New York nomination of Philip Schuyler, he and Connecticut congressman Silas Deane rode to the falls of the Schuylkill for breakfast. The two men discussed plans that evidently included the capture of HMS *Asia* at New York City, a plan that Deane described as "another bold stroke like the Ticonderoga affair," which was the 10 May seizure of the British outpost on Lake Champlain by forces under Ethan Allen and Benedict Arnold. The Connecticut Yankee found the Yorker to be most agreeable, although many New Englanders frequently displayed little love for their New York neighbor. However, Deane found "This gentleman is the soul of Albany county, and tho' he may have faults, he is sincere, well bred, and resolute, and I think a valuable acquaintance."[3]

The value Deane found in Schuyler's company was not exactly that which others perceived in making him a major general. The hostage-ship implicit in his appointment rested upon his property and kindred and connections, and these were no trivial considerations in assigning a man to wage a war or rebellion. Rich enough to maintain his new military status, Schuyler as major general acting in a separate department was to be paid a mere $332 per month. The New York Department of which Schuyler was made commander contained the sprawling acres of his personal estate, a growing family, and an even vaster network of relations and political connections. Although he possessed no manor nor patroonship, Schuyler ranked with those who were so entitled. Like his relations, the Van Rensselaers and Van Cortlandts, whose semifeudal "lordship" did not amount to much in legal terms, Schuyler's power was rooted in his ownership of a sizable acreage—a modest estimate would be perhaps ten to twenty thousand acres. It had placed him "at the top of the provincial class hierarchy and brought" him into public offices. A militia colonelcy, justiceship of the peace, and particularly his membership in the provincial assembly indicated the Albany squire's growing influence.[4]

Not to be overlooked are Schuyler's inheritance from his mother of part of Cortlandt Manor and his wife's interest in her father's estate at Claverack, or the "Lower Manor" of Rensselaerwyck. His mother's portion of Cortlandt Manor was about eighty-four hundred acres, but Schuyler shared this with his sister Gertrude (1724–1813) and brothers Stephen (1737–1820), John (1725–46), and Cortlandt (1735–73). Although by the opening of hostilities in 1775 they had sold three quarters of their share, about twenty-seven hundred acres evidently remained in the family's hands.[5]

Rents from tenants were modest and frequently in arrears for years. Neither Schuyler nor his land agents pressed tenants with threats of reprisal. Despite his proud sense of personal prerogatives, his gentlemanly sense of honor and his value of a public image more than sufficed to prevent him from immoderate or cruel behavior, a certain way of exciting odium instead avoiding opprobrium. And no purpose would be served by "sueing a beggar only to catch a louse."[6] The loss of one tenant was not easily offset by the gain of a new one. Moreover, the improvements of the property were security to the owner who had the right of distraint.

Aside from some as yet largely undeveloped lands in the Mohawk River valley, Schuyler's principal property lay at Saratoga, about thirty-five miles north of Albany, where stood his solid and stately Georgian house. There tenants rented his neighboring farms while slaves and hired labor operated Schuyler's mills. In addition to his two sawmills, the creek powered a gristmill and a hemp-and-flax mill. Attached to the substantial country house and its extensive outbuildings was a country store, the whole supervised by a young bookkeeper or clerk, Daniel Hale.[7]

Presiding firmly and adeptly over his households at Albany and Saratoga was Philip Schuyler's wife Catharine, the daughter of John Van Rensselaer of Claverack and Greenbush and Engeltie (Angelica) Livingston. A year younger than her husband, Catharine was forty when Schuyler rode off to war. Already she had borne twelve children of whom but half were alive in 1775; the thirteenth, Cornelia, would be born in December that year. The three eldest were Angelica (nineteen), Elizabeth (eighteen), and Margaretta (seventeen). Three sons, John Bradstreet (ten), Philip Jeremiah (seven), and Rensselaer (two), were the other surviving children, and the fourteenth and fifteenth (Cortlandt and Catherine Van Rensselaer) would appear in 1778 and 1781 respectively. In an era when women averaged six to eight pregnancies between the ages of twenty to forty, Mrs. Schuyler was not typical. Her twelve pregnancies came between the ages of twenty/twenty-one and forty-seven. She not only managed a large brood of children but a sizable household that included both servants and slaves. In 1790 the latter numbered as many as thirteen at Albany and fourteen at Saratoga, but in 1775 the Schuylers had perhaps as few as nine.[8]

The standard of living for such a household establishment must have been high. The minimum income required for any well-to-do colonial was £500 per annum, and wealthy property owners who had at least "£5000 worth of real and personal estate" were "at most 3 percent of the population." There is little doubt that Schuyler's estate was worth £5000, probably much more. One glimpses the extent of his riches and style of life from accounts of his expenditures for food, drink and clothing; silver and household furnishings; and the education of his children. Between June 1761 and March 1762, for example, he spent over £900 while in England, two thirds of it for glassware, silver, china, and other furnishings for his Albany house. Built during 1761–62 for more than £1,400, the cost of the house did not include some materials such as lumber, which Schuyler furnished from his own mills. Two quarters of tutoring for Margaret Schuyler and one for Elizabeth at William C. Hulett's school in 1774 cost £16.12. In May 1775 and January 1776 the cost of making and mending shoes for Schuyler, his children, and eleven servants (of whom at least nine were slaves) totaled £9.10.00, which came to an average of about 11 shillings 3 pence per person.[9] Similarly, glimpses of the Schuyler's standard of living are evident in receipts like those of James Ponpard, who engraved crests on four pieces of silver plate and two sauceboats and mended a large silver basket with a flower design. Other family expenses between October 1775 and September 1776 totaled more than £750. After the enemy destroyed the general's Saratoga house and outbuildings, the defeated British commander estimated the extent of the damage at no less than £10,000, which two hundred years later may be stated as the equivalent of $400,000![10]

The risk of losing all or part of such a stake in the prevailing order prompted Philip Schuyler to think more than once of the prospects of going to war with Britain, and then of the outcome, especially when military success seemed elusive. If the rebellion succeeded, and Britain redressed American grievances, he might not only escape retribution but also win fame for contributing to the security of liberties that colonials argued were being violated. If the war dragged on or failed, could he not be punished as a traitor? Or if he failed to join the patriots, could they

Fig. 1. Schuyler House, Albany, New York. Watercolor by Philip Hooker, 1818. Schuyler built his mansion in Albany in 1761–62 with lumber from his own mills. Contemporary household receipts indicate the Schuyler family's high standard of living. Courtesy, The New-York Historical Society, New York City.

not seize his property and banish him and his family? Could the radical forces of revolution and finally independence be constrained, and could Schuyler help conduct "a civil war with mildness and a revolution with order"?[11] What kind of revolutionary was he?

Schuyler joined the rebellion in 1775 as much because he was disappointed and frustrated with royal provincial government as because of any commitment to political principles. On the one hand Thomas Gage, the British commander in chief, would no longer accept Schuyler as an aide to John Bradstreet in the quartermaster department, which was curtailed after the Great War of 1754–63. And Schuyler must have been disappointed in his patron Bradstreet's interests in developing a colony in the Detroit area after Pontiac's Indian uprising. These, with the promise of attendant civil and military patronage, were "frustrated by a combination of poorly placed friends at 'home,' well-placed foes in America, and the prevailing hesitancy and instability within British administrations" during the period from 1763 to 1774. Also, Schuyler's cousins, the DeLanceys, had been able to thwart many of his ambitions to share their influence if not to replace it. Since 1768, when Schuyler had been elected to the assembly, his factional partisanship ranged over both local issues and the wider imperial questions of taxation and regulation of trade. In short, if the issue was home rule for New York and the other colonies, for Schuyler it was also very much of a question of who would rule at home. Along with manor lords like the Livingstons, Van Cortlandts, Van Rensselaers, and Morrises, Schuyler turned patriot because the king and his ministers meddled in his affairs. Theirs was the "spirit of the feudal barons who had exacted [the] Magna Carta from King John at Runnymede."[12]

Not to be overlooked as another probable motivation for Schuyler's resistance to British rule is the government's reduction of his father-in-law's Claverack territory by sixty-six thousand acres because of a long dispute over land titles. The problem boiled up into a "Great Rebellion" in 1766–67, and when it was solved in 1772–73, John Van Rensselaer's Lower Manor had been cut to a mere 120,000 acres, an estate in which Schuyler's wife shared an interest but with a considerably diminished portion since her father had relinquished more than a third in order to safeguard the remainder.[13]

Yet real estate, with all its entanglements with political issues, and revolutionary rhetoric about liberty and property alone were not what propelled Philip Schuyler away from the royal standard. Unable to swing New York's assembly to the causes undertaken by the First Continental Congress in 1774, he and his Livingstonian allies used the extralegal maneuvering of local committees of correspondence to convoke a special provincial congress that chose delegates to the Second Continental Congress in April 1775. Ostensibly such methods were employed in the name of preserving and reestablishing American rights and privileges and of restoring harmony between Britain and the colonies. But through them Schuyler plunged deeper into the rising tide of revolution, swam with it as a congressman, and then accepted appointment as a major general in the "army of the United Colonies," as his commission stated. It was also specified that his duty was to defend American liberty and to repel every hostile invasion of it, and this made him subject to the orders of Congress or its committees or the commander in chief and any other superior officer.[14] This double chain of command to which Schuyler was responsible must not be forgotten if his wartime career is to be properly understood.

A month before the explosion at Lexington and Concord Schuyler's views toward the mother country remained optimistic. At New York City, where the provincial assembly was still meeting, he wrote to his Albany constituents that "there is no doubt but we shall have our Grievances redressed." Then with the opening of hostilities in April, Schuyler revealed his motives as a rebellious subject of King George III. Preferring peace and professing a high regard for his freeborn status as a British subject, he would not "tamely submit to an insolent and wicked ministry" or to be "ruled by a military despotism." With Joshua, he said, "[A]s for me and my house, we will serve our country."[15]

In August 1775, about to signal the beginning of his army's invasion of Canada, Schuyler again lamented that the British had trampled upon their own admirable constitution. Force must be met with force if true English law and liberty were to be retained. The American cause "has only in View a Restoration of those Inestimable Rights, which she claims by the Laws of Nature, & the Principles of the Constitution." Should anyone oppose that aim, "It will then be the Duty of every Servant of the Public to prevent him. Nor shall I [in] such a Case hesitate one moment to make Use of Coercive Measures, and in which I trust, my Country will justify me."[16]

However, following the capture of Montreal on 13 November Schuyler expressed a lingering wish that the conquest of all Canada might bring the "Ministry of our Sovereign to reasonable terms—" and that heaven might still "reunite us in every bond of affection and interest; that the *British Empire* may become the envy and admiration of the Universe and flourish until the Omnipotent Master thereof shall be pleased to put his fiat on all earthly empires."[17] As the possibility of restoring harmony within the empire faded, Schuyler found himself obliged to accept independence, first with the challenge of constructing a new state and then with the labors of creating a republican union of states.

Following his election as a major general on 19 June, Schuyler promptly absented himself from Congress. His attention had to be given to preparations for leaving Philadelphia and taking up new responsibilities as Continental commander of the New York Department.[18] Congress and the commander in chief acted accordingly. And after July when Schuyler was also appointed to the Commission for Indian Affairs of the Northern Department, the description of his military jurisdiction became that of the Indian department rather than the province.

The general paid for his and a servant's board and lodgings at Philadelphia on 23 June. At daybreak that Friday morning Schuyler rode off with Washington, Maj. Gen. Charles Lee, and Brig. Gen. Horatio Gates, accompanied by a parade of militia, a troop of light horse, and a string of politicians in carriages. Among the latter was John Adams, who observed the spectacle with envy: "Such is the pride and pomp of war. I, poor creature, worn out with scribbling for my bread and liberty, must leave others to wear the laurels which I have sown; others to eat the bread which I have carved; a common case."[19]

Washington's party included his secretary Joseph Reed and aide-de-camp Thomas Mifflin. As the Virginian "surveyed his companions—Lee, Gates, Schuyler, Reed and Mifflin—on this journey to the true start of his adventure, he could not know that, before the adventure was over, four of the five would prove his enemies." Only Schuyler, the Hudson valley grandee, proved steadfastly loyal. Similar in temperament and interests, he and Washington were bound by a common heritage of rank and fortune, sharing much the same code of honor and devotion to duty. Less than two years separated them in age. At forty-one Schuyler's presence was as striking as Washington's; slender and well proportioned, although, not quite six feet tall, he did not equal the Virginian in physical stature. Even though some thought that the Yorker deemed "social inferiors tolerable only if they kept their lowly distance," his manners were warm and gentlemanly; his proud carriage was usually tempered by kindness and courtesy, and a grandson remembered him as one who entered with great pleasure into children's amusements. The assessment that "he had the solemnity of a grotesquely ugly man" is surely wide of the mark. Serious and ever attentive to business, Schuyler conveyed nothing offensive in appearance, although enemies naturally found his behavior unpleasant and obnoxious. Endowed with a brown complexion, piercing black eyes, and a prominent nose, which was distinctly straight and long, he inspired trust in those who knew him but disquietude in others who were less familiar with him. His deportment and dress were impeccable. His voice was raspy but clear, and the words that came from his prominent lips "revealed the hard headed worldly knowledge of a seasoned handler of great affairs."[20]

Washington and his companions were indeed in the midst of great affairs with much to consider as they rode toward New York. For five days they consulted on strategy and the myriad details of assembling armies, provisions, and arms. If Schuyler and Horatio Gates had not become acquainted earlier when they both had served in the Mohawk valley and north of Albany during the Great War of 1754–63, they now had an opportunity to take one another's measure. Little could they have imagined what troubles they would cause for each other or the difficulties they would suffer as the new war drew them into jurisdictional disputes, mutual rivalry, and animosity. Between Trenton and Newark the generals' retinue paused at New Brunswick on 24 June, where Schuyler probably introduced his brother-in-law Dr. John Cochran to the Continental commander. Cochran volunteered his medical services and ultimately became director general of the army's medical department in 1781.[21]

From New Brunswick Schuyler sent word to the president of the New York Provincial Congress that Washington's party would arrive at Newark on 25 June. Both courtesy and the presence of British warships at New York City suggested the need for precautionary measures. The return of the royal governor of New York, Sir William Tryon, with a naval detachment coincided with the approach of these rebel leaders to the city, and Schuyler requested that a number of gentlemen of the provincial congress come out to advise them upon the safest crossing into New York.[22]

Schuyler and his companions entered New York City on Sunday afternoon, 25 June, and the crowds that welcomed them then moved off to greet Governor Tryon later in the day. At the house of Leonard Lispenard, where there were speeches with dinner, Washington opened a dispatch from Massachusetts to the Continental Congress. The message carried news of the battle of Bunker Hill, the cry for gunpowder, and the plea for the commander in chief's own presence. Washington could not tarry, and on the following day he pressed forward to New Rochelle. Schuyler accompanied him for further discussions and instructions and then returned to New York City on the evening of 27 June to face the burdens of his own command.

2

Advantage is a better soldier than rashness.

—*Henry V*, 3. 6. 120

Schuyler's commission, as I have noted, specified that his orders would be given by Congress or its committees, by Washington, or by any other officer superior to a major general of the united colonies. He was now also armed with instructions of the commander in chief. Directly accountable to both civil and military superiors, Schuyler was not deprived of political office as an army officer. The significance of this cannot be overemphasized if his efforts are to be properly appreciated.

When Washington indicated that Schuyler held command over all troops in the New York Department and must execute the orders of Congress as precisely as possible, he was stating what had been obvious from the moment the Yorker was made a major general. A copy of the Virginian's own orders from Congress indicated what Schuyler might do within his own jurisdiction: take charge of the forces assembled, fill vacancies in officers' ranks, victual and equip volunteers at Continental expense, and use all power with prudence to destroy or capture all who might appear in arms against the united colonies. Much had to be left to the general's discretion, but he was to act with the advice of a council of war. More particularly Washington urged Schuyler to occupy all New York posts as recommended by the provincial congress, to secure the stores already removed from New York City and from the reach of royal authorities, and to frustrate any activity of Governor Tryon that might be deemed inimical to the American cause. Without dictating the mode, Washington advised Schuyler to use force against Tryon if necessary and if Congress were not sitting at the time. The posts on Lake Champlain must be supplied with provisions and ammunition in the most economical manner, and information collected about Col. Guy Johnson, British agent to the Six Nations, and about the disposition of both Indians and Canadians. Schuyler must seek to conciliate these people and to prevent Johnson's efforts to influence the tribes. No invasion of Canada was as yet warranted. The information Schuyler might acquire would help determine "a proper line ... to conciliate their good opinion or facilitate any future operation." Monthly returns of Schuyler's forces must be submitted to the commander in chief and to Congress and done so more often as needed.

Likewise, Washington expected to be informed promptly of any news the Yorker could glean. Schuyler's secret service work proved to be one of his most substantial contributions to the war effort during both his active command and his retirement from the army. As Washington came to value his colleague's abilities and loyal services, he was fully justified in advising that Schuyler's "own good Sense must govern in all Matters not particularly pointed out, as I do not wish to circumscribe you within too narrow Limits." In some sense, then, Schuyler had an independent command.[23] But he never acted without consulting or at least informing the commander in chief; even in exercising initiative he evinced no notion that he was free of the directions of Washington or Congress.

On the night of 29 June Schuyler received the first of a stream of orders that would come from the Continental Congress. These included directions for the invasion of Canada, which was the principal campaign of 1775. Congress had decided to adopt the idea of "making an Impression into Canada" partly because of the urgings of the Albany committee of correspondence, which feared British influence over the Indians in the north and west, and partly because of the arguments by Ethan Allen and Seth Warner of the Hampshire Grants territory. The prospects for a successful invasion seemed good because the British forces along the Saint Lawrence were reported to number only about one thousand. The governor of Canada, Sir Guy Carleton, was reported to be inciting the Indians and preparing to invade New York. But Congress cautiously gave the general considerable discretion in launching the scheme; he was to seize Saint John's and Montreal and pursue other measures to promote colonial peace and security only if he found it *practicable and not disagreeable* to the Canadians. And he was to "observe as much Secrecy as the Nature of the Service will admit." Gov. Jonathan Trumbull of Connecticut was requested to furnish money, ammunition, and other supplies if the New York congress proved unable to raise what Schuyler needed. Congress insisted that the general visit Ticonderoga and Crown Point as soon as possible; survey the conditions of the fortifications, the troops, and supplies; and report on the navigation of the lakes as well as any news of the disposition of the Indians and Canadians. Because a dispute over the command of Yankee troops at Ticonderoga had arisen, Schuyler must confer there with colonels Benjamin Hinman and Benedict Arnold and report the state of those affairs to Congress.[24]

The decision to invade Canada in an effort to make it the fourteenth colony "was a strategic decision of the first magnitude" and an indication that overall American strategy was to be aggressive or offensive and "to run all risques." But the Second Continental Congress's interest in winning Canadian support for their rebellious protest was seriously undermined; in 1774 the First Continental Congress had denounced the Quebec Act with exaggerated fulminations against its provisions for the religious liberty of Roman Catholics, the use of French law, and a military style of government. French Canadians were right to question the allegations that the British act threatened their interests as much as their Protestant neighbors to the south argued. Suspicious of the colonial rebels' anti-Catholicism, they were not especially enamored of the glories of representative government either. There were elements in British Canada—some of them merchants and ambitious fortune seekers from New York and New England—who might favor colonial invasion, the seizure of Canada, and bringing her into union with the Continental Congress; but it was problematical whether the bulk of the inhabitants, who were fundamentally French, would welcome an army led by Philip Schuyler or by anyone else.[25] Therefore it was with utmost good judgment that he delayed the invasion until reasonable assurances could be given that Canadians would not oppose it.

It is also entirely understandable that some of the delay was necessitated by the monumental effort required to launch a suitable invasionary force. Schuyler found that he could agree with Frederick the Great's complaint that "It is not I who commands the army, but flour and forage who are the masters."[26] Castigated for cowardice, lack of energy, timidity, incompetence, or conservative indecisiveness,[27] he encountered his responsibilities with careful and thorough administration.

Schuyler could not leave Manhattan before 4 July. There were many arrangements to make after he had left Washington at New Rochelle on 27 June. Brig. Gen. David Wooster and Col. David Waterbury brought their Connecticut regiments to the edge of the city to assist with preparations against the British regulars. Orders for the troops must be given, accounts of their disposition collected, and consultations taken with members of the New York congress about tents, fuel, and straw, and the recruiting of the first five Continental regiments to serve in the northern campaign. Supplies of all kinds must be ordered, and military appointments issued. Congress should specify, Schuyler insisted, the allowances for each man so that all his troops "may be equally provided for to prevent uneasiness." His department needed commissary and quartermaster generals, and he recommended the appointment of agents who could deal effectively with the northern Indians and wean them from attachment to the Crown's agents. With these suggestions Schuyler observed that should he be found "unfortunate" in the discharge of his many responsibilities, he hoped that Congress might impute it "to that want of abilities which I . . . avowed previous to my appointment." But his orders to Colonel Hinman at Ticonderoga, to the Albany Committee of Safety, and to the commissary Elisha Phelps had already demonstrated his ability to act with foresight and with dispatch. Similarly, Schuyler called upon the Albany committee to promise friendly Oneida tribesmen that a conference would be held later to deal with their request for renovating and garrisoning Fort Stanwix. He recommended that they offer presents to the Indians visiting Albany and hire thirty of the best ship carpenters to begin building boats on Lake George and at Ticonderoga.[28]

Increasingly Schuyler focused his attention upon the northern reaches of his department. Uneasy about his discretionary authority to move troops up the Hudson from Manhattan, he posted an express rider to Congress on 30 June, asking for its approval. Men were needed at Albany, he argued, for the transport of stores and the construction of boats and carriages. Simultaneously he hurried his nephew-in-law Walter Livingston to Jonathan Trumbull, requesting some six tons of powder, a quantity of ammunition, and £15,000 to £20,000 for assembling the army at Albany. Livingston was also charged with the purchase of two hundred fat cattle. Turning to the New York delegates in Congress, Schuyler sought their influence for Livingston's appointment as commissary general. Without him Schuyler insisted that he would "otherwise be in the highest Distress. Controversies between different Commissaries and Committees have already arisen."[29] The appointment duly secured, Livingston unfortunately became the focus of the very kind of trouble that Schuyler wished to avoid.

Congress's answer to Schuyler's request for shifting troops northward came on 1 July. David Wooster and his Connecticut forces were not to be removed from New York City. The department commander must raise the Green Mountain Boys, whose officers were democratically chosen except for an appointed lieutenant colonel and major. Other men from the Ticonderoga neighborhood were to be similarly enlisted. With President Hancock's notification came a promise of fifty quarter casks of powder from Philadelphia and instructions for Schuyler to use his own discretion about allowances of provisions to individual soldiers.[30]

Meantime Schuyler had issued detailed orders for the discipline and training of Wooster's notably youthful and agile troops.[31] Although he became notorious among Yankees for insisting upon drill and discipline, he was no more rigorous nor exacting than was appropriate for any conscientious officer—and certainly no more zealous than Washington, who became famous for his ardor in punishing refractory soldiers.

By 1 July, when Schuyler sent his first report to Washington, he had managed to collect troop returns that indicated that forces in the New York Department had reached 2,857. Wooster's and Waterbury's regiments at New York numbered 576 and 929 respectively. Col. Benjamin Hinman's Connecticut regiment was divided among Ticonderoga (478), Crown Point (293), the landing at Lake George (98), and Fort George (104). There were also 174 Massachusetts troops scattered at these posts and 205 Yorkers at Fort George. Two weeks later Schuyler's return of the army showed little improvement; the total rank and file was 2,958, of whom 2,419 were actually fit for duty. And over half the troops were still posted on the lower Hudson. The department had two brigadier generals, Wooster and Richard Montgomery; a chaplain; surgeon and two mates; and Schuyler's aides-de-camp were John McPherson and James Van Rensselaer, who was Mrs. Schuyler's youngest brother. As his secretary he appointed Richard Varick, who only a few days earlier had enlisted as a captain in the First New York Regiment. The twenty-two-year-old lawyer was a partner of John Morin Scott, and Schuyler soon found him to be an admirable manager, trustworthy personal friend, and ultimately a reliable political ally.[32]

Schuyler may not at first have expected that his responsibilities would remove him from New York City so soon or for so long, but on 1 July he was obliged to inform his commander in chief that Congress had ordered his northward. Accordingly, he planned to set out on 3 July. The threat of British troops landing at Manhattan had lifted as eight transports (at Sandy Hook since 29 June) were now setting sail. Moreover, Governor Tryon's conduct had been "unexceptionable," and Schuyler thought that the governor showed no signs of leading a vigorous opposition to rebel activities. But there could be danger if the New York convention failed to find the ammunition needed for seizing and occupying the position in Highlands of the Hudson.[33]

Although the New York convention was energetic in responding to his call for supplies, Schuyler asked the Continental Congress for more gunpowder and a few fieldpieces. As for using the Green Mountain Boys, it appeared that they could be made a separate corps instead of being included in regiments whose officers Congress had already designated. With an eye to probable Indian threats to the Pennsylvania, New Jersey, and New York frontiers, Schuyler suggested that two more regiments, each 740 strong, be raised by New York and stationed in the back country along the Pennsylvania-New Jersey border and the Oneida carrying place. There they might keep the tribes in awe, which would force them to refrain from attacking.[34]

On Monday, 3 July, Schuyler hurried preparations to leave Manhattan. Messages were posted to both the New York and Continental congresses, to Gen. David Wooster, and to Congressman Silas Deane. The general had wished to take Wooster's corps to the lake country because without them his army would be inadequate to accomplish anything decisive; the thirteen hundred-odd troops there were scattered among several outposts. Schuyler preferred to do without Wooster himself. *"Entre nous,"* he told Deane, he could wish "that the good old General was at home or near Boston." Because he still needed an adjutant general, Schuyler asked Deane to arrange the appointment of Benedict Arnold. "I dare not mention it to Congress, and would not have it known that I ever hinted it as it might create jealousy. Be silent therefore with respect to me."[35] Schuyler failed to have Arnold made adjutant general. By August he was assigned to lead the assault on Quebec via the Kennebec River, which was perhaps an "ill-conceived and ill-executed" maneuver inspired by Arnold's own "misdirected enthusiasm." But what remains undeniable is that "there was no planning or coordination between" Schuyler's forces under Montgomery and the Arnold expedition.[36] Perhaps William Duer's opposition to Arnold's candidacy proved decisive. Congress decided to allow New York's provincial congress to make the appointment. Later, after Schuyler's Saratoga neighbor Duer declined the post, Edward Fleming was finally chosen in late August.[37]

As for the collection of men and provisions, Schuyler turned to the New York congress with an estimate of military stores and a request for hastening provincial troops to Albany. The need was especially pressing because of Congress's order that Wooster's men must remain at New York City. On 28 June the New York congress authorized recruitment of the first Continentals—five regiments to be raised for service until 31 December. Not until early August, however, did Col. Alexander McDougall have part of his regiment armed and equipped for dispatch to Schuyler's northern service.[38]

Meantime, upon the recommendations of both Schuyler and the Continental Congress, the New Yorkers agreed to permit the enlistment of an independent regiment of the Green Mountain Boys led by Ethan Allen and Seth Warner. This was a delicate business because these men of the Hampshire Grants had long disputed New York's jurisdiction over them. Schuyler could not but have been cheered when he received word that the Green Mountain Boys were happy to be organized as an independent battalion. Subject to the New York congress's regulations respecting the nomination of their own officers, men of the Hampshire Grants and the Bennington committee recommended both Ethan Allen and Seth Warner; they in turn could signify what junior officers Schuyler should commission. Schuyler made it clear to Allen that disputes must not arise about the election of officers; he would permit the nomination but not the election of field officers. The New York Provincial Congress would make the final decision, and in the end Seth Warner became their commander.[39]

Envisioning an army of at least four thousand, Schuyler called upon the New York congress for about six hundred tents, three months of food supplies, and a variety of tools. Thirty barrels of pitch and a ton of oakum for boat building were also wanted, and two tons of musket balls or lead and "what powder can be spared" and "whatever arms can be spared" were also requisitioned. In addition he listed two tons of bar iron, 500 weight of steel, thirty-five millsaws, "[n]ecessaries for a hospital," fifty swivel guns, fifty small truck carriages, and ten dozen carriages for field-pieces. The body that nominated him for the command was now to advise him, and Schuyler deftly reminded the members how dependent he must be upon their "aid and countenance" in promoting the public service. With characteristic diplomacy he averred that he would never be able to equal their confidence in him, but he would strive to deserve it "that I may not draw disgrace on you, my country, or myself."[40]

Within a week Peter Curtenius promised to send most of the articles

Walter Livingston waited for Governor Trumbull and the Connecticut general court to respond to requisitions of troops, funds, gunpowder, and provisions. Two regiments (seven hundred men each) were to be raised in Connecticut, and shortly after reaching Albany, Schuyler received Trumbull's promise that £15,000, not £20,000, would be provided as quickly as possible. By 18 July, however, Livingston indicated that he had raised £20,000 in "York" currency. But instead of the six tons of powder that Schuyler had requested, Trumbull was able to ship only forty half-barrels to Albany. Yet he furnished Schuyler with some of the first direct news that the Yorker was able to collect from Canada. James Dean (1748–1823), a protégé of Eleazar Wheelock and a 1773 graduate of Dartmouth, had left Montreal in mid-June. Having learned Iroquois languages while living with the Oneida, Dean was to become a valuable servant of congressional Indian commissioners. For the moment his news suggested that the Caughnawaga and Saint François Indians were none too cooperative with Governor Carleton's efforts to arm them except for defensive purposes. After the May incursions from Ticonderoga to Saint John's, they seemed not to wish to be involved in the colonial struggle for liberty. Only out of fear of being dispossessed of their lands had they agreed to Carleton's demands for help in defending Montreal should it be besieged by the southern rebels. Dean clearly believed that the tribesmen were fickle, but he suggested that American seizure of western posts like Oswego, Niagara, Detroit, and Michilimackinac would secure both the peace and trade of the tribes. Montreal's fortifications were in disrepair, and Governor Carleton was concentrating his defenses at Saint John's and Chambly.[46]

Had it been possible to launch a proper American invasion quickly, before British reinforcements had reached Canada, Schuyler might have been heaped with laurels. Instead, the delays in preparations, largely dictated by circumstances beyond his control, prevented the winning of an early advantage. Not until late August was the American invasion of Canada actually ready to commence. No sensible plan of operations could have been set in motion earlier without its being foolhardy or irresponsible. Yet Schuyler has been charged with lacking dynamism, for being "better qualified to lead a quadrille than an undisciplined mob of men."[47] In fact it was his energetic efforts to build an invasionary force and to create a system of organization and supply that finally enabled the campaign to begin. Prudence also dictated that he create safeguards against possible Anglo-Indian activities in the west. Plans for defenses and an intelligence system for the Mohawk valley and negotiations with the Iroquois were also time-consuming. And his main enterprise in the northern

lake country demanded the thorough arrangement of a line of communications over which slowly assembled troops, provisions, and equipment
could be moved.

Shortly after Sunday noon on 9 July, Schuyler's sloop eased into the
Albany landing. With his secretary Richard Varick he was greeted by the
Albany Committee of Safety, Correspondence, and Protection; with them
were a city troop of horse, an "association company," and a crowd of
citizens. Escorted to the city hall, Schuyler received an address by the
acting chairman of the committee, Dr. Samuel Stringer, who was the
Schuyler family physician. A week earlier he had written Schuyler his
congratulations with hints of difficulties: Would the general's constitution "be equal to the arduous Task you have to engage"? Yet he noted
that Schuyler's firm hand was sorely needed at Albany, "& unless you
arrive soon," he wrote, "you will find the Business altogether in greater
Confusion than you conceive."[48]

Stringer's speech of welcome noted Schuyler's abilities and aptly summarized the work to which they must now be applied. Raised to an
envious position of opulence and known for principles "invariably opposed to power," Schuyler was expected to use his knowledge, prudence,
and experience in the defence of liberties now threatened by a deluded
and despotic ministry. When Stringer had completed his brief encomium,
Schuyler professed that he was unable to offer an adequate response.
Requesting the assistance of his neighbors in the work now looming
before him, he deplored "the unhappy occasion which has forced America
to have recourse to arms for her safety and defence." His orders for the
"impression into Canada" made him "Ambitious only to aid in restoring
her violated rights," and he would "most cheerfully return my sword to
the scabbard, and, with alacrity, resume the employment of civil life,
whenever my constituents direct, or whenever a happy reconciliation with
the Parent State shall take place." His warmest wish, he insisted, was that
heaven might guide men to a speedy restoration of peace, harmony, and
mutual confidence in all parts of the British empire. The exchanges made,
the company adjourned to Cartwright's Tavern to dine—perhaps in the
usual Dutch civic tradition of public entertainments.[49]

Did these sentiments suggest that Schuyler was deliberately dilatory
in launching the campaign into Canada? Can it be that he "lacked both
energy and decisiveness in his preparations" or that he "was vastly deficient in assembling and training an offensive army"?[50] No. The work at
hand required time to execute. Fully organized armies do not spring from
the earth. Armaments and food supplies, clothing, wagons and livestock,
bateaux and felling axes, picks, shovels, and the money to pay for every-

thing are not plucked from the air. A sparsely populated wilderness could not easily furnish abundant manpower; its lakes and other waterways together with poor or nonexistant roads determined not only the lines of communication and movements of armies but the speed of traversing them. And there were problems of relations between civil and military authorities, the local authorities and the emerging national government, and the lines of jurisdiction in formulating and executing strategy. Sometimes there was meddling or lack of timely support, sometimes envious behavior and rivalries that threatened successful decision making; and there were questions of priorities in action to which cautious answers seemed to betoken timidity. How far to proceed with armed force? When to seek mediation and reconciliation? Amidst the welter of such questions strategy emerged piecemeal. Initially, military action was aimed at limited ends: the British to force a settlement, restoring the colonies to a peaceful position in the empire; the colonists to force a recognition of their rights and liberties.[51]

Schuyler labored mightily to discharge his orders to accomplish these ends. Nor did he cease when sometimes he was forced temporarily to a sickbed. Tireless even when given to fits of despondency or exasperation, the Yorker expended energies that amaze anyone who takes the trouble to read the record and who appreciates the circumstances that lie beyond even the best commander's control.

The Albany to which Schuyler returned in July was by all comparisons a small city and still bore noticeable marks of its Dutch heritage in language, architecture, religion, foods, and family customs. Its population was about four thousand (Philadelphia's was twenty-three thousand and New York's thirteen thousand), of which half were probably children and about four hundred were black slaves. But English notions and local political rivalry between fur traders and merchants had come to alter Dutch Albany's affairs considerably; divisions between local leaders had arisen between those who thought their "city's greatest advantage lay in preserving its independence from British interference" and those who believed in cooperation. The merchants Volkert P. Douw and Jacob C. Ten Eyck, both of whom were former mayors, and Douw's Gansevoort relations were among the former; the lawyer Abraham Yates, Jr., and the fur trader and mayor Abraham C. Cuyler were among the latter. Now, however, they seemed unusually united for the struggle to which Philip Schuyler had committed himself.[52]

On 1 May, at a public meeting called by the committee of correspondence, a new Committee of Safety, Protection, and Correspondence of the City and County of Albany had been chosen to act for the "weal of the American Cause" and to oppose the "Ministerial Plan now prosecuting against us." The crowd that assembled at the market house in Broadway chose twenty-one men from the three city wards; nearly all of them were of the existing ruling class and representative of the earlier political divisions. Included were Douw and Ten Eyck, Yates and Dr. Samuel Stringer, Schuyler, and his boyhood friend Abraham Ten Broeck. As brother-in-law of the patroon Stephen Van Rensselaer II, and agent-guardian of his son, Stephen III, Ten Broeck represented a landed interest much as Schuyler did.[53]

It was this committee upon which the general was now to rely for much of the assistance he needed to collect craftsmen, wagoners, and provisions for the army, not to mention aid in dealing with the Indians and persons disaffected from the rebel cause in Albany County. Through the local committee Schuyler also had ties to the provincial congress, which included members elected by the Albany group. Even before his return to the city Schuyler and other New Yorkers in the Continental Congress had looked to the Albany committee for provisioning the New England forces holding Ticonderoga. And it was through the promptings of the committee that the delegates urged Congress to seek the friendship or neutrality of the Iroquois in the great struggle now begun. Fears that Sir Guy Carleton was inciting Indians against the colonies prompted the Albany committee to insist upon a countermove. And because of its urgency Congress altered its sentiments about "making an Impression into Canada." Thus Schuyler had been ordered first to seek information and counsel, to make preparation to secure the waters of Lake Champlain, and then to seize Saint John's and Montreal "if practicable, and not disagreeable to the Canadians." With these orders he now proceeded to act before leaving Albany on 12 July for a tour of the northern posts.[54]

Unlike Washington, who already had a sizable army some 16,700 strong and ready to command in a largely stationary position, Schuyler started with a mere 2,800, and he was obliged to enlarge, provision, and move it toward Canada.[55] He had learned logistics from John Bradstreet in the previous war, especially in the 1758 campaign against Fort Frontenac, but now the preparations were more complicated. Problems of prying men, equipment, and provisions from congresses and committees, not to mention raising the money to pay for them, and coordinating supply lines and troop movements were considerably more vast than those he had encountered during the earlier campaign. The difficulty of relieving and strengthening Ticonderoga from the south was of particular significance because the French-built fort had been more conveniently accessible by water from the Saint Lawrence River valley. The so-called communication between Lake Champlain and Albany included links of both land and water carriage. Bateaux could navigate the Hudson north to Stillwater, Saratoga, Fort Miller, and Fort Edward, where their cargoes had to be carried around rapids now marked by locks of the Champlain Canal and forward along a trail barely deserving of the name "road" to Assembly Point on Lake George. There was also a trail stretching northeastward from Fort Edward toward Fort Ann at the source of Wood Creek and on to Skenesborough (now Whitehall), which lay at the south end of Lake Champlain, called South Bay. Easiest for packhorses and men on foot to traverse, this route required extensive improvements if baggage and supply wagons were to travel along it. The last thirty miles to Ticonderoga from either Lake George or South Bay on Lake Champlain, which lay like parallel prongs of the northern waters, could be more easily crossed by boat. Schuyler was well acquainted with this forested territory, and he was to become even more familiar with it in the coming years as he passed through it repeatedly. In September 1775 he would move his army north of Ticonderoga along the smoother water passage of the lake and the Richelieu River. From Isle aux Noix and Saint John's, the Richelieu ran to Chambly, almost directly east of Montreal, and north to Sorel, where it joined the Saint Lawrence River some one hundred miles above Quebec.

Between 10 and 12 July Schuyler grappled with a variety of business. Local merchants and the committee of safety were directed to acquire and ship hundreds of barrels of flour, peas, and rice to Ticonderoga. Schuyler asked for carriages to haul the supplies and promised reimbursement for the merchants' extension of credit. Likewise, he called for drovers to move cattle now expected from Livingston's foraging in Connecticut. As some men of the country had refused to serve as Continental officers because of dissatisfaction with proffered ranks or because of timidity in joining the rebellion, Schuyler suggested that other appointments be made so that officers could enlist their units. The Albany committee must not delay the creation of an army by waiting for the provincial congress, which had now adjourned, to issue new commissions. Thus with Schuyler's prompting, men like Peter Gansevoort (1749–1812), and Goose Van Schaick (?–1789) began their military careers, each of them ultimately rising to the rank of brigadier general.[56]

Warning them to make preparations for his coming, Schuyler hurried orders to the commanding officer at Fort George and to Col. Benjamin Hinman at Ticonderoga. Troop returns must be compiled, specifying the numbers of sick; the officers and effectives; and smiths, wheelwrights and carpenters; along with an inventory of arms and ammunition. Intelligence must be obtained from Canada. Hinman must act decisively to promote the troops' health; cleanliness was imperative, as was care in dressing victuals. Men not posted on guard or fatigue duty must constantly exercise, for sloth would invite the "most fatal consequences." With thanks to Governor Trumbull, whether for the promise of funds or for the small supply of powder, Schuyler wrote wishfully that Connecticut might furnish "more [of that] necessary article in military operations." Without it business would slow to a threatening halt. Trumbull proved invariably cooperative and usually could be relied upon for considerable support, a situation that was in a marked contrast to the lingering Yankee-Yorker animus that occasionally flared into dangerous proportions. Nor was Schuyler's New England neighbor less responsive to the Yorker's calls for help than his own province's authorities. To them, too, he turned repeatedly for assistance of all kinds.[57]

Concluding his brief halt at Albany before riding northward, Schuyler posted a final round of orders to Livingston; Brig. Gen. Richard Montgomery, his second in command; and several other officers. His strictures against the plundering of fields, orchards, or other property revealed the canny landlord's belief that military necessity was no license to violate the sanctity of property; he also rightly anticipated the behavior of men under arms.[58]

At practically every stage of his military career Schuyler managed to send reports to his superiors, thus enabling us to follow his movements with as much care as he applied to the energetic discharge of his duties. Aside from the general's concept of responsibility that these reveal, the record may of course vindicate his honor against the censorious charges of incompetence, maladministration, misconduct, and even disloyalty. Typical of these accounts was the Yorker's letter to President Hancock, written on the eve of his departure from Albany. Explaining that he would have tarried longer in the city to supervise preparations but for the reports of disruption at Ticonderoga, Schuyler was determined to end the officers' dispute over command at the fort, which had "thrown everything into vast confusion." Unless he quickly imposed some order and discipline among them, the turmoil would swell beyond remedy. (Washington had encountered similar disorders when he assumed his command at Cambridge.) Few provisions were on hand; some troops, he feared, had been dismissed and others refused to serve "if this or that man commands"; and more vessels were essential for commanding the lake and ferrying troops across it. The general's information about the Indians seemed sparse; James Dean's report, received through the hands of Governor Trumbull, was enclosed. Reputedly friendly, they were by all reports and probabilities being incited by the British. Schuyler noted evidence of great waste or embezzlement of rations at the northern outposts, which was good cause for his furious determination to end carelessness and fraud. Carefully explaining his orders for the purchase of flour at Albany and cattle in Connecticut (to save the expense of transporting salt meat), he reviewed his current shortages of powder and money. Again he repeated the necessity for better administration and urged appointments of a muster-master general and his deputies and of New York officers in the Continental line. A quartermaster general, which he had requested on 28 June, was also vital to proper management of transportation, which must be both economical and reliable. How could he execute his command without properly qualified subordinates? Crying also for copies of Congress's articles of war, Schuyler reported a scandalous lack of subordination in his army; the "low treatment" of some officers and similar behavior by them to their subordinates he thought merited exemplary punishments. Such despicable behavior was both destructive of the service and a disgrace to those in command.[59]

A partial answer to the general's impatience with the delay of some appointments came on 17 July. Congress approved his recommendation of Walter Livingston as deputy commissary general of stores and provisions in the New York Department; Capt. Donald Campbell was named deputy quartermaster general for New York's Continental forces, and Gunning Bedford deputy muster-master. Congressman Samuel Chase was pleased that Schuyler had agreed to his nomination of Bedford and invited the general to command his good offices for anything else that might remotely "contribute a mite to your happiness or Ease."[60] Chase's exchange with Schuyler proved to be but one strand in a growing bond of sympathy and support between the general and other New York congressmen and delegates from the South. Drawn through personal rapport, these ties were no doubt partly reinforced by mutual social and economic interests of slaveholders and landed gentry. And in part they were an expression of sectional uneasiness about the more radical members of Congress, especially the New Englanders.

With the first of his duties discharged at Albany, Schuyler was finally prepared to tour the northern outposts of his command. Everywhere he turned he encountered challenges to his skills as an organizer and to his determination to prepare a campaign with thoroughness and dispatch.

Organizing the Northern Army

1

A Tour of Inspection

Schuyler intended to reach Ticonderoga by mid-July, but other business delayed him along the way from Albany until 18 July. Issuing a constant stream of orders to various subordinates as he moved, the general received news at Saratoga late in the evening of 14 July that suggested he might be obliged to ride west to Tryon County. Expectations of Indian raids were rumored in the Mohawk valley. A quick exchange of news between him and the Albany and Tryon County committees prompted Schuyler to divert fifty men intended for Lake George to the west. If four to eight hundred Indians joined Scottish Highlanders and other disaffected Tryon County settlers, civil war would erupt in the valley and the line of supplies he was stretching to his troops in the north would be endangered. Promptly he sent word of these apprehensions to Congress, reiterating his need for men and ammunition and urging that it lift its restrictions on the Connecticut troops, which represented more than half of his entire army, so that these men could be sent north. Congress first directed General Wooster to rush one thousand of his Connecticut forces to Albany and then empowered Schuyler to dispose of all troops in the New York Department "in such Manner as he may think best for the protection & Defence of these Colonies."[1]

Schuyler's reactions to rumors from the west were prompted by sound suppositions.[2] Pausing at his country house to decide whether to proceed north or west, Schuyler waited for further intelligence. His presence was required at Ticonderoga to settle disputes among officers and to establish order in the supply system, but should he give the Mohawk valley his

25

immediate superintendence? The authenticity of early reports that the settlers and Indians of Canada were favorably disposed to an American invasion could not be trusted. But then word came from Montreal and Oswego that the British were not succeeding in efforts to persuade various tribes in Canada and western New York to take the hatchet against the "Bostonians," which was an Indian reference to colonial rebels. Ultimately the "savages" might not be able to withstand British pressures. Scouts could be posted against further alarms, and the Iroquois might be less provoked to war if troops were not sent further into their territory. While approving these proposals of the Albany committee, Schuyler urged that a strict watch be set near Fort Stanwix and warned Congress that little reliance could be placed upon the peaceful professions of the tribes or of Guy Johnson, who had declared that he was warmly attached to the colony's inhabitants and intended no destruction of them.[3]

Schuyler's suspicions were not misplaced. After reaching Montreal on 17 July Johnson conferred with tribesmen there and won their declaration of support; he also disputed with Governor Carleton, who opposed sending the Indians to war outside Quebec. Peace in the Mohawk valley remained precarious at best. Having raised several hundred men to overcome the patriot settlers, Alexander White of Tryon County was forced to flee to Sir John Johnson, and from his protection he was reported to have escaped toward Canada with designs of rousing Indians against the rebel cause. When Schuyler learned of probable threats to the frontier at Caughnawaga (south of Montreal), he quickly ordered Capt. Cornelius Van Dyke to take his company from Ticonderoga back to post at Schenectady. And, finally, early in August Sheriff White and several confederates, including three Mohawk Indians, were captured at William Gilliland's house at Willsboro on the south shore of Lake Champlain. Schuyler then sent them under guard to the Albany committee with the warning that they not be permitted to return to the Mohawk valley. The three Mohawks, however, were given gifts as an enticement to others before the general conference with all of the Iroquois could be assembled.[4]

Before leaving Saratoga on 16 July Schuyler again pressed the New York congress to hasten reinforcements and supplies for the Ticonderoga and Crown Point garrisons. The provincial committee of safety reported only qualified success in their efforts to furnish powder, tents, and entrenching tools or to provide enough arms, ammunition, blankets, and clothing for even a regiment. With their treasury empty, Schuyler was left to manage a miniscule army as best he could.[5]

By 17 July the general reached the southern end of Lake George. What he found in the little garrison there—a mere 334 men—provoked a veritable deluge of orders. Some sought to regulate the sutlers' movements and their charges for rum, others to stop their sales except by order of one of the purchaser's commissioned officers. More important were Schuyler's strictures on wasting and embezzling stores and his regulations for the cleanliness and sobriety of troops, their exercise, diet, drills, roll calls, and work. Systems of scouting, message delivery, repair of roads and bridges, and transport of stores were instituted. Roll calls were to be held twice daily; garrison work hours were established.[6]

Although the incidence of courts-martial may be a measure of successful command, Schuyler's record as a disciplinarian contains relatively few cases of legal proceedings but many instances indicative of his constant concern for control of his troops. Evidently other means of enforcing discipline were used or many offenses went altogether unpunished.[7] The general, however, seldom relaxed his penchant for orderliness and system. He could not abide subordinates whose jurisdictions and personalities clashed, especially if they challenged his own authority or interfered with efficient administration. Thoroughly capable of organizing and managing a department under the worst conditions, he recognized that a smoothly running system of logistics was the lifeline of any sustained military mission. Without it even the best strategy or tactics were unlikely to succeed. Often he was forced to deal with petty insubordination that compromised effective administration.[8]

Although Schuyler felt obliged to supervise the smallest details in all corners of his department, he was not averse to the use of initiative by subordinates. Those who were able to take advantage of unexpected opportunities were to be commended for improvising as necessity dictated. His work with Brig. Gen. Richard Montgomery demonstrated the bond of trust and mutual respect that any first-rate leader relies upon. Montgomery wondered at the time of Schuyler's commissioning whether he had "strong nerves" for so important a trust as department commander.[9] He soon discovered that his chief not only had energy and pluck, but a great many other qualifications as well. In July, as Schuyler prepared to leave Fort George, Montgomery had reached Albany to execute the general's orders for organizing troops and supplies destined for Ticonderoga. The two generals began their common task as it ended when the invasion of Canada failed—with mutual trust and goodwill and a reliance upon one another's energies and judgment. When Montgomery, for example, announced his decision to move a company of men from Schenectady northward to escort a shipment of Connecticut gunpowder, Schuyler happily approved because the alarms from the west had dissipated. And he phrased his orders with the tone of a colleague more than the pitch of a superior officer.

The two men found themselves similarly exasperated by the difficulties of ordering their army. Appreciating Montgomery's concern "that the levies go on so tardily in our Colony," Schuyler made no quibbles when Montgomery reported deviations from orders. On his side, Montgomery trusted Schuyler's understanding of the propriety of making them. No evidence suggests that Schuyler was ever dissatisfied with Montgomery's performance or that Montgomery ever executed orders in a way that challenged or thwarted Schuyler's command. Moreover, Montgomery sympathized with his chief's troublesome ill health and recognized those difficulties—the provision of manpower and supplies—that were beyond his control. "Melancholy as it is," Montgomery wrote, "I wish to partake of & alleviate your burden."[10]

From Fort George Schuyler moved on to the Landing at the north end of the lake, where he paused before ferrying across to Ticonderoga. At 10 P.M. on 17 July he found the hundred-man garrison woefully lacking in alertness. Upon hearing that the general was in the boat, a sentinel left his post to awaken three guards. These made no stir, and when Schuyler "walked up and came to another, a sergeant's guard," he discovered that the sentinel allowed him to advance without rousing his sleeping fellows. "With a penknife only I could have cut off both guards," he fumed, "and then have set fire to the blockhouse, destroyed the stores, and starved the people here." That previous exhortations to maintain constant vigilance were ignored annoyed him mightily. Still, Schuyler found the officers and men otherwise attractive in appearance and decent in their deportment. Once he got "the better of this inattention . . . this nonchalance of theirs," he believed they could be made into good soldiers.[11]

Repeatedly, however, Schuyler discovered that the combating of confusion and disorder was a never-ending challenge. Not only Yankees but civilians from all colonies resisted the discipline so vital to successful military organization. Armies of course reflect the societies from which they spring, and the existing militia system by its very nature "reinforced the provincialism that was a salient characteristic of the colonial period." Americans were also notably hostile to any hint of militarism or threat to the subordination of the military to civilian control. Within this framework Schuyler, as did many other officers, struggled against great odds to discharge his duty.[12]

Early on 18 July, Schuyler at last reached Ticonderoga. Finding the old French fortifications in poor repair, he was amazed that Col. Benjamin Hinman had done nothing beyond his orders to reinforce the garrison and to wait for the general. At least Hinman's arrival there had halted the jarring disputes between Ethan Allen and Benedict Arnold over who should command the outpost, but a surprise attack from Canada would leave the poor troops defenseless. The garrison had fallen from 535 men to little more than 300. Although entrenchments had been commenced at Crown Point, none were yet begun at Ticonderoga. At once Schuyler ordered that the works proceed, and in the next few days he issued a small avalanche of directives while inspecting every corner of the place. Fortunately for Schuyler the British position in Canada was scarcely stronger than his own, nor would it be when his own army was ready to invade the north late in August.[13]

Immediately posting word to Washington of his arrival on Lake Champlain, Schuyler indicated that four hundred of Carleton's men were entrenching Saint John's. A Canadian informant thought neither the settlers nor Indians of Canada would support Carleton (but Schuyler remained uneasy about the prospects that Carleton might persuade some Indians to attack the lake posts); he would need time to prepare adequate defenses.[14]

In orders issued on 19 July Schuyler proceeded to deal with the garrison in both general and particular terms. If the troops were to remain in good health, their officers must supervise the proper dressing of victuals, the airing of bedding, and the prevention of drunken disorders. Arms and ammunition must be properly tended. The virtuous, obedient, and orderly soldier would enjoy the general's "smiles and be cherished with the fond attention of an indulgent parent." Others, he warned, must suffer his frowns and contempt, and repeated offenders could expect punishment and disgrace. Orders must be read aloud to the men so that "none be ignorant" of them. No soldier must leave the garrison without permission of his immediate commander or the general. At soundings of alarm all troops must immediately assemble on parade.[15]

Hitherto the comings and goings at Ticonderoga had quite obviously been too free, for Schuyler issued further directives about the movement of personnel and of sutlers' and commissaries' provisions on 20 July. Necessary for the promotion of security against spies, these orders were also designed to inculcate proper record keeping and accountability and to prevent loss, waste, and embezzlement. All commissaries must report regularly the provisions they received and dispersed, times of transactions, and the identity of personnel bringing or taking the shipments. Guns were not to "be fired nor ammunition wasted in any way whatsoever."[16]

Expecting accountability of subordinates to himself, Schuyler never forgot to practice it with superiors. Frequently and carefully he explained to Congress and Washington his movements and efforts, seeking where necessary the advice for plans or the authority to act and proposing measures that largely depended upon the will or aid of others for effective execution. Such were his attempts in his first letter written from Ticonderoga to President John Hancock.

No reliable news had yet been received from Canada, he told Hancock, but the inhabitants were reputedly friendly and the Indians inclined to neutrality. The time was ripe to press forward to Saint John's (where fortifications were being constructed); the rebels must demonstrate that they aimed only to prevent British regulars from achieving a naval power to interrupt friendly intercourse between the colonists and their Canadian brethren. But nothing had been done to enable Schuyler to make such a move. More boats were needed and also materials to build them. Powder, ammunition, and provisions were scarce, and the few guns on hand lacked carriages. Since his earlier return of troops only one armorer was available to repair weapons, and two hundred men had disappeared. With poor barracks badly crowded, Schuyler asked for tents to relieve the shortage of shelter as well as to prevent the onset and spread of disease.

Continuing his explanation of other problems for the benefit of Congress, the general described how he had acted or proposed to act in order to solve them. The governor of Connecticut had been asked to send tents for the troops of his province; but the Yankees' daily subsistence allowance had been so large as to cause other units to expect a similarly generous allotment. Schuyler urged Congress to declare a standard and to order the colonies to provide none greater. Finding a variety of persons engaged in handling commissarial services, he now complained of the resultant confusion.[17]

2

Those who would carry on great public shemes must be proof against the worst delays, the most mortifying disappointments, the most shocking insults, and what is worst of all the presumptuous judgment of the ignorant upon their design.

—Edmund Burke

Between 18 July and 17 August Schuyler steadily pushed preparations at Ticonderoga for launching an army into Canada. Despite a violent attack of scurvy, he grappled doggedly with a dozen organizational difficulties, gradually creating a system of departmental operation that proved both his abilities as a strategist and his mastery of logistics. Without formal training or even extensive practical military experience beyond his quartermaster service with John Bradstreet in the war of 1754–63, he drew upon his background as landlord and merchant and upon his knowledge of the countryside and his connections with its inhabitants to begin what in fact was the first campaign of the American War of Independence and the major rebel effort of 1775. And he knew that in order to succeed he must not act prematurely and without the means of supporting an army once it had been set in motion. A Connecticut visitor to Albany in late August aptly testified to Schuyler's vigorous efforts to commence the campaign of 1775. Finding the city bustling with preparations, John Pierce noted that the general had had "almost every difficulty to surmount." Schuyler, he said, was "active enough and a sincere lover of the Cause. I hope he may curb the impetuosity of his temper, to the genius of his troops."[18]

Among those difficulties were the assemblage, movement, and placement of troops; the creation of a lake fleet and construction of dozens of bateaux; the repair and building of roads and bridges; and the marshaling of wagons, livestock, and teamsters. While the work went forward Schuyler wisely sought intelligence from Canada and assurances that his northern line of march would not be endangered by attacks on his western flank. Beginning what became an extensive and enduring secret service system, he sent spies and other messengers into Canada to collect news from contacts in the northern province. Convinced of the desirability of obtaining New York and Canadian Indians' pledge of neutrality, if not their support of the rebel cause, Schuyler finally turned to negotiate with Iroquois tribesmen in August. This mission took him back to Albany while Richard Montgomery was left to initiate the army's first movements north from Ticonderoga and Crown Point.

Although critics have wondered at Schuyler's delays in opening the Canadian campaign, the marvel is rather that he succeeded in making the necessary preparations as quickly as he did. Unlike Washington, who found an army at hand when he took command at Cambridge, Schuyler was obliged to wait for his to be assembled. But it must not be forgotten that both men encountered tremendous tasks in creating a military machine and hard work first in setting it in motion and thereafter in maintaining it in running order.

Two parts of Schuyler's initial work in organizing the campaign of 1775 illustrate both the problems of parochialism that he faced and the abilities that he brought to their solution. In his handling of Philip Skene's confiscated property at Whitehall and in his diplomacy with the Green Mountain Boys, seeking to organize an army corps on the New Hampshire Grants, Schuyler revealed not only his true character and considerable talents but also the extent to which they could or could not be reasonably expected to change the circumstances.

Skene, the founder of a settlement now known as Whitehall, New York, was lieutenant governor of Crown Point and Ticonderoga and surveyor of His Majesty's woods near Lake Champlain. Apprised on his arrival at Ticonderoga that a "set of people" acting as a committee of war had seized Skene's estate under pretense of using it for the patriot cause, Schuyler quickly intervened. By whose authority? Schuyler asked—And was it not in fact embezzled? Schuyler demanded that the property be surrendered to Skene's agent, Patrick Langan, insisting that "no disgrace ... be brought on our cause by such lawless proceedings." He ordered a reckoning of the accounts of Skene's property and issued general orders to his entire army that the course of war was as yet defensive; neither persons nor property must be injured any further than was absolutely necessary for the safety and protection of the troops.[19]

Skenesborough was not the only site ravaged by plundering rebels. After capturing Ticonderoga in May, Benedict Arnold's forces had roamed as far north as Saint John's. Claims for eight barrels of flour that they had taken there were filed with Schuyler in August. It was then that one of the victims, Lachlan Mackintosh, appealed to Schuyler for compensation, referring to the Yorker's reputation for generosity and moral rectitude. "Your known Merit & fortune," he wrote, "setts you far superior to sordid Views[;] it gives lustre to the cause of Liberty & secures Individuals in their property. May your health be restored & [may you] long remain an ornament to your Country & a Terror to Evil doers."[20]

While Schuyler dealt scrupulously and evenhandedly with problems like Skene's and Mackintosh's, he also managed to steer a course by which inhabitants of the Hampshire Grants could be encouraged to raise military forces for the Continental cause. Stretching east of Philip Skene's estate, the territory had long been the subject of jurisdictional disputes between New York and New Hampshire. Settlers of Yankee stock, rampageously democratic and also contentious about their land claims, were not only devoted to their own cause of independence but also frequently unwilling to cooperate with one another. Soon to create the state of Vermont, these men were led by Seth Warner and Ethan Allen, and already they had been credited for the seizure of Ticonderoga and Crown Point from the small garrisons of British regulars on 10–12 May. In these circumstances it is not surprising that Schuyler faced difficulties in following Congress's orders to organize a troop of five hundred Green Mountain Boys, especially when the men fell into disputes over the choice of their own leaders.

During a visit to Ticonderoga, Allen and Warner informed Schuyler that men would not serve without popularly elected officers. They also confirmed his suspicions that recruitment of so large a body depended upon enlistments from other parts of New England and that it was not likely to be raised before September.[21]

In mid-July, however, one of their leaders at Bennington, Stephen Fay, reported that some Vermonters were willing to form an independent battalion subject to the regulations of the New York Provincial Congress; but field officers of their own choosing were to be nominated to Schuyler and to the congress for the receipt of their commissions. Soon thereafter, William Marsh of Manchester urged the general to consider carefully the issuance of warrants or commissions to officers for the enlistment of troops. Schuyler replied by posting the directives of both the New York and Continental congresses to Fay.[22]

Alerted by these warnings of disputation, Schuyler turned to Col. Ethan Allen to explain the constraints placed upon him. It did not appear to him that the field officers could be elected by their men, but rather that they must be nominated to the provincial congress.[23] When Allen and Seth Warner visited him at Ticonderoga on 20 July, Schuyler informed them that the Continental Congress would not permit the appointment of all their own officers. But their enlistment of troops continued to be delayed by disputes over the officers, and Schuyler accurately conjectured that because Warner could not raise five hundred men without recruiting many from other parts of New England, the regiment would probably not be assembled for action until September.[24]

On 27 July town committees on the Hampshire Grants chose Seth Warner lieutenant colonel by a vote of forty-one to five. Their list of lesser officers did not include the redoubtable Ethan Allen! If Schuyler was surprised by this notable omission, he was probably also relieved. But immediately he urged the officers to enlist their men without waiting to receive their commissions or the warrants to act from New York's provincial congress.[25]

Meantime, tying loose ends in army formation apparently required attention even to the most minor details. Because remnants of New England militia that had seized Ticonderoga and Crown Point in May continued to loiter at those posts until August, Schuyler finally ordered their discharge unless they had enlisted in some Continental regiment. Again, there were questions of accounting for the proper location of men in particular units.[26]

In mid-August the New York congress finally authorized Schuyler to appoint both a lieutenant colonel and a major for the Green Mountain Boys. Each soldier was promised a green coat with red cloth facings.

Materials were also ordered to make tents for 225 men, which was less than half of the 500 that originally had been designated. Schuyler then furnished Warner the necessary warrants duly made out for six of his captains and twelve lieutenants. Several blanks were also provided with a pledge of £500 credit drawable upon the department commissary. On 23 August he handed Warner orders to march each company of his regiment to Ticonderoga as soon as it was completed and properly enrolled. But he declined to inform Warner of his recent authorization to name the field officers; he felt that the delicacy of the strain between New York and the people of the Hampshire Grants made it necessary for the provincial congress to fill up the warrants for the officers. In sum, internal disputes over the choice of the officers more than dilatoriness in actually commissioning them were responsible for the American army's march northward without the Green Mountain regiment.[27]

Although Schuyler's army began its trek from Crown Point on the last day of August without the Green Mountain Boys, Ethan Allen had appeared to offer his services. Rejected by fellow Yankees as an officer, Allen made no favorable impression upon Brigadier General Montgomery. Schuyler's able lieutenant laconically referred to the *"great General"* and his easy talk "of going a Volunteer." Brash, impulsive, potentially insubordinate, and disruptive, Allen was not particularly welcomed, but evidently Warner and others persuaded the general to accept him as a civilian volunteer on the promise of his good behavior. Within weeks he proved Schuyler's suspicions were anything but ill placed. Exceeding orders from Montgomery that he persuade French and Indians to support the rebel invaders, Allen prematurely attacked Montreal and was captured. His removal was probably more of a benefit to the American ranks and the commanders' interests than it was a positive loss to them all.[28]

3

Paymasters and Physicians

By contrast, Schuyler's association with New Englanders like Gov. Jonathan Trumbull of Connecticut and his son Jonathan Trumbull, Jr., was much happier and wholly free of the Yankee-Yorker animus. The governor readily supported Schuyler's army with manpower, money, provisions, and equipment, and his son proved to be one of the general's trusty subordinates as paymaster for the New York Department.

Establishment of the department paymaster's office was one of a multitude of details that Schuyler faced in organizing his army for the campaign of 1775. Until it began to function the general managed military finances through the commissariat. But the Second Continental Congress almost adjourned for a month's recess on 2 August without adequate appropriations for Schuyler's military chest. However, at the last moment fellow New Yorker James Duane won a motion to deposit $200,000 with the department paymaster; Schuyler was authorized to draw an additional $100,000 if the initial appropriation was expended before Congress reassembled. Duane also proposed young Trumbull as paymaster general because New York congressmen believed that no qualified Yorker would accept the post.[29] In view of Connecticut's contributions to Schuyler's army, it was of course politic to make appointments with some attention to geographical balance as well as to individual qualifications.

Schuyler registered no objection to Trumbull's appointment and soon found the young man to be able and efficient. Always ready to execute the general's orders, Trumbull however was much delayed in discharging his duties in the department. Anticipating his need for direction, Schuyler urged Trumbull to hasten to Albany with as much gold and silver currency as he could get in exchange for Congress's paper dollars.[30]

On 8 September, more than a week after Schuyler's army began its march into Canada, Trumbull finally reached Albany. Some of Montgomery's troops accepted their mission with only a promise of their pay at the end of the campaign. But others, notably New York recruits, proved more reluctant to move without it. The commissary Walter Livingston filed his claim account for salary advances with Trumbull and, informing Schuyler that he needed a fresh warrant to draw funds from the treasurer of Congress or from Trumbull, he offered to fetch more funds from Philadelphia if Schuyler would issue the orders.[31]

As Trumbull traveled north in pursuit of Schuyler's army, he continued to provoke complaints. At Ticonderoga, for example, he exasperated Capt. Nathaniel Buell, who was already worried by artificers' claims for pay, and Buell grumbled to Schuyler that Trumbull had no orders to leave any cash behind as he moved northward. Unless the general issued these, workmen's discouragement could turn into malingering and the service would suffer; others were sickening "and discharging" and wanted money to carry home.[32]

Buell's complaint was probably resolved when Schuyler returned to Ticonderoga on 18 September. There he found Trumbull fallen into "indisposition" and agreed that he might go home to recover his health.

Although Schuyler urged that Trumbull provide a deputy until he was again ready to "attend" the general, the paymaster's business was for a time placed in the hands of the deputy commissary general Walter Livingston. Not until November was Trumbull able to choose a deputy, John Winslow, a man who had been bred to business in Boston. On 23 November Trumbull also filed a report to Schuyler of cash that he had issued after receiving $100,000 at the Continental treasury on 24 August. After three months a balance of only $8,474 remained in the military chest. Most of the $91,526 expended had been issued on Schuyler's warrants to Walter Livingston, although sizable sums totaling $20,444 were paid to General Montgomery and a modest $2,000 had been paid to Dr. Samuel Stringer for medical expenses.[33]

Congress had instituted a paymaster's office for Schuyler's army, but it fell to the general to take the initiative in organizing an equally important division of his department—that of a director of medical services. It was to this post that Schuyler named his personal physician, Dr. Samuel Stringer. Unaware that Congress had already recessed without providing for hospitals and physicians, Schuyler urged their provision, the collection of medicines, and the appointment of a superintendent. But he did not wait for a response before acting upon his own proposal. Trusting that Congress might approve his use of initiative and vote a salary for his appointee, he announced that he was sending a physician to the Ticonderoga garrison where a fifth of the five hundred troops there were sick, their needs too pressing to wait until an appointment could be regularly made. Conscious of the risk of being charged with insubordination, Schuyler carefully added that he would discharge his appointee if Congress failed to approve him.[34]

Congress supported Schuyler's initiative by approving Stringer's appointment as hospital director and chief physician and surgeon on 14 September. Stringer was allotted a salary of $4 per day and authorized to appoint up to four surgeon's mates at a salary of 66⅔¢ a day. Retention of the latter in constant pay, however, would be warranted only by an unspecified number of sick and wounded! Livingston was also authorized to pay Stringer for medicines already purchased for the army and to order more as Schuyler's warrant might direct.[35]

Stringer's activities proved the wisdom of Schuyler's confidence in him. Their work of creating hospital housing, collecting medical supplies and food for patients, and providing personnel for the care of the sick and wounded is illustrative of but another facet of Schuyler's responsibility for managing an army in the field. Such day-to-day activities are reminders that there were "ragged gaps in the pageant" of a "great war waged by a successful nation." The panorama of heroic struggles is not so much full of resplendence as it is of the commonplace.[36]

4

Enterprise and Liberty

Timing for the invasion of Canada in 1775 depended not only upon the collection of an army, provision of its supplies and equipment, and the assurance of a friendly or neutral reception by northerners, but also upon arrangements of transportation. Once forces were assembled on Lake Champlain—a feat requiring movement over land and water some hundred miles north of Albany—a sizable fleet was needed to ferry men down the lake to Isle aux Noix and then along the Richelieu or Sorel River to Saint John's and Chambly, which lay almost due east of Montreal. Between the time Schuyler arrived at Ticonderoga on 18 July and the end of August, when his army was nearly ready to move, he had enlarged the size of his fleet dramatically. By the end of July the number of vessels constructed had risen from about ten to thirty, and their capacity for carrying only 200 men increased to a capability of accommodating 550. During the following month the number more than doubled, making it possible to move 1,300 troops with a three-weeks' supply of provisions. Most of the craft were bateaux, primarily of French design, which were rugged "double-ended" boats about thirty feet long, with a cargo capacity of three to seven tons. They could be fitted with sail but were usually paddled by an eight-man crew.[37]

Concentrating the boat-building work on Lake George, Schuyler ordered the construction of dozens of bateaux and larger vessels more suitable for naval warfare. By the end of July one boat capable of carrying about 300 men was on the stocks and a second was ready to go up. Even so, intelligence gleaned from Saint John's led Schuyler to expect that British naval power would outstrip his own and prevent his army from approaching that fort on the Richelieu River. With more carpenters and materials, he might be able to equal the enemy's naval force, but as of early August he feared that the want of ammunition would prevent the Americans from gaining the advantage.[38]

Naval construction required vast quantities of lumber, nails, pitch, and oakum, not to mention the millhands and carpenters to perform the labor. Despite shortages of men and material, Schuyler bent every effort to create a small flotilla. In addition to a sloop and a schooner that were already available on Lake Champlain, he was offered a number of boats and a "beautiful cutter" with a thirty-foot keel by William Gilliland of Willsboro. Gilliland's mills on the western shore had already furnished about five thousand feet of boards and plank for Schuyler's little navy, and he promised that he had enough pine logs to supply another ten to fifteen thousand board feet of lumber.[39]

Meanwhile the sloop *Enterprise,* captained first by John Halsey and subsequently by Maj. "Commodore" James Smith, and the *Liberty,* a schooner commanded by James Stewart, were employed in exploring the lake and seeking information about the strength of enemy positions in the north.[40] By 27 July Schuyler had the reports of the *Liberty's* findings at the north end of Lake Champlain. It appeared that the Canadians would either support an invading army or remain neutral. The fort at Saint John's was garrisoned by about 450 regulars, and British scouts were ranging southward to within thirty-five miles of Ticonderoga. Both sides were probing each other's lines. As other reports confirmed the news from the *Liberty,* Schuyler thought it was time to move on Saint John's to test the Canadians' response. But how to get there? he asked. For the moment there were only enough bateaux to carry about half the army across Lake Champlain, and Schuyler was not ready to move his troops without adequate stores. He could only promise to "make all the dispatch I possibly can, and move the moment I am in a condition for it."[41]

Properly cautious, Schuyler endeavored to follow Congress's directives to launch the invasion only if assured of favorable Canadian sentiment. He also had to be satisfied that his manpower, provisions, and transportation were adequate to begin it. Accordingly, while pressing for these preparations, he again ordered the *Liberty* to cruise toward Isle la Motte, Windmill Point, and Pointe au Fer.[42]

As the sloop and schooner prowled Lake Champlain gathering intelligence, the carpenters slowly expanded his little fleet of bateaux and Schuyler groped for a decision about when to move his small army out of Ticonderoga. Between 2 and 6 August he notified John Hancock and Washington that he would be ready to act only if Congress or the commander in chief did not stop the invasion. They might judge the propriety of a decision to begin it by considering the latest intelligence brought from Saint John's. Governor Carleton's resistance to an invasion might prevent approach by water to Saint John's, but it would not be insurmountable. Canadians seemed disposed to neutrality. Three armed schooners were lying off Sorel in the Saint Lawrence River. Col. Guy Johnson and Col. Daniel Claus had brought about five hundred Indians to Montreal and Lachine, and there were reports that others would come up the lake country to fight the colonists when the regulars were ready to engage them.[43]

In the face of his own army's limitations and the reports of Carleton's naval strength, which seemed capable of preventing movement down the Richelieu River to Saint John's, Schuyler was understandably reluctant to move. Although by early August the Yorker was heartened by the speedier flow of provisions to Ticonderoga and the progress made in boat construction, the time to strike must be considered with due regard to shortages of ammunition and to the sickness of almost a fifth of his five hundred-man army. His forces were at best a barely even match for the Saint John's garrison, which also held an advantage in having more artillery. Partly on the strength of Maj. John Brown's 23 August report and recommendation of speedy action to secure command of the lake, Richard Montgomery decided to take the fateful step.[44]

Montgomery, however, did not choose to move until 28 August. When he did so he acted according to Schuyler's own inclinations, confident that his chief trusted him to exercise his own best judgment and initiative. There is no evidence that Montgomery had grown impatient with Schuyler's delays or that he overreached his superior's commands, much less violated his wishes to open the campaign. Their association was perfectly harmonious. In Schuyler's absence from Ticonderoga, necessitated by a conference of Indian commissioners of the Northern Department with Iroquois tribesmen at Albany, Montgomery was bound by no orders to stand fast. What Schuyler could not determine by reason of his distance from the field, Montgomery was free to decide. While the former endeavored to safeguard the northern line of action by forestalling possible Anglo-Indian attacks in the west, the latter could be trusted to decide when the army might best commence the assault upon Canada.

5

The Labors of a Hercules

Montgomery's decision to move the army from Ticonderoga toward Canada was taken only seven weeks after Schuyler's return to Albany on 9 July. Within six weeks of his arrival at Ticonderoga, about twenty-four hundred men were finally assembled along the lake posts; at least half of these, however, were held as reserves and garrisons of the forts while Montgomery led the others north to the Richelieu valley.

Assembling that modest army at Ticonderoga, the initial positioning of various units and the inauguration of a reliable supply system at scattered stations west and north of Albany were neither easily nor suddenly accomplished. Moreover these tasks were complicated by the variety of officials and government agencies with which Schuyler was obliged to deal. Governor Jonathan Trumbull of Connecticut provided considerable support, and Schuyler valued the willingness of his able Yankee neighbor to help him.[45] The commander in chief and the Continental congress were of course distant supporters but also limited by other responsibilities for matters beyond Schuyler's immediate command. Closer at hand were local committees of safety at Albany and Schenectady, the New York provincial congress, and of course Brigadier General Montgomery, the post commanders, and the department's deputy commissary general, Walter Livingston.

The collection of troops proceeded at so slow a pace that it is a wonder that enough men were on hand by late August to begin the invasion of Canada. Indeed, by 26 July Schuyler assured President Hancock and Congress that despite indications of the need for the army to seize the offense, he was chagrined that he dare not move toward Saint John's without enough manpower. Nor did he have enough boats to carry them and their supplies. Tardiness in raising New York levies was hindering even the maintenance of four necessary military posts. Nor could he expect further reinforcements, he was told, in less than a month. Besides garrisons at Ticonderoga, Crown Point, the Landing at Lake George, and Fort George, there were others at Skenesborough, Schenectady, and Albany to be manned. Were the enemy to move south from Canada, the consequences at Ticonderoga, Schuyler warned, would be "easier conceived than described." The tardiness in raising New York levies was so embarrassing that he urged the Albany committee to encourage recruitment lest other colonies or counties outstrip them in the effort.[46]

By the end of July, Schuyler was expecting the arrival of a thousand Connecticut reinforcements who had been pried from David Wooster's command on the lower Hudson. He continued to plead with the New York congress for the stores he had requested of them three weeks earlier. About the same time Washington offered the Yorker a few more Yankee troops, but with a disquieting warning. Although Schuyler might order three New Hampshire companies to join his command, he must accept the units and their own officers (Timothy Bedel, James Osgood, and John Parker) as non-Continentals. The commander in chief would neither agree to the New Hampshire congress's requests that the three companies be made Continentals nor approve their location at several frontier posts along the Connecticut River between New Hampshire and Connecticut. But he wanted Schuyler's troop returns.

Troop returns—the rosters of officers and enlisted men—proved to be not only difficult to compile with accuracy but also a challenge to keep current. Ultimately, a muster-master general could be expected to discharge this business, but Schuyler did not wait for the arrival of Gunning Bedford, who had been named to the office. One of his first efforts as a department commander had been to establish a system of regular report-ing. Periodically and repeatedly he issued orders for the proper submis-sion of information.[47]

When Brigadier General Montgomery reported from his camp at Half-moon, north of Albany, on 5 August, he was unable to give Schuyler a proper return of the Connecticut forces there. At best estimate there were 850. At this time some of New York's second battalion, still in the process of recruitment, were moving forward although they lacked all kinds of accoutrements, including camp kettles. Col. David Waterbury's regiment, which had finally arrived from Manhattan, would be sent in two divisions to Skenesborough, the first moving on 7 August and the second following on 10 August. Intending to accompany the rear, Montgomery was invited by the Schuylers to bring his wife and "Miss Caty," her companion, to Saratoga. Upon her return from Ticonderoga Mrs. Schuyler wished to offer the ladies the hospitality of her country house.[48]

The routing of men through Skenesborough and thence by water to Ticonderoga suggests that alternative approaches to Lake George from Saratoga were not yet so easy to follow. A party assigned to repair the road between Fort Edward and Fort George had been diverted to the work of carrying provisions across Lake George for the Lake Champlain forts; consequently little had been done to facilitate the movement of men and baggage wagons by land. But pressing to inaugurate the invasion of Canada, Schuyler was quick to summon every available unit to his side.[49]

Bit by bit Schuyler's army grew and with it myriad orders for the movement of supplies and service personnel: hospital stores, boards, plank and nails for boat building, surgeons, carpenters, oarmakers, and wagoners. The scarcity of manpower and some commodities were matched by a surfeit of other articles. Distressed by the difficulties of equipping the men, he remained unable to execute Congress's directives for the campaign without the necessary equipment. Similarly he urged provincial authorities to fill Congress's orders for an adjutant general or brigade major. An active disciplinarian must be chosen, and he also wanted a competent commander of artillery.[50]

Struggling against time and a variety of inadequacies, the general no sooner found the solution to one difficulty, or a partial alleviation of it, than another appeared. The succession of these seemed unending. Al-though the Albany committee succeeded in engaging a master carpenter and nine workmen for him on 18 July, six days later Schuyler grew im-patient when the craftsmen failed to appear at Ticonderoga. Moreover, he wanted twenty more and an overseer who was a knowledgeable boatbuilder.[51]

While awaiting the arrival of Congress's appointee, Donald Campbell, Schuyler meticulously worked as his own quartermaster, tirelessly supervising practically every detail of that vast service. Included were directions for the movement and recovery of livestock.[52] Lacking for a time a deputy quartermaster general for his department and then finding that the appointees who were named to the office required constant supervision, Schuyler was relieved to have the services of his able nephew-in-law Walter Livingston as deputy commissary general of stores and provisions. Livingston also functioned initially as the department paymaster. His marriage to the general's niece Cornelia afforded the kind of easy intimacy that suited Schuyler. And it provided a convenient connection to one of the province's great families. A son of the third lord of Livingston Manor, Walter could draw upon his own family's connections for a variety of assistance. From them as well as Schuyler's coterie of friends in the merchant-gentry community, men like Jacob Cuyler and John N. Bleecker, and from relations like the general's brother-in-law, Henry Van Rensselaer, he found both assistants and the contacts necessary for collecting provisions and other supplies needed by the army.

Livingston's first assignment had been to collect funds in Connecticut and to order a supply of cattle. By 17 July he had collected £20,000 in "York money" and a promise that within a few days a herd of sixty cattle would be brought to Albany. It was principally there that Livingston expected to execute the general's orders and to coordinate the collection and movement of provisions and other supplies.[53]

Although Livingston had general oversight of a variety of business, Schuyler found it difficult to limit his orders for supplies to a single channel like the deputy commissary general. And in the course of the summer of 1775 there were particular problems in establishing proper lines of jurisdiction between commissary officers of the department. Most notable was the question of Elisha Phelps's subordination to Livingston and Phelps's relation to other deputies Livingston needed to discharge his responsibilities at various outposts in the department.

Phelps, appointed commissary for Connecticut troops by Governor Trumbull and for Massachusetts soldiers by the bay colony's provincial congress, had begun functions well before Livingston was commissioned as the department officer on 17 July. But as soon as Livingston learned of his official appointment, he sought Schuyler's advice about organizing his operations. Should he assign deputies to function at Ticonderoga, Albany, and New York City? And at what wages?[54] Pleased to have succeeded in having his kinsman appointed, Schuyler simply ordered Livingston to take charge of the department. Almost immediately he was at loggerheads with Elisha Phelps.

Schuyler rightly assumed that Phelps must continue to serve; from him Livingston could obtain information respecting contacts in Connecticut and accounts of the stores he had already handled. Schuyler thought that Phelps should be posted to Fort George, and he approved Livingston's suggestion that Jacob Cuyler and John N. Bleecker be made his assistants. As members of the Albany merchant-gentry community these men had more than personal talents to offer; they could be expected to use their valuable connections with a network of suppliers of provisions. The general also expected Livingston to oversee the shipment of stores from the deputy quartermaster general Campbell at New York City. And he further insisted that Phelps must account for all persons he had hitherto employed in order that proper payments could be made when Continental funds were issued.[55]

Livingston's altercation with Elisha Phelps over their respective positions in the commissariat not only revealed a curious difference in personalities but also illustrated how intercolonial tension affected the war effort. More important, it tested both Schuyler's ability to establish a workable supply system for his department and his capacity for managing the officers of his army. When Livingston showed Phelps his commission as the department's deputy commissary general, Phelps argued that his own commissions from the governor of Connecticut and the Massachusetts provincial congress made him commissary "at Albany and Places adjacent" and that consequently Livingston must be his deputy! Phelps was determined to continue his operations as before and to write Governor Trumbull for advice, but both men appealed to Schuyler.[56]

Convinced that his commission from the Continental Congress entitled him to head the entire departmental commissariat, Livingston allowed that Phelps's commission together with a congressional resolution entitled him to manage the forwarding of provisions from Albany. But Livingston wanted John N. Bleecker to assist him in Albany, Jacob Cuyler at Fort George, and some other assistant at Ticonderoga. The general, however, proposed that Phelps take the Fort George post, which was a fortuitous suggestion because Cuyler proved unable to serve there.[57]

Phelps assured Schuyler that the volume of work confronting Livingston and himself was so great that there need be no difficulty in dividing it between them; yet the general's nephew seemed to insist that he must have all of it or none. Phelps refused to abandon his post because no faithful soldier could do so before he was properly "superseded or regularly dismissed." And his interpretation of both his own commission and Livingston's was that Livingston should purchase and deliver supplies to Phelps as commissary of issues. Phelps announced that he would refer his case to the Continental Congress, the congress of Massachusetts, and the governor and congress of Connecticut.

Schuyler responded by issuing orders to Phelps on 30 July and then a letter on 31 July. The Yorker's interpretation of the rivals' commissions emphasized that Congress had made Livingston "D[eputy] Commissary *General*"—never mind the distinction that Phelps had drawn between "commissary" and "deputy." Therefore "[t]he whole of the Commissary business in every branch thereof is under his immediate controul and direction," and Phelps and all others "employed in it are to obey such orders as he shall give and to be moved to such places as he shall think best for the service." Schuyler told Phelps that he seemed "to be little acquainted with Military Distinctions, not to know that a Deputy Commissary-*General's* commission supercedes a meer Commissary's." The commanding general must have "only one Person to apply to, to furnish him" with provisions and supplies, "and that Person must then be accountable." Also, although a deputy quartermaster general was to forward all stores, Schuyler wanted Livingston to supervise this work until such an officer appeared. Assuring Phelps that he could continue in the service, Schuyler announced that he had no wish to discharge anyone who performed necessary services "from whatever Colony he may be, for I make no Discrimination of Persons." However, if Phelps failed to obey Schuyler's orders, he "must answer for It."[58]

Thinking he had settled the business, Schuyler sent Livingston a copy of his orders to Phelps. But there was another dimension to the problem that caused Schuyler additional trouble. This was Phelps's introduction of Jedediah Strong of Litchfield, who had been appointed commissary of the Fourth Connecticut Regiment before Congress had made other commissary appointments. In mid-July Phelps sent Strong to the northern forts with stores and livestock, advising him to consult Schuyler about complaints of both shortages and waste of provisions. Phelps also requested that the general appoint a local overseer in the north who would be able to satisfy Connecticut authorities of proper management of the commissariat for their troops. And finally Phelps had commissioned one Josiah Norton to handle provisions at the Landing between Lake George and Ticonderoga. In writing Schuyler to explain his position as regimental commissary of the Connecticut troops, Strong complained that Walter Livingston "professes a Design to discharge" Phelps and his Connecticut assistants. He begged Schuyler not to permit this to occur because Phelps had already established a workable system of supply; and appealing to Schuyler's reputation for candor, justice, and generosity, he asked that the general remove all jealousies tending to alienate any colony's affections to the patriot cause. Strong, however, went too far in displaying his own candor. "God forbid," he wrote, "that any overgrown Colony or over-bearing Man should at this critical Juncture use such pernicious Partiality as to attempt to monopolize every Emolument & enslave any Instrument of publick Service for no other Accusation or Complaint than that he belongs to the most patriotic free & generous Colony on Earth." Here was an accusation that Yorkers were hogging the enterprise of supplying the army and depriving Yankees of an opportunity to share the profits; mention of an "overgrown Colony" reflected New Englanders' long-standing dispute over New York's eastern boundary claims against Massachusetts and to the Hampshire Grants.[59]

Schuyler promptly retorted that if Livingston had employed men to buy Connecticut livestock with Connecticut funds, it was nevertheless by the Continental Congress (in which Connecticut was represented) that he had been commissioned. Moreover such purchases were made at the joint expense of all the colonies and according to Congress's assignment of quotas to them. What did Strong mean by "monopolizing every emolument?" Schuyler insisted that he had done no such thing, for Congress was responsible for appointments, and he would refer Strong's letter to that body. No commissary would be dismissed provided he was necessary and adequate to the service. Captain Phelps was clearly both and would be assigned to Fort George. Schuyler assured Strong that he had high regard for the virtue and patriotism of Connecticut. But "what you intend by using the Epithet 'overgrown' is best known to Yourself," he snapped; "my Construction of it is not very favorable to You." Agreeing, however that causes of jealousy in the army and between provinces must be removed, Schuyler noted that none should prevail between "any Colonies, *overgrown* or not." Unaware that he was responsible for any such difficulty, Schuyler suggested that "If I have [been], I wish you would complain of me to the Congress. If not, you might have spared the observation."[60]

More than five months later Strong found occasion to apologize most abjectly when Phelps's accounts were referred to Congress. For the moment, however, as far as Schuyler was concerned, the question of jurisdiction was closed and the preparations for supplying the army for its invasion of Canada were clearly in Livingston's hands. Although Phelps was not finally persuaded to submit to Schuyler until October, the commissariat seems not to have suffered beyond some question of the Yankee's overcharges of almost £1,200 in his accounts. These led to accusations that Schuyler was negligent in refusing to pay them and to Schuyler's rebuke to Phelps: "You are then, Sir, a most wretched calculator" and "incompetent to the charge that was conferred on you." Schuyler's work to supply his army was so repeatedly plagued by personal altercations that it is a wonder that his system of provisioning the army worked at all. But it is notable that even after Schuyler lost his command, the fruits of his efforts from 1775 to 1777 "remained and made possible the victory which changed the entire course of the Revolution."[61]

Meantime, in 1775 Schuyler's army required provisions to enable it to begin the march into Canada. Livingston proceeded with his duties in August as best he could. The work of the commissariat was arduous. Herds of cattle were driven from Connecticut to Albany and Fort George. Flour had to be stocked and shipped, and wheat purchased for milling. In early August, however, Livingston found flour to be so scarce in the Albany environs that he feared he would be unable to supply any but Col. David Waterbury's regiment. Hoping to obtain five hundred barrels of it from New York City, he also ordered five hundred barrels of pork, which was both scarce and much in demand. "Don't forget Molasses & Rum," Schuyler wrote Livingston on 1 August, for "I cannot get the People here to do any thing without these Articles." Sweetening tempers and inspiriting sluggards were obviously as important as filling bellies or clothing and arming the troops.[62]

In attempting to collect provisions Livingston ranged far and wide purchasing cattle, flour, and pork wherever he could find them and in quantities however small. In addition Schuyler pressed him for miscellaneous articles such as nails, paper, lime juice, raisins, and brandy. Between August 1775 and October 1776 Livingston's disbursements for food alone totaled more than £47,000, most of which passed through the hands of Philip and Henry J. Van Rensselaer, Leonard Van Buren, and Teunis Van Vechten.[63]

The nature and extent of Schuyler's commissariat operations may be further illustrated by John N. Bleecker's reports to the general on 5 and 10 August. Between 26 May and 3 August the Crown Point garrison had received 172 barrels of flour and 221 of pork. After issues to the troops and loans to neighboring inhabitants had been made, only 27 barrels of flour and 155 of pork remained in stock. In two months' time four hundred persons had consumed 145 barrels of flour and 66 of pork, not to mention various quantities of fresh beef, peas, and rice. At Fort George, which Bleecker inspected along with Ticonderoga, commissariat business had been passed through so many different hands that Bleecker could find no regular entries for receipts and issues. With news that an additional

twenty wagonloads of flour were then en route to Fort George, it appeared that the train of foodstuff was well under way. Between 6 and 16 August Walter Livingston was able to announce that he expected to be able to supply the garrisons with enough flour and plenty of cattle. By 10 August the deputy commissary general's only anxiety about obtaining more meat stemmed from the fact that Schuyler needed it in order to signal the start of the invasion of Canada.[64]

As the time approached for launching the army northward in August 1775, it is apparent that however limited its manpower, its stores of powder and lead were ample. And because Schuyler lacked artillery officers he found little prospect for using many cannon. For almost two months the work of assembling troops, supplies, and bateaux had proceeded slowly but steadily. Painstaking in his preparation, he has been wrongly accused of "a strange and almost fatal patience" and his caution attributed to "his Dutch blood perhaps" or the result of a "patrician habit to order and not to do" or of "his lack of physical stamina."[65] In fact he was often impatient. Untiring in both ordering and doing the work of a departmental commander, he did not lack the stamina to prepare the campaign or to lead it until after he had joined the army north of Lake Champlain. Wisely, he refused to rush into a campaign with inadequate manpower, equipment, provisions, or means of transportation. Admitting inadequacies, the Yorker later vowed to "atone for [them] by assiduity," and this he most surely did as he labored to promote the rebel cause, sometimes even from a sickroom.[66]

Like the most energetic and able commanders, Schuyler encountered circumstances beyond his control or power to alter. However it was he who collected the army that Richard Montgomery led into Canada. It was Schuyler who had had to create, organize, and supply it, an accomplishment that none could have done more quickly or better. He knew, as few others did, the countryside in which the work had to be done, and he employed both the advantage of his connections and his considerable energies and talents unreservedly. It is difficult to imagine that anyone could have excelled him either in abilities for the task or in actual achievement. Silas Deane of Connecticut sympathetically observed that the general was not properly supplied and supported "from below."[67]

After two months of work Schuyler's department contained about 2,500 men present and fit for duty; a regiment of 500 Green Mountain Boys proved to be more of a promise than a reality. The troops were scattered between Manhattan and Lake Champlain, and not all could be sent crashing into Canada because of the need to garrison a variety of posts along the routes of march and supply. Between 17 and 21 July the garrisons included about 1,200 men divided among Fort George (334), the Landing at the north end of Lake George (102), Ticonderoga (335), and Crown Point (412).[68]

New York's enlistment of four regiments was tardy, and because of the difficulty in procuring arms the provincial congress could not immediately equip them all or rush them forward. On 8 August only four companies of Col. Alexander McDougall's regiment were finally able to leave New York City for Albany. Led by Lt. Col. Rudolphus Ritzema, they set out in the van of Col. James Clinton's regiment, which though completed remained largely unarmed. Ritzema's contingent reached Albany by 10 August, but not until eight days later did it arrive at Saratoga. Schuyler found that their movement was impeded by excess baggage, enough he said for three regiments instead of one. Already fourteen men had deserted, and expecting more to follow, Schuyler thought that "if those gone, are like some that remain, we have gained by their going off."[69]

Another regiment of New York Continentals, the first, commanded by Col. Goose Van Schaick, long remained uncompleted and scattered, and when Schuyler summoned them to Ticonderoga on 15 August he provided for an officer of each company to tarry in Albany to fill their ranks and then march the recruits to the lake. Van Schaick's reports of delay were but one example of the widespread difficulties Schuyler had in forming his army.[70]

Not until near the end of August did James Clinton reach Albany with six of his companies, and even then only half of these had serviceable weapons; one had none, and "two had guns needing repairs." By 29 August Lt. Col. Philip Van Cortlandt brought five more companies of the Fourth New York Regiment to Albany, but they lacked clothing, blankets, and weapons; indeed, only one of the companies had been even partly armed. Not until 22 August did the first New York units under Lieutenant Colonel Ritzema reach Ticonderoga. Yet Schuyler had been urging Ritzema's haste as early as 22 July when he asked General Montgomery to push troops up from Albany. Moreover, Brig. Gen. David Wooster's thousand men from New York City moved slowly at best. Led by Col. David Waterbury, the first four companies did not reach Albany until 27 July; they were obliged to delay their march to Ticonderoga while adequate supplies could be stocked and necessary road work was completed between Halfmoon, Fort Edward, and Fort George. The operation of an orderly transportation system for troops and baggage wagons moving from Skenesborough and Lake George required continued improvement of roads as well as arranging a relay system for the movement of bateaux. But by 12 August Waterbury and the advance party of his regiment had reached Ticonderoga, having traversed the waters of Lake Champlain from Skenesborough by boats. This last segment of their journey was but a day's effort after almost two weeks of trudging overland from Albany.[71]

Schuyler drew other troops into Ticonderoga from neighboring posts and from greater distances. Col. James Easton (who had helped capture the fort in May) was summoned to return with his Massachusetts regiment on 13 August. Commanded by Col. Timothy Bedel, three companies of New Hampshire rangers would join the march to Saint John's, but it was not until 19 August that General Montgomery sent orders to Bedel to hasten to the mouth of the Onion River. Thus despite his best efforts to move quickly Schuyler found the collection of an army remained time-consuming; both delays and the effectiveness of forces deficient in arms and constantly in need of provisions nagged his anxiety. The army embarked by Montgomery from Ticonderoga on 28 August was only about twelve hundred strong. A similar number remained behind.[72]

6

Thoniyoudakayon

In Schuyler's absence from Ticonderoga Montgomery did nothing but execute a plan for which Schuyler had made careful preparations. Called to Albany to confer with Iroquois tribesmen, the Yorker was on the verge of leading the army north toward Saint John's two weeks before Montgomery actually did so.[73] Although he left Montgomery with the initiative to proceed and hurried to Albany, the army inched forward only as far as Crown Point. By 31 August, when Montgomery again set the troops in motion, Schuyler returned to Ticonderoga in hot pursuit of his forces.

Schuyler's presidency of the Northern Department's board of Indian commissioners obliged him to exercise responsibilities larger than those of a field commander. Congress had wisely combined both in a single individual. Deciding that negotiations with Iroquois tribesmen demanded his presence at Albany during the period from 23 to 27 August, Schuyler relied upon Montgomery's discretion to manage the army while he and his fellow commissioners dealt with the Indians. Long acquainted with the Six Nations, he recognized that his forces could not safely move north or west of Albany without establishing an Iroquois alliance or at least a pledge of their neutrality.

The Continental Congress's organization of Indian departments emerged from the necessity of countering British influence on the various tribes.[74] In New York that influence had been rooted in the career of Sir William Johnson, whose tribal dealings and vast estate were headquartered at Johnson Hall (Johnstown) in the Mohawk valley. After Johnson's death, his nephew and son-in-law Guy Johnson became Indian superintendent, and Sir William's deputy for Canada, Daniel Claus, another son-in-law, served Guy as an assistant.

Congress decided to seek Indian neutrality, a policy that was to remain unchanged for a year. Only if British officials induced Indian hostilities were the colonists to seek alliances with various tribes. Through Schuyler's arrangements the Reverend Samuel Kirkland, a missionary to the Iroquois, principally to the Oneida and Tuscarora, testified to Congress on the means and methods of dealing with the tribes. On 12 July Congress created three geographical departments, northern, middle, and southern, for the management of the business. The Northern Department would deal with the Iroquois and "all to the Northward and Eastward of them;" the Southern Department covered the Cherokee and tribes southward, while the Middle Department managed those in between. Each department was given a commission to conduct negotiations and empowered to seize royal officials who attempted to turn the natives against the colonists.[75]

Placed at the head of the Northern Department's commissioners, Schuyler was joined by Joseph Hawley, Turbutt Francis, Oliver Wolcott and Volkert P. Douw. Douw, like Schuyler, was an Albanian, and both he and Timothy Edwards, who replaced Hawley when illness prompted him to decline the post, were merchants. Edwards lived at Stockbridge, Massachusetts. Francis, who was from Philadelphia, like Wolcott of Litchfield, Connecticut, was interested in the Susquehanna Company's claims to territory along the borders of New York and Pennsylvania.[76]

After he received notification of his appointment Schuyler promptly called upon Volkert Douw and the Albany committee to summon the Indians to a conference. Because he was then at Ticonderoga (on 26 July) he was forced to rely upon his Albany associates to establish a date for the parley and to prepare the necessary provisions and accommodations for the conferees. Insisting that no time must be lost, he instructed Douw to apply to Walter Livingston for funds to pay messengers to the tribes and to notify the other commissioners of the conference date.[77]

It was at the end of July as these orders were given that an Indian scare in the Mohawk valley was also ended. Sir William Johnson's heir, Sir John Johnson, apparently agreed to take no action against the patriots, but whether he could be relied upon not to rouse Loyalist retainers and Indian friends again was questionable. Although reports that Schuyler had received from Canada suggested that Governor Carleton would not be able (or willing) to incite the Indians to war and that "the Canadians [were] averse to enter into the controversy, the noblesse and very lower order excepted," he knew that there could be no substitute for a general conference with the tribes. Nor dare he relax a constant surveillance of them or continual probes for intelligence into Canada. Moreover, the general expected that much of the Indian commissioners' work must be entrusted to the Albany committee.[78]

Like the preparations for the army itself, the Indian conference was considerably delayed. The commissioners needed time to assembly at Albany and to collect a variety of gifts for the Iroquois.[79] Although the members of the Albany committee did not deem themselves competent to conduct the Indian commissioners' work, their chairman, Abraham Yates, Jr., promised Schuyler their aid. Accordingly they issued Samuel Kirkland a pass to carry messages to the Oneida and served as a clearinghouse for the general's exchanges with the commissioners. Others, too, volunteered services. From Dartmouth College Eleazar Wheelock wrote Schuyler to recommend a young student as Indian interpreter. James Dean had learned the Iroquois tongues and customs and had proved to be prudent, faithful, honest, and well esteemed by the Six Nations.[80] Indeed, Dean proved to be more than a match for the task that the commissioners gave him to perform among the tribes.

Meantime at Ticonderoga Schuyler chafed at the lack of evidence that arrangements for the Indian conference had been made. Not until 10 August were commissioners Douw and Francis able to write him that they were at last ready to journey west of Albany and send messengers to the New York and Canadian tribes. They were the only members of the commission present and able to function. Already they had consulted some of the Iroquois who were in Albany and learned that they welcomed the proposal of a conference.[81]

But Douw and Francis's proposal for a conference at Ticonderoga was scotched when Schuyler indicated that his invitations to Canadian tribesmen had failed because his messengers had been intercepted. Writing from Ticonderoga on 14 August, he urged Douw and Francis to hasten their messages to the Caughnawaga and other Canadian tribes. Speed was important, he said, because he intended soon to begin the army's move upon Saint John's, which was a plan they must keep secret. Various reports had tended to assure him that the Canadian Indians were friendly.[82]

Schuyler would have been cheered had he known that Governor Guy Carleton had rejected the urgings of Guy Johnson and Daniel Claus to rouse the Indians against the New England and New York frontiers. Carleton's instructions were to avoid this, and his strategy was to prepare to block the Americans at Chambly and Saint John's and then to regain Crown Point and Ticonderoga. Schuyler would also have been comforted to know the exact extent of Carleton's military restraints. With other forces drawn from Canada to Boston, and only unreliable militia to guard much of the countryside, the governor had concentrated his strength at Saint John's. When the American army finally reached Saint John's on 17 September, Carleton had no more than seven hundred regulars to defend the entire province.[83]

Arriving at Saratoga on 18 August the general found Mrs. Schuyler still dangerously ill with perhaps some malady associated with her pregnancy of some five months' standing. But on the next day the crisis had passed. Intending to return to Ticonderoga on Sunday, 20 August, where he expected to open the assault on Canada, the general delayed on Monday and then turned instead toward Albany.[84] Relieved that commissioners Douw and Francis had finally initiated steps for holding the treaty, he may have decided that he should use his own ability to impress the tribes. His reputation with them was high; and the Albany committeemen had declined to share their work beyond providing incidental assistance. Perhaps he was not wholly confident of his colleagues' competence to deal with the Iroquois, and his proximity to Albany now made it more convenient to ride south than north. Also, General Montgomery could be trusted with the Ticonderoga forces, and perhaps it was news that the Indians expected Schuyler's personal attention that finally prompted his visit to Albany.

Douw and Francis had opened the Indian commission's proceedings halfway up the Mohawk valley at German Flats on 15 August. This, however, served to assure the Iroquois of Americans' pacific intentions and to invite them to assemble at Albany, where the commissioners continued their sessions from 23 August to 1 September. By then messengers had spread word of the conference, and tribesmen—mostly Oneida, Tuscarora and Mohawk—trekked into the city, although about eighty Oneida had arrived as early as 18 August, asking for aid. With the Reverend Samuel Kirkland and young James Dean as their interpreters, and Tench Tilghman as secretary, Douw and Francis welcomed Schuyler on 23 August. The Albany committee and other gentlemen of the city joined them in greeting the conferees at 5:00 that afternoon. By next day Oliver Wolcott was also on hand for the first confrontation with the sachems at Cartwright's Tavern. There were smokes and drinks all around, and the Indians danced with what one Yankee visitor thought was hideous noise.

Even preliminaries for the conference were time-consuming, but the council fire was kindled on 25 August behind the old Dutch church.[85]

The sachems' spokesmen approved the colonists' desire for peace, indicating that their own union with allied tribes to the west and with the Caughnawaga was designed for the same end. They hoped that neither the Americans nor the British would close the trading area of Fort Stanwix and that both sides would confine their struggles to the east. Fearing that the British might capture Kirkland, they asked that he be withdrawn from the frontier. Following a round of the peace pipe, the commissioners rehearsed the terms of old treaties and the interests of the Continental Congress, carefully referring to Schuyler as a descendant of the Indians' seventeenth-century friend, Queder (his grandfather's brother Peter). After the general left the conference, the sachems requested that he be appointed as watchman for the council fire and tree of peace; nor did they forget to stress the importance of maintaining the long-standing links with Dutch traders from Albany and Schenectady. Those, too, had been a part of Schuyler's family heritage.

Like Quedor the general had learned how to deal with the natives of New York, and he had earned a reputation for honesty and fairness in his relations with them. The Mohawk had also given him the name Thoniyoudakayon, the meaning of which remains something of a puzzle. James Dean's *T* transcription may have been an attempt at tho'nikonhraká:'on, or "his mind is old." If so, the Mohawk assessment of Schuyler as a wise man accords very well with the judgments of others like the Marquis de Chastellux, who later noted, "He knows well what he is speaking of, and speaks well about what he knows."[86]

On 26 August, Schuyler's last day at the conference, the commissioners delivered the address that Congress had sent to the general on 18 July. Although "much altered by the Commissioners," the essential message it conveyed was a call for Indian neutrality. The king had broken a covenant, and the colonists' dispute was with the king's counselors who were accused of slipping their hands into Americans' pockets without their consent. The king's soldiers must now be driven away, but the Indians should refrain from joining either side. Yet there was a closing warning: If the British seized American property, they would do the same to the Iroquois; let them so inform their allies.[87]

The conference was recessed for the following day, which was Sunday. Before beginning his long ride to rejoin his army in the field Schuyler piously attended "the Dutch church and desired the Prayers of the Congregation for himself and the Army under his Command which he received." Leonard Gansevoort wrote his brother Peter, "I sincerely lament that you was [*sic*] not present that you might have heard it." Dominie Eilardus Westerlo's prayer was "so very pathetic and so well adapted that he drew Tears from the Eyes of almost all there present."[88]

As Schuyler hastened north to Ticonderoga, General Montgomery began to move the army to Crown Point, and the Indian commissioners pursued their work with the conferees for four more days. Their exchanges were lengthy and repetitious—a style that was of course in keeping with an oral tradition that depended much on memory. The sachems were told again of the colonists' unity and their desire for a free intercourse with neutral tribes. The Mohawk leader, Abraham, insisted that Col. Guy Johnson at a conference at Oswego had also asked for neutrality and that such promises must be scrupulously kept. While requesting that John Stuart, the Anglican missionary to the Mohawks at Fort Hunter, be left unmolested, Abraham also reproached Albanians for their landgrabbing.

On 1 September the commissioners offered gifts and answered that Americans would spill no blood in the Indian country unless their enemy invaded it. Stuart might remain at Fort Hunter and both Quedor's descendant and Volkert Douw would tend the Albany council fire and tree of peace. The Indian trade from Albany and Schenectady would be resumed, but the land disputes with the Albany corporation and those of Connecticut and Pennsylvania over the Susquehanna were matters referable to Congress. A request for a minister to the Stockbridge (Massachusetts) Indians would likewise be referred to Congress. Except for the Albany committee's address to the sachems on 2 September, the conference was ended. Dismissing the Indians' land grievance, the committee insisted that Albany's claim to territory was based upon the municipal charter granted by the king; no tribesmen had been driven off it. However, in November, while approving opening of Indian trade at Albany and Schenectady, Congress also ordered that two tracts of land near Albany be restored to the Mohawk.[89] Meantime, the Iroquois were content that both Guy Johnson and the Americans had pledged to keep the peace and to maintain the lines of trade.

Through the Albany Indian conference Schuyler executed the Continental Congress's initial policy of neutrality between the rebellious colonies and the Six Nations, and the treaty may be regarded at least as a temporary success. At most the general's attendance at the conference perhaps delayed the 1775 invasion of Canada by as much as two weeks. But his responsibility as an Indian commissioner was vitally related to the discharge of his duties as a general. His army could not be certain of victory in Canada unless the Indian power there and in the Mohawk valley was neutralized. For the moment he had succeeded in gaining assurances that there would be no Iroquois war at his rear. To be sure, this accomplishment was in part due to the disadvantageous position in which the British found themselves. An army besieged at Boston and a small Canadian garrison threatened by an American invasion were not inducements to winning the Indians to their side. Moreover, the Iroquois' own internal divisions worked to the American advantage. The Mohawk ties to the Johnsons were made tenuous by the inability of Col. Guy Johnson to persuade Governor Carleton to enlist them in the war or otherwise to launch early attacks upon the Tryon County settlements. Bound to Samuel Kirkland, the Oneida were drawn by him to the patriot side, and they resisted Guy Johnson's efforts to separate them from the missionary's allegiance. Others, bewildered as to which side to take, could feel only relief that the rebels wanted and promised friendly commerce, peace, and neutrality.[90]

7

Intelligence and Initiative

Obliged by circumstances to delay the invasion of Canada, Schuyler also chose to wait for intelligence collected by Indians, scouts, Canadian correspondents, and others traveling south, and by spies who might indicate the extent to which Canadians would welcome and assist the army or resist its advance and support Governor Carleton's crown forces.

The questions of whether to invade Canada, and when, had been raised by Washington and the Continental Congress late in June, but the answers depended in some measure upon influential forces in Canada itself: leaders of the Anglo-American community, the British governor and his regular troops, the Iroquois allies in Canada (especially the Abenaki and the Caughnawaga), and a variety of officials who assiduously worked to enlist the tribes for the British cause. The latter included Louis St. Luc de La Corne, formerly the French superintendent of Indian affairs; Col. Guy Johnson, the British superintendent; Joseph Brant of the Mohawk tribe; and Col. John Butler and Daniel Claus, Johnson's assistants. Armed with complete discretionary authority to decide whether to make "an impression into Canada," Schuyler had been ordered by Congress to do so only if he found it "practicable and not disagreeable" to the Canadians. And like Congress, the commander in chief trusted Schuyler's "own Good Sense" to "govern in all Matters not particularly pointed out, as I do not wish," the Virginian assured him, "to circumscribe you within too narrow Limits."[91]

Ever since 1775 critics have carped that Schuyler dawdled or otherwise could not be prodded to make a decision when Canadian sentiment and circumstances proved ripe for an invasion. The critics have also imagined that Brigadier General Montgomery finally took matters into his own hands.[92] But in view of Schuyler's and Montgomery's judgment and their sense of mutual responsibility, the junior commander's initiation of the march was really unexceptional—and unexceptionable. Whether Schuyler should have been on the spot instead of at the Albany Indian conference when the army moved is a point of little consequence. Montgomery had no sooner begun the march when Schuyler caught up with his forces to lead them. Moreover, Schuyler had been eager to commence the invasion and decided that it must begin at least a fortnight before Montgomery acted; there is no evidence that there was any disagreement between the two leaders or that Montgomery was doing anything but beginning what Schuyler intended to do but could not because of his absence from Ticonderoga. Although Montgomery wrote a courteous apology for lacking Schuyler's explicit or specific orders to move the army, he was confident of his superior's trust. And there is no indication that Schuyler was anything but enthusiastic about accepting Montgomery's initiative.[93]

In reaching the decision to open the campaign in August, however, Schuyler gave considerable attention for a month or so to the question of what the army would encounter north of the border. It is impossible to believe that Montgomery was not equally attentive to this issue. As with many of his other labors, the general's collection of information about British troop dispositions, Indian support, and Canadian attitudes toward an invasion could not begin in earnest until he reached Ticonderoga on 18 July. Given the necessity of making other preparations for the army and the time required for spies and others to traverse the northern forests and waterways, it is noteworthy that his intelligence operations moved as rapidly as they did. He was also properly cautious in seeking more than a few sources of information and in demanding corroboration of the reports that did come to him. And for several weeks after 21 July he set in motion a considerable secret service operation.[94]

Schuyler wisely made haste slowly, seeking the necessary intelligence of Canadian conditions as well as making thorough preparations. Even Montgomery did not deem these adequate before 25 August. For the Yorker it was not a question of "insisting upon optimum conditions within his command" before striking against an "outnumbered, confused or nearly defenseless enemy," nor was he simply sluggishly permitting weeks to slip by, indifferent to the loss of a timely advantage. That Schuyler was unimpetuous or "painfully deliberate and methodical" should not be deemed a fault, nor is it true that he "obviously" lacked "the power of decision, perhaps because he sensed what many others knew—that he was at best a second-rate leader of men." Montgomery after all thought that Schuyler's presence would "give the men great confidence in your spirit and activity." Moreover, from the beginning critics have been less acquainted with the man's real abilities and virtues than with his flashes of temper and his penchant for complaining or justifying his every move. Doggedly he pursued his duties with both energy and steadiness, and there were some, like Samuel Chase of Maryland, who feared that Schuyler's zeal for action or impetuosity were potentially more dangerous than delaying the campaign. Chase cautioned him that the envious or indiscreet might urge him to undertake what his own prudence might condemn.[95]

Schuyler's army could neither walk on water nor be expected to succeed without sufficient supplies and equipment. No "more forceful leadership might have managed to obtain faster and better results" because the record of his activities shows no lack of energy or vigor. And there were some circumstances beyond his control. His accomplishments were amazingly prompt despite the constraints of both time and circumstance. Quite properly he chided Brigadier General Wooster for suggesting the ease of marching to Canada as if the obstacles to that were no greater than those Wooster had encountered in moving between Greenwich, Connecticut, and Manhattan. It was easier said than done to take Montreal and Quebec; could troops swim the hundred-mile lake? The building of boats since mid-July required a little more time than Wooster seemed to be aware of and the task was not yet completed.[96]

Schuyler's performance in fact exceeded what his written reports have suggested to some readers; suspicious of his caution and thoroughness, critics have dwelt too much on one or a few statements betokening hesitation or indecisiveness. On 6 August, for example, he indicated readiness to move against the enemy unless Washington or Congress ordered otherwise. Yet he quickly added that soon he would determine the action. Enough boats would be ready to move twelve hundred troops to Saint John's if he were ordered to that place; but Schuyler also wished to know whether Congress expected him to build a naval force on Lake Champlain superior to the enemy's.[97] On the other hand, the general had to consider his duties as Indian commissioner that finally pulled him to Albany, obliging him to leave Richard Montgomery in command of the field. Meantime he continued to press for the troops, supplies, artillery carriages, and powder that seemed all too slow in reaching his Ticonderoga headquarters. And in five weeks the number of boats for moving his army had risen from a carrying capacity of two hundred men to thirteen hundred and with twenty days' provisions. In addition two flat-bottomed boats had been launched; sixty feet long, each would carry five twelve-pound artillery pieces, although for lack of carriages only one gun could be mounted.[98] These, then, were ample testimonies to both Schuyler's success and his vigor in preparing the first campaign of the American rebellion.

On 14 August Schuyler learned of Congress's adjournment without ordering or stopping the invasion of Canada. Regretting only that he had been left to act upon his "own Ideas" in such a critical situation, he was grateful for the advice and assistance of so trusty a subordinate as Montgomery. By 27 August Schuyler fully expected that Montgomery might decide to move without the department commander but that he would be able to overtake the army at Crown Point.[99]

Responding to Washington's proposal that an auxiliary expedition be sent into Canada via the Kennebec River, Schuyler thought that a two-pronged attack would increase the prospects of success because his own army would not exceed seventeen hundred men—a number he believed to be inadequate for the conquest of Quebec because a number of posts along the route of march would have to be garrisoned. Although Washington promised to move the second army through New England as soon as he heard that Schuyler meant to proceed with the first, he did not indicate that Benedict Arnold would be its leader. The Yorker readily signaled Washington to proceed with the second expedition, assuring him of the imminent departure of the Northern Army from Ticonderoga. The two-pronged invasion would surely force Sir Guy Carleton to divide his forces, thus affording Schuyler's army a freer passage north. But it is remarkable that the project was launched at the last moment with so little consultation between the Virginian and the Yorker, and with no further coordination. Although Schuyler thought that the scheme must succeed, he aptly requested Washington to avoid one possible difficulty. He suggested that the officer placed in charge of the auxiliary forces should be instructed of his subordination to the Northern Department's commander "that there may be no clashing, should we join."[100]

Eruption into Canada

1

Strain every nerve . . .

—Brig. General Richard Montgomery

O n 28 August, as Montgomery began to move from Ticonderoga to Crown Point, Schuyler hurried his horse north from Albany, expecting to find his army somewhere along Lake Champlain. About 2,000 men were quartered at Ticonderoga and another 550 at Crown Point. Allotting about half the troops for garrison duty and as standby reserves, Montgomery's orders had set the others in motion. Receipt of fresh news from Saint John's indicated to him that speed was vital if the enemy were to be prevented from launching their vessels onto Lake Champlain.[1]

Montgomery's movement was, however, not particularly rapid, and Schuyler, despite a growing illness, quickly caught up to his able lieutenant. Upon reaching Ticonderoga on 30 August the general was already "much indisposed," but he pushed on. That very day about a thousand men embarked from Crown Point for the long bateau ride along Lake Champlain to the Richelieu River.[2]

From Crown Point Schuyler posted orders to Montgomery to encamp the army at Isle aux Motte until he could overtake them. Promising that he was not more than twenty-four hours behind, the commander explained that illness had confined him to bed in a bateau. On 3 September Montgomery reached Isle aux Motte; next day at noon Schuyler joined him there. Pausing only because of high winds and driving rain, they proceeded together toward Isle aux Noix. Not only was the season wet, but the weather was already growing chilly in the north country, and

59

neither his brief stay abed on 1 September at Crown Point nor his boat travel in a bed did much to abate the onset of Schuyler's "bilious fever, & violent rheumatic Pains." Still he refused to leave the field and made "every Effort to bear up agt." what he called the "Inflexible Severity of my Disorders."[3]

At Isle aux Noix the general fired three cannons as a signal to Canadians to join his forces. On 5 September he ordered the troops to put their arms in good order and to cook provisions for a three-day march, and he issued a declaration to the "Messieurs les Habitants du Canada." Asserting the necessity of taking arms against British tyranny, Schuyler proclaimed the Continental Congress's belief that their northern neighbors would not endure such offenses and outrages as Britain had already committed. Congress would protect Canadians and restore their rights within the empire. Expulsion of royal troops was the remedy proposed. Insisting that Congress would not dispossess the settlers or the natives, Schuyler carefully reassured the Caughnawaga and other tribes that the recent killing of some of their New York brothers had been in contravention of express orders to the contrary and that the Iroquois leaders had concluded a treaty of neutrality with the rebels at Albany. Copies of this proclamation were scattered through the north country by Ethan Allen. Residents of Chambly evidently responded well to the message and the Caughnawaga promised neutrality, as did settlers in the Richelieu valley. Governor Carleton had fewer than a thousand troops to defend the entire province; and although Canadians along the Saint Lawrence might welcome the invaders with sympathy, their willingness to volunteer for the rebel cause depended upon a show of superiority by American forces.[4]

On 6 September Schuyler's army moved toward Saint John's, and within two days reinforcements had raised the invaders' strength to about seventeen hundred men, but these he believed would be insufficient for a final assault upon Quebec. Because Saint John's, Chambly, and Montreal would require garrisons once—and if—they could be conquered, Schuyler remained dissatisfied with the size of his forces. Reporting to Washington, Schuyler cheerfully noted his hope that a catalogue of all his wants would "serve for an evening chat at some future day." Without a dependable return of his own forces, he managed to estimate enemy strength fairly accurately: 350 to 400 men at Saint John's; 150 to 200 at Chambly; about 50 at Montreal; a company of regulars at Quebec; and 350 to 500 Indians, Scots, and Canadians at La Chene with Col. Guy Johnson.[5] Considering the necessity of scattering manpower among several garrisons in enemy territory along the way and the prospects of losses by death and illness, one cannot conclude that the American invasion enjoyed an advantage even by the addition of Arnold's expeditionary forces, which labored for weeks along the Kennebec and then over to the Chaudière River and the Saint Lawrence.

Within two miles of the fort at Saint John's Schuyler's men encountered the first enemy firing, but they proceeded by bateau to within a mile of the outpost. There on 6 September they landed in the midst of a swamp and then moved to reconnoiter. That evening a "gentleman" whom Schuyler would not name in his report to Congress informed him that the army's prospects in Canada were gloomy. The visitor was Massachusetts-born Moses Hazen, who had settled in the Richelieu valley after the war of 1754–63. Claiming that only a single regiment of British regulars was present in all of Canada, Hazen indicated that all but fifty of these were poised with about a hundred Indians at Saint John's and Chambly where fortifications were strong and a well-armed schooner was nearly ready to be launched against the invaders' Lake Champlain approaches. This news prompted Schuyler to retreat because Hazen offered no promise of support for the army by Canadians. At best he deemed them neutrals professing a willingness to allow the invasion of their countryside.[6]

Although Schuyler decided to withdraw to Isle aux Noix, he first held a council of war on the morning of 7 September. The "great forwardness" of the enemy's vessel with gun mountings posed a considerable threat; two pieces of artillery could not outfire a ship equipped with sixteen. They decided unanimously to retreat to Isle aux Noix where a thousand men might better be able to block the ship's entry to Lake Champlain. Then, depending upon more promising news from Canadians and the arrival of more reinforcements, a strong detachment might again be sent overland to Saint John's.[7]

Through general orders Schuyler carefully explained that the advance to Saint John's had been attempted in order to test the "disposition" of Canadians and to give them an opportunity to join the invasion. Now the return Isle aux Noix would serve to check the enemy's chances of entering Lake Champlain. The general hoped that the fallback would not dispirit the troops but Col. Rudolph Ritzema thought that Schuyler's poor health was a major difficulty. Ill since "he joined us," Ritzema wrote, "he continues so & in my opinion is in a dangerous Situation. this is very detrimental to us."[8]

Was Schuyler's decision to retreat to Isle aux Noix "an incredible performance" that "revealed his limitations" and caused such a delay in the invasion that the initial victories were canceled by the ultimate American defeat at Quebec? Perhaps so, if one discounts the reality of British artillery superiority, which might have demolished the American bateaux

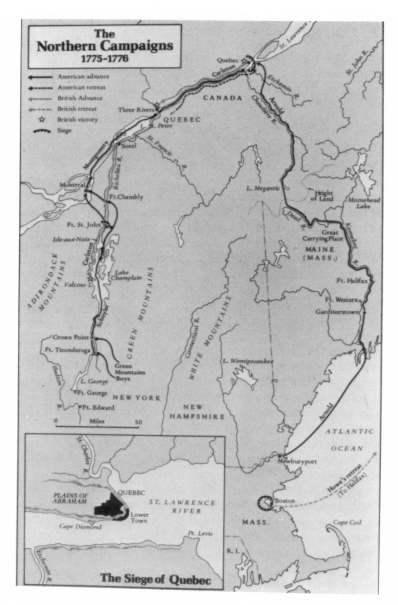

The
Northern Campaigns
1775–1776

→ American advance
⊷⊶⊷ American retreat
← British Advance
⊶⊷⊶ British retreat
☆ British victory
∿ Siege

CANADA

QUEBEC

Quebec
Carleton

St. Lawrence
St. John R.

Three Rivers
L. St. Peter
Sorel
St. Francis R.
Richelieu R.
Montmorency R.
Montreal
Ft. Chambly
Ft. St. John
Isle-aux-Noix
Carleton
Valcour I.
Lake Champlain

ADIRONDACK MOUNTAINS

Schuyler R.

Crown Point
Ft. Ticonderoga
Green Mountains Boys
L. George
Ft. George
Ft. Edward

0   Miles   50

GREEN MOUNTAINS

NEW YORK

NEW HAMPSHIRE

WHITE MOUNTAINS

Connecticut R.

L. Winnipesaukee

L. Megantic

Dead R.

Height of Land

Chaudière R.
Etchemin R.
Arnold

Great Carrying Place

Kennebec R.

MAINE
(MASS.)

Ft. Halifax
Ft. Western
Gardinerstown

Moosehead Lake

Arnold

ATLANTIC OCEAN

Newburyport

Howe's retreat (To Halifax)

Boston

MASS.

Cape Cod

R. I.

PLAINS OF ABRAHAM
QUEBEC
Lower Town
Cape Diamond

St. Charles R.

ST. LAWRENCE RIVER

Pt. Levis

Etchemin R.

The Siege of Quebec

Fig. 2. The Northern Campaigns, 1775–76. The "Inflexible Severity" of
Schuyler's illnesses forced him to direct the campaign against Montreal
from Fort Ticonderoga. From *The Glorious Cause: The American Revolution, 1763–1789*, by Robert Middlekauf. Copyright © 1982 by Oxford University Press, Inc. Reprinted by permission.

and gondolas. Schuyler, however, insisted that it would have been a waste of time to try to silence the enemy guns guarding their vessel. Perhaps he could be held culpable if the delay and hesitation had really enabled Carleton to strengthen Saint John's for a siege that might otherwise not have dragged on until 2 November. Perhaps so, if Schuyler's illness, which finally forced his own withdrawal to Ticonderoga, did in fact mean "permanently relinquishing the army's direction to Montgomery."[9] However, Schuyler's major officers agreed with his decision, and it was not necessarily foolish to pause until more artillery could be dragged up to strengthen the army's chances of seizing Saint John's. Also, the unruly troops performed no better for Montgomery than for Schuyler; they insisted upon retreat after the second march to Saint John's was attempted during 10–11 September.

Interestingly, too, the Continental Congress found no fault with Schuyler's report of the 7 September retreat to Isle aux Noix but commended his conduct as "highly expedient and necessary." But President Hancock warned that the foothold at Isle aux Noix was not to be abandoned without the "most mature consideration or the most pressing necessity." Congress also promised to spare neither men nor funds for the invasion; the venture must surely succeed even though Canadians remained "neuter."[10]

Was the American invasion of Canada (in both 1775 and 1776) an aberration in the general strategy of a war that was defensive? Did the spirit of '76 and American generalship really win the war? Neither that generalship nor the quality of American troops under Schuyler or Washington was demonstrably superior to the British, who also were at no disadvantage in employing European methods of warfare in the new world. The answer lies on the British side with their own fumblings and failures in policy and generalship; it is against these that the leadership of Philip Schuyler as well as the performance of his armies must be measured.[11] If either seems deficient, one must remember the odds and wonder at the magnitude of the effort expended in the circumstances.

Meantime at Isle aux Noix on 8 September Schuyler dictated a report to the president of Congress, explaining that he was then too ill even to hold a pen. Commending Montgomery's great services, he urged Congress to issue directions if the army was not to be moved from the wet and unhealthy terrain at Isle aux Noix. Schuyler promised otherwise to order the move if decisive action in Canada proved to be unlikely. Next day, with a message from James Livingston, another American merchant and informant in the Richelieu valley, he did not hesitate to exercise his command of the department. Livingston called for a detachment of troops to block enemy communications between Saint John's and La Prairie and Chambly. Urging the necessity of seizing vessels at the mouth of the

Richelieu in order to prevent enemy troops from escaping from Chambly and Montreal to Quebec, Livingston and also Ethan Allen reported that Canadians had responded well to Schuyler's 5 September manifesto, but that they would not actually support the American invasion until it was more visibly under way. Although not many Canadians enthusiastically flocked to the American army, some eventually did so and others proved to be far from committed supporters of Sir Guy Carleton's government and army.[12]

Schuyler promptly responded to James Livingston's request for troops by ordering five hundred men to cut off communications between Saint John's and La Prairie. Lt. Col. Rudolph Ritzema was to prevent the movement of supplies from Chambly to Saint John's, to procure provisions and tools from Canadians for the necessary entrenchments and to keep strict discipline among his men lest their unruly behavior offend the Canadians. Schuyler also demanded frequent dispatches, the collection of information, and the establishment of correspondence with Montreal.[13]

Ritzema's detachment accomplished none of Schuyler's objectives. Ambushed and scattered on 10 September near Chambly, they suffered no losses. After managing to reassemble the men, General Montgomery exhorted them to try again on 11 September. Again they were checked by the enemy's fire from swivel guns, and again Montgomery and other officers tried to persuade the mutinous soldiers to repeat the effort to block the route between Chambly and Saint John's. Frightened by word of the enemy's armed vessel moving along the river, the troops refused and then embarked for Isle aux Noix. Nor could Montgomery persuade them to march back after he stopped their panicked flight eight miles from Saint John's. They insisted upon returning to Isle aux Noix.[14]

In response to this disgraceful display Schuyler appointed a court-martial headed by Col. David Waterbury with Capt. Richard Varick as judge advocate. Three days later, when the court completed its work, Schuyler confirmed its decisions, which included more acquittals than convictions. Among the former were two men accused of running from the enemy (insufficient evidence), and thirteen sailors from the sloop *Enterprise* who were charged with "notorious behavior." One man was sentenced to thirty-nine lashes for cocking and presenting his firelock at a Lieutenant Hurst; one was fined 20 shillings for stealing rum; a sergeant was reduced in rank for deserting his post during action, and another man was sentenced to fatigue duty for the duration of the campaign because he confessed to having fled in fear of enemy pursuit. Here then were some of the "many difficulties" Schuyler found in the army's failure to invest Saint John's.[15]

On 12 September Schuyler discovered that over 600 of the troops then at Isle aux Noix were sick. During the following week the 1,394 rank and file who were counted "effectives" were reinforced by about 400 new arrivals including two companies of New Yorkers, Connecticut men, and about 100 New Hampshire troops belonging to Col. Timothy Bedel's regiment. Capt. John Lamb's company of New York Artillery were at last expected to join the army on 19 September. Further attempts to approach Saint John's were delayed until 17 September, but upon hearing Montgomery's report that his troops were unable to bear reproach for their recent "unbecoming behavior," Schuyler ordered that his artillery be embarked for Saint John's on 14 September, and the army and a schooner were to follow on 15 September.[16]

Heavy rain delayed the movement of the cannon, but feeling an improvement in his health, Schuyler hoped to be able to move with the troops once again. Suddenly, however, on the evening of 14 September, he was wracked with rheumatic gout. Two days later, despairing of a speedy recovery, he was carried from his tent to a covered boat that bore him to warmer and drier quarters at Ticonderoga. Despite his relapse, the general laid careful plans with Montgomery to renew the assault before leaving him to execute them.[17]

On Sunday, 17 September, as Schuyler's boat glided across Lake Champlain carrying him to the healthier confines of Fort Ticonderoga, Montgomery's forces headed north. Numbering about fourteen hundred effective men, the army approached Saint John's that evening, and next day Montgomery followed the plans for cutting off the approaches to Saint John's from Chambly and Longueuil. The siege of the fort then lasted until 2 November, but Chambly first succumbed to American attacks in mid-October.[18]

Meantime, as September waned, Schuyler remained confined to his quarters. Solicitous about her husband's care, Catharine Schuyler rushed to his bedside to nurse him. When she finally left Ticonderoga to return to Saratoga on 12 October, not only had the general shaken off the fever, but he also had recovered to the point of thinking that he might soon return to the field. Several days later his hopes were dashed by renewed attacks of his old disorders. Violent fluxes weakened him again, and recurrent sweating proved debilitating. Yet through October and November he probably contributed more to the Canadian campaign at Ticonderoga than he could otherwise have accomplished at Montgomery's side. It was there that he revealed his unflagging attention to the business of furnishing reinforcements for his senior lieutenant.[19]

Schuyler's continual supervision of reinforcements and the movement of provisions and other supplies was not the only valuable part of his work as a commander forced out of the field. Keeping open the line of communication between Albany and the Saint Lawrence required the unraveling of snarls and confusions at one point or the setting to work of hands idled by nothing to do at another. It is difficult to underestimate how much Schuyler's management contributed to Montgomery's success at Chambly, Saint John's, and finally at Montreal.[20]

With an eye always upon the future, Schuyler urged Congress to consider the questions of stationing troops in Canada in the event of American victory. Which would remain, and how were those in Canada and at Ticonderoga to be reenlisted? (Only Congress could authorize suitable inducements.) What of supplies of winter clothing and arrangements for hospital services? Where could gold be procured for the purchase of provisions in Canada? Paper was unacceptable. Even as Schuyler wrote, Richard Montgomery was clamoring for specie. What line of conduct should be taken with the Canadians respecting their civil government? And should the invaders ultimately be repulsed, did Congress wish him to prepare for the construction of a superior fleet to guard the lake country in the spring? Reporting similarly to Washington, Schuyler further noted the various concerns to which his attention was constantly given. Claiming again that he felt an improvement in his illness, Schuyler hoped soon to "return where I ought and wish to be": at the head of his army.[21]

What Schuyler wrote the commander in chief was perhaps not as accurate a revelation of his personal condition as what he told Col. Goose Van Schaick when he ordered him to inspect and repair the road between Albany and Lake George. "Reduced to a Skeleton with a Complication of disorders, I have been under the distressing necessity of returning to this place [Ticonderoga], to procure, if possible a restoration of my Health, which is greatly impaired." A month later the general found that his illness was so inflexibly stubborn that repeated signs of improvement were invariably ruined by fresh attacks of "a Violent Flux." By mid-October he could only hope that he might remain at Ticonderoga, poor as it was for his health, so as not to inconvenience Montgomery irremediably.[22]

However unable Schuyler remained to direct business in the field, his admirable qualifications for assisting the army by work at Ticonderoga and ultimately at Albany were proven again and again during the remainder of 1775 and then in 1776. At the end of September, for example, Montgomery found that despite limited artillery, manpower, and ammunition, Schuyler's "provisions came seasonably, and have given no small relief to my anxiety." While begging for haste in the sending of specie, iron, steel, and turner's tools, as well as more powder and well-provisioned reinforcements, Montgomery commended his chief for his diligence and foresight; they had saved the army from threatening difficulties and on 6 October he no longer feared starvation. Schuyler's assessment of his own role was a just one. Regrettable as his return to Ticonderoga had been, he was convinced that "[i]f I had not arrived here, Even on the very Day I did, as sure as God lives the Army would have starved."[23]

Schuyler's success in maintaining a flow of men, provisions, and other supplies northward was in part due to his help from sources like the Albany Committee of Safety and the New York Provincial Congress.[24] The powder shortage was largely solved with the first substantial American victory in Canada. When Chambly was taken on 18 October, captured stores included six tons of powder—enough to finish the bombardment of Saint John's, Montgomery thought. But he wanted rum. "Let us have rum, my dear General," he wrote, "else we shall never be able to go through our business."[25]

During the following weeks until the fateful attempt to reduce Quebec in December, Montgomery's reports to Schuyler contained no more pleas for provisions or artillery stores. With successive victories (Saint John's on 2 November and Montreal on 13 November), the troops in Canada managed their supply needs through conquest and purchases. Montgomery's requests to Schuyler were largely for specie to pay for food and clothing and for reenlistments or reinforcements.[26]

Manpower remained a serious problem, particularly when about 450 British reinforcements arrived at Quebec in early November and Montgomery feared that it would be difficult to reenlist his own men even for six months. Those who reengaged he promised to reward with clothing. But the First New York regiment and Lamb's artillery company had nearly mutinied because he refused to stop clothing the Saint John's garrison. Having coaxed the army to Montreal, he wondered whether they would go on to Quebec. That key point must be taken before Britain sent sizable reinforcements in the spring. If it could not be captured by then, the Saint Lawrence would have to be blocked in order to prevent its relief by forces moving upstream from the gulf.[27]

Like many of his rank and file (whose enlistments would expire by year's end), Montgomery was tempted by thoughts of going home. Would Schuyler's health permit him to come to Montreal? If not, might Gen. Charles Lee be sent to take the command there? Weary of power, Montgomery professed a lack of patience. Thinking that the presence of a congressional committee would have a salutary effect upon his turbulent troops, he also surmised that such a committee should direct the political arrangements necessary for organizing civil government for Canadians and providing the election of delegates to the Continental Congress.[28]

However dwindling, the army in Canada held, and Montgomery welcomed Benedict Arnold's contingent from Massachusetts early in November. Arnold's eleven hundred men had shrunk to about half the number during their arduous march through Maine, but Montgomery found them well disciplined and their leader both energetic and intelligent. He joined them at Point aux Trembles on 3 December. Next day they began maneuvering against Quebec, to where Governor Carleton had fled from Montreal. In order to persuade his own troops to join Arnold's and to extend their enlistments to 15 April, which was the time for planting spring crops, Montgomery had promised them clothing. He asked Schuyler to inform Congress of this necessity, hoping that the issue of both winter garb and monetary payments for extended service would not greatly exceed congressional authorization of bounties.[29]

Without much expectation of the arrival of further augmentations for his army in December, Montgomery suggested that a force of ten thousand must be provided by spring if Canada was to be held. British reinforcements would surely arrive with the first thaws of the Saint Lawrence, and at least ten thousand troops with artillery and row galleys must be ready to block the enemy at the Rapids of Richelieu above Quebec. Canadians would remain friendly to the American invaders only for so long as they could hold the ground won from the British.[30] Accordingly Schuyler expended much of his energy during the winter of 1775–76 trying to maintain garrisons in the north, laying in provisions and other supplies, and forwarding necessary troops to Canada.

In what was evidently his last missive to Schuyler before he made the 31 December attack on Quebec, Montgomery pleaded again for men and money. On 26 December he begged Schuyler to "[s]train every nerve to send a large corps of troops down the instant the Lake is passable." Quebec must be taken before the British relieved it. The plan of attack must be altered because three of Arnold's companies refused to risk a coup de main; their enlistments were within a few days of expiring. Without a fresh supply of specie to purchase provisions, Montgomery was nearly at wits' end, for he had almost exhausted his credit with James Price at Montreal. The troops, too, wanted their pay, and they were not inclined to take paper because the Canadians would not accept it. Trusting that steps had been already taken to replace him, Montgomery told Schuyler that he must assume that Congress wished Brigadier General Wooster to succeed him, and that should the assault in Quebec end "in Blockade" he would feel free to go home.[31]

Acknowledging Montgomery's letter of 5 December, Schuyler expressed relief of considerable anxiety because there were rumors that Montgomery had been killed (which was a strange sort of premonition), Arnold made a prisoner of war, and their little American army totally defeated. The rumors included allegations that Schuyler knew of these disasters but dared not publicize them. The general tried to assure Montgomery that he had informed Congress of the pressing need for clothing the army in Canada and of his request to Montgomery to purchase clothes. On 31 December, the very day Montgomery died in the swirling snows at Quebec, Schuyler wrote again, saying that he had been urging Congress to provide the reinforcements necessary to assemble a "formidable" army in Canada by spring. With respect and affection, he also rejoiced that Congress had promoted Montgomery to major general in response to news of his victory at Montreal. Both the contents and closing salutations of his letters reflect a fond regard, and they squared with his own recommendation to Congress on 11 November that Montgomery should be given a separate "command in *Canada*." Again, on 8 January 1776, responding to Montgomery's 18 December dispatch, Schuyler was obliged to admit that his efforts to send more specie to Canada had failed. But not until 13 January did the general know that the northern army had suffered grievous losses: 51 killed and 36 wounded; 387 taken prisoner, including Daniel Morgan; Montgomery dead; and Arnold wounded.[32]

2

Contretemps with "the old Genl. of Connecticut"

Richard Montgomery's death left Benedict Arnold to maintain a weak blockade of Quebec throughout the winter. Arnold's own report of the forces remaining on 2 January 1776 indicated that he had not more than 800, including Col. James Livingston's local regiment and some 200 other Canadians.[33] For the moment, Brig. Gen. David Wooster, whom Montgomery has posted at Montreal, was the ranking American officer in Canada, and Wooster now confronted the same difficulties that for so long had bedevilled both Montgomery and Schuyler, not least of which were the shortage of troops and poor discipline. With perhaps 500 to 600 men scattered in garrisons at Montreal, Saint John's, and Chambly, Wooster at first felt he could spare no troops for Arnold, especially because the garrison units were dwindling by desertion and the expiration of

enlistments. By mid-January, however, he relented and sent 120 reinforcements for the siege at Quebec until others might enter Canada.

Wooster experienced the very kind of insubordination and uncooperative behavior that he and his own regiment, officers and enlisted men
alike, had earlier displayed to Schuyler at Ticonderoga. The tone of his
reports to Schuyler on 5 and 14 January 1776 sound curiously like Schuyler's
earlier laments about Wooster and the Connecticut troops: " Something
must be done, and that speedily, or I greatly fear we are ruined." Aside
from the everlasting uncertainty of adequate numbers of men, there were
invariably the problems of soldierly misconduct, and in the face of expiring enlistments Wooster had dared to order that no man must leave his
post in Canada.[34]

Not a man to bear grudges, even against one who had given cause for
offense, Schuyler bent as much effort on Wooster's behalf as he had on
Montgomery's. He readily approved Wooster's orders to his men and
assured him that he had urged Congress to send more troops and that
he had also asked Washington for three thousand reinforcements. Beyond
that and supplying funds to enlist more Green Mountain Boys, he could
but pray heaven to free Wooster's army from peril. Schuyler refused to
dictate measures to him from so great a distance; only Wooster could
properly determine what was appropriate for his circumstances.[35]

An unknowing or unsympathetic reader may imagine that Schuyler
was indulging in sarcasm when he wished Wooster a heavenly deliverance.
But careful consideration of the general's voluminous correspondence and
a willingness to appreciate his own qualities and efforts and those of
others will bring us closer to a proper understanding of his behavior and
character. His dealings with David Wooster, like those with so many
others, are of course instructive for what they reveal of both men's frailties
and virtues. They began earlier in 1775.

As department commander, Schuyler rightly regarded the various officers and their respective corps as subordinate components of his army.
When Congress had ordered Wooster to station his Connecticut troops
at Manhattan, Schuyler hesitated to call him north with reinforcements
in September without congressional direction. Moreover, Wooster's rank
was a problem. Would he, if sent to Canada, claim to outrank Brigadier
General Montgomery? In June Wooster held the rank of a Connecticut
major general, but Congress named him a mere brigadier in the Continental army after selecting an inferior, Israel Putnam, as one of the four
major generals.[36]

Despite Congress's order of choice in which Montgomery was second
and Wooster third, Schuyler was justifiably apprehensive about Wooster's
subordination because the Yankee seemed to consider his rank as a Con-

necticut major general to be superior to that of a Continental brigadier. For example, he had refused to muster his men as Continentals while he had been left in southern New York. And "a similar attitude prevailed among the Connecticut troops" serving with Schuyler in the north who were loath to sign the Continental articles of war. But so long as the troops were not pledged to Continental regulations, they could not be court-martialed or otherwise disciplined except under Connecticut rules and by Connecticut officers. This was a situation that Schuyler found intolerable, although for a time he did not press the issue for fear that Connecticut soldiers would simply abandon his army.[37]

With the approach of Wooster and the remainder of his contingent in October, Schuyler found that he could no longer compromise the demands of order and discipline for the sake of maintaining an army in the field. After Congress finally responded to his calls for reinforcements by ordering both New York's forces and the remainder of Wooster's men at Manhattan to march to Albany, Schuyler might direct their disposition, but "Wooster's status remained unclassified" because Congress had not properly settled it. Its "order sending him north ... clearly indicated he was a Continental officer," but Congress had waffled. Instead of having the governor of Connecticut warn Wooster against disputes over rank or command, the delegates apparently decided that their own order to Wooster was sufficient indication of Wooster's subordination to both Schuyler and Montgomery.[38] Yet Wooster continued to behave like an officer of independent provincial troops rather than a brigade commander within the Continental system.

In September Congressman Thomas Lynch of South Carolina promptly warned Schuyler to expect trouble from the Connecticut Yankee. Lynch predicted there would be difficulties "about the old Genl. of Connecticut" and suggested the wisdom of limiting him to the command of Fort George.[39]

By October George Washington was also perturbed by news suggesting that Schuyler's illness would open the way for Wooster to take command of Montgomery. The Virginian feared that the grizzled Yankee was not active enough to press through difficulties and that consequently Arnold's auxiliary expedition through Maine to the Saint Lawrence might be left to perish if Wooster abandoned the entry to Canada. The main army must at least feint or create an appearance that would "fix Carleton" and prevent the whole country from focusing its force against Arnold. Should Schuyler be obliged to permit Wooster to command, Washington urged that Wooster be forcefully impressed with the need to proceed and to assist Arnold in making a safe retreat at the least.[40]

At first Schuyler considered retaining Wooster and his troops at Albany, or perhaps moving them no farther than Fort George. At least he might be able to keep Wooster at arm's length. As he told Congressman Lynch, he "should not dare to trust this Post [Ticonderoga] to the Old Gentleman." Wooster was sixty-four, Schuyler forty-two, and Montgomery only thirty-seven, and doubtless the eldest of the trio felt "the incongruity of his subordination to men so much his junior in years." But Schuyler's concern for establishing a proper order in the management of military responsibilities would not permit him to make concessions to age or mere expediency. The commander of an army courted disaster if he failed to establish and maintain a suitable system of discipline or chain of command. Schuyler also emphatically agreed with Montgomery's description of one of the greatest threats to the whole military enterprise: "Troops who carry the Spirit of Freedom into the Field & think for themselves will not bear either Subordination or Discipline." Too much independence of spirit, whether in old men like Wooster or young ones like Ethan Allen, could become calamitous. However, in view of the numbers of sick men filtering down to Ticonderoga from Canada in early October, Schuyler decided to order Wooster's corps north from Albany. At least they might replace the losses that Montgomery sustained because of the growing ranks of the ill.[41]

With the arrival of the first 250 of Wooster's troops at Ticonderoga on 15 October without their commander, Schuyler discovered that they would not march farther until Wooster had caught up with them or had given them orders to proceed! "Do not chuse to move!" Schuyler snorted. "Strange language in an Army,—but an Irresistible Force of Necessity obliges me to put up with It." In another instance Lieutenant Colonel Ward questioned the general's order to send men with two bateau loads of powder, rum, and other supplies to Montgomery's army: Would Wooster blame him for obeying? Schuyler responded by explaining the necessity of moving the cargo, and after begging the men to go on he could only hope that they would do so.[42]

Although a few such vexations might have been borne, Schuyler found a multiplication of them to be acutely annoying. Moreover, he felt that his ill health was aggravated when he later discovered that Wooster had dared to send some of his troops home and to convene a court-martial at Fort George while he paused there on his way north from Albany. On both counts Wooster had presumed to do what only a department commander had a right to do. Confirmation of the justice of Schuyler's resentments was furnished by the commissary Walter Livingston and the muster master Gunning Bedford. Bedford reported Wooster's refusal to have Connecticut soldiers mustered as Continentals. Wooster also provided his own commissariat, which not only rejected the department commissary Walter Livingston's aid but also brushed aside his jurisdiction. Connecticut commissary officers like Elisha Phelps had for too long created arrangements that clashed with the main army's commissariat, providing multiple collection and disbursement systems.[43] Wooster now had added another. Such bureaucratic diversity produced confusion, complicated the work of accounting, and perpetuated intercolonial distinctions and jealousies so destructive of a unified war effort. This too was a part of Schuyler's problem with Wooster. And the department hospital director at Fort George encountered still another difficulty.

In exchanges with Dr. Samuel Stringer, Wooster insisted that he was "*Major Genl. of the Connecticut Forces,* & that no man on this side [of] Connecticut had a right to discharge one of his Soldiers but himself." This was a pointed warning that even a physician's recommendations for the discharge of sick Connecticut troops must be referred to the Connecticut commander, not to the Continental one. Gunning Bedford found such circumstances "almost incredible"; that slander had "delighted your enemies, by poisoning your fame therewith. They would wish the contagion to spread, but their tools are too insignificant & your upright conduct must ever check its progress," he told the Yorker.[44]

Schuyler's "upright conduct" did check the contagion, but not without certain strains. While inclined to save Montgomery from Wooster's views of his respective provincial and Continental ranks, Schuyler felt obliged to reinforce him with Wooster's troops. Although Wooster told Schuyler that the men would not move without him, he did promise to follow Montgomery's commands for the good of the public service. But there was further difficulty.

After Schuyler learned of Wooster's orders for a court-martial while he had stopped at Fort George, the general immediately told Wooster that he could not understand such conduct "unless You consider Yourself my Superior." Wooster must make an explicit written acknowledgement of his subordinate status, otherwise Schuyler could not permit him to join Montgomery's forces. Confusions and disagreements between the two brigadier generals could only harm operations in Canada. There must be no future "misapprehensions." Did Wooster consider himself and his regiment to be in the service "of the United Colonies" and did he regard himself a "younger" brigadier general than Montgomery?[45]

Wooster explained that because his officers had declined to sign the Continental articles of war he had felt obliged to administer discipline according to the martial law of Connecticut. On the same principle he had ordered the court-martial at Fort George without ever designing to contradict or counteract Schuyler's authority as department commander. As to his intentions, Wooster asserted that he would not have continued in Congress's service if he had not decided to observe the rules of the Continental army. Devoted to his country's cause, Wooster clearly promised not to dispute Montgomery's command. As for his regiment, Wooster regarded its service as being intended for the defense of Connecticut; but acting in conjunction with troops of other colonies, it would also serve to defend the common cause, and Wooster would try to promote the strictest union and harmony among all officers and their men.[46]

Schuyler quickly and candidly reported the Wooster affair to Washington, and he also submitted copies of his and Wooster's exchange of letters to Congress. Far from simply regarding the old man's "insubordination as a personal insult, rather than as the serious breach of military discipline it was," Schuyler made his sentiments quite clear. As a man of honor he was keenly sensitive to the insults of a general officer, but "the critical Situation of our Public Affairs at this Period require[s] that I should sacrifice a just Resentment to them. And I would wish to have It remembered that to that Cause only must be imputed, that I have suffered a Personal Indignity to go unpunished." Without the issue of military discipline there could be no personal affront, no cause for just resentment, and it is to Schuyler's credit that he realistically considered Montgomery's need for troops and did not use a breach of military discipline or personal affront as excuses to keep Wooster and his regiment from marching into Canada.[47]

Between 19 and 22 October Wooster and his troops were delayed by violent gales and heavy rains. The unpleasant weather reminded the shivering Yankees of the approach of winter, which was a season they dreaded to endure in Canada, where they imagined they might be left to perish. On 21 October Schuyler learned of these fears from Wooster's secretary and chaplain; there were also rumors that if the army were forced to retreat from Saint John's it would not have enough boats to bring it safely away. Schuyler endeavored to assure them that there were more than enough boats—enough in fact to carry an army of 1,000 men larger than then existed in the north. Finally, at 1:00 p.m. on 22 October Wooster reluctantly set sail with 335 troops. "The Parson," Schuyler noted, had "been indefatigable to persuade them to move." Another 98, however, left for home, and 51 who were sick or feigning illness remained behind.[48]

Schuyler fired a parting shot at the Yankee general, but except for this display of witty sarcasm mitigated by notes of somber concern for the safety of the troops, he showed no sullen malice then or afterwards. The parting shot was a letter that Schuyler sent to Montgomery, who was asked to read it and then to give it to Wooster or destroy it as Montgomery chose. Shortly after Wooster had embarked from Ticonderoga, Schuyler was told that the old man had boasted of his regiment's superiority to all others. Were he at Saint John's, Wooster had said, he would boldly march into the British fort at the head of his troops—a bit of bravado that suggested that Montgomery's siege there had been prolonged unnecessarily. Therefore Schuyler invited Montgomery to allow Wooster to demonstrate his prowess, to offer him the challenge in the presence of proper witnesses, and "give him Leave to make the Attempt if he chuses." Writing with practically the same terminology to Wooster, Schuyler stated that he had heard of the officer's boast and thought it "just that you should have an opportunity of showing your prowess and that of your regiment." Montgomery therefore was "desired ... to give you leave to make the attempt if you choose." But Schuyler also advised Wooster not to "be too lavish of your men's lives, unless you have a prospect of gaining the Fortress."[49]

Montgomery evidently decided to give Wooster the letter, but Wooster did not react to it until months later when other tensions developed between him and Schuyler. For the time being he was mollified by Montgomery's attentiveness and considerate attitude. For his part, Montgomery welcomed Wooster's help with the siege of Saint John's, especially because another brigadier general was now on hand to replace him. "For I must most earnestly request to be suffered to retire," Montgomery wrote, "should matters stand on such a footing this winter as to permit me to go off with honour." Having been warned by Schuyler of the Yankee's crustiness, it seems that Montgomery carefully avoided giving Wooster offense. When Wooster responded to Montgomery's query about troop returns, he explained directly to Schuyler that he had discharged none of his men on the march from Albany to Ticonderoga. He had merely granted furloughs because the soldiers' enlistments had not yet expired.[50]

Wooster assisted in the conquest of Saint John's, which capitulated on 2 November, but his regiment then resisted Montgomery's orders to proceed to Montreal until he promised them winter clothes and the freedom to go home after Montreal was taken. The city surrendered on 13 November without resistance. Thereafter Wooster's activities proved to be unexceptionable. Neither Yorker nor Yankee seems to have been uncooperative. Certainly Philip Schuyler was unfailingly courteous, considerate, and supportive so long as officers did their duty and shared the commander's responsibilities for the common cause without challenging or thwarting their superior's jurisdiction. Moreover Schuyler used every means in his power to break down sectional jealousies, which the Wooster case exemplified, and he strove always to promote a sense of intercolonial unity, even, for example, in a case of the distribution of a shipment of watchcoats. In a continental army there must be no discriminations among men from various colonies.[51]

One footnote may be added to the Wooster-Schuyler contretemps. Apparently there were no further difficulties between the two men. Washington "much approved" of Schuyler's conduct of the affair. And Gunning Bedford wrote the Yorker on 9 November that most members of Congress were pleased to hear that Schuyler "managed Genl. Wooster as you did." For the moment, at least, congressmen sympathized with Schuyler's "disagreeable situation," and they were confident that restoration of his health and the issuance of new army regulations would soon make him more comfortable at the head of a more obedient army.[52] Beyond these assurances Congress had at last answered Schuyler's pleas for a committee to assist the commanders in the field.

The General Holds the Rear

1

A Committee with "full powers"

*W*ith his confinement at Ticonderoga stretching from mid-September until early December 1775, Schuyler had become determined that Congress should send a committee to share his responsibilities for reinforcing the army in Canada. Perhaps such a body could assist the work of forwarding supplies and provisions, persuading the Canadians to join the rebel cause, and making a variety of other decisions preparatory to the war effort for the coming year. The idea of a committee seems to have originated with Schuyler in early August when the defenseless state of Ticonderoga suggested that a small group of congressmen might inspect the fort and surrounding area and decide whether any place in it should be fortified.[1] Congress, however, adjourned during August and one month passed before it could even consider Schuyler's request; another slipped by before it was persuaded actually to name a committee.

Meantime, reasons for repeated requests for a committee multiplied. Schuyler's "[b]ilious Fever, & violent rheumatic Pains" were one. Also, if the army succeeded in Canada, what troops were to be stationed there and at other posts? What line of conduct with Canadians was to be followed in civil matters, especially if they were persuaded to join the thirteen colonies and send delegates to Congress? In the event that the army was repulsed, was Schuyler to prepare timber for the construction of lake vessels to defend the northern waters the following year? Richard Montgomery asked similar questions and clearly wished "exceedingly to have the burden [of political arrangements] off my shoulders."[2]

Late in September Schuyler reinforced the pleas to Congress by hinting that his illness limited the chances of accomplishing the work with which a congressional committee might assist. The barbarous complications of his physical disorders, he wrote, "prevent me from reaping those Laurels for which I have so unweariedly wrought since I was honored with this Command." A committee, properly empowered, might relieve the anxiety and strain that were retarding his recovery of health. "If Job had been a General in my Situation," he sighed, "his Memory had not been so famous for Patience." Only "the Glorious End we have in View and which I have a Confidential Hope will be attained will attone [*sic*] for all."[3]

Again, on 18 October, with the army's need for replacements for sickening forces and a variety of other problems in mind, Schuyler repeated his request for a congressional committee with "full powers" to direct the operations in Canada. "Much, very much is to be done" whether the army succeeded or failed in its immediate mission. Specie was wanted for purchasing provisions and clothes, especially because Canadians were as reluctant to accept paper as "a burnt Child dreads the Fire."[4]

Hancock's reply did not reach Ticonderoga until 21 October. Congress had appreciated Schuyler's difficulties and diligence. Lamenting the general's loss of health, Hancock flatteringly observed that the country's obligations to him rose in proportion to the sacrifices he made. But trusting that his care and prudence rendered unnecessary the dispatch of any committee to the northern outposts for the moment, Congress insisted that Schuyler must try to attach Canada to the colonial union by having the parishes elect a convention that in turn could send delegates to Philadelphia. He must assure the Canadians that their rights would be respected; their liberty, property, and freedom of religion duly recognized. Should the invasion succeed, Schuyler might consult his officers about what troops to station at various posts; he was also to enlist a Canadian regiment for which Congress would furnish the funds. In all events Lake Champlain must be held, and Schuyler should proceed to construct a fleet to guarantee this; accordingly, he would be expected to obtain the necessary articles and craftsmen from the New York convention, the Albany committee, and the governor of Connecticut.[5]

To follow these instructions properly Schuyler should have gone to Canada, but he could not leave Ticonderoga in his weakened condition. From late September until mid-October the general's redoubtable consort, who was already six months pregnant, and his two daughters, Elizabeth and Margaret, nursed him after making the difficult fifty-mile journey north from Saratoga.[6] Schuyler had recovered from fever by 12 October but subsequently suffered "violent fluxes" and recurrent fits of rheumatic gout. But his presence at the Lake Champlain outpost probably served the needs of the army best, because that was the strategic assembly point for manpower, provisions, and other supplies to be forwarded to Montgomery. Here, too, a fleet of bateaux and other vessels could be constructed and maintained to keep lines of communication open; here the care of the sick could be managed and proper defenses raised against the possibility of an American retreat.

When Schuyler received word of Congress's refusal to assign a committee to visit his army, he notified Montgomery to do the best he could in discharging Congress's orders without one. But in replying to President Hancock he reported a variety of problems to demonstrate again why a committee was needed. The commander of a well-ordered army could of course devote time to the proper weighing of measures instead of to the problems of discipline, but Schuyler insisted that he had hitherto seldom enjoyed half an hour to himself since the campaign began because of extraordinary difficulties with insubordination. And if Congress expected to garrison Crown Point, it must realize that no fort existed there; the barracks might be enclosed by constructing a picket, but better defenses were more vital for Ticonderoga. Perhaps Congress could properly comprehend the situation if several of its members inspected the north country. As to its orders that Schuyler consult his officers about the enlistment or reenlistment of troops, Congress had said nothing about their pay. The general could conclude only that no changes were intended in the pay schedules, but he warned that officers would refuse continued service at rates that denied them a gentleman's subsistence. And were the rank and file expected to reenlist when their pay remained in arrears? Finally, with the news of Montgomery's first success at Chambly (on 18 October) there were the disposition and maintenance of prisoners of war to consider.[7]

Schuyler's proposal for a congressional committee to assist the army enterprise thus remained a sensible one. Moreover, there was already a precedent for it. Three congressional delegates visited Washington's headquarters in October to assist in planning and other arrangements.[8]

On 2 November the committee to Washington's headquarters returned to Philadelphia and Congress agreed to appoint the committee that Schuyler wanted to assist in military and civil arrangements for Canada. As yet unaware of the selection of John Langdon, (New Hampshire) Robert Treat Paine, (Massachusetts) and Eliphalet Dyer (Connecticut), Schuyler repeated his request for a committee on 7 November. Announcing the 2 November victory at Saint John's, he reiterated the arguments that a committee could manage various business that neither he (for want of health) nor Montgomery (for the burdens of other work) could do. Again on 11 November he wrote President Hancock, insisting that a committee must be sent to Ticonderoga.[9]

Fig. 3. Robert R. Livingston, 1746–1813. Oil on canvas by John Van-
derlyn. Livingston was one of three members of the congressional fact-
finding committee whose mission was to survey the condition of the
Northern Army. The committee's recommendations bore out Schuyler's
convictions about the direction of the army. Courtesy, The New-York
Historical Society, New York City.

Meantime, on 8 November, Congress agreed upon instructions for the committee. Gunning Bedford of Delaware and others thought the committee should have included Southerners; not only might they better serve the purpose of the mission, but Schuyler would find them more agreeable than Yankees. In the end one of the three Yankee committee members was replaced. When Eliphalet Dyer asked to be excused, Robert R. Livingston of New York was substituted.[10]

Directed to move speedily to Ticonderoga, Livingston, Paine, and Langdon were to consult Schuyler on a variety of points: the number troops needed to hold Canada, the best method of obtaining and keeping them during the winter, and ways and means of persuading Canadians to join the rebellion. They were also authorized to direct the procurement of provisions for an army of three thousand for six months, to settle arrears in pay, and to offer two months' pay as bounties for reenlistments. Promising to procure as much specie as was needed for the success of the Canadian venture, Congress indicated that officers' salaries were to be increased. Regimental organization was described in detail. Likewise, daily rations were specified down to the last pound of food, candles, and soap. Fortifications at Ticonderoga and Crown Point must be repaired, and arms purchased from the sick for use by the able-bodied. With Schuyler's cooperation the committee was authorized to raise reinforcements in Canada, New York, and New England and to induce Canadians to send delegates to Congress with assurances that their political and religious rights would be respected. On their way up the Hudson the committee members were also to survey fortifications for the Highlands (a subject upon which Schuyler had been asked for advice in October); and all cannon and military stores for Canada not required there must be shipped to Albany to await Congress's disposition.[11]

On 11 November Congress added instructions that any two members of the committee could transact business should one be disabled or prevented from making the journey. They also must consult the generals of the department about the propriety of sending artillery and all or parts of their armies to Quebec for support of Benedict Arnold's expedition, which was then moving through northern New England, or for renewing an attack on that fortress city should Arnold's have failed.[12] The committeemen left Philadelphia on 11 November but did not reach Ticonderoga until two-and-a-half weeks later. Part of the delay was caused by their inspection tour of the Hudson Highlands. Fortifications then under construction there were found to be insufficient to withstand an enemy attack, and they recommended the installation of obstructions at the narrows. Indeed, the recommendations confirmed what Schuyler had urged earlier when asked for advice about securing the lower reaches of the Hudson against possible British naval incursions.[13]

With winter approaching, enlistments expiring, many soldiers returning from Canada, and Montgomery wishing to retire, it was not surprising that Schuyler grew impatient when Livingston, Langdon, and Paine failed to appear promptly at his headquarters. Their presence was vital, for much must be done to promote reenlistments. With Arnold's dwindled forces added to Montgomery's, Schuyler estimated that the entire army by the end of November would number approximately nineteen hundred; later the committee at his headquarters reported only seventeen hundred, which was more than a thousand short of the total he proposed for the winter.[14]

Writing the committeemen on 22 November, Schuyler requested pardon for presuming "to press You not to make the least Delay. Pray bring beds," he added, " ... I have only one here." Four days later the three congressmen reached Fort George, but severely cold temperatures deterred their passage across the lake, and not until the evening of 28 November were they able to reach Ticonderoga. By then a schooner and row galley captured at Saint John's had appeared with an American sloop and schooner, laden with baggage and prisoners of war. Arrangements for moving the prisoners elsewhere now became necessary.[15]

In many respects Schuyler happily found that the committee's instructions coincided with most of his own proposals and that the members were agreeably responsive to his various suggestions. But they declined to go beyond Ticonderoga. Schuyler's and Montgomery's hopes for their presence in Canada to arrange the election of delegates to Congress and otherwise to promote the army's welfare were dashed. Livingston, Paine, and Langon recommended that Montgomery arrange for Canadian parishes to elect a convention, which in turn could send delegates to Philadelphia. As far as the prisoners from Canada were concerned, Schuyler was relieved to learn from the committee that his proposals coincided with Congress's orders that such captives be sent to Pennsylvania. Included were Brig. Gen. Richard Prescott and several officers who had been taken with three schooners, two sloops, a brigantine, and several other vessels. Welcoming the acquisitions, Montgomery's forces found that the cargoes of these craft included several pieces of artillery, arms, tools, and a variety of provisions. These had been with Governor Carleton's forces when they fled from Montreal to Quebec.[16]

Their stay with Schuyler at Ticonderoga was brief, but after the committeemen left the fort on 1 December, Schuyler followed them to Albany, where they remained until 10 December. Doubtless there were further consultations in the interval. The report they submitted to Congress on Schuyler's behalf just before Christmas was pressed with "utmost earnestness."[17] Having witnessed the difficulties otherwise described only in pen and ink, the three delegates could represent them more forcefully and sympathetically than Congress could otherwise perceive them from afar.

The committee's official account contained a variety of information gleaned from the members' travels; recounting their own activities, it offered detailed recommendations for action by Congress. Montgomery, they said, had been obliged to coax Connecticut troops from Saint John's for his assault on Montreal by promising them that they could go home once Montreal had been taken. Seth Warner's regiment of Green Mountain Boys also ran off, although their enlistments would not expire until 1 January. Only about 200 Yankee troops reenlisted with Montgomery, and those of his army who were willing to remain in Canada totaled about 1,000. Benedict Arnold's contingent was estimated to contain about 550, bringing the total of all American forces in Canada to perhaps 1,700. These included noneffectives, but Schuyler had no accurate count for any of them. Obliged by pragmatic foresight to begin reenlisting soldiers before receiving congressional directions thereon, the committee found that Schuyler had not been able to make arrangements exactly as specified. Acting upon Congress's general promise to furnish clothing, he and Montgomery, for example, had decided to procure it at Montreal and to issue it as a bounty. The committee urged that funds for reenlistments be diverted to cover the clothing bounty. The reenlistment of troops was too serious a problem to quibble over all particulars.

The committee's report went on to say that the Canadian regiment authorized by Congress had been enlisted even before the order had reached Montgomery. In response to complaints by soldiers in the lake country that they would not reenlist if they must labor as boatmen and carpenters, the committee proposed the hiring of civilian laborers, especially because this would be more economical. With respect to the army's Canadian food supply, the committee deemed provisions to be adequate until spring; then, except for bread, more would have to be furnished from New York or adjacent colonies. The transportation of cannon from Saint John's and Ticonderoga to Washington's army at Cambridge had by now been arranged, but Schuyler had found it impossible to purchase more than a few arms from men who had quit the service. He and the committee also agreed to provide a storekeeper and barracksmaster for each garrison; and because of a shortage of blankets they fell upon the expedient of cutting damaged or worn-out tents into sacks— one for every two men—for barracks "cribs."

Other parts of the committee's report touched upon matters of administrative detail as well as general aims for the future. Because Schuyler had persuaded them that repairs of Crown Point fortifications would be more costly than useful, efforts should be concentrated upon Ticonderoga; but even there little could be accomplished during the winter unless new troop levies were sent up. Even for the winter Schuyler wanted at least four companies of ninety men and officers each stationed there and at Fort Edward in addition to three thousand men in Canada. The committee concurred and proposed that three regiments (each consisting of eight companies) be raised at once and sent to Lake Champlain where they would be ready to march into Canada in the spring. And to facilitate the future movements of men and supplies they suggested that Schuyler clear the course of Wood Creek for bateau navigation, thus opening a "communication" between Fort Ann and Skenesborough. The committee lamely argued that Montgomery could manage the political organization of Canadians without it, but that Montgomery might "pave the way for the reception of any Committee" Congress might later decide to send when ice-covered waters could "render the Journey more practicable, and when it may probably be attended with Salutary effects."[18]

By the time Congress considered its committee's report, Schuyler, too, had furnished information with which to buttress it. Commenting upon the committee's rather general references to some problems, Schuyler typically noted the particular details that must be considered. With respect to clothing, for example, he cited the need for Canadian moccasins, not ordinary shoes; and he specified that every soldier should have a woolen cap, mittens, and a pair of "Indian stockings." Administrative procedures also warranted refinement. Officers' commissions should be reworded so that those who in fact left the service could be discharged; otherwise they might claim salaries for the entire period for which their units had been enlisted. Moreover, accounts of funds supplied by various colonies could not be settled without Congress's orders to submit them. The cost of supporting prisoners of war was proving to be so great that the general asked whether the British commander at Boston might be asked to pay for them. Hinting again that he intended to resign his command, Schuyler suggested that in order to avoid further trouble with the turbulent, mutinous spirit of the army, Congress must take action on the subject of military discipline.[19]

Schuyler's reference to his intended resignation may have been designed to reinforce the report offered by the congressional committee on his behalf. However, it was clearly qualified by his pledge not to surrender his command until the campaign was ended and until preparations were made for an ensuing one. Still, the proposal of resignation prompted anxious responses from both Washington and President Hancock.

Washington begged him not to think further of resigning unless he had been so unequivocal in his notice to Congress as to be unable to "recede" from the inclination. Like Schuyler, he had encountered difficulties that he had never expected. But these must be borne. The American cause was just and righteous, and officers must surmount the obstacles thrust in their path.[20]

Hancock, too, expressed Congress's wish that Schuyler not deprive the country of the benefits of his zeal and abilities—nor should he lose the honor of completing a glorious work already so successfully begun. Congress had unanimously resolved that his "[c]onduct, Attention, and Perseverance, merit the Thanks of the United Colonies." Already the Yorker had "risen superior to a Thousand Difficulties . . . reaped many Laurels, but a plentiful Harvest still invites you. Proceed therefore," Hancock urged, "and let the Footsteps of Victory open a Way for Blessings of Liberty, and the Happiness of well-ordered Government to visit extensive Dominion." Schuyler must "Consider that the road to glory is seldom strewed with Flowers," and that he would "receive an honourable Compensation for all your Fatigues, in being able to leave the Memory of illustrious Actions, attended by the Gratitude of a great and free People, as a fair, a splendid, and a valuable Inheritance to your Posterity." Hancock's florid encomiums were supplemented by Nathaniel Woodhull, president of the New York Provincial Congress.[21]

In the ensuing months Schuyler retreated from his inclination to resign the department command. Committed to the call of duty and lured by the chances of grasping glory, he was also reassured by the prospects of what Hancock had reminded him might be "the Happiness, or Misery, of Millions yet unborn." The response from Congress to his leadership, his proposals, and to the recommendations of the small committee so completely supportive of his own ideas proved to be encouraging if not altogether prompt.[22]

2

Another Round with the Iroquois

For several months after the Indian conference in August 1775 Schuyler was little troubled by concerns for the Iroquois. Upon his return to Albany on 7 December, however, he was confronted by about sixty tribesmen who insisted upon further talks. Since the fall of Montreal, the sachems were ready to offer congratulations. Obliged to listen to them for a full day on 8 December, Schuyler and Volkert Douw then set 11 December for the conduct of various business with the delegation. The absence of three members of the Northern Department's board of Indian commissioners prompted the general to suggest that Congress add two or three Albanians to the board in order to facilitate future proceedings by more than a minority of its members.[23]

The meeting scheduled for 11 December was evidently postponed to the following day in order to await the arrival of a third commissioner, Timothy Edwards of Massachusetts. Apprised of difficulties that had lingered since the August conference, the commissioners endeavored to clarify the business of the old Wyoming land controversy. The subject had been raised by an Onondaga, Tiahogwando. At issue was an Iroquois cession of territory in the Susquehanna valley to Pennsylvania and the claim of Connecticut settlers to the land. The latter was based on a fraudulent treaty made earlier between a Yankee agent and some Mohawk tribesmen. "These land grievances rankled the Iroquois and stood as an impediment to a sincere friendship between them and the Americans." The commissioners had been able only to promise to refer land problems to Congress, but since Commissioner Turbutt Francis had prompted Tiahogwando to raise the subject on behalf of Pennsylvania interests, it now seemed necessary to determine whether other sachems supported him in voicing a grievance. Interpreters James Dean and Samuel Kirkland had reported that the sachems had disapproved of Tiahogwando's remarks. The tribesmen now in Albany indicated nothing beyond the fact that Francis had promised them presents if the Susquehanna land matter were raised without mention of his involvement. Yet the clashing claims of Connecticut and Pennsylvania were not the proper business of the Indian commissioners, whose concern for treaty making was centered on the Indians' response to the Anglo-American hostilities.[24]

More significantly, on 12 December Schuyler and commissioners Douw and Edwards learned more about Col. Guy Johnson's summer conferences with the tribes, which had culminated in a meeting at Montreal. There the British officer offered them war belts and the hatchet. Canadian Indians had accepted and feasted on a "Bostonian"—a roasted ox. The belt was now surrendered to Schuyler and his colleagues. Reporting to Washington and the president of Congress, the general used it as proof of the British government's effort to engage the Indians as allies instead of making them neutral. However he was happy to discover that the American seizure of Montreal on 13 November had convinced most of the Six Nations that they could not do without American friendship or trade. The rebel victory, he noted, had rendered them "all humiliation."[25]

With the surrender of Colonel Johnson's war belt the December conference served to reconfirm the August promise of Iroquois neutrality, and in early January 1776 these assurances were supplemented when thirty Caughnawaga visited Albany and pledged Schuyler their peace and friendship on the basis of neutrality. They, too, testified to Johnson's "infernal invitation" to eat a "Bostonian" and drink his blood.[26]

The general then endeavored to reinforce the commitment of these tribesmen to their decision by sending thirteen of them to visit Washington's headquarters, where they might be impressed by the display of American military might. Except for the attendant expense, both Schuyler and Washington were willing to engage Indians who volunteered enlistment. But not until June 1776 did the Continental Congress reverse its neutrality policy and permit the employment of Indians wherever the commander in chief found they might be useful.[27]

3

Cannon from Lake Champlain, Christmas, and Cornelia

Prompted by Lt. Col. Henry Knox, Washington decided to ask for Schuyler's artillery that the army invading Canada had left behind at Saint John's and Lake Champlain. On 16 November he wrote of his plans to dislodge the British at Boston by bombardment. Knox would fetch the artillery with whatever powder and lead might be spared.[28] The Yorker was expected to make the necessary preparations, and indeed it was largely his efforts that enabled Knox to execute his mission. The only notable delay was caused by the weather, which proved unusually moderate until Christmas Eve. The artillery convoy was forced to tarry until rivers froze in early January and enough snow had fallen to facilitate the movement of sleds.

Washington's call for artillery reached Schuyler at Ticonderoga on 26 November. After the congressional committee arrived there two days later, the Yorker consulted them, and it was they who directed the transfer of artillery from Saint John's as well as Ticonderoga. On 5 December, in view of his departure for Albany, Schuyler gave directions for the shipment of the heavy equipment to proceed by water, not ice, at least as far as the fort at the south end of Lake George.[29] But long stretches of overland transportation depended on frozen ground and snow-covered trails, and considerable labor was required just to move the fieldpieces from Ticonderoga to the Landing at the north end of Lake George and on to the point where they could be shifted from boats to sleds.

Henry Knox reached Albany on 1 December, and by the evening of 4 December he had reached Fort George, where he stayed the night in the company of one of the British prisoners of war, Lt. John André. There he also encountered Schuyler, who was riding south toward Albany. Having already arranged for Knox's collection of equipment, the general promised further assistance in moving it beyond Albany as soon as snow made sledding possible. In the following days Col. James Holmes, commandant of Ticonderoga, executed Schuyler's orders for moving the cannon and other arms to the Landing by sled and thence across Lake George.[30]

The collection of ordnance taken from Ticonderoga included several brass guns from a schooner, a variety of mortars taken from Saint John's, five eighteen-pound cannon, one nine-pounder, two thirteen-inch mortars, and one nine-inch mortar collected from the bridge and shipyard. Other pieces were evidently collected from Crown Point and Fort George. By 9 December the first of the guns were moved by water toward the fort at the south end of Lake George. The shipment was sizable: fifty-nine pieces in all, weighing almost sixty tons, together with a barrel of flints and about two dozen boxes of lead. The enterprise of crossing the lake required about a week and evidently tied up most of the available boats, which, as Colonel Holmes noted on 16 December, were all "employed for important purposes."[31]

Meantime, having reached Albany on 7 December, Schuyler began to organize the further movement of Knox's artillery convoy by engaging drivers, teams, and sleds. Busy with other duties such as conferring with the Iroquois sachems, moving prisoners of war, and calling for reinforcements for the northern garrisons, the general waited to learn of Knox's progress.[32]

A week before Christmas Knox notified Schuyler that the mortars and cannon had been assembled at Fort George. Capt. George Palmer of Stillwater had agreed to furnish teams and conveyances for the train by 21 December, but Knox anticipated difficulties in crossing the Hudson at Albany for want of a proper scow. Ignorant of the roads south of Halfmoon, he asked Schuyler whether it would be practicable to follow the east bank of the Hudson south to Kinderhook. As witnessed by his request for a speedy shipment of five hundred fathoms of rope with which to lash the cannon and mortars to sleds, Knox depended upon Schuyler for more than advice and direction.[33]

Anticipating Knox's needs, Schuyler notified him that he had already taken steps for moving the artillery train from Albany to Boston. Only the snow was lacking. But he urged Knox to countermand any arrangements with Palmer; the expense was unnecessary and there were ten times as many available sleds as were necessary to drag the fieldpieces out of Albany County.[34]

By Christmas Eve Knox had moved his artillery train to Saratoga, and that day he halted eight miles south of Schuyler's country house. By Christmas Day the Albany area was covered with about two feet of snow, and drovers spent the holiday dragging the equipment as far as Lansingburgh, about nine miles north of Albany. On the evening of 26 December Knox, who had "almost perish'd with the Cold," enjoyed the comforts of Schuyler's fireside and the bounties of his table.[35] The corpulent colonel loved to eat, and perhaps he also enjoyed the sight of his hosts' teenage daughters and their little brothers, ten-year-old John; Philip, who was nearly eight, and Rensselaer, almost three. Holiday festivities in the Schuyler household were heightened by the safe delivery of a daughter on 21 December. Named for her paternal grandmother, Cornelia Van Cortlandt, the infant was the thirteenth in the line of fifteen offspring, of which only eight survived birth or infancy.

In the last few days of the month Schuyler helped Knox make the final arrangements for his long trek to Boston. They hired men, sleds, and the oxen and horses to drag the artillery across the Hudson and through New England. By New Year's Eve, 124 teams of horses were straining to move the train of ordnance forward. On New Year's Day practically all of Albany's available "carriages" were employed in moving the cannon and mortars toward the banks of the Hudson. In order to thicken the ice, holes were cut in the river's surface to induce flooding, and on 3 January 1776 the first cannon were brought to the city. Because of a thaw it was not until four days later that Schuyler witnessed the first pieces crossing the river by sled. Even so, there was one final difficulty.[36]

Two of the heaviest cannon broke the ice. About to sit down to dinner on 4 January, Knox was alarmed by Schuyler's news that a twenty-four-pounder had sunk into the river at the Halfmoon ferry. While workmen labored to move their weighty cargo forward, Knox spent his time viewing the falls at Cohoes, bright with ice and glittering snow. At about noon on 9 January, after seeing "all the Cannon set out from the ferry opposite Albany," Knox took leave of Schuyler and other friends he had made during his stay in the city. Although one of the fieldpieces had been rescued from the broken ice, on 10 January the general reported that the other had yet to be pulled from the water. Knox was obliged to leave this piece behind; weeks later it was retrieved and returned to the lake country.[37]

Save for that single piece of artillery, all the others scraped across the icy countryside south to Kinderhook and Claverack and then east to Great

Barrington and to Washington's headquarters at Cambridge.[38] With Schuyler's assistance Knox's mission enabled Washington force the British out of Boston. Meantime, the early months of a new year brought no surcease in Schuyler's responsibilities; the completion of one task led only to a succession of others for him to discharge. And the end of the 1775 campaign meant only the preparation of another.

4

1775 in Retrospect

With Richard Montgomery and Benedict Arnold's assault upon Quebec on New Year's Eve, the campaign of 1775 faltered, leaving only remnants of the army to maintain a cordon around the city during the winter. In a sense the campaign had ended, and the invasion seems to have failed because the Americans had been unable to take Quebec. Failure, indeed, may be the verdict if success is measured by the goals of winning the colony to the rebel cause and of removing the British threat from Canada. On the other hand the enemy had not yet reinforced Quebec, nor was it yet clear that they would actually be able to do so or that they would be able to push the rebels back into New York. And it is noteworthy that Schuyler's army was responsible for less than half of all American losses in military engagements during the first year of the war. A grand total of 1,340 killed, wounded, captured, missing, and deserted included 625 from the Northern Department. This is not a particularly discreditable record when one considers that except for Washington's army at Boston, Schuyler's was the one that accounted for most of the rebels' military effort during 1775. Of the 625, most (436) had been captured; and of the latter most were taken prisoner at Quebec. Similarly, most of the killed and wounded also fell during the attack on Quebec. Curiously, 55 of the 57 American deserters also came from the Northern Army.[39]

Moreover, a verdict of failure in 1775 cannot be rendered without qualifications. Victories had been won at Chambly, Saint John's, and Montreal with very few losses, and Schuyler's army was not finally forced to retreat until the middle of the following year.[40]

Could the campaign have succeeded in 1775 had it moved more rapidly? And how much faster could it have been executed? Was Schuyler or any other single leader responsible for the delay that made the difference? Or were Congress, the wary Canadians, and the various army contingents also accountable for the slow progress of the enterprise? Was Schuyler himself directly guilty of indecisiveness or procrastination? Answers to such questions are not easily given with the advantage of hindsight. But it seems fair to conclude that the general alone was not culpable. He had proceeded sensibly with both initiative and thoroughness in assembling an invasionary force, carefully seeking assurances of Canadians' neutral if not friendly reactions, and guarantees of a similar sort on the part of the Indians of New York and Canada. A combination of men and circumstances made these tasks difficult, as his story has shown. The initiation of the war was a complicated business and also time-consuming. The wonder is that so much was accomplished or even attempted as speedily as Schuyler, his colleagues, and revolutionary bodies like the Continental Congress managed to do. To a large extent the general was obliged to rely on others to create his army and to furnish it adequately with provisions and equipment. But the Northern Army did not lack energetic and courageous commanders. Where Schuyler urged haste or applied his energies to the creation of organization and discipline, others did not; but neither could they invariably respond with equal fervor or effectiveness. Even when ultimately forced out of the field by illness, he labored relentlessly to provide Montgomery's troops with as many reinforcements and provisions, with as much specie and other assistance, as it was possible for any man to have done.

It is practically impossible to calculate what effect Schuyler's absence from the army had upon the morale of its officers and men. He has been criticized for so long for ineptitude, procrastination, indecisiveness, and especially for unpopularity with the rank and file; but one wonders why the performances of other commanders like Richard Montgomery, who experienced the same kind and degree of insubordination and lack of discipline as Schuyler himself, have not been criticized for the very parts they contributed to Schuyler's own record of alleged failures?

The Canadian campaign might indeed have succeeded if Congress or the New York and New England governments had been more generous and prompt in sending men and supplies. But were they more capable of doing so than their performance indicates? The campaign might also have succeeded had Carleton's British forces been outnumbered by both American troops and their Canadian sympathizers.[41] But Canadians were little more committed to the rebels than to the British. Moreover, American soldiers were hostile to discipline, and many were unwilling to persevere under undeniable hardships or beyond short enlistments. These circumstances of course affected the outcome of the campaign, as indeed contemporaries like Gouverneur Morris and George Washington realized well before its conclusion. Morris noted that Schuyler's best efforts had not saved him from an "undisciplined and ill provided" army. And Washington observed in late November that "[i]t grieves me to see so little of that patriotick Spirit, which I was taught to believe was the Characteristick of this people."[42]

The American army in Canada was of course obliged to move in stages, and at every step it suffered the dimunitions of deaths, sickness, desertion, and ultimately the refusal of many soldiers to extend their service or to reenlist. That refusal was really no more affected by the caliber of Schuyler's leadership than by the quality of Montgomery's or others'. Had Arnold's original forces reached the Saint Lawrence largely intact instead of losing about half their numbers, or had they arrived a month earlier than they were able to do, Montgomery might have been more successful, and both he and Schuyler would then have gathered laurels. But the physical obstacles of the New England wilderness were underestimated, and the delay of more than a month made a crucial difference. Ironically, Washington's removal of much of Schuyler's artillery and all of his heavy cannon from Ticonderoga later proved to be disadvantageous for the besiegers of Quebec. Although Washington was thereby able to force the British to evacuate Boston, Arnold and Wooster's forces were deprived of the means to succeed at Quebec. General Wooster reported on 20 January that Arnold needed artillery for the bombardment of the citadel; what he had was simply inadequate to the task. The guns remaining in the department—four-, six-, nine-, twelve-pounders, and but one eighteen-pounder—were not large enough to fulfill the needs of the little army at Quebec. And Schuyler correctly surmised that the siege must fail if indeed its success depended upon mortars and heavy cannon, which he could not supply to his men on the Saint Lawrence. Washington lamely apologized to Schuyler late in February, explaining that when he had sent Knox for the artillery he had not intended that Schuyler should be "disfurnished."[43]

However, even a victory at Quebec could not have guaranteed that Schuyler, Montgomery, and Arnold would not face the challenge of British reinforcements in the spring. And it is doubtful that Congress would have been able or even willing to commit an army as large as ten thousand men, which is what Montgomery and Schuyler proposed to hold Canada in 1776. The events of the winter of 1775–76 suggest, however, that Schuyler and others worked hard to prepare for a new campaign. The British could be expected to attempt a reassertion of their sway beyond Quebec and to push the ragged rebels out of the fourteenth colony. They might also attempt to reverse the invasion entirely by carrying the war south into the province of New York.

The Challenge of 1776

1

Something must be done, and that speedily, or I greatly fear we are ruined.
　　　　　　　　　　　　　　　　　—Brig. General David Wooster

*S*chuyler's preparations for a fresh onslaught in 1776 began months before the new year's campaign. Plans were dictated by the turn of seasons as well as by his sense of strategy and his firm command of logistical principles. "Effective supply and administration is a first condition of success," and like Washington, Schuyler appreciated that point as much as he observed the principal objective of eighteenth-century warfare: preserving one's force.[1] The Yorker also realized that effective supply and administration both governed and limited overall strategy, and it is to his credit that he was both early and accurate in anticipating the British plans for 1776 and 1777 and that he acted accordingly.

For 1776 the overall British strategy proved to be basically straightforward. After taking Manhattan, Sir William Howe's main army would push north along the Hudson while a lesser one moved south along Lake Champlain and Lake George. Or if Howe could pin down Washington's forces in southern New York and New Jersey, a British invasion from the north might simply be allowed to advance. Washington must then either retreat from the Hudson River and leave New England isolated from the middle colonies, or he must risk his raw troops in a decisive battle. Either way, the rebels *could* be defeated. However, the British effort in Canada proved to be an "example of wasted manpower and time," for it diverted thousands of troops to Quebec, "far off on the edge of the battle scene,"

93

and it encountered the determined labors of Philip Schuyler to prevent a juncture of royal forces moving from opposite ends of the Lake Champlain-Hudson valley highway.[2]

The Northern Department commander first tried to reinforce the American army in Quebec and then managed to impede the British invaders as they pursued the fleeing rebels across Lake Champlain. Here was the great rehearsal for the 1777 campaign, which ended as it did because of what Schuyler and a few colleagues accomplished. In short, there were "determined and convinced men in every level of the rebellion who kept their comrades at the job." Schuyler no less than Washington persevered in his and persuaded others to do likewise. Together they enabled Continental forces to survive. As long as the patriot army existed, the British had not won.[3] That the British were unable to destroy the Continental army was in part due to Schuyler's overall success both in timely preparation and adeptness in defensive maneuvering even in retreat, as his forces skirmished with the enemy, harassed him, interrupted his transportation, and removed food and supplied from his reach.

The general's timeliness in preparing for 1776 was evident in the report of the congressional committee that visited Schuyler and viewed the northern outposts late in November 1775. Although the small contingent besieging Quebec was first deemed sufficient for the winter, Schuyler proposed that at least three thousand reinforcements be stationed in Canada before spring broke the ice of the Saint Lawrence. By the end of February thawing could begin. Earlier, he had informed the committee that it would be prudent to add three thousand men to the army in Canada by 8 December and he expected Congress to advise him to issue more warrants for the enlisting of a regiment while four companies of men were being recruited for winter service at Ticonderoga and Fort Edward. Aside from the need for Canadian moccasins, Indian leggings, woolen caps, and mittens with which to cope with the northern winter, there were real discouragements to the work of recruiting new forces.[4]

One such impediment was reenlistments—a business that was complicated by unsettled accounts. There were, however, some matters upon which the general could act without waiting for congressional approval. Because the visiting committee had agreed, he decided to hire carpenters to mend the Albany barracks, which were then in such disrepair as to discourage enlistment of the men who must be quartered in them. But by mid-December Schuyler was hardly reassured by news that recruiting officers were finding little success with enlistments. It was questionable that once the terms of troops at Ticonderoga and Fort George expired on 31 December they would agree to extend their enlistments.[5]

The report of the committee that had conferred with Schuyler at Ticonderoga contained other points, revealing not only his recent difficulties but also his current needs and his requirements for operations in 1776. Their firsthand acquaintance with his circumstances in the field prompted the three congressmen to endorse Schuyler's recommendations with particular impetus.

First, the report noted the need to survey the Hudson River to the north end of the Highlands with a view to obstructing the Narrows. Without this the construction of other defenses would be inadequate to block the British from moving up the valley. Next came a resumé of the problem of maintaining the army. American forces then in Canada did not exceed seventeen to nineteen hundred, including those not fit for duty. Necessity had obliged Schuyler to order the reenlistment of men before he could obtain congressional directions, and the committee explained that this was accomplished on terms at variance with Congress's provisions. But troops stationed on Lake George and Lake Champlain were not inclined to reenlist, partly because of their disgust with having to serve as laborers. Accordingly, the committee recommended authorization to hire men to work as boatmen. Finally, persuaded by Schuyler that the usefulness of Crown Point would not justify the high cost of repairing the post, the committee agreed that Ticonderoga should be the focus of all efforts to improve fortification. And with regard to improved transportation of troops and supplies to Ticonderoga the committee directed Schuyler to open a "communication" between Fort Ann and Skenesborough by clearing Wood Creek of obstructions. The movement of bateaux might be improved along this waterway, which emptied into the lake at Skenesborough, thereby facilitating access to Ticonderoga. The committee also endorsed both Schuyler's call for four companies to be stationed at the lake forts during the winter and his recommendation that at least three thousand men be sent to Canada. Meantime, other reinforcements—at least three regiments—must be collected at Ticonderoga at once and prepared for movement in the spring.[6]

Schuyler's proposals for reinforcements of the army in Canada were also supported by generals Montgomery, Arnold, and Wooster. In early January 1776, just after Montgomery's death, Arnold insisted that Congress must not think of sending less than eight or ten thousand men if a lasting connection with Canada was to be secured. And Wooster echoed these sentiments. "Something must be done, and that speedily," he urged, "or I greatly fear we are ruined." There were but five to six hundred men to maintain three garrisons at Montreal, Chambly, and Saint John's. Many were expected to flee for home as soon as their enlistments expired, and others had already run off. Canadians, eager to ally with the winners of the struggle, were unreliable—almost like savages, he said. Moreover, Roman Catholic clergy had warned their flocks to arm against the invaders, and they refused sacramental absolution to parishioners who were friendly to the Americans.[7]

Almost a month before Wooster penned his report to Schuyler, the general had informed Washington that if Congress agreed to his proposals for reinforcements and sent three thousand men to Albany at once, he believed they could be pushed into Canada by mid-January. But he hoped in vain because Congress did not act until 8 January. As December waned he repeated his importunities to President Hancock.[8]

While Schuyler waited, hoped, pleaded, and fretted about the tardiness in obtaining reinforcements, Congress did not receive its committee's report on the Northern Department until 23 December. Robert R. Livingston sent condolences for what he deemed was Congress's neglect of the general.[9] Dismayed by the inability to obtain action from Congress for more than a month, Schuyler finally wrote Washington to explain why he had contemplated retirement from public life. He agreed with Washington that virtuous Americans must exert themselves in the cause of liberty and sacrifice the sweets of domestic felicity. He had made the "firmest resolution to sink or swim" with his country, "unanxious how I quit the stage of life, provided that I leave to my posterity the happy reflection that their ancestor was an honest *American*." Personal difficulties had not been his reasons for thinking of retirement; rather he believed that the good of his country should not be prejudiced. He could overlook the disagreeable nature of his responsibilities "were it not that it has chiefly arisen from prejudice and jealousy." It had been argued that the department commander ought to be of the colony providing a majority of the troops, and Connecticut soldiers apparently would not bear with a general not of that province. On the other hand such notions tended to alienate even New Yorkers' affections. In the end Schuyler persevered, but with fresh reports of the weakness of Arnold and Montgomery's combined forces and fears of what might happen to them, "I tremble" he noted, "lest *Canada* should be lost."[10]

The Continental Congress began to act upon the Yorker's November proposals with a series of resolves on 8, 9, and 10 January 1776. Most of them fit his specifications, but several matters were delayed: not until February was he told to proceed with arms inspections, repairs, and replacement; and not until almost a year later did Congress make provision for the regimental paymasters' accounting.[11]

Most significant of the congressional resolutions were those regarding manpower for Schuyler's department. Shipwrights from New York and Philadelphia were to be sent to Ticonderoga to build up to a hundred bateaux, and Schuyler was to hire enough men to row them, thus obviating soldiers' complaints about being treated as mere laborers, which had been an impediment to their reenlistments. However, on 6 January Schuyler had already signed an agreement with Jacob Hilton of Albany to employ a company of men to construct bateaux, other vessels, and buildings. The battalion of Canadians already raised under Col. James Livingston was approved. In addition, eight other battalions were to be maintained for the defense of Canada in 1776. Two were to be formed of the troops already there. Three more were to be raised in New Hampshire, New York, and Connecticut. One of five such units recently ordered to be raised in Pennsylvania was also to be sent to Canada; Colonel Bull's First Pennsylvania and Col. William Maxwell's Second New Jersey regiments were ordered to march immediately to Schuyler's command at Albany.[12] With a net gain of six new regiments the general might expect between a thousand and fifteen hundred more men than the two thousand he had requested—if the units were completed instead of being sent only partially formed. The remainder of Congress's twenty-two resolutions covered a variety of subjects, no less indicative of Schuyler's labors than of Congress's interest in what he or others had proposed.[13]

Beset by illness and then by the diversion of leading militia into Tryon County to deal with the inhabitants' fears of a Tory menace, Schuyler was unable to acknowledge President Hancock's notification of Congress's provisions for his department until 22 January. But he had not been idle; seldom could he snatch a moment's relaxation from a variety of demands upon his attention. During the first week of January he completed arrangements for Henry Knox's relay of artillery between Ticonderoga and Boston. He consulted the Indian commissioners and a band of Caughnawaga from Canada who visited Albany and agreed to a peace treaty. Thirteen of the tribesmen were sent to visit Washington's headquarters in an effort to further impress the Indians with the power of the rebel forces. Again he appealed to Congress to deal with troublesome officers who claimed pay beyond the time of quitting the service. And many accounts remained unsettled because the requisite papers had not been submitted, although claimants—some of whom were the troops who had been responsible for the seizure of Ticonderoga and Crown Point during the previous May—wanted payments. In response to Connecticut's generous allowances for travel and billeting charges, the general suggested that no colony should be permitted to make allowances for its troops beyond what Congress deemed proper for men in the Continental line.[14]

About six in the evening on 13 January Schuyler received dispatches carried by Edward Antill and Moses Hazen from General Wooster. The blow had fallen: "[t]he affectionate the gallant Montgomery" was dead. Schuyler's note to Robert R. Livingston revealed how intimately his sympathies flowed to men with whom he shared a real measure of trust, respect, and congeniality. Similarly, he rushed word to Washington that "[m]y Amiable Friend the Gallant Montgomery is no more." Arnold had been wounded, and "we have met with a severe Check." Nothing might prevent the "most fatal" consequences to the American troops in Canada unless Washington could immediately send reinforcements. The resurgence of danger steeled Schuyler to the necessity of remaining in the public service.[15]

The Yorker also appealed to Congress, proposing that Washington immediately send three thousand men to Canada via the Onion River and Lake Champlain. Again he urged that a "full-empowered committee" be hurried to Albany to assist in the current crisis; and he proposed to march local militia west to deal with a Tory menace in Tryon County.[16] To David Wooster, Schuyler could only send assurances that he was struggling to find three thousand reinforcements for the little army on the Saint Lawrence—and prayers that Heaven bring the men out of peril. God must give Wooster the guidance that Schuyler, not knowing the particular circumstances, would not presume to offer from so great a distance.[17]

Despite Schuyler's pressing cry for troops, Washington had no men to spare, especially because of the dissolution of the old army and the recruiting of a new one that proceeded but slowly. The Yorker must wait the results of Congress's resolutions for the raising of new regiments in Connecticut, Massachusetts, and New Hampshire for a year's service. Meantime, perhaps Arnold could obtain reinforcements from Connecticut and the Hampshire Grants. But Schuyler had already recognized this possibility and had posted a request to Col. Seth Warner for all the men he could raise on the Grants.[18]

As news spread from Albany of Montgomery's defeat at Quebec, the committees of nearby Massachusetts communities responded to Schuyler's alarms by offering to raise troops for Canada.[19] Congress also reacted by supplementing their resolutions of 8, 9, and 10 January for the support of Schuyler's department. A second regiment of Canadians was to be enlisted by Moses Hazen and Edward Antill, who had brought the news from Canada. Moreover, Congress issued orders for rushing troops to the north, collecting specie, and paying special gratuities for recruiting and bonuses for enlistments. Washington was directed to appoint a replacement for Montgomery, and a new address was hurried to the Canadians, assuring them of American protection against the British. Again Congress urged them to establish associations in their parishes and to elect a provincial assembly that might then send delegates to Philadelphia.[20]

Thus armed, Hazen and Antill returned to Montreal. But their recruiting efforts proved to be largely unsuccessful. Only a few hundred Canadians were willing to serve, and others refused to risk their skins when the American army obviously lacked manpower, specie, or credit.[21]

By mid-January, Schuyler found little else to do about the crucial affairs of Canada but wait for Congress's newly ordered regiments to be enlisted, equipped, and marched on their winter venture. Weeks would pass before the general could push them through the northern forests and lake country. Although a considerable stir was made to collect more men for Continental service, the actual execution of the business, reflected in a week's exchange of correspondence, required more weeks to bring to fruition. And questions invariably arose for which the answers entailed still more delay.[22]

Momentarily, however, Schuyler was obliged to turn his sights from Canada to the Mohawk valley. Responding to alarms of a Tory menace and the threat of Sir John Johnson's influence among the Iroquois, the general roused himself from the discomforts of recurrent asthma, which portended an onslaught of gout in both limbs and lungs. At the head of a contingent of local militia he would disarm the Loyalists, quiet the Indians, and secure Johnson's pledge of neutrality.

2

"A Triumphal Carr with Tories dragged behind"

The presence of Sir John Johnson, British superintendent of Indian affairs, his Loyalist tenants and neighbors, and the Iroquois in the Mohawk valley constituted a lingering threat to Philip Schuyler and the rebel cause. It was not only a distraction to him, but also created tactical and strategic problems on the western flank of his vast department. These he now attempted to settle only to discover later that his solution would not endure. Yet his "genius and determination" did serve to weaken the British hold on the Six Nations. By overawing the Indians even temporarily Schuyler checked the influence of the late Sir William Johnson and his heirs. And by providing American respect for Indian territory his efforts to persuade the Iroquois to stay out of the Anglo-American quarrel were not wholly unsuccessful.[23]

The seven hundred militia whom Schuyler summoned to disarm Tryon

County Tories swelled to an army of three thousand shortly after he marched west from Albany on 16 January. This popular surge of support was not altogether gratifying, for it caused Schuyler much anxiety and trouble. The Mohawk valley Loyalists he found were no more of a challenge to his generalship than was preventing "so large a body of men, collected on a sudden, with little discipline, from running into excesses." But it was a second military excursion to Johnson Hall that Schuyler ordered in May that ran "into excesses"—and these were committed by regular Continental troops, not the militia. Referring to outrages committed by Col. Elias Dayton's New Jersey regiment, Loyalists jibed at their foray as the "peacock expedition" because apart from rough behavior and some plundering, the soldiers decorated themselves with feathers plucked from Sir John Johnson's peacocks.[24]

The story of the first of these forays along the Mohawk in 1776 began in December 1775 when a committee of the Continental Congress discovered that Tryon County Loyalists were armed and being enlisted in the king's service. Testimony that a store of weapons and ammunition might be seized for the American army prompted Congress to direct Schuyler to take the speediest measures to secure them, disarm the disaffected, and seize their leaders.[25] South Carolina congressman Thomas Lynch later wrote that he did not doubt but that Schuyler's "Slay [sic] will return a Triumphal Carr with Tories dragged behind to attend your Ovation at least if the Prayers of some honest Whiggs . . . can avail any thing." However, the general acted with such prudence and restraint that his lenience toward Johnson and other Loyalists later raised both suspicions and accusations that he was at least a Tory sympathizer. Upon receipt of the congressional committee's missive—perhaps before 11 January—Schuyler referred the business to members of the Albany Committee of Correspondence. Without disclosing more than a general need for defense against enemy attacks, the committee summoned seven hundred militia. And on 12 January Schuyler received affidavits from the Tryon County committee that six to seven hundred Tories at Johnstown were indeed preparing some action against the patriots.[26]

Within four days of the Albany committee's call Schuyler's forces were assembled to march but with very little powder and at first no cannon. With an eye toward staving off unfavorable Indian reaction to his march toward Johnstown, Schuyler posted messengers to Mohawk tribesmen at Fort Hunter on 15 January, a day before he actually began the trek. Urging them to take no alarm and to spread word to the other Iroquois tribes, the general assured the Mohawk that no action against them was intended, and that the treaty made at Albany in 1775 would be respected. Schuyler meant only to inquire into the truth of reports that people at Johnstown were raising men in order to cut patriots' throats or to help enslave them and block the route of trade and communication into Indian territory. Johnson and his family would not be molested if they had not committed hostile actions.[27]

By the evening of 16 January, when Schuyler and his forces reached Schenectady, a Mohawk delegation encountered the general with protests that he had not heeded their answer to his message. In that reply they had proposed that only three or four men should visit Sir John to request that he observe peace and neutrality. If the troops pressed forward, the Mohawk refused to relay Schuyler's assurances to the western tribes. They insisted that the uneasiness that prevailed at Johnstown should be settled without recourse to the militia incursion; the people there they said feared that Yankees and Albanians intended to destroy them—a fear perhaps as legitimate as that which the latter entertained about the former.[28]

At Schenectady the Mohawk sachem Abraham spoke in tones that Schuyler regarded as extremely haughty. Requesting Schuyler to avoid all bloodshed or molestation of Sir John, Abraham asked why the general had cannon if he intended to keep the peace and had promised no aggression. Sir John had given them his pledge against bloodshed, but he had also vowed to defend himself. The Indians, however, denied that he had any artillery or that he was making any military preparations. And they insisted upon being present at any encounter between Johnson and the general. What perhaps neither the Mohawk nor Schuyer actually *knew* at the time was that Sir John Johnson had been corresponding with Governor William Tryon about raising a battalion for the king's service and rousing the Indians against the rebels. But the general's action was justified by well-grounded *suspicions* of Johnson's preparations to oppose the patriot cause.[29]

In their wintry and windy encounter on 16 January, Schuyler told Abraham and his companions that he was pleased by their candor. However, he was disappointed that they had not deemed his own initial message to be candid and that they had refused to carry it to their western neighbors. Insisting that he had adequate cause to suspect Johnson of preparing hostilities, Schuyler again promised to observe the 1775 treaty of neutrality and argued that his expedition was designed to prevent Sir John from severing the American-Indian connection. No blood would be shed unless Johnson's people did so first, and there would be no intrusion upon Indian lands. The Iroquois must remain neutral, and Schuyler would not tolerate the presence of enemies at his rear when he might be obliged to face battle in the east. However, he agreed to write Johnson to request an interview; and the Mohawk might attend the encounter together with the interpreters Rutger Bleecker and James Dean. But should hostilities erupt and the Indians engage in any of the fighting, they must suffer the consequences.

"Brother Schuyler, the Great Man," the Mohawk delegation responded, "attend!" The general's proposition was acceptable. What time would he meet with Sir John? The warriors would be calmed.[30]

Before marching from Schenectady on the morning of 17 January, Schuyler hurried Rutger Bleecker and Henry Glen with a message to Sir John Johnson. Announcing his intention to investigate reports that Tryon County settlers were engaged in dangerous designs against the liberties and property of His Majesty's subjects, the general promised to make his inquiry as peaceably as possible. Johnson might choose to meet him at any point along the route to Johnstown. His personal safety was guaranteed, and Lady Johnson should be assured that she would suffer no indignity. Accordingly, Schuyler also rushed a note to the Tryon County committee, informing them of his message to Johnson and asking several of their members to join him as soon as possible. The Tryon militia, however, were to remain at Caughnawaga (south of Johnson Hall) until Schuyler joined them or summoned them elsewhere.[31]

Sir John and a number of Scots supporters met the general sixteen miles beyond Schenectady on the evening of 17 January. There Schuyler proposed that he and his neighbors must surrender all cannon, army, and military stores, specifying by inventory which were privately owned and which were Crown property, so that appropriate restoration or reimbursement might be made. Sir John must accept a parole of honor not to leave Tryon County unless Congress ordered him to move elsewhere. The Scots of the county—who were mostly Johnson's tenants—must surrender all their arms and promise to engage in no hostilities for the remainder of the war; moreover, they must give Schuyler six hostages. Other Tryon County people who had resisted the united colonies' efforts must likewise surrender arms, pledge their peaceability, and grant six hostages. All Crown supplies, blankets, and other Indian articles must be given to an American commissary for distribution to the tribesmen. If Sir John and his supporters agreed to the terms and observed them, Schuyler pledged that they would not be molested; indeed, they would be protected in their quiet neutrality.

Johnson asked for time to consider the terms, and the general agreed to wait until the following evening. Schuyler warned that if he resisted with the Indians' help, blood would be shed. Following their encounter, Schuyler learned from the sachem Abraham and a fellow Mohawk that

Johnson had lied about the Indian support; the Mohawk, they insisted, were not Sir John's defenders but only mediators.[32]

On 18 January Schuyler moved his troops to within four miles of Johnstown. At Caughnawaga the militia had grown to three thousand strong. Several gentlemen were sent to Johnstown to await the answer from Sir John and his retainers. During the day the general notified Johnson of the presence of the waiting messengers.[33] By early evening Johnson and Allan McDonell had sent their reply to Schuyler's terms, but the general found it "imperfect" and unsatisfactory. Johnson insisted upon retaining his own armaments; said that there were no Crown supplies, Indian blankets, or other articles of trade to surrender; and declined to be confined to Tryon County. The Scots would deliver their arms and promised no hostilities, but they refused to give hostages.

At 5:00 P.M. Schuyler fired off a rejoinder, demanding reconsideration of his terms and warning that although he would observe the laws of humanity in executing his orders for totally disarming the Loyalists, there must be no resistance whatsoever; otherwise the consequences might be "most dreadful" indeed. If Lady Johnson was at Johnson Hall, she must leave at once with the general's passport; Schuyler intended to march the militia to the hall immediately. Robert Yates, Henry Glen, and William Duer were sent to receive the final capitulation. After midnight he would accept no further proposals from Johnson and McDonell. This delay was the final "condescension" he could make in the interests of avoiding bloodshed or risking the safety of the county or violating his orders from Congress.[34]

Again the Mohawk interceded. Sachems and warriors from several Mohawk towns called upon Schuyler to indicate that Johnson had explained to them what Schuyler had offered. Persuaded that the baronet intended only to defend himself, the tribesmen begged Schuyler to accept Johnson's terms. The general finally agreed to the Mohawk's plea to extend the deadline to 4:00 A.M. Until then they might try to persuade Sir John to submit. Schuyler later reported to Congress that this concession was designed to impress the Mohawk leaders with his leniency and to convince them that requests for favors were more likely to be efficacious than threatening utterances.

Schuyler, however, did receive Johnson and McDonell's reply at midnight. Their surrender of arms would not be complete as they wished to retain a few family weapons. Sir John promised not to raise hostilities against America but resisted a full submission; although he promised not to travel west of German Flats and Kingsland district, he insisted upon freedom to move anywhere to the south. No hostages would be given, but prisoners of war might be taken if they were permitted to go to Pennsylvania or New Jersey, whichever Congress might direct, and provided their families could be properly provisioned. Johnson and McDonell declined to pledge to disarm or surrender hostages from other Tryon County Loyalists over whom they claimed no influence; yet they would try to persuade such people to surrender arms. Again, Johnson insisted that he had neither blankets nor trading goods to surrender for the use of the Indians. And were he finally to sign the terms, Schuyler must be held responsible for protecting unarmed people.

In the early hours of 19 January Schuyler informed the Indians that a peaceable solution had been reached, and they withdrew with thanks. Still at Caughnawaga, he then wrote Johnson and McDonell a final version of terms to which Sir John agreed. Conceding that they might retain some of their favorite weapons, the general nevertheless demanded an inventory of them. Johnson's freedom to travel south was approved save for the exception of seaport towns; he might also ask Congress for permission to go elsewhere. Six Scots would be made prisoners—not hostages—and Congress might determine where to send them after they reached Reading or Lancaster, Pennsylvania. Schuyler made no promises of maintenance for the prisoners' families, but he offered to recommend this to Congress. All the Scots must surrender their arms at noon on 20 January; otherwise the general would consider himself freed from all promises.[35]

With signatures affixed to the agreement Schuyler went to Johnstown on 19 January. From there he sent messengers throughout the countryside to exhort other Loyalists to bring in their weapons. The arms and military stores delivered that afternoon by Sir John were fewer than the general expected. Next morning his troops were drawn up on Johnstown's main street and between two and three hundred Scots Highlanders grounded their arms. Included were several pieces of artillery (six- and four-pounders), swivels, and blunderbusses. The general harangued the clansmen to observe the peace and then dispatched a party of officers to inspect the spot where an informer had alleged a supply of arms had been hidden. Nothing was discovered. His suspicions aroused by talk that the informer was an imposter, Schuyler clapped him into jail to await the Continental Congress's directions.[36]

Before returning to Caughnawaga on the evening of 20 January, Schuyler answered an appeal from several Albany patriots who were alarmed by Tory prospects in local elections. So many Whig electors were away from the city on militia duty that their opponents might outpoll them. The letter from Albany explained that the local committee had endeavored to nominate candidates for the New York Assembly. The royal governor, William Tryon, had called fresh elections in an effort to obtain an assembly amenable to reconciliation with the mother country. Local Whigs feared that Loyalists or men with Tory leanings would be elected, and therefore they endeavored to keep the polls open until Schuyler's militia could return to Albany to vote.[37]

The general promptly reacted by sending a plea to Henry Ten Eyck, high sheriff of Albany City and County, to adjourn the polling from day to day if necessary until the electors in his militia forces could reach Albany to vote. By election day, 22 January, Schuyler's militia had returned to Albany. The general himself had reached the city by the previous evening, and the polling resulted in the election of two Albany Whigs, Abraham Yates, Jr., and Robert Van Rensselaer, who swelled the number of patriots elected throughout the colony, and left four Loyalist winners vastly outnumbered despite the fact that moderate and conservative victors might have dominated the assembly. So potentially hostile was the composition of the new assembly, however, that Governor Tryon never summoned it into session.[38]

Meantime, until he could lead the militia back to Albany, Schuyler withdrew from Johnstown to Caughnawaga to complete the final arrangements of his sortie. There about 110 Tories were escorted to surrender their arms. Leaving Col. Nicholas Herkimer and the Tryon County committee to seize weapons from English and German inhabitants and to obtain six prisoners or hostages, the general supposed that over 600 men had been disarmed. But not satisfied with the size of the cache of weapons and ammunition surrendered by Sir John Johnson, Schuyler asked him why the Scots had brought in no broadswords, dirks, or ammunition. Preferring to construe this as a matter of inattention rather than of willful omission, he noted that whatever it was would be ascertained by the Highlanders' immediate compliance with the treaty specification that all arms of whatever kind be surrendered.[39]

Finally, Schuyler gave James Dean a belt of peace with a parting message to carry to the Six Nations. As interpreter and agent of the Northern Department's board of Indian commissioners, Dean would explain how Congress had ordered the general to investigate the "wicked men" of Tryon County and to secure their leaders and disarm the others. The terms arranged with Johnson proved his kindness and leniency much as the Mohawk had requested. Dean would speak of the general's kind intentions toward all of his Iroquois brothers, and of his expectation that they would abide by the 1775 treaty.[40]

Schuyler succeeded admirably in executing Congress's orders to disarm

Johnson and his retainers, and President Hancock commended his "prudence, zeal, and temper" in doing so. But "the issue thus resolved was in actuality only temporarily settled. The next encounter with Sir John would result in a complete rupture of relations." While Schuyler worked to keep the Six Nations neutral, British agents like John Butler sought their friendship with a view toward obtaining their outright support. Because Butler's Mohawk kindred resented the moves against Johnson as an apparent breach of the 1775 treaty of neutrality, it "would be increasingly difficult to control" warriors' propensities to answer British inducements to take the warpath. Once Schuyler could not prevent a British invasion from Canada, the enemy could more easily persuade the Iroquois to choose sides instead of maintaining friendly relations with both.[41]

3

"My country may justly claim my last services."

Indisposed even before his sortie up the Mohawk valley, Schuyler was confined to his room for eight days after his return to Albany on 21 January. His "Antient Enemy" had attacked him "in the foot and Supported by an Auxiliary now formidable . . . made a lodgement in my Lungs and threatens destruction." He could only hope that milder weather would again enable him "to Act Offensively." Spring might bring relief, for, as Schuyler diagnosed his suffering to the governor of Connecticut, "[a] close attention to business in the closet I find more prejudicial to my cough than the fatigues of out-door work."[42] The mission to Johnstown had indeed been "out-door work," but now more "business in the closet" demanded considerable attention. A multitude of details must be tended if his winter army was to be reenforced; and preparations must be laid for the spring offensive. Making his house his headquarters until early April, he did not venture beyond the city environs save for a brief ride to Halfmoon and Saratoga at the end of March to direct the movement of artillery north toward the lakes and to the army in Canada, which he struggled to reenforce.

The Canadian enterprise remained important to the American war effort in more ways than one. Victory for independence was not yet the point. As Thomas Lynch, congressman of South Carolina, observed late in January, recent consideration of peace through reconciliation with Great Britain must wait until congressmen's tempers cooled and military actions established "our selves on a Footing in Canada."[43] American success there might create a position from which Congress could bargain advantageously—or press on for independence. Increasingly, however, separation from the mother country became the goal after Thomas Paine's famous pamphlet *Common Sense* was published in that selfsame month. It was a passionate diatribe, riling tempers that men like Lynch wished to cool instead.

For his part Schuyler worked steadily to achieve a "proper footing" for the American forces in Canada. Upon returning from Johnstown he had no news to indicate that the situation in the north was worse than when Edward Antill had brought word of Montgomery's death on 13 January. The general was cheered by the prospects of Col. Seth Warner's dispatch of Hampshire Grants forces to Canada—perhaps a total of about seven hundred men. And a Berkshire County, Massachusetts, regiment of militia, enlisted to serve until 15 April under Col. John Fellows, was also on the march. Because Washington was unable to send any reinforcements, Schuyler was glad to accept Fellows's corps despite its short enlistments. Schuyler knew, too, of Congress's orders for the two Pennsylvania and New Jersey regiments to march to Albany. Yet he thought that the general state of public affairs had worsened; undisciplined troops and his "very bad state of health" had tempted him to think of retiring. Without prospects that his health "will ever mend," but with hope that order would improve, Schuyler assured President Hancock that "[m]y country may justly claim my last services." Moreover, Hancock's recommendation had encouraged him. "That my little service should have attracted the notice of Congress, so far as to merit their thanks," he wrote, "I can only attribute to the conviction which ... that respectable body entertains of my wishes and endeavors to serve my country in this hour of danger."[44]

Continuing his long report to Congress on 22–24 January, Schuyler reviewed a considerable variety of business in which he was then engaged or would be occupied with during the weeks ahead. An engineer was needed if General Wooster was to determine places where the Saint Lawrence could be fortified or obstructed against a British naval incursion. Would the New York convention issue officers' warrants for completing the new regiment, or did Congress intend that Schuyler should do so? During the winter Wood Creek could not be cleared as ordered for improved communication between Skenesborough and Ticonderoga, so preparations must be made for bateau construction at Fort George; but the supply of nails at Albany he feared would be insufficient. All his heavy cannon had been sent to Washington for the siege of Boston; where could he obtain new pieces that would be needed if Quebec did not otherwise surrender? The general also needed to settle payments for the Johnstown expedition. If provincial authorities were to hire men for bateau work, Schuyler proposed to engage them at Albany, but what wages would Congress provide? And finally, would Congress please "to attend the Naval Department in this quarter?" There were questions about the construction of lake vessels and their staffing.[45]

Had Schuyler simply awaited answers to all of these inquiries or requests for authorization to act in such matters, he could never have accomplished what he did in meeting the Northern Department's requirements. In some of the business he could wait, but he also knew when to seize the initiative, trusting that what he did might be approved by military or civilian superiors or otherwise adjusted or corrected. The case of Col. John Fellows and the Berkshire County committee's offer of a regiment of militia is perhaps instructive here, as is Schuyler's late January correspondence with Governor Trumbull of Connecticut and his son Jonathan, Jr., the department's paymaster general.

In the latters' case Schuyler indicated that weapons and accoutrements collected from former Connecticut troops had been assembled for repair, but he promised that they would be reissued to the Connecticut regiment newly levied according to Congress's orders for reinforcing the Northern Army. In addition there were difficulties with accounts of funds advanced to the new Connecticut regiment and to Massachusetts forces serving in Schuyler's army. Yet he found no alternative but to pay the officers and men according to rolls duly attested by company commanders, provided the latter furnished a certified account of funds received for their companies. Until Massachusetts submitted accounts as ordered by Congress, Schuyler directed paymaster general Jonathan Trumbull, Jr., to adopt this modus operandi. And he closely monitored young Trumbull's labors, reporting them in turn to Congress.[46]

When John Fellows proceeded to raise the Berkshire County militia regiment, volunteered in response to news of the campaign losses in Canada, he encountered several difficulties that Schuyler did not wait for others to answer. On 22 January the general promptly sent funds for bounties to the men and pay advances for the officers; and Fellows speeded the recruitment. Then came word that Washington had asked Massachusetts to raise a regiment for Canadian service from both Berkshire and Hampshire counties, and Fellows wondered whether he should endeavor to complete his own regiment (in Berkshire County) and march them up or halt enlistments. Perhaps Hampshire County would recruit the balance of the corps, but Fellows had no return completed for his own enlistees when he wrote to Schuyler for directions.[47]

Sent by express, Fellows's queries were answered by Schuyler on the following day. Careful to commend his Yankee neighbors for their zeal and alacrity in stepping forth at a critical moment for the country, Schuyler explained that the Massachusetts assembly's order to enlist a regiment for one year's service had superseded the need for more recruits as Schuyler had previously arranged with Fellows. Warning him not to permit men already enlisted in the regiment provided by Massachusetts' government to act unless they engaged for a year's service, Schuyler invited the colonel to march with his recruits, but in any event to send them forward without delay.[48] Perfectly amicable as was this exchange between Yankee and Yorker, Schuyler found others with David Wooster to be far less agreeable.

4

"Not upon the most friendly terms"

A repetition of tensions between Schuyler and Brig. Gen. David Wooster, which had marred their initial encounter in the autumn of 1775, once again developed in the early months of 1776. The clash of two proud personalities seems on the surface to have reflected the long-standing Yankee-Yorker animus. In fact it was mostly if not wholly personal. Although the effects of such strains upon the success or failure of the war effort are difficult to measure, it is clear that both men were resolved to do their duty in the public interest and that they managed to cooperate to that end. This time, however, with congressional intervention, Schuyler had the satisfaction of seeing Wooster replaced in the command of that part of the Northern Army remaining in Canada.

Wooster began the fray in January with complaints about prisoners of war. Expelled from Canada, a number of captives returned by Schuyler's direction. Despite the Yorker's humanitarian considerations and his determination that the captives were not inimical to the patriot cause, Wooster found their behavior suspect. And he insisted upon returning some of them to Schuyler on the charge that they were Tory ringleaders.[49]

Schuyler referred Wooster's complaints to Congress, explaining those instances in which he had allowed but a few captives to return to Canada; and he sent Wooster a stiff rebuke. From Wooster's letter, he wrote President Hancock, "one would be led to imagine that I'd sent back vast Numbers of dangerous persons"; moreover, "he has before wrote to me on the occasion with an unbecoming Subacity [sic.]." Perhaps fearful that he would be accused of Loyalism or of undue leniency toward Tories, Schuyler was determined to show that he had complete command of the Northern Army both by rank and personal capability. Accordingly, he carefully reviewed the cases for his congressional superiors.[50]

The general's rebuke to Wooster contained a copy of what he reported to Congress and an order. Resolved to be treated respectfully as a gentleman and officer, he gave "positive" directions that Wooster call in all the persons returned to Canada with Schuyler's permits. He must confront them with accusers who could testify to their Tory activities; if they were guilty, Wooster could send them "in close confinement" with affidavits of their guilt to Schuyler. All other prisoners of war and other persons deemed too dangerous to the American cause to be left in Canada must also be sent to Albany. Long frustrated by the lack of troop returns, Schuyler also ordered Wooster to submit these together with the names of the officers of each unit and other similar data on reinforcements.[51]

In subsequent dispatches to Wooster between 29 January and 9 February, Schuyler hammered away at his need for information about the officers then in Canada, for rolls and accounts long since requested of Wooster's predecessor, General Montgomery. Without lists of discharged and furloughed troops Schuyler could not issue warrants for their pay. And he was determined to prevent the payroll confusions that had arisen in 1775 because of poor accounting.[52]

On 2 February Schuyler wrote two more letters to Wooster. Having by then received the old Yankee's list of prisoners of war, the general noted that it contained the name of only one man whom he had allowed to return to Canada. Why, he sarcastically asked, did it not include others who had his permits to return and whom Wooster had believed were so dangerous? Touching also upon the subject of reinforcements, Schuyler announced that Col. Moses Hazen and Lt. Col. Edward Antill would enlist and command a new Canadian corps. Wooster was instructed to give Hazen a warrant on the paymaster general for the rest of the bounty due him and to send troops at Montreal to assist Arnold at Quebec. Demanding a list of all officers engaged under the reorganized regiments, Schuyler stipulated that it must contain the dates of their commissions.

In his second letter to Wooster, on 2 February, the general furnished a list of field officers then in Canada and instructed Wooster to offer regimental positions according to their ranking order. All but two were Yorkers. If these officers declined, Wooster must go down the roster of "eldest" captains: first New Hampshire, then Massachusetts, Connecticut, and finally New York. Aiming to "prevent those jealousies which are so dangerous in an Army, and so prejudicial to the common cause," Schuyler promised to accept any other mode of appointment that Wooster could demonstrate was better designed to achieve it.[53]

Wooster answered Schuyler's 26 January salvo with one of his own on 11 February 1776. "I also claim a right to be treated with the respect due to me" as a gentleman and an officer commissioned by the Continental Congress, he wrote. "Why, sir, are these positive mandates? Have I ever disputed your orders?" Wooster insisted that he had always encouraged unity among his officers and had tried to avoid the creation of jealousies. How ungenerous for Schuyler to take advantage of Wooster's conciliatory disposition! Referring to Schuyler's 23 October letter, which jibed him for an alleged boast of the prowess of Connecticut soldiers in assisting with the siege of Saint John's, Wooster protested that the letter was "founded in falsehood" and that Schuyler could only have meant to insult him. Once vowing to take no notice of it, Wooster now decided that because Schuyler had complained to Congress, he too would appeal to that body by submitting copies of his correspondence with Schuyler. Congress might judge which man had better reason to complain of ill treatment. This was no time for altercation, Wooster continued; but he then added fuel to the flames by asserting that "the commanding officer who is with the Army is to give out orders, and is the only competent judge of what is proper ... for the regulation of the Army, and for the immediate safety of this country." This was a point that Schuyler had often conceded to Montgomery—and to Wooster—but he would do so upon his own initiative and not in response to contentious demands or bristling challenges. Wooster should have remembered this when he alluded to Montgomery's friendly and respectful behavior toward him, but instead he boldly asserted that he would now issue orders as he saw fit. Those people deemed to be dangerous to the cause he would expel from Canada. And he would send army returns and execute Schuyler's orders and Congress's insofar as he found it possible. "I will just observe further," he added in a postscript, "that I think it would have been much more generous in you, to have pointed out to me the exceptionable part of my letters, before you complained to Congress."[54]

Wooster now felt no compunction about carrying his case beyond Schuyler's jurisdiction, although had he followed his advice to the Yorker, he might have privately settled their differences, and Schuyler would have had no further cause for complaint. Politely, he sent the general a copy of his letter to Congress; in it Wooster rehearsed his case for the delegates in Philadelphia, reported on Canadian affairs, indicated the need for more manpower because the Canadians were undependable, and voiced fears that it would be difficult to conquer Quebec without proper artillery and ammunition. No personal ill treatment would prevent Wooster from discharging his duty, he said, but the whole American cause would be better served if Schuyler "could learn to bridle his Passions."[55]

Supplementing this appeal to Congress, Wooster also wrote to Connecticut delegate Roger Sherman. In tone this was anything but bitter; copies of his correspondence with Schuyler, he said, would simply show that "we are not upon the most friendly terms." Unhappy that the two men could not agree, Wooster was conscious of no fault or neglect on his part as a cause of the coolness between them. In conclusion, he argued, Sherman would perceive the terrible consequences of an army's lack of confidence in Schuyler as its commanding officer; it would be difficult to raise recruits for such an army, and new soldiers would be infected by veterans' disregard for the commander. Wooster, however, revealed a degree of suspicion as infectious as that of others. Having heard that Congress had promoted him to major general, he found nothing in the extracts of Congressional resolutions that Schuyler had sent to him, and noting that the general had said nothing of a promotion, he asked Sherman to send some word of the matter.[56]

By 13 February Wooster had received Schuyler's directions regarding the formation of new regiments from among the various units then in Canada. Judging by his officers' talk, he thought the general's plan would not work. It would be hard to place younger officers ahead of older ones, nor would men of various colonies serve in companies composed of a mixture of them. Alternatively, he suggested that New Yorkers be made into one regiment, the Yankees another, and that their respective officers be ranked according to seniority. The remainder of Wooster's letter contained no hint of the feuding that hitherto had occurred. Promising to tend the orders sent by Schuyler and the Congress, Wooster suggested that those for constructing gondolas be executed at Montreal, where lumber and nails were available, but noted the need for good carpenters and pitch, tar, oakum, and turpentine.[57]

On his side Schuyler said nothing more to Wooster that would aggravate their altercation. Like Wooster, he pledged that their conduct of public affairs must not suffer because of it. He accepted Wooster's advice on boat construction in Canada, assuring him that he had requested the necessary shipwrights and supplies. As for Wooster's call for cannon and artillerists, Schuyler feared Congress's orders for artillery companies would not produce the help that was needed at Quebec—at least not in time. Failing the receipt of orders of what to do with cannon at Ticonderoga and Crown Point in the next ten days, he was resolved to send these arms to Canada by sleds. If Wooster could not buy beef and pork in Canada, he would probably suffer shortages before Schuyler could send these supplies from the lake posts.

The general accepted Wooster's criticisms of the plan for creating the two regiments in Canada with good grace. He had foreseen the difficulties of appointing the officers, and he was willing to accept a "more eligible mode." Because Wooster was "on the Spot, you will be best able to judge," he said. Reminding Wooster of a multitude of his own difficulties as department commander, Schuyler noted that troops coming into Albany in late February as reinforcements for Canada had put him "at my Wits End to supply them." They were half naked and as poorly armed as clothed.[58]

Except for these epistolary exchanges the two generals labored together with no apparent difficulty. But Schuyler again pressed the problem of David Wooster upon Congress. On 20 February he wrote President Hancock that copies of their recent correspondence would show "that matters are got to such a height between us, that either he or I must immediately quit this department, for I cannot, consistent with my honour or my feelings, serve with an officer, who, very early in the campaign, witnessed a contempt for my orders, and ... offer[ed] insults of the grossest kinds ... I must therefore, request that Congress will order an inquiry to be immediately made." Congress must remove one of the two. Schuyler became especially relentless because Wooster had claimed in his letter of 11 February that as the commander in Canada only he was competent to decide what actions were proper to be taken there. If Wooster was correct, Schuyler fumed, Congress must have erred in its resolves "which clearly signify that I had something to do with the regulation of the army in Canada." Convinced of the necessity of discipline and good order in the army from bottom to top, he was invariably jealous of the rights—and duties—of rank. So long as no one ordered instead of requesting or advising him, Schuyler was perfectly generous and cooperative with subordinates and colleagues. Now, however, he insisted that Congress rule upon Wooster's assertion which, if accepted, would have made him autonomous in his command in Canada.[59]

Hitherto Schuyler's public life had revealed his "principles on the present unhappy contest." Having no ambition but to serve his country, he wrote, he would "never court the favour of either officers or men, unless they are deserving; such as are not, I shall always freely and indiscriminatingly censure. If this gives umbrage, it can never be remedied whilst I am in command, because I cannot hesitate a moment between giving offence and doing my duty."[60] This statement of principle was perhaps a bit grandiose, but it rings with a certain nobility. Proud, too, perhaps, but it was at least consistent with most of his behavior in military and political life and also in his conduct as a landlord and paterfamilias. And for the moment he bent every effort to discharge those duties as both Wooster and he pledged to do, mindful that personality clashes must not harm the war effort.

In the fleeting days of February, as yet ignorant of congressional re-arrangements of army departments and command assignments, Schuyler and Wooster continued to demonstrate that they were men of their word. Wooster regularly reported his army's wants: specie—not paper money—was needed for the purchase of firewood and food and the settlement of debts; meat supplies, shot and shells, and flour.[61] When his secretary reached Albany on 26 February to plead for money, Schuyler replied that he sincerely pitied Wooster's situation; perhaps he could persuade Montreal merchants to accept bills drawn on Schuyler for payment in specie for thirty days. The general offered his own credit as a merchant with a store at Saratoga, and by mid-March Wooster had taken advantage of his offer, drawing upon his credit with a Mr. Blake for £866.14.0 in order to buy blankets and acquire some cash for other uses.[62]

Meantime, despite the costliness of sledding, ($7.50 per barrel) the general pushed four hundred barrels of pork off to Canada and promised that whatever cannon and artillery stores were available at the lake posts would likewise be shipped north. Surmising that a great deal of waste of provisions must have occurred in Canada, Schuyler guessed that otherwise expenditures had been made without his knowledge; how else to account for the many supplies that had been captured at Chambly and Saint John's in addition to the purchase of still others? Certainly the commissaries were not as exact in their accounting as the general wished.[63]

Schuyler's persistent efforts to collect hard cash succeeded. With much difficulty, he said, he "collected on my notes, payable in like money, on demand," and raised £2,139.18.10. Uncertain when more might be sent from Philadelphia, Schuyler could only promise Wooster to continue his efforts to obtain more. Dispatching these funds to Wooster on 28 February, Schuyler also announced that Congress had resolved the altercation of the two generals. Maj. Gen. Charles Lee had been ordered to take the command in Canada, and Schuyler was assigned to New York. Recognizing that because of his health and his duties as Indian commissioner the Yorker could not be expected to go to Canada, Congress was confident that he could cooperate with Charles Lee to secure the "communications" through the lake country and facilitate the transportation of "necessaries" that Lee must have to accomplish the goal of holding the northern province. As soon as his health permitted Schuyler was to go to New York City "to take command of the forces" there.[64]

The new arrangement suited Schuyler. But even if he were well enough he did not think he could leave Albany until all the troops destined for Canada had passed the city, bateau construction had been completed at Fort George, and everything put in order for Lee's campaign to commence. There was much to be done. Forced to seek artillery ammunition and carriages for the cannon, Schuyler also confronted the need for more meat to augment the dwindling supplies just sent into Canada. The commissary general must be asked to order one thousand barrels of pork in New Jersey, and if it was discovered that fresh meat was cheaper, Schuyler would have to drive livestock to the Onion River and forward it by vessels to Saint John's.[65]

With expectations that Charles Lee would soon arrive in Albany, Schuyler sent word to alert him for the task awaiting him. His presence in Canada was "much indeed, wanted." Schuyler calculated that the troops in Canada should have received enough provisions to last until June. If the New York Committee of Safety could not provide gun carriages, Schuyler surmised that he might have them built at Albany within ten days' time. Lee must bring as much hard money with his as possible. And with eight tons of powder already ordered for shipment north, the supply in Canada would not exceed twelve tons. As for manpower, Schuyler noted that neither the new Massachusetts nor Connecticut regiments had yet left for Canada. Four companies of Col. John De Haas's Pennsylvania Regiment had marched on 5 February and another was scheduled to leave Albany on 1 March. Three companies of Col. William Maxwell's New Jersey regiment had marched, as had about a thousand from New York and Massachusetts (which included the Berkshire County enlistees). Unfortunately Schuyler found that all of the troops hitherto reaching Albany had arrived only half armed and without moccasins, shoes, stockings, mittens, and caps to withstand the late winter weather.[66]

5

"perfecting the work so conspicuously begun"

Hardly had Schuyler responded to the announcement that Lee was to have the command in Canada than Congress changed its mind. On 1 March Lee was ordered to the Southern Department, and President Hancock's notification of this new arrangement, although dated 7 March, did not reach Schuyler for almost two weeks. The general did, however, learn of Lee's reassignment by mid-March, evidently by word of Leonard Gansevoort, a fellow Albanian.[67]

The reassignment of personnel was prompted when Congress restructured the military districts of the country on 27 February. New England became the Eastern Department, and Canada the Northern Department. Lee was shifted to the Southern Department, composed of Virginia, the Carolinas, and Georgia. With a promotion to major general, John Thomas would go to Canada, where Brig. Gen. David Wooster was to remain, and Schuyler was given the Middle Department—New York, New Jersey, Pennsylvania, Delaware, and Maryland. William Thompson and the Earl of Stirling were to be his brigadiers. The whole scheme was posited on a belief that the British were shifting their efforts from New England and would campaign against the middle and Southern colonies.

President Hancock explained to Schuyler that Congress would still "rely greatly on your efforts for perfecting the work so conspicuously begun, and so well conducted under your orders last campaign." Schuyler "should, for the present, or until you receive further orders, fix your Headquarters at Albany; there, without being exposed to the fatigues of the camp, until your health is perfectly restored, you will be in a situation to direct the proper arrangements for supplying the Army in Canada, and to superintend the operations necessary for the defence of New-York and the Hudson's River . . . and also the affairs of the whole Middle Department." Generals Thompson and Stirling in the lower reaches of the department would respond to his orders, but he must be ready to bring down to their aid the entire force of the colony of New York. More particularly, Schuyler's tasks would include the erection of fortifications "both in New-York [City] and on Hudson's River." Because the general had long asked for a committee to manage political affairs in Canada and otherwise to assist the military effort there, Hancock sent promising news that such a committee would soon be leaving Philadelphia. They would visit Schuyler along the way, "invested with full powers not only to settle the affairs of that Province, but to adjust those matters that have given you uneasiness."[68]

For a month and a half before 20 March, when Schuyler received Hancock's notice of his new assignment, the general worked at his Albany headquarters to discharge most of the duties described for him as commander of the Middle Department. Shifting department boundaries altered only their scope but little of their weight or variety. Those duties included management of Indian affairs and supervision of prisoners of war, the stockpiling of naval stores and timber and the coordination of a transport system, the supply of artillery and other arms, troop discipline, the commissioning of officers, the organization and movement of reinforcements for Canada, and, finally, the first of Schuyler's directives to officers on the lower reaches of the Hudson.

6

"I am overrun with Indians"

In the aftermath of the Johnstown campaign Schuyler of course kept constant watch over Indian affairs lest Sir John Johnson and others endeavor to entice the tribes from neutrality. The party of Caughnawaga whom Schuyler sent to Cambridge to be impressed with the rebel army's power there prompted Washington to comment that he was relieved that these tribesmen would "joint the forces in Canada" whenever Schuyler called for their assistance. Circumstances might determine the occasion for Schuyler to employ them. But in February the Yorker was more concerned about the Indian commissioners' lack of stores, which were constantly needed to bribe the tribes for their continued neutrality. "Tormented" by their frequent importunities for clothes, hunting ammunition, and other goods, Schuyler feared that Tories were encouraging the Indians to clamor for various supplies in order to embarrass him and thereby prove that the rebels could not satisfy the tribesmen's wants.[69]

On 15 February Schuyler reported to Congress his decision to react to Col. John Butler's efforts to make mischief among the Iroquois. He would request a friend at Niagara to report the state of the garrison there. Schuyler suggested that the Iroquois be requested to permit several regiments to march through their territory to invest Niagara; the Indians' aid might be assured by promising them all of the Crown stores in the fort, and the occupation of Niagara would also stop the flow of supplies beyond it to Detroit. But nothing appears to have come of Schuyler's ploy or proposal. Had it been pursued, the Iroquois may indeed have turned hostile whereas the "Americans had done no violence" to them "and had been careful to offer no threats to their territory."[70] Other tribesmen—not the Iroquois—posed other questions, especially those of using them to fight the enemy or of keeping them neutral.

Washington was reluctant to arm the Caughnawaga partly because of fears of the expense. Yielding only "in Appearance to their Demands" to join the fight, the commander in chief reserved to Schuyler the decision to regulate their numbers and movements. The Yorker replied in mid-February that it was difficult to decide what to do, but he was inclined to avoid their offers of help because the expense would be "amazing." Moreover, the value of their actual help would be inconsequential unless other nations also took the American side. Their hauteur had diminished since the rebel army's seizure of Montreal; that victory had seemingly demonstrated to the Indians that they must depend upon the rebels instead of the British for gifts and trading goods.[71]

The Stockbridge Indians of Massachusetts presented another ticklish problem. To refuse their offer to fight for the rebel cause in Canada was a delicate business, but the general sidestepped it by referring it to Congress. Confident of the justification for using the "savages" against the British because they had tried to rouse them against the colonists, Schuyler however feared that once employed, the Indians would be led to believe that their help was so valuable that they could increase their demands for maintenance and other goods. Still other details in the management of Indian affairs Schuyler felt obliged to refer to Congress in late February. James Dean had discovered questions among the Iroquois concerning rumors that Governor Penn had invited them to a treaty or conference at Philadelphia. Schuyler insisted that a reply to Dean and the tribesmen must come from Congress. From Andrew Allen, congressman from Pennsylvania, Schuyler obtained an answer a month later. Upon committee investigation Allen could discover no foundation for the rumor about Governor Penn.[72]

Continuing to watch the course of Indian activities, Schuyler tried to replenish the stock of goods that were constantly being drained from the Board of Indian Commissioners. "I am overrun with Indians from the six Nations," he wrote Timothy Edwards, "and have expended whatever was in store." By early March he expected that the Iroquois would soon request a new conference at Albany. Dreading their coming, Schuyler feared that without presents to give them the Indian commissioners would encounter the beggars' "disgust." He proposed that Congress allow traders to remain active in Canada. Characteristically, Congress responded on 6 April by requesting the commissioners of the Northern Indian Department to assure the tribes that they would do everything in their power to provide goods for them.[73]

Meantime, as March wore on the general found that even small groups of tribesmen coming into Albany required much of his attention, and that frequently his meetings with them went unrecorded because he could spare no time to write minutes. Seeking a measure of relief from such onerous responsibilities, he asked Congress for the appointment of a secretary to the commission and recommended Robert Yates as a particularly sensible, facile, virtuous, and loyal candidate. Young Yates's appointment relieved the general of many routine chores, but Schuyler was never freed very long from more important business of the Indian department. As of mid-March, for example, he once again encountered rumors of an Indian threat. The Reverend Samuel Kirkland reported that some of the Oneida believed that Col. John Butler would rouse western tribes to hostilities in the spring. Could Schuyler preserve the friendship of the Six Nations without capturing "a certain post at the westward [Niagara]?" As Sir John Johnson too was accused of inciting the tribesmen, he and his accusors were summoned to Albany for Schuyler's inquiry. And caught between the demands for trade from both the Indians and a score of Albany merchants, Schuyler agreed to permit a resumption of the western trade in April.[74]

7

Of Ships and Sleds and Sawing-Mills

Although winter was not the most auspicious season for lumbering, Schuyler did not overlook opportunities for cutting timber, which was always needed to repair or construct fortifications, bridges, and bateaux. Hoping that he could obtain forage for the horses required for the task, the general decided to hire timber cutters in February when their work would be less expensive than in spring or summer.[75] Stocks of logs could be ready before the creeks thawed and spring freshets could again power the mills.

Owners of a few sawmills scattered in the countryside between Saratoga and Skenesborough were glad to find the army a ready customer for boards and planks. Neighbors like William Duer at Fort Miller, a few miles north of Saratoga, enjoyed both a lucrative business and convenient access to Schuyler to whom they looked for reimbursement for their sales. Nor was the general's Saratoga overseer idle. A bit delayed because of his sawmill's need for repairs, John Graham managed to have a Captain Vanderberg put it in order, and by 19 March sawing had commenced.[76]

Carpenters in the Albany area also found employment, and Schuyler hired dozens of them to prepare timber for bateau construction. At Fort George they found work aplenty with Harmanus Schuyler, the assistant deputy quartermaster general. No close kinsman of the general, Harmanus was at first most occupied with bateau construction, supervising both the procurement of materials and the work of the carpenters, and reporting his progress from time to time to the general. Between early February and mid-March sixty-eight bateaux were finished under his direction, and another thirty-two scheduled for completion in the following week. In April his work carried him to Skenesborough where old boats were repaired, a road was opened, and bridges mended. Thereafter, Harmanus superintended the Skenesborough mills and proceeded to execute Schuyler's orders for construction of a lake fleet of larger vessels— gondolas and galleys—which was to be part of the ultimate strategy of staving off the British invasion from Canada.[77]

These operations naturally prompted Philip Schuyler's growing concern for the acquisition of naval stores, oakum, cordage, pitch, and tar; not to mention iron and steel for bolts and bands, nails, and tools; and of course shipwrights, carpenters, and blacksmiths. Whereas this great enterprise remained but a prospect in the opening months of 1776, the general aptly took timely steps to avoid subsequent delays. He prodded the New York Provinical Congress for naval stores and for enough men and officers to staff two lake schooners and a sloop. These were vessels that had been seized from the British on Lake Champlain and at Saint John's in 1775. Already he had obtained the Continental Congress's approval for Capt. Jacobus Wynkoop to serve under "Commodore" William Douglass, and to take the command if Douglass declined. Thus, the construction of the famous fleet that did battle under Benedict Arnold on Lake Champlain in October was no mere summer project. Nor were men like Arnold more responsible for preparing and executing it than the department commander and his assistant deputy quartermaster general.[78]

Similarly, Schuyler's work in maintaining and extending a network for transportation remained steady, but there were seasonal variations in the amount required and the methods used for moving troops and supplies. *Bateaux* were employed while waterways were navigable, and *sleds* when they and the ground were frozen and snow covered. "Carriages" or *wagons* were used at other times, and these of course required manpower and draft animals such as horses and oxen. And for the latter quantities of forage were vital.

Schuyler hired local sledders and wagoners for his army, purchased oxen for the department's quartermaster operations, and hired carpenters to build boats and the men to navigate them. Aiding him were not only various military personnel but also civilian authorities like the local revolutionary committees of safety and correspondence whose function shifted from prewar political agitation to the practical work of government administration. In mid-February Schuyler himself appealed to the inhabitants of Schaghticoke (a district northeast of Albany) for hay. The response was generous, and by early March Schuyler managed to acquire twenty-three and three quarters tons of hay for the public service. He paid £187.5.0 for the hay, and each of fifty-seven sleds employed in hauling it to Fort George cost fifty shillings.[79]

From nearby Schenectady the general's calls for bateaumen and carpenters brought slightly different responses. While offering work in the public service, he insisted upon economy. Consequently there were difficulties in arranging acceptable terms and wages. Despite delays Schuyler was able to report to Congress on 19 March that within little more than a week he would have enough boats (save for the pitch and oakum needed to caulk them) to move the troops that were then ready at Albany north. And although the enlistment of Schenectady carpenters also proved to be something of a problem, it was settled with greater dispatch than was the hiring of bateaumen. Schuyler's memorandum of terms reveals not only the working conditions of the day but also the minutiae of his military administration. Overseers were paid ten shillings (in New York currency). Their wages began on the day of departure from Schenectady and were to run until two days following completion of work at Fort George, but four days following the conclusion of such at Ticonderoga. These extra days were calculated as travel time for returning home, but if the men happened to be at some farther distance from Albany, they were to be allowed extra days' wages calculated at a rate of twenty miles' travel per deim. Their contract included rations of meat, flour, and rum. In return for the wages and rations the carpenters agreed to construct bateaux or other vessels and buildings at Fort George, Ticonderoga, or at other places as Schuyler might direct. Each man furnished his own tools; the workday ran from sunrise to sunset, except for one hour for breakfast and an hour and a half for dinner. Anyone who left his post without permission forfeited all his wages, and none would be paid for days of illness.[80]

While boatmen and carpenters figured significantly in operating his transport system, a variety of other individuals also assisted the general in the work of extending and improving it. On 18 March, for example, Schuyler called upon George Palmer of Stillwater and the local highway commissioners to assist a company of soldiers who were mending roads in that vicinity. More particularly he wanted Palmer's help in constructing a causeway over some low ground along "Mr. Bemus's" farm (the man whose name is remembered because of the battle of Bemis Heights, 7 October 1777); a number of bridges also wanted strengthening to bear the weight of heavy cannon that were to be sent northward.[81]

Ranging even farther from the Albany environs, Schuyler found some assistance for improving his transport work as far away as Philadelphia. Although carpenters and boatbuilders were closer at hand, good wagon makers evidently were not, and in this Carpenter Wharton's offer of services proved most welcome. Wharton had met Schuyler at Albany in February, and upon his return to Philadelphia obligingly furnished the general with several small luxuries like newspapers and pipe tobacco. Seizing upon Wharton's offer to execute any commission the general might give him, Schuyler decided to order four of the largest and best Pennsylvania wagons available, complete with harness. Somewhat diverted by his work as commissary of provisions for Pennsylvania troops that were sent into New York in March, Wharton finally managed to send the vehicles by water from New City. That they were constructed in "an extraordinary manner" for strength was testimony to the heavy work for which they were intended and to the rough and muddy roads over which they must roll between Albany and Lake George.[82]

8

"next to Nothing of any Kind of Military Stores"

In his efforts to facilitate the flow of men and supplies, whether by rude roadways or water, in sleds, wagons, or bateaux, Schuyler particularly worried about the movement of artillery. Heavier cannon called for reinforcing bridges, extra road work, and sometimes the construction of causeways across low and marshy terrain. The availability of armaments loomed large upon his agenda of responsibilities. The burden remained constant for leaders responsible for one campaign after another. But in the early months of 1776, as was the urgent need to assemble reinforcements, it was one of Schuyler's most pressing concerns.

Following Henry Knox's removal of much of the Fort Ticonderoga artillery in December, neither the northern lake posts nor Schuyler's army in Canada were equipped with any heavy fieldpieces. In an effort to furnish the besiegers of Quebec with cannon suitable for an effective bombardment of that city's solid fortifications, Schuyler naturally turned to Congress. Noting that Ticonderoga should also have heavier artillery than the array that was then located at the various northern forts, he catalogued the ninety-odd pieces on 1 February. Although suggesting that he should have an engineer to help determine what cannon should be collected, Schuyler was certain he must have the largest ones that were available.[83]

Weeks later, as February was fading, the general was further convinced that the various artillery on Lake Champlain should be forwarded to the army in Canada; however, this would be of little use to the army unless adequate supplies of powder were sent with the weapons. While Schuyler could not be expected to manufacture gunpowder himself or attempt the casting of cannon, at least he was diligent in making these needs known to authorities who could provide them. In collecting other necessaries, provisions, specie, and forage that were obviously within the range of his grasp, he did not hesitate to act. In some matters, however, he was constrained by circumstances rather less amenable to his powers. Even Washington did not fully appreciate the Yorker's shortages of artillery or other arms; in late February he wrote of his pressing need for muskets: "Can you, my dear Sir," he pleaded, "assist me with any from your Parts?" Somehow the Virginian had heard that a store of three hundred of the king's arms was available at Schenectady.[84] His colleague, however, faced no less a deficiency for his own army.

Schuyler was "pained" that he could not supply the weapons. Indeed, in early March he had employed a number of people to buy every firearm they could lay their hands on—and at high prices, too; but no mortal yet knew how four New York regiments were to be armed. No, there were no muskets stored at Schenectady. More happily, Schuyler was now able to tell Washington of reports that a dozen heavy cannon were on their way up the Hudson. Yet what might be done with these—in Canada or in New York—without powder and ball was also a cause for wonder.[85]

On 7 March Schuyler learned of still other difficulties with regard to the transportation of artillery. Sleighmen had refused to carry heavy cannon north of Fort George. This was but one of a myriad of details preventing the relaxation necessary for recovering the general's health. Frequent bloodletting wearied him, and he could not "with any propriety" yet assume his new command at New York, for the train of supplies and reinforcements for Canada must first be set in motion. The change of seasons signaled by thawing ice made it dangerous to venture over the ice with heavy cargoes, and fearful sleighmen deserted their assignments.[86]

Apart from worrying over adequate artillery and the movement of heavier cannon into the north country, Schuyler's distress for want of other weapons continued unabated for weeks. Apparently all of the troops were being sent to Albany with the promise of obtaining all of their equipment there; but, exclaimed Schuyler, "God knows we have next to Nothing of any Kind of Military Stores here." To Col. Alexander McDougall's question of the destiny of "poor Canada" if the army lacked cannon, ammunition, tools, and other supplies to win it, Schuyler answered that he had "long observed with the deepest Chagrin that Indolence & Non Challance which so unhappily prevails in almost Every Part of this Colony, will sink Its Reputation so as to become the Contempt of the Confederacy."[87]

Although eight of the fifteen tons of powder requested by Schuyler early in February finally reached Albany on 15 March, the long-awaited heavy artillery did not arrive until five days later. After several weeks of river passage and a delay at Poughkeepsie, the cannon, which had been sent up by General Lee, would not likely be moved with much dispatch. Schuyler assured Wooster that he would forward them as rapidly as possible, but the spring thaw impeded the shipment at the very moment when the Northern Army wanted both the powder and the artillery. Despite his recent altercation with Schuyler, Wooster continued to rely on the Yorker's talents for collecting and moving provisions and equipment; aware that Congress had assigned Schuyler to move to New York, he did not relish the loss of the department commander's reliable presence in the rear.[88]

9

"business in the closet ... the fatigues of out-door work"

While Schuyler juggled Indian and prisoner affairs; the direction of carpenters, commissaries, and bateaumen; the collection of artillery and powder; disciplinary problems; and the business of commissioning officers, perhaps no task loomed larger for him than that of reinforcing the Northern Army. Collecting and equipping the men whom Congress had summoned for service in Canada in 1776 was scarcely easier than the launching of the 1775 campaign. In both those years, as in 1777, Schuyler's efforts illustrated the very "nature of a revolutionary culture, the heroic demands it imposes on all who are swept up in it."[89] As the work proceeded in February and March the waning of winter threatened to delay the reinforcements' movement north; spring thawing made sledding and wagon travel extremely difficult, and boats could not safely or easily navigate the rivers and lakes until the ice had largely disappeared. Initially there was much "business in the closet" for Schuyler to accomplish before he could confront "the fatigues of out-door work"—a prospect he welcomed because he thought the former was "more prejudicial" to his health than the latter.[90]

In response to the news of American setbacks at Quebec, Connecticut's council of safety agreed to furnish a regiment to reinforce Schuyler's Northern Army and immediately named officers to enlist the men. Much as he welcomed these early initiatives, the general was obliged to deal with several attendant perplexities. As Congress had given no directions about paying even the old troops when it called on Connecticut and other colonies to raise new regiments, Schuyler decided to order a rate to cover the time between their discharge or expired enlistment and the date of their arrival at home: an allowance of a day's pay for every fifteen miles of travel. Hoping that Congress would give its approval in due course, Schuyler took this step because Governor Trumbull had suggested that the settlement of pay for troops in the 1775 campaign was necessary to stimulate fresh enlistments. Conversely, recruiting would suffer unless arrears were paid. Yet the long delay in submitting regimental rolls for Connecticut troops left Schuyler's work of settling their accounts especially onerous, particularly when enlistees were promised a month's pay in advance. It is not surprising therefore that Schuyler wanted accounts of all the funds advanced to his department units to be sent to the deputy paymaster general Trumbull. The confusions arising in 1775 accounts must not be repeated![91]

As for Schuyler's long unfinished business of settling accounts and payments that were owed to troops engaged in the May 1775 conquest of Ticonderoga and Crown Point, not until April 1776 did the Continental Congress propose a way of relieving him. It then asked the Albany committee "of Inspection & Observation" to determine a settlement based upon whatever papers Schuyler could lay before them and to report their action to Congress. In the meantime, the Connecticut governor also thrust several other chores upon the Yorker: the arming, provisioning, and transportation of Connecticut troops.[92]

Turning to the enlistment of New York's new regiment, Schuyler left the provincial congress to discover whether several companies he had begun to recruit as garrisons for the lake posts were to be included. Commissions were finally given to fifteen men whom he had authorized to enlist the new units. As for the two regiments that Congress expected to form from various New England and New York troops still in Canada, Schuyler forwarded to General Wooster a plan for arranging their respective staffs of officers, asking that he send authorized recruiters south to help fill up the ranks. Returning to Canada to enlist his own regiment of Canadians for the American service, Col. Moses Hazen carried the scheme to Wooster. This proposal contributed to the two generals' altercation, as noted earlier.[93]

Not a part of New Hampshire's response to the call for reinforcements, and more than a little troublesome, however welcome, was Seth Warner's collection of recruits, which were the earliest to reach the remnants of the Northern Army. Schuyler's promise of bounties for those who would accept service in Canada encouraged Warner's recruitment enlistments in the Hampshire Grants, but the general was dubious about reports of their numbers. When Schuyler later reported Warner's recruiting to Congress, he noted the discrepancy between the 736 men returned as "engaged" and the 417 who had arrived in Canada on 5 March. Although the general had issued a warrant to pay bounties for the 736, he did little more than observe that Warner's conduct was "extremely outré."[94]

As the various regiments were organized and began to assemble, Schuyler repeatedly found their ranks incomplete and ill equipped. The reinforcements, however, were marched out of Albany as rapidly as they could be prepared for their long trek to Canada. Amidst supervising their arrivals and departures Schuyler occasionally fell victim to indispositions like "internal imposthume," a bothersome distraction. So it was not surprising that he turned to the Albany committee for help with other tasks that were repeatedly thrust upon him, such as the organization of Goose Van Schaick's regiment.[95]

Aware of the urgent need for reinforcements at Quebec, Schuyler did not wait to forward completed regiments northward. Instead he marched them off in scattered companies, which was a tedious and worrisome business. As February turned to March, he feared that not even half the new army could reach Canada until April; by 9 March only about a third of the Pennsylvania and New Jersey regiments had as yet passed through Albany. Of Connecticut's (only one company of Col. Charles Burrell's regiment) and Massachusett's—about one thousand in all—had gone north, and all of them Schuyler found to be poorly equipped. Part of New Hampshire's new regiment had begun their march overland on 24 February. As they plodded northwest to Lake Champlain Schuyler providently instructed the Ticonderoga garrison to send provisions to the Onion River for the Yankees. Spring thaws however threatened delays in travel. As of 10 March the upper Hudson remained frozen, but Schuyler surmised that by the time the river became fully navigable the ice on the lakes would be too weak to carry the troops, and boats would not be usable until the waterways were largely cleared of ice.[96]

By mid-March with sloops from down river able to reach Albany, the transportation of reinforcements and artillery remained primarily a problem for the remainder of the route to the lakes.[97] But Schuyler was obliged to pay some attention to the territory south of Albany as well as the state of the northern terrain. Although entrusting him with superintendance of the relief of forces in Canada, Congress had assigned him to oversee the Middle Department, which included lower New York, New Jersey, Pennsylvania, Delaware, and Maryland.

10

Eyes on Both Ends of the Hudson

Schuyler's initial directions for the defense of lower New York in 1776 coincided with the British evacuation of Boston. Expecting General Howe to shift his forces to New York, patriot leaders erred only in anticipating Howe's timing. Preparations for the encounter there thus became a matter of some urgency for Schuyler as he considered the needs of forces both north and south of his headquarters.

Trying to decide how to dispose of a regiment being recruited at Albany, Schuyler demanded a return of troops then on the lower Hudson from General Stirling. While the Hudson was clear of ice on 16 March, the northern lakes remained impassable. As soon as the various corps could be embarked at Lake George, Schuyler intended to join Stirling and Brig. Gen. William Thompson at Manhattan. His health he now found to be "much reestablished," and he hoped he would suffer no relapse.[98]

As Schuyler penned his message to Stirling, he as yet had not received the earl's first appeal for directions. Admittedly a novice, Stirling felt perplexed; yet he was convinced that the defense of Manhattan and Long Island would require a minimum of eight thousand men by early May. As Schuyler exchanged correspondence with Stirling it appeared that the latter's estimate met with the general's approval. From afar, however, Schuyler would not presume to make particular suggestions. And pending further directives from Congress, he saw that he must remain at Albany to superintend the movement of supplies and reinforcements to Canada. He did, however, propose that Stirling try to prevent Connecticut troops from marching home until Congress considered the circumstances.[99]

Rejoicing over news of Washington's success with the siege of Boston, Schuyler confided his thoughts of a possible turn of events to Governor Trumbull. Aside from impressing the Indians to remain neutral, the effects of the British evacuation of Massachusetts would surely be salutary in other ways. Europe must now see that the rebels' martial abilities deserved respect. But would the British "[m]inistry . . . recede from their diabolical plan"? Sensing the increasing momentum toward independence, he concluded that the ministry "seem to be seized with an infatuation, that leads them on to the ruin of Old England, which, I think, must inevitably happen whenever we are driven to the necessity of declaring ourselves an Independent State." Such sentiments suggest that colonists had increasingly sensed both an opportunity to shape the future and also that God could not permit Britain's immoral power without undoing the moral order of creation.[100]

The course of the war itself favored the cause of independence. Its center was shifting from New England to the middle colonies, and toward the close of March 1776 both the upper and lower reaches of the Hudson River were increasingly the foci of this transition. Leaving Brig. Gen. William Thompson and Lord Stirling to act in New York City, Schuyler found that the tempo of activity around Albany and along the routes northward was increasing. By 21 March five companies of Burrell's Connecticut regiment had reached the city, and the other three were expected daily. One company of St. Clair's Pennsylvania regiment had appeared, and by 27 March about six hundred men were ready to be moved beyond Albany. On 22 March the cannon and shot so long awaited had at last been delivered. Schuyler pushed these on their way, issuing detailed instructions about the route. On 28 March he was obliged to ride to Halfmoon to superintend their further movement. Forage shortages created difficulties in obtaining working cattle to drag the heavey equipment, and land travel was unavoidable between Halfmoon and Stillwater and again from Little Falls to Fort George. Bateaux could be employed only between Stillwater and Little Falls.[101]

At last, weeks of preparations were giving way to a harvest of results. By 27 March thirty-five new bateaux were ready at Fort George, and another sixty-five had been finished there except for caulking. The necessary pitch and oakum had yet to arrive from New York City, and Schuyler might have ordered the construction of more boats except that Congress had "stinted" him. Everlastingly, it seemed, there were the shortages of arms and the threat of undisciplined troops with which to contend.[102]

During his brief foray north of Albany to direct the shipment of nine new pieces of artillery to Saratoga and beyond, the general received welcome news that Maj. Gen. John Thomas had finally reached the city. As Congress's replacement for Charles Lee, Thomas promised to relieve Schuyler of much of the anxiety over the Northern Army. Yet at the end of March troops could not yet traverse Lake Champlain. The ice would not bear them. Boats could not yet push through ice-choked waters, and several companies remained stalled about forty miles above Ticonderoga. A few warm days with southerly winds must remove the obstacles. Arranging for the first of the cannon to reach Fort George on 30 March and the remainder by the middle of the following week, Schuyler anticipated his return to Albany for consultation with Thomas. By then, with preparations well in train, he might comfortably hand Thomas the reins.[103]

When Schuyler arrived in Albany on 1 April he found reinforcements filing off daily toward Lake George. Together he and Thomas laid plans to launch them in seventy bateaux, thus speeding them on to Quebec. To race the reinforcements against the enemy's, Schuyler urged Thomas to take the water route along the Richelieu River to the St. Lawrence. It would save two hundred miles of overland marching on bad roads; and bateaux might also save the considerably greater cost of wagons. Deciding that a fleet of seventy bateaux on Lake George and Lake Champlain would be insufficient to maintain a continuous movement along the line of communication, Schuyler ordered thirty more boats constructed, and with Thomas's consultation he also proposed that Congress increase its allocation of reinforcements for Canada. Otherwise Thomas would have only five thousand troops, of which about one thousand must garrison and maintain the line of supply from Saint John's and Chambly to Montreal. Another five regiments would be none too many for Congress to add. In Canada after all, there were no local militia upon which to rely, nor could Schuyler raise such troops to send there. Congress responded by allocating four of Washington's regiments for northern service. In mid-April, while promising that these units would soon be on their way, Washington warned Schuyler to prepare subsistance for some two thousand men and officers.[104]

By the end of the month the first of the new troops had passed through Albany; others soon followed: three Massachusetts regiments under colonels John Patterson, John Greaton and William Bond; Col. Enoch Poor's New Hampshire battalion; and the Second Pennsylvania Regiment under Col. Arthur St. Clair. In May as these units—about twenty-two hundred in all—were led into Canada by Brig. Gen. William Thompson, another half-dozen regiments—about thirty-five hundred strong—followed under Brig. Gen. John Sullivan. Except for Col. Elias Dayton's New Jersey men, whom Schuyler diverted to the Mohawk valley as a guard for his western flank, all of these regiments were destined for the Canadian theater: two from New Hampshire (under colonels James Reed and John Stark) two from Pennsylvania (under colonels Anthony Wayne and William Irvine), one other from New Jersey (under Col. William Wind). All told an army of ten thousand men in Canada was a sizable force, obliging

Schuyler to meet increased demands for provisions. By early May he estimated their daily rations would include twelve thousand pounds of flour and a like amount of meat.[105]

The successive enlargements of troop allocations for Canada came none too soon. Since January only about 1,200 American troops had struggled up to Quebec in parties of 15 to 100 men. By 1 April, with Wooster's move from Montreal, Arnold had some 2,800 soldiers, but about 800 of these suffered from smallpox and fell unfit for duty. With Quebec's sizable population, its strong garrison, and formidable fortifications replete with almost 150 cannon, the odds against the invaders were tremendous. Smallpox continued to flourish, and the threat of British reinforcements loomed large. Canadians were growing increasingly hostile. The patriot army lacked order and subordination. With enlistments expiring on 15 April, no artfulness or craft or even money would persuade men to extend their service. Montreal merchants grew disaffected by General Wooster's circumscription of their western trade with the Indians. Indeed, the general tenor of Wooster's administration was a principal reason for Schuyler's wish that Congress send a committee to forge political ties with the northern provincials and to oversee the military efforts in their midst.[106]

For all of his labors and those of Congress to push men, clothing provisions, equipment, artillery, and gunpowder into the Canadian maw, it is not surprising that Schuyler feared the worst. Soon after General Thomas reached Quebec on 2 May, the army there, which had been slowly built up to twenty-five hundred to twenty-eight hundred men, was quickly reduced to nineteen hundred by desertions, death, and discharges. Because of smallpox and other illness only one thousand of these were fit for duty. Thomas himself eventually succumbed to the dread contagion and died. With three hundred lost because of expiring enlistments and another two hundred incapicitated by inoculation, Thomas could count on no more than five hundred effectives to challenge the strong fortifications of the city with its five thousand inhabitants, sixteen-hundred-man garrison, and 148 cannon. Although he was aware that more American troops were not far behind him, Thomas got word on 2 May that fifteen British ships had entered the mouth of the Saint Lawrence. Within five days they were in sight of Quebec, and the siege was over. The straggling American army gradually gave way to Gen. John Burgoyne's eight Irish and English regiments and two thousand German mercenaries.[107]

Meantime, during April other rebel leaders, as did Schuyler himself, continued to race against time and against the odds that they did not doubt would be raised against them. British reinforcement of Quebec was to be expected as were enemy activities elsewhere. At the south end of the Hudson preparations to check a British incursion by sea were under way. Forced to summon local minutemen to respond to new threats from western Indian tribes, Schuyler insisted that these made his cries for gun-powder even more urgent. With fresh news from Tryon County the gen-eral again grew anxious lest the Six Nations turn hostile. Affidavits from Tryon County inhabitants indicated that several Mohawk tribesmen had uttered ominous warnings. Within six weeks inhabitants of the Mohawk valley were to be ravaged and scalped; ranging east toward Schenectady, the Cherokee would perform a "fine Dance" for the Yankees.[108]

Schuyler doubted that a general Indian uprising was likely to occur, but he could not afford to relax his vigilance. That agents like James Dean and Samuel Kirkland had registered no alarms was reassuring, but he alerted Gen. Abraham Ten Broeck and the Albany committee to the need to consult on proper responses to the fears of Tryon countians. Following Ten Broeck's deliberations with the committee, Schuyler posted word to the Tryon committee on 5 April that no troops would be sent to them lest the Iroquois deem this a breach of their treaty. However, he promised that those forces raised in Tryon County by order of the provinical con-gress would remain there for local protection. The committee must assist to recruit them while Schuyler would furnish gunpowder and provisions through the army storekeeper, Philip Van Rensselaer, at Albany.[109]

Local committees like those of Albany, Schenectady, and Tryon County had for almost a year proved to be ready supports in Schuyler's work of military management. They provided of course the core of local revolu-tionary government, and he relied upon them for a vast variety of services such as collecting provisions; hiring carpenters and bateauxmen; furnish-ing oxen, horses, and wagons; recruiting troops; arousing the militia; maintaining a surveillance of the Indians and Tories; and even overseeing prisoners of war. And just as he relied upon this system of local manage-ment, he expected Congress to send its own committees to inspect his administration, offer their counsel, and witness both his own labors and the condition of his army. The first committee stopped short of entering the northern province when it visited Schuyler's army in the fall of 1775. Now, in April 1776, a second was to appear in answer to the Yorker's repeated pleadings.

Canada Evacuated

1

A "full-empowered Committee"

*A*lthough it had not ventured into Canada, the congressional committee sent to confer with Schuyler at Ticonderoga in November
1775 proposed that General Montgomery should "pave the way, for the
Reception of any Committee, that the Congress might think proper to
send, when the ice should render the Journey more practicable, and when
it may probably be attended with Salutory effects." After Montgomery's
death Schuyler repeatedly asked for a "full-empowered Committee" to
assist in the campaign for Canada. Although Congress seemed oblivious
to the need for haste in dispatching a special committee, South Carolina
congressman Thomas Lynch supported the general's plea for one, promising him that "I will be at them 'till tis done" yet warning that his efforts
might not succeed.[1] Schuyler did not relent. On 10 and 13 February he
wrote President Hancock that only a congressional committee could manage affairs in Canada, where David Wooster seemed unable to persuade
provincial leaders to join the rebellion. Wooster's administration at Montreal turned Canadian sentiment against the American cause. And this
together with the press of Schuyler's other work and his altercation with
Wooster in January and February over their respective jurisdictions further justified the Yorker's desire for a committee to participate in the
direction of the campaign.[2]

On 15 February Congress decided that Schuyler should have his committee because it might win Canadians to the cause if it could "counter
the hostile and growing influence of the clergy among the habitants and
restore faith in American ideas."[3] The committee, which was carefully

selected, included Benjamin Franklin, Samuel Chase, and Charles Carroll. Franklin's reputation for liberal views and diplomatic talents might help. Carroll's brother John, a Roman Catholic priest, was asked to accompany the three delegates, specifically to offset the influence of Canadian clergy who threatened to deprive American supporters of the sacraments. Because both Carrolls were Roman Catholic, their selection was an admission by Congress that it "had injured its own cause by its attack on the Quebec Act and its other anti-Catholic activities and utterances."[4]

Congress's instructions to the committee for Canada were designed to assure Canadians of the rebels' devotion to their neighbors' freedoms; of France's favor to the Americans; and of the need for Canadians to organize their own government to secure their religion, liberty, and property. United by common interests, all the colonies must cooperate to bring the war to a speedy end. Ordered to proceed to the northern province "with all convenient dispatch," the committee (or commissioners) were authorized to settle disputes between American troops and Canadian civilians, to reform abuses, and establish regulations for peace and order. All officers and soldiers were subject to their commands, and officers' commissions might be suspended, pending a final decision by Congress. Here perhaps was some remedy for the long-standing evils of undisciplined troops. The commissioners were to be included in councils of war, and they were entitled to draw upon the Congress for sums of up to $100,000. Significant, too, was their instruction to establish the credit of Continental currency because Canadians were averse to accepting anything but specie. On 23 March Congress also authorized the commissioners to raise up to six independent companies of troops, to appoint their officers, and to fill all vacancies in the army while they were in Canada. Finally, a sum of paper and specie currency was provided to meet the commissioners' expenses.[5]

Even before Congress had agreed upon the commissioners' instructions, Schuyler was alerted to prepare to receive the delegation. Writing on 11 March, Franklin requested transportation beyond Albany for the deputation and several servants. They did not, however, set out until weeks later, and it was 1 April before they managed to leave New York City. Hancock's notice to Schuyler announced that congressional commissioners were "invested with full powers not only to settle the affairs of" Canada but also "to adjust those matters that have given you uneasiness."[6]

An inveterately attentive host, Schuyler greeted the Carrolls, Franklin, and Chase at the Albany landing on Sunday morning, 7 April. Accompanying them were the Baron de Woedtke and Fleury Mesplet, a Philadelphia printer, whose talents and press were to be employed in providing newspaper propaganda in Canada. The Prussian baron's military service had won him a commission as brigadier general and—incidentally—an assignment to improve the discipline of the ragged American forces in Canada. After almost six days aboard a sloop, the commissioners welcomed Schuyler's invitation to dinner, and promptly they began their consultations about the Canadian campaign. Carroll in particular was impressed by the general's "great civility," his "pretty style" of living, and two of his "pretty" daughters. Sunday entertainment aside, Schuyler's work was scarcely interrupted by his visitors. Arrangements for the committee's travel on Tuesday were made.[7]

After almost two days of rest the congressmen were ready to resume their long trek toward Canada. Early on 9 April Schuyler led their entourage out along the north road from Albany. Accompanying them were Maj. Gen. John Thomas, the new commander for Canada; Mrs. Schuyler; and two of her daughters. Shaken over rutted roads and delayed at two ferries, the party reached Saratoga shortly before sunset. There the Schuylers once again offered their hospitality and the general grew expansive as Charles Carroll inquired about his lands and their management. Farm leases, Schuyler explained, produced income from both produce and the penalties of the quarter sale. Sales of lumber were also profitable, and six miles from his Saratoga house Schuyler had four mills powered by the waters of the Fishkill: a grist mill, two saw mills, and one for hemp and flax. Acquainted with the countryside stretching north to Quebec, the general also explained his views on inland waterway transportation. Almost twenty years later he would attempt to realize them, but for the moment Carroll recorded Schuyler's estimate that water carriage could link the cities of New York and Quebec.[8]

Projections of easier and speedier travel stood, however, in stark contrast to reality. The turn of seasons proved to be a hindrance, too. Thawing worsened ruts and mire through which sleds or wagons must now be dragged. Ice jams delayed bateau movement, and the committee was not able to reach Montreal until 29 April. While the congressmen tarried at the general's house for a week, Schuyler and Thomas pushed on toward Lake George on 11 April—Schuyler to superintend the movement of military supplies and Thomas to prepare for the first chance to cross the lakes.[9]

At Fort George on 12 April Schuyler found everything in readiness to launch the expedition once the lakes opened. After a severe snowstorm that day the weather began to clear and a high northwest wind, Schuyler hoped, might break the ice. Thomas would then be able to press forward in bateaux with six remaining companies of Burrell's Connecticut regiment, two of De Haas's Pennsylvanians, and three of Maxwell's New Jersey regiment. Except for two companies halted below Crown Point, other parts of these corps had already managed to reach Canada. Some units remained scattered or incomplete.[10]

On the afternoon of 12 April, the post from Canada brought alarming news; promptly Schuyler wrote Washington that he must have more troops at once. Following the snowstorm, the courier from Canada was sent back with promises of immediate reinforcements under Thomas and of another three to four thousand to follow soon thereafter; Washington's express rider, Bennett, set off southward, bearing letters for Congress, General Thompson, and the commander in chief. Having never received a proper return of the forces in Canada, Schuyler could not tell Washington what their strength was. But he was convinced that more reinforcements were desperately needed. The Virginian's 3 April offer and Congress's order to send four more battalions to Canada depended upon his being convinced that New York had been safely garrisoned; that, in turn, depended upon knowing whence Howe's troops had sailed after withdrawing from Boston. Happily, by 19 April, Washington had reached Manhattan, and on that day he sent four more regiments sailing up the Hudson. In the meantime Schuyler could do little but wait and struggle with the collection and transportation of provisions. Painfully he wrestled with another "copious scorbutick eruption," a frequent occurrence of late, which led him to hope that "it threw off some other more disagreeable disorder" and would not confine him or otherwise prevent the discharge of his duties.[11]

In his message to Congress, Schuyler noted his request to Washington for reinforcements and pointedly referred to a variety of reports from Canada. These were letters that revealed threats that an Indian uprising might cut off the garrison at Montreal; growing Canadian disaffection; and skirmishes of Canadians, British regulars, and Indians with the invading army. Fearful that soldiers' misconduct would turn Canadians against the army and the American cause, Schuyler now recommended that Congress provide a stricter military code of discipline and allowance for harsher punishments. Hancock's reply carried a note of exoneration for the general, which is perhaps especially significant in light of Congress's quest some months later for answers to the question why the Canadian campaign failed. Making soldiers, Hancock observed, required much time and labor; although officers were expected to maintain discipline, even "the utmost vigilance could not have totally prevented all irregularities." Perhaps the committee visiting Canada could succeed with

Congress's remedy—"sundry resolves"—to quiten local fears and orders for moving a total of ten battalions north to impress them with patriot force.[12]

On 13 April Schuyler summoned the congressional commissioners from Saratoga. Lake George was now open in so many places that the general thought they might soon be able to embark. General Thomas was ready to move twelve hundred reinforcements across the lakes and more would follow. But the days passed without marked improvement in the weather, and the expedition moved slowly. Thomas inched forward to Ticonderoga, whence he finally departed on 21 April. The congressional delegation lagged behind. On 18 April the others joined Chase and the general at the Lake George garrison, and "Doctor Franklin and the other gentlemen" dealt with Schuyler's vile ague. They "administered such a number of doses of Peruvian bark" to him that the malady disappeared and he could hope to "last at least this campaign."[13]

Like the ague, the work of the Indian commissioners also pursued Schuyler to Fort George. Traders wanted permission to deal with the western tribesmen, and James Dean brought several Caughnawaga sachems from a meeting with the Iroquois at Onondaga. The latter intended to carry the commissioners' speeches at the 1775 Albany treaty conference into Canada. Schuyler obliged by giving Dean a letter of introduction to all officers and commissaries, instructing them to furnish food and boats for the agent and his Indian companions. And in response to news that an Iroquois deputation would soon visit Albany, the general asked Robert Yates, the commission secretary, to assist with preparations for them. As for a request for opening a communication between Lake George and Quebec, however, Schuyler replied that the Indians must be content with the western route to Fort Stanwix and Montreal. Once Quebec had been conquered, the entire Saint Lawrence valley would be opened for trade.[14]

Before escorting the congressmen beyond Fort George, Schuyler issued orders for moving troops forward with provisions and baggage. He instructed Walter Livingston, deputy commissary general, that if wagon teams were lacking, he must use the oxen that had been procured to replace the livestock that Schuyler had already moved from Saratoga to Ticonderoga, "as I would rather that not a Foot of my Farm should be cultivated than that the Service should suffer." Schuyler's personal sacrifices contrasted starkly to the behavior of some people engaged in the public service. Teamsters hired by the day, for example, were dawdling between Fort Edward and Fort George, taking nearly two days to make a round trip of only thirty to thirty-five miles.[15]

On the afternoon of 17 April Schuyler escorted the committee from

Fort George toward the Landing at the north end of Lake George. There was time for conversation as their bateau glided across the lake. Charles Carroll proved interested in the general's plans for surveying Wood Creek and estimates of the costs for building a canal and locks along that waterway. At the Landing another portage was required to reach Lake Champlain and Ticonderoga. Here Carroll was fascinated by Schuyler's machinery for lifting boats from the water and swinging them onto carriages for the trek to Ticonderoga. Thence they could cross Lake Champlain and move down the Richelieu River to the Saint Lawrence.[16]

For about a week Schuyler busily superintended the movement of artillery, stores, and provisions between Lake George and Lake Champlain. The congressional committee followed in the van of General Thomas's reinforcements, whose embarkation at Ticonderoga had commenced on 21 April. There was good news, too, to pass on to Thomas. On 25 April Schuyler had learned that his appeals to Washington for more reinforcements had been answered; five more regiments were en route from New York City, the first of which he expected were already moving north of Albany.[17]

Moving to and fro between the Landing and Ticonderoga during those final days of April, and thence south again to Fort George and Saratoga, Schuyler applied his energies to the task of keeping the line of communication bustling. Few boats could be returned soon from General Thomas's Northern Army, so it was imperative that bateau builders work with speed to construct more. In addition to the carpenters, Schuyler assigned all hands and available wagons at Fort George to the enterprise.[18]

Indicating a constant attentiveness to detail, Schuyler's orders clearly reveal how his system of transportation was designed to function with efficiency. Each bateau would carry thirty-five men without provisions as far as Ticonderoga. Thereafter, for the route along Lake Champlain and the Richelieu River, each must proceed with twenty-eight men and five barrels of pork. Between various points like Skenesborough and Ticonderoga, or Fort George and the Landing, bateaux were to run in relays, moving back and forth across the lakes.[19] Similarly, they shuttled up and down the Hudson between Albany and Fort Edward with occasional interruptions for portaging or sometimes because of the lag that occurred when wagoners or boatmen failed to maintain an even flow in their activities.

Several weeks of field work interrupted Schuyler's usual correspondence with Washington and Congress. Recounting his movements of the troops, he explained that despite Congress's orders for only a hundred bateaux, he was now obliged to build more lest new reinforcements be detained for want of transportation. Without a suitable contingent of sailors, it was questionable whether other lake vessels could proceed with reinforcements to Saint John's. With crews, however, the schooners and sloops could carry five hundred men. The army in Canada might well face shortages of pork before fresh supplies could reach them, especially because there were but 150 barrels of meat then at Fort George and Ticonderoga to be shipped. And as always, more funds were needed, and there were sizable claims outstanding. Ten thousand pounds "will hardly pay what I am personally bound for on the publick account," he told Washington. Because the Virginian was now present in the Middle Department and in effect had superseded him, Schuyler asked how funds might be drawn from the chest once Congress replenished it. If he must obtain the commander in chief's approval for warrants, the Yorker feared that necessity would force him to trespass upon that jurisdiction before Washington furnished instructions.[20] Before Schuyler learned of Washington's arrival at New York City, he had issued orders for the disposition of certain other troops; now he felt obliged to seek approval for these, or at least to apprise Washington of them.

The discipline of an army, Schuyler continued to complain, was almost invariably bad. The regular work of maneuvering men with provisions, baggage, artillery, and other supplies might be alleviated were it not for the indescribable licentiousness of the troops. For all of his efforts nothing seemed to halt their "scandalous excesses," malingering, pilferage, and destruction of private property, the waste and embezzlement of public stores, and desertion. His only recourse was to continue to issue barrages of pointed orders and trust that the threat of courts-martial might improve the conduct of men and officers alike. Not least of his worries was Benedict Arnold's recent letter from Montreal containing the first return of troops Schuyler had yet received from Quebec. Arnold had been forced to retire to Montreal after his horse fell on him and aggravated the leg wound that he had received in the New Year's assault on Quebec. The picture he painted of the army besieging Quebec—small; with enough food to last only until 10 May; and insufficient artillery, gunpowder, and shot—was truly dismal. It was doubtful they could succeed without eight to ten thousand reinforcements, good artillery, and a full military chest. Endorsing Col. Moses Hazen's 1 April warning to Schuyler about the Canadians' growing disaffection, Arnold further reviewed the defenses needed at the Richelieu rapids (above Quebec) if British ships appeared there.[21]

In fact, General Thomas and the first American reinforcements did not reach Quebec until about three weeks after Arnold had written his prognosis for Schuyler. Within a few days of Thomas's arrival there the British fleet appeared—too soon for their progress up the Saint Lawrence to be blocked.

In contrast to his report to Washington, Schuyler's letter to Congress on 28 April was penned in broader generalities. Washington's presence in the department, he explained, rendered it improper to address them on military matters except through him. Information from the west now indicated that Sir John Johnson had broken his parole and intended to march several thousand men from New York and New Jersey to the relief of Quebec. The threat also of Johnson's arousing the Iroquois to support him in this venture prompted Schuyler to take action against "the diabolical designs of those miscreants." Proceeding with efforts to apprehend Johnson's supporters, he hoped to be able to mete out capital punishment to any of them who might be captured in arms.[22]

Except for safeguarding the Mohawk valley in the spring of 1776, Schuyler's focus of attention, like Washington's and Congress's, was on Canada. As more troops poured northward, he and the congressional committee attempted to prevent the northern province from slipping back into British hands. Having reached Saint John's on 27 April, Franklin, Chase and the Carrolls moved quickly to Montreal (29 April) but then proceeded no farther.[23] What they witnessed along the route of their long journey and at Montreal soon convinced them that they had come too late and could accomplish too little to guarantee an American victory.

General Thomas arrived at Quebec on 2 May, but within a few days he was forced to abandon the siege. Expecting to find nineteen hundred men, Thomas discovered that because of smallpox there were only a thousand fit for duty, and with enlistments expiring he was left with only about seven hundred effectives. Moreover, on 6 May the approach of a fleet of fifteen British ships bearing reinforcements up the Saint Lawrence made it clear that if the rebels were to continue the struggle for Canada, they must choose other ground and collect sufficient reinforcements and supplies with which to carry on. Thomas first moved the army west to Point de Chambeau (Deschambault) and then to the mouth of the Richelieu River.[24]

Despite Schuyler's struggle to obtain the necessary reinforcements and supplies since November 1775, neither Congress nor Washington responded quickly enough to make an effective winter or early spring offensive possible. Otherwise Quebec might have been reduced before British reinforcements could have rescued it from the besiegers.[25] The commissioners in Canada saw and heard enough at Montreal to learn that the American miscarriages were mainly due to circumstances quite beyond Schuyler's control. These included, especially, short enlistments, the scarcity of specie, and smallpox. And for all of his strenuous activity in moving reinforcements into Canada, they simply arrived there too late to be able to do more than fight a rearguard action. With the abandonment of Quebec, General Thomas endeavored to hold the territory along the Saint Lawrence from the mouth of the Richelieu southwest to Montreal and southeast to Saint John's—a sort of triangular tract that was the last defense against enemy penetration and the ultimate invasion of New York.

As yet unaware that the retreat from Quebec had commenced in early May, Schuyler busily concentrated upon preparations to launch Brig. Gen. William Thompson's five regiments across Lake George and Lake Champlain. For the moment he ordered John Sullivan's brigade to be held in Albany; wagons and bateaux must first carry baggage and provisions for the advance contingent of reinforcements. Anxiously seeking more carriages, Schuyler called on the Albany committee and their Schenectady neighbors to furnish them, and he pressed the commissary Livingston into quartermaster service until someone like Henry Glen or Christopher Yates would agree to assume the task. "I am at my Wits end," he told Livingston, "to rectify the Blunders and make up for the Negligence of a certain person here" [Fort George]. After an eight-day absence he had returned to the fort only to find no bateaux completed nor any boards collected to ensure that the work of his carpenters would be uninterrupted.[26]

Responding to the wishes of a delegation of several hundred Indians seeking an interview at Albany, Schuyler set out from Fort George on the evening of 7 May. Although commissioners Volkert Douw and Timothy Edwards had begun to confer with the tribesmen on 29 April, they needed Schuyler's advice about permitting traders to range as far west as Niagara and Detroit. Some of the Indians themselves warned that they should not be permitted beyond Oswego. But because Schuyler had already agreed to the request of a score of traders to resume their operations along the Mohawk River, some decision must be made about the limits of their travel, and the commissioners did not wish to counteract Schuyler's orders unless he withdrew them. Moreover, Schuyler was expected to provide some gifts for the visiting Indians.[27]

On the evening of 8 May, when the general rode into Albany to consult his colleagues, there were also military affairs that immediately demanded his attention. Brig. Gen. John Sullivan wanted directions for marching his brigade to the lakes. The shortage of bateaux had temporarily delayed further movement. Seeking to prevent soldiers' theft, destruction, and abuse of wagoners, bateaumen, and carpenters, Schuyler demanded a close-order march. Regimental officers were instructed to guard against straggling and looting by threatening confinement of offenders. None of the rank and file must pile his pack into boats or wagons otherwise loaded with provisions and other baggage.[28]

The movement of troops was of particular concern to the Indian delegation, too, and Schuyler decided to post Col. Elias Dayton with three hundred of his New Jersey Continentals in the Mohawk valley. In order to pave the way for the tribesmen's acceptance of Dayton's contingent, the Indian commissioners' secretary, Robert Yates, and interpreter, John Bleecker, were sent west along the Mohawk to spread the news and to invite the Iroquois to another conference at Johnstown. The presence of many troops in Albany duly impressed the representatives of the Six Nations, who watched Schuyler's review of Sullivan's brigade and then witnessed the staggered march of five of the regiments out of Albany during 11 to 16 May.[29]

Again the general found that the movement of several thousand men with baggage and provisions strained his transport system. But his prediction that all of Sullivan's troops should be able to reach Quebec by 1 June was fairly accurate. Sullivan's brigade passed Chambly on 3 June, moving along the Richelieu River to join the army then led by Brig. Gen. William Thompson. Meantime Schuyler had found a new assistant deputy quartermaster general, Christopher A. Yates of Schenectady, to relieve him of some of the chores of managing the line of communication.[30]

While Schuyler superintended the renewed effort to hold Canada in the spring of 1776, the committee from Congress endeavored to augment his work by echoing pleas made earlier by the Yorker. The committee's messages to Philadelphia warned that unless funds were provided, Canadians would suspect that Congress was bankrupt. On 6 May, for example, they noted that without money it would be advisable to withdraw the troops and to concentrate upon protecting the New York lake passages, and British reinforcements would surely attempt an invasion. Similarly, they alerted Schuyler to the probable retreat to the Richelieu. More reinforcements would only add to the army's difficulties; it was provisions that were wanted, and plenty of bateaux to facilitate a withdrawal without abandoning supplies and artillery to the enemy. Upon receipt of this news on 13 May, Schuyler at once agreed to halt the further movement of troops; immediately he set to work shipping more provisions. Unable to entrust the business of managing the communication south of Lake George to anyone else, he rushed to Saratoga to superintend the movement of wagons and bateaux along the route.[31]

By 10 May the committee in Canada was ready to leave Montreal, for its members discovered they could perform no further services there. The committee's return to New York was in some respects—like the army's own movements—disjointed. Chase and Charles Carroll remained with the army until early June. Franklin and Father Carroll set out from Montreal on 11 May; at Fort George, Schuyler equipped them with directions for the roads south of Albany and for the use of one of his carriages. Pressing on from Albany on 22 May with Schuyler's post chaise and driver Lewis, the priest and the Pennsylvanian arrived in New York City on the evening of 26 May. Franklin's letter of thanks to the general reveals not only the generosity of Schuyler's hospitality, but also Franklin's regard for his military labors, and it hints at the committee's later report to Congress. Franklin began by explaining that he would have driven himself, "but good Mrs. Schuyler insisted on a full Compliance with Your Pleasure as signified in your Letter, and I was obig'd to submit; which I was afterwards very glad of, part of the Road being very Stoney & much gullied, where I should probably have overset & broke my own Bones; all the Skill and Dexterity of Lewis being no more than sufficient. Thro' the Influence of your kind Recommendation to the Innkeepers on the Road, we found a great Readiness to supply us with Change of Horses." Commenting on threatening news of the approach of mighty reinforcements from England and Germany, Franklin concluded with a touching encomium: "May God bless & preserve you *for all our Sakes,* as well as for that of your dear Family."[32] Indeed, much of the continuing effort to prevent the Northern Army's complete failure depended, as Franklin realized, upon Schuyler's abilities and perseverance.

2

"I believe we shall lose Canada"

Although Franklin and Father Carroll beat a hastier retreat from Canada than did the American army, Samuel Chase and Charles Carroll tarried at Montreal for another three weeks. With Benedict Arnold the two Marylanders relayed information to Schuyler, echoing Arnold's own alarms about the size of British reinforcements and the importance of the general's supply system: "our whole dependence is on you," Arnold wrote. If enemy frigates passed the falls of the Richelieu, not only would American forces be cut off from provisions, but from a route of retreat by water. Food shortages and smallpox were also lingering threats to their survival. For the moment the army needed provisions more than more reinforcements; with General Thompson's brigade the commissioners estimated the army's strength would rise to about five thousand—enough at least to block the enemy at Saint John's and Isle aux Noix.[33]

After his brief and hurried trip to Albany, Schuyler rushed back to Fort George on 12 May. It was a hard day's journey. Even without Chase and Carroll's urgings he had been forced to delay Sullivan's brigade at Albany in order to push the shipment of provisions ahead of their line of march. With every man needed to withstand the expected British reinforcement of Canada, Schuyler was chagrined to see soldiers daily returning to Fort George, homeward bound, their enlistments expired and unrenewed. The remedy was to engage soldiers either for the duration of the war of for three years of service. Fearing now that the small army at Quebec, riddled with sickness, would be obliged to retire before reinforcements could bolster them, Schuyler was not yet cognizant that the retreat had already begun despite the arrival of John Thomas's troops. "Some amongst you," he wrote Robert R. Livingston, "will ridicule me for this apprehension but a push will be made by the Enemy to get up [the Hudson River] and If their Commander has any resources In himself he will find the means altho Ships should not be able to come up." Schuyler's perception was, however, exactly correct.[34] The British plan for 1776, after Howe moved to New York, included movements at both ends of the Hudson River-Lake Champlain waterway.

While shifting momentarily from his work of rushing Sullivan's brigade of reinforcements into Canada—this one some three thousand strong—Schuyler found that not all of his problems were those of shortages. Informing him of the confusions that increasingly threatened the last-ditch effort to hold Canada, General Thompson cited the shameful retreat of General Thomas's troops from Quebec without their artillery and provisions; the consumption of food as rapidly as it was acquired; and soldiers frightened of their own shadows because of smallpox, although they had already had the dread disease. About to move his sixteen hundred men from Sorel to Deschambault, Thompson urged Schuyler to send more: "For God's sake my dear General send on the Jersey and Pennsylvania Regiments," he wrote, "or this Country is gone." New England troops like Colonel Greaton's Massachusetts regiment, whom Thomas ordered to Deschambault with Thompson, were largely unfit for duty because of smallpox inoculation.[35]

Despite temporary alterations in scheduling, Schuyler soon resumed the shipment of both troops and provisions north from Fort George, where he maintained headquarters for most of April and May. The current spate of troubles in Canada Schuyler attributed principally to the failure of Connecticut's troops there to reenlist and to Congress's long delay in meeting his calls for more reinforcements. "Although I believe we shall lose Canada, which will be attended with many disagreeable consequences," he warned the commander in chief, "yet I am not under the least apprehensions that they will be able to penetrate into this Province." Events proved Schuyler's first point to be correct; on the second he was simply too sanguine.[36]

However Schuyler imagined the campaign might end, he worked hard to make it succeed. Whether the army could maintain a foothold in Canada, or only attempt to check the enemy's push into New York, it needed supplies and reinforcements, and the general steadily endeavored to move both to the front. By late May his fears that the army might starve had vanished. Still, the general fell short of the numbers needed for garrison duty, clearing Wood Creek, cutting roadways, and repairing fortifications. He also lacked an engineer to direct the works at Ticonderoga. And Col. Elias Dayton's regiment, divided between Albany and the Mohawk valley, might be obliged to maintain defenses in Tryon County. If so, they could not follow Sullivan's brigade to Canada. Accordingly, he begged Washington for further reinforcements; if reports of the numbers of British troops poured into Canada were true, he said, the American army there would have to be further augmented.[37] The flow of supplies, Schuyler promised, would continue as long as he could collect them and the reinforcements to move them—provided that he was "not obliged to appear before a Court Martial to answer a Charge of High Treason."[38]

The general's strenuous efforts to provision the Northern Army had, in fact, given rise to slanderous rumors that first emanated from settlements south of Albany. It was alleged that the enormous quantities of foodstuff that he had shipped into Canada were intended to fall into enemy hands. Although affidavits for the charge had been given to the committee of King's District, the persons who had made them were not to be named. Conscious of the integrity of his conduct and "ever resolved to sink or swim with my dear Country I reflect," Schuyler wrote, "with Contempt on the idle tales" thus spread about him. However, they must be noticed! Creating jealousy and distrust, prejudicing "our righteous Cause," their authors, he insisted, should be exposed to public derision.[39]

The slanders coincided with even more astounding allegations that Washington's express rider, Elijah Bennett, picked up in western Connecticut. There it was charged that Schuyler intended to launch an attack on patriots with the help of Tories and several regiments recently raised in New York. Affidavits against him had been sent to Washington, and

Schuyler was of course incensed. "I hope the scoundrels may be secured and held up to publick contempt," he wrote. "Ungrateful villains! to attempt to destroy a man's reputation who . . . by fatigues that nothing but a wish to be instrumental in procuring liberty to my country would make me undergo."[40]

Washington regarded the King's District slanders merely as evidence of diabolical Tory schemes to sow dissension and distrust in patriot ranks. With the utmost confidence in Schuyler's integrity, and incontestable proof of his attachment to the patriot cause, the Virginian "could not but look upon the Charge against" his comrade "with an Eye of Disbelief and Sentiments of Detestation and Abhorrence." Washington might have spared Schuyler further notice of them but for the King's District committee's dissemination of the charges to Governor Trumbull and several other local committees. Failure to inform these authorities might be interpreted as "Distrust by them of their Zeal" and would further "promote the Views of the Tories," whose design was to involve high-ranking leaders in their plots. Others, too, informed Schuyler of the rumormongering that flourished against him in May.[41]

Schuyler was not disposed to brush such outrageous popular rumors aside. Once libelous charges had been presented to ranking officials, he sensed that duty to himself and to the country obliged him to expose the perpetrators of calumny. More than a scheme to confuse and disunite patriots, the charges he believed were specifically designed to ruin his reputation and therefore the effectiveness of his command. Washington must give him a court of inquiry; the public at large could not otherwise know the general's exertions for the American cause.

Reflecting, of course, Schuyler's jealous regard for his honor, his demand for a formal inquiry also reveals the extent of the proud commander's anxiety and dismay. He must not be proclaimed "through all America a traitor to my country." His unremitting labors on behalf of the rebel army and his actions to disarm and secure Loyalists were proof of his patriotism. And what of the risk to his very life? Although silent upon the subject of his repeated illness aggravated by the strains of his exertions, the Yorker felt particularly aggrieved because "assassins and incendiaries are employed to take away my life and destroy my property." A hundred New Hampshire Grants people were reported to "have had a design to seize me as a Tory, and perhaps still have. There never was a man so infamously scandalized and ill treated as I am." Were Congress convinced of Schuyler's zeal for his country's cause, they must, he hoped, afford him the same public justice as Washington had—a clear announcement of disbelief in the detestable charges.[42]

Hysteria during wartime could of course prompt critics to charge a general with doing too much or too little in the face of shifting military circumstances. In disarming Tryon County Loyalists or supervising the disposition of prisoners of war Schuyler appeared to some patriots to have been excessively lenient. His scrupulous regard for the demands of civility, courtesy, and humanity simply did not suit zealots whose hatred and fears of Loyalists led them to clamor for reprisals and vengeance. And as Alexander McDougall observed, "caution by some (especially the New England Gentlemen) is considered as signs of fear or evidence of Tor[y]ism."[43] Having mentioned to Congress the court of inquiry that Schuyler had requested, Washington professed that he had "only discharged the Duties of Justice and of Friendship." He would not, however, pursue the business unless Schuyler remained certain of its necessity and could indicate some modus operandi. "The Matters objected to you, appear so uncertain, vague and incredible, that there is nothing to found the Proceedings on," the Virginian argued.[44]

By mid-June Schuyler decided to relent. He accepted Washington's opinion that a court was "absolutely unnecessary" and agreed to "rest satisfied." He would, however, appeal for the Virginian's assistance "whenever it may be necessary." Yet Schuyler was incapable of such contentment. The suspicion lingered that enemies would resurrect insinuations that he was disloyal to the patriot cause.[45]

For the moment, however, Schuyler's uneasiness was focused less upon himself than upon the fate of the Canadian campaign. At Fort George on 31 May he again posted assurances to Charles Carroll and Samuel Chase that troops and food supplies were being rushed northward as rapidly as they could be brought up from Albany. The army would lack neither provisions nor boats. It was at this juncture that Schuyler received Congress's resolutions of 22 May and posted them to General Thomas. Jolted by news of the reverses at Quebec, Congress insisted that it was absolutely necessary to hold Canada; the army must contest every foot of ground there and cut off all communications between the enemy in the upper country and the south. Although the commander in Canada was deemed responsible for the execution of these orders, Congress expected Schuyler "to take Care that the Army in Canada be regularly & Effectually supplied with Necessaries"—an order that was practically superfluous in view of the general's energy and foresight. While readily promising his execution of it, Schuyler urged Thomas to furnish estimates of articles needed and asked whether flour was procurable in Canada or must more be sent.[46]

Encouraged by the promises that $500,000 would be sent "as soon as possible," Schuyler could not have been cheered by the warning that Congress could not assure him or Chase and Carroll of enough specie to maintain the army in Canada. Similarly, to the general and the commissioners, other parts of the resolutions were little more than palliatives. One blithely exhorted them not to despair of purchasing supplies with paper. Another announced that Washington and the commanding officer at New York City had been asked to send light artillery to arm the vessels on Lake Champlain. In everything, Schuyler must consider two "great objects." First was "the Protection and assistance of our Canadian friends," and the second, Congress insisted, was "the Securing so much of that country as may prevent any communication between our enemies and the Indians."[47]

The solemn tone of Congress's resolutions was reinforced by Hancock's missive to the general. Schuyler's response was tinged with irony; he claimed that Congress's resolutions "have given me new life." Perhaps he was more pleased with the tenor of their approval of his efforts or the expressions of confidence in his abilities than he was dismayed by the burdens implicit in Congress's enlargment of his powers. However, he forthrightly proposed that another brigade be dispatched to join the three installments of reinforcements hitherto raised for Canada since the year began: Thomas's, Thompson's, and Sullivan's. In anticipation that a new brigade would soon appear he had already managed to construct sixty additional bateaux. There should be no fears, he said, that supplies for the army would prove inadequate as long as they continued to flow into Albany and thence to the lakes. Admittedly, the quantity of flour shipped to Canada had been limited, but only because Schuyler believed it might be more economical to procure it there; since learning that the army wanted it, he would send more. With his health restored, the general pledged his best efforts as always. Briefly, but emphatically, he alluded to his request to Washington for a court of inquiry; "branded ... with a Character which my soul abhors," he said, he expected to have his innocence publicized.[48]

With the arrival of fresh dispatches from Canada on the morning of 1 June Schuyler promptly passed the news to Congress, noting that although the army's position was still precarious, the danger was not due to any shortage of provisions and powder. Now believing that American fortunes in Canada were not irretrievable, the general hoped soon to receive happier accounts of them. Wooster, he complained, had sent no returns of his troops or provisions; had it been otherwise, "I should not have been (as I have to this very day) left in the dark with respect to everything in Canada." In the interests of order and discipline Congress should also stiffen the military code: "thirty-nine lashes are not an adequate punishment for a wretch who, by laying down to sleep on his post, exposes a garrison to be cut off," Schuyler growled.[49]

During the early days of June, while his secretary Richard Varick and his commissary Walter Livingston endeavored to enlist crews of bateaumen and continue shipments of provisions, artillery stores, tents, and other supplies from Albany, Schuyler supervised the transport work at Fort George. The flow of food and materials was almost constant. In the week preceding 2 June alone, for example, Livingston had shipped 1,515 barrels of provisions.[50]

In the early hours of Monday, 3 June, Charles Carroll and Samuel Chase reached Ticonderoga, where Schuyler himself appeared to hear their dismal news of the army. The substance of what they had to say was reflected in a letter that he addressed the next day to General Thomas "or the Officer Commanding the Army in Canada." Thomas had been expected to die of the smallpox, although neither Schuyler nor the two Marylanders yet knew that he died on 2 June. The general did, however, think that word had reached Thomas that Congress expected the army to dispute every foot of ground with the enemy. But he repeated the order. Should retreat become unavoidable, the army must bring all the goods, especially nails, they could collect from Montreal. Without the nails, Schuyler's naval construction would suffer. Receipts, however, were to be given for confiscated property, together with pledges that the United Colonies would pay for it. Chase and Carroll's recommendations were to be executed: Anyone opposing the American cause must be captured and sent south on parole or under guard as circumstances dictated. Because Schuyler now knew that the army could not procure enough flour in Canada, he would supply it. Bateaux must, however, be sent to Ticonderoga to fetch it, and all provisions were to be especially well guarded because they were expensive and difficult to obtain.[51]

While Schuyler resumed activities at Lake George, Carroll and Chase made a remarkably speedy return to Philadelphia. The winds and current bore them quickly down the Hudson. By 9 June they reached New York City, and two days later they were again in Philadelphia.[52]

What Carroll, Chase, and Franklin, with whom they were now reunited, were able to report to Congress of Schuyler and the Northern Army did not prevent other delegates from wondering about news of reversals in Canada either then or in subsequent weeks. While the three commissioners' earlier communications to Philadelphia had echoed many of Schuyler's own anxieties and demands, Congress had replied with promises that simply failed to materialize except for tardy dispatches of reinforcements and supplies. It had not been able to guarantee that enough specie could be obtained for army purchases in Canada. And yet hard money could have saved the time and expense of shipping many provisions into Canada.[53] It could also have rescued the fiscal reputation of the revolutionary government, which Canadians came increasingly to distrust.

Congress's prompt reaction to the report of the special commission was to appoint another committee to inquire into causes of the "miscarriages" in Canada. Franklin, Carroll, and Chase's testimony, supplemented by further reports from the north, finally produced an answer on 30 July. Apparently neither Schuyler nor any other particular individual nor group could be deemed culpable. The reverses, Congress decided, were due primarily to the short enlistments of troops, the scarcity of specie, and a smallpox epidemic.[54]

Such pronunciamentos did not, however, satisfy captious critics who wanted scapegoats, not impersonal or impartial assessments of military leaders and the trying circumstances of a distant army. Nor could they prevent murmurings about Philip Schuyler's responsibility for the retreat from Canada. With the subsequent spread of rumors and insinuations the general finally found it necessary to demand a thorough investigation. Congress *must* inquire how far the miscarriages in Canada could be directly charged to him. It *must* specify his guilt or clearly exonerate him of all such imputations. Meantime, in June 1776, the Yorker's entire efforts were bent to bolster the army and to check the British pressure that finally obliged American forces to retreat.

3

"In every Vicissitude of Fortune"

With commissioners Chase and Carroll speeded on their return to Philadelphia, Schuyler remained at the little fort on Lake George long enough to give final directions before hastening south to Albany. The ague, which he thought had been finally eradicated by stiff doses of "the bark," reappeared, and for several weeks more it lingered; despite the discomfort he managed to discharge his duties without interruption.

As the work of forwarding provisions ground on, Schuyler was especially eager to make up the short supplies of flour. Relying upon Gen. Israel Putnam at New York City to furnish powder, cannon, and entrenching tools, Schuyler also asked Putnam for clothing and more provisions to enlarge the commissary's magazine at Albany. There was no danger that too many supplies might be accumulated for the needs of the coming months. For the first week of June, Schuyler reported that 450 barrels of pork, 187 barrels of flour, and 40 of corn had been forwarded from Fort George. Since 13 May a total of 2,180 barrels of pork had been sent to the army in Canada—enough, he calculated, to last until 7 July if expended at the rate of ten thousand rations per diem.[55]

On 7 June the general likewise prodded the assistant deputy quartermaster general Harmanus Schuyler to push the construction of gondolas at Skenesborough. Once the sawmill there was repaired it must be run day and night. The log supplies must be tallied at sunset and again at sunrise to make certain the sawyers did not "play Tricks" and claim to have cut more lumber than in fact they had. Thus, the construction of a lake fleet was commenced in early anticipation of the naval encounter that did not occur until October. By 20 June the first gondola 500 feet long with a beam of 15 feet and a depth of 4 ½ feet was ready for caulking, and a second was being planked. In the ensuing months Harmanus Schuyler's reports to the general reveal the slow but steady accumulation of a dozen gondolas and row galleys.[56]

Persuaded by the Albany committee, the Reverend Samuel Kirkland, and the Indian commissioners that defenses of the Mohawk valley required his attention, Schuyler decided to leave Fort George. Fresh from his travels through Oneida country and Johnstown, where Col. Elias Dayton was posted, Kirkland visited Schuyler at Lake George to press his case. The "impudence" of some of the Mohawk who forsook their pledges of neutrality seemed ominous, and the Oneida and Tuscarora were deeply concerned with Col. John Butler's growing strength at Niagara. Butler, he said, had persuaded most of the Seneca, Cayuga, and Onondaga to join the royal cause and also offered the war hatchet to the Chippawa and Ottawa. As the frontiers were increasingly endangered, the Oneida lamented the patriots' apparent lack of resolution and their forbearance with the faithless Mohawk. A new treaty might determine which tribes would choose neutrality or friendship, and Kirkland proposed that five hundred troops be stationed at Fort Stanwix for defense of the frontiers. The gesture would both annoy the enemy and display American mettle.

Schuyler quickly asked Congress to approve a series of proposals for dealing with the western frontier. Before troops were assigned to Fort Stanwix, a conference with the Six Nations should be held at German Flats; there the necessity for this move would be explained to the tribesmen. By consulting them first the commissioners might demonstrate forbearance and argue that their confidence in the Indians—not the lack of power—had occasioned a delay in a show of force. Although several of the tribes had proven false to their promises of neutrality, all of the Mohawk Indians should now be challenged to join the enemy or to observe their pledge of neutrality. Because some had been enticed by British agents, they must return to their homes and give hostages for the future good behavior of the tribe. Schuyler further suggested that the Mohawk be warned that if they joined Sir John Johnson, they would never be permitted to return to their lands. Nothing less than this would persuade them or the Seneca, Cayuga, and some of the Onondaga to maintain neutrality, and it might, as Kirkland suggested, even prompt them to take the patriot side. The Ochgugue and Caughnawaga of Canada and the Oneida and Tuscarora had already made a defensive league against the others, but the Oneida begged that the league be kept secret lest they be attacked by the other nations. Schuyler decided that in order to avoid delays, he would advise the Indian commissioners at Albany to summon the Iroquois for a meeting as soon as possible. It was urgent, therefore, that Congress make a speedy response to his proposals.[57]

On 9 June, just before his departure from Fort George, Schuyler received news of General Thomas's death a week earlier. Immediately he dispatched word to John Sullivan to assume the command in Canada, encouraging him to hold the ground against further enemy advances from Quebec. While Sullivan's army dealt with the enemy in the north and Col. Peter Gansevoort maintained the flow of provisions to him from Lake George, Schuyler would endeavor to erect safeguards against any incursion by Loyalists, regulars, and Indians from the west.[58]

Arriving at Albany at 9:00 on the morning of 10 June, Schuyler fell immediately to work with the committee of safety and his fellow Indian commissioners. The Iroquois were summoned to a conference at German Flats at the beginning of July, but Schuyler was obliged to tell the Tryon County committee that he could send them no reinforcements. As their own militia must suffice for a time, he urged them to deploy their forces beyond Fort Stanwix. A systematic scouring of the woods might deter the enemy from launching surprise attacks.[59]

Although Schuyler had received Washington's news that Congress had voted to raise six thousand militia to reinforce the army in Canada and to authorize the use of two thousand Indians against the enemy, he refused to be satisfied. If, indeed, the New England militia turned out, many of them would be needed to guard the communication north into the lake country. Should they thereafter desert that duty, it would be increasingly difficult to forward more provisions. And "So far from being able to procure two thousand Indians to join us," he said, "I shall be extremely happy if we can prevent them from acting against us." Indeed, by the end of May the Iroquois were divided, and Samuel Kirkland had brought news that many of the Oneida and Tuscarora were increasingly disinclined to maintain a policy of neutrality. Others of the Six Nations seemed to believe that neutrality was desirable, and in late May a delegation of their spokesmen had urged Congress to continue that policy, but to no avail.[60]

Schuyler soon found reason to doubt the rumors of threatened Indian uprisings in the west. Between his letter writing to Washington on 10–11 June, he was given information by James Dean that contradicted Samuel Kirkland's earlier alarms. Nevertheless, the general secretly pursued preparations to establish an outpost at Fort Stanwix. Once the Indian conference had ended, he hoped to have enough troops to settle a garrison there. Should the Mohawk, Onondaga, and Cayuga clearly turn against the patriot cause, Schuyler proposed to cut off the latter two tribes by deploying a detachment from Fort Stanwix and to fall upon the Mohawk, who were the most proximate threat. The Seneca, however, lived so far west as to be beyond the Americans' reach.[61]

Schuyler took one further step in anticipation of both the July conference with the Indians and the establishment of a garrison at old Fort Stanwix. On 18 June he ordered Colonel Dayton to prepare to move most of his troops from Johnstown to German Flats, where two companies of Col. Cornelius Wynkoop's New York regiment were to join him. At the Flats Dayton was to prepare a picket fort and entrenchments for suitable cover and a rendezvous for Tryon County militia. After the Iroquois could be informed of the necessity of posting troops beyond the Flats, Dayton's men would be moved on to Fort Stanwix.[62]

The speed with which provisions, powder, and ammunition could be dispatched remained as constant a worry to Schuyler as was the very availability of the supplies. The receipt of fresh news from Arnold and Sullivan on 12 June left the general with decidedly mixed feelings. While fearing that the next messenger would bring word of the evacuation of Canada, Schuyler remained confident that the enemy could be stopped at Lake Champlain if only Sullivan's army could make its way up the Richelieu River—and if enough food and ammunition could be forwarded to the north end of the lake. On the other hand the dispatch of more bateaux north to Saint John's was limited by the numbers of men who could navigate them. And others must be reserved at Ticonderoga to fetch militia whenever they reached Skenesborough. Schuyler also feared that the Northern Army could not be evacuated without serious losses because his advice about collecting boats at Saint John's had not been followed. Now more pressing than ever was the need to speed up the construction of a fleet of barges that could be mounted with small artillery. Again he begged Washington for a dozen whipsaws and files to enable the mills to provide more plank; and he still wanted at least twenty more shipwrights and some expert craftsmen who could properly direct the building of the gondolas.[63]

Little suspecting how close the American army was to the verge of further retreat from Sorel, which began on 14 June, Schuyler responded to Arnold's and Sullivan's dispatches on 13 June. Instead of trying to rush more bateaux to Saint John's, where they might be ready to facilitate the army's retreat, Schuyler ordered the retention of 120 boats at Ticonderoga where they might carry militia reinforcements across Lake Champlain. With Sullivan's hope for renewed Canadian support, the army might yet be able to hold Canada. If only for this campaign, that would settle the contest, Schuyler thought. And if the construction of armed barges, already begun at Skenesborough, could continue, the command of Lake Champlain might yet be assured at the very least.[64]

On 13 June the general met with Volkert Douw and Timothy Edwards to decide how to proceed with the business of the Indians. The board of Indian commissioners approved his call for the 1 July meeting at German Flats and summoned absentees Turbott Francis and Oliver Wolcott to join them for the conference. As the Iroquois could not yet be invited, Schuyler and his two colleagues decided to enlist only two companies of "Mohekander" and Connecticut Indians at Continental wages. Each company was to consist of three officers and eighty-one men—a handful in view of Congress's authorization to "employ in Canada" up to two thousand tribesmen.[65]

The commissioners' decision to enlist Indians in Connecticut and Massachusetts did not, however, meet with Congress's approval. Their resolution for employing the natives had been so broadly phrased as to lead the commissioners to think that they might be recruited anywhere. On 27 June Washington instructed Schuyler that Congress had intended to use Canadian Indians for the Canadian theater. Accordingly the Yorker was obliged to inform Governor Trumbull and the commissioner Timothy Edwards to halt work of organizing the tribesmen in Connecticut and Massachusetts.[66]

Fortuitous in part, Schuyler's return to Albany in June proved to be especially fortunate in several respects. Prompted as it was by considerations of western defenses and Indian affairs, the move allowed the general to assuage his suffering from recurrent fits of ague with the comforts of his family and hearthside. Once there, he was also conveniently positioned for overseeing the work of subordinates at a variety of posts in a vast department.

Increasingly, too, the Yorker's attention was perforce drawn from northern operations to affairs in the west, and even to the east and south. Yet to be sure the transportation of provisions to Lake George and Lake Champlain required almost constant supervision, as did the work of naval construction and searching for sufficient garrisons for Fort George and Ticonderoga. For the moment, however, he found utterly impossible the execution of Congress's orders for improved fortifications at Lake George and Ticonderoga or for opening a new roadway along Wood Creek. Lacking an engineer and manpower, he also discovered Congress's 17 June resolves to be stupendous and impracticable; these included orders for a good wagon road between Fort Edward and Cheshire's on Wood Creek, the clearing of the creek, and construction of a lock at Skenesborough for the continuous navigation of bateaux between Cheshire's mill and Lake Champlain. All available hands were concentrated upon bateau work, and because Washington could spare no more troops, Schuyler was obliged to wait for New York, Massachusetts, Connecticut, and New Hampshire to answer Congress's call for eight militia battalions.[67]

The need for reinforcements, whether Continentals or the militia, was obviously pressing. Heeding Washington's suggestions that he inform provincial governors of routes of march and places of rendezvous for their militia, Schuyler promptly posted notices to the executives of Connecticut, Massachusetts, and New Hampshire. Weeks were to pass, however, before the various governments managed to set their militia in motion, which was too late, in fact, to prevent the final evacuation of Canada. Meantime, the army's internal disorders also threatened the success of the Canadian campaign. Schuyler asked the president of New Hampshire for the arrest of a large number of men who had deserted Col. Timothy Bedel's regiment and who presumably had fled homeward. Both Bedel and Maj. Isaac Butterfield were also in serious trouble for their roles in a shameful retreat from the Cedars a month earlier.

After consulting Washington, whom Schuyler regarded as the proper authority to approve court-martial proceedings since the Virginian had arrived in his department, the general gave orders for the trial of Bedel and Butterfield. Upon reaching Isle aux Noix in his retreat from Burgoyne's forces, Sullivan proceeded with several courts-martial while his army paused to reassemble and to rest. Because it had been officers' cowardice as well as lack of discipline in the rank and file and a smallpox epidemic that had ruined the American campaign in Canada, Sullivan wasted little time in using Schuyler's orders to make examples of Bedel and Butterfield.[68] The two officers' cases were not, however, finally settled until 1 August. Although both were cashiered, never again to hold an American commission, Bedel later won reinstatement and also rose to the rank of major general in the New Hampshire militia.

Meantime, at Albany, Schuyler waded through a variety of business. Occasionally he found it necessary to intervene in affairs that were neither strictly those of the army nor of the Indian commissioners. On 18 June, for example, he responded to rumors of Charlotte County inhabitants about his friend and neighbor William Duer. Writing to the Reverend Thomas Clark and several other principal leaders of the county, the general denied that he had made any insinuation that Duer was not to be trusted with public office because of his English birth and relations. Well acquainted with the effects of rumormongering, he deprecated the report as wicked, false, and infamous. Duer's conduct, and especially his efforts to expose Tory machinations, proved his warm attachment to the American cause. As the next provincial congress would probably consider forming or recommending some mode of government for the colony, Schuyler recognized the necessity for all counties to choose "the most sensible of their Inhabitants on so great an.Occasion." The "most sensible" were to him those who would keep the framework free of too much innovation. Were the voters of Charlotte County to elect Duer their representative, the general was certain that he would serve them well. And he asked that his letter be read at the first general meeting of the county electors as an antidote to the calumny that Duer might have suffered. In the end Duer was elected to the Fourth Provincial Congress, which opened its session on 9 July. Having approved the Declaration of Independence, the delegates then converted themselves into a Convention of Representatives of the State of New York, and it was this body that not only proceeded to govern the new state but to draft its first constitution.[69] Conservatives like Duer managed to produce a form of government that was as close to the old forms as more liberal leaders would allow.

Again during the week of 17 June the ague struck, largely confining Schuyler to his house and sometimes to his bed. Still he managed to issue orders, remain abreast of the endless round of correspondence, and once at least he ventured out to attend a meeting of the Indian commissioners. On 18 June he was called to a session with Volkert Douw and the commissioners' secretary, Robert Yates, to hear a report of thirteen Oneida tribesmen who had just returned from a visit to Canada. The Oneida had consulted with the Caughnawaga, Scawenedee, Arondax, and Annongonga, and although the latter three tribes had surrendered Guy Johnson's "bloody axe," others were joining the British cause. Complaining that several American officers had been inattentive to their needs for provisions while on their journey, the Oneida heard Schuyler's promise that the insult would be punished and were mollified by a supply of powder and ball.[70]

Suffering another violent attack of the fever, Schuyler could neither write nor dictate letters. Attempting to answer one of Washington's dispatches, he was obliged to desist until 20 June. That morning an express letter from John Sullivan arrived, indicating that the retreat from Canada had finally begun. Sullivan began to withdraw from Sorel on 14 June. Rather than retain bateaux for the movement of militia reinforcements across Lake Champlain, Schuyler now decided to order all boats sent to the rescue of Sullivan's troops from Saint John's. It was of course more important to save the army than to risk its facing General Burgoyne's superior forces. Schuyler did not despond; once Sullivan's men reached the safety of Crown Point, the general thought, the enemy could not proceed so far for the remainder of the campaign. So long as the army was not lost, the enemy's further penetration into the country could be prevented. He instructed Sullivan to halt them at Lake Champlain and explained to him the preparations to block a western assault by taking post at Fort Stanwix. Yet the Yorker also knew that he must speed up the work of naval construction to guarantee American mastery of the lakes.[71]

While noting the urgency of hastening naval construction at Skenesborough, Schuyler discovered that Charlotte County officials were actually hindering the work by ordering fines and arrests for Sunday laborers. Coaxing the county committee to rescind their orders as far as they were applicable to men in the public service, the general apologized for the violation of the Sabbath, but he reminded the zealots that the perilous state of affairs dictated that no time could be lost in the construction of lake vessels. Similarly, he instructed Harmanus Schuyler to press the work at Skenesborough by close supervision of loggers, millhands, and carpenters. After the first gondolas were completed and sent to Ticonderoga, another five must be built at once.[72]

After a week of fluctuating fever Schuyler welcomed signs of his recovery together with news that Congress had authorized the proposed conference with the Iroquois. On 14 June the Indian commissioners had been instructed to engage the Six Nations in the rebel interest on the best possible terms, and Schuyler's preparations to garrison and fortify Fort Stanwix were also approved. With appropriate bounties to enlist the tribesmen's services, Washington hoped that they would prove adept at capturing British regulars, and he asked Schuyler to promise them the wages of Continental officers and enlisted men. As Congress heaped other orders on Schuyler, he had already anticipated some of them and had begun to act. Provisions and various supplies for the new garrison at Fort Stanwix, for example, were already collected. Already, too, the erection of a sawmill at the head of Wood Creek was almost completed, and row gallies were being constructed at Skenesborough. By 24 June one gondola was finished and a second was being planked. Once he could complete his negotiations with the Indians at German Flats, he intended to turn out one such vessel every six days. As soon as he had the requisite manpower he would finish the road to link Fort Edward and Cheshire's on Wood Creek.[73]

Late in the evening on 24 June Benedict Arnold and his aide-de-camp, Capt. James Wilkinson, reached Albany with news of the American retreat from Canada. Burgoyne's army had forced them south toward Isle aux Noix, the northern tip of Lake Champlain. Despite the debilitation caused by smallpox, the troops managed to carry off their supplies and equipment, burning Chambly on their way and destroying bridges in their rear. With the loss of only ten bateaux, Sullivan was nevertheless "mortified" by the necessity of withdrawing. But the abandonment of Quebec, the spread of smallpox, the affair at the Cedars in May, and the appearance of superior British forces had thoroughly demoralized the army; even forty officers had offered to resign their commissions rather than continue the effort.[74]

Seeking orders to make a stand on Lake Champlain, Arnold sent Sullivan's dispatches to Schuyler's house where the general received them at midnight. After preparing a report of the crisis to Washington, Schuyler issued instructions for General Sullivan. The danger of allowing him to remain at Isle aux Noix was too great to wait for Washington's orders. He must at least move on to the broad part of Lake Champlain, perhaps to Point-au-Fer or the Isle-la-Motte. However, should he retire as far as Crown Point he might employ the armed sloop and schooner commanded by Capt. Jacobus Wynkoop to cruise about Isle-la-Motte. These vessels, together with some bateaux mounted with swivel guns, might be used to prevent enemy harassment of lakeside settlements. Schuyler's brief instructions to Sullivan carried the date and time of 25 June, 5:00 A.M.— an indication of his prompt response to the news he had received at midnight and his sense of urgency in advising Sullivan to take some more advantageous position against a pursuing enemy.[75]

Reporting his and Arnold's visit with the general, James Wilkinson discovered Schuyler to be a man with "a strong, fertile and cultivated mind; with polished manners he united the most amiable disposition and insinuating address, and his convivial pleasantry never failed to interest and enliven his society: in the discharge of his military duties, he was able, prompt, and decisive, and his conduct in every branch of service marked by active industry and rapid execution; but he excelled in the departments of commissary and quartermaster general." Wilkinson's assessment of Schuyler's accomplishments as a supply and transportation officer has, unfortunately, been better remembered and accepted than his judgment of the general's "conduct in every branch of service."[76]

Having armed Arnold with orders for Sullivan on 25 June, Schuyler turned at once to Massachusetts and Connecticut authorities for help in improving his naval construction at Skenesborough, for ship carpenters, and speedy replies. Governor Trumbull did not respond until 2 July, but he again proved to be one of Schuyler's most sympathetic supporters. Remarking that the Northern Army seemed plagued by "some strange fatality," the governor saw cause for rejoicing that at least "the Lord reigns." Schuyler would soon have General David Waterbury's militia, and captains J. Winslow and Jonathan Lester were collecting crews of ship carpenters. Winslow was to set out for Albany in the following week. By 12 July Lester's men were also on their way. Meantime, Schuyler was again obliged to divide his attention between Sullivan's Northern Army and the strengthening of naval forces on Lake Champlain, and the impending Indian conference at German Flats.[77]

On 26 June Schuyler discovered that the German Flats conference, scheduled to begin on 1 July, might be delayed. Receipt of an unsigned letter from Oneida Village requesting a two-week postponement prompted him to post an express rider to ask for clarification from John Frey of the Tryon County committee. Had the Oneida and Onondaga request for delay come from Frey or someone else? Immediately, Schuyler alerted Col. Dayton, now stationed at German Flats, that the Indian commissioners would put off their journey west until they had heard from Mr. Frey. Should the tribes assemble on 1 July, they must be given apologies for the commissioners' tardiness.[78]

Dayton quickly traced the source of the letter proposing the postponement of the treaty session to a Mr. Spencer at Fort Stanwix. With assurances that the request for delay had been no enemy ruse and other reports that the Indians did not expect to assemble for another fortnight, Schuyler was obliged to accept the delay. Although he had hoped to use the German Flats conference to explain to the Iroquois the necessity of garrisoning and refortifying Fort Stanwix, the general was inclined to wait no longer. Sullivan's retreat from Canada had increased the importance of the old fort as a watchpoint in the west, for the enemy might choose to follow the Americans south and also, with Indian allies, launch an invasion from Lake Ontario. At the strategic linkage between the lake and the upper Mohawk River, any incursion might be checked; even the enemy's navigation of Wood Creek could be blocked by felling trees into the waters. And the Reverend James Caldwell supplied another reason for Schuyler not to delay moving forces to Fort Stanwix: the inhabitants of German Flats were anxious for the protection that a more westerly garrison could afford. On 30 June Schuyler issued orders for marching Dayton's regiment from the Flats to Fort Stanwix.[79]

Amidst the flurry of these preparations the Albany committee grew apprehensive for Schuyler's safety. Alarmed that he intended to travel so deeply into Iroquois country while the dangers in the north were mounting, the committee feared that individual tribesmen might not heed their sachems' collective pledge of neutrality. Might they not seize some opportunity to capture the Yorker on his ride to German Flats or during his return to Albany? Perhaps the meeting should be scheduled at Caughnawaga (now Fonda), a point just south of Johnstown and only half the distance between Albany and the Flats.[80]

Schuyler promised the committee to consult with the other Indian commissioners about moving the conference to Caughnawaga. Knowing of no certain safeguards against assassins or kidnappers, he agreed to necessary precautions for his life and safety. There are but few traces of general philosophizing in Schuyler's writings, but in answering Abraham Yates, Jr.'s, warnings, he did refer to several principles by which he was clearly guided. It was deplorable, he said, that presumably civilized men—and especially those among whom "the social Religion of Christ is taught"—should wish to instigate barbarians to attack others. But "civil Discords are commonly marked with Crimes of the deepest Dye, especially by such as would destroy the Liberties and trample on the Rights of Mankind."[81] These were no extraordinary sentiments for men of the Enlightenment, but unlike some, Schuyler did draw distinctions between waging a moderate revolution and avoiding the excesses into which it could degenerate.

While civil discords were often marked, as Schuyler recognized, "with Crimes of the deepest Dye," they were also opportunities for selfless service. The cause of liberty required endurance and perseverance, and as he withstood the hardships and frustrations of an army commander, he did not hesitate to exhort others to do likewise. His own physician and the department director of hospitals, Dr. Samuel Stringer, was a case in point. In late June, Stringer despaired at the task of caring for three thousand sick men of Sullivan's army. With only five assistants to help him the doctor was also annoyed that Sullivan had treated him "with as little civility as his orderly Sergt. would be" and had faulted him for refusing to give the soldiers medicines and stores whenever they requested them. Falsely accused of selling medicines (meaning wine and molasses) at two shillings a dose, Stringer found his situation so irksome that on 22 June he announced that he would quit the service as quickly as Schuyler could name a replacement.[82]

Schuyler sympathized with Stringer, but he begged him not to "let [his] Resentment run so high as to quit the Service." Well acquainted with ill treatment himself, Schuyler insisted that "in this critical Day of my Country I put up with Matters that at another Time I would sooner lose my Life than not resent." Could Stringer not do as much? To resign would but gratify the physician's enemies and aggrieve his friends—especially Schuyler. "I hope for better Times," the general concluded, an obvious note of optimism and of wearied pleading.[83] Stringer was persuaded to stay on; doubtless his bond of friendship with Schuyler thus strengthened was in part responsible for the general's later row with Congress. In 1777 after Stringer was suddenly ousted as hospital director, Schuyler roared in protest because Congress cavalierly offered him neither the courtesy of advance consultation nor an explanation for the dismissal.

4

"punctilios with General Gates"

While mollifying Dr. Stringer Schuyler came to the verge of succumbing to his own resentment of the claims of Maj. Gen. Horatio Gates. Gates arrived in Albany on 26 June armed with Congress's 17 June orders to take command of the forces in Canada. Now there were no longer any forces *in* Canada for Gates to command, but Schuyler welcomed his arrival and expected Gates to function simply as John Thomas's successor. With no inkling of Gates's inclination to assert independence of his own command, he saluted him "with every friendly and affectionate wish" that they might consult on methods to prevent any "increase of our misfortunes in this unlucky quarter." Generously he offered Gates the hospitality of his Albany house. "Be so good as to take a bed with me, that, whilst you remain, we may be as much together as possible," he added.[84]

What passed between the two generals in the next few days, however, somewhat upset Schuyler's calm expectations. Although their initial clash had no immediately baleful results, it probably poisoned his relations with

Gates in the long run. And a proper appreciation of his recurrent difficulties with Gates requires careful consideration of the most important
facts about their origins. Most significant of these, perhaps, was Schuyler's sense of order and rank. His June 1775 commission as major general
made him senior to Gates, who had only recent been promoted to that
rank on 16 May. Schuyler's command of the Middle Department also
entitled him to claim a superiority, for Gates had been given command
of the army *in* Canada. Now there was no such army for Gates to lead
unless Canada were reinvaded. Gates, however, seemed to think that his
orders entitled him to command the army that had come out of Canada,
and in this his interpretation was strained.[85]

Temperamentally—and perhaps ideologically too—Gates and Schuyler were poles apart. Gates's views tended to be decidedly more radical
or democratic than Schuyler's. As the Revolution wore on, their personal
quarrel may well have reflected the fundamental split between those patriots who became determined to establish a strong national government
and those who fought to retain the federal principles of the confederation.
Gates, "the figure of a strong clumsy bear," was popular, especially with
New Englanders, but Schuyler was invariably caricatured as a proud aristocrat, stiffly pompous, and insistent upon a disciplined army whose
Yankee contingents resented regularity and restraints. Elegant, distant,
and courtly, the general seemed much less accessible than Gates; he was
also less eager to argue and less willing to give in. Happy to swear, Gates
was only superficially aggressive, whereas Schuyler carried himself with
cool dignity and unrelenting determination to persevere and to triumph.[86]

It has been charged that Schuyler "suffered from a neurosis derived
from a sense of being pursued, even hounded. The foundation of his state
of mind has not been fully explored, though it is pretty certain that back
of it was a high-powered ego conscious of its limitations."[87] In fact,
Schuyler was untouched by neurosis. His state of mind was undoubtedly
affected at times by actual illnesses, rheumatic gout; sometimes "scorbutic
eruptions," which indicate the effects of scurvy; and fevers. By late June
1776 he had barely recovered from recurrent onslaughts of the ague, which
had lingered for about a month. But in his contest with Gates he only
revealed his consistent adherence to a sense of the responsibilities and
prerogatives of all military commanders.

Although Schuyler and Gates' brief altercation in 1776 partly reflected
the long-standing animus between Yankees and Yorkers, it cannot be
deemed as serious or as virulent as the dispute between the two men and
their partisans in 1777. Yet as John Adams later recalled, Gates's appointment as a major general "soon Occasioned a Competition between him

and Schuyler, in which I always contended for Gates, and as the Rivalry occasioned great Animosities among the Friends of the two Generals, the consequences of which are not yet spent. Indeed they have affected the Essential Interests of the United States and will influence their ultimate Destiny." Adams's 1802 assessment is an intriguing, if curious, tribute to the effects of Schuyler and Gates upon the politics of an emerging nation. The Yorker's partisans, especially John Jay and Alexander Hamilton, proved to be political enemies of Gates, Aaron Burr, and John Adams. And Adams believed that his own role as a supporter of Gates rankled in Hamilton from 1776 until the famous secretary of the treasury wrote his "libel" of the Yankee president in 1799. "I had never in my Life," Adams insisted, "any personal Prejudice or dislike against General Schuyler: on the contrary I knew him to [be] industrious, studious and intelligent." Yet Adams felt the "necessity of supporting Gates" because New England Continentals and militia were reluctant or refused to serve under the Yorker.[88]

As early as April 1776 Adams proposed to make Gates a major general and to give him a command of New England troops who presumably would serve him better than they would Schuyler. The opportunity arose in May after Gen. John Thomas died and it became necessary to name a successor. However, it was not until 17 June that Congress finally acted. Reacting to news of American reverses at Three Rivers and the continued retreat from Quebec, it ordered Washington to send Gates "to take command of the forces in that province."[89]

Specifically, the issue of which general would command the army now retreating to Lake Champlain was raised because Gates proposed to have his own deputy quartermaster general (Morgan Lewis) and his own commissary (Elisha Avery). Avery was commissioned for the Canadian service by the commissary general Joseph Trumbull, and Avery claimed that Trumbull had instructed him to replace Walter Livingston, who might otherwise function as a contractor for military provisions. When Gates introduced Schuyler to Avery on the morning of 30 June, Schuyler sent for Livingston, who produced a letter from Trubmull to show that he was the department commissary. Avery insisted, however, that Congress had empowered Trumbull to name or dismiss any deputy as he saw fit, and that Trumbull wished Avery to take Livingston's place. Livingston argued that Trumbull could not replace him without specific approval of Congress, and Schuyler ruled that Avery must function as Livingston's subordinate if he was to remain with the army. Because of Livingston's proven experience and great "family connexions," Schuyler did not intend to lose him. Explaining this to Gates and Avery, the general first deduced that Gates had acquiesced. But he was soon surprised to hear that Gates had informed Avery that once he "came to the Army he would employ him." Uncertain of what Gates might do next, Schuyler drafted a memorandum of their conversation in the presence of Walter Livingston and sent a copy of it to Washington with a request that Congress settle the matter. Gates, he said, agreed that it contained the gist of their talks: the army in Canada that Gates was to command was now within Schuyler's department and therefore Schuyler claimed it to be under his own command. He would "not suffer" appointments to be made by Gates. "General Gates Conceived the Contrary, upon which G. Schuyler observing that he meant to be Clear and Explicit on a point of such Importance, declared that he Conceived the Army to be Altogether under his Command when on this side of Canada subject however to the controul of G. Washington. In his [Schuyler's] Absence Gen: Gates Commanded the Army in the same Manner as G. Sullivan did now. . . . If he [Schuyler] was with the Army which he always would be when his health, or other Indispensible public business did not Call him from It and ordered It to remove from one place to Another that he Expected to be Obeyed." Schuyler granted that if Gates faced any emergency with the army in the field while Schuyler was not present, Gates or any other such commander might properly exercise his own judgment and take appropriate measures to deal with it. But if Congress meant to supersede Schuyler with Gates, Schuyler would not remain with the army. Congress might move Schuyler "wherever they pleased," but "they could not put him under the Command of a Younger [i.e., junior] officer, nor oblige him to be a [junior] & Stab his own honor." Recognizing Gates's superior qualifications, the general promised that he would always consult him and other brigadier generals of his department so long as he held the command. Should Congress choose to name a successor, he would be greatly pleased to be replaced by a gentleman of Gates's character and reputation. And until it decided the matter, both men pledged to cooperate for the good of the service; neither wished their dispute to produce "evil consequences" during the "critical moments" that they and the army now faced. Indeed, Schuyler proved his willingness to cooperate by issuing general orders whereby Elisha Avery was temporarily appointed deputy commissary and superintendent of issues at Crown Point. Much of Sullivan's army gathered there early in July.[90]

In forwarding his appeal to Washington on 1 July, the general pointedly argued that if Congress intended that Gates command the army, Schuyler should have been so informed, and he would have then surrendered it; but without such instructions he could never do so. The line must be clearly drawn; until it was Schuyler would "stand upon punctilios with General Gates that I would otherwise with pleasure waive." Meantime, he was reassured by Gates's agreement to his plans for building a stronger lake fleet and fortifying some advantageous point on the east side of Lake Champlain, either opposite Ticonderoga or somewhere between it and Crown Point.[91]

News of the generals' dispute quickly spread before Congress settled it on 8 July. Joseph Trumbull acidly observed that Gates should not be obliged to take a subordinate position, for Schuyler "is willing to let anybody fight the battles that will, under him, but let him command the chest, the commissary and quartermaster departments and he is pleased." The Connecticut Yankee was plainly suspicious that Schuyler and other Yorkers were profiteering from the army—and was envious of their business advantage over New Englanders in a major theater of the war. Gates of course could be expected to favor Yankees over Yorkers. Trumbull urged the Massachusetts congressman Elbridge Gerry to get Gates the command or have him return to Washington's army; "if you keep him there," he advised, "don't keep him in sha[c]kles, let him be ABLE to ACT, and then if he doesn't act, blame him." Another Connecticut patriot, Col. Jedediah Huntington, who was Trumbull's brother-in-law and was then serving in Washington's army, characterized Schuyler as an "unhappy obstacle" that had fallen in Gates's way. Schuyler's insistence "on holding the supreme Direction as General & Commissary" he found to be particularly annoying; not only could Gates proceed no further, but Trumbull's "Deputies are returning [from Albany] or will be soon. I hope Congress will see fit to call Genl S: as well as Genl Woorster [sic] to Philad[elphia]," he wrote.[92]

While Congress finally ruled in favor of Schuyler's claims against Gates, it did not support the Yorker's efforts to retain Walter Livingston as deputy commissary general. Instead, it gave Trumbull "full power to supply both armies, that upon the lakes as well as that at New York; and also to appoint and employ such persons under him, and to remove any deputy commissary ... it being absolutely necessary, that the supply of both armies should be under one direction." Here was the origin of further difficulties between Trumbull and Schuyler. Livingston, who was the general's appointee, would be subject to replacement by Elisha Avery or to a position subordinate to Avery. As for Gates, it was Congress's pleasure to say that it had not intended to vest him with a command superior to Schuyler's while the troops were on this side of Canada. Rather, as Schuyler had rightly interpreted the language of Gates's orders, Congress wished "to give ... Gates the command while the troops were in Canada, but no longer." However, the two generals were urged, as President Hancock put it, "to cultivate a harmony in your military operations," because it was "expedient" for Gates to remain in the north and not to return to Washington's army. And both officers were commended for their patriotism and magnanimity in deciding to cooperate rather than allowing a difference of opinion to harm the public service.[93]

For the remainder of the campaign of 1776 the two men clearly demonstrated that their pledges to cooperate were not idly given. As Schuyler saw it, seldom did gentlemen find disagreeable consequences from acting with candor. His difference with Gates had been such that neither could be disgraced; "the most perfect harmony subsists between us," he wrote. And he assured Washington that he intended to cultivate it by paying "every attention" to his colleague. Moreover, Gates seemed to be genuinely regretful that the general was obliged to leave the army in order to negotiate with the Iroquois at German Flats in July. Perhaps Gates discovered the value of congressmen Charles Carroll and Samuel Chase's advice that he place "the most unreserved and unlimited confidence" in the Yorker.[94]

With the Gates issue momentarily in abeyance as June turned to July, Schuyler first thought he should remain at Albany to superintend the department while Gates proceeded to Lake Champlain to direct preparations for meeting a British invasion. The two men agreed that the lake fleet must be augmented and new fortifications constructed opposite Ticonderoga or on the east side of Lake Champlain somewhere between the fort and Crown Point. Because the Iroquois had deferred the German Flats conference until mid-July, Schuyler waited no longer to order Col. Elias Dayton to take post at old Fort Stanwix. Dayton's scouts discovered no indications of warlike activities in the west, and the Iroquois conference had been delayed for another fortnight, so Schuyler succumbed to the urging of Gates and Arnold to accompany them to Crown Point. Together they might determine where and how to proceed with additional fortifications on Lake Champlain.[95]

Before leaving Albany, Schuyler replied to an express message from Washington, indicating what steps had been taken to improve Mohawk valley defenses and noting that he was still waiting for responses to his calls for militia and ship carpenters. He was grateful for Washington's promises that every effort would be made to ship powder, cannon, and other equipment for outfitting the Lake Champlain navy. The schooner, sloop, and row galley would soon be supported by new barges mounted with small artillery. Two gondolas had just been completed at Skenesborough, and Schuyler expected that millhands and carpenters could soon turn out two such vessels every week. Disappointed that Washington himself had been able to collect only about a thousand militia reinforcements for his New York army, the general recognized that his army, too, might be as poorly augmented from New Hampshire, Massachusetts, and Connecticut. "What can they be about?" he wondered.[96]

5

Contretemps over Crown Point

As Schuyler rode north from Albany with Horatio Gates and Benedict Arnold, on 2 July Gen. Sir William Howe began to land British forces on Staten Island. If he could push up the Hudson River while Sir Guy Carleton and Gen. John Burgoyne pursued Sullivan's army south into New York, the American cause might indeed be ruined. On the same day most of Sullivan's eight thousand men safely reached Crown Point. About three thousand of these had been barely able to travel because of illness. About six hundred of his troops remained in his rear to escort the last boats from Isle aux Noix; some assisted Capt. Jacobus Wynkoop's little fleet of armed vessels, cruising the lake waters to scout for signs of any enemy pursuit.[97]

Horatio Gates now began to learn something of Schuyler's heavy responsibilities of managing an army in the field, the difficulties of operating a long line of communications and supplies smoothly, and the energies required to improve fortifications and to build and equip the navy that was intended to be a major part of the lake country defenses. Already John Sullivan was busily collecting boards and timber from Otter Creek and the Onion River and setting hands to run the sawmill near Crown Point. His officers, he was pleased to find, were determined to fortify the place and to retreat no further. Like Colonel Campbell, he begged Schuyler for supplies, but for food more than clothing—peas, beans, and sauce for meat—and soap for his lousy army![98]

But it was not to be Crown Point that Schuyler's army fortified in the summer of 1776. Instead, Ticonderoga became the command post of his department—a hospital for the diseased mob of soldiers who had been forced out of Canada; the seat of courts-martial; a rendezvous for Moses Hazen's Canadian regiment and their families, most of whom were French; and a depot of supplies, replete with workshops and barracks— in short, the "nerve center of the whole" Northern Army.[99]

For Americans the war passed from its initial phase of taking the offensive to a second stage, that of attempting to defend the country just as Congress declared independence. By July it was apparent that Burgoyne and Carleton were expected to press south from Canada while Sir William Howe maneuvered against Washington, endeavoring to press northward along the Hudson valley. Having guessed that the British would send 22,500 troops to Canada (10,000) and New York (12,500) in 1776, Washington and Congress agreed to raise 55,00. In the end not half that number could be mustered, and the British and German forces totaled about 48,000! Despite their numerical superiority the enemy failed to move resolutely and speedily at both northern and southern ends of the province, thus saving Schuyler, Washington, and New York from conquest. Neither of course was then assured of the final outcome as together they confronted the enemy's two-pronged attack. When Washington proposed a broad strategy of defense later in the summer of 1776—"a war of posts" in which general actions were to be avoided unless absolutely necessary—his "masterpiece of strategic thought" was already familiar to trusted subordinates like Philip Schuyler. In 1776, and again in 1777, the Yorker followed this line without the need of the Virginian's promptings; despite the risks of a protracted war he, too, recognized the means by which a weak force could combat a powerful opponent.[100]

During the first week of July 1776, as Schuyler led Gates and Arnold across the terrain from Saratoga to Fort Edward and Skenesborough and between Crown Point and Ticonderoga, it became increasingly clear to all three men that they must adopt a defensive posture that at least could prevent the enemy from penetrating beyond Lake Champlain. At nearly every step along the route Schuyler demonstrated for Gates and Arnold his careful attention to details. On 4 July at Skenesborough, for example, the general reviewed Harmanus Schuyler's superintendency of the rudimentary naval yards. Anticipating the arrival of four companies of Massachusetts and Connecticut carpenters, he prepared instructions for their officers to work their men diligently. Fearful of the effects of jealousies between Yankees and Yorkers, he exhorted the men to live and work together in harmony for the sake of their country.[101]

The realization of lofty sentiments and aspirations for colonial independence that Congress approved on 4 July very much depended upon the practical success for which Schuyler labored as he introduced Gates and Arnold to their impending tasks. Although they, too, were to share his responsibilities for the creation of the Lake Champlain navy, it was Schuyler who began the enterprise and it was he who must be credited with providing the direction as well as the materials and manpower needed to bring it to fruition. By the time Gates and Arnold appeared on the scene, Schuyler's fleet consisted of one large schooner mounting twelve guns, two smaller ones with four to six guns, a sloop with eight guns, and three gondolas. By the Battle of Lake Champlain almost three months later, the little navy had been augmented by five more gondolas and five row galleys.[102]

From Skenesborough Schuyler and his companions made their way down South Bay River to Ticonderoga on 5 July. That evening they reached Crown Point to survey the fortifications and the state of the army. Brigadier General Sullivan did not, however, welcome the arrival of Maj. Gen. Horatio Gates. In view of his own services he was disappointed that Congress had not promoted him to the rank and position now held by Gates, who had not been superior in rank or service to him; and because he felt that his conduct had not otherwise been impeached, Sullivan asked leave to visit Philadelphia and to tender his resignation.[103]

Schuyler did not wish to discuss the merits of Sullivan's arguments, and he wanted him to remain with the army. But Schuyler intended to show the "utmost tenderness to the feelings of every gentleman who conceives himself injured," and he therefore approved Sullivan's request to leave.[104] Perhaps when Sullivan and his aides visited the commander in chief, Washington would dissuade him from resigning his commission to Congress.

John Sullivan did not immediately rush off; he chose first to attend Schuyler's council of general officers. On 7 July with Gates, Arnold, and Brigadier General De Woedtke, he and Schuyler decided that Crown Point was not tenable, nor was it worth the great exertions required to render it defensible. The healthy troops must be moved to the east side of the lake, opposite Ticonderoga, while those with smallpox and other illnesses would be taken to Fort George. Without this segregation the militia could not be expected to join the army. The generals further agreed to bend their efforts to complete a fleet of gondolas, row galleys, and armed bateaux; and a road must be laid out between the high ground opposite Ticonderoga and another stretching from Skenesborough toward the northern settlements.[105]

Schuyler's decision to abandon Crown Point was protested by Col. John Stark and twenty other field officers on the day the general returned to Ticonderoga. Like Stark, most of them were New Englanders (Enoch Poor and James Reed of New Hampshire, William Bond and John Greaton of Massachusetts, Charles Burrell of Connecticut), but Col. William Maxwell of New Jersey also signed the remonstrance. Arthur St. Clair and John De Haas of Pennsylvania evidently did not carry their objections so far as to put their names to the list. These officers disavowed any intention to disobey orders, nor did they presume to dictate measures to their superiors; but they believed the decision to retreat to Ticonderoga was contrary to the spirit of Congress's orders to "dispute every inch of the ground in Canada." Convinced that they could hold Crown Point against any enemy assault, they also argued that it was the only place where a naval superiority might be maintained against the British. To allow the enemy to reach Crown Point would destroy American communication with lower parts of Lake Champlain and open a way for the penetration of both New England and New York. The army's further retreat would leave Crown Point a haven for savages and would force local inhabitants to abandon their homes and crops. Finally, the remonstrants argued that Ticonderoga was simply an unhealthy location for an army already riddled with diseases.[106]

John Sullivan handed the officers' remonstrance to Schuyler at Ticonderoga on the evening of 9 July. Within an hour the general penned a reply, which is clearly an indication that in dealing with fellow officers he was not averse to the employment of persuasion and mollification. Congress, he said, had recommended the location of strong fortifications in the vicinity of Ticonderoga *or* Crown Point. The council of general officers had unanimously chosen Ticonderoga, but Schuyler could not discuss particular reasons without their consent. However, he accepted the ultimate responsibility for the decision and remained convinced that it was both prudent and necessary. Unhappily, the twenty-one officers did not see fit to let the matter rest but forwarded a copy of their protests to Washington. Later in July the Virginian himself protested the evacuation of Crown Point to both Gates and Schuyler. Although Gates explained that the decision was not his own, he was quick to support the reasons for it and to defend Schuyler's judgment in having made it. Washington's queries to Schuyler were, however, carefully couched; the protesters' arguments seemed persuasive to the Virginian, but he gingerly conceded that Schuyler and the others must be trusted to consider their options, and he hoped that they had reached the best possible decision.[107]

That Schuyler and his colleagues had properly assessed the army's situation cannot be doubted. During his visit to Crown Point the general had left John Trumbull (Gates's deputy adjutant general) to reconnoiter the ground opposite Ticonderoga. It was Trumbull's report that had persuaded Schuyler's council of war and confirmed the Yorker's belief that this was the best place at which to block an enemy incursion. Then, on 9 July, he and Gates with both Trumbull and the army's chief engineer, Col. Jeduthan Baldwin, minutely surveyed the terrain on the east side of

the fort. It was there that entrenchments and other fortifications were to
be built; and after Col. Arthur St. Clair read the Declaration of Independence to the troops on the site on 28 July, the place was duly christened
Mount Indpendence. Judging it to be tenable against even a superior
force, Schuyler decided that the militia would be stationed on Mount
Independence while regulars held Ticonderoga and the sick were moved
south to Fort George. What he had seen of the army at Crown Point had
also convinced him of the prudence of concentrating upon the defenses
of Ticonderoga.[108]

On 10 July Schuyler left Ticonderoga and the army now entrusted to
Horatio Gates. He was not to visit the Lake Champlain fort again until
June 1777. In the long interval the fortunes of war and a variety of other
duties called him as far west as German Flats and south to Philadelphia.
There were also stretches of illness that confined him to Albany or prevented him from moving beyond his country house at Saratoga except in
November, when he briefly ventured as far north as Fort Edward and
Fort George.

As Schuyler went off to confront the Iroquois, Gates promptly pursued
the Yorker's directives to prepare for an enemy onslaught, improving the
fortifications and constructing the lake fleet. Gates, however, expected
Schuyler to continue directing the work at Skenesborough, for he asked
the general to issue appropriate instructions to the commanding officer
there. And Gates fully trusted that Schuyler's zeal would somehow produce all of the tools, ammunition, and equipment that he knew to be
wanted at Ticonderoga.[109]

Remarkably, Schuyler traversed the seventy miles between Fort George
and Albany within about twenty-four hours with only a pause at his
country house on the morning of 12 July. Somewhere along the rough
road north of Saratoga he encountered his overseer, John Graham, and
six men whom Mrs. Schuyler had dispatched to escort him safely home.
Except when accompanying troops or groups like a congressional committee or the Indian commissioners, he apparently never traveled with
guards or an entourage of more than one or two aides. On this occasion,
however, Mrs. Schuyler had become "very much alarmed" for her husband's life. Graham bore a letter from the general's daughter, Angelica,
explaining that her mother was "under great distress"; a certain "Indian
Joe" had threatened that Schuyler "shall not ride this road a fortnight
longer." The women begged for news to relieve their "alarming apprehensions" and wished for the general's speedy return. Reminding her
father that his family's happiness depended on his very life, Angelica
touchingly closed her note, "Adieu my dear papa, God bless and preserve
you."[110]

Apparently the general did not encounter the danger so much feared by his wife and daughter, but threats to his life and safety were by now not new to him. Nor were they unrepeated or unheeded. On 13 July he requested the Schenectady and Tryon county committees to furnish escorts for himself and commissioners Volkert Douw and Timothy Edwards, which was a precaution he deemed necessary at least to spare Mrs. Schuyler any further anxiety.[111] Still, there was another reason for his precaution.

On the very day Schuyler reappeared in the city the Albany committee discovered "some desperate" Tory designs, and early in the afternoon on 14 July four conspirators were arrested about three miles out of the city. The incident prompted Schuyler to order two companies of Col. Goose Van Schaick's regiment back from Fort George to guard his house and family and also to reassure his fellow townsmen of their safety against further disturbances, arson, or even armed uprisings.[112]

Between his arrival at Albany on the afternoon of 12 July and his departure two days later, Schuyler had little time to complete preparations for the conference at German Flats. The draft of his speech to the Indians was ready, but travel arrangements and the shipment of camp equipment, baggage, and supplies required considerable attention. The general's thoughts remained largely fixed on the fate of the Northern Army and the race to strengthen its hold on Lake Champlain against the invasion that was sure to come once the British had built enough boats and other vessels to move from Saint John's. Amidst other preparations for his trip to the Flats, Schuyler posted final instructions to General Gates for the evacuation of Crown Point and the additional fortification of Ticonderoga. By 13 July he also had the first news of independence to relay to Gates. Noting only that Congress had voted to declare the colonies free states on 2 July, and that no colonial delegation had dissented, Schuyler revealed nothing of his sentiments about this fateful step. And when he received Washington's orders to read the declaration to the troops on 18 July, he merely forwarded Gates a copy of the document together with the Virginian's instructions that it be "proclaimed throughout the northern Army."[113]

Perhaps anticipating Washington's questioning the propriety of the army's retreat from Crown Point, Schuyler carefully explained his reasons for the move before he left Albany on 14 July. Noting the wretched state of the troops and the need to separate the sick from the able-bodied, he fully reviewed the course of his actions at Crown Point and Ticonderoga, the council of war, the survey of the terrain, and the necessity of fortifying the most tenable position on Lake Champlain. He also asked that the commander in chief request Congress's approval of the decision to enlist six companies of Hampshire Grants men as regulars and proposed that Congress order an abatement of the charges for soldier's clothing. Without this, the high prices would only "disgust" the troops; conversely, a better display of attention to the men would improve morale—the essential ingredient in creating good discipline and a preventative of one of the worst of all threats to an army—desertion. Obliged to repeat his calls for other supports, the Yorker noted that as yet no ship carpenters had arrived from New England, nor had the long-requested naval stores yet appeared at Albany. His fears that a shipment of anchors and cables had been mistakenly landed at Poughkeepsie were confirmed when Washington replied to Schuyler's letter on 17-18 July. It was then that the commander in chief questioned the wisdom of abandoning Crown Point, but the Virginian was unable to say more than that he trusted that Schuyler had done what was best. By now carpenters from Connecticut and Pennsylvania were indeed on their way to help construct the navy projected for Lake Champlain; those from Philadelphia would be delayed because they had missed the boat and so were obliged to move overland instead. Although the quartermaster was sending a quantity of naval stores, Schuyler would be constrained to obtain others elsewhere as best he could. The anchors and cables that had been mislanded at Poughkeepsie were to be found and shipped on to Albany. Surprised at Schuyler's reports of food shortages, Washington correctly ascribed them to what the Yorker had long since discovered by firsthand observation as well as from officers' reports: the extravagant wastefulness of soldiers, bateaumen, and wagoners.[114]

Struggle for Lake Champlain

1

Interlude at German Flats

Diverted momentarily by the work of the Northern Department's Indian commissioners in July 1776, Schuyler had already commenced the campaign to check a British advance beyond the waters of Lake Champlain. His role in this momentous struggle actually began with efforts to reinforce the American forces retreating from Canada and to create a navy for the lake as an effective auxiliary force for the army. The projected negotiations with the Iroquois and other tribes were but another part of the grand design to halt the British incursion into New York. While the main body of forces remained in the north, the general sought safeguards for them by blocking any enemy movement on their western flank.

On Sunday, 14 July, Schuyler set out from Albany to meet the Six Nations at German Flats. Accompanied by commissioners Volkert P. Douw and Timothy Edwards, and two aides, Maj. James Van Rensselaer and Maj. Henry B. Livingston, the general wondered whether he could ask the Iroquois to join the American war effort or whether he must be content with a reaffirmation of their neutrality. Fearing that the tribes would be tempted by the blandishments of Col. John Butler to ally with the British, especially after their show of force in pushing the American army out of Canada, Schuyler had decided to display his own strength as a warning to the Iroquois. The posting of Col. Elias Dayton's New Jersey regiment of Continentals at old Fort Stanwix, for example, might effectively demonstrate to the tribes that they should be wary of breaking the neutrality that they had pledged in the Albany treaty of 1775. Moreover,

Mohawk valley settlers might be encouraged not to abandon their homes nor to turn Loyalist and join the enemy.[1]

In the larger context of the British campaign for the Hudson in 1776, Schuyler's military and diplomatic maneuvers in the Mohawk valley were particularly significant; American forces had to be protected from assaults from the west if they were to concentrate their efforts on both ends of the Hudson. For the time being the enemy in Canada were not ready to begin a penetration of the lake country. But between mid-July and mid-August 1776, while Schuyler confronted the Iroquois, the British managed to sail several of their ships beyond New York City, seeking to sever Washington's communications with the north. At the very moment Schuyler arrived at German Flats a British squadron had reached Peekskill, posing a threat to Albany and to the rear of the American army on Lake Champlain. Should the British pass the Highlands, they might also destroy two Continental frigates being built at Poughkeepsie and even provoke a Loyalist uprising. Leading Orange County and Ulster County militia down from the Highlands, Brig. Gen. George Clinton prevented British landings, but for several weeks after 19 July the maneuverings on the river continued.

News of these activities on the Hudson moved the New York convention to alert Schuyler to the danger and to appeal for help. In answering their request for a heavy chain with which to obstruct the river, he advised making casoons by sinking sloops filled with stone, instead. The chain, he said, might better be used for the defenses of Ticonderoga, but he suggested that the enemy would be hard put to force a passage through the Highlands if proper obstructions were sunk near Fort Montgomery and well-entrenched troops were positioned at a narrow passage just beyond the first house in the Highlands.[2]

On 18 August patriot forces finally managed to chase the British squadron south to New York harbor. The enemy's activities had demonstrated that American fortifications at New York City were incapable of stopping superior British naval forces, and that greater efforts would be required if the province was to be defended successfully.[3] It also illustrated the importance of both Schuyler's army's role in checking an invasion from Canada and Washington's efforts to prevent an enemy incursion from the south. And, finally, it made Schuyler's efforts to safeguard the west especially significant, for disturbances in that quarter could endanger the Northern Army's efforts to hold their ground against a British drive across Lake Champlain.

When Schuyler reached German Flats on the morning of 16 July he was disappointed to find that only about 150 of the Iroquois had as yet appeared. Having sent Samuel Kirkland and James Dean to urge the tribesmen to hurry to the conference, Schuyler was still obliged to wait more than three weeks for the sachems to assemble. Lured to Niagara for parleys with John Butler, the Seneca proved to figure principally in the delay in the conference. Schuyler remained hopeful that they and the other tribes might at least be kept "neuter." Increasingly he doubted the wisdom of engaging the Iroquois as full-fledged American allies, although Washington urged him to try. They might at least be incited to capture enemies of the cause, Washington insisted. Should this fail, the Virginian still trusted the Yorker's ability to maintain the Iroquois' neutrality—"an important Point to you," he concluded.[4]

Until he could open the Iroquois conference there were other matters for Schuyler to press, which constituted a variety of important points for him to consider as he tarried on the upper reaches of the Mohawk. From a distance he continued to do what he could to direct General Gates's work at Ticonderoga and the naval project at Skenesborough. Closer by was the business of fortifying Fort Stanwix, where Colonel Dayton's regiment and the Tryon County militia needed provisions, artillery, and engineers' stores. The shipment of these supplies Schuyler had ordered from Henry Glen of Schenectady, and Glen had commenced the task before the general himself began his western tour.[5]

Upon reaching German Flats on 16 July Schuyler issued instructions to Dayton for a system of scouting against surprise attacks from the west. Sutlers must proceed no further lest their supply of trading goods be sold to Tories. Dayton should extend his defenses by obstructing Wood Creek against any enemy approach from Lake Ontario. When Dayton could discover no signs of British activity along Lake Ontario, he asked whether he should dispatch men to attempt to burn Fort Ontario (Oswego). The venture, Schuyler thought, was one that he could not yet determine, but he feared that it would annoy the Indians at a time when they should not be aroused.[6]

Like Dayton, Congress also proposed schemes for the western frontiers, which Schuyler must have found to be singularly grandiose. On 11 July they recommended construction of forts at Oswego and Presque Isle, Le Boeuf and Kittaning, and a number of galleys to guard the waters of Lake Ontario. A battalion of troops was to be raised to execute these designs, and the Indian commissioners were asked to determine the size of naval forces required to secure Lake Erie for the United States as well! When Schuyler received these proposals he calmly replied that he regretted that there was no prospect of accomplishing such tasks during the current campaign; he simply had no equipment and supplies to attempt them. And whether troops could be spared from New York or the Mohawk valley outposts was a question that could not be answered for a few weeks more. Already concerned that the delay of the Indian conference was keeping him from being more directly helpful to General Gates and the Northern Army, Schuyler feared that the affairs of his department would suffer. The "incessant begging of drunk and sober" Indians was a torment to him. But for one consideration, he told Hancock, "I would infinitely prefer being a Team Driver in the Green Mountains" than an Indian commissioner, "but *vive la courage*." On some happy winter's evening, he hoped, there would be laughter at all past pains, and cheer from "the enlivening but untaxed Juice of the Grape."[7]

As Elias Dayton proceeded with his scouting and the repair and extension of the works at Fort Stanwix, he was able to inform Schuyler of the continued peace of the frontier throughout July. Dayton renamed the post Fort Schuyler and his accomplishments were a testimony both to his own energies and to the general's able direction of strategy. But there were several officers in the New Jersey regiment at Fort Schuyler whose activities proved to be less than commendable. In response to reports of their embezzlement of Sir John Johnson's property at Johnstown while the troops had been stationed there and had searched Johnson's house for "warlike papers," Schuyler ordered an investigation that promptly led to the court-martial of Lt. William McDonald on 30 July. McDonald was brought to German Flats for trial, and on 1 August the general approved the verdict and sentence of the court. McDonald was dismissed from the service and his pay was declared forfeited.[8]

McDonald's trial, however, proved only the beginning of a series of investigations and trials that dragged on for months. Other men were implicated, including two of Dayton's young captains, Thomas Paterson and John Ross, and even his second-in-command, Lt. Col. Anthony W. White. Although Paterson and Ross confessed their folly and imprudence, they tried to excuse themselves by pleading that they had vented their youthful enthusiasm against an "obnoxious" enemy and the "baseness" of Johnson's conduct. Their minds, they told Schuyler, had been inflamed "with Blind Resentment" at Johnson's efforts to ruin their country and to "murder your self together with other Supporters of American Freedom." Throwing themselves upon Schuyler's "well known Clemency and Mercy," they feared that legal proceedings would ruin their careers.[9]

Schuyler agreed to postpone further action until Paterson and Ross filed a full report about everyone who had been involved in plundering Johnson Hall; meantime they must issue a public statement of contrition at the head of their regiment. Urging other officers who had taken part in the episode to do likewise, Schuyler decided to refer the question of further proceedings to the commander in chief and to allow Ross and Paterson to retire to Schenectady to await the answer.[10]

The two captains immediately implicated Lieutenant Colonel White; another captain; seven lieutenants, including the already convicted McDonald; four ensigns; and several other men. They further offered a detailed list of articles that various individuals had taken from Johnson Hall. As the entire business of the thefts unfolded, Schuyler feared that were so many officers to be publicly convicted, their regiment or perhaps the entire army would be disgraced. He decided to refer the problem to Washington, suggesting that the officers' confessions together with their pledges of restitution and future good behavior might be accepted and the affair buried. Or trials might be ordered for all of them.[11]

Washington advised Schuyler to follow his own judgment in the case but suggested court-martialing the officers. Meantime Schuyler diligently pursued the evidence that was necessary for a proper disposition of the case. Not until the first week of October was the case of the plundering of Johnson Hall finally settled. After a court of inquiry at Fort Schuyler on 13—17 September, a general court-martial was held in Albany on 1—7 October. On charges of breach of orders and involvement in embezzling Sir John Johnson's property, Lieutenant Colonel White was found not guilty, as was a Lieutenant Gordon. The charges against Captain Ross and Captain Paterson, judged to have been malicious and vexatious, were dismissed. But apart from the delayed and formal proceedings, Schuyler had already executed what may be regarded as more substantial justice. His requirement that Captain Ross and Captain Paterson confess their misconduct at the head of their regiment was a salutary piece of discipline for their entire corps. And the restitution of many if not all of the articles that had been plundered was perhaps as effective a retribution as the verdict dismissing Lieutenant McDonald from the service.[12] All in all the behavior of such officers with whom Schuyler served illustrated a general malaise in the army of which he so frequently complained; and they proved the legitimacy of his concern for discipline throughout the army's rank and file.

Between his arrival at German Flats in mid-July and the opening of the conference with the Iroquois on 6 August, Schuyler directed Colonel Dayton's activities at Fort Stanwix with a minimum of effort. Most of his attention remained fixed upon generals Gates and Arnold's efforts to fortify Lake Champlain. Again he demonstrated a capacity for supervision at a distance and for managing the work of various subordinates by cor-respondence. By constant prodding, repeated inquiries, and steadily relaying information, he coordinated the efforts of Congress, Washington, Arnold, and Gates to prepare the army for the British invasion that was certain to be launched from Canada. Like Washington, he recognized the enemy's intent to subdue them by focusing their campaign on the colony of New York.[13]

Largely with the cooperation of the commander in chief and Governor Trumbull of Connecticut, Schuyler collected carpenters, tools, and a variety of materials for the construction of the fleet on Lake Champlain. With Congress's help some shipbuilders were also sent from Massachusetts, Pennsylvania, and Rhode Island. Noting that American naval strength initially exceeded Burgoyne's, he expected Burgoyne to create his own fleet; "we shall," he promised, "certainly build as fast as he can," and he steadily endeavored to guarantee that Gates and Arnold got the manpower and materials needed to accomplish it.[14]

Although obliged to rely heavily upon these two subordinates, Schuyler did not hesitate to press them to their tasks. With Arnold, however, he was noticeably less abrasive and enjoyed a more spontaneous rapport. Confident that Arnold agreed with him, the Yorker noted that twenty years of experience had convinced him that nine men out of ten required shoving to do their duty even when they were properly interested. But Schuyler was pleased with Gates's decision to assign Arnold to supervise the boat construction at Skenesborough. Arnold could be relied upon to "push matters" there as avidly as Schuyler would himself.[15]

While the general was forced to tarry in the Mohawk valley, his secretary, Richard Varick, maintained a clearinghouse at Albany for his correspondence, daily supervising the execution of Schuyler's orders for the movement of men and supplies, ammunition, nails, livestock and even paper. The general drove Varick with an avalanche of instructions to obtain and to ship nails, tools, blacksmiths, and anchors, cables, sailcloth and rigging for the shipyards at Skenesborough. Although Arnold reported at the end of July that two hundred carpenters had finally arrived to speed construction work, he was convinced that Schuyler's presence at both Ticonderoga and Skenesborough was much needed.[16]

As Schuyler's surrogate, Varick was expected to see that the collection and transportation of supplies for the Northern Army did not falter. On 27 July he and Philip Van Rensselaer, the public storekeeper, had run about the entire morning collecting blocks, rigging, cables, and anchors from Albany shipowners. "Neither the Love of Money, Virtue to their Country or the persuasive Eloquence of officers will induce some Persons to part with a single Article," he wrote.[17]

Benedict Arnold commended Varick's industrious efforts when on 8

August he reported to Schuyler that many of the naval articles had arrived at Skenesborough. Largely, too, because of Varick's assistance, Schuyler managed to acquire a quantity of light artillery and supplies of shot for the lake fleet. Armed with the general's orders, the faithful secretary obtained these from Col. Robert Livingston's ironworks and Connecticut suppliers like Governor Trumbull and Joshua Porter of Salisbury.[18]

As of early August the list of armed American vessels on Lake Champlain included two schooners, *Royal Savage* and *Revenge;* the sloop *Enterprise;* and three gondolas, *New Haven, Providence,* and *Boston* (the names are suggestive of the origins of the carpenters who built them). The schooner *Liberty* and the gondola *Spitfire* had yet to be completely rigged, as were also another gondola and a "Spanish-built" row galley. The ten craft were manned by 350 sailors and mounted with about 50 carriage guns and 70 swivels. The guns ranged in rize from two (10) to twelve-pounders (2), most of them (30) four-pounders. Arnold began his command of the yet unfinished fleet by reporting to Schuyler on 8 August that he would soon inaugurate cruises down the lake to watch for the enemy's approaches. The latest news from Saint John's included no indication that the British had as yet completed construction of large vessels, and for the moment it appeared that Schuyler's promise to outbuild them was being realized. When the fleet finally did battle at Valcour Bay in October it had been augmented by seven more vessels, all of them gondolas and row galleys. The seventeen craft were armed with a total of 102 guns, 176 swivels, and 900 men. In addition to its own crew each vessel carried a contingent of soldiers acting as marines. Although Schuyler hoped that enough seamen might be discovered among New England militia reinforcements, he did not simply trust that such would appear to man the little fleet. At the end of July when he learned that there were only 70 sailors to be found in the Northern Army for naval duty, he applied to Governor Trumbull to raise another 200 to 300 of them.[19]

While Schuyler and Gates prepared the defenses of Lake Champlain they were chagrined to learn that the commander in chief and his retinue at headquarters disputed the necessity of the Northern Army's abandonment of Crown Point. Although Washington protested to both generals, they vigorously defended their action and insisted that as commanders on the spot they were the proper judges of such decisions. In the face of their explanations Washington finally relented.[20]

The "Crown Point affair" was not, however, the least of Schuyler's problems in the summer of 1776. Although it occasioned questions of his competence as a strategist and tactician, there were also fresh rumblings about his management of the commissariat. Tension between the deputy commissary Walter Livingston and the new commissary general, Joseph Trumbull, continued after Trumbull had sent a new deputy to serve the army in Canada. Although, like Gates himself, Elisha Avery first had been obliged to accept a position subordinate to Schuyler, and therefore to Livingston, Congress decided in favor of Trumbull's power to direct both deputies as he saw fit. As Trumbull proceeded to assert his jurisdiction over the commissariat, he began to question Schuyler's and Livingston's administration, hinting to Washington that the army's food shortages were inexcusable. On 22 July, in asking Schuyler to remove aspersions upon his conduct, Livingston announced that "To avoid such treatment for the future I shall resign."[21]

The general begged his nephew-in-law not to think of it nor to be alarmed by Trumbull's charges about the waste of provisions. People "at a distance," he said, did not understand the soldiers' responsibility for the prodigal consumption or squandering of stores. Nor could Livingston be blamed for the army's lack of provisions in Canada. While he must justify himself vigorously, Schuyler would vouch for his integrity, prudence, and diligence. In inspecting his assistants at the various posts, Livingston should enforce Schuyler's standing orders to post commissaries to make regular returns. Clearly intending to keep Livingston employed, the general urged Washington to inform Trumbull of his fears that Livingston would resign if anyone were appointed to act independently of him, which was a warning that he must not provoke the Yorker into quitting the service.[22]

When Washington insisted that Congress had given Trumbull "supreme Direction" of the work of supplying all Continental forces and that Trumbull's appointments "must be regarded," Schuyler replied that he did not doubt that Livingston was Trumbull's subordinate. Only Elisha Avery's appointment could not be accepted because it had been made for the army in Canada. Since the army had left Canada, Avery had been accommodated in Schuyler's department, for he had been given a temporary appointment to serve as commissary of issues at Lake Champlain. In early August when he learned that Trumbull finally decided to order Avery to return to New York, Livingston agreed to follow the advice of Robert R. Livingston and James Duane and to defer his resignation until Schuyler returned to Albany from the Indian conference. Surmising that the general himself might soon resign, Livingston wrote Schuyler that the government might then discover how valuable their work of provisioning the army had been—and could yet become.[23]

Schuyler was indeed again considering resignation of his command. On 7 August he wrote Livingston, "I believe I shall very soon leave the

Army, unless the most Ample Justice is done me. General Gates has informed me of the Insult offered to him, to me & to all the General Officers, who held the Council of War at Crown Point [7 July], he has resented It in a spirited Manner, & I hope I have done Justice to my Injured Honor in What I have said xxxxxxxx on the Subject to General Washington." Meantime, Livingston should do everything in his power to provide ample supplies for the army.[24]

Schuyler's consideration of Livingston's grievances, together with his weariness with waiting for negotiations with the Iroquois, had clearly aggravated his sense of outrage over the challenge to his decision about Crown Point. Had he known of the sentiments then being exchanged among New Englanders, he would have been even more incensed. Having searched the July 1775 journals of Congress, Samuel Adams discovered a way of countering Livingston's claims that he was answerable only to Congress. The Yorker's appointment, Adams said, had been as deputy commissary "for the New York department during the *present* campaign." Therefore, his authority had expired in 1776, and if Schuyler intervened on Livingston's behalf, Joseph Trumbull should lodge formal protests with both Congress and Washington.[25]

Still another barb was aimed at Schuyler. On 7 August William Williams notified Joseph Trumbull that Congress had decided to scrutinize Schuyler's fiscal administration. Trumbull's brother, Jonathan, had been ordered to make a complete report of all funds that had passed through his hands as deputy paymaster general for Schuyler's army. More generally Congress had resolved (on 16 July) that commissioners of audit be appointed to inspect *all accounts* of the Northern Department—not merely the paymaster's, but also the quartermaster's, the commissary's, and the hospital director's. This, Williams reported, had been designed "to find out what Schuyler has done with his money." Yet he did not "see at present that it would be possible to remove him, if the utter ruin of the Continent was to be the known consequence of his continuence [sic] in office." However, in promising that "endeavors will not be wanting," Williams registered perhaps one of the earliest steps taken in a protracted effort by New Englanders to get rid of Philip Schuyler. For some of his critics the only questions were the means and the timing for accomplishing their ends; if they could not win an outright dismissal, the general could be provoked into resigning.[26]

Schuyler was of course aware that his character was traduced within Congress as well as elsewhere. Within Congress the general's friends, men like Samuel Chase and Charles Carroll, who had become acquainted with him during their visit to the army, did not hesitate to speak on his behalf or to warn him "how egregiously" he had "been represented to the Members of Congress. You have many Enemies," Chase wrote, after news of the army's retreat to Ticonderoga had been announced. But Chase also assured Schuyler that he had friends. Shortly after taking his seat in Congress on 22 July, Benjamin Rush heard Chase "insinuate from the floor that New England troops had caused the failure of the Canadian invasion." The Marylander had of course witnessed the army's behavior in Canada firsthand, but that did not stop John Adams from jibing that the failure was due entirely to Chase's own "impudence." Such remarks of course revealed the acidity of some of Congress's debates and the animosities among colleagues that were to damage both Schuyler's standing and his capacity to serve effectively as a department commander.[27]

Responding with gratitude for Chase's expressions of esteem and for his recent services on the committee that had visited the Northern Army, Schuyler hoped for a formal inquiry into the discharge of his duties; thereby an impartial world would be persuaded to censure those who had censured him. "Envy my dear Sir that blackest Fiend of the Human Race is ever active," he sighed. Selflessly, Schuyler wished Congress or Washington would reassign him to New York and put his department into abler hands. It would advance the service, he said, not because of any considerable aid that he might render elsewhere, but because of the "injurious Report that I am unfriendly to the American Cause [that] has been so industriously propagated." Suspecting that much of the army believed such rumors, Schuyler was willing to surrender his position, but not to sacrifice his honor. For the moment, however, he must stick to his duty, and that meant work with Horatio Gates in improving the defenses on Lake Champlain, and also negotiations with the Iroquois.[28]

2

"haughty princes of the Wilderness"

Distressed "beyond imagination" by the delays in convening the Indian conference after a week's wait, Schuyler considered returning to Albany; there he might better conduct the military business that followed him by post to German Flats. But neither commissioners Douw and Edwards nor the Iroquois sachems would hear of his leaving. As tribesmen trickled into the campgrounds their growing numbers put a strain upon the general's food supplies. The arrival of each new party required a ceremony of congratulation and drinking. By 24 July Schuyler found there were enough of them present "to make one weary of Life; patience is a virtue above all others necessary for a Commissioner of Indian Affairs, [and] they have an ample field for the Exercise of it," he wrote. To Samuel Chase he observed, "Entre nous, ... I would rather be the proprietor of a potatoe Garden & literally live by the Sweat of my Brow, than be an Indian Commissioner at a Time when you cannot prudently resent an Insult given by these haughty princes of the Wilderness."[29]

By 28 July there were more than a thousand Iroquois encamped for the treaty, half of them women and children. However, only part of the Onondaga delegation had arrived, and but few of the Cayuga and Seneca, who were yet expected to attend in force. The sooner he could finish negotiations, Schuyler felt, the sooner he might "get relieved from the incredible Trouble these people give me on such Occasions." Anxious for the state of the army at Ticonderoga and the progress of boat construction at Skenesborough and again "indisposed" by symptoms of recurrent fever, he feared that another fortnight of waiting to settle the Indian business would prove even more harmful to his health. Moreover, by 1 August the nine hundred-man garrison at Fort Schuyler would have had a six-months' stock of provisions laid in save for the diversion of supplies to feed the tribesmen. By the time the last laggards appeared and the commissioners were able to commence conference formalities, there were more than seventeen hundred men, women, and children at German Flats, and their appetites for food, drink, and gifts seemed insatiable. Schuyler estimated that they consumed more than twice as much as an equivalent body of soldiers.[30]

The problem was aggravated because while the Seneca delayed their arrival, the negotiations could not proceed, and the other tribesmen ate on. Having sent two Oneida messengers to ask the Seneca why they did not appear, the commissioners learned that Colonel Butler had called them to another meeting at Niagara. Douw and Edwards agreed with Schuyler's proposal to open the treaty with a speech threatening revenge for such faithless conduct. They would wait to see how the Indians replied before deciding whether to offer them the hatchet.[31]

On the evening of 6 August, Schuyler finally opened the conference at German Flats with ceremonial formalities. All of the Six Nations were represented, as were the "Delawares and Mohegans." Schuyler and commissioners Douw and Edwards stiffly refused a proposal that they begin with public condolences for one of the sachems who had been killed in attacking Americans at the Cedars in May. Such a gesture would have been inconsistent with their intention to rebuke the Indians for violating their 1775 pledge of neutrality.[32]

Exchanges between the commissioners and the tribesmen dragged on for a week. Only on Sunday, 11 August, were the talks suspended. Thus, the pace was leisurely but to some degree it was forced by the use of interpreters and the frequent pauses required for consultation and the preparation of the spokesmen's rejoinders. Customarily, too, each speaker prefaced his remarks with a summary of what he had previously heard. While the exercise was time-consuming, it was also a valuable way of avoiding misunderstandings and exercising the memory. This was especially important for a people whose oral tradition, supplemented with wampum belts, differed so notably from the white man's reliance upon written records.

Impressively, Schuyler delivered the commissioners' opening speech, accusing some of the Iroquois of violating their pledges of neutrality. "With this string we open your ears," he began, presenting a belt of wampum, "that you may plainly hear What the Independent States of America" wished to say. Reconciliation with the king, so long hoped for, was no longer possible. The family quarrel had begun with an agreement that the Iroquois would stand aloof. Yet there were instances since 1775 that proved that some had broken their word not to interfere in the contest. Had not some warriors aided Sir John Johnson in fomenting danger in the Mohawk valley? More recently had not the Seneca been listening to the blandishments of Col. John Butler? Yet Americans had taken no revenge, roasted no Englishmen, nor asked their Indian brothers to drink his blood. Would peace and friendly intercourse be maintained? What did the Six Nations intend? Were they to decide on enmity, they might leave the conference in peace, but thereafter Americans would retaliate rather than tolerate belligerancy, for they did not fear the tribesmen. Schuyler's tone was firm throughout, accusatory, and as one commentator later observed, "very warm."[33]

On 9 August Abraham, A Mohawk sachem, offered but a brief reply. Thanking Schuyler for calling the council at a place where the Indians need not fear the dangers of smallpox infection, he acknowledged the general's claims that Americans' quarrel with the king had been justified because their petitions to him had been scorned. Similarly, the Iroquois recognized the thirteen states as independent. But in order to speak of peace they asked for a postponement until the following day.

In the proceedings of 10 August it became apparent that Iroquois leaders were ready to promise a renewal of peaceful neutrality. During Sunday's adjournment of the council, Douw left Schuyler and Timothy Edwards to resume the talks on Monday. On 12 August the general commended the Oneida and Tuscarora for abiding by their agreements and remaining neutral. But he repeated his rebukes to the entire Indian confederacy and singled out each tribe for a stern reprimand. The Mohawk, he warned, must no longer plead drunkenness as an excuse for their crimes. Nor must they be misled by Sir John Johnson's evil intentions. They had been wrong to claim that Sir John had made no preparations hostile to the Americans, and that he had acquired no cannon to threaten them. They must abide strictly by the covenant of neutrality and concede the right of patriot forces to pursue their enemies through Indian territory. To the Onondaga and Seneca sachems Schuyler insisted that they must restrain their warriors from making further forays into Canada; bellicose leaders must be punished for attempting to set their tribes at variance with their best friends. The general then commended the Cayuga for advising the rest of the confederacy to rectify their conduct and for or- dering their warriors to return from Canada. As for the Cayugas' com- plaints that they had been deprived of American trade, Schuyler cast the blame on the British Indian agent, John Butler. Since Butler had enticed some of their tribe into Canada, traders had not been permitted into the west lest they be "knocked on the head." Finally, turning to the other tribes present, Schuyler warned that what he had said to the Iroquois also applied to them. They must not allow their warriors to go astray. For the Americans' part Schuyler promised to prevent them from injuring the rights of the Indians and to punish those who did so. Tribesmen were not to take their own revenge but to request their patriot brothers to execute justice. Content with the Indians' professions of repentance for misconduct, the general announced that the confederacy as a whole would not be blamed for individuals who had struck the hatchet into American heads. Now if any of the Six Nations joined the enemy and fought against the independent states, the entire peace would be broken and retaliation taken.[34]

One further round of speeches followed on 13 August. The ancient covenant "made in the time of Queder" (Schuyler's great uncle, Peter Schuyler) was reaffirmed. Should differences arise between tribes and settlers, they must be settled speedily and amicably. As for complaints that white men had encroached on the boundary established by the 1768 Treaty of Fort Stanwix, the commissioners announced that this would not be countenanced. Noting that although the treaty had been the king's agreement, Schuyler pledged that Congress would honor it by stopping the encroachers and punishing them. However, the Indians must bring offenders to "the Minister"—the well-known missionary, Samuel Kirk- land; and upon his information the Indian commissioners would proceed to deal with interlopers.[35]

With the reaffirmation of peace Schuyler concluded the council by distributing presents. Convinced that the Indians regarded American offers of neutrality as an indication of the strength of the rebel cause, he decided not to press for an alliance or even to offer rewards to warriors taking prisoners for the newly proclaimed independent states. To do so, he thought, might actually have turned the Indians against them. While he could now believe that there would be no frontier hostilities to threaten the major campaign effort at Lake Champlain, he did expect that at least a few of the Indians in Canada would join General Carleton and General Burgoyne. As for the Iroquois, not until the campaign of 1777 would there be a major threat to the policy that they and Schuyler had first established in 1775 and then reaffirmed in 1776. However, in the month after the German Flats treaty, several Seneca leaders took the first step toward abandonment of Iroquois neutrality. Meeting in secret council at Niagara they and a number of Cayuga, Onondaga, and Mohawk declared their loyalty to the Crown, thus in effect splitting the confederacy, although their actual decision to take up the hatchet was postponed until the summer of 1777.[36]

3

"very Expeditious in this business"

In the final weeks before Sir Guy Carleton and Gen. John Burgoyne moved their fleet and army to Lake Champlain, Schuyler worked with Horatio Gates and Benedict Arnold to prepare defenses much as he did with lesser officers of smaller contingents in the Mohawk valley. Protecting the army's western flank was not, however, as arduous a task as were the preparations for a major assault by both land and water in the north.

The general's return to Albany from German Flats on 15 August put him squarely into his secretary Richard Varick's scramble to collect seamen, cordage, blocks, swivel guns and shot, sailcloth, and other naval supplies for the lake fleet. While at their end of the department Gates and Arnold could be trusted to manage the defenses of Ticonderoga and the completion of a lake fleet, Schuyler's presence at Albany ensured the steady coordination of the work required to equip and provision their forces and crews of carpenters and other workmen. But Gates, preoccupied at Ticonderoga, seemed unable to accomplish certain tasks like the repair of roads along the communication between Albany and Fort George, or the shipment of lumber from Cheshire's mill on Wood Creek to Ticonderoga and the Skenesborough shipbuilders. For these and others, like the movement of bateaux and wagons full of provisions, Schuyler repeatedly proved to be an effective director.[37]

In their race to prepare their army and navy to meet the enemy's, Gates found Schuyler's cooperation to be effective even when the general himself depended on others to meet his requisitions. "Pray strain every nerve to supply us," Gates begged on 15 September as he presented a list of cables and rope needed for the new row galleys; without them the craft could not sail from Skenesborough. Two days later Schuyler answered that after searching for the articles at Albany, he had been obliged to send to Poughkeepsie to procure them. Hoping for speedy success, the general ordered the boatmen to travel day and night. This mission accomplished, the galleys were able to sail before the month was out even though they lacked the eight-inch cables that Gates had asked for. Convinced that the commander had done everything possible to obtain the cordage, Gates was quick to proffer thanks for Schuyler's prompt efforts even before the rope had arrived. "I must gratefully acknowledge," he said, that "you have constantly done, to send every supply demanded for the troops here."[38]

Whether a victory over a British invasionary force could yet be won in 1776 remained highly problematical. By early October Schuyler was confident that the enemy would not be able to accomplish much if they soon attacked on Lake Champlain. Although still lacking a variety of stores and ammunition, long since requested of Congress, Schuyler was certain that the Northern Army was well supplied with provisions, and that its reinforcements by militia, together with the nearly completed lake fleet, would prove to be effective in checking any British advance. But Schuyler could not be so sanguine were the enemy to delay until American enlistments expired, and the troops went home rather than reenlist. Nor was he very hopeful of quick results from Congress's authorization for raising eighty-eight battalions of Continentals by the states' legislatures in September. "For God's sake," he urged Gates at the end of September, "try to keep the Pennsylvania and New-Jersey regiments in service until every possibility of the enemy's crossing the Lake this campaign disappears."[39]

Gates's return of forces at Ticonderoga on 29 September revealed just how pressing the need for manpower yet remained and why neighboring militia reinforcements would have to be called the moment the enemy's approach could be signaled. His rank and file of 11,180 included 3,583 present but sick, 851 sick and absent, 2,212 "on command," and 192 on furlough. Another 1,383 men, including 103 artificers, were scattered among other posts to the south like Skenesborough and Fort George.

Thus Gates had only about 6,500 effectives to confront Carleton and Burgoyne's forces, which outnumbered them almost two to one. And in the end the enemy's naval force proved to be superior, although the Americans' had something of an edge in manpower and artillery. Capt. Thomas Pringle commanded twenty-nine vessels under sail; these carried 89 guns and almost 700 seamen. Arnold's fleet of seventeen mounted 102 guns and 170 swivels with crews of almost 900.[40]

No less attentive to the needs of Washington's troops far down the Hudson than to those of Gates's far to the north, Schuyler answered the commander in chief's call for lumber, which he wanted to prepare winter barracks for his army at Kings Bridge. Zealous in everything that he undertook, Schuyler issued detailed directions to his overseer, John Graham, and quartermaster officers about rafting the lumber and the necessity of promptly meeting the army's needs. "Pray be very Expeditious in this business," he told Capt. Ephraim Van Vechten, who was to construct the rafts in six-board thicknesses. To his overseer Schuyler gave orders to cut four-inch square timbers of pitch or white pine. Both of his mills must be kept running: "they must saw on Sundays As well as Other Days & then You must pay the Negroes for It," he instructed Graham on 21 September.[41]

The business ran on into October. By 6 October the general informed Washington that he could supply at least forty thousand boards of the one hundred and sixty thousand that the Virginian asked for. Another twenty thousand could yet be obtained by the Albany committee, and as late as 17 October Schuyler's secretary Richard Varick was urging the committee to continue their work of collecting lumber—a project by which they would both oblige the general and help "our bleeding Country."[42]

The preparations to strengthen the defenses on Lake Champlain were momentarily jeopardized in mid-August by the march of New England militia reinforcements to Skenesborough. This and a clash between "Commodore" Jacobus Wynkoop and Benedict Arnold over command of the lake fleet were the kinds of disturbances that, when added to Schuyler's more serious complaints of congressional neglect and a damaged reputation, propelled him to a decision to resign his commission. The Yankee militia and also a company of Rhode Island carpenters had inoculated themselves for smallpox, thus threatening to incapacitate themselves for as long as six weeks and endangering other troops with whom they might come in contact. Outraged by "a Conduct so wicked and so evidently destructive to the Army," Schuyler ordered Gen. David Waterbury to quarantine the infected men. It was, after all, smallpox that had so debilitated the Northern Army that it had been forced to retreat from Canada, and efforts to promote recovery must not now be ruined by a fresh outbreak of the disease.[43]

The Wynkoop-Arnold clash was another annoyance, but more easily settled because only a few individuals were involved. Wynkoop had been made "commodore" by Schuyler's request in March 1776, but by mid-August, when Gates instructed Arnold to begin maneuvers with the growing fleet, Wynkoop was determined that as "Commander of Lake Champlain" he would take no orders but those of the commander in chief. Anxious to proceed with scouting the lake against enemy approaches, Arnold ordered two schooners to sail north from Crown Point on 17 August. Wynkoop fired a warning shot to bring the vessels about. After an exchange of notes failed to persuade Wynkoop to obey Arnold's command, Arnold showed him Gates's instructions and threatened him with immediate arrest unless he obeyed orders. In the end Gates ordered Wynkoop to Albany and Schuyler not only accepted his removal, but also Gates's proposal to replace him with Gen. David Waterbury, whose courage, experience as a seaman, and familiarity with Arnold would enable him to serve more effectively than Wynkoop. "As you are on the spot," he told Gates, he must judge the propriety of sending Wynkoop down, but Schuyler intended that Congress should settle the case. The general, however, had little to say on Wynkoop's behalf but to commend him for his bravery. As the "commodore" seemed no longer equal to the responsibilities of directing an enlarged fleet, Schuyler unhesitatingly commended Gates's assignment of Arnold to the command. As far as he was concerned Wynkoop's assignment by the New York congress had been temporary and conditional until another appointment could be made. Even had an officer inferior in rank to Arnold been named, Wynkoop had no justification to complain of being superseded.[44] The affair, however, was a reminder to Schuyler of more serious altercations that had arisen among officers of the army—disputes of jurisdictions—and suspicions sometimes rooted in regional or provincial jealousies. Even in the Wynkoop case there were overtones of the latter, for he was a Yorker, Arnold a Yankee, and Gates a known partisan of New Englanders. The general, however, neither supported nor opposed any man because of his regional origins. His criteria were personal ability and merit and willingness to serve the common cause with honor and self-sacrifice.

4

"fired with Resentment" and "a matter of moonshine"

It was a sense of honor as well as exasperation with Congress's failure to respond to his demands for vindication of his record of self-sacrifice that finally drove Schuyler to resign his commission as a major general and Indian commissioner in September 1776. Rumors of the Yorker's misconduct and Congress's decision that General Wooster had not been responsible for the reverses in Canada led Schuyler to insist that he too should be publicly exonerated from any blame for the retreat from Canada.

The general's sense of injury was further aggravated not only by the continuous clashing of the commissary general Joseph Trumbull and the department's deputy commissary general, Walter Livingston, but also by criticisms of Schuyler's management of his department hospital system. In the latter instance Dr. John Morgan, the director general of hospitals, confided in Samuel Stringer, Schuyler's friend and departmental hospital director, and Stringer promptly informed the general of Morgan's allegations of malfeasance. Schuyler's difficulties with both the commissary general and the director general of hospitals were particular variations on the theme of his growing disenchantment with Congress and additional reasons for his determination to resign his congressional appointments.

The need for medicines and an adequate hospital staff for the Northern Army were long-standing, but in July 1776 they had become crucial because the ranks of the sick had swollen to several thousand. Gates agreed that Dr. Jonathan Potts and his eight-man staff could manage the Fort George hospital while Stringer went to New York City to procure medicine. Stringer also was determined to visit Congress in order to persuade them to enlarge both his own powers to act and the size of the hospital staff.[45]

During Stringer's travels in August, Dr. Potts reported the sorry state of affairs at the Fort George hospital to Dr. Morgan. Impatient with Stringer's absence, General Gates became suspicious that "instead of fulfilling his promises and returning with all dispatch to his Duty, [he] is gone Preference Hunting to the Congress" while the soldiers suffered for lack of medicine. Bypassing Schuyler, Washington, and Congress, Gates finally wrote Dr. Morgan for help, and Morgan proceeded to ship medicines as a personal favor to the general. But Morgan also tried to assert a jurisdiction over Stringer, which the doctor resisted. After Congress first attempted to make Stringer subordinate, in August it was persuaded to allow him the autonomy that he demanded and to authorize all hospital directors to appoint their own surgeons and other staff officers.[46]

Having at last returned to Albany, Dr. Stringer visited Schuyler on 1 September to report the results of his mission. When he recounted Morgan's charge that Schuyler was "making a Fortune out of the public," the general immediately denounced the assertion as "equally false & injurious." Quickly he dashed off a letter that he sent to Washington for perusal before it was forwarded to Morgan. Refusing to tolerate insults from anyone "worthy of my notice," Schuyler reminded Washington that such false and scandalous allegations were further proof that Congress should afford him the opportunity to restore his damaged reputation.[47]

To Morgan himself the general issued a challenge to prove his assertions if he could. "My patrimonial Estate," he wrote, "afforded me a genteel Competency ... and that Man is both a Scoundrel & a Lyar that insinuates that it is since encreased by either dishonest, dishonorable or any indirect practice." Schuyler claimed that by accepting military office he had forgone many advantages that with "strictest Regard to Justice and Honor I might have made, but which I have not, from a Delicacy of Sentiment, that I might not give the least Colour for such scandalous Assertions as you stand charged with, and for which as an officer I shall order you under arrest as soon as I can conveniently be at New York." Morgan might thus be forced to prove his charges.[48]

Although it is evident that Schuyler sold a variety of foodstuff, lumber, livestock, and other articles to the army, it is also clear that he was not a greedy profiteer. Indeed, the commissioners of audit who inspected his accounts, and Congress itself, found no evidence of peculation or any other mismanagement. Illustrative of the general's dealings is his account with the public between 15 July 1775 and 16 July 1776. When compared with other evidence of prices then current, the items do not suggest that Schuyler took advantage of his public office to make a private fortune.[49]

The general's remonstrance that he was innocent of "dishonest, dishonorable or any indirect practice" rings true. But Morgan tried to wriggle out of the unpleasantries by suggesting that Stringer had not accurately reported Morgan's views. Perhaps Schuyler had overreacted to what Morgan had not himself charged but to what he merely reported as the accusations of others. But Schuyler believed Stringer, not only because they were old friends, but especially because Stringer had noted that Morgan wanted a "seal of secrecy" for what he said about the general's misconduct. Did Morgan imagine, Schuyler asked, that the general was so unfeeling as not to be "fired with Resentment" or as not to insist upon measures to cleanse himself of infamous imputations? When Stringer returned from his search for medicines in New England, Schuyler promised, he would examine the doctor further. If, in view of Morgan's letters, Schuyler discovered that Stringer had perverted Morgan's words and "made one or more 'black Crows' where none existed," the general promised that Morgan's resentment would be no more misplaced on Stringer than Schuyler's had been on Morgan. "A Man's Character ought not to be sported with," Schuyler fumed, "and he that suffers Stains to lay on it with Impunity really deserves none nor will he long enjoy one."[50]

The altercation with Morgan in fact helped Schuyler to decide to resign. Noting the army's continued distress for lack of medicines and hospital stores, the general complained on 9 September that "As every misfortune and want they labour under is imputed to me, so is this." He reminded Congress that he had begged for medicines since 10 February. And he announced that he would soon resign his commission, warning Congress to prepare to replace him.[51]

Schuyler's intention to resign was partly prompted by the annoyances created by the commissary general Joseph Trumbull and the deputy commissaries Walter Livingston and Elisha Avery. Trumbull had succeeded in establishing his jurisdiction over Schuyler's departmental commissaries in July, but the general insisted that Trumbull's appointee, Avery, must submit returns of provisions at Ticonderoga to Livingston, who had served long before either Avery or Trumbull had appeared on the scene. Avery, however, refused to accept subordination to Livingston, thereby foolishly challenging Schuyler's superior authority to direct his department's commissariat. Not only did Schuyler have every right to supervise the departmental commissaries, it was also impractical for anyone else to do so because Joseph Trumbull was himself in no proximate position to oversee Livingston and Avery.[52]

Horatio Gates's thoughts on the commissariat imbroglio were remarkably diffident. To Schuyler he merely observed that he would see that returns of men and provisions were duly furnished. "As to Mr. Avery," he wrote, "I desire not to be concerned in the dispute between him and Mr. Livingston. It is a matter of moonshine to me who is Commissary, so [long as] the troops are well supplied."[53]

Having fought to retain Livingston in office, Schuyler did not regard the business as mere moonshine. But once his kinsman made up his mind to quit, Schuyler proceeded to inform Avery of his good intentions. The commissariat must not be further disrupted or the army would suffer. But he also insisted upon explaining to Avery why he had found his behavior so exceptionable. By clearing up misunderstandings he might establish a more agreeable rapport with the deputy commissary.

Avery's quotation from Schuyler's 20 August letter to Gates, the general began, contained the positive order that he must submit returns to Walter Livingston. How could he therefore claim that he might report to Schuyler instead of to Livingston? Moreover, Schuyler knew of no instructions from Trumbull that could militate against such an order; those which Avery had displayed "are out of the Question," Schuyler said, "For by them You are not empowered to act at all on this Side of Canada." Perhaps Avery had forgotten that, like Gates, he had been intended to serve the army *in* Canada. Since the American retreat, Schuyler himself gave Avery a temporary appointment to serve with Gates at Ticonderoga. As for Congress's 8 July resolution, Schuyler argued that that had not altered his order because it only allowed the commissary general to appoint and remove *deputy commissaries*. Livingston had been appointed as a deputy commissary *general* for Schuyler's department, and until Livingston resigned or Congress revoked his commission, he must be regarded as senior and superior to every commissary or deputy commissary general in the department.

Proceeding next to a review of Avery's other erroneous suppositions, Schuyler observed that he had not distinguished between returns and supplies. The congressional resolution for Trumbull's centralized direction applied to the supplying of both Schuyler's and Washington's armies. The commissary general had the right to employ whomever he pleased to furnish the supplies. But such persons who applied to Schuyler for money with which to make the purchases the general must strictly refer to the deputy commissary general of the department. In the commissary general's absence, only the deputy commissary general could issue a warrant for funds. Perhaps when Trumbull told Avery that it was not necessary to make *returns* to Livingston he had not meant to suggest that Schuyler could not order these reports submitted to whomever he wished.

However, because Livingston had submitted his resignation, Avery could expect to be appointed in his stead. So long as he commanded the department, Schuyler promised, Avery would receive the same support that Livingston had had. Again the general insisted that he had never charged Avery with malpractice. His complaints had been of other commissaries' conduct—not of Avery's nor Livingston's. Perhaps Avery would one day learn that Schuyler had held him up in quite a different light to his superiors; perhaps he would also discover that once Livingston was determined to resign, Schuyler had taken steps to make Avery his successor.[54]

The Avery-Livingston-Trumbull affair was practically concluded when Livingston's resignation was laid before Congress on 12 September.

Eleven days later Schuyler received Trumbull's announcement that Avery had become the department's deputy commissary general. Trumbull's notice of Avery's appointment was brief, but it politely solicited Schuyler's aid to the new deputy. The general quickly summoned Avery to Albany, asking Livingston to continue his labors until Avery arrived and to cooperate by furnishing his successor with appropriate information and advice.[55]

Having lost Livingston's services, Schuyler did not begrudge Joseph Trumbull his victory. Characteristically, however, he felt obliged to offer the commissary general one further note of explanation of their difficulties. With that he promised to assist and advise Avery "on every occasion, when he stands in need of it." This, he said, would be in keeping with the requirements of his own honor, the good of the service, and the pleasure of obliging Trumbull, too.[56]

5

Resignation Refused

Although the blowup over the commissariat was finally settled with a degree of amicability, its denouement dovetailed with Schuyler's decision to resign his commission. Having for so long failed to obtain a congressional inquiry before he resigned, he decided that only by this act could he force Congress to give it.

Following the army's retreat from Canada, and then from Crown Point in order to concentrate defenses at Ticonderoga, Schuyler complained that the clamors of both military and civilian critics entitled him to a public inquiry. Because his character had been "most infamously aspersed in every part of the Country and all the Misfortunes in Canada attributed to" him, the general insisted that Congress must determine whether any blame could properly be placed upon him. Unless "satisfaction is given," he promised, "I shall most certainly retire from the army." Sympathetic friends like Benedict Arnold urged him to disregard the censures of rumormongers and insisted that he not think of leaving the army at so critical a juncture of the campaign. Schuyler insisted that resignation might at least force an investigation, and that must surely find him not guilty of any misconduct as commander of the Northern Army.[57] Perhaps the general also considered the advice that his old friend, William Smith, Jr., had offered on 17 August. The New York convention had named a committee to draft a state constitution on 1 August. Smith told Schuyler that "as a great Landholder ... your Interest at this tremendous Moment of forming a new Government calls you rather to the Cabinet than the Field." But beyond hints that Leonard Gansevoort, a convention delegate, and Robert R. Livingston and Robert Yates, members of the drafting committee, solicited the general's views about their work, it is impossible to determine exactly what Schuyler's counsels might have been.[58] While trusting others to frame a government as close to old forms as would serve to protect liberty and property, he remained preoccupied with military responsibilities and the failure of Congress to clear him of all implications of his mismanagements of the Canadian campaign.

Although Congress long ignored Schuyler's demands for an investigation, it did not much dawdle over the similar request of Brig. Gen. David Wooster. After the latter's return from Canada in June, Congress agreed that a committee should determine the extent of his responsibility for the military reverses in that province. On 17 August Congress approved the committee's findings that "upon the whole ... nothing censurable or blameworthy appears against" him—but not "without a great Struggle." Some delegates wished to blame Wooster for their "own misconduct" in Congress; after "embarrassing and starving the War in Canada," they had seemed willing to pronounce Wooster incompetent and cowardly.[59]

As yet unaware that Congress had cleared Wooster of responsibility for Canadian reverses, Schuyler voiced fears that should the army be obliged to retreat farther into New York he would be blamed for that as well as for the Canadian reverses. Already, Connecticut troops who had returned to their homes were spreading their complaints of the army and "jealousies" of Schuyler to their neighbors. Certain that even a congressional inquiry would not stop the tide of malevolent slander, he was determined, he told Washington, to quit the army once an investigation had proved him an "honest Man and faithful American." He would, he said, "Evince Myself in private life what I have strove to do in public [as] the friend of my injured Country."[60]

Similarly, Schuyler informed General Gates that he would retire once Congress exonerated him from charges of malconduct. The two men had worked most amicably once their clash over the command of Canadian forces had been settled. And as of late August 1776 Schuyler seemed to be preparing the way for Gates to succeed him once he had gained a hearing and could then resign.

Congress continued to ignore Schuyler's demands for an inquiry but it did decide to audit his military accounts. When two of three commissioners of audit, John Carter and James Milligan, reached Albany on 7 September, Schuyler promptly notified General Gates to have officers submit reports to Jonathan Trumbull, deputy paymaster general. Gates was also instructed to allow any officers at Ticonderoga to come to Albany if they must confer with the commissioners.[61]

The work of the auditors in fact required months to complete, partly because of the need to collect evidence of disbursements made by commanding officers in Canada and regimental records of a variety of units and officers no longer with the Northern Army. Complicating their labors were lacunae in the late General Montgomery's papers, which Schuyler had had examined. Because no records had been found of Montgomery's receipts, he could be charged only with the amounts Schuyler had furnished him. While the auditors pored over military accounts in Albany during the autumn months, one of them found the opportunity to meet Schuyler's family. John Barker Church, then using the alias John Carter, evidently became acquainted at this time with the general's eldest daughter, Angelica.[62] Their elopement the following June does not suggest that Schuyler or his wife found Carter to be much to their liking.

For the moment, however, the auditors' activities and the accounting for public funds were the least of Schuyler's worries. Confident that no fault would be found with his fiscal administration, the general was rather more concerned by his altercation with the commissary general Joseph Trumbull. And the business of directing the commissariat remained at the heart of the question of whether or not Congress would pronounce the general innocent of the charges of peculation and other misconduct. Submitting another copy of his 16 August letter to the president of Congress, he wrote on 8 September that he feared his earlier missive had miscarried. In it he had asked that the committee assigned to investigate causes of military reverses in Canada (or a separate committee) be charged "minutely to inquire how far, if at all, any of the miscarriages in Canada are to be imputed to me." In repeating this request Schuyler now argued that "however little the public may be interested, it is of some moment to a man conscious of the rectitude of his conduct, that he should be justified and his character cleared from aspersions that may involve him and his family, in this jealous day, into a variety of difficulties."[63]

On 9 September Schuyler decided to fix a deadline for resigning. Promptly he advised Washington and both Congress and the New York convention that he would resign his commission as soon as he could complete a journey to Ticonderoga or Tryon County. Having become so heartily tired of abuse that he could "no longer suffer the publick odium,"

Schuyler also notified Horatio Gates on 11 September that because Gates would soon be in command he should decide what general officer should manage the army's business in Albany.[64]

Gates relished his prospects to succeed. Although continuing to report to the general as a subordinate, the tone of Gates's letters became increasingly imperative. "You will consider," he wrote, the provision of winter quarters for the troops at Albany and Schenectady and if more were needed, "you will give orders accordingly." Because no serious attack north of the Mohawk River could possibly be launched before next summer, "you will," Gates insisted, "order Colonel Dayton's regiment to this post." Unruffled by Gates's succession of "you wills," Schuyler replied without the slightest hint of resentment. Colonel Dayton could not yet be moved from Fort Schuyler because a garrison must be maintained in the west. And were there any troops to spare, Schuyler announced, more would be sent up the Mohawk because the latest intelligence suggested that the enemy might yet strike a blow in the valley.[65] Unoffended by Gates's tone or language, Schuyler was content to practice what he preached—a willing service for the common cause and the army's welfare. And with proof of Gates's cooperation in that service as well as his own resolution to retire, Schuyler saw no need for quibbles.

In announcing his intention to resign, Schuyler had expected that he might first be obliged to visit either Ticonderoga or Tryon County; rumors of impending attacks by the enemy dictated that he should not attempt to quit in the midst of an imminent crisis. But the alarms from both the west and the north quickly passed. And on 14 September he was free to reverse his summons of the militia and to write President Hancock that he was quitting the public service. Resigning not only his commission as major general but "all and every other office or appointment" by Congress, he explained that he still expected Congress to make formal inquiries into his military record. Generously he offered to promote the country's weal in other ways and to assist his successor by other means at his command. He would "continue to act as usual until such a reasonable time is elapsed in which" a general officer could be sent to Albany. Surmising that a fortnight would suffice, Schuyler proposed then to attend his "duty in Congress without delay." Observing that other general officers like Arnold were being slandered, Schuyler found it regrettable that he was not the only one to be so maligned. Considerate as ever of men of proven capability and loyalty, he recommended various subordinates like his secretary Richard Varick for appointments or other marks of congressional attention. And because the other Indian commissioners resided so far from Albany and Volkert Douw had moved from the city, it was vital that Congress name others to carry on the commission's work.[66]

Having thus attempted to prod Congress into vindicating him, Schuyler turned to others like Abraham Yates, Jr., president of the New York State convention, to press the merits of his claims. The stir of protest against Schuyler's resignation by fellow Albanians spread elsewhere. William Smith, Jr., heard of their "great Discontent" weeks later. And John Pierce, Jr., feared the results of Schuyler's and Walter Livingston's resignations: "their families are & always have been the only Support of our Cause in this Province; their Connexions will all resign—an Interruption in the course of business creates at any time confusion—Much more will be the Confusions as the Genl has done more than any other can or will."[67]

Meantime, Schuyler sought to allay suspicions evidently emanating from Connecticut. On 21 September he sent an "express" letter to the committee of safety of Salisbury in an effort to "undeceive the public" and "ward off their Resentment." At issue was the charge of a Mr. Blagden or Blackden who had served with General Wooster in Canada during the previous winter. Blackden accused Schuyler of detaining specie funds for the army and of using the money for himself. The general explained in detail the disposition of his personal funds to pay for intelligence work and Indian gifts and how the remaining monies (£469.3.8) were given to Richard Montgomery. He had retained no specie for himself but rather had adavnced private funds to supply the army with currency more acceptable to the Canadians than was American paper. Consequently, he was still owed over £900 for these advances, which the commissioners of audit would be able to determine as they proceeded to settle accounts. If Mr. Blackden could prove his accusations, let him present his case to the commissioners. Schuyler urged the Connecticut committee to act either to expose robbery or to clear him of the charge of theft.[68]

How effectively Schuyler silenced the Connecticut rumormongers is difficult to know. But the Salisbury committee responded through its chairman, Joshua Porter, on 7 October, agreeing that Blackden ought to try to prove his charge if in fact he could. The public had long relied upon Schuyler's great "Abilities and Inclination, to serve Them," and the Connecticut men hoped the suspicions of him were as groundless as they had been common. Wishing that his continued good services would merit the applause and respect of his country, Porter advised Schuyler to remember that "on Eagles Wings immortal scandals fly, while Virtuous Actions are but born to die."[69]

Connecticut's governor also expressed "deep concern" over news of the general's resignation. Schuyler could doubtless justify himself, but he should not publish a narrative of self-justification, as he had proposed. Trumbull feared that delicate matters might thereby be exposed to further misinterpretation, and he urged him "to suspend your publication a little while" because the Yorker's reputation might be cleared from another quarter in a manner more honorable to him. Ultimately the congressional commissioners of audit would be able to answer the suspicions that the general was a peculator. Agreeing to defer publication of his statement, Schuyler persisted in his determination to flee all public office rather than endure "insult added to injustice."[70]

By 25 September 1776 Schuyler learned that Congress had finally referred his complaint of 16 August to the committee investigating the Canadian reverses. Immediately he wrote President Hancock, sarcastically expressing his thanks "with a sincerity equal to the attention they have evinced in their resolution" of 14 September. "Permit me to entreat the favour of a farther resolution," he snapped—one allowing him to defend his conduct and point out other causes of the miscarriages— "causes ... so obvious, that I could not but wonder that they passed unnoticed." There were other points that nettled the Yorker: Why had he received no replies to his letters of 20 July, 16, 18, 25, and 29 August and 2, 8, and 9 September? Was it not a "little improper" for Congress to have ordered (on 14 September) powder sent to General Gates instead of to the department commander? Congress could not have by then received Schuyler's letter of resignation as a justification for directing the shipments to his successor. And why did Congress vote the resolution of 12 September repeating its order for Joseph Trumbull's supreme authority over the commissary department? If it was because Schuyler had intervened in commissary affairs, the general insisted, Congress should know that he had "acted in such a manner as not to repent of what I have done; returns must and shall be made [to] me, through the proper channel, or I will punish the offender ... and I will always interfere in every department under my command, when it becomes necessary for the good of the service."[71]

Perhaps Schuyler's sense of injury was exaggerated. Washington assured him that the resolution to send stores to Gates could not have been "calculated or designed in the smallest degree to give you offence." Because Gates had requested them, was it not reasonable that they be sent to him? Nor could any slight have been intended to Schuyler as department commander when Congress voted that the stores be sent "for the use of the Northern Army." Supplies allocated for any department were similarly designated, Washington noted. Still, the Virginian's arguments did not dissolve the legitimacy of his colleague's other complaints, the demands for a committee inquiry, and a variety of other correspondence that had been neglected for weeks on end. Nor could Schuyler be persuaded by Washington's reasoning when he learned that on 25 September Congress had dispatched a committee "to confer with General Gates with respect to the army under his command." Was it not insulting for Congress thus to have ignored the commander of the department to whom Gates was subordinate?[72]

Perhaps the general was fortunate that Congress did not hear his 25 September letter read until *after* it voted to refuse his resignation on 2 October. Prickly delegates may well have taken offense at the tenor of his missive. But by then the New York State convention had prompted its delegates to assist Schuyler's efforts to lift the clouds of suspicion under which he had fallen. And the committee to which Congress assigned the matter of his resignation comprised men who suited Schuyler's supporters. Philip Livingston was confident that the report would, "without question, be satisfactory."[73] And when Edward Rutledge, William Hooper, and Thomas McKean proposed their resolution on 2 October, it was promptly passed.

Although Congress declined to accept Schuyler's resignation, it failed to proceed with the business of a formal inquiry. Instead, it voted assurances that "the Aspersions which his Enemies have thrown out against his Character have had no Influence upon the Minds of the Members of this House, who are fully satisfied of his Attachment to the Cause of Freedom, and are Willing to bear their Testimony of the Many services which he has rendered his Country." And there were promises that "in Order Effectually to put Calumny to silence, they will at an Early Day appoint a Committee of their Body to enquire fully into his Conduct; which they trust will establish his Reputation in the Opinion of All Good Men." Robert R. Livingston thought that the unanimity by which this resolution carried indicated the highest marks of respect and honor for the general. Edward Rutledge, who had penned the resolution, asked Schuyler to remember that "the friendship of some people is not to be purchased but at a price which" he "would scorn to pay." President Hancock suggested that the resolves "fully expressed their sense of your past conduct" and a determination to do Schuyler's character justice. "Congress cannot ... consent to your retiring from the army in its present situation." To do so would prompt the general's enemies to exult in thinking that their charges must be true. Schuyler must not allow calumny to deprive the country of services he might still render.[74]

Meantime, on 25 September Congress decided to send George Clymer of Pennsylvania and Richard Stockton of New Jersey to Ticonderoga to confer with General Gates about the army under his command. But when President Hancock wrote Schuyler on 27 September, enclosing a variety of resolutions including that concerning Clymer and Stockton, he suggested that the two men would confer on the state of "the army &c." with Schuyler. Thus it is not surprising that the Yorker became suspicious when he discovered that the congressional inspectors were actually authorized to confer with a subordinate instead of himself. Nor was he particularly mollified by Hancock's apologies for the failure to answer a number of earlier letters or by news of Congress's favorable response to a variety of his recommendations. Although some of the resolves of Congress were welcome, others were not, for they included acceptance of Walter Livingston's resignation and reaffirmation of Joseph Trumbull's centralized power over the commissariat.[75]

Schuyler continued to fret over the long delays in Congress's direct responses to his letters. On the evening of 5 October he received a variety of dispatches, including Hancock's letter of 27 September and some news he had otherwise gleaned only in part from other correspondence. At this point he still had not heard of Congress's rejection of his resignation; but by reading the resolves of 25 September he deduced that Congress had "Already implicatively declared" that he was "no longer in command." These resolutions contained references to clothing to be shipped to "General Schuyler or the Commanding Officer at Albany" and to instructions that Clymer and Stockton should confer with General Gates without mention of any consultation with Schuyler. Quickly complaining both to Gates and to President Hancock, Schuyler grumbled that Congress might have informed him of his replacement "in a manner less liable to objection." Still, the general could not bring himself to "fly to Philadelphia" for he considered his duty was to remain with the army until it was absolutely clear that his resignation was accepted and that a successor had been chosen. The "implicative" congressional resolutions of 25 September were "extremely insulting" to him, and he struggled to answer Hancock "with Temper" while making it clear that he "resented the Indignity." As for Congress's investigation of his record, Schuyler now expected that all judgment of his case would be suspended until he could appear before the committee of inquiry.[76]

By 11 October, when Benedict Arnold's notable naval encounter with the British at Valcour Island began, Schuyler was still in Albany, still ignorant of Congress's refusal of his resignation, and still endeavoring to superintend the business of military supply and troop disposition. Briefly interrupted by a violent rheumatic attack in his head and stomach, the general recovered in time to entertain congressmen Clymer and Stockton, who arrived in Albany on that very evening. The duo at first remained tight-lipped about their mission, apparently unwilling or hesitant to ask Schuyler about his work at Albany or at Saratoga, whence they accompanied him on 14 October. But the general did not intend to rely upon his visitors to present his case to Congress. Within a fortnight, he hoped, he would set out for Philadelphia, and he promised General Gates that "if I am in Congress, you, or whoever may command in this department, will have more attention paid you than I have had, if I can in anywise induce others to be of my opinion."[77]

Although Clymer and Stockton ultimately reported to Congress (on 27 November) many of the Yorker's concerns, needs, and recommendations, most of which were favorably received, the presence of the two men was not at first reassuring. On 13 October, for example, the general wrote Robert R. Livingston of his lingering resentment that the committee had been ordered to confer only with Gates. Having dined with Schuyler on 12 October, they spoke of no public business "that is to be transacted with my inferior officer, under my very Nose." Schuyler thought a more "brutal Insult could not be offered" and vowed not to "bear with Impunity from any Body of Men on Earth." Admitting he was "fired with the highest Resentment at the ill usage," he entreated Livingston "not to be alarmed, as I shall steadily make the Good of my Country my first Object and thus heap more Coals on the Heads of my Enemies."[78] In fact, he was as good as his word. Sticking conscientiously to his departmental duties until March 1777, Schuyler repeatedly postponed plans to visit Congress while the business of the army continued to demand the attention of a devoted commander. Few men matched or excelled the proud Yorker's perseverance or labors in making the good of his country his first object.

6

After Valcour Bay

On Monday morning, 14 October, as yet unaware of the Anglo-American naval battle on Lake Champlain and only barely recovered from a severe attack of rheumatic pains in his head and stomach, Schuyler escorted congressmen Clymer and Stockton to Saratoga. There they were obliged to remain until the end of the month, unable to confer with Gates until the British threat to Ticonderoga had subsided. In the interval the two men had ample opportunity to observe Schuyler's work of moving men, provisions, gunpowder, and other supplies along the communication to the lake country.[79]

The first news from Gates about the initial encounter between Arnold's fleet and the British navy at Valcour Bay was delivered to Schuyler on the road halfway between Albany and Saratoga. Immediately, he summoned militia reinforcements from New York and the neighboring states, lest the troops at Ticonderoga find themselves unequal to the task of blocking Carleton and Burgoyne's penetration. Gates he instructed to send frequent dispatches with as much detailed information as he could, for without it, Schuyler said, he could not "regulate my motions in such a manner as to be of most service."[80]

Two days later the general learned of Arnold's defeat at Valcour Bay, but happily it had not been a total disaster for the Americans. In fact, most of Arnold's men had escaped to Ticonderoga with a sloop, two schooners, two galleys, and a gondola—six of the seventeen sail. And Carleton released Gen. David Waterbury and 110 American prisoners of war on parole. As the Northern Army contained about nine thousand effectives at Ticonderoga, an enemy assault by land and water might still be repelled if Gates could be supported. Although Arnold wrote Schuyler that Gates and Arthur St. Clair wanted eight to ten thousand militia reinforcements, in passing on the alarm to the New York convention the general announced that Gates wanted ten to twelve thousand! Whatever could be spared must be sent in time to fight or to help cover possible retreat.[81]

Schuyler also alerted the Berkshire County, Massachusetts, committee that British mastery of the lake threatened Ticonderoga; the army must have the aid of militia. Asking that the committee spread the call to neighboring counties in Massachusetts and Connecticut, the general also summoned the Albany County militia commanded by his old friend, Brig. Gen. Abraham Ten Broeck.[82]

Ten Broeck responded with alacrity, and the first of his troops reached Saratoga five days later on 21 October. But for Gates's insistence upon having the militia, Schuyler would not have called them. How exactly he would manage them as reserves was a question that was difficult to answer; without tents or other shelter he knew that they could not be relied upon to remain for long in the field. The sooner they could be discharged, he told Gates, the better—the more so because they were notorious wasters of supplies and malingerers who resented being employed as wagoners, bateaumen, or road workers.[83]

To assist in the direction of militia reinforcements and to provide for recruitment of four new state regiments of Continentals in mid-October, the New York convention dispatched a special committee to visit Schuyler's headquarters. Robert Yates, Jacob Cuyler, and James Duane found him at Saratoga on 20 October. For the next few days they consulted Schuyler about the implementation of Congress's resolutions of 8 October. Officers must be named to enlist new regiments to serve for the duration of the war. At least two of the four regimental commanders commissioned by the state committee of safety a month later, Goose Van Schaick and Peter Gansevoort, were recommended by the general. Having marked a list of colonels and lesser officers, the committee then assigned several to proceed with recruitment; and they were obliged to borrow over a thousand dollars from Schuyler in order to furnish enlistment bounties. Schuyler immediately issued instructions for the recruiting officers, specifying the clothing and money to be offered as bounties and Congress's promise of a hundred acres of land to every soldier who served to the end of the war.[84]

For the remainder of October the convention committee tarried in Albany. While it continued to exert an authority to summon militia from various counties, it also "devoted an important portion of its time and energy to the apprehension of loyalists." Disturbed by evidence that the Mohawk valley would soon be attacked, the committee lamented Schuyler's decision to move Colonel Dayton's regiment from the west to Ticonderoga, but Gates had been so insistent upon having Dayton's reinforcements that Schuyler "could not prudently refuse" him. A few days later the general agreed to halt Dayton's troops at Canistighena or Halfmoon until the committee could decide whether to order them to retrace their steps or proceed to Gates's army. After further exchanges between Schuyler and the committee, Dayton was ordered on to Ticonderoga and Schuyler withdrew four hundred militia from Fort Edward for service in the Mohawk valley.[85]

Schuyler valued the services of the New York convention's committee, perhaps because a citizens' army responded best to a civilian authority. And he did not wish the committee to leave Albany at the end of October while the "critical juncture" of affairs lingered. But the committee did not ease or simplify his labors because while it functioned, it demanded much of his attention. Moreover, its authority did not relieve much of the distress caused by the unruliness and unreliability of militia forces. Although Yankees had usually proved to be most troublesome for him, Schuyler discovered that even Albany County's troops were less than a real comfort and hardly more reliable. After the first of them appeared at Saratoga, it became obvious that they were reluctant to serve, especially because others marched in so slowly.[86]

Reports from Fort George prompted Schuyler to fear that Carleton's army, poised at Crown Point, would endeavor to reduce Ticonderoga by cutting its line of supplies and communications to the south. Already apprised by Washington's aide, Robert H. Harrison, that Howe's forces were also trying to get round to the rear of the American army on the lower Hudson, Schuyler anticipated that the same kind of maneuver might be tried by Carleton and Burgoyne. Expecting attacking parties to strike along the route that linked Fort George and Fort Edward, Schuyler quickly ordered Ten Broeck to rearrange his militia assignments by doubling the reinforcements dispatched to the lake post and erecting breastworks for a larger party to be positioned on a hill above Fort Edward.[87]

In the waning days of October the Yorker doubted not only that many militia would appear but also that they would agree to march as far north as Ticonderoga. Those who had already proceeded as far north as Fort Edward seemed unwilling even to help reinforce Fort George. Having managed to send some to the Lake George post, Schuyler discovered that the men then refused to accept guard duty or to help construct fortifications, do road work, or haul provisions.[88]

Like Washington, who found the "humours and intolerable caprice of Militia" a positive liability, Schuyler longed for the opportunity to send them home. Although they might fight well enough, as compared to regulars, they were too difficult to manage between engagements and could not be trusted to tarry long enough to be employed in significant battles or skirmishes. While offering some of the men extra allowances if they would agree to repair the road north of Fort Edward between Jones's and Cheshire's mills, Schuyler decided to solve part of the problem of militia recalcitrance by sending some of them to the Mohawk valley.[89] Fresh alarms of possible enemy incursions there gained credence because Carleton's army at Crown Point hesitated to attack Ticonderoga. Could it be that the British intended a diversion?

Schuyler's secretary, Richard Varick, and Brig. Gen. Nicholas Herkimer, who commanded the Tryon County militia, indicated that the danger was indeed mounting in the west. Similarly, Capt. Lathrop Allen at Fort Dayton registered rumors that Indians and Tories had been prompted by news of Arnold's Lake Champlain reverses to join the enemy. Varick reported that four hundred of Maj. Robert Rogers's rangers had been defeated and routed at Mamoroneck in the Mohawk valley on 22 October. Herkimer wrote from Canajoharie that several settlers had set out for Oswego to join the enemy, and from thence a major force was sure to be launched against the valley. Herkimer expected that Sir John Johnson at the head of six hundred British regulars would be joined by twenty-two Indian tribes. Unable to resist such a power, Herkimer begged Schuyler for troops; without them many Tryon countians would surely surrender to it.[90]

Although thinking that the westerners' fears were exaggerated, Schuyler promptly ordered General Ten Broeck to push two of his Albany County regiments and part of a third from Fort Edward into Tryon County. Urging the New York convention committee at Albany to send out other militia units as well, the general rushed a message to Col. Elias Dayton, advising him to halt his regiment momentarily in case the committee decided to order them back to the Mohawk valley. Fortunately, enough militia were sent west from Albany to save Dayton's regiment from retracing their steps to Fort Schuyler. After they reached Stillwater on 27 October, Schuyler ordered them forward to Skenesborough and then to Ticonderoga, where Gates had been impatient to have them.[91]

The appearance of the militia in the field complicated the functions of the commissariat not only because of their demands for provisions but also because they were wasteful and unwilling to assist in the maintenance of a steady system of transportation. And Schuyler also found that the new deputy commissary general of his department was a stranger to the neighborhood and required the assistance of others more knowledgeable about the local sources of supplies like flour and meat.[92]

As with his former commissary, Walter Livingston, Schuyler did not hesitate to take a direct hand in Elisha Avery's work. He asked the Albany committee and others to purchase flour for Avery. John Lansing, Jr., his aide-de-camp, issued the general's orders for the movement of provisions along various stages of the route north from Albany to Skenesborough, Fort George, and Ticonderoga, and also west from Schenectady to Fort Schuyler. Having inspected the line of communications as far north as Saratoga, on 23 October Schuyler complained to Congress that Avery's inexperience and unfamiliarity with the neighborhood had caused a variety of disorders in the transportation of supplies. When another "painful scorbutic eruption" prevented the general from hastening to "every part of the communication" to remedy the difficulties, he prodded others like Harmanus Schuyler to unsnarl the stoppages and resume the motion of bateaux and wagons along the river and portages stretching from Halfmoon to Lake George.[93]

By contrast, Schuyler was happier with the services of Maj. Richard Varick, who proved as adept an assistant in the work of commissaries and quartermasters as he did a personal secretary. After sixteen months of service Varick sought both a promotion and an appointment as muster-master, which were rewards that Schuyler obtained for him but that did not exempt him from the general's demands that he assist Elisha Avery at Albany and serve as Schuyler's surrogate in directing the movement of wagoners and bateaumen along the northern communication. While Schuyler remained at Saratoga in October, he depended upon Varick to help Avery discharge his responsibilities in Albany. It was to Varick that he turned when he wanted Philip Van Rensselaer to send spades and axes from the public storehouse or Henry Glen to supply bateaux from Schenectady.[94]

Deciding to return to Albany to lend Avery a hand and to prevent a halt in the flow of provisions, the general dispatched both his aides, Major James Van Rensselaer and Varick, north to inspect the line of communications and to make certain that stocks of provisions were properly forwarded from point to point along the route. Varick found confusion everywhere, rebuked Harmanus Schuyler and others for "want of proper attention," and found one assistant commissary a "truly Incapable *Yankee*." Others, like Jacob Wendell, he deemed spirited and active, but Wendell complained that Elisha Avery intended to replace him for refusing to sign certain receipts specifying the exact quantities of flour he had handled. Without scales to weigh the commodity, Wendell was unable to do as Avery wished, but Varick urged Schuyler to "interpose" on Wendell's behalf.[95]

Varick's whirlwind tour of the posts along the communication during the first week of November won the general's hearty approbation. With his help, Schuyler soon was able to overcome the difficulties caused by Elisha Avery's replacement of Walter Livingston as deputy commissary general. The change had simply interrupted the business of the commissariat until Avery could get the hang of its operations. Between late September and the end of October, for example, the army's stock of flour had dropped from forty days of supplies to sixteen and then to seven. But by early November Schuyler's intervention and Avery's cooperation improved the flow of flour and meat to the northern posts, and the general could again be sure that the army would not lack food.[96]

Meantime, the watch on Lake Champlain, like that on the Mohawk valley, continued until early November. The enemy was not, however, confined to these two frontiers. Loyalists at Schuyler's rear threatened disruptions of the civilian scene, defections to the enemy, and infection of the militia. More significant a part of the Loyalist threat, however, were the movements of Tryon County inhabitants to join enemy parties in the Mohawk valley, and of settlers west of the upper reaches of the

Hudson who were close to Carleton's army on the western shore of Lake Champlain. Again, the Albany committee had collected reports that Sir John Johnson would descend upon the valley with British regulars and Indian allies. And if Carleton assigned some of his forces to the Mohawk valley, Schuyler feared that they would be aided by disaffected settlers and Indians. Unwilling to rely upon only the militia, Schuyler decided to send Col. Goose Van Schaick's regiment from Fort George to Johnstown. In order to discover the activities of local Tories and whether Carleton intended to divert some of his troops from Crown Point, Schuyler ordered generals Ten Broeck and Gates to mount careful watch on the upper Hudson countryside west of Fort Edward and Ticonderoga. Similarly, he instructed Colonel Van Schaick and other officers to post scouts into the wilds west of the Hudson and north of the Mohawk as far as Sacandaga. Should Gates's scouts discover signs of any movements to the southwest, Schuyler insisted that he must then dispatch at least three regiments— more as he judged feasible—for service in the Mohawk valley. Emphasizing that the militia were absolutely undependable, Schuyler ordered that once these detachments were made from Gates's Continental forces, they must travel rapidly and leave their baggage behind.[97]

Although few signs of enemy and Loyalist movement from Carleton's lakeside position came to light, there was evidence that British sympathizers in the Albany environs were eager to join the royal invasionary forces at Crown Point. That Schuyler was alerted to their intentions at least indicates the kind of threats with which he was compelled to deal behind the lines; similarly, his fears of attacks that could be launched at points along the long route linking Albany to Ticonderoga cannot be regarded as trifles.[98]

While the British remained poised north of Ticonderoga, reconnoitering Gates's defenses and gradually deciding that the risks of opening a frontal attack so late in the season were too great to take, Schuyler continued to suspect that Carleton intended to strike at his flank in the Mohawk valley or somewhere along the communication between Saratoga and Lake George. By the first of November the general had carefully redeployed several militia and Continental regiments, preparing to parry an enemy thrust wherever it might be made. On 30 October two more of Colonel Van Schaick's companies and Captain Bradt's rangers had been sent westward, Captain Hager's Schoharie militia were instructed to follow Van Schaick's orders, and General Herkimer was being notified to detach a thousand of his best militia for Van Schaick's service. Colonel Van Ness's unfilled regiment would be retained in Albany.[99]

Coincidentally, on 28 October, while Carleton's fleet and army maneuvered toward Ticonderoga, Sir William Howe encountered Washington's forces at White Plains. But whereas the sharp battle ended with Howe's capture of a key position from which to attack Washington again, Carleton's forces quickly pulled back when Gates's troops fired at them from their redoubts. Three days later, when Gates dispatched news of the aborted engagement to Schuyler, it appeared that Carleton had settled back into position at Crown Point and encampments at Putnam's Point and Chimney Point.[100]

Relieved to learn of the British withdrawal from Ticonderoga, Schuyler deduced that Carleton's maneuver had been made to test American strength so that he could report to his superiors why he dared make no actual assault upon the fort. But the general was not yet willing to think that Sir John Johnson could make no strike along either the Mohawk or the line of posts south of Ticonderoga. Accordingly, on 2 November, he urged Gates to rush one of his regiments to Fort George and two to the Mohawk valley to join Colonel Van Schaick. And while informing Van Schaick of the enemy's probable withdrawal to Canada, Schuyler warned him to maintain a vigilant watch for Sir John Johnson.[101]

Schuyler was inclined to think that Johnson's expedition had not been merely delayed; perhaps it had turned back. And Carleton's failure to move decisively against Ticonderoga, together with the advancing autumn promised an end to the dangers that had hovered so long over both the northern and western ends of Schuyler's vast department. The general now wished that Carleton would venture an attack, for he might be beaten. But the Yorker was already thinking of shifting the troops from crowded quarters at Ticonderoga. As soon as it was certain that Carleton's troops had fully retired to Canada, much of the Northern Army could be moved to winter barracks at Saratoga, Stillwater, Albany, and Schenectady.[102]

On Monday, 4 November, the British forces began to withdraw from Crown Point, and by the end of the week Schuyler had received Horatio Gates's assurances that Sir John Johnson had also retreated with them. When Goose Van Schaick reported that he had discovered no threat to the peace of the Mohawk valley and that his militia auxiliaries were not inclined to tarry longer at Johnstown, Schuyler ordered him to dismiss them "with my best Thanks for their Services." The relief of the pressure upon Ticonderoga now made the desertions from General Ten Broeck's Albany County militia less bothersome too, but it was still too early to be confident that Carleton's withdrawal had totally freed Ticonderoga from all danger.[103]

Schuyler's army had failed to win Canada in 1775–76, but it did check the enemy's advance into New York. The British plan of invading the province had also failed, principally because the Yorker's Northern Army had managed to block Carleton and Burgoyne's progress while Washington concentrated on the lower Hudson. The Virginian's forces, however, were not so fortunate or successful as Schuyler's, for Sir William Howe had driven them from Manhattan. Thereafter even Howe's halfhearted efforts continued to pose a considerable threat to the commander in chief's army. With the danger over Lake Champlain now lifted, Washington did not hesitate to summon parts of Schuyler's army to assist his own. Unlike the northern campaign now ended, the Virginian's struggle continued as the British drove him from White Plains, Fort Washington, and Fort Lee, and then across New Jersey toward the Delaware River.

Prelude to Ticonderoga

1

"the glory of completing this work"

*T*he British invasion of 1777 from Canada was no surprise to Philip Schuyler; he expected it because he knew well the history of the Mohawk valley and the Lake Champlain basin up and down which "had gone the tides of war for almost a century." And if the British army was to subdue North America it must hold the Hudson valley, "the chief strategic highway of the continent"; it could divide the rebellious colonies, dealing with them "separately and at leisure."[1]

"The British plan of campaign for 1777 was quite simply an extension and elaboration of the campaign of 1776." In 1776 only the first stages of a plan to seize the Hudson valley had been completed. Sir William Howe failed to press north and instead diverted his forces toward New Jersey; and Sir Guy Carleton, having pushed Philip Schuyler's invading army out of Canada, failed to win control of Lake Champlain until so late in the season that he chose to withdraw northward for the winter. Logistical problems hindered him from rapidly pursuing the retreating Americans. It was largely through Schuyler's efforts in collecting forces and constructing the lake fleet so ably captained by Benedict Arnold that Carleton was delayed and was then prompted to withdraw after the famous naval engagement on Lake Champlain on 11–13 October 1776. Because the season was so late, Carleton hesitated to undertake anything further that year. Not so Schuyler.[2]

From his experience as military commander since June 1775, and as chief of the Indian commissioners, he had demonstrated awareness of possible threats to the Hudson valley both from the north and from the west along the Mohawk valley. Because negotiations with the Iroquois to secure the latter route from any hostile incursion occasioned some delay in launching the American invasion of Canada in 1775, carping critics continued to slander him as inactive, procrastinating, irresolute, and even cowardly.[3] Beginning in November 1776 Schuyler proposed to seize the initiative rather than wait indefinitely for a legislative imprimatur before he acted. Congress had requested New Hampshire, Massachusetts, and Connecticut to send forty-five hundred men to Ticonderoga and urged Governor Trumbull to furnish Schuyler with twenty pieces of artillery (eighteen-pounders). The commissary general had been asked to send an eight-months' stock of provisions for five thousand men to Fort Ann, and a like amount to Albany. Hancock assured Schuyler that the "glory" of checking any incursion into New York and New England would "be reserved for you"; his wisdom and abilities fitted him to execute the task.[4]

But all was not harmony. Congress was to dismiss Dr. Samuel Stringer, Schuyler's appointee, without so much as the general being informed of the reasons. Almost as galling to him was the altercation that arose over another appointment, that of Lt. Col. Jonathan Trumbull, Jr., as his departmental deputy adjutant general.[5]

By early 1777 Schuyler turned his thoughts to the coming campaign. From various agents he expected "that the Enemy intend to open next Campaign by an Attempt to penetrate up Hudson's River, whilst General Carlton will press on us from the Northwards, and cause a Diversion to be made by the Way of Oswego and another on the Sea Coast of the Massachusetts Bay." Here were the essential points of what became the famous 1777 campaign, and upon them Schuyler continued to base his exertions.[6]

Except for a trip to Fishkill to consult the New York convention during 7–20 January, Schuyler spent the early months of 1777 at Albany where he could most conveniently direct preparations for both western and northern approaches to the Hudson valley. He continued to fear a winter assault from the enemy, yet luckily none came. His voluminous correspondence reveals how attentively he dealt with a multitude of responsibilities. News of Washington's victory at Trenton was quickly passed to the Six Nations to impress them with the necessity of observing their pledges of neutrality. While ordering presents for the tribes and establishing fair prices for their furs and skins he instructed the Reverend Samuel Kirkland to warn the Oneida and others against the blandishments of the Mohawk to join the Seneca and follow Chief Joseph Brant and the British.[7]

As in the direction of affairs of the board of Indian commissioners, so in the command of his military department Schuyler bent every effort to

collect men, provisions and equipment, construction materials and workers, artillery, and powder and shot for the coming spring and summer.
His visits to the New York convention at Fishkill failed to turn up any
artificers. But the convention did lend him £10,000 ($25,000) to relieve
his depleted military chest until Congress could supply the funds that
were needed by Governor Trumbull to pay Connecticut army recruits.[8]

Despite these promising developments, Schuyler, to some who observed him, seemed dismayed with the current state of American affairs.
William Smith, Jr., thought he despaired of the colonies' abilities, said he
declared against the disunion of the empire, and wished "Negotiations
were opened for Peace." As reliance upon France seemed delusive, "Schuyler said the convention ought to do something" such as "promote ...
some Application in the Continental Congress for a Treaty of Reconciliation" with Britain. Upon Schuyler's return from Fishkill, Smith recorded that he had made "no Impression on the [New York] Convention"—which dared not propose to Congress a negotiation for
reconciliation. "He laments his Situation," Smith wrote, "Thinks it impossible to raise an Army upon the Scheme of Independency," but that
"If he refused to act, (as they will not accept his Resignation) [Schuyler]
is confident they would make him a Prisoner." According to Smith,
Schuyler thought the colonies were exhausted and that nothing could save
them in the coming summer unless France declared war and assisted the
rebels fully.[9]

Such sentiments, if true, were not reflected in Schuyler's continued and
energetic efforts to prepare for the coming season of warfare. On 13 January he wrote Benedict Arnold that within a fortnight he expected to
begin the work of obstructing the water passage between Fort Ticonderoga and Mount Independence. Shortly thereafter he sent Capt. Frederick
Chappel to New England to recruit a company of seamen for service on
Lake Champlain and issued orders for lumber to build bateaux, for salted
meat and flour to be carried to strategic points, and for reports and
"returns" of all provisions at posts along the "communications" north
and west of Albany. The general was energetically preparing for the impending military campaign.[10]

But the collection of foodstuff and lumber was hindered by enterprising monopolists. Schuyler appealed to the New York convention for legislation empowering his deputy quartermaster and commissary general
to seize supplies at the usual price, "or what would be better such a price
as Convention may please to order." The suggestion was rejected for fear
of popular outcry.[11] Thus Schuyler was left to struggle against these additional odds in collecting provisions and material.

The difficulties of raising and maintaining, let alone augmenting, an army were indeed sizable. By the end of January Schuyler was forced to report to Congress that Ticonderoga was still inadequately garrisoned. The few troops raised in New York were still at Albany, many half-naked and dying. Some had already deserted. The New England states had not fulfilled their quotas except for seven hundred Massachusetts militia, who were to replace the regulars at Ticonderoga, and even they were much reduced by death and desertion. The enlistment of Lt. Col. Nathaniel Buell's regiment, already reduced by deaths from 370 to 250 men, would expire on 1 February. Anthony Wayne's Pennsylvania Continentals were marching home after staying almost a month beyond their enlistment, which had expired on 5 January.[12]

Until Washington could order new levies raised in New England and communities nearest the lakes to move north, the commander in chief expected that Schuyler "must contrive to make a shift, as I have done [at Morristown], with temporary supplies of Militia." Neither the Yorker nor the Virginian much relished the use of militia because they were unreliable, but both indeed "made shift" with them. Expecting Carleton to push his way out of Canada by late April, Schuyler wrote Washington on 30 January that the army at Ticonderoga should be at least ten thousand strong; another thousand should be posted along the route north of Albany, and a thousand more at posts along the Mohawk River. The vast territory of Schuyler's department acquired a sizable force with cannon, ammunition, and food sufficient to block a British invasion. He also suggested that his army include men from as many different states as possible. "The Southern people who have a greater Spirit of Discipline & Subordination," he thought, "will by Degrees influence the Eastern people, who without such a Mixture will never acquire it."[13]

In February 1777 John Burgoyne submitted to Lord Germain and the British cabinet plans for a major thrust along Lake Champlain and a secondary invasion from Oswego east along the Mohawk. Expecting such an attack, Schuyler feared the consequences of the American loss of Ticonderoga, for Albany then would be vulnerable, and people would defect out of "Fear and ... Attention which most Men pay to the Security of their property." News from Col. Anthony Wayne indicated that Ticonderoga was in disarray because of the imminent departure of two regiments. Ordnance and stores were insufficient, ammunition had been carried off, and a smallpox outbreak had forced the quarantine of eastern troops at Fort George. Wayne had to act not only as commandant but as quartermaster general, commissary, and engineer; his own health impaired, he was "worried with Wretches Applying for Discharges or Furlows—*as you used to be* until I am become a mear Skeliton."[14]

At Albany Schuyler was constantly importuned by Mohawk, Oneida and Onondaga begging for clothes and other goods. He deemed a treaty with them before the new campaign began vital to offset enemy efforts to negotiate one at Oswego. Having borrowed $50,000 from the New York government and other large sums from individuals, Schuyler lamented that all funds were spent, and he begged Congress to send more. Unable to begin reinforcing the works at Ticonderoga and Fort George until artificers arrived, he could not safely send cannon north of Fort George. Ammunition had not yet reached Albany and Washington was unable to supply it.[15]

As spring approached Schuyler's anxiety increased. By 16 February he had Colonel Wayne's report of scouts who had estimated the disposition of enemy troops in Canada. The largest concentration of some fourteen hundred scattered among various points was five hundred fifty who were at Saint John's; another three hundred were reported to be at Isle aux Noix. About eight hundred Canadians were building four large vessels for Lake Champlain to augment four others already fitted with sail and twelve guns each, and two row galleys. All Schuyler could tell Wayne was that he had no regular troops to spare him, but that militia of Hampshire and Berkshire counties were en route to him as were part of four regiments from Massachusetts and one from New Hampshire; about one-fifth of the militia from Albany, Tryon, Charlotte, Cumberland, and Gloucester counties were under orders to prepare to reinforce Ticonderoga at a moment's notice.[16]

The state of the northern garrisons remained grossly inadequate despite General Washington's expectation that Ticonderoga had been properly reinforced and despite his orders that Massachusetts and New Hampshire regiments march to its support. Lt. Col. Richard Varick wrote Schuyler on 16 February that he had mustered 1,045 troops at Ticonderoga, but these included the sick and would shortly be reduced to 723 once Col. Dayton's regiment of 322 left. In all a total of 1,200 militia, artillerymen, and scouts were available, but many of these had not a month left to serve their enlistments.[17]

Neither Schuyler nor the Northern Army received full support. John Adams, for example, thought that he and other officers like Israel Putnam, Joseph Spencer, and William Heath were not "capable of the great commands they hold. We hear of none of their heroic deeds of arms. I wish they would all resign," he confided to his wife. But war is more drudgery than heroics, and if Schuyler's merit was not apparent to the cranky congressman from Massachusetts, it was perhaps because Adams was not so much cognizant of the Yorker's day-to-day preparations for a major campaign as he was a romantic dreamer of the clash of arms and the flourish of one army parading in surrender to another. As for the commander in chief, Washington expected the war would soon enlarge in his own quarter; he could not believe that Carleton would attempt any southern movement from Canada before spring. Perhaps, he told Schuyler, the British would withdraw from Canada and join Howe's challenge to the main American army. But in any event Schuyler must rely upon only Massachusetts and New Hampshire regulars and in an emergency use the militia. However, the Virginian pointedly requested Schuyler to call for no more New York regulars to join his army![18] This would not be the last time Washington miscalculated military situations and deprived Schuyler of troops that the commander in chief deemed more important to his own efforts than to the Yorker's.

By late February 1777 Schuyler increasingly turned his thoughts to a visit to Congress. But he felt constrained to postpone the journey until a competent garrison had been raised for Ticonderoga and until some general officer had arrived to take charge of the department. And not until 26 March did Schuyler set out from Albany to Philadelphia. In the meantime he plodded on with his work of preparing for the new campaign and of collecting the papers necessary for vindicating his record of military and financial administration against charges of peculation and mismanagement. For a general and Indian commissioner, the volume and variety of Schuyler's duties were indeed impressive, and anyone who reads the remains of his papers covering the years from 1775 to 1777 must admire his grasp of all affairs and wide-ranging attention to details.

In the first days of March 1777 Schuyler's fears of an early British eruption out of Canada disappeared. The season now was so far advanced that it was unlikely that Lake Champlain would freeze and permit an easy crossing on the ice. However, he did expect Guy Carleton to press south when he had accumulated enough bateaux and other craft to transport an army. Wayne's garrison was still inadequately manned because New England troops were amazingly tardy in reaching the post. He feared they would not appear until May, and even then their ranks were likely to be "deficient." Washington himself lacked reinforcements, and judging by his own experiences, Schuyler likewise feared they would not soon be forthcoming.[19]

Washington did not offer much encouragement when he wrote Schuyler on 12 March. Indeed, he so badly misjudged the prospects for the 1777 campaign that responsibility for the weakness of Schuyler's department seems to be the Virginian's more than the Yorker's. Washington thought a defensive war to which he was now committed required the drawing of troops together at the opening of a campaign. They might later be dispersed where needed; otherwise it was impossible to guard against every likely incursion or satisfy every commander's request for reinforcements. Moreover, he expected the enemy's main objective would be Philadelphia, and that the operations of his own army would largely govern the motions of the British in Canada. If he could hold the enemy at bay in the middle states, no force would dare penetrate New York from the north. Supposing the enemy might attempt such a move—which he much doubted—Washington insisted that they could not succeed if the forts were properly garrisoned and supplied, and cattle and carriages were removed from the invader's path. And if a large force were concentrated at Ticonderoga, and the enemy made no move on the lakes, that army would be useless while his own would suffer. It would do no good, he insisted, to guard the northern frontiers so strongly while his own army was so weak. Accordingly the commander in chief decided to divert eight of the ten New England regiments earlier assigned to Ticonderoga; these would be concentrated at Peekskill whence they might move up or down the Hudson as circumstances might direct. Five New York regiments were likewise to be assembled at Peekskill under Alexander McDougall.[20]

This decision and line of thinking indicate Washington's failure either to assess correctly the military prospects or to follow Schuyler's superior judgment. The loss of Ticonderoga in July is therefore attributable in some measure to Washington himself. The fort that so many imagined to be impregnable simply remained inadequately garrisoned. And while the commander in chief shrewdly coached the Yorker general "to let the forest fight for him," the advice was gratuitous, for Schuyler was fully acquainted with the wooded territory north of Saratoga and the possibilities of using it to obstruct an invasion. Nor did he much agree with the Virginian's calculations however loyally he bowed to the advice. Confiding to Robert R. Livingston that although it was generally believed "below" that Howe's push for Philadelphia would be the heart of the enemy campaign, Schuyler had reason to think otherwise. Events proved the accuracy of Schuyler's estimation. Unhappily for him, Washington's offensive strategy in 1775–76 had now given way to one of defensiveness. Schuyler consequently suffered not only the difficulties of waging a war to check the invasion from Canada but also the ultimate damage of his military reputation.[21]

Shortly before setting out to make his long-intended visit to Congress, Schuyler replied to Washington's directions, agreeing that the concentration of forces at Peekskill would be judicious *if* Howe intended to draw most forces from Canada and merely guard against an American invasion there. But *if* Washington's intelligence proved unfounded and that which Schuyler had already received was corroborated by British attempts to penetrate from the north, Ticonderoga would fall before any troops from Peekskill might reach it. And that is exactly what occurred! Schuyler feared that many inhabitants in the neighborhood of Albany and northward would then defect, the enemy would be able to acquire supplies and carriages from them, and the Indians would move readily to join the invaders. That too was to come to pass. The general remonstrated against Washington's design to divert part of New York's troops from Ticonderoga and other stations north and west of Albany. He needed small garrisons to guard military magazines at a variety of posts like Skenesborough, Fort Ann, Fort George, and Fort Edward, and Saratoga. Moreover, he had been obliged to divert Col. Peter Gansevoort's men from Skenesborough and Fort Ann to the Mohawk valley, where Col. Samuel Elmore's Connecticut regiment at Fort Schuyler required replacement; their enlistments expired on 15 April and they would not remain beyond the term. Gansevoort's troops in "this quarter" were fewer than two hundred. Several companies of eastern troops had in turn been ordered to Skenesborough and Fort Ann. Because hostile Indians and Canadians had already begun depredations on Lake George and the area south of Fort George by 20 March, Schuyler felt obliged to try to strengthen that post as well as Fort Edward and Saratoga. No wagoner or teamster would stir beyond Saratoga without a good convoy of soldiers, and small units were scattered among a variety of outposts for such service. Col. Goose Van Schaick's regiment containing less than four hundred men was divided among Fort George and Fort Edward, Saratoga, and Albany. Col. Henry Beekman Livingston's regiment had fewer than one hundred rank and file for service at Fort Dayton and Johnstown. Seth Warner's uncompleted regiment at Ticonderoga was less than fifty strong, and Schuyler had no hope that these units could recruit sufficient manpower to fill their depleted ranks. Fearing that the regiments expected from the eastern states would also be incomplete and noting that he also had too many boys in the ranks, the troubled Yorker expected that he must soon visit Washington for further consultation on these and other problems.[22]

Within a day or so of writing his expostulation to the commander in chief, Schuyler left Albany for his long-awaited encounter with the Continental Congress. Events proved both the accuracy of his expectations for the 1777 campaign and the seriousness of the mistake of drawing too much of the army toward the Jersies. By late April even Horatio Gates agreed that the conquest of New York State would be the enemy's "First and Main Object of their ensuing Campaign."[23]

That Schuyler chose this moment to absent himself from command of the Northern Army was no sign of failure in responsibility. With the restrictions now imposed upon his forces by Washington there was little that could not be managed by any subordinate. Having waited since November 1776 for a general officer to be sent to serve in his absence, Schuyler decided on 21 March that Goose Van Schaick must take the command as the eldest ranking colonel in the department. Four days later the Continental Congress finally responded to his call for a general officer to assist him. Horatio Gates was "directed immediately to repair to Ticonderoga, and take command of the army there."[24]

In one of his last efforts to procure reinforcements for the Northern Army before he departed Albany on 26 March, Schuyler posted "express" letters to the presidents of Massachusetts and New Hampshire, requesting that they hasten the march of their promised troops to Ticonderoga. Colonel Wayne had reported the weakness of his garrison and begged Schuyler to rouse the officials of those states from their "shameful lethargy" before it was too late. Four hundred militia would end their enlistment by early April, and their departure would reduce the garrison to about eight hundred men. The need for replacements was indeed urgent, for even then Sir Guy Carleton was collecting troops at Saint John's, Chambly, and Montreal; Lake Champlain would be navigable in two or three weeks, and the way would be open for invasion.[25]

Late in March 1777 Schuyler finally set off for Philadelphia. He would seek "an opportunity to Justify himself to Congress, and if necessary to the world, as his Administration has been faulted by some," as John Pierce, Jr., of Albany put it. Thinly veiled hints that Schuyler had mismanaged the 1776 campaign had been aggravated by suspicions, rumors of maladministration and peculation, and most recently by a clash with Congress over military appointments. The general was determined to brook the assaults upon his reputation and prerogatives no longer. If he could not resolve his grievances with Congress he would resign his commission.[26]

The general's seat in Congress proved to be an effective lever in achieving vindication. Following his election to the Second Continental Congress by New York's provincial convention in April 1775, Schuyler had been launched into military duties during his service as delegate in May and June 1775. But he had not relinquished that post when he became a major general, even though he could not attend the Congress. Furthermore, on 13 May 1777 the New York convention would again elect him a delegate together with William Duer, James Duane, Philip Livingston, and Gouverneur Morris.[27]

2

"resolved that Justice shall be done me"

By March 1777 the most long-standing of Schuyler grievances—that he had been wrongly blamed for the 1776 reverses in Canada without an appropriate investigation to clear him of suspicions of incompetence—remained unsettled. They had been aggravated by popular suspicions of peculation, difficulties with the commissary general Joseph Trumbull over jurisdictional lines in Schuyler's Department, and finally by a clash with Congress over the removal of his hospital director without proper consultation. More threatening, perhaps, to the general's position was the presence of Horatio Gates. After accompanying troops from the Northern Army to Washington's command in December 1776, Gates avoided military duties in the Trenton-Princeton campaign; instead he visited friends in Congress, which had fled to Baltimore. And while Schuyler remained attentive to his martial responsibilities at Albany instead of mending political fences in Congress, his besmirched reputation went unredeemed. Gates, on the other hand, "lost no time in playing politics for military gain," for he began a "successful intrigue to replace the Yorker as head of the Northern Army."[28] Although the scheme did not succeed until August 1777, evidence of its progress appeared in the early months of the year. The dismissal of Samuel Stringer from his post as director of hospital and chief physician of Schuyler's department and Congress's vehement response to Schuyler's moderate protest were signals of the advancing intrigue. The Stringer affair proved to be one of the final provocations for Schuyler to confront Congress in person if his reputation was to be cleared and his administrative record shown to be honest and responsible.

Stringer began his onerous duties when Schuyler seized the initiative to obtain the physician's services in August 1775. Nearly a fifth of the five hundred troops then at Ticonderoga were ill. Dr. Stringer's work proceeded apace for a year without cause for particular notice, but by the summer of 1776 certain antagonisms developed between him and Dr. John Morgan, whom Congress had made director general of hospitals. Like the clash between Walter Livingston and Joseph Trumbull over the commissary department, this was a jurisdictional dispute involving the general himself.[29]

Indirectly Stringer involved the general in strained relations with both Horatio Gates and Congress and prompted further rumors of Schuyler's fiscal malfeasance. Gates accused Stringer of going "Preference Hunting to the Congress" instead of "fulfilling his promises and returning with all dispatch to his Duty"—a remarkable charge to be made by a man who was so adept a preference hunter himself.[30]

Bickering between Stringer and Morgan continued until January 1777, when Congress dismissed both men from the service and opened the way for reorganizing the medical bureaucracy. Stringer's dismissal was voted on 9 January—curiously enough the very day that Samuel Adams noted Gates's presence at Baltimore and asked, "How shall we make him the head of that [Northern] Army?"[31] One way was to aggravate Schuyler's irritated sense of injury. Gates's partisans seem to have calculated that they might egg Schuyler on to resign or create a commotion by which his own dismissal could be justified.

Although some complaints against the administration of the medical department had been made earlier and Schuyler had insisted upon an inquiry into his conduct, on 15 March there came a veritable explosion. Congressmen like the Adamses and partisans of Horatio Gates, who had hoped for Schuyler's resignation or dismissal, voted resolutions that were manifestly calculated to achieve their goal.[32] Almost blatantly Congress demonstrated the pettiness of its politics, the meanness of its members.

First of Congress's March blasts was its assertions that decisions like Stringer's removal were made "upon reasons satisfactory to themselves" and that "General Schuyler ought to have known it to be his duty to have acquiesced therein." Then followed a denunciation of his suggestion that Congress owed him the "compliment" of an explanation; such was "highly derogatory to the honour of Congress," and "it is expected his letters, for the future, be written in a stile more suitable to the dignity of the representative body of these free and independent states, and to his own character of their officer." Moreover, Schuyler's appeal for justice against the libel of Joseph Trumbull's letter to William Williams provoked Congress to even greater wrath, although all it needed to do to afford that justice was to issue a simple announcement. Congress might merely have proclaimed that Schuyler was *not* responsible for the delay in delivering John Trumbull's commission as deputy adjutant general and that as the Yorker had recommended the appointment he could hardly be charged with trying to thwart it. Instead Congress huffily refused to interfere in disputes among army officers on the grounds that they might be settled by military rules or courts-martial. Schuyler's complaint "that he confidently expected Congress would have done him that justice, which it was in their power to give, and which he humbly conceives they ought to have done" was now deemed "to say the least illadvised and highly indecent." When President Hancock posted these resolves on 18 March he warned

Schuyler to "write in a stile better adapted to" Congress's "rank and Dignity, as well as [to] your own Character."[33]

Finally, at the end of March, Congress responded to Schuyler's long-standing and repeated request for a general officer to command the Northern Army while he visited Philadelphia. It resolved simply "That General Gates be directed immediately to repair to Ticonderoga, and take command of the army there." The meaning of this language is debatable, for it seemed to make Gates Schuyler's successor. But the army at Ticonderoga was not coterminous with the Department of which Schuyler was commanding officer. Nor was Ticonderoga Schuyler's headquarters; on 6 March 1776 a Congressional resolution had established those at Albany. And by remaining there Gates seemed to assert a jurisdiction over the entire department instead of merely the army at Ticonderoga.[34]

It also must be noted that Gates cannot have been regarded as Schuyler's successor until August 1777 because in June when Gates appeared in Congress to protest the "disgraceful Manner" in which he had been "superceded," his behavior provoked a clamor of denunciation. James Duane reported that few congressmen had supported Gates's claim and that most decided that he had no reason to suppose that the departmental command "ever had been invested in him."[35] Schuyler received no notification of Congress's 25 March action respecting Gates nor of its cranky outburst of 15 March by the time he left Albany about 26 or 27 March. However, he soon encountered a rumor that suggested the existence of an intrigue for Horatio Gates to supersede him.

Well before Schuyler left the city he neither imagined nor intended to return a major general, much less the commander of northern Continental forces. Nor did he need to read Congress's nasty resolutions of 15 March to reach that conclusion. Uncertain how long he would sit in the national assembly, he informed young John Trumbull on 16 March, "I am something more Certain on another point—that is I shall not return a General. I find Congress will have no Occasion for me." Schuyler grumbled that "It does not Even appear necessary to Consult me on any Matter whatsoever." But he professed to relish the prospects of his retirement to Saratoga; there he could indulge "in rural amusements unperplexed by business, undisturbed by laws and freed from the disagreeable Importunity of their Mightenesses [sic.] the princes of the Wilderness"—the Indians.[36]

Schuyler was ready to confront Congress when he arrived to take his seat on 7 April. He had paved his way by submitting his report on the disposition of specie to President Hancock on 24 February, claiming that he was "still in Advance £1362.7.2" for monies he had furnished the army by his personal borrowings. He had prepared his accounts and was armed with the audit of special commissioners James Milligan, John Welles, and John Barker Church (alias John Carter, who in a few months was to become his son-in-law). This summary of their findings indicated an accountability for almost $890,000 since August 1775; and as of 20 March 1777 a balance of $4,964.30 was still owed to the general.[37]

Finally, Schuyler went to Philadelphia armed with the support of fellow New York delegates. This he had arranged with Robert R. Livingston, asking that John Jay and James Duane might favor him "with their Company both because they could say more than would perhaps be proper for me to do, and that they receive the fullest Conviction of the unjust and Injurious treatment I have sustained." If these men could not be spared by the New York State convention, Schuyler wished it would send William Duer and Gouverneur Morris as delegates. By the time the general reached Kingston he learned that the convention had obliged him; Philip Livingston and James Duane had been directed to follow him to Congress and William Duer had been named to accompany him as a new delegate.[38]

Not far along his way to Philadelphia, Schuyler heard a rumor that he referred to his secretary, Col. Richard Varick, who was remaining in Albany, to investigate. The information he wanted might be of use in his dealings with Congress. Dr. Jonathan Potts, who had succeeded Samuel Stringer as hospital director, had alleged that Congress intended to replace Schuyler with Gates or had actually done so, evidently on the basis of Schuyler's proffered resignation in 1776. Potts supposedly had such information from Gates himself.[39]

Varick reported that Potts insisted that he had not learned this from Gates, and Morgan Lewis could not or would not tell Varick to whom it was reported, or whether ir was in any way authentic. Varick suspected that there was "more on the Carpet" than either Potts or Lewis chose to mention; and because both were "most *Violently* attached to" Gates, Varick could not expect to discover much from them that would satisfy Schuyler's curiosity. According to Lewis, Gates had "declared he will not be Obliged to receive Orders from an Officer who is an hundred Miles from the Army." That clearly suggested that if Gates accepted assignment to the Northern Army during Schuyler's absence, he would not do so as Schuyler's subordinate but only as his successor.[40]

From Kingston Schuyler rode on to Philadelphia, skirting British-occupied New York City and pausing at Washington's Morristown headquarters. It was during these early days of April 1777 that he and Alexander Hamilton probably met for the first time—a fateful encounter indeed, because Hamilton became his son-in-law in 1780 and subsequently a staunch ally in Federalist partisanship and statesmanship. By then Schuyler must have learned that a general officer had been sent to serve in his absence from the Northern Army if not to supersede him. Accompanied by Maj. James Van Rensselaer and Maj. Henry Brockholst Livingston, his aides, and John Lansing, Jr., as secretary, Schuyler took up lodging in Philadelphia with Mrs. Sarah Clarke.[41]

The journals of Congress for 7 April record simply that "Major General Schuyler attended, and took his seat ... as a delegate from the State of New York."[42] But much of his time was not devoted to service as a delegate. Indeed, most of it was given to a special military command under directions of both Congress and the Pennsylvania state government. Doubtless this afforded him the opportunity to display his splendid administrative abilities and energies under the very noses of critical fellow delegates. Their demonstration doubtless contributed to a restoration of his reputation with Congress, perhaps as much as did the official investigations of his fiscal affairs.

Within three days of taking his seat as a delegate, the general was assigned further military responsibilities. "An excellent man of business, of wide experience and knowledge, he was useful and impressive." On 10 April Congress ordered him to execute a series of resolutions: To form a camp on the west side of the Delaware River for Continental troops then at Philadelphia and for others marching from the south and west and to hasten them to Washington's army; To recommend to Pennsylvania's supreme executive council the preparation of three thousand militia to be assembled there on the shortest notice; To send proper officers to determine the number and condition of troops between Annapolis and Philadelphia and to hasten their march northward. From 14 April until 27 May the general was busily engaged as "Commander in Chief" of Pennsylvania forces under orders of the state's board of war.[43]

Schuyler's special assignment involved him in extensive exchanges with Washington, commissary and quartermaster officers, and various local authorities. His steady stream of orders revealed his invariable attention to a host of details: sentinels posted, supplies, clothing and equipment collected and dispersed, food and troops moved, Fort Island entrenched, boats built, reports and troop returns compiled, warrants drawn to pay arrearages in militia wages, courts-martial set and sentences executed, prisoners of war quartered, rolls called, inspections held, shipments of cash escorted from the treasury board, forage purchased, arms and clothing requisitioned, troops inoculated for smallpox, and more resolutions of Congress executed.[44]

Drawn into some awkward exchanges with the Quakers toward the end of May, Schuyler found them resisting efforts to collect blankets for the army. Exasperated, he threatened coercion unless they offered at least a thousand. "This Jesuitical Set do us much injury," he exclaimed to Washington. But the commander in chief reminded his colleague that his efforts to procure blankets must "be founded in the strictest propriety." And after an explanation from Israel Pemberton that the Friends had already made contributions in accord with their religious scruples, Schuyler pressed them no further but did order a forced requisition from others. Pemberton used the occasion to press some book upon the general who promised to read it and admitted that it might "mend his heart," although he could not fully subscribe to every part of the doctrine it contained.[45]

While Schuyler discharged his special military responsibilities in and around Philadelphia (too busy even to write Mrs. Schuyler of his safe arrival), the wheels of Congress turned steadily toward satisfying his demands for an official investigation and exoneration. Three days after the Pennsylvania Board of War vested him with authority as "commander in chief in this State," Congress appointed a committee to inquire into his conduct since his appointment in 1775. Some opposed this move, speciously arguing that no particular charges or complaints had been made nor anything said against Schuyler on the floor, and that therefore any inquiry would by implication be a censure. Schuyler's colleagues silenced them by asking why the general's authority had been pared away and the command of his army "in effect" transferred to Gates. James Duane vowed that hostility to the Yorkers' interest in defending their general could be cured by good manners and sociability.[46]

Convinced that he would never return home a general because congressional resolutions passed before his arrival in Philadelphia pointed to his downfall, Schuyler at least was determined to make his exit without dishonor. To this end his secretary, John Lansing, Jr., became engrossed in arranging the materials for submission to the congressional committee.[47]

On 30 April Schuyler wrote Washington that in a day or two he would resign his major general's commission and then give the commander in chief his reasons. Washington's reply gave the Yorker no particular encouragement. The Virginian blandly expressed sorrow that the circumstances were such as to dispose Schuyler to quit, "but you are the best judge of the line of conduct, most reconcileable to your duty in a public and personal view," he wrote, "and your own feelings must determine you in a matter of so delicate and interest a nature."[48]

Whether Schuyler intended only to promote his case for exoneration or also to prepare the way for an invitation to resume the Northern Army command remains unknown. On 7 May he conveyed a memorial to President Hancock. No abject apology for the missive of protest concerning Dr. Stringer and the Commissary Joseph Trumbull, the memorial was conciliatory but a manly, reasoned, and decent explanation of why Congress's violent reactions on 15 March were mistaken and misplaced. He had intended only to be candid—not disrespectful of the "Grand Council" of the United States. To Congress's assertion that he ought to have acquiesced to its decision to dismiss Dr. Stringer, Schuyler replied that he did indeed obey its orders by delivering the notice to Stringer; if his request that Stringer continue to function until his successor arrived was deemed disobedience, he must of course plead guilty. As to the reference to military rules for inquiry and courts-martial for settling disputes, Schuyler argued that he had not received Congress's 29 November 1776 order for a medical department inquiry until 12 January 1777—four days after Stringer had been discharged. Never questioning Congress's right to dismiss its servants, he nonetheless believed that it was objectionable to do so without formal inquiry; men of worth and ability would otherwise hesitate or refuse to serve the public for fear of mistreatment. Furthermore, their requirement of "acquiescence" surely must not prevent officers like himself from answering directives with suggestions and information. In a number of cases, Schuyler noted, he had objected to congressional proposals with decency and candor, and Congress had acquiesced and approved his views. Had he not merely behaved similarly in Dr. Stringer's case? Certainly he never meant "to wound *the Dignity of Congress* or dispute their Authority."

The next portion of Schuyler's memorial dealt with commissary Trumbull's intercepted and publicized letter to William Williams. It had injured the general's honor, and Congress might have vindicated him by a simple testimonial that he had not been responsible for the failure to deliver the deputy adjutant general's commission to Trumbull's brother. Should Schuyler really have attempted to clear himself by court-martialing Joseph Trumbull for slander as Congress seemed to suggest? What, for example, would have been the consequences had Schuyler "immediately arrested Major General Gates, when on the Retreat of the Army from Canada he disputed" Schuyler's command? Was not the appeal to Congress rather the more proper means of settling the dispute? Indeed, Congress had settled it in 1776. Why might it not have acted similarly in the Trumbull imbroglio? Schuyler closed the memorial by noting that he had studied to deserve the previous thanks of Congress for his zeal and attention to duty; he was deeply wounded to think he had been "recorded as an intemperate Person, who has acted in Contempt of that Body Whose Dignity he has endeavoured to maintain with his Life & Fortune." Therefore he hoped "that the Honorable Congress will reconsider the Resolutions" of 15 March and adopt such measures as justice and wisdom might dictate!⁴⁹

The response was almost immediate—and favorable. On 8 May Congress declared Schuyler's explanation of his 4 February letter to be "satisfactory" and professed to "entertain now the same favorable Sentiments concerning him, which they entertained before that Letter was received."⁵⁰ So far, so good. But the questions of the general's alleged peculation and overall military management still remained for the treasury board and the special committee of inquiry to settle. And with a variety of usual delays, this required more effort and management—and more than the week Schuyler had once thought would be required once the committee began its work.

On 13 May the board of treasury reported its examination of the slain Richard Montgomery's accounts as well as those of Schuyler's (to 20 March 1777); of the paymaster general John Trumbull, Jr.; and of the deputy commissary general Walter Livingston. It certified them as properly filed and adjusted by the auditing commissioners whose work was approved, and Congress duly resolved that the report be confirmed. Minutes of the board of treasury specified a final discharge for Schuyler "on the public Account, of all Demands of the United States of America against him and in any wise concerning the same, down to" 20 March 1777. Suggestions of Schuyler's fiscal mismanagement were squelched. And on that very day the New York convention struck another blow for Schuyler's vindication by reelecting him a delegate to Congress, He, James Duane, and Philip Livingston were the only members of the original dozen delegates chosen in April 1775 to be reelected. Gouverneur Morris and William Duer were named to serve with them. Thus, even if Schuyler no longer merited Congress's trust as an army commander, it must continue to admit him to a seat in the house. The significance of this political maneuver was further delineated by William Smith, Jr., who noted that Schuyler had first received the fewest votes for delegate (fourteen) and Francis Lewis the most (twenty-one). The Albany members expressed disappointment that their native son, who had been recommended to Congress for high military rank in 1775, should now fare so poorly, and to mollify them a second vote was taken. Schuyler then outpolled Lewis. This, Smith thought, would produce great discontent because of Schuyler's congressional inquiry "on Aspersions imputed to the N[ew] E[ngland] People."⁵¹

Between 15 and 22 May Congress debated the final issue of Philip Schuyler's case: Did his military record merit their continued trust? It was the recommendation of the board of war that he be directed "forthwith to proceed to the Northern department, and take upon him the command there." Horatio Gates might choose between remaining in a subordinate position or accepting the adjutant generalship "in the Grand Army" of Washington.[52] The choice of language may be instructive. Congress's order of 25 March to Gates was to "repair to Ticonderoga, and take command of the army there," but the proposed order to Schuyler now referred more carefully to the Northern Department of whose command Schuyler was never deprived until more than two months later. For the moment he was only absent from it, and Gates as the general officer on the scene was naturally in charge but had not yet properly or completely replaced the Yorker.

As Congress considered the board of war's recommendation, the New York delegates labored to prevent what might have been their colleague's ultimate humiliation. The recommendation that he return to the army had occasioned warm debate on 16 May. Three days later his old adversary Joseph Trumbull, who had finally discovered that President Hancock—not Schuyler—was responsible for the failure to forward his brother John's commission as deputy adjutant general, wrote Jeremiah Wadsworth that "Every Act is Using here to get Genl Gates recalled. . . . Genl Schuyler is here, with his mirmedon's [sic]." Trumbull feared they would succeed because the Rhode Island delegation was absent and only Roger Sherman sat for Connecticut, which was a significant hint at the nature of the vote that finally determined the issue.[53]

On 22 May Congress finally passed the board of war's recommendation and also repealed their 6 March 1776 resolution that Schuyler establish his headquarters at Albany. It was more reasonable to permit him to move his headquarters as circumstances dictated. And the Northern Department was generally defined to include Albany, Ticonderoga, Fort Schuyler (Stanwix), and their dependencies.[54]

James Lovell explained to General Gates something of the argument against returning Schuyler and letting Gates choose between the subordination to him and the adjutant generalship under Washington. It was futile to expect Gates to command at Ticonderoga under "absolute orders of another at 100 miles distance, in treaty with Indians or busied in the duties of a provider." Although he had been ordered to command the army at Ticonderoga, Gates never left Albany until Schuyler returned in early June. If Gates learned anything about the diverse and onerous duties of a department commander, he hardly demonstrated much capacity to deal with them. And Lovell's remarks were perhaps an inadvertent admission of the variety of labors that Schuyler had long performed and now would be expected to resume.[55]

The Connecticut congressman Roger Sherman revealed another detail of the congressional maneuverings: New Englanders suggested appointing Schuyler second in command to Washington, thus leaving Gates in the north. The move "would probably have been carried if Rhode Island had been represented," but its delegates were absent, as were Delaware's.[56]

Philip Livingston and James Duane merely reported to the New York convention that Schuyler was "fully reinstated in his Command, every point being adjusted entirely to his and our Satisfaction. This Business with which more than the *Reputation* of our State was so closely connected required address and great attention for Reasons which the General" who was to carry their message could explain in person. William Duer, in another account to the new chancellor of New York, Robert R. Livingston, explained his attentiveness "in defeating the Designs of a Mischievous Combination and in cultivating the Friendship" of southern delegates; "in Spite of all the Arts, and Influence made Use of by the Eastern delegates in conjunction with the Members from New Jersey," he wrote, "we have got Genl. Schuylers Conduct fully justified, and himself reinstated ... in as extensive a Manner as before. There was never I believe a more Difficult Card to play. Genl. Gates had the address whilst at this Place to insinuate himself into the good Graces of even the honest Part of the House, and the Unkindness to poison the Minds of most with Prejudices ... which operated so strongly that nothing but Time, and great Temper and address could have dispelled the Mist of Error which had clouded the Eyes even of those who were Friends to ye great Cause, and to the State of New York." Duer also revealed that Delaware and Rhode Island delegates had been absent from the vote, Georgia's and New Jersey's were divided, and Richard H. Lee of Virginia supported New Hampshire's, Massachusetts's, and Connecticut's votes against returning Schuyler to the army. Only the delegates of New York, Pennsylvania, Maryland, Virginia, and the Carolinas had voted for him—all of which Duer thought was a fair reflection of the political complexion of the states.[57]

As Duer saw it, the general's victory was not an overwhelming one, and Congress was not as generous as Schuyler, who penned sincere thanks to President Hancock for the attention and justice obtained since his arrival in Philadelphia. As the general rode northward on 28 May to resume his duties, John Burgoyne's invading forces were sailing south from Saint John's, and the great campaign of 1777 began to unfold, much as Schuyler had expected it would.[58]

3

"the Spirit of Electioneering"

The clearance of his reputation by the congressional resolves on 8, 13, and 22 May were enough to mollify Schuyler. The pull of duty and his sense of public responsibility were too great for him to resist the opportunity of military service. Moreover, he could not really be content to retire to life as a country squire in the midst of the political and military maelstrom that was swirling around him.

Having left Philadelphia on 28 or 29 May, Schuyler reached Kingston by 1 June. That evening he consulted the New York Council of Safety and especially John Jay and Robert R. Livingston. As a consequence, Jay began a letter-writing campaign for Schuyler's election as governor of New York.[59] Next day through John Lansing, Jr., Schuyler issued the first of his general orders for the final months of his active command. Within the next few weeks the general completed a remarkable military record, replete with almost constant movement in the field between Albany and Lake Champlain, and minute supervision of a host of responsibilities both as department commander and Indian commissioner. Moreover, he sustained a variety of setbacks—but with commendable spirit—the army's retreat from Ticonderoga, the frustrations of rallying regulars and militia to resist invasion, a fresh tide of acrimony and suspicion that led Congress to recall him, the loss of the first state gubernatorial election, and even the elopement of a daughter with a bridegroom of whom the general and Mrs. Schuyler knew little and therefore did not approve of him. Yet in the midst of all his troubles Schuyler helped lay the foundations for ultimate victory at Saratoga, where the enemy finally destroyed much of his estate. Aided by time; circumstance; and men like Benedict Arnold, Benjamin Lincoln, and Daniel Morgan; and even disgruntled Yankees like Seth Warner and John Stark, Schuyler may have otherwise gained the laurels that devolved upon Horatio Gates had Congress not been so choleric and impatient as to remove him.

Plunging into the work of reestablishing his direction of military responsibilities, Schuyler first notified Horatio Gates to supply copies of all orders he had given to post commanders and to report the number of troops on hand. On 4 June he invited Gates to consult on the best way of executing their orders and to share information and Gates's observations for the future direction of business. Gates, however, was largely uncooperative, leading Schuyler to complain to fellow delegates in Congress that he was unable to procure copies of Gates's orders and even very little verbal information. On 9 June he granted Gates's request to leave Albany, although he had wished him to take the Ticonderoga command.[60]

Only incidentally did the general take time from resuming his army business in June to correspond about politics, although the subject of the first elections under the new state constitution was of considerable concern to him and his allies. Schuyler became a leading contender for the governorship, and the choice of a legislature was likewise a matter of considerable importance. Politics in the Hampshire Grants territory were also taking a turn that could not please New Yorkers who defended their state's claim to the area. Delegates from various towns assembled at Windsor on 4 June to begin forming the state of Vermont and the work of framing a constitution that continued well into July.

By early June it appears that people at Albany considered both Schuyler and John Jay to be candidates for the governorship. Jay, however, preferred the office of chief justice. "When I consider how well General Schuyler is qualified for that important office," he wrote John Ten Broeck, "I think he ought in justice to be preferred to Your most obt. humbl. Servt."[61]

Schuyler was probably not alone in his dismay that so many candidates were nominated. Included were Philip Livingston, Jay, John Morin Scott, and himself for the first place; and George Clinton, James Duane, Abraham Ten Broeck, and a Mr. Snyder for the lieutenant governorship. By 9 June two slates were circulating in Albany County, one for Livingston and Ten Broeck and the other for Schuyler and Duane. The general professed a preference for Livingston and Duane, but as Robert R. Livingston put it, Schuyler finally "consented to take it upon him" with the chancellor's support.[62]

The Livingston interest was usually powerful and helpful, but in this case Schuyler's candidacy seemed not to profit by it. Noting the arrival of an Albany committee letter to the Livingston Manor committee, touting Schuyler and Ten Broeck for the two high offices, the indefatigable diarist William Smith, Jr., recorded a Schuyler animus in Cambridge and also that John Morin Scott was charging the Livingstons with greed for office. Scott, a notorious sot, was reputedly campaigning energetically in Dutchess, Orange, and Ulster counties, deceitfully hinting (Smith thought) that Chancellor Livingston and Chief Justice Jay were improperly using the state council of safety to campaign for Schuyler. The chancellor also perceived that politics had "taken a strange turn" as "Genl. Shoulders [a nickname for Scott] & his Agents ... contrived ... to blow up a flame about the impropriety of having two brothers Governors"— a reference not only to Philip Livingston of New York and Governor William Livingston of New Jersey, but also to a rising democratic prejudice against aristocratic family politics. This, the chancellor reported to William Duer, "unaccountably opperating very strongly with some other party matters, made it absolutely necessary to change our battery or to see our government drowned in a bowl of grog." Hence the determination to concentrate efforts upon Schuyler.[63]

In quarters like Rhinebeck, where several hundred people met on 12 June to ballot for governor and lieutenant governor, there was "No Mention of Mr[.] Scott, only of Schuyler & [George] Clinton." William Smith, Jr., observed how popular the electioneering was and how unalarming the British military presence seemed to be, and he was clearly disgusted with the failure to restrict the candidacy for higher offices in the state to the ranking men of property. "Amongst us," he wrote, "a Beggar may be Govr. a Senator or Assemblyman."

Evidence of the electioneering and the results of several days' polling during the week of 15 June are fragmentary, but several contemporary observations are particularly noteworthy. Smith remarked that Dutchess County and Ulster County voters were persuaded to name no Livingston or anyone connected with that family, and therefore George Clinton was preferred to Schuyler. The tenants on Livingston Manor proved that their landlord could not invariably direct them although on occasion he had been able to carry 400 votes in Albany County, where Schuyler garnered 589 to Clinton's 125. Schuyler himself attributed his defeat to the low vote in Albany County, and a major reason for this seems to have been a tenants' uprising in May that had the effect of continuing an antiaristocratic sentiment into the elections. William Duer in Philadelphia deduced as much when he wrote Schuyler on 19 June: "I am extremely sorry to hear that the Spirit of Electioneering has gone forth in our State. I dread the Consequences which may too probably ensue from that Sourness of Mind which is the natural Result of contested Elections ... Mr. Scot I am informed rails at an *Aristocratic Faction* which he pretends has form'd and Organised the new Government; his disappointed Ambition will lead him to make use of every Act however gross or wicked which he thinks will serve to make himself popular."[64]

When Chief Justice Jay wrote Schuyler at the close of the election he told him that pollings in the Middle District were such that if a "tolerable degree of unanimity" prevailed in the upper counties where Schuyler was expected to gain a heavy vote, he little doubted that ere long he would be addressing Schuyler as "Your Excellency." Jay thought that Clinton's "being pushed" for both offices of governor and lieutenant governor might well result in his loss of both. And on 22 June William Smith also recorded that the elections below Livingston Manor had run to Schuyler's and Clinton's favor. But George Clinton won both posts, and Smith also indicated that this was undoubtedly due to the fact that Dutchess, Ulster, and Orange counties had largely favored Clinton.[65]

Not until early August did Schuyler congratulate the new governor in a letter begging for militia reinforcements to meet the growing threat of Burgoyne's invasion. In the face of such dismal circumstances the general then assured Clinton "I shall embrace every oppertunity [sic] to make you sit as easy in the Chair of Government as the Times will admit. Your Virtue; the Love of my Country and that Friendship which I have always and with great Truth professed are all so many Inducements to it."[66] For the remainder of the war Schuyler and Clinton enjoyed an easy friendship that indeed was a continuation of their cooperation in the old colonial assembly. But with the advent of peace they came to a parting of the ways as partisanship and serious differences over political philosophy and programs developed between them.

Schuyler suffered not only a political setback in the summer of 1777, but also military and familial reverses. Ticonderoga fell to the enemy, and his eldest daughter, Angelica, ran off with John Barker Church, alias John Carter, one of the special congressional commissioners of audit. Mrs. Schuyler was so furious at the elopement that even her parents, the John Van Rensselaers, found it difficult to mollify her and to affect a reconciliation.[67] Martial duties prevailed over paternal ones as Schuyler valiantly directed efforts at Fort Edward to block the march of Burgoyne's invading army. His own small forces had only recently been augmented by St. Clair's troops, which escaped from Ticonderoga, and by Gen. John Nixon's brigade, which came from Peekskill. The most immediate beginning of those efforts came between Schuyler's resumption of his command on 3 June 1777 and the abandonment of Ticonderoga on 5–6 July, although in a larger sense they stretch back into 1776.

4

"Every Exertion to get Affairs in decent Train"

When Schuyler returned to Albany on 3 June he found that little had been accomplished during his absence to put the department in readiness for the campaign. During April and May, Horatio Gates had not stirred beyond Albany (although Congress had directed him to take charge *at* Ticonderoga). And contrary to allegations that "the Northern Army began to hum, the moment" Gates "took over his post," the evidence is that he accomplished nothing more than a holding action. In reviewing the state of affairs for a committee of Congress in October, Richard Varick noted that neither Gates nor anyone else had "thrown into" Ticonderoga more than a "very small" quantity of provisions while Schuyler had been absent from the department.[68]

While Gates served in Schuyler's absence, the number of troops available in the department remained low. In March 700 were stationed at various posts in addition to Anthony Wayne's return of about 1,200 at Ticonderoga. Between late May until 13 June fewer than 2,300 men were at Ticonderoga. Worrying that "my Yankees" were tardy and convinced that the enemy would field more than 11,000 for the campaign, in April Gates had called on Congress for an army of 13,600. Although he applied to Massachusetts for militia on 30 May, by mid-June only about 250 Massachusetts militia were reported at Ticonderoga.[69] Gates had had no better fortune in collecting and retaining an army than Schuyler had had even earlier; neither general could be accountable for superiors' withdrawing Continentals from the north or for state authorities' failure to replace and augment them or the militia until the most serious danger became too transparent for further hesitation in reinforcing the main army.

Nor was manpower the only problem. Fortifications and the shipment of food supplies, equipment, and ammunition all needed attention. These Gates seemed to have been none too adept or energetic at handling or even attempting to settle. And because of Tory activities the Albany County Committee of Safety was obliged to work double time to apprehend and imprison the troublemakers, some of whom were evidently part of the tenant uprising on Livingston Manor.[70]

Gates himself had been anxious about such matters. Recent destruction of magazines at Danbury and Peekskill were striking confirmation, he told the president of Congress, of the enemy's designs to move up the Hudson. The lookout at Ticonderoga became increasingly uneasy as enemy scouting parties ranged south from Canada, preparing the way for the invasion of John Burgoyne, who had arrived at Quebec on 6 May.[71]

But Gates evidently felt no urgency about visiting Ticonderoga, and by 12 May Richard Varick reported that he was not inclined to leave Albany until satisfied that enough troops had been collected for his support at the northern outpost. Everything at Albany remained in the same state as when Schuyler had left except for the forwarding of some artillery and hospital stores. Most of the cannon still at Albany had not been moved forward because of spring rains and bad roads. Perhaps Gates now knew that "a General at Albany had not set Idle, as It was thrown Out by some persons not very friendly to" Schuyler.[72]

Schuyler's discoveries of failures in departmental administration were soon noted in his reports to Congress and in his orders to the deputy commissary general Elisha Avery and the deputy quartermaster general Morgan Lewis. Within two days of his homecoming, he called upon Avery and Lewis for accounts of provisions, articles and bateaux in the department and their locations. On 6 June he directed Lewis to hasten a variety of foodstuff from Fort George to Ticonderoga and likewise to send all the supplies he could procure from Avery to Fort Schuyler. Bricks must be made for Ticonderoga, and large stocks of wood were to be cut all summer in preparation for the ensuing winter. Blacksmiths were constantly to make entrenching tools when not otherwise occupied.[73]

With considerable detail Schuyler explained to Congress the difficulties presented at Ticonderoga and at Mount Independence, where fortifications were unfinished and the number of troops inadequate. They could not be manned even if the entire force intended for the department could be collected there. At least two thousand men were needed at various other posts both north and west of Albany. But it would be imprudent for the greater part of the army to occupy a post like Ticonderoga should the enemy invest it and manage to cut off its communication. And two or three thousand men must maintain Mount Independence and secure the passage against enemy entry into Lake George. But the entire army could not be risked at the mount lest they be forced to abandon it for lack of provisions.[74]

When Brigadier General St. Clair reached Ticonderoga on 12 June he found the fortifications weaker than they had been in the fall of 1776 because the garrison had burned the abatis as firewood during the winter. The troop strength even by the end of the month consisted of barely two thousand rank-and-file infantry fit for duty and fewer than three hundred artillerymen. Stores were low, and the rainy spring had made transport more difficult. By mid-June very little had been accomplished to make Mount Independence defensible, and the pontoon bridge between it and Ticonderoga was little more than half-finished. Continuous rainfall prevented much progress on the work. Varick estimated a total of perhaps twenty-three hundred men were on hand, but many of them were boys and some were old men. Of the New Englanders he observed that if they were at war for fifty years they could not be disciplined even by officers of their own states. None but Maj. Ebenezer Stevens's artillery seemed to understand simple manual exercises.[75]

Like Richard Varick's, St. Clair's report to Schuyler rang similar changes: 1,576 Continentals fit for duty, some artificers and 52 rangers, three regiments of Hampshire militia dwindling by desertion, and two regiments of Massachusetts militia consisting of 250 fit for duty and serving for two months (with three weeks of their term already past). St. Clair did not think that militia could be called in to Ticonderoga in view of the inadequate food supplies; there seemed to be little prospect of collecting new provisions except from a limited stockpile at Stillwater, nor of fresh meat except from New England. The bridge construction was progressing fairly well, but it entailed heavy work, especially as timber had to be hauled from the woods by hand. Draft animals were lacking, the powder magazines were in a wretched condition, cartridge paper nonexistent, and everything out of order. St. Clair's intelligence of the enemy forces gathering at Saint John's suggested that Burgoyne would have about 10,000 men, including Canadians and Sir John Johnson's Indians, who were expected to penetrate the state by way of the Mohawk valley.[76]

By the end of June, when the vanguard of Burgoyne's army approached Ticonderoga, St. Clair's troops totaled about 3,000, including 571 sick and 937 "on command." In addition his artillerymen and artificers numbered 238. Burgoyne's army of 7,000, although smaller than St. Clair suspected, was still far superior to the American forces.[77]

Schuyler could rightfully claim, as he reported to Washington on 28 June, that the department's scanty provisions were "in a great measure, if not altogether, to be imputed to a want of attention in persons whose duty it was to supply this department" before and after Schuyler returned to its command. Although his criticism was largely aimed at the commissary general Joseph Trumbull and his deputy Elisha Avery, it was in some measure applicable to Horatio Gates as well; the latter had not been able to move stockpiles north from Albany. As Schuyler pointedly noted later, not "much, if anything, was done" while the department had been in Gates's hands.[78]

At best Schuyler conducted a holding action, but the Yorker displayed a great deal more energy than Gates in augmenting the forces north of Albany, collecting and moving supplies and equipment, and maintaining a watchful eye on the Indians in the Mohawk and Cherry valleys.[79] The deputy commissary general Elisha Avery also had to be prodded, exhorted, and rebuked. Reports from Ticonderoga and Fort George indicated that St. Clair had provisions enough for only seven weeks, and that there was little more at Fort George to feed its own garrison. To fellow congressmen Philip Livingston, James Duane, and William Duer, the general observed that during his absence from the army "such a Chaos has been formed that It will require Every Exertion to get Affairs in decent Train." Schuyler wrote both Avery and the president of Congress on 14 June that if orders he had issued the previous winter had been obeyed, the army would not now be so distressed. Had Schuyler not told Avery to lay in foodstuff for three thousand men at Fort George and Fort Ann and Skenesborough, and a like amount at Albany? "I charge you in the most positive manner," he wrote Avery, "to hasten what Beef and pork you may have to Albany or to any of the Posts on Hudsons River between Albany & Fort Edward, and to procure as many fat Cattle as possible" for speedy driving to Ticonderoga. "If we are obliged to abandon Ticonderoga for want of provisions," he warned, "I leave you to judge of the consequences to yourself."[80] Unhappily, the consequences fell upon Schuyler rather than Avery or others.

Elisha Avery was of course not wholly to blame for the shortages of all provisions. In one instance, for example, Schuyler was obliged to appeal to the president of New Hampshire to intervene in the state legislature's prohibition against the deputy quartermaster general's moving rum, which was purchased for the army's artificers and bateaumen.[81] And if Avery's performance was inadequate, Morgan Lewis's quartermastering was scarcely more satisfactory. At Saratoga the general was exasperated to learn that St. Clair had no working livestock at Ticonderoga and that timber had to be hauled by hand. Forced to issue Lewis more detailed instructions, Schuyler was obliged to give attention to a series of congressional resolutions on the commissariat.[82]

In forty-five enactments on 10, 11, 16 June and 2 July Congress limned out a system of a commissary general of purchases with four deputies and a commissary general of issues with three deputies, which was a vast bureaucracy with detailed instructions for securing and issuing, reporting, and paying for provisions. Amounts and values of daily rations for soldiers were stipulated. It would take time to set all of this in motion, and Schuyler's remaining weeks in command of the Northern Army were probably too brief for him to have been much affected by it—or to affect the workings of it. But in one particular, that of personnel, Schuyler felt the results of Congress's actions immediately. And the general's recent complaints to the delegates of commissarial deficiencies brought on renewed altercation with Joseph Trumbull.

Under the reorganized commissarial system, on 18 June Congress named Trumbull commissary general of purchases and Charles Stewart commissary general of issues. The deputy commissary general in Schuyler's department, Elisha Avery, was now shifted to Stewart's jurisdiction, and through the influence of Schuyler's fellow New York congressmen Avery was replaced by Jacob Cuyler as Trumbull's deputy for the Northern Department. The Yorkers saw that the business of purchases was so influential upon the state's economy, affecting as it did the prices of agricultural produce, that they were determined to have it conducted by one of their own.[83]

Nor was this all of the battle. Three days after Joseph Trumbull's new appointment he penned Schuyler a biting statement of self-justification against the general's charge of months of negligence in Trumbull's department. Obviously the Yankee was embarrassed by the criticisms of his administration. On 29 June the Yorker replied with a devastating and detailed list of particulars, squelching Trumbull point by point. It filled almost ten pages of one of Schuyler's letter books. Similarly, he exhorted and remonstrated with Trumbull's deputy, Avery, to get on with the crucial business of supply.[84] Then as the tempo of other events quickened, Schuyler's attention was increasingly drawn from such detailed instructions of administrative subordinates to the business of troop movements and Indian affairs.

5

One Eye on the North and One on the West

Tactical arrangements for Schuyler's far-flung department included Indian relations and the disposition of garrisons in the Mohawk and Cherry valleys. With a shortage of manpower, these were as pressing as the problems the general encountered with commissary and quartermaster business.

Hoping to keep the Indians from falling into the enemy's orbit, Schuyler invited Canadian tribes to a treaty with the Iroquois to renew the convenant of neutrality at Albany in July. Having established commerce with the Iroquois at Fort Schuyler, the general used the fort as a listening post as well as a center to cater to them with trade. And while principally concerned with his northern defenses, Schuyler kept a watchful eye on the western flank of his department. Toward the middle of June he learned that Joseph Brant had been rousing various Indians to steal livestock and threaten frontier settlements like Tunissdilla. Through the young agent James Dean, Schuyler hoped to have the Oneida intervene in Brant's efforts, which in effect were designed to pave the way for the British invasion from Niagara. By the end of the month Dean passed on information gleaned from Indians who had been in Canada: Montreal was full of British regulars, and Sir John Johnson was expected to reach Oswego by 1 July to join John Butler and a party from Niagara. While the main forces moved against Ticonderoga, this auxiliary maneuver was aimed at Fort Schuyler at the west end of the Mohawk valley.[85]

In response to Joseph Brant's frontier incursions Schuyler also decided to send Col. Goose Van Schaick from Saratoga with 150 men to protect Cherry Valley settlers. Disgruntled that Congress had preferred other men for promotion, Van Schaick threatened to quit the service, but Schuyler prevailed upon him to lead the force into the valley and promptly interceded with Congress for Van Schaick's promotion. He argued that a general officer was needed at Fort Schuyler and Van Schaick was particularly suited because of his steady reliability and his acquaintance with the Iroquois.[86]

Important as the western defenses were, Schuyler's chief concerns were with the northern posts. Proceeding to his Saratoga country house on 12 June, he moved on to Fort Edward, Fort George, and on 18 June to Ticonderoga. He had not visited the key outpost since July 1776, when the army had retreated from Canada. There Schuyler consulted Arthur St. Clair and his officers, inspected the works, issued a variety of orders, and laid plans to meet the British invaders who were even then poised at the northwest reaches of Lake Champlain.

Schuyler found that St. Clair had been busy with improving the works on Mount Independence, which was necessary to hold with Ticonderoga. The cassoon bridge between them was not yet completed, but almost all of the timber was ready for it. The two posts were interdependent, but St. Clair feared that both could not be held with so limited a garrison and that ultimately he might have to retreat to Mount Independence.[87]

During Schuyler's inspection of the fortifications, he drew Col. James Wilkinson aside, saying, "Young gentleman, I have a crow to pick with you." Wilkinson had been a member of Horatio Gates's entourage, but he had not chosen to leave the department when Gates refused to continue as Schuyler's subordinate. The "crow" to which the general referred was a letter Wilkinson had sent Gates on 9 June. In it he commiserated with Gates for Congress's insult of returning Schuyler to the army, an action Wilkinson believed was a sign of "fellest Ingratitude." Although addressed to Gates, the letter had been opened at Schuyler's office because it was not marked private and was deemed to be the department commander's business. The general now told Wilkinson, that "You have not treated me with great civility in that letter," but he professed admiration for Wilkinson's display of warmth and affection toward his superior. According to Wilkinson's account of the conversation, Schuyler expressed a hope that the colonel "may find cause to give me a share of the regard you now bear General Gates." Charmed by such liberality, Wilkinson hesitated to give any opinion of the fortifications when Schuyler invited him to do so. But finally he proposed that save for fifteen hundred selected troops the army should be sent to Fort George to guard against a possible enemy feint; there they might better be able to maneuver freely should a serious attack by the enemy materialize. According to Wilkinson, Schuyler agreed but said that without orders from Congress "he dare not take on himself the responsibility of a measure which would excite a great outcry."[88] In that Schuyler was perfectly correct, for the pettiness of political critics was again to be demonstrated. St. Clair's subsequent abandonment of Ticonderoga provoked much suspicion, puzzlement, dismay, and anger throughout military and political circles.

For the moment, however, decisions for dealing with the stand to be taken at Ticonderoga had to be made. On 20 June Schuyler held a council of war with St. Clair and brigadier generals Roche de Fermoy, Enoch Poor, and John Patterson. Considering the number of men required to hold the post and how they were to be deployed, the generals unanimously agreed that the barely twenty-five hundred effective rank and file were insufficient to defend both Ticonderoga and Mount Independence. They would maintain stands at both as long as possible, consistent with the safety of the men and stores. Should it be necessary to evacuate one place, Ticonderoga must be left. Therefore cannon stores not absolutely necessary for that post were to be moved to Mount Independence, where the engineers were to proceed with repair and construction of fortifications. Obstructions of the passage from Lake Champlain into Lake George were to be finished speedily, although it was calculated that the task would require six weeks! Despite his slow movement, Burgoyne did not permit the defenders more than two weeks of the six to complete it. In other unanimous decisions Schuyler's council of war agreed to ask Washington for reinforcements at once and to call for more provisions of meat from all available sources. The patriot forces might be numerically adequate to hold their ground at Mount Independence; but unless more provisions were brought in to withstand a siege, even this could fail. And to avoid capture of their army the generals provided a means of retreat; they ordered the repair of all bateaux and called for such that could be spared from Lake George to be brought close at hand.[89]

The decisions of the council of war are perfectly understandable. Schuyler might have taken but one alternative—that mentioned by James Wilkinson—but he rightly judged that he had no congressional authority for such a move and that the political as well as military consequences of taking it would indeed be unnecessarily risky. If the army did not stand to fight, or if it fell back for the purpose of feinting, its moves would be questioned. And the small garrison might yet be the nucleus around which militia and other reinforcements could rally. Schuyler's seven hundred other Continentals scattered at posts south of Lake Champlain were needed to guard supplies and the line of communication south to Albany. Perhaps the men at Ticonderoga could at least cripple the invaders before being obliged to retreat.[90]

Thus matters stood when Schuyler departed Ticonderoga on 22 June. But before he went he devoted his customary attention to several details of logistics and supply, some of which were nagging and some petty, as the need to establish rank for field officers; the almost total lack of drums, fifes, and colors; and a memorial of nine battalion commanders, including colonels Seth Warner and Alexander Scammell. The statement complained that officers and men alike wanted reimbursement for baggage transportation and asked for mileage rates for soldiers' travel, payment of recruiting officers, and issuance of clothing allowances. Schuyler referred them to the deputy quartermaster and paymaster generals.[91]

At Fort George on 23–24 June, Schuyler superintended the shipment of stores and the work of carpenters and bateaumen. And as ever there were court-martial verdicts to review. For repeated desertion Schuyler approved the sentence of Private Robert George of Van Schaick's regiment, who was to be shot to death on 1 July. On the morning of 24 June two other deserters were each given a hundred lashes and then ordered confined in irons and fed on bread and water for two weeks.[92]

By the afternoon of 24 June Schuyler rode on to Saratoga, where he hoped to supervise the movement of men and materiel along the communication. There he discovered, however, that on the night of 22–23 June some miscreants had attempted to burn down his house. Happily the fire was "discovered and extinguished before it got to any great Head."[93]

From Saratoga Schuyler continued efforts to support St. Clair, whose first letter since the general left Ticonderoga arrived on the evening of 25 June. Signs of the enemy's movements north of Crown Point indicated they were gathered at a large camp on Gilliland's Creek. Schuyler urged St. Clair to leave nothing at the Lake George landing and to bring up bateaux to protect all necessary means of escape. Scouts should be kept posted on the east side of Lake Champlain to watch for enemy movements toward New Hampshire. If Burgoyne did not intend a full attack on Ticonderoga, he might cover attempts in that direction and along the Mohawk River or try to cut the link between Fort George and Fort Edward. Or he might make all three moves. Schuyler intended to hasten to Albany where he might better direct the speedy movement of regulars and militia northward, and on 25–26 June he fired off appeals for help to Pierre Van Cortlandt of the state council of safety for militia from Dutchess and Ulster counties, and to Congress. To the latter the general explained that although St. Clair's troops were barefooted and poorly clothed and armed, he imagined that Burgoyne's army would press into New Hampshire while attempting only to keep the Americans diverted at Ticonderoga. Provided that Washington sent reinforcements and no full attack came at Ticonderoga, the general seemed confident that British penetrations into New England or the Mohawk valley could be checked.[94]

Before his departure for Albany on 27 June, Schuyler directed last-minute arrangements from Saratoga. As he and his wife rode the thirty-odd miles between their Saratoga and Albany houses, they first learned the disconcerting news of their daughter's surreptitious marriage. At Stillwater they met a messenger bearing a letter from the newlyweds, but the angry parents sent no reply until two days later, when they asked their daughter and son-in-law to come home.[95] Amidst these family tensions, Schuyler spent the last few days of June and the first of July in a flurry of effort, trying to provide support for his forces at Ticonderoga and in the Mohawk valley. Except for 27 June these days were particularly hectic, but the general stretched considerable energies to meet the impending crisis.

Pressing his secretary, John Lansing, Jr., with extensive correspondence beginning on 28 June, Schuyler sent express carriers scurrying with pleas for aid to Major General Putnam at Peekskill; the governor of Connecticut; the president of Massachusetts; and the Berkshire County, Massachusetts, committee. Reporting his receipt of two letters from Arthur St. Clair within two hours of one another, he announced that the enemy had reached Crown Point, and that two parties seemed to be moving to cut Ticonderoga from connections with Skenesborough and to threaten Fort George. The general insisted that he could not take the offensive without militia reinforcements; these should be marched quickly to Fort Edward or Fort Ann. The time had clearly come for a display of spirit; without it patriots and their posterity would suffer the worst of consequences.[96]

Similarly, Schuyler issued orders to Albany County's militia commander, his old friend Abraham Ten Broeck; to Maj. Christopher Yates at Fort George; and to the commander at Fort Edward. Warning the latter to keep a sharp watch against the enemy's approach, Schuyler expected Yates to defend his post to the bitter end, and he promised to hasten to his relief as soon as any troops could be collected. Turning his attention again to the west. Schuyler ordered General Ten Broeck to prepare his militia to answer any call from Colonel Gansevoort at Fort Schuyler. Nicholas Herkimer must also prepare the Tryon County militia for immediate march. Urging the New York Council of Safety to forward his plea for regulars to Maj. Gen. Israel Putnam at Peekskill, the general begged for militia from Dutchess and Ulster counties. The Yorker's plea to Putnam was also based upon a fear that he would be unable to obtain a sufficient number of militia.[97]

It has become a commonplace judgment of historians that Philip Schuyler was a poor choice to rally the New England states, especially the militia, to meet the invasion of 1777. But even the Yankees' hero Horatio Gates did not accomplish more than Schuyler until the danger became so transparent that politicians and militia alike realized the necessity of reacting in order to defend their homes and close neighbors as well as the greater common cause. Gates's record in the spring of 1777 certainly shows no evidence of his particular ability to collect an army, whether of regulars or militia. But it was the Continental line, not the militia, that won the battles of Saratoga, and some of the units appeared in the field while others were en route to the army even before Gates replaced the general.[98]

Much of Schuyler's difficulty in collecting forces in the summer of 1777 came not only from reluctant or dilatory militia, but from the Continental commander in chief. The record of the two men's correspondence in June has hitherto been overlooked but is particularly instructive on this point.

In the frequent exchange of letters between the Yorker and the Virginian, one senses Schuyler's resolute and unflagging activities, the progression of his problems, and how energetically he labored to solve them. On 9 June, for example, the Yorker expressed doubt as to two spies' account of the number of troops gathering in Canada or that General Burgoyne had arrived there as early as 10 May. But if the account of the movement of four regiments toward the Little River, eighteen leagues below Montreal and toward Quebec, was correct, Schuyler thought it probable that they were intended as reinforcements for General Howe on Manhattan. Having proposed that Congress approve the removal of part of his army from Ticonderoga to Mount Independence, Schuyler now asked Washington for his directions in the matter.[99]

Washington's reply on 16 June is a remarkable revelation of his miscalculation of both the intended and actual British movements in 1777. Schuyler's news reinforced his opinion that if Howe was not certain of adequate reinforcements from England, part of the Canadian forces would surely be sent by sea to the middle colonies. Having learned of the British movement into New Jersey, Washington ordered the troops that were collected at Peekskill to join him, thus leaving only a thousand Continentals and the militia there to guard the Hudson. The latter he deemed to be a force superior to any the enemy then had at New York or its dependencies and therefore enough to prevent any surprise! Little did he realize that the army about to penetrate northern New York numbered approximately 10,000, including auxiliaries and camp followers. And whereas Schuyler was rightly suspicious of the information brought to him from Canada, Washington was not nearly enough so. Moreover, he informed the Yorker that he must wait still longer for a supply of artillery and also that he must try to create his own troop of horse rather than depend on any being sent.[100]

The commander in chief could not see further than his own immediate circumstances, and he long continued to withhold support from Schuyler, whose repeated requests for reinforcements beginning in mid-June evoked little response until July. Only one brigade was ordered from Peekskill to Schuyler's support on 2 July, and after long delays in its actual movement, Washington failed to send another until 22 July. As of 16 June the Virginian revealed no suspicion of an invasion from Canada.[101]

As it became increasingly obvious that the British were preparing to launch into Lake Champlain, Schuyler turned to other possible sources of aid. Of the New York Council of Safety he expected both advice and tangible help in meeting the military crisis. Of Congress he asked little except what his account of developments might prompt them to offer by their own initiative. But he hoped that proper concentration upon Mount Independence would enable the garrison to hold the pass between it and Ticonderoga. Inadequate stores of provisions were the result of commissarial negligence and the quartermaster general's languor and want of attention in collecting working cattle and in building and repairing bateaux. But Schuyler hoped that the steady exertions he had made since early June would eventually overcome these difficulties.[102]

On 14 June the general sent express riders to the executives of Massachusetts and New Hampshire, entreating them to hasten the Continentals already ordered for the service and warning that delays were extremely dangerous. The latest dispatches from Arthur St. Clair, he told them, as he did the president of Congress, indicated that the enemy would soon be moving down Lake Champlain as well as along the Mohawk River. Because the New Hampshire militia had already returned to their homes, St. Clair's Ticonderoga garrison was reduced to approximately twenty-two hundred men, including those not fit for duty. All regiments were deficient in composition. In one case only officers had appeared; Gen. Ebenezer Learned and his brigade major had reached Saratoga on 14 June without any men. Learned was sent to organize militia as they gathered at Fort Edward and Fort Ann.[103]

Washington's response to Schuyler's pleas afforded little comfort to the anxious northern commander. Washington could not believe the enemy could execute a plan such as a spy named William Amsbury had suggested to Schuyler. Still, the Virginian indicated that he had ordered Gen. Israel Putnam to hold four Massachusetts regiments at Peekskill in readiness and to call sloops down from Albany to carry them north faster than they could otherwise march. He further speculated that unless Burgoyne had brought reinforcements from England, he could not have more than five thousand men, and if the British besieged Ticonderoga, instead of bypassing it and leaving it to endanger their rear, Burgoyne could not have enough men to attack from Oswego in the west and also to menace Fort Edward and Fort George. Believing the Ticonderoga garrison sufficient to withstand conquest, Washington insisted that it was not politic to send Schuyler more troops, for they would only consume supplies without serving any particularly useful purpose. Maneuvers against his own army on 19 June seemed to demonstrate to the commander in chief that it would be unwise to weaken the defenses on the North River, especially on the strength of what he deemed to be the "uncertainty" of Schuyler's situation. Washington simply could not see that reinforcements were yet "really wanted." While evidently expecting the Massachusetts and New Hampshire regiments of Continentals ordered for the Northern Army to suffice, the Virginian could not "imagine" why they were so delayed in reaching Schuyler.[104]

Had Washington responded speedily and affirmatively to the first of Philip Schuyler's calls (16 June) for reinforcements, it might have been possible to prevent the fall of Ticonderoga—and the downfall of Schuyler himself, for his removal from command was largely predicated on the loss of the overrated fort. Or failing that, the timely arrival of troops might have provided an earlier check to the invasion instead of a succession of retreats. But it was not until 2 July that Washington relented when he received Schuyler's dispatches of 28 June with copies of reports written by St. Clair on 25–26 June. The enemy had reached Crown Point, not far north of Ticonderoga. Should any "accident" now occur there, Schuyler warned, and the way opened for Burgoyne to push farther south, "I know of no obstacle to prevent him; comparatively speaking, I have not a man to oppose him." Schuyler's seven hundred men scattered at posts between Lake Champlain and Albany could not be spared from their positions, and strong reinforcements were needed without delay—and appropriately equipped with a suitable artillery. Therefore he had sent an express to General Putnam to hasten the march of troops from Peekskill. "I am in pain about Fort George," he wrote, "but have no troops to throw in," and it would take time before militia could be summoned and moved.

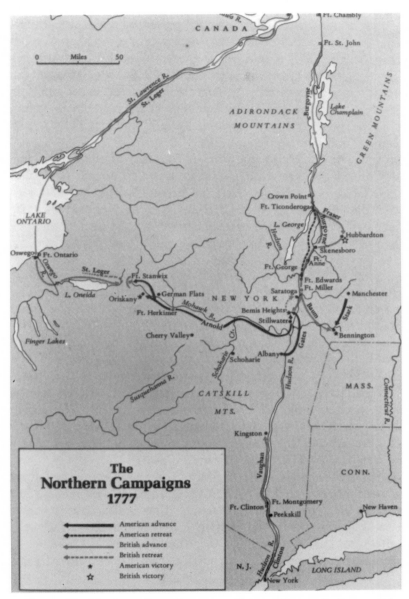

Fig. 4. The Northern Campaigns, 1777. By 1777 the war had expanded
to the western frontier of New York State. But Schuyler's major concern
was still directed to the north. From *The Glorious Cause: The American
Revolution, 1763–1789,* by Robert Middlekauf. Copyright © 1982 by Oxford
University Press, Inc. Reprinted by permission.

Moreover, news written on 25 June by James Dean confirmed Schuyler's suspicions that the enemy would soon launch an attack in the far west. He had, accordingly, taken steps to beg for militia not only from New York counties but also from Connecticut and Massachusetts.[105]

Washington received Schuyler's 28 June letter on the evening of 1 July at Morristown. Thinking that if Burgoyne's move toward Ticonderoga was not a diversion, the Virginian suspected it was proof that Howe's army would turn up the Hudson valley.[106] Next morning he replied to Schuyler that some troops were leaving his camp to return to Peekskill and that General Putnam was ordered to set four Massachusetts regiments in motion toward Albany. All of these men belonged to John Nixon's Continental brigade, and Nixon himself could be expected to follow them from Peekskill by 5 July at the latest.

Mistaken in his belief that Howe would move north toward Burgoyne's southern thrust, Washington also erred in thinking that Ticonderoga would not soon succumb to its besiegers. But the commander in chief was of two minds. He could not, he told Schuyler, be certain what Howe's maneuvers from New Jersey to Staten Island on 30 June meant—perhaps a plan to "amuse" Washington's army until Howe could hear from Burgoyne. If the two British generals intended to cooperate, Howe must soon move up the Hudson. If he failed to do so, Washington thought Burgoyne's forces would only "amuse" Schuyler's army on Lake Champlain! And yet—and yet he was inclined to think that Burgoyne would make a strong effort to break through Ticonderoga because it was difficult to believe the Englishman would return to America to execute only an auxiliary, diversionary plan for which he could gain no particular credit or honor. Promising to hold his army in readiness to move northward, Washington assured Schuyler that he had asked for the Orange County and Ulster County militia to turn out and for General Putnam to summon the Connecticut militia as well. If Howe could be kept below the Highlands, the enemy's schemes could yet be baffled. His final advice to remove all livestock and carriages from the invaders' path was gratuitous; Schuyler was as fully aware of the necessity of such safeguards as he was familiar with the terrain and strategy necessary to employ upon it.[107] And he had already begun to assemble the necessary tools for laying obstacles across the invaders' path.

St. Clair's most recent reports left Schuyler with little doubt that Ticonderoga would be attacked head-on, not merely harassed and bypassed, and that he saw no prospect of defending his post without reinforcements. His garrison would be ruined either by protracted enemy operations or direct "investment." St. Clair foresaw the abandonment of both Ticonderoga and Mount Independence. The woods were full of Indians. Work on Mount Independence was continuing, and the most valuable stores and provisions had been moved to it from Ticonderoga; but construction of the bridge between the posts had not advanced much beyond the state it was in when Schuyler had left it on 22 June; and although set, the boom was only feebly secured because of a shortage of rope. If all the bateaux were not brought up from Lake George soon, there would be no use in sending them at all, for St. Clair feared the enemy would capture the landing place and seize the boats. The arrival of some of Col. Gameliel Bradford's regiment of Massachusetts Continentals had inspired the garrison a little, but St. Clair still could not guess what the enemy's strength was; either they were in full force or very weak and were using the Indians to intimidate the Americans. The beleaguered general promised Schuyler to make the best show of resistance possible, perhaps enough to cripple the invaders if not to defeat them or to hold the fort.[108]

As the month of June waned Schuyler hoped that responses to his efforts would be sufficient to block the enemy before the invasion progressed much farther than Ticonderoga. Except for Albany County and Tryon County units he found that the militia response was uncertain, but at least St. Clair had received a few Continental reinforcements, so by 28 June his troop returns indicated a total of 2,842, including militia; 238 artillerymen and artificers; and 532 sick; 937 "on command"; and only 2,089 rank and file fit for duty.[109]

On 28 June at Albany John Lansing, Jr., issued Schuyler's orders for Col. John Bailey's Second Massachusetts Regiment of Continentals to move up to Fort Edward on the following morning. Two of the four Massachusetts regiments ordered from Peekskill were under way (Bailey's and Bradford's), but not until 12 July, a week after the fall of Ticonderoga, did Washington finally order the remainder of John Nixon's brigade forward. Even that could not have augmented Schuyler's forces by more than about seventeen hundred, if that many.[110] Had the general known what history reveals by hindsight, he must have despaired of ever collecting men enough to turn back Burgoyne's mighty invasion until it was diminished by extended lines of communications, rear guard posts and auxiliary engagements like those in August at Bennington and in the Mohawk valley.

Schuyler feared that the militia would not march unless inspirited by the presence of more Continentals. The point of morale was well taken. Since the spring uprising of tenants on Livingston Manor, signs of Toryism in northern New York had been rife. Schuyler therefore suggested that "It would greatly Inspire the people with Confidence to See the whole Council of Safety" at Albany. If not the council at least a committee might help at Albany with the direction of militia movement. More news indicated that the enemy would menace Tryon County from Oswego, and

General Herkimer had been alerted to prepare his militia to support Fort Schuyler at the west end of the Mohawk valley. If Ticonderoga fell, Schuyler feared the enemy would seize Fort George before he could begin to resist them. He begged the president of the state council of safety to send Ulster County militia on the sloops dispatched from Albany to carry the Peekskill Continentals. But the council had no militia to send Schuyler since many had been diverted to the Highlands at Washington's request, and the council deemed itself too small a body to send Schuyler a committee.[111]

Misconceptions and misinformation of Schuyler's efforts abounded. William Smith, Jr., recorded a rather sour note about his summoning a brigade of Continentals from Peekskill. General Montgomery's widow Janet sharply censured Schuyler's action "as discovering Weakness." She further claimed there were six thousand men at Ticonderoga—a force large enough for the northern defense! And she blamed Schuyler for remaining at Albany instead of taking to the field. Her carping criticism has been repeated by historians who seem not to realize that a commanding general has more things to do than confine himself to a particular part of his army when his command responsibilities are diverse and geographically extended.[112]

6

"in a most violent Passion"

In the press of military duties Schuyler found himself confronted by family troubles when Mrs. Schuyler's parents, the John Van Rensselaers, crossed the Hudson from Greenbush to promote a reconciliation between his runaway daughter and her newly acquired husband and the Schuylers. John Barker Church, alias Carter, wrote that "the General scarcely spoke a dozen Words all the Time. Mrs. S. was in a most violent Passion and said all that Rage & Resentment could inspire; Mrs. R[ensselaer] was very hard upon her" and Mr. Rensselaer told his daughter "that he did not know who she took after he was sure not after her Father & Mother." The Schuylers "might do as they pleased, but if they would not be reconciled" Rensselaer vowed to protect his grandchildren. Typically, the grandparents were more indulgent than the parents. Schuyler took his wife aside to calm her, but he "would promise nothing" to his father- and mother-in-law because he thought that Church and Angelica should have come home the day before. Indeed, on 29 June he had sent for them, but when Church and his wife crossed the Hudson and saw the Schuylers along the lane leading from their house to the river, the young couple turned back. Because the general and his wife retreated to their house rather than advance to greet them, neither Angelica nor her husband cared to risk further rebuffs by proceeding.

The next step in the negotiations came through an exchange of letters between the Schuylers and Churches. On 2 July the Churches received what they regarded as a cold answer to their morning missives. They were told that "Mr. and Mrs. S will hope the Declarations in Mr and Mrs. C's Letters are sincere, and that their Conduct will be correspondent thereto, they yield to the Feelings of Nature, and wish that no Occasion may be given to repent that they have indulged them, on these Principles they permit them to come in Person and make their Peace." The Schuylers then coolly received them in their simple but elegant parlour. Church begged pardon for his wife, and Angelica's mother retorted that she and the general had been greatly pained by the elopement. When at last Mrs. Schuyler relented, Church promised always to treat her with the "most respectful attention." He found the general "in the Hall, and begg'd him to forget what was past." Schuyler "said he wish'd Things had not been carried on in the Manner they had, but that he should forget it all and that he restor'd his Daughter to his full Confidence, that he was now my Father," Church wrote, and that the general would "take the Freedom of giving me his Advice when he thought I stood in need of it with the Candour of a Parent." During the remainder of the day and the following morning, the Churches felt the cutting coolness of the proud Schuylers; but time dampened passions and warmed affections, and the difficulties vanished.[113]

Philip Schuyler must have been annoyed and dismayed with family discord in the very midst of his difficult military responsibilities. Neither he nor his wife could have wished to have their daughter elope or even to be properly married in those unsettled summer days. But more particularly they did not approve of John B. Church, whom they then knew only as John Carter, one of the officers Congress sent to audit Schuyler's departmental accounts in 1776. Schuyler shared his own sentiments with William Duer: "unacquainted with his Family, his connections, and Situation in Life the match was extreamely disagreeable to me ... but as there is no undoing this Gordian Knot I took what I hope you will think the prudent part. I frowned, I made them humble themselves forgave and called them home." The discipline might be corrective—a warning for the future—when it could not be preventative. How much the awkwardness and strain of the reconciliation was natural and spontaneous and how much it had been orchestrated by Schuyler for this effect it is difficult to know. But happily, the adventurer Carter became Church the successful entrepreneur and business partner of Jeremiah Wadsworth. Together they grew prosperous by selling supplies to Rochambeau's army and by land speculation. And after the war Church took his family back and forth across the Atlantic several times, reestablished himself in his native England, and even sat as a member of Parliament for Wendover from 1790 to 1796. The Schuylers found no call to frown upon a son-in-law who achieved such eminent respectability.[114]

7

"a desperate game ... without a trump in hand"

On the last day of June 1777, as the Schuyler-Church clash came to its denouement in Albany, an observer with Burgoyne at Crown Point recorded a splendid invading British army led by the Indians in canoes; gunboats, followed by the *Royal George* and the *Inflexible* towing large booms; then brigs and sloops; with Burgoyne and his chief officers, Phillips and von Riedesel, in pinnaces. "We are now within sight of the enemy," he wrote. Ticonderoga would be besieged as soon as artillery stores could follow.[115]

Arthur St. Clair was hopeful that his own troops had been positioned for the best possible efforts, and he expected they would be able to give a good account of themselves. The Americans seemed in good spirits. By 1 July St. Clair himself did not think the invading army was particularly large because Burgoyne's flotilla standing off Three-Mile Point included only two ships, eighteen gunboats, and three sloops. But he was indeed ignorant of the full force of Burgoyne's army, which outnumbered his by more than three to one. Nor had he seen the full complement of the British lake fleet and their impressive, indeed oversized, train of artillery.[116]

Schuyler's was the more realistic assessment. Indeed, he had "great cause" to believe that the fortress would be lost because its garrison was insufficient, the fortifications were imperfect, and the troops lacked discipline. His hope was placed on reinforcements from Peekskill.[117] For the next five days until he could ride north into the field (on 7 July) the general continued the business of preparations at Albany.

During the first week of July 1777 as he observed the enemy's campaign develop "in every quarter" of his department, Schuyler impatiently waited for militia and Continental troops from Peekskill. But both he and St. Clair waited in vain for sufficient reinforcements that might have prevented disaster on Lake Champlain. On 3 and 4 July about eight hundred New Hampshire militia did reach St. Clair, but Schuyler continued to wait to lead Continental reinforcements north as soon as they could arrive from Peekskill. As days passed without news from Ticonderoga, Schuyler could not impute the silence to the enemy's isolation of the garrison. The fort could not, he thought, be so closely invested as to prevent messengers from leaving it, especially as lake vessels could enable them to pass by way of Skenesborough. On 3 July Schuyler wrote William Duer that the militia were on the march although they were not moving with all the speed possible. Yet he dared not call out more than half of the available forces closest at hand lest Tories take advantage of defenseless Albany environs. A fair wind on 3 July promised the arrival of sloops from Peekskill with Continentals that very day, and the general intended to lead them on; everything had been placed in readiness to do so. But the regulars did not appear, and for several days Schuyler busied himself with lesser details, such as Indian affairs and local and Continental politics. When he finally left Albany on 7 July, he was obliged to go without the long-expected reinforcements.[118]

Meantime, Ticonderoga had been evacuated the night of 5–6 July. Relief for the Americans, although it was not apparent at the time, came at the far southern reaches of the Hudson River. On 5 July Sir William Howe embarked his troops, turning his sights to Philadelphia instead of Albany. Although eighteen days elapsed before the fleet had favorable winds to move, and Sir Henry Clinton argued that Howe should first move north to assist Burgoyne, Howe set sail on 23 July, believing that Burgoyne was able to fend for himself. The most he would concede to Clinton was enough men to prevent Washington's seizure of New York City. Clinton's arguments that Washington would be freer to send relief to the American forces in the north, and that the river should be opened to British shipping, which could drive Americans from the Highland forts, all fell upon deaf ears. Admitting the validity of Clinton's warnings, Howe yet refused to act accordingly.[119]

By contrast St. Clair's decision to evacuate Ticonderoga was contrary to Schuyler's expectations and made without Schuyler's orders or direct approval save for the general agreement that had been reached on 20 June: Ticonderoga and Mount Independence must be held as long as possible, consistent with the safety of the troops and stores. But Schuyler's disappointment that St. Clair fled without a fight was by no means as great or unreasoned as that of Congress and even of officers like Washington when they first heard of the event. Although he could understand the necessity of the retreat, the Yorker was furious and vexed at rumors that he had actually ordered the move. Against other rumors that he had deliberately lost ground to the enemy, who paid him for his treason by firing silver cannon balls into his camp, Schuyler fought an almost losing battle to restore luster to his reputation thus foully tarnished.[120]

Because of the vulnerability of Ticonderoga and of Mount Independence to artillery on Sugar Loaf Hill, the question of why Schuyler and his subordinates failed to secure this prominence is really the only important one in the assessment of responsibility for Burgoyne's momentary success. The possible threat had been noted a year earlier by Horatio Gates and Col. John Trumbull, who proved that a cannon shot could reach the fort from the hill. In May 1777 Thaddeus Kosciuszko reported the possibility of placing cannon there, but Gates had done nothing about it before Schuyler resumed command of the department.[121] Burgoyne's guns may not have been "powerful or accurate enough to render" Ticonderoga indefensible, but "they threatened the bridge; they could destroy the boats brought up to evacuate the garrison; they could undermine the morale of the defenders."[122] After Schuyler resumed command there had been neither time nor manpower with which to grapple with all the work of improving and defending extensive fortifications, nor artillery enough for both Sugar Loaf Hill and Mount Independence. And he insisted that without orders from Congress for dividing forces between Ticonderoga and Fort George, "he dare not take on himself the responsibility of a measure which would excite a great outcry." Similarly, the variety of options like mounting cannon on Sugar Loaf Hill, which Congress had not ordered, and the strengthening of Ticonderoga, which it had specifically directed Schuyler to hold, was in fact not wide. And if the wrong choice had been made, it was nonetheless taken with a view of holding off the invaders by blocking their passage between Mount Independence and Ticonderoga within the limits of both time and means. The mounting of artillery on Mount Defiance was no threat to the fort but to St. Clair's line of retreat; the distance would have inhibited the effectiveness of artillery fire. More important probably was the enemy's ability to cannonade Ticonderoga and Mount Independence from closer ranges. And finally it must be noted that practically no one had seriously imagined that an enemy *would* attempt to drag artillery up the hill's steep and heavily wooded slopes. The stand at Mount Independence, James Wilkinson decided, was a "desperate game played for popular applause, without a trump in hand . . . and the losers were left without the consoling reflection that they had exercised their best judgment."[123] All criticism notwithstanding, while Horatio Gates had been left in charge of Schuyler's department earlier in the spring, he had displayed less energy and initiative to prevent the reverses now suffered than either Arthur St. Clair or Philip Schuyler.

Knowing that he could save his character by sacrificing the army to bloody honors, St. Clair decided, according to James Wilkinson, that were he to do so, he "should forfeit that which the world could not restore, and that which it cannot take away, the approbation of" his "own conscience." Neither he nor Schuyler were practitioners of the art of popularity. Moreover, St. Clair had less than a fourth of the troops required (ten thousand) to hold both Ticonderoga and its outlying works. His strength in relation to that of the British was only half. If he tried to hold Ticonderoga, the enemy could cut him off from routes of withdrawal and supply, for Brig. Gen. Simon Fraser, outflanking the fort on the west, could block the route to Lake George. And Gen. Friedrich von Riedesel on the east side of Lake Champlain outflanked Mount Independence and blocked the route to Skenesborough along the Hubbardton road and the Lake Champlain narrows, which lay just south of Mount Independence. Fortunately for St. Clair, von Riedesel was delayed because the swampiness around East Creek and his soldiers' heavy uniforms and equipment slowed their movement. Finally, Burgoyne's artillery was vastly superior to St. Clair's. And with 128 cannon, howitzers, and mortars for approximately seven thousand British and German troops, the British commander far exceeded the normal ratio of about 100 guns per ten thousand troops.[124]

The British, although experiencing difficulty with their gunboats and other vessels in passing the bridge between Ticonderoga and Mount Independence, broke through to pursue the Americans by South Bay within three miles of Skenesborough. St. Clair moved quickly to avoid being cut off.

Burgoyne may have erred by failing to return to Ticonderoga to move his forces south by water; instead he continued overland from Skenesborough to Fort Edward, which was a distance of only twenty-three miles but one that covered territory that was difficult to traverse because of marshes, streams, and a dense forest of pine, spruce, and sycamore. Schuyler seized the advantage of the time and terrain to throw further blocks into Burgoyne's path, forcing the British to labor twenty-four days to traverse the twenty-three miles. Perhaps Burgoyne further erred by failing to rush a lightly equipped column to seize Fort Edward before it could be utilized as a rendezvous point for the rebels. But he was determined to move only as fast as his baggage, supplies, and equipment could be kept close in train. Having suffered heavy casualties at Hubbarton, even his light infantry needed rest and supplies.[125]

As St. Clair began his retreat, Schuyler had not been able to leave Albany as he had intended. Reinforcements from Peekskill still had not appeared, and the general continued preparations for forwarding provisions to Ticonderoga and for an impending conference with the Iroquois. By 6 July Schuyler decided he could tarry at Albany no longer, and he prepared orders for Brig. Gen. John Nixon when he should reach the city with reinforcements to collect ammunition from the storekeeper, apply to the deputy quartermaster general for bateaux or carriages, and march his men as rapidly as possible. Schuyler did not know that Washington had ordered but a portion of Nixon's brigade from Peekskill to his relief. The commander in chief could spare no more troops but hoped that Schuyler would have adequate manpower to prevent the loss of Ticonderoga. With Howe's army on Staten Island preparing for embarkation, Washington could but wonder at its destination.[126]

Retreat and Retribution

1

"in high spirits and ... hoping for the best"

*A*t dawn on 7 July, Schuyler hurriedly prepared to leave Albany. At about five in the morning an express messenger reached him with news of St. Clair's evacuation of Ticonderoga and of the progress of his retreat to Skenesborough. Immediately the general posted orders that St. Clair scatter detachments of his troops throughout the countryside to evacuate all inhabitants north and northeast of that settlement. Their livestock and wheeled carriages must also be brought off or destroyed. By eight o'clock Schuyler had mounted his horse to ride off once more from the comfort of his wife and home. A full month of ceaseless movement awaited him in the field. His first day's hard journey carried him about forty-five miles to Fort Edward with stops at Stillwater and his Saratoga estate. At Stillwater he decided to send word to Lt. Col. Richard Varick to assist the quartermaster in all his business and to inform General Nixon of the urgency of moving his troops on to Albany and beyond.[1]

Pausing briefly at Stillwater, Schuyler posted dispatches to Washington and Pierre Van Cortlandt of the New York State Council of Safety. Having received messages from Gen. Ebenezer Learned as well as St. Clair, Schuyler naturally pressed once more for the militia to be rushed north from all quarters. For the moment Schuyler's own power to resist the British pursuit of St. Clair was limited to about seven hundred Continentals and no more than fourteen hundred militia, a few small field-pieces, and artillery insufficient to arm the two schooners on Lake George. Expecting that all of St. Clair's artillery had been abandoned, he warned Washington that the area north of Albany would soon be under the invader's sway unless he was speedily reinforced; again he urged that the New York council of safety or some of its members come to Albany to support him.[2]

Once Schuyler had managed to reach his Saratoga house, he paused long enough to consult his overseer John Graham and to post more messages to St. Clair and Washington. His mind must have teemed with plans for action as he rode. Graham had only just written that the garden was so overrun with weeds that he would "be sorry the Genl or maddam Should see it till such times as we have it in better order." Schuyler managed to sort out Graham's affairs as he put his secretary, John Lansing, Jr., to work dashing off a variety of orders and letters. Bearing directions to take post in the vicinity of Fort Edward and Fort George, a messenger was sent to find General St. Clair; a stand must be made against the enemy. Perhaps Nixon's brigade would come forward in time if it could but reach Albany that evening, as Schuyler still hoped. Penning other orders to the Albany public storekeeper Philip Van Rensselaer, Lansing demanded that he employ all available hands to make musket balls and send them to Schuyler with stocks of cartridge paper and thread. An Ensign Sharp was sent with a party of men to guard provisions at McLarin's mill at Saratoga Falls.[3]

Having met Lt. Col. Udny Hay, deputy quartermaster general, between Stillwater and Saratoga, Schuyler gleaned more particular news to relay to Washington. Colonel Long with some six hundred men, including the sick, had moved over the waters of Lake Champlain and were overtaken before reaching Skenesborough. They abandoned their craft and ammunition in order to hasten to Fort Ann. St. Clair's whereabouts was still unknown, although Hay thought he would move his men by way of Skenesborough and would encounter the enemy there. Schuyler had hurried orders to St. Clair to march toward Fort Edward, but he did not yet know exactly where he would attempt a stand; that depended upon the enemy's route of march. With little prospect of preventing Burgoyne's further penetration with a well-equipped army now flushed with victory, Schuyler insisted that Washington send him more help than Nixon's brigade.[4]

On 10 July Washington answered the first of the Yorker's 7 July letters without offering much encouragement. The commander in chief thought that Schuyler's news from General Learned was insufficient ground for fear; had not Schuyler construed Learned's message about the prospects of Burgoyne overtaking St. Clair more unfavorably than it warranted? Was it not a reference to a mere misfortune to Seth Warner's men instead of to a total defeat of St. Clair's army? Washington promised that Nixon's brigade, replete with artillery, would reach Albany by 15 July. Presuming that Howe and Burgoyne intended to cooperate from opposite ends of the Hudson, he also promised to move the main army toward Peekskill in readiness to act. If the worst had happened to St. Clair, Schuyler would be able to maneuver with the militia and Nixon's brigade on the south side of Lake George and still assist Washington in checking the enemy.[5]

Then on 12 July, after moving from Morristown to Pompton Plains, Washington responded to the second of Schuyler's 7 July messages. He would suspend judgment upon the "very extraordinary" surrender of Ticonderoga until he heard from St. Clair, but "in truth, it is altogether unaccountable," he wrote. He also was unable to meet all of Schuyler's demands for tents and a variety of other equipment. And more reinforcements were out of the question. Washington could not spare a man lest Howe's forces disembark and catch him unawares. At best he could promise that if St. Clair's forces had been lost, Brig. Gen. John Glover's Massachusetts Continentals would be ordered north from Peekskill. Otherwise Washington expected Schuyler to have enough men to stop Burgoyne's advance.[6]

The commander in chief may have made the best decision to fit his own circumstances, but it proved to be a disastrous one for Philip Schuyler's. And even on 22 July, when at long last Washington decided to send General Glover's brigade (although St. Clair's army had not been lost!), the Virginian's support of the northern commander was too late to prevent further retreat. Glover's thirteen-hundred-man brigade did not reach Albany until 27 July, and by then Schuyler had been obliged to fall back from Fort Edward to Moses Creek, and, on 31 July, to Saratoga.

Occupying the territory around Fort Edward between 7 and 23 July, Schuyler attempted to rally St. Clair's men and other reinforcements while stretching every nerve to improve his position with still more manpower and other maneuvers. With but a mere six-to-seven hundred Continental troops and fourteen hundred militia as against an enemy three times as numerous and only twenty-three miles away, Schuyler did not succumb to despair, nor did he lose his head. The hope of Nixon's brigade as reinforcements, the militia, and St. Clair's arrival would enable him "to do a little more than merely keep [the British] at Bay." The Yorker also hurried Col. Robert Van Rensselaer and a detachment of New York militia to Fort Ann to the rescue of Col. Pierce Long, whose New Hampshire militia were accompanying the sick from Ticonderoga separately from St. Clair. Schuyler finally received a message from St. Clair at about ten o'clock on the morning of 10 July. The retreating general was then about fifty miles east of Fort Edward, but Schuyler feared he might lead his men toward Bennington instead of toward the fort.[7]

Between 8 and 12 July the Yorker's army grew as reinforcements joined him at Fort Edward. Beginning with approximately 2,100 militia and Continentals, his ranks expanded with St. Clair's remaining 1,700 men and Nixon's brigade of almost 600. After Ten Broeck's 1,600-odd Albany County militia were added on 18 July, a "return" of the troops at Fort Edward registered a total of 6,359 (2,434 militia and 3,925 Continentals); but only 4,467 of these were fit for duty (1,625 militia and 2,842 Continentals). Thereafter desertions reduced his ranks until the end of the month, when Col. Seth Warner brought in about 800 Hampshire Grants men and John Glover's Continental Brigade of 1,300 reached Albany.[8]

Having finally pulled back from Fort Edward to Moses Creek on 23–24 July, Schuyler painted a discouraging picture of his forces for the governor of Connecticut: a third of his 2,700 Continentals were old men, boys, and Negroes who were poorly armed, almost naked, and mostly sick, and he thought them a perfect disgrace to the army. General Ten Broeck's Albany County militia now were reduced to about 1,050. It was not surprising, therefore, that the general begged Governor Trumbull and Massachusetts authorities for fresh levies. Asking Trumbull for at least 2,000, he admitted that desertions and failures to augment his army were prompted by a variety of difficulties: the spreading clamor against the loss of Ticonderoga and other retreats; accusations that he had sent too many provisions to Ticonderoga, where they had been lost to the enemy; and the dismounting of cannon and their replacement with light field-pieces. Moreover, every act seemed to Schuyler to be employed to destroy confidence in his generalship.[9]

The critical situation confronting the general, however, was offset by a fatal mistake of John Burgoyne, which testified not only to the Briton's generalship but also to Schuyler's. Having "advanced to Fort Ann in pursuit of Long's men fleeing Skenesborough," the British failed to occupy the post. Instead, Burgoyne ordered his forces back to Skenesborough, and the "military vacuum this maneuver created allowed the Americans to destroy the road" between Skenesborough and Fort Edward within a few days. Schuyler seized the initiative to begin the destruction when Burgoyne did not press "his initial advantage with the vital road clear and open, Wood Creek unimpeded, and the disorganized and demoralized Americans running before him."[10] With alacrity and foresight the patriot commander systematically slowed Burgoyne's subsequent advance, deliberately buying time to reorganize and augment his army. The

Yorker could not have done so had Burgoyne's forces not retired from Fort Ann, and of course this last-ditch effort of Schuyler did not occur until after the British fell back to Skenesborough. But the effort that he did make was of vital significance to the ultimate outcome of the entire campaign.

Fortunately for the Americans, Burgoyne pressed his invasion slowly for several reasons, not least of which was Schuyler's effective campaign of blocking his path with the aid of nature. Spring rains had swollen the swamps and streams, the forest was heavy, and roads and bridges were easily ruined. The Yorker's general orders for 9 July directed a thousand men of John Fellows's brigade and of the New York militia to parade at 8:00 A.M., armed with felling axes. North of Fort Edward they sent trees crashing down in tangles across the roadways, broke up bridges, diverted streams, and impeded the invader's paths with water and boulders. In contrast, Burgoyne did not bother to thrust forward with a flying column to force his adversary to retreat faster and farther. Schuyler, however, followed the important dictum of the great Clausewitz: "all time not turned to account serves the defense." And he also made certain that crops were burned and that livestock which the British might otherwise employ for their own sustenance were driven beyond their reach. So effective were these tactics that Burgoyne was unable to reach Fort Edward for over three weeks, taking twenty-four days to cover twenty-three miles. And five days after he arrived there (on 29-30 July) he also learned the disappointing news that Howe was not advancing to meet or even assist him but had set out for Philadelphia instead. All in all, Burgoyne's delay impaired the effect of his victory at Ticonderoga, and more than anything else he did it "laid the foundation of his ultimate failure." Conversely, Schuyler's responsibility for seizing the advantage and buying time for his own army made him the leader most responsible for the ultimate American success at Saratoga.[11]

In the meantime, the Yorker spent day after day in much anxiety. The pressures never paralyzed him, and the variety of his effort never ceased. Although critics have often argued that his military abilities were limited to those of a good quartermaster or commissary, Schuyler was adept at tactics and strategy, and the record of his performance suggests that his generalship was markedly better than what has usually been credited to him. The flow of messages to and from his subordinates and superiors testifies to his energy and ability, not to failure or limitation. Above all, the American cause "at the lowest point of despair, was upheld by" Schuyler's firmness.[12] Whatever may be said of his faults and failings, it is difficult to argue that he could have performed more nobly or effectively.

On 8–9 July Schuyler repeatedly called on St. Clair to hasten to Fort Ann or Fort Edward; already some of the enemy were probing the lines at Fort Ann. Colonel Warner's regiment, he advised, should be left on the Hampshire Grants to drive cattle and carriages away from the British and to destroy what could not be removed. General Nixon was likewise repeatedly urged to hasten his march north to Fort Edward. And in ordering Nicholas Herkimer to clear the road between Fort Dayton and Fort Schuyler of timber and to augment Colonel Gansevoort's garrison at Fort Schuyler, the general had not forgotten the British threat that he expected would come along the Mohawk.[13]

Deputy quartermaster and commissary generals were expected speedily to supply carpenters and carpenters' tools to replace those lost by St. Clair's retreat, as well as carriages, meat and fat cattle, and ammunition. Turning his attention to Fort George, Schuyler likewise ordered the commander there, Maj. Christopher Yates, to remove stocks of gunpowder and musket balls to Fort Edward, retaining only enough for his small garrison and the guns of the schooner on Lake George. Spare cannon, entrenching tools, salt, flour, and rum were also to be moved. As soon as St. Clair's men reached Fort Edward, he would send reinforcements to Fort George. But Schuyler warned Yates that if the enemy should approach his post with overwhelming strength, Yates must abandon it, bringing away all the provisions and equipment he could carry. The rest, together with the buildings, must be destroyed, and above all the cannon and tents must not be lost. "Keep the Contents" of this letter "a profound secret," Schuyler cautioned, "for fear of Dispiriting the Troops."[14]

The general's warning about dispiriting the troops pointed to a serious problem—one so explosive in fact that its growing magnitude ultimately was an excuse, if not a real justification, to remove him from command of the army early in August. In the first place, the popular as well as private and official response to the loss of Ticonderoga was one of dismay and great wonderment. Who ordered it? Why had St. Clair fled without resistance? Was not Ticonderoga nearly impregnable? Why were so many provisions stocked in the fort and then left to fall into enemy hands? Such questions led to suspicions of the loyalty and competence of both Schuyler and St. Clair.

Schuyler was chagrined by some of the answers that began to circulate no less than he was first disturbed about St. Clair's moves and infuriated by actions like Col. Long's. On the night of 8–9 July, in direct violation of the General's orders and despite his own success in repulsing an enemy party there, he evacuated Fort Ann. To the rumor then spreading "in the Country" that he had ordered the evacuation of posts above Fort Edward,

Schuyler retorted that none of his letters carried so much as a hint to support such a notion. Denying that he had even hinted that St. Clair might evacuate his position, he insisted that his last two letters never reached St. Clair but had been returned to him. The missives were directly "repugnant" to the orders Schuyler was "so unjustly accused" of giving. And he expected his correspondents to help dispel the falsehood of popular rumors to the contrary. It was St. Clair's council of officers who had finally decided to retreat, and Schuyler still was uninformed of their reasons for doing so.[15] Schuyler persisted in hoping that St. Clair could help him prevent Burgoyne from reaching Albany, and that is precisely what he finally accomplished. For the moment, however, militia deserted almost as rapidly as they reached him. And repeatedly Schuyler carped in his letters, as he did in one to Washington on 9 July, that "what adds to my distress, is, that a report prevails that I had given orders for the evacuation of Ticonderoga." Also bothersome was a proclamation just circulated by Burgoyne.[16] It was an invitation to inhabitants of towns like Castleton, Hubbardton, and Rutland, and neighboring districts along White Creek to send deputations to meet Col. Philip Skene at Castleton on 15 July or risk military execution. Evidently the invader intended to intimidate settlers to declare loyalty to the Crown.

To counteract Burgoyne's proclamation Schuyler issued a manifesto of his own. Announcing how the enemy had barbarously treated Jersey people by burning, pillaging, butchering, and ravishing them, Schuyler asserted that Providence had enabled the patriots to drive the British from New Jersey, thus leaving Loyalists to the mercy of a new occupation army. The same fate could befall New York frontiersmen if they assisted Burgoyne's forces, he warned; all civil and military officers had been ordered to apprehend traitors and to march them to his army for reprisal.[17]

Washington's response to Schuyler's report of 9 July was merely to notify him of orders that had been issued for forty barrels of powder and lead to be sent from Peekskill. Washington found it to be "astonishing beyond expression" that Schuyler had heard nothing of St. Clair, and "it even baffles conjecture," he wrote. But the commander in chief offered no further reinforcements; John Glover's brigade would not be sent from Peekskill unless St. Clair's forces had been already lost to Burgoyne. Yet the Virginian continued to hope that Schuyler would leave nothing undone to check the enemy.[18]

Washington's hope was not misplaced, and it is difficult to detect anything left undone by Schuyler in the work of stopping the invader. "If the Enemy gives us a little time," he wrote on 10 July, and "I am joined by General St. Clair they will not see Albany this Campaign." Again and again Schuyler fired off orders to General Nixon to hurry his lagging reinforcements forward; they must march night and day to reach Fort Edward. Having an inadequate force himself, Schuyler had no Continentals to spare the Tryon County committees of safety. Trying to allay their fears, he told the westerners, "For God's Sake, do not forget that you are an Overmatch for any Force the Enemy can bring against you, if you will act with Spirit." Similarly, the general asked Abraham Ten Broeck of the Albany County militia to encourage the Schoharie committee. Unable yet to spare any troops for their assistance either, Schuyler suggested that the people of Schoharie take the initiative, seize Tories, and so remove one source of their difficulties. Having managed to collect about forty pieces of cannon and fifteen tons of powder at Fort Edward, he asked Ten Broeck for wagons to carry the unmounted artillery to Saratoga, where carriages could be made for them. Ship carpenters were removed from Lake George and sent to his country house to help fashion the gun carriages. Offering the use of his mills to cut the necessary oak timber if none other was in stock nor could be pulled off the covered bridge at Saratoga, Schuyler stipulated that wagon wheels be used for the carriages, and that blacksmiths forge the ironwork.[19]

Again reporting his activities to Washington on 10 July, Schuyler announced that he had just received the first word that St. Clair had sent in several days. He not only feared that St. Clair would have no more than a thousand men left, but that they would be marched to Bennington instead of to Fort Edward. And he began to expect that Nixon would bring fewer than a thousand Continentals. Therefore, the general's force would be less than four thousand, including about a thousand militia. General Fellows, with a small body of the latter, was breaking up the road between Fort Ann and Fort Edward. While keeping Fellows busy felling trees, collecting livestock, and posting scouts, Schuyler promised to reinforce his party with some of Nixon's brigade after it reached his headquarters.[20]

Washington was no less relieved than Schuyler to discover that St. Clair's men had not been captured, but despite the gloomy appearances of the northern situation, the commander in chief offered no further help. Persisting in hope that a spirited opposition would stop Burgoyne, Washington cautioned against despair; dismal prospects had been dispelled before. In light of the lingering uncertainty of operations, Schuyler should send all available river craft to New Windsor and Fishkill, there to be ready to move troops up the Hudson if necessary. Speculating also about the necessity of evacuating Fort George, as Schuyler was preparing to do, Washington noted that some of his officers seemed to think that the fort was too important and defensible to abandon. But whatever the possibilities, the Virginian could only trust Schuyler to do his best and take the most appropriate actions.[21] Seldom presumptuous in giving the Yorker particular directions, Washington sometimes offered gratuitous advice, and occasionally it was actually unsuitable to the conditions with which Schuyler had far better knowledge and wit to deal.

Meantime, to offset the dangerous intimations of Schuyler's incompetence and disloyalty—for even officers like Nathanael Greene and Alexander Hamilton questioned the loss of Ticonderoga—a few friends like John Jay spoke out to defend Schuyler's generalship. "The stroke at Ticonderoga is heavy, unexpected and unaccountable," Hamilton wrote to Jay. If the fort was untenable, why had this not been discovered earlier and remedied? If tenable, what in the name of common sense could have prompted the evacuation? Armed cowardice or treachery? "All is mystery and dark beyond conjecture," he wrote.[22]

Even before Jay had received Hamilton's missive, the New York Council of State had taken steps to publicize their confidence in their fellow countryman. "The Evacuation of Ticonderoga appears to the Council [to be] highly reprehensible, and it gives them great pain to find that a measure so absurd & probably criminal should be imputed to the Direction of General Schuyler in whose Zeal vigilance & Integrity the Council repose the highest confidence." And Jay urged Schuyler, "Let not the hasty Suspicions of the ignorant or the malicious Insinuations of the wicked, discompose you. The best & greatest Men in all Ages have met with the like hate, and gloriously risen superior to Calumny." Moreover, the New York State Council of Safety made it clear to New Hampshire authorities that the "alarming and critical" condition of Schuyler's array was partly due to their own inability to supply much aid because troops were assigned to check revolt in three counties and to defend others against British incursions from the lower Hudson.[23]

While military reverses bred suspicion and calumny, Northern Department headquarters at Ford Edward continued to hum with activity. Schuyler's secretary and aide-de-camp received the steady flow of his directions. In Albany another aide, Richard Varick, found that offering his services to the quartermaster general Morgan Lewis was coolly received, perhaps because Lewis took it as a reflection upon his own capacities. Mrs. Schuyler and her family were more receptive to Varick's attempts to cheer and help them in their distressing business of packing belongings. Should the British invasion reach Albany from the south, everything would be ready to move from their grasp. Everyone in the city was alarmed by rumors of British approaches up the Hudson and also from the west.[24]

With the appearance of Arthur St. Clair's and John Nixon's forces at Fort Edward on 12 July, Schuyler quickly integrated them into his preparations for Burgoyne's approach. St. Clair's men were posted at Fort Miller. John Patterson's Massachusetts Continentals were to guard William Duer's house at Fort Miller, while John Nixon's were moved north to Fort Ann, where they could scout the size of Burgoyne's forces. Schuyler also directed Nixon to burn all sawmills and to fell trees into Wood Creek. If the enemy forced the patriots to retire, he must also cover their retreat and destroy all bridges. Finally, John Fellows's Massachusetts militia was annexed to Nixon's brigade.[25]

Gradually placing matters at Fort Edward "in tolerable train," Schuyler expected to save everything that had been stored at Fort George if only a hundred wagons could be collected there within two days. Necessity seemed to oblige the enemy to delay, and that would ultimately help the army to prevent their penetration further southward. "Notwithstanding the variety of cares" that engrossed his attention, Schuyler claimed to be in high spirits. Almost exultantly he thanked God for "full health, hoping for the best and not doubting but that our affairs will soon wear a better face and take a more favourable turn and in the fullest confidence that America cannot be conquered by Brittain [sic], why should we dispond?"[26]

2

"If we act vigorously we save the country"

Burgoyne remained at so great a distance for so long that it was difficult for American scouts to discover his army's strength, especially while it was not strung out or observable in separate parts along a line of march. On 13 July Schuyler's aide, Henry Brockholst Livingston, indicated that there had been no signs of enemy scouts probing the patriots' positions. Vigilance, however, was maintained constantly against surprises. Until 24 July Burgoyne's main army remained at Skenesborough, awaiting the collection of provisions, bateaux, and gunboats at Lake George before pushing on to Fort Edward. A number of Loyalists came to his aid in clearing roads and bridges that Schuyler's axmen had so rapidly blocked or ruined.[27]

While collecting his army at Fort Edward, Schuyler found his men's spirits recovering despite desertions and their lack of almost everything but provisions. His whole strength, he told Gen. William Heath in mid-July, was not more than 4,400, including Nixon's brigade, which consisted of but 575 effective rank and file. His usable artillery consisted of two iron fieldpieces, and ammunition supplies were down to fifteen reams of cartridge paper and less than three tons of lead. Accordingly, he appealed to Heath for "whatever you can think of for an army," especially blankets, camp kettles, arms, flints, clothes of all kinds, rum, coffee, chocolate, sugar, and axes. With advanced posts at Fort George and Fort Ann, Schuyler considered his rear and proceeded to plan for a fallback four miles south at Moses Creek.[28]

On 14 July the Yorker ordered Enoch Poor to march his brigade to a point where Col. Thaddeus "Kuskusko" would direct their construction of fascines and other entrenchments. Other units were directed to keep watch against enemy approaches at Lake George and along White Creek.[29]

Having sent word to commissary Cuyler and others to hasten the cattle being driven to Fort Edward, where the army needed fresh meat, Schuyler again considered the western flank of his department. To Major Badlam at Fort Dayton he wrote, advising the officer to counsel with the Tryon County committee about the best defensive position to take in the Mohawk valley. Pausing briefly from his official correspondence and other labors on 14 July, the general set his thoughts in order for his friend and political ally, John Jay. Grateful for the state council of safety's recent expression of confidence in him, Schuyler felt himself superior to malicious enemies because he had done his duty while their calumnies would bring only shame and confusion to them. The loss of Ticonderoga, the general confided, "was an Ill judged measure not warranted by necessity, and carried Into Execution with a precipitation that could not fail of erecting the greatest panic In our troops and Inspiriting the Enemy. I am confident," he added, "that with a moderate degree of foresight and Exertion, the far greater part of valuable Stores might have been saved." Evidently not even St. Clair's arrival at Fort Edward on 12 July had yet led Schuyler to change his views of the evacuation, for he told Jay that even if it was necessary to abandon the fort, St. Clair had had reason to believe that Schuyler would reinforce him. Together they might have had an army of four to five thousand, "but let all this be *Entre nous,*" he wrote. Also disdaining George Clinton's gubernatorial election, Schuyler hoped that Clinton's victory would not cause any divisions among patriots. "Altho his family & Connections do not Intitle him to so distinguished a predominence yet he is virtuous and loves his Country, has abilities and is brave, and [I] hope he will experience from Every patriot what I am resolved he shall have from me, Support, Countenance & Comfort."[30]

In a letter thanking the state council of safety for their support, Schuyler further noted that his general officers had unanimously agreed that he was not responsible for the loss of Ticonderoga; if the evacuation were deemed reprehensible, "they only [were] guilty," for the Yorker had given no order for it.[31]

Meantime, the New York Provincial Convention, still in office until the newly elected state legislature could replace it, had assigned Gouverneur Morris and Abraham Yates to investigate Schuyler's command. From Albany on 14 July, Morris was able to report only rumors of the enemy's attacks on St. Clair's retreating army and at Fort Ann, where Col. Henry Beekman Livingston's militia had twice repulsed invading parties. Detained by steady rains at Albany, Morris finally reached Fort Edward at noon on 16 July. Schuyler's command, he found, consisted of twenty-six hundred Continentals and two thousand militia, in addition to the five hundred men at Mohawk River outposts.

Like the New York convention, the Continental Congress, too, was inclined to investigate Schuyler's activities, especially the loss of Ticonderoga. President Hancock informed the general that the eastern states as well as New York authorities had been urged to send militia to both him and Washington. Copies of Schuyler's 7 and 9 July letters to Washington, reporting the loss of Ticonderoga, had reached Hancock on 13 July, and "Their interesting Contents" were to be "immediately laid before Congress." As soon as the delegates could reach a decision on these, Hancock would notify the Yorker.[32] Probably neither of the men could have suspected how outraged Congress was to be.

Riding from Albany toward Fort Edward on 14 July, Gouverneur Morris followed the tracks of Mrs. Schuyler's team and wagon closely. Accompanied by Col. Richard Varick, the general's wife reached the family estate by five thirty in the afternoon; her trip to Saratoga had begun at six in the morning. Morris and several companions arrived an hour and a half later. With her they found her youngest daughter, Cornelia, a mere year-and-a-half old, and a slave, Jenny. The other five children, Elizabeth (twenty), Margaretta (nineteen), John (twelve), Philip Jeremiah (nine), and Rensselaer (four and a half) had been left in the safety of Albany while their mother ventured into the country, probably to pack belongings for removal from danger.[33]

When Schuyler learned that his wife had reached Saratoga he was too busy to respond except by a hurried note to Varick, asking that he show her the letter. "I am In good health and good Spirits and with great hopes that the worst is passed," he wrote. "My Love to all at my house which I trust will remain so [,] Burgoyne, Howe & all their abettors not withstanding." The enemy had left Fort Ann, and Schuyler's axmen were ob-

structing their communications. Forty pieces of unmounted cannon sent
to Saratoga might well be made useful if carpenters and blacksmiths hurried to make carriages for them. The general thought Burgoyne "pretty
near the length of his Tedder,—he will not reach Albany this Campaign,"
he promised.[34]

Perhaps the general's letter reassured his wife enough so that she could
halt preparations for removing possessions from Saratoga. Or she must
not have wholly completed her work when she returned to Albany on 19
July, for she was again at the country house by 29 July. This time she was
doubtless convinced of the need to rescue her family's belongings, for she
witnessed the further retreat of her husband's army to the premises on
30 July.[35]

Although Schuyler continued to make Fort Edward his headquarters
until 23 July, he wrote Washington of the reasons that finally forced still
another withdrawal to Moses Creek. Nixon's brigade was only 575 strong;
some were mere boys, others Negroes, and some were sick and otherwise
deemed unfit to fight. In all the confusion St. Clair could only guess that
he had about 1,500 men. Colonel Warner's remnant had been ordered to
remain in Hampshire Grants territory to help militia there carry off all
cattle and carriages. Schuyler thought many inhabitants of the countryside had turned Loyalist, and Learned's and Webb's regiments of Massachusetts militia had gone home. Provisions were short, and daily rains
without shelter for the men discouraged them from staying. Despite having fifteen tons of powder, Schuyler's shortage of lead had reduced his
soldiers to but fifteen rounds of ammunition apiece. Thirty pieces of
cannon were still useless without carriages, and two fieldpieces dragged
up by General Nixon were his only artillery. Unable to obtain others from
Springfield, he begged Washington for both cannon and troops. Alarming, too, was his news that an express messenger from Burgoyne to Howe
had managed to slip through his lines, and he expected that Howe would
soon be coming up the Hudson. Four miles south of Fort Edward a likely
site for further defenses was being occupied. Schuyler would remain at
Fort Edward until Fort George had been safely emptied of men and stores,
and in the meantime Nixon's brigade and 600 militia (over 1,100 men)
were felling trees into Wood Creek and across the road between Fort Ann
and Fort Edward.[36]

When Washington replied four days later, he declined to send more
help to Schuyler except for the remainder of Nixon's brigade, for he dared
not weaken his army more. However, he promised that six tons of ball,
cartridges, and ten pieces of artillery as well as some camp kettles had
been sent to the Northern Army. No tents were available, and no partic-

ular directions were offered beyond that of safekeeping of the thirty pieces of light artillery, which lacked carriages. Again Washington trusted Schuyler simply to do his best and make a vigorous defense, but he did provide the help of an able officer by sending Benedict Arnold to the Northern Army. Congress had passed him over for promotion, but Arnold waived his claim to a rank superior to St. Clair's so that he might return to service. The energetic Yankee proved to be a welcome addition to the Yorker's staff as well as a loyal supporter.[37]

On 15 July Schuyler rushed men toward Fort George in response to an alarm that wagons evacuating the post had been attacked by enemy soldiers and Indians. Heading the relief party himself, the general received a report from Col. John Ashley, who had chased off the marauders toward South Bay, which is an extension of Lake Champlain that parallels Lake George. The Yorker then resumed his directions for the removal of the last stores from Fort George. Simultaneously he ordered Colonel Simmons to divide his militia regiment, sending four to five hundred to reinforce Seth Warner in the Hampshire Grants and the remainder to Fort Edward.[38]

Sending Warner word of his intended aid, Schuyler again urged the removal of all cattle and carriages in the Hampshire Grants from Burgoyne's grasp. Extending thanks for the brave performance of the Yankee troops at Hubbardton, Schuyler promised Warner clothes and funds. The general's message of encouragement was doubtless a calculated one, especially because Vermonters had vigorously contested New York claims to their territory. But Schuyler was no crabbed or petty localist, and his patriotic advice was anything but ill-humored or patronizing. "If we act vigorously," he wrote, "we save the country. Why should we dispond? Greater misfortunes have happened and have been retrieved. Cheer up the spirits of the people in your Quarter."[39]

While the general continued preparations to meet the approaching British thrust from the north, Nicholas Herkimer reported growing difficulties in the west. When he attempted to send two hundred of his Tryon County militia to reinforce Fort Schuyler, members of the county committee of safety interfered with their departure for fear that the diversion of troops would weaken home defenses against the "savage" allies of the British. Some settlers were abandoning their homes, others simply expected to "render themselves over to the enemy" and "think it worthless to fight ... if the County is not Succour'd with at least Fifteen hundred More Continental Troops. The loss of ... Ticonderoga & Mt. Independent [sic] made the greatest Number of our well affected Inhabitants downhearted," he wrote, "and maketh the disaffected bold with threatnings,

Fig. 5. The Plan of the Position which the Army under General Burgoyne took at Saratoga, 10 September 1777. Map by William Fadin. Courtesy, The New York State Library, Albany.

disobedient and their Number increasing." Men who had been staunch patriots had grown discouraged and suspicious that "by all Appearances, ... this River is sold alike, as Fort Ticonderoga." Thus Schuyler's problems were misunderstood and his effectiveness hindered by popular ignorance and rumormongering no less in New York State than in New England.[40]

Schuyler's first response to Herkimer's alarming report was to inform the Albany County Committee of Safety of his inability to send troops west and to ask Abraham Yates and Gouverneur Morris to inform the state convention of the urgent need to meet the growing crisis. Morris promptly reported to the state council of safety that Schuyler's strength at Fort Edward consisted of twenty-six hundred Continentals and two thousand militia, and at western posts the troops numbered about five hundred. "Excepting the General [Schuyler] and Genl. Sinclair, you have not a general officer here worth a crown," he wrote.[41]

By 18 July Schuyler concluded that he would have to divert some troops to Tryon County and decided that part of Col. James Wesson's 9th Massachusetts Regiment of Continentals, then in Albany, could be ordered west. Except for thirty men to guard his Albany house, Schuyler sent Wesson's regiment to German Flats, where he might be able to respond to calls from several directions. If Colonel Gansevoort discovered an enemy approach that endangered Fort Schuyler, Wesson must hasten there to assist him. Schuyler speeded word to General Herkimer, too, urging him to revive the Tryon County people's spirits with news of Continental reinforcements. Better morale would save the westerners from danger that he deemed still "inconsiderable."[42]

If Schuyler believed what he told Herkimer about the prospect of an invasion from the west, he was, however, not blind to the threat. His main concern was, properly enough, to deal with Burgoyne, whose presence was immediate and indisputable, whereas an enemy force from the western lakes might be confronted when it had clearly become more immanently dangerous. The general simply had more time to prepare for that eventuality than he could spare from his present task at Fort Edward.[43] And it was early August before enemy forces under Col. Barry St. Leger finally menaced Fort Schuyler and Oriskany.

Meantime, the committee from the New York State Council of Safety visiting Fort Edward observed Schuyler's constant movement as he traversed the countryside and prepared his defenses. The general hedged against the possible loss of ground by preparing works four miles south at Moses Creek. There Col. Thaddeus Kosciuszko was directed to position generals Roche de Fermoy's and John Patterson's brigades as he saw fit. The Polish patriot proved his engineering skills at various places between Ticonderoga and the mouth of the Mohawk as Schuyler's army repeatedly established defenses against the invaders. Upon hearing that New Hampshire militia were en route to Fort Edward, Schuyler ordered them east on 16 July to assist Colonel Warner instead. Despite his own need of reinforcements, the general decided that it was more dangerous to expose New Hampshire to the enemy and that Warner must be assisted if he was to attack them or at least rescue patriots and capture defectors from Burgoyne's line of march. The time had also come for Schuyler's order for the garrison at Fort George to escape.[44]

Schuyler issued general orders for 17 July from Saratoga as his headquarters moved with him. Doubtless his quick ride from Fort Edward enabled him to see his wife before she returned to Albany, but his main business was to inspect the progress of artificers who were constructing gun carriages. Disturbed by news that Col. Seth Warner was so ill supported that he was obliged to avoid an encounter with a small body of the enemy, Schuyler issued instructions to colonels Robinson and Williams to lead their Massachusetts militia toward Bennington. Such militia as had not yet marched or arrived at Albany and those who were north of the city must also reinforce Warner. A hundred of the militia then moving north must stop when they reached Saratoga and await further orders.[45]

Before returning to Fort Edward on 18 July, the general hurried off a seven-page answer to the commander in chief's letter of 15 July. Having received Washington's missive at three o'clock in the morning, Schuyler took further pains to explain the controversial loss of Ticonderoga. By now the Virginian must have received other evidence of the reasons for evacuation. Schuyler admitted his earlier mistake in estimating St. Clair's numbers at fifty-five hundred instead of something above two thousand. And the commissary's returns had been "fallacious" in suggesting that a greater supply of provisions had been laid in than was the case. But to Washington's officers, who claimed to have seen Fort George and deemed it defensible, Schuyler sharply retorted that if they had been there, "they were blind" or they had forgotten that it was merely part of an unfinished bastion of an intended fortification! If Washington or his subordinates imagined that Burgoyne could be lured into following a more circuitous route southward, Schuyler wished to know what that could be. Noting that all distances between the British and Fort George were but twelve to fifteen miles, Schuyler also announced that no batteries could be raised on the lake without artillery. Advising the commander in chief to relay this intelligence to Congress, the general wished them to be prepared should "the same ingenious Gentlemen give that respectable Body the same Information, they have presumed to afford you." Finally, Schuyler lamented that although rumors that he had ordered the evacuation of Ticonderoga were largely stopped, he was now being accused of having "at least connived at it." But he was resolved to carry on, "smiling with Contempt on the Malice of my Enemies; doing my Duty, and attempting to deserve your Esteem."[46]

When Washington replied, he did so with little challenge to Schuyler's remonstrance and complaint. In the first of two letters sent on 22 July the Virginian expressed pleasure that Schuyler had discovered better ground for making a stand at Moses Creek than doing so farther north. Attacking Burgoyne's detachments seemed the best course of checking the British advance. As for Howe's conduct, Washington professed puzzlement and embarrassment; ships moved up and then down the Hudson as if to suggest indecision about aiding Burgoyne. While proposing that Schuyler not place too much confidence in constructing defenses on Moses Creek lest they become a kind of trap for his own army (unless they were placed at passes that the enemy could not avoid), Washington exhorted Schuyler to prevent popular defections to the invaders and advised that there was no need to send Congress reasons for the evacuation of Fort George!

The second of Washington's 22 July letters revealed a change of mind that must have been as encouraging to Schuyler as it was too late to prevent yet another retreat of the Northern Army. The commander in chief decided to send him further reinforcements consisting of Glover's thirteen-hundred-man brigade from Peekskill.[47] But only reluctantly had he given way to Schuyler's long-standing pleas for help. The only other reinforcements he had ordered after the fall of Ticonderoga had been the remaining part of Nixon's brigade; the first had been sent on 2 July in response to the Yorker's 28 June request.

By 22 July, the day of Benedict Arnold's arrival at Schuyler's head-quarters, members of the Continental Congress had become increasingly agitated about the Ticonderoga affair. Lacking "proper Information," John Hancock wrote that Congress regarded it nevertheless as "very mys-terious," and after beginning a letter to Schuyler on 18 July he added a postscript on 22 July. Congress had finally received a copy of Schuyler's 14 July report to Washington and a letter from St. Clair with a copy of minutes of his officers' council of war and other reasons for the evacua-tion.[48] Although these papers clearly indicated that Schuyler was not culp-able, the Yorker's enemies promptly attacked St. Clair, and within little more than a week they had proceeded to develop their opportunity to replace the New Yorker with their old favorite, Horatio Gates.

3

Patience and Fortitude

In traditionally anti-Yorker territory a train of events developed, beginning in mid-July, which soon provided substantial albeit indirect help to Philip Schuyler and his army. And it was the sort of aid, coming as it did, that proves both the baseness and falsity of the canard that Yankees would not help fight the enemy while the proud Yorker remained at the head of the army. On 18 July the New Hampshire legislature commissioned John Stark a brigadier general, making no mention of any relationship between Stark and the Northern Army *or* the Continental Congress. Stark remained hostile to Congress for passing him by in promotions made in March 1777, and he had had little confidence in Schuyler since their disagreement about the evacuation of Crown Point in 1776. But neither he nor the New Hampshire legislature failed to see the necessity of defending their territory from invaders. Nor did they refuse all action required to do so. Stark was authorized to cooperate with Seth Warner's Hampshire Grants militia, the Continental Army, and other states' troops, or to act independently, as he saw fit. Such provincialism resulted in recruitment of over four hundred men within two days and ultimately in a total of almost fifteen hundred.[49] Moreover, Schuyler's command did not prevent the cranky Stark from aiding Warner and trouncing the British at Bennington several days before Horatio Gates actually replaced the Yorker on 19 August. Nor must it be forgotten that Stark's activities began even before Congress had desposed Schuyler and before the countryside had any news that a presumably more popular idol would supersede him.

Not all of Schuyler's trouble with the militia was by any means the result of Yorker-Yankee animosity. Nor was it probably due to a popular, personal dislike of the general at all. Even fellow Yorkers would not stand fast when ripening grain and hay fields beckoned. In July the general permitted half of the Albany and Berkshire counties militia to go home for harvest in an effort to discourage others from deserting the army. He then found it necessary to beg the governor of Connecticut to send replacements. Still another difficulty with militia reliability was the popular fear of Tories that prompted militiamen to run home to defend their families and property. For such reasons eastern militia were seldom very prompt to answer Schuyler's summons to reinforce even their fellow Yankee officers like Seth Warner.[50] But New Englanders like Benedict Arnold, who joined the Yorker on 22 July, and Benjamin Lincoln, who reached him a week later, were able to offer their substantial services by leading troops who were perhaps more confident in officers of their own states or region. Provincialism had not yet yielded to national sentiment or vision.

Patience and fortitude were Schuyler's watchwords; his general orders for 19 July designated these as the day's parole and countersign respectively. Residents of the countryside north of his army were not permitted to enter his camp for fear they might be Tory spies. Col. Goose Van Schaick, who had served at Fort Dayton, was ordered to Albany to command forces there and in Tryon County. Schuyler instructed him that if any sizable enemy force was reported in the west, he must summon the militia of Schoharie, Duanesburg, Schenectady, and Tryon County and lead them out. And any Continental regiment arriving at Albany thereafter must be ordered to follow.[51]

Further readying his Fort Edward forces, Schuyler ordered conveyance of field artillery from Albany as soon as it arrived there from the lower Hudson. Attentive to Col. Kosciuszko's engineering project at Moses Creek, Schuyler sent eight carts and forty-eight oxen with drivers and an overseer to assist the Polish officer. General Learned's brigade was moved forward along the Hudson toward Lake George and General Nixon's toward Fort Ann, South Bay, and Skenesborough. These advanced units were to scout the enemy's approach and determine Burgoyne's invasion route.[52]

By 20 July a general return of the Continentals and militia under Schuyler's immediate command indicated grand totals of 3,925 Continentals and 2,434 militia. Of the Continentals in brigades led by John Nixon, Roche de Fermoy, Enoch Poor, John Patterson, and Ebenezer Learned, along with Maj. Ebenezer Stevens's artillery, there were only 2,842 present and fit for duty. Eight regiments of militia contained only 1,625 men present and fit for duty; hence, Schuyler's effective fighting force totaled little more than 4,400.[53]

Realizing too well his relatively precarious position because of the weakness of his army, the vulnerability of his Saratoga estate, and even that of his Albany house, Schuyler nevertheless remained unwavering in his devotion to the American cause. On 19 July Col. Philip Skene sent him an offer of Burgoyne's protection. Armed with Burgoyne's commission to make concessions to Americans who "wish to see themselves once more united to that Country from whence they derived their existences," Skene announced he would be happy to help accomplish "an undertaking so important and upon which, the Happiness of Thousands immediately Depend." Only hinting at the reward for Loyalism, Skene was "inclined to believe, that the prosperity, and not the distruction *[sic]* of your Country is the ultimate object of your wishes. Our former knowledge [acquaintance], and the present destracted *[sic]* state of Independency makes me extremely Desirous to converse with you upon matters of the highest consequences." Quickly rebuffing Skene, Schuyler observed that such correspondence must be conducted between commanders of the opposing forces. Or "if a Conference is desired and an Officer appointed one of mine of equal Rank will meet him."⁵⁴

Other north country inhabitants and Mohawk valley people were not so resolute as Schuyler in withstanding the threats of invaders or enemy agents' blandishments to confirm their land titles or make Vermont a British province. Still, the general's enemies continued to blame him for the loss of Ticonderoga, and some suspected him of treachery because of the want of clear evidence to the contrary. John Jay wrote Schuyler from Kingston on 21 July that his general officers were not alone the objects of suspected treachery, "it reaches you," he said. Gen. Israel Putnam at Peekskill had raised doubts and seemed not to notice the state council of safety's recent letter expressing its confidence in Schuyler. "This kind of reserve," Jay thought, "is not friendly." There were rumors that St. Clair had blustered justification for his flight by alluding to orders for it from Schuyler. Dissatisfied ships carpenters had returned from the northern lakes with complaints about the seizure of their tools on Schuyler's orders. The general's distance from Ticonderoga when the enemy approached it occasioned further suspicion. Yet Schuyler's friends were not idle in arguing on his behalf: they were quick to point out that the general could not deprive the entire department of his services by confining himself to one place, nor had he ordered or even known of St. Clair's evacuation until after it occurred. Jay suggested that subordinate officers furnish a certificate that Ticonderoga was abandoned without Schuyler's direction, advice, or knowledge, but this had in effect already been given when minutes of St. Clair's council of officers were sent to Congress. The New York State Council of Safety might also issue a statement of facts to vindicate the general, but this must be done without appearing to be a defense. Jay suspected that at least one member of the council was Schuyler's enemy, for while professing respect he had voiced a wish that Schuyler had been closer to Ticonderoga. Although not doubting the general's spirit, the unnamed councillor hoped that Schuyler would be able to justify himself. Jay urged the general to observe great caution with his letters; their contents should not be susceptible to wrong inferences. Moreover, his letters to Washington had often reached Kingston with their "flying seals" broken and bearing telltale signs of another color of wax.⁵⁵

News like Jay's offered little comfort to Schuyler. But the general neither relented in doing his duty nor relaxed his determination to obtain
vindication for his actions. In a variety of reports to Washington, the
governor of Connecticut, and to the president of New York's council of
safety he carefully explained decisions or offered counsel on matters that
might be misinterpreted or mistaken. The Yorker told Washington, for
example, of Philip Skene's overtures and of his decision to allow half the
militia to go home for harvest; again he asked for reinforcements, for his
army was inferior to Burgoyne's, and he noted that no New Hampshire
militia reinforcements had yet reached Seth Warner. Burgoyne's army was
now cutting a road from Skenesborough to Fort Ann, and they could be
expected soon to move as far as Fort Edward.

Schuyler painted no favorable picture for his correspondents when he
indicated that he now had fewer than three thousand Continental troops
to oppose an enemy whose ranks were swelling with Tories. Should the
Indians turn against the patriots, Schuyler was convinced that the difficulties would be "inextricable," yet he hoped the Iroquois would confer
with him at Albany in a week or two. If they did so, he was confident
that they could be persuaded not to join the enemy.[56]

Late in the evening of 21 July Schuyler replied to a message from General Nixon, whose regiment was positioned five miles north of Fort Edward. Sent but an hour and a half earlier, Nixon's letter indicated that a
large party of Burgoyne's army had reached Fort Ann the evening before.
Schuyler replied that if that was true, not enough scouts had been posted
for early warning, and he ordered Nixon to remedy the failing at once.
That same day Gen. Sir William Howe persisted in a fault that proved
to be far more dangerous to the British campaign than Nixon's mistake
was to the American one. Howe received the first of Burgoyne's messages
with detailed news of his capture of Ticonderoga. Expecting Burgoyne
to reap further successes, Howe refused to be diverted from his plans to
move against Philadelphia. It is difficult to avoid the conclusion that when
Howe's fleet sailed from New York City on 23 July, "the invasion from
Canada lost its last chance of success."[57]

Of course, neither Burgoyne nor Schuyler could then have imagined
how much their future would be thus affected. And as Schuyler yielded
at Fort Edward on 23 July, and then at Moses Creek (31 July), at Saratoga
(3 August), and finally at Stillwater in mid-August, the invasion from
Canada seemed anything but unsuccessful to all the contestants. The
punishments meted out in Schuyler's general orders on 22 July suggest
the infection of discontent within his army as Burgoyne inched forward.
That same evening the disappearing militia provoked Schuyler to further
alarm. His express message to Washington reported that he expected not

even five hundred of the half of the militia who had not gone home for harvest would remain within a few more days. And John Nixon's Continental brigade probably would not contain two thousand even when the last men Washington ordered from Peekskill on 18 July were added to it.[58] Nixon himself appeared to lack attentiveness. Almost frantically Schuyler ordered him to send scouts over a variety of specified routes after hearing that Nixon had failed to heed orders issued earlier. That the general characterized his subordinate's omission as merely extraordinary was in itself more than a little remarkable.

Having ordered a detachment of Continentals under Major Badlam (who earlier had been posted to the Mohawk valley) to proceed to Fort Schuyler on 21 July, Schuyler continued to make every possible attempt to assist Tryon County defenses. But the themes of disaffection, suspicion, and dismay swelled more and more as July passed into August. Everywhere there seemed to be doubts, questions, and fears more than patience, confidence, or hope. Far from the scenes of Schuyler's endeavors even the general's future son-in-law, then aide-de-camp to Washington, seemed surprised by news from the Northern Army. Alexander Hamilton found Gouveneur Morris's report that Fort Edward was indefensible contrary to the representations of some of his fellow officers who had traversed the ground. From the halls of Congress Samuel Adams voiced suspicion not only of Schuyler's and St. Clair's ability but of their loyalty.[59]

At Kingston the state council of safety recalled their committee from Schuyler's army because Gouverneur Morris and Abraham Yates, whom they had sent to confer with the general on measures for assistance, had displeased them. Yates and Morris had written a "disrespectful and unsatisfactory" letter, objecting to council demands that they discover and explain the loss of Ticonderoga. When Morris reached Kingston to report on 28 July, he completely endorsed Schuyler's call for reinforcements if Burgoyne's army was to be stopped. The militia were unreliable and restless, and little help could be expected from Loyalist territory like Gloucester, Cumberland, and Charlotte counties. Consequently, the council of safety agreed to send Morris and Jay to confer with Washington about reinforcing the Northern Army.[60]

If New York's own militia seemed unreliable in supporting the New Yorker commanding the Northern Army, it was not merely because of mistrust of Philip Schuyler. Perhaps others with whom the general was associated were more the cause of suspicion because of reasons like that given by John Chester of Wethersfield, Connecticut. News from Peekskill, he wrote, indicated that the army there "very much Resent[ed] the Conduct of the Northern Army and that the Officers all say that America must have a *Byng*." Similarly, John Adams remarked to his wife, "I think we shall never defend a post until we shoot a general"—pour encourager les autres. But Chester also revealed how fantastic rumors could be. "An Acc't came yesterday to town [Wethersfield]," he wrote, "that General Schyler was in Goal [gaol] on acc't of having Order'd Ticonderoga to be evacuated. I believe it to be false."[61] But few people proved to be as healthily skeptical as this Connecticut Yankee.

More than popular suspicion of Schuyler and discontent with his army's movement harmed the general's efforts. More than self-interested farmers who valued their harvest above their duty to the American effort caused him anxiety and even interrupted his sleep. Outright bungling, slow-moving reinforcements, and witless subordinates hampered his effectiveness. And of course malice and petty partisanship finally dictated the downfall of the man who acted so heroically to frustrate Burgoyne's campaign. A striking example of Schuyler's justifiable exasperation with stupidity is his account of the return to Fort Edward of General Fellows with some Berkshire County, Massachusetts, militia. On his way Fellows had observed the movement of Howe and Burgoyne's express messengers who exchanged missives somewhere on Livingston Manor. Instead of capturing these emissaries, Fellows sent one of his colonels on a thirty-six-mile ride to ask Schuyler what to do. Evidently wakened in the middle of the night, the general issued orders (dated 3:00 A.M., 23 July) that the officer return at once to Halfmoon, pick up the trail of one of Burgoyne's messengers who passed there the day before, and capture him.[62]

As the general reported his efforts to interrupt the Howe-Burgoyne line of communication, he told Washington that General Fellows had discovered a vital piece of information. Burgoyne's express rider had revealed to a friend of Fellows that the British invasion would indeed be made from both north *and* west, and that Howe would attempt a diversion on the eastern American coast and also send forces north to Peekskill to divide the rebels' army. Thus the Yorker would surely need more reinforcements, and he further illustrated his case by announcing that all but three hundred of the twelve hundred Berkshire militia had left his army.[63]

Washington answered the Yorker's cry of alarm with reassurances that there seemed to be no danger on the Hudson. One of Howe's letters to Burgoyne had been intercepted, but Washington suspected that it was meant to fall into his hands. In it Howe professed to be making a maneuver southward while intending to strike off toward Boston and assist Burgoyne from that quarter. Washington did not believe this because Howe had given no account of other occurrences and no date for his sailing. The Virginian made Schuyler no promises of more aid for meeting either northern or western invasions, but he expected that Gen. Benjamin Lincoln's arrival would influence the collecting and retaining of New England militia.[64]

In a previous letter, too, Washington had answered Schuyler's message of 21–22 July concerning the serious shortage of troops in the face of Burgoyne's approach. John Glover's brigade was absolutely the last of the reinforcements the Virginian said he could spare, and Glover's artillery must surely suffice. Benjamin Lincoln, whose popularity in Massachusetts would enable him to draw out the Yankee militia and keep them in the field, would soon reach Schuyler's army. Perhaps Benedict Arnold or some other sensible but energetic officer should be sent to Fort Schuyler to inspirit the westerners and cultivate the savages' inclination against a Mohawk valley invasion. Indeed, there appeared to be an increasing need for the kind of leadership in the west that Arnold could provide, and about two weeks later Schuyler sent him rushing out to rescue forces beleaguered by Barry St. Leger. Meantime, Lt. Col. Marinus Willett gave evidence of his ability to direct defenses in that quarter.[65]

Time was running out. Barry St. Leger reached Oswego on 25 July with a force of some fourteen hundred regulars, Loyalists, and Indians. The following day his expedition began to move against Fort Schuyler, where the main army arrived on 2 August. Col. John Butler with about two hundred Seneca joined them on 5 August, but by then the fort had been well provisioned to withstand a siege for six weeks; the last convoy of supplies from Schuyler was hauled inside the walls only moments before St. Leger's advance force reached the post. The British found the fort "too strong to rush, and its garrison too large to bypass."[66]

Meantime Schuyler had moved his army four miles from Fort Edward to Moses Creek on 23 July as Burgoyne's army began its approach to Fort Ann. And when the British moved closer to Fort Edward on 28 July, Schuyler again inched rearward toward his Saratoga estate. The Yorker simply was not yet certain that his army was strong enough to hold fast. At Moses Creek, for example, he reported his situation to the presidents of Massachusetts and the Continental Congress, the New York State Council of Safety, and to Chief Justice Jay, begging for reinforcements. Promising to dispute every inch of ground with Burgoyne, Schuyler also warned that he could not stop him without either Washington's reinforcements *or* a sizable militia. Unable to obtain the former, he knew not from where the latter could be had.[67]

Schuyler's report to John Hancock on 24 July rang in similar changes and also alluded to Congress's concern for Ticonderoga. Now the general warned that if another "accident" occurred, the popular outcry would doubtless be that he and his officers had an army of ten or twelve thousand and were traitors or cowards as indeed they had been charged after Ticonderoga fell. Unwilling to believe that Congress would condemn them without a hearing, Schuyler requested an inquiry for himself as soon as possible. Had he published a report of his letters to St. Clair, he could have easily exculpated himself, but he had not wished to harm the public interest by doing so.

Aside from John Jay, Schuyler expected other friends like Gouverneur Morris to defend his reputation. He begged Morris to inform the council of safety of what he had learned by visiting the army in the field. On 25 July General St. Clair obligingly wrote Jay that he, and he alone, was responsible for the decision to evacuate Ticonderoga. Claiming that the loss of the post was necessary in order to save the state, St. Clair suggested that Jay publicize his letter to convince the suspicious public that Schuyler was blameless. Jay promptly did so in Holt's *New York Journal* (on 28 July), but the gesture was not to save Schuyler from the partisans of Horatio Gates.[68]

The endless torment Schuyler suffered for his maligned reputation did not paralyze him. The press of responsibilities was more preoccupying. Within two days of Benedict Arnold's arrival at his headquarters, the general wisely divided his army. St. Clair's division embraced New York and Massachusetts brigades led by Roche de Fermoy, Enoch Poor, and John Patterson, together with any militia then with them and other militia that might arrive. Arnold's command include John Nixon's and Ebenezer Learned's Massachusetts Continental brigades and Abraham Ten Broeck's Albany County militia.[69] With these lines of command Schuyler proposed to stop the advance of John Burgoyne.

4

Two Women in the Field

The work of removing cattle and forage from the reach of the enemy also continued. Expecting his neighbors north and east of Saratoga to remove or destroy their crops and other property rather than permit the enemy to capture them, Schuyler did not exempt himself from the requirement. And a family legend traced to the general's daughter, Catherine Van Rensselaer, suggests that her father not only directed Mrs. Schuyler to fire their own wheat fields, but also that she did so with her own hands as an example to tenants and neighbors. Remarkably, too, the legend prompted one artist to commemorate the event on canvas in 1852. Better known for his portrayal entitled "Washington Crossing the Delaware," Emanuel Leutze painted "Lady Schuyler Burning Her Wheat Fields on the Approach of the British."[70]

There is no doubt that the general's wife was a woman of great spirit and determination who was perfectly capable of taking the initiative even without her husband's prompting. She had, after all, made a long and difficult trip through the wilderness to reach Ticonderoga in September 1775, where she nursed him back to health from a violent attack of fever and gout. And the running of a large household of children, slaves, and servants suggests that she was more than equal to the task of destroying the crops.

Mrs. Schuyler visited Saratoga at least twice in July 1777. The first trip took place between 14 and 19 July, and it was a twelve-hour ride by wagon. Evidently she returned to Albany without finishing her work of packing the furnishings of the country house. Again she traversed the thirty-six miles between her Albany and Saratoga houses sometime before 29 July, perhaps in the company of Gen. Benjamin Lincoln, who rode on to meet her husband at Fort Miller. A formidable collector of gossip, William Smith, Jr., noted in his journal on 24 July that while the people of Albany were bracing themselves against a possible invasion of their city, it seemed "unusual" that Schuyler's family were going to Saratoga. Perhaps it was a gesture of confidence to animate the populace, but Smith noted that it was interpreted otherwise by some people who alleged that Schuyler would throw himself, his family, and the army upon the mercy of John Burgoyne! Popular criticism of the military desolation of the countryside had also arisen, and Schuyler was blamed for that as well, although he issued certificates whereby farmers could later claim reimbursement for their losses.[71]

Faced with the ultimate necessity of losing much of his own property at Saratoga, Schuyler did no more than flinch at the sacrifice. But there is no really satisfactory evidence that Mrs. Schuyler did fire the ripening wheat fields on their country estate. Instead, the general's directions to Col. Udny Hay, deputy quartermaster general, on 28 July suggest that he wished to save his crops for the use of his army, and that it is unlikely that much if any of his wheat was destroyed by Mrs. Schuyler's torch or anybody else's.[72]

Whether the emergency harvesting was accomplished is not certain. Thomas Anbury reported that when Burgoyne's forces camped on the "plains of Saratoga" as late as 13 September, "great quantities of fine wheat" were found and "also Indian corn," which fed the British and their horses.[73] So Mrs. Schuyler's activities at Saratoga probably had little to do with destroying crops. Aside from packing furnishings in preparation to move, she took care to send food and drink and fresh linen to her husband at Moses Creek. When he, in turn, ordered her taken to safety, she was "not at all pleased with leaving Saratoga so soon." Henry B. Livingston reported that "the alarms we have had have but little effect on her, she is only uneasy for you and has enjoined me to entreat you not to expose yourself unnecessarily." The alarms to which Livingston referred included the discovery of four Indians nearby and a constant firing all the previous night by sentries who saw or pretended to see Indians.[74]

Schuyler's prospects in the field brightened but little after 26 July, and in far-off Philadelphia they grew positively bleak as congressmen glowered uneasily over reports from the Northern Army. The general was momentarily encouraged by news that Seth Warner had raised eight hundred men on the Hampshire Grants and that still more militia were reported on their way to join him. But other militia with Schuyler at Moses Creek continued to dwindle away. The first contingent of John Glover's thirteen hundred-man brigade at last arrived at Albany on 27 July, and welcome as they were, when they finally reached the Yorker's army at Saratoga, it was too late to prevent the American retreat from Moses Creek. Benjamin Lincoln's arrival at Schuyler's headquarters promised substantial encouragement to New England regulars or militia who might more readily serve a Yorker commander if a fellow Yankee led them in the field. For the moment Schuyler did not expect to be able to attack any of Burgoyne's detachments because the British seemed too knowledgeable of the patriots' moves.[75]

Popular rumors that Schuyler and the general officers who had been at Ticonderoga were "all a pack of Traitors" continued to roll across New England and into his army. Fearing what else would be said of his retreat from Fort Edward, Schuyler wrote Washington that the place was little more than a ruin and he had galloped his horse through the site with ease.[76] Under the circumstances he considered the prudence of risking an engagement with Burgoyne closer to Albany; the British might finally be cut to pieces if Schuyler delayed and drew them further south while giving Washington time to march his army north.

The murder and scalping of Jane McCrea by a party of Burgoyne's Indians near Fort Edward on 26 July has long been thought to have sparked a popular realization of the great danger of Burgoyne's invasion and encouraged Yorkers and Yankees alike to provide militia assistance to the Northern Army as never before. The killing is supposed to have "fanned the hatred for the advancing enemy more than any other incident of the campaign," and allegedly Burgoyne worsened the impact by failing to execute the reputed murderer, Wyandot Panther, for fear his Ottawa cohorts would desert the British ranks.[77]

However, the militia who appeared in arms under John Stark to check the British at Bennington had other incentives for acting: pledges of payment for their services, Stark's popularity, and New Hampshire's authorization for him to act independently or cooperatively with United States forces as he might determine. There is no evidence that Jane McCrea's death was used to appeal to the militia to act, although there was plenty of time for the news of her murder to have spread, and it is probable that the men who fought at Bennington knew of the incident. The Vermont Committee of Safety did not use Jane McCrea's death or the British Indian allies "as a propaganda tool to draw out the militia" during the first weeks of August. And "there is no available evidence that her memory was invoked to draw the militia into battle at Bennington." New England newspapers made no prominent mention of her when the incident was reported weeks later. In light of the circumstances, which "were ideal for the use" of her story, it is remarkable that "the desperate men of the Hampshire Grants" did not do so. The young Tory woman "holds an undeserved place in the annals of the American Revolution."[78]

It was above all the threat of imminent invasion of home territory that provided militia manpower to Schuyler's army before he was deprived of his command, and he would as surely have benefited from this or popular reaction to Jane McCrea's death as did his successor, Horatio Gates. Direct evidence of the impact of her murder is simply lacking, and there seems to be no indication of how Schuyler himself viewed the effects of it. The only reference he appears to have made to her was a passing one in his 26–27 July letter to Washington: Indians and British regulars had attacked a picket at Fort Edward, he wrote, killing and scalping four men and capturing another four; "They also scalped a woman and carried off another."[79]

Whether the McCrea murder of the general threat of invasion provided a military reaction in Schuyler's favor, political moves at Philadelphia and Kingston on 26 July proved decidedly less auspicious for his immediate future. New Jersey congressman Jonathan Sergeant introduced a motion to recall both Arthur St. Clair and Philip Schuyler, and to send Horatio Gates to command the Northern Department. The debate that followed echoed the old charges that Schuyler was long unpopular with Yankees, but now both he and St. Clair were said to lack the confidence of all of the army. Gates's partisans insisted that only Gates could keep the army intact. Schuyler's defenders, like James Duane, rightly argued that conditions, not men, were to blame for northern reverses, and that Schuyler should be left at his post until such time as an inquiry into St. Clair's record might implicate the commander enough to warrant his recall. While the debate rumbled on a vote on the recall motion was put off for several days.[80]

5

"Tardiness . . . Boys, aged Men and Negroes . . . disgrace our arms"

During 28–29 July Schuyler shifted back and forth between Moses Creek and Saratoga while Burgoyne's army inched south toward Fort Edward. The British occupied the pitch pine plains between Fort Ann and Fort Edward, and on 30 July Burgoyne reached the latter post, prompting Schuyler to move his army on to Saratoga. In the American rear inhabitants were ordered to carry their possessions from Stillwater to Albany, and both army carriages and bateaux were employed in assisting their movement. Without much hope of collecting reinforcements in time to make a stand, Schuyler felt obliged to retreat, thinking that he might hold the ground about eight miles north of his country house. Almost daily he reported his circumstances and his fears to officials like Washington, Pierre Van Cortlandt, and William Heath. Inadequate manpower and insufficient provisions continued to plague him. To General Heath, for example, he wrote that "Very timely and repeated orders have been given for the latter, and frequent applications made for Troops to the States that were to furnish them. A shameful Tardiness has prevailed in making the Levies, and one third of the few that have been sent are Boys, aged Men and Negroes, who disgrace our arms. Is it consistent with the Sons of Freedom," he cried, "to trust their all to be defended by Slaves? Every effort of the Enemy would be in vain if our Exertions equaled our Abilities; If our Virtue was not sinking under that infamous venality which pervades throughout and threatens us with Ruin. America cannot be subdued by a foreign Force; but her own Corruption may bring on a fatal Catastrophe."[81]

Schuyler's reference to venality was more particularly demonstrated when he answered Lake George carpenters' complaints against his order for seizure of their tools. Without tools, gun carriages could not be built or repaired, and yet he had provided compensation for the workman's confiscated property.[82] These, then, were but a sample of the circumstances that conspired against the general's effectiveness and added to the popular clamors against him.

These outcries and a growing, widespread uneasiness about Schuyler after the fall of Ticonderoga were not limited to New England. Even the New York State Council of Safety became critical, and it was not only the intrigue of Horatio Gates's supporters that finally brought the Yorker down. From the last days of July until 4 August, when the effect of those clamors reached a climax in the halls of Congress, Schuyler's critics, especially New Englanders, bombarded his reputation and his record of competence with slurs and slanders. When James Duane accused them of a combination to attack the general by mere resentment and "private views," William Williams of Connecticut denied it but admitted that the eastern states had no confidence in Schuyler or St. Clair. Openly, they asserted "that their troops [had] no Confidence in General Schuyler and assign[ed] this as the Reason that they have not marched to his Assistance." But Jonathan Sergeant of New Jersey and Daniel Roberdeau of Pennsylvania, who had moved to recall the two generals on 26 July, hotly denied being in any combination or that they were acting from any motive but the discovery of truth. The debates of 26 and 28 July resulted in a resolution that an inquiry be made into reasons for the evacuation of Ticonderoga and Mount Independence and into the conduct of the general officers in the Northern Department at that time. An investigatory committee was also named, including Roberdeau and three New Englanders: John Adams of Massachusetts, Eliphalet Dyer of Connecticut, and Nathaniel Folsom of New Hampshire.[83]

The drift was now unmistakable, and William Duer promptly wrote Schuyler not to be surprised if Congress asked him to appear for the inquiry. The general's enemies, he said, had left "no means unessayed to blast your character, and impute to your appointment in that Department, a loss which, when rightly investigated can be imputed to very different causes. The friends to truth find an extreme difficulty to stem the torrent of calumny." And the torrent raged on. Congress ordered St. Clair to headquarters on 30 July. On 1 August it likewise voted that Schuyler be "directed to repair to Head Quarters" and that Washington be requested to name his replacement. But the Virginian refused to be embroiled in what was so obviously a partisan maneuver to involve him in Schuyler's disgrace. When he warily declined, Congress voted on 4 August to appoint Gates. The majority against Schuyler was large, despite the staunch loyalty of his fellow New Yorkers and some southern congressmen who "violently opposed" his replacement.[84]

In writing Schuyler of his recall on 5 August, President Hancock did not deign to indicate who would succeed him but merely enclosed copies of the congressional resolutions of 29 July and 1 August. Indeed, the general did not discover that Gates would replace him until 14 August. No wonder, then, that he resented the discourtesy of this failure to inform him almost as much as he did the bare notice of his dismissal.[85]

As yet unaware of Congress's blows, Schuyler grappled with the question of how to ward off Burgoyne's and to strike some of his own. At first the Yorker rather overestimated the size of Burgoyne's army, but by 11 August he had reasonably accurate estimates of the opposing army, and he reported Burgoyne's forces to be about sixty-six hundred strong.[86] But the strength of the enemy was not his only problem.

Schuyler's trouble with Yankee militia bore a remarkable resemblance to General Herkimer's problem with Tryon County militia. Whether Yankees or Yorkers, militiamen were reluctant to serve more than brief terms in the field, and they were determined not to remain there when they thought their homes were defenseless, or when hay must be made and their wheat harvested. They either deserted or refused to extend their enlistments. Those considerations were probably more cogent explanations of the Schuyler-militia question than any suspicions that he or his officers were incompetent or even disloyal. Herkimer, for example, warned Col. Peter Gansevoort at Fort Schuyler on 29 July that he must not try to detain the Tryon militia longer than the three weeks agreed upon, including travel time from and to their homes. By Thursday, 31 July, they must be discharged or they would desert and then refuse to serve again after harvest time.[87]

By 30 July with the appearance of Benjamin Lincoln, Schuyler had good reason to hope that difficulties with New England militia would diminish. He immediately notified Seth Warner that Lincoln would assume overall command on the Hampshire Grants, where he hoped John Stark's New Hampshire volunteers would make a substantial addition to Warner's reputedly small number of militia and serve amicably under a fellow Yankee general. Although Massachusetts men left Warner's forces no less readily than they abandoned Schuyler, the Yorker expected that Lincoln's "great good Sense," combined with his bravery, activity, and influence in Massachusetts would soon draw a "very respectable body" of troops to make a powerful diversion against Burgoyne. On 31 July Schuyler ordered Lincoln off to maneuver Burgoyne into stationing a sizable detachment of his army at Skenesborough. And having discovered that the British commander had at last reached Fort Edward, that day Schuyler followed the unanimous decision of his council of general officers to move the army another step south to Saratoga. With daily desertions of militia, he knew that another retreat would follow. Without sizable reinforcements he could be forced all the way to Albany. And if that was not enough cause for worry, there was the threat that able leadership would be lost; Benedict Arnold wished to retire if Congress would not improve his rank, and already Arnold had requested leave to do so. Schuyler did, however, manage to persuade him to wait.[88]

The first days of August marked the opening of Barry St. Leger's three-week siege at Fort Schuyler and also a scene of much agitation and confusion at Saratoga. Although Schuyler reacted promptly to the first news of the western assault when it reached him on the early morning of 8 August, his immediate task was to find the ground for the best defenses against the northern invasion and to keep his shifting forces in some semblance of order. He directed the organization of scouting parties and pickets by forming companies of light infantry from each brigade of Continentals. His secretary posted orders to Col. Goose Van Schaick to raise a variety of militia units near Albany and to lead them into Tryon County, where the enemy were soon expected to appear. Reacting to Morgan Lewis's request to remove quartermaster supplies from Albany to places of greater safety, Schuyler insisted that this would worsen the panic of the townsmen, whose imagination of danger was much more exaggerated than was warranted. Instead, he advised Lewis to inculcate "an opinion that the Retreat of our Army is only a Finesse to induce Burgoyne to precipitate himself into Ruin." No better summary of Schuyler's Fabian tactics is to be found than in that brief request.[89]

6

"a good man in ye cause"

On the afternoon of 3 August Schuyler once again led his army away from the skirmishing vanguard of Burgoyne's forces. While British headquarters remained at Fort Edward between 4 and 13 August, the Yorker established his at Stillwater until 14 August. Receipt of news from Sir William Howe on 3 August evidently prompted Burgoyne to pause, for Howe's 17 July letter had given no indication that British forces would move up the Hudson to assist the northern invasion.[90]

Despite Burgoyne's halt, Americans grew more dismayed that their own retreats seemed relentless. Schuyler's aide, Maj. Henry B. Livingston, provided a glimpse of more than his own sentiments on the day of the army's departure from Saratoga. "We are busy at packing to move off and of course in confusion," he wrote. "Destruction and havoc mark our steps . . . I feel more sensibly at leaving Saratoga than any place we have yet passed. I hope we shall be able to make a stand at Stillwater . . . God only knows where we shall stop retreating." Schuyler himself could not have been less dismayed with the abandonment of his country house or with the need to withdraw again from the enemy's reach. After arriving at Stillwater late in the evening without loss of men or stores, Livingston was surprised that the army had escaped harassment since its vanguard had been attacked that morning. But the devastation along the line of retreat was shocking to him, and he was not sanguine about the general's prospects for holding the new position unless Burgoyne "politely" afforded the time for him to erect defenses and for his soldiers to recover from panic.[91]

Schuyler's move to Stillwater had been decided by a council of his general officers, and again with the aid of Thaddeus Kosciuszko he attempted to fortify a position, hoping the reinforcements might finally reach him in time to hold the ground. However, militia would not remain more than a week, he noted on 4 August, and even the Continental forces daily decreased by desertion, skirmishes, and sickness, while Burgoyne's army was increasingly aided by Tories. Repeated requests for Massachusetts and Connecticut militia had as yet apparently gone unanswered. When the officers of Fermoy's brigade again requested annexation to another Continental unit, Schuyler finally confronted the Frenchman about his difficulties in communicating with them. Unable to persuade Fermoy to take command at Albany, Schuyler agreed to let him leave the army altogether. With Benedict Arnold, Schuyler was more persuasive.

Arnold had proposed to resign his commission after learning that Congress had refused to remedy his complaints that other brigadier generals' promotions in February left him junior in rank, although he was their senior in service and his record had been equal, even superior, to theirs. Schuyler managed to convince Arnold that by remaining with the army he might better demonstrate the rectitude of his intentions. And his faithfulness cemented "a mutual friendship that only the supremest infamy could destroy." When the position at Stillwater grew precarious and the need for sending forces west to the relief of Fort Schuyler became urgent, Schuyler found Arnold to be one of the most dependable and energetic of his officers.[92]

For about ten days Schuyler's army remained at Stillwater, a pleasant point on the Hudson where the river still merits that placid name. There the general regrouped his forces, hoped for reinforcements, and continued to apprise superiors and subordinates of the critical state of his affairs. Massachusetts militia who were still present would insist upon returning home by 10 August, when their enlistments expired. Impossible as it was to obtain a return of the troops, he insisted that he had no more than four thousand, "If men one third of which are Negroes, Boys and Men too Aged for Field or indeed any other Service can with propriety be called Troops," he wrote. Yet these were the men recently raised by the states for Continental service. Many had taken the field poorly armed, inadequately accoutered, naked, and without blankets.[93]

Sending a copy of his letter to Congress to the state council of safety, Schuyler suggested that his own countrymen might lend him their aid in overcoming the alarming situation at Stillwater. He also appealed to George Clinton, who had taken the oath as first governor of the state on 30 July. If Clinton were to take the field as New York's commander in chief, perhaps the militia would turn out in sufficient numbers to enable Schuyler to hold ground against Burgoyne's further advances. And if the militia from the eastern states would only arrive in time, Schuyler felt that they "should then, in all probability, be able to ruin General Burgoyne's army." Attempting to impress upon his old assembly colleague the urgency of his request, Schuyler warned the governor that if Albany County and Dutchess County units did not reach Albany before 12 August, they would be too late. And he reminded the governor of his patriotic duty, assuring Clinton that he would "embrace every opportunity to make you sit as easy in the Chair of Government as the Times will admit. Your Virtue, the Love of my Country and that Friendship which I have always and with great Truth professed are all so many Inducements to it.[94]

In desperation Schuyler also posted an express message to Benjamin Lincoln on 4 August, ordering him to rush all but Seth Warner's regiment to Stillwater. Lincoln must, if he could, move in such a way as to appear to attack Burgoyne's rear. And having heard nothing from Lincoln since he had left to take command of Yankee militia in the Hampshire Grants territory, Schuyler begged for an answer by the messenger whom he sent speeding to find the Massachusetts general. His final prod was to warn Lincoln that Howe's sailing from Manhattan was but a diversion and that Sir William would surely soon return and proceed up the Hudson.[95]

Lincoln was at that moment at Manchester, New Hampshire, where he had arrived two days earlier. Between five and six hundred militia had already assembled, and he expected to have two thousand within three or four days. He then intended to lead forces toward Skenesborough and

Ticonderoga, harassing Burgoyne's rear and inspiriting the people who were abandoning good crops and moving off their farms and hurrying their families to safety. Lincoln had received promises of about fifteen hundred New Hampshire militia for two months of service, and word had reached him that a Massachusetts regiment of seven hundred men was also marching to join him. Thus New Englanders were bestirring themselves even before news had spread of Schuyler's dismissal and of Gates's appointment; and the Yorker's continued command of the Northern Army had not prompted Yankees to refuse to serve the cause for which he fought no less than they.[96]

The problem of rallying New England militia to an army led by a man as allegedly unpopular as Philip Schuyler has long been exaggerated. The allegations of congressmen alone are not proof that Yankees were universally as hostile to Schuyler as has been claimed. Ira Allen, for example, wrote for Vermont's committee of safety, asking Schuyler's information about the use of the new state's regiment of rangers. More to the point of the difficulty were the realities that civilians in a "citizens' army" resented all military regimen, and that provincials did not fully appreciate that the defense of their territory required fighting beyond it or that their interests in the seasonal work of planting or reaping crops must be sacrificed to the larger public welfare. Yankee rumors of Schuyler's behavior of course existed. But not all New Englanders scorned or mistrusted the New York general. Expressing his hope that thousands of them would flock to Colonel Warner's aid and cut off Burgoyne's line of retreat, John Sergeant of Stockbridge, Massachusetts, wrote Eleazer Wheelock about some people's "ill opinions of Genl. Schiler." But Sergeant believed "him to be a good man in ye cause—politically virtuous—& a brave general his conduct the other day was somewhat proved. he stop[p]ed and attacked about 2000 of the enemy who wer[e] pursuing him—he beat & drove them back—he has burnt his own Mills and destroyed his own Grain—They off everything & leave nothing for the enemy—his army increases & [I] fancy he will with ye divin[e] blessing give a good account of them within a month."[97]

In early August 1777 it seemed to Schuyler that the New England states had given up the cause as lost, but that the British might suffer fatal reverses if Burgoyne could be checked at Stillwater. Contemplating the depressing prospects of his army at Stillwater, Schuyler continued to urge other officers to raise their spirits and to encourage public support of the patriot effort. When the Schenectady Committee of Safety reported the growing fears of people west of Albany, the spread of disaffection, and the need for at least sixty good soldiers and officers to defend the town,

Schuyler retorted that he blushed for his countrymen. How could they be so despondent or expect him to furnish soldiers when his own army lacked manpower? Let the local militia do their duty and the enemy would regret their invasion! Local leaders must simply exert themselves.[98]

By 6 August no Connecticut militia had yet appeared, and again Schuyler complained to their governor that his little army at Stillwater was continually neglected by those whose duty and interest it was to help him. Again he begged Trumbull for haste in sending reinforcements, warning that if the enemy were allowed to reach Albany, they would grow even stronger with Indian and Tory reinforcements and with the army invading the Mohawk valley. The general also insisted that Governor Clinton and the New York legislature or at least the state council of safety must come to Albany to lend their assistance and boost the inhabitants' morale. People were despondent, and Schuyler feared that not even a few of the Albany County militia would turn out otherwise.[99]

7

Oriskany and Bennington

Far to the west the British siege of Fort Schuyler was punctuated on 6 August by the bloody engagement at Oriskany. Marching 800 of his Tryon County militia from Fort Dayton and supported by some Oneida Indians, Nicholas Herkimer was ambushed on his way to aid the besieged. His attackers were a contingent of Barry St. Leger's 800 regulars, Tories, and 600 Indians. Brave old Herkimer directed the fierce battle from the cover of a beech tree after he had been mortally wounded. Although British forces were finally repulsed, the Americans were too weakened to pursue them and withdrew, having lost perhaps as many as 160 to 200 dead, 75 wounded, and at least 17 captives. Colonels Peter Gansevoort, Marinus Willet, and James Wesson were left to face St. Leger's siege with about 750 men; the remnants of Herkimer's forces retreated unpursued, for St. Leger was determined to concentrate his efforts at Fort Schuyler. The engagement was particularly significant as the first major battle outside of Canada in which so many of the Iroquois fought the patriots. Schuyler's efforts to maintain a policy of Indian neutrality had largely failed, but up to this point only the Seneca and Cayuga had proven particularly hostile. Now the Six Nations were noticeably divided; the Oneida and some of the Tuscarora and Onondaga nations supported the patriots, while Joseph

Brant's Mohawk Indians, the Seneca, and the Cayuga stood with the British. The danger remained real. "If St. Leger got past Fort Schuyler, the Iroquois and Loyalists would run wild down the Mohawk, and Schuyler would be trapped between St. Leger and Burgoyne. With the Tryon militia shattered, Schuyler must somehow defend both the Hudson and the Mohawk."[100]

While news of the savage civil war in the western reaches of the Mohawk valley was sped to Schuyler's headquarters, the general ventured to leave Stillwater for a visit to Albany, where he expected to confer with representatives of some of the Iroquois. Before riding south, and for some unexplained reason, he had been obliged to request Brig. Gen. John Nixon to reconsider the submission of his resignation; the times were too critical, Schuyler insisted, for the acceptance of such a gesture. Despair, perhaps disgruntlement, infected the highest ranks of the army as well as the lowest levels of the public.[101]

But circumstances had a brighter side in August 1777, and if Schuyler had not been so summarily dismissed, he must clearly have been their beneficiary as much as was Horatio Gates. These included a whole series of events set in motion before notice of Schuyler's removal reached Albany on 10 August or even before Gates himself arrived in the city on 18 August. In a sense they began with the bloody blow struck by Nicholas Herkimer at Oriskany, or perhaps even with the arrival of Benedict Arnold and Benjamin Lincoln at Schuyler's headquarters (on 22 and 30 July respectively). After Lincoln was sent scurrying to the Hampshire Grants territory, evidence of New England militia support to the Northern Army's efforts gradually became apparent. And already John Stark was leading a body of New Hampshire volunteers west to harass Burgoyne's left flank. Although Stark refused Lincoln's call to march to Schuyler's army on the Hudson, he did agree to maneuver against the British left and rear while Lincoln obeyed Schuyler's summons to Stillwater. The crusty Stark was soured by Congress's failure to accord him suitable rank as much if not more than he was annoyed by Schuyler; but his services proved to be invaluable if indirect aids to Schuyler's efforts.

On 8 August Stark proceeded to maneuver his men southwest toward Bennington to guard sizable stores of flour and livestock for Schuyler's army. By 13 August, when he prepared to march toward Cambridge, which lay to the southeast of Schuyler's Saratoga estate, he received news that prompted him to change his course. This was the information that Lt. Col. Friedrich Baum's dragoons were searching for horses and supplies and were moving toward Bennington with artillery and Tory, Canadian, and Indian auxiliaries. Between the skirmishes of 14 August and the engagements of 16 August at Bennington, Stark's brigade not only defeated Baum but also a reinforcement led by Col. Heinrich von Breymann. Against about 30 Americans killed and 50 wounded, Burgoyne had lost perhaps 200 killed and 696 captured of Baum's and Breymann's troops (which had totaled almost 1,200).[102] Thus another telling blow was delivered to the British invasion before Horatio Gates took command of the Northern Army.

Still confident of his ability to reach Albany by 22 or 23 August, Burgoyne wrote Howe of his progress on 6 August. Bennington was his first serious setback except for the major difficulty that Schuyler had created for him by forcing his slow movement of provisions and artillery along tree-choked roads, marshy terrain, and ruined bridges.[103] St. Leger's failure at Fort Schuyler proved another sizable reverse for the invaders. The beginning of their failure in the west was the clash at Oriskany; its denouement continued with Schuyler's response to news of Herkimer's gallant action of 6 August.

Schuyler received a report of Herkimer's disaster at about six in the morning on 8 August. After a twenty-five mile ride from Stillwater he had reached Albany the previous evening in order to meet with a delegation of Indians and had risen early to begin preparations for the conference and other duties. Interrupted in writing a letter to Congressman William Duer, he noted the arrival of the express messenger from the west and bemoaned his inability to furnish relief to Fort Schuyler because no militia had yet appeared at Albany; nor did he believe he had a single Continental soldier in the city to send. Asking Duer and other friends to press for an inquiry into his conduct, Schuyler insisted, "be assured my Dear friend that if a General Engagement takes place whatever may be the Event you will not have occasion to blush for Your friend."[104]

The general wasted little time in reporting the fresh news from Tryon County to the president of Congress. The Oneida Indians and Caughnawaga from Canada who had come to Albany to see Schuyler estimated Burgoyne's strength at eight thousand, including tribesmen and Canadians. Other Indians—Mississauga, Huron, Chippawa, and some Iroquois—were following Sir John Johnson in the west. The invaders were spreading allegations that General Howe had occupied Philadelphia and then had proceeded to move up the Hudson. The purpose of such rumors was obviously to encourage Indians and frontier settlers to defect to the enemy. With no reinforcements to spare for Fort Schuyler, the general also indicated that Massachusetts and New Hampshire militia refused to extend their terms of service despite his offer of twenty dollars' bounty if they would remain until 1 December. Connecticut and Massachusetts militia were refusing to advance if they were to be commanded by the general officers who had served at Ticonderoga. He heard that the northern invaders had reached Saratoga. The business of the commissary of issues was in utter confusion because Elisha Avery was indisposed and refused to discipline his assistants.[105] Such were the dismal colors added to the picture that Schuyler had for so long painted of his department; little did he realize that congressmen had viewed them as justification for his removal, of which he as yet had no inkling.

The press of affairs at Albany delayed Schuyler's return to Stillwater until 10 August. He agonized about the need for reinforcing Fort Schuyler. Several days earlier a detachment of Col. James Wesson's 9th Massachusetts Regiment of Continentals had set out toward Fort Dayton, which lay about forty miles east of Fort Schuyler. On 8 August he ordered Wesson to join Herkimer's forces if the latter returned to German Flats. However, if Herkimer had managed to hold ground near "Orisko" or anywhere above Fort Dayton, Wesson must join him there and relay news of Fort Schuyler by express carrier as frequently as possible. Schuyler then hurried messages for help to Benjamin Lincoln, governors Clinton and Trumbull, General Putnam at Peekskill, the Berkshire County committee, and Ira Allen. Lincoln must not tarry long for the Massachusetts militia at Bennington but leave orders for them to follow him to Stillwater.[106]

The missive to Lincoln must have crossed paths with Lincoln's news to Schuyler of John Stark's arrival at Manchester and his disgruntlement with Congress. If he did decide to lead his New Hampshire volunteers to Stillwater, Stark insisted that he would act independently of any officer except Schuyler. On 8 August Lincoln was still uncertain about the number of Massachusetts troops collecting at Bennington. The shifting of army forces provided other curious problems for Schuyler, who remonstrated with Governor Trumbull about his offer to send Connecticut militia to Washington. If Trumbull imagined that this would enable the Virginian to release other troops for the northern service, he was mistaken, for Schuyler was convinced that this would not bring him a single man from the commander in chief. Pointedly, the general warned the Berkshire County committee that if the enemy reached Albany, their own country would soon be invaded.[107]

With some of Benjamin Lincoln's reassuring news from Bennington in hand, Schuyler wrote more confidently but urgently to him, and to generals Herkimer and St. Clair on 9 August. Having reported John Stark's situation to Congress, Schuyler told Lincoln to entreat Stark to waive his rightful authority to act independently; Stark might then claim greater honor for refusing to allow anything to interfere with his country's welfare. Lincoln must beg Stark to march to Stillwater at once. As Burgoyne's vanguard was now reported to be at Saratoga, Lincoln could not move too quickly in the effort to reach Stillwater himself.[108]

Acknowledging Nicholas Herkimer's message of 8 August, Schuyler commended his gallantry and hurried his reply that a party of Continentals had set out from Albany three days earlier. More would leave for the west that very day, he said, and asserting that militia reinforcements were on their way, the general promised to send still more men to the relief of the Mohawk valley. Schuyler wrote similarly to Arthur St. Clair, indicating that Lincoln should reach the main army on 10 August and that he had ordered bateaux to begin evacuating stores from Abraham Fort's which was a position five miles below Stillwater. Thus the bustle of preparations continued.[109]

8

"the Indignity of being relieved"

Sunday, 10 August, brought bitter news to Schuyler's Albany house. About to mount his horse to return to the army at Stillwater, the general paused as dispatches from the Continental Congress arrived. He reentered his office to answer John Hancock's 5 August letter containing the resolutions Congress had passed on 29 July and 1 August. The first provided an inquiry into reasons for the loss of Ticonderoga; the second ordered Schuyler to Washington's headquarters. Not a hint of who would succeed him had been sent, although Hancock might as well have written that Horatio Gates had been chosen on 4 August.

"I am far from being Insensible of the Indignity of being relieved of the command of the army at a time when an Engagement must soon take place," Schuyler began. But he was consoled by his confidence that an investigation would vindicate him, for he deserved the thanks of his country, not its censures. Recounting the variety of his most recent difficulties, he also emphasized the pressing need to obtain reinforcements for Fort Schuyler. He had promised Colonel Gansevoort to send them but admitted that as yet he knew not where to obtain them. The Albany County militia were everywhere "borne down" by Tories; and in the midst of the crisis Massachusetts and Connecticut seemed inert, for there was little sign of the appearance of their militia.[110]

When compared with his speedy reply to Hancock, Schuyler's letter to Col. Peter Gansevoort, which was also dated 10 August, indicates that the general was desperate enough to stretch the truth. As he agonized over Gansevoort's pressing need for reinforcements, he could not escape the fact that he had none to spare, so he tried to encourage the commander of the distant post then besieged by Barry St. Leger and hoped that somewhere, somehow, he might yet find the men to send west. Promising Gansevoort that "a body of troops left this [Albany] Yesterday and others are following to raise the Siege," Schuyler wrote that "Every Body here believes you will Defend" Fort Schuyler "to the Last and I must strictly enjoin you so to do."[111] It was true that a detachment of Col. James Wesson's regiment had been sent to Fort Dayton to join their unit, but what "others" were "following" were as yet no means assured.

Schuyler found the means to hasten reinforcements to the western reaches of the Mohawk after he returned to the army at Stillwater. But before he rode north from Albany on that August Sunday he quickly penned a notice to the nearby Berkshire, Massachusetts, committee. No time must be lost in seizing any opportunity to strengthen the army that another would soon command. Suggesting that Nathanael Greene would probably lead the Northern Army, Schuyler merely observed, "I need not suggest the Reasons why I wish these Resolutions should be made as public as possible. You will easily see my Motive."[112] If indeed any Yankee militia had refused to come to Schuyler's aid, they must surely not withhold their support now that he was superseded.

Schuyler, of course, saw no license in the letter of his dismissal to lay down his command or report to Washington's headquarters until his replacement had reached the army. He would surrender office to his successor before obeying Congress's other orders. What his biographer said of Benjamin Rush is unmistakably applicable to Schuyler: "Every man who perseveres when cut down deserves respect."[113] Schuyler did persevere, and when Gates finally appeared to assume the reins of the Northern Department, he volunteered his services without hesitation.

Gates, however, cavalierly made his way to the Northern Army slowly despite Congress's directions that he move speedily. His leisurely journey did not bring him to Albany until 18 August—a full two weeks after his congressional appointment. Whether supremely confident of his abilities to rescue the country from Burgoyne's invasion in his won good time or ignorant of the urgency of the crisis in the north, Gates evidently enjoyed his stops along the Hudson while others labored in the field to guarantee the very existence of the nation that had declared but had not yet won independence.[114]

As Schuyler rode to Stillwater on 10 August, Burgoyne's main force was at Fort Miller. Washington, considering the whereabouts of Howe's seaborne army, soon discovered that it would not likely return to New York City for a rush up the Hudson, nor was it probable that Howe was merely trying to draw Washington away from the river in order to allow Sir Henry Clinton the freedom to cooperate with Burgoyne. The commander in chief therefore decided that he could send more aid to the Northern Army. Two New York regiments of Continentals were ordered to proceed from Peekskill, and Daniel Morgan was directed to march his regiment of five hundred Virginia riflemen north as well. Although these reinforcements strengthened the army led by Horatio Gates, they could have served as well under Schuyler had he been retained in command.[115]

Within the next several days Schuyler determined upon a bold course of action; contrary to allegations that a council of general officers opposed it, the general claimed their unanimous agreement. Perhaps he was encouraged to take this action because of news that Burgoyne's vanguard had fallen back from Saratoga toward Fort Edward.[116]

First, Schuyler sent orders for Col. James Wesson's garrison at Fort Dayton to speed to the relief of Fort Schuyler. Issued on 11 August, these were quickly supplemented by orders that posted Gen. Ebenezer Learned's Continental brigade into the Mohawk valley. Then on 12 August Schuyler sent a messenger flying to General Herkimer and the Tryon County committee alerting them to the reinforcements and exhorting them to raise the county militia and join Learned's brigade. When Benedict Arnold volunteered his services, Schuyler quickly gave him command of all forces along the Mohawk. And on 13 August Arnold was armed with orders to hasten west. On 21 August he reached Fort Dayton with Learned's 950 Continentals. Despite the lack of New England reinforcements and the murmuring of some of his subordinates against thus weakening his main army, Schuyler acted with courage in sending forces west. "A lesser man would have left Fort Stanwix [Schuyler] to its fate and concentrated on Burgoyne."[117]

On 13 August Schuyler's council of officers agreed that it was necessary to retreat from Stillwater. Their destination now was the mouth of the Mohawk River, where the army would be directly in a position to move against either northern or western invasionary forces. The withdrawal, of course, conveyed the impression of weakness, even cowardice, for with half of his forces scattered at positions both east and west of the core of Schuyler's command, they could give him only indirect support. Retaining thirty-five hundred Continentals and about forty New York militia, the general again begged the president of Massachusetts and the New York State Council of Safety for more state militia.[118]

The risks of weakening his main force and of raising more popular alarm by abandoning Stillwater were properly taken. Despite the demoralization of frequent retreats, Schuyler would have been foolish to attempt a stand against the British with an army barely half the size of Burgoyne's. The more he could oblige them to extend their lines, the more the invasionary force could be weakened. Moreover, there was no certain danger for the moment that Burgoyne would launch a large-scale battle. And in the face of so many uncertainties Schuyler might still hope for the arrival of reinforcements for the success of both the Yankee maneuvers against Burgoyne's left flank to the east and Arnold's rush to check St. Leger in the west. Should such auxiliary actions prove effective, the army's morale could be raised and Mohawk valley forces could yet be recalled to assist against Burgoyne, whose own delays continued to work to the American advantage.[119]

Meantime, at Stillwater Schuyler dealt with the ordinary and continual round of difficulties. Included was the deputy quartermaster general's failure to furnish bateaux for the removal of stores from Abraham Fort's place south of Stillwater to Van Schaick's Island. And there the general officers made a formal request to Schuyler that he use his influence with New York militia to rally them to their army's support. Facing their commander's imminent withdrawal to Washington's headquarters, brigadier generals John Nixon, Enoch Poor, John Glover, John Patterson, and Ebenezer Learned petitioned Schuyler not to leave the county without first affording this kind of assistance. The attendant delay in Schuyler's obedience to Congress's orders that he report to headquarters, they hoped, would be excused as a necessity. It was perhaps poetic justice that if New England militia—or at least many of them—declared they would not march while Schuyler and other officers responsible for the fall of Ticonderoga remained in command of the Northern Army, the Albany County militia almost unanimously declared that they would not serve if Schuyler quit the department! Accordingly, he agreed to "risk the censure of Congress by remain[ing] in this quarter after [he was] relieved and bringing up the Militia to the support of this weak Army." As of 14 August he still did not know who would succeed him, but whoever he might be Schuyler vowed to pity him "altho he should be my Enemy for he will find a choice of difficulties to Encounter."[120]

Despite long-standing Yankee-Yorker tensions, Schuyler appealed to John Stark to hasten his New Hampshire volunteers to the support of the army. Grateful for news of their movement in his direction, Schuyler suggested that Stark march by way of Schaghticoke, which was the shortest route. In such a critical hour his sacrifice of his feelings to a great cause would win him greater honor than he could gain by fighting alone. Sympathetically, he reminded Stark that he was not the only officer who had been so injuriously treated by Congress.[121]

Schuyler's orders for the army to march from Stillwater were issued on 13 August, and as they prepared for this final withdrawal toward the mouth of the Mohawk, the news must have spread quickly southward. The retreat from Stillwater was systematic and unhurried. John Patterson's brigade with Col. Gamaliel Bradford's regiment formed the vanguard, followed by John Glover's and Enoch Poor's brigades in the center. And John Nixon's brigade guarded the rear, assisted by Col. Jeduthan Baldwin's detachment of engineers and artificers, who were to destroy bridges. No soldier was permitted to break ranks to enter any habitation "under Penalty of immediate Death," and Schuyler expected all officers to "shoot any Person detected in plundering the Inhabitants."[122]

Between 14 and 18 August Schuyler's headquarters shifted as he moved from Stillwater to Abraham Fort's, then to Halfmoon, and finally to Van Schaick's Island, Again the process of denuding and blocking the countryside in the army's rear was repeated—routes of transportation were broken up, cattle were driven out of the enemy's path, and scouts were sent ranging to keep watch against the British advance. The quartermaster's bateau service required additional boats from Albany as the work of moving public stores to Van Schaick's Island proceeded.[123]

Posting General Poor's brigade to Louden's Ferry, Schuyler ordered him to cross the Mohawk and march five miles up its south bank to establish headquarters at Jacob Cluet's farm. Smaller parties were ordered to throw up works farther along the river at the fords, thus guarding aginst any enemy attempt to cross the river. East of the Hudson the enemy was to be diverted by a troop movement northward to Cambridge led by General Lincoln. Having done what he could to harass the enemy's rear, Lincoln might find it necessary to retreat toward the "New City" (Lansingburgh), but he must bring Col. Seth Warner's regiments and the Hampshire Grants militia with him.[124]

Just before the middle of the month Burgoyne's army had built a bridge of rafts to cross to the west bank of the Hudson, and the British advance corps passed over to encamp on the heights at Saratoga. But a few days later, on 15 August, a heavy rain washed away the rafts and temporarily cut the British advance party from the main body, and then on 16 August John Stark sent Baum's and Breymann's forces reeling at Bennington. Both man and nature seemed to conspire against the invaders.[125]

By 15 August, when he had established headquarters at Abraham Fort's house, Schuyler learned that Horatio Gates was soon to arrive. (However, it was not until the evening of 19 August that Gates in fact appeared in Schuyler's camp on Van Schaick's Island.) The general was determined that Congress's treatment of him would not so far get the better of his judgment as to embarrass the new commander. "I am Incapable of Sacrificing My Country," he generously vowed, "to a resentment however Just, and I trust I shall give an Example of what a good Citizen ought to do when he is in My Situation." The Yorker's resentment grew as it became more likely that he could finally withstand the enemy and seize an opportunity to show that he did not lack one of the first qualifications of a general officer. Moreover, he had finally found the position against which Burgoyne would be most disadvantaged. With a mind cast upon both military and political affairs, he gave James Duane a hint of one of his defenses against Congress's suspicions: every movement of his army since the fall of Ticonderoga had been taken only with the advice of his general officers, and he claimed that no resolution had been executed without their unanimous consent. Ready to share the credit for success when it was warranted, he was determined to share the blame for reverses when that was required. "Although they are natives of States whose Inhabitants have no prejudices in my favor," Schuyler was pleased that his officers—most of them Yankees—were very unhappy with news of his replacement. And only men who were familiar with his personality seemed to see the nobility of character behind the aristocratic—even haughty—mien.[126]

On 16 August, while John Stark led the rout of Burgoyne's forces, which had been seeking provisions and horses at Bennington, Schuyler continued his preparations for a stand at the junction of the Mohawk and Hudson rivers. That Saturday morning he pushed some four hundred Massachusetts militia under Benjamin Lincoln from Halfmoon to join Stark in an effort to divert Burgoyne's left flank north of Cambridge. And the general fired off answers to the Massachusetts Council of State, which had expressed "disbelief" that his Continentals included so many old men, boys, and Negroes. Because he was to lose the command and his performance would be investigated, the general hoped that militia would now hasten to the army. The only reason for its repeated retreats was the neglect of those whose duty it was to furnish reinforcements.[127]

Strangely enough on that fateful August Saturday, Sir William Howe received dispatches that the colonial secretary, Lord George Germain, had written three months earlier on 18 May! Germain had never sent Howe inflexible instructions but only hints that he cooperate with John Burgoyne on the Hudson, and now it was too late for Sir William to act upon Germain's suggstion. "I trust," the secretary had written, "that whatever you may meditate, it will be executed in time to cooperate with the Northern Army." Howe used his freedom to act with discretion so irresponsibly that he too contributed to the multifarious circumstances that marked the turn of both Philip Schuyler's fortunes and those of the army whose command he had lost.[128]

By 19 August Schuyler had received General Lincoln's report of the great American victory at Bennington, and he promptly sent his aide Henry B. Livingston with the news to Washington and Congress. Initial estimates of enemy killed, wounded, and captured were too high, but the impact of the blow to the British was incalculable. Burgoyne's Indian and Tory auxiliaries began to dwindle after the sobering experience of such a defeat. The British had failed to plunder much-needed livestock and provisions at Bennington and had also lost a considerable amount of baggage and four brass fieldpieces. The campaign had reached its turning point. The farther Burgoyne penetrated the territory that Schuyler had left barren of support, the more attenuated were his lines of communication and succor. With the well-placed hope that Arnold could soon raise St. Leger's siege of Fort Schuyler, the General expected that that would enable him to engage two to three hundred Indians for the patriot army. He spent much of his last day with the army hurrying the good news of Bennington to Arnold, the Albany and Schenectady committees, and the New York State Council of Safety. If on occasion he made dismal reports to warn others of grim dangers, he also recognized the value of spreading news of a more encouraging kind. The Yorker did not overlook Brig. Gen. John Stark in his last-minute flurry of letter writing. Congratulating him upon the Bennington victory, he offered Stark his "best thanks" and promised that salutary effects of his accomplishment were assured; the enemy could now surely be retarded and expelled.[129]

Schuyler's high spirits on 19 August were not dampened by news that Gates had arrived in Albany the previous morning. His last orders reflected not bitterness but generosity and hope. A few days earlier he had approved the court-martial dismissal of Daniel Hale, James Lamb, and Allan Durant for neglect of duty and other offenses; he now sanctioned the appointment of the three offenders by the deputy commissary of issues as his assistants. A Captain Page, who had been court-martialed for disobeying orders and making a false report to the general, was sentenced to be cashiered. But with the court's recommendation of mercy, Schuyler ordered him returned to duty. These orders formed the last entry that Henry Brockholst Livingston entered in his orderly book as Schuyler's aide-de-camp.[130]

Despite Congress's wishes that he relieve Schuyler "with all possible

Expedition," Horatio Gates had made no haste to assume his new command. Arriving at Albany on 18 August, Gates evidently waited for a good night's rest before proceeding to Van Schaick's Island. On the evening of 19 August in the solid brick mansion of John G. Van Schaick he finally received the command from Schuyler's hand. The American position had now been stabilized. Only two days later upon the receipt of news that Schuyler's reinforcements were fast approaching the post the British lifted the siege of Fort Schuyler. And by the evening of 23 August, when Arnold arrived at the fort, St. Leger's forces were in full flight.[131]

9

"the luck of reaping harvests sown by others"

Not until 8 September did the general's successor decide to turn the American army northward, for Gates, like Schuyler, preferred to wait for reinforcements before taking the offensive. But what the Yorker had so laboriously wrought and what circumstances accomplished for him were now the good fortune of Gates to inherit.

On 20 August Schuyler reported to Washington the surrender of his command. That morning he had shown Gates his papers and explained the disposition of all the forces together with their standing orders. The generals' meeting had been cool but courteous, "and then" writing from the comfort of his Albany house, Schuyler tersely added, "[I] came down to this place." There was little else for him to tell the Virginian, but appearances still suggested that Burgoyne expected aid from Howe. Encouraged by word from Benedict Arnold that a number of Oneida were expected to join his forces at German Flats, the general suggested that if Arnold succeeded at Fort Schuyler, the Indians would be favorably impressed. Schuyler hoped then to be able to raise two or three hundred of them for service with Gates's army.[132]

At the end of his active military career Schuyler might now relax in the bosom of his family and enjoy the comforts of his wife and fireside. And he could concentrate upon the labors of accounting for his stewardship. Impatiently he waited for Congress to act upon its intended inquiry. But he did not cease all efforts to assist in winning the victory that finally came in October. Gates seems to have spurned all but the most initial and incidental of Schuyler's offers of aid and counsel, but the erstwhile commander deemed no matter too inconsequential to be of help to the army.

When, for example, his Saratoga overseer and bookkeeper, Daniel Hale, evidently hesitated about continuing his useful services as deputy commissary of issues, Schuyler prevailed upon him to do so.[133]

What he intended to have done had he remained in command and been reinforced, Schuyler fully revealed to Gates on 20 August along with his orders to generals Lincoln and Arnold. But he clearly knew Gates was less familiar with the northern terrain than himself and he wished to share his intimate knowledge of all its passages and defiles so that every advantage might be wrung from them for the sake of ultimate victory. Gates might have had the services of the man who best knew the countryside through which his army must move, but he had neither the wit nor the grace to invite his predecessor to his side. Petty men do not enlist the support of men they know to be their superiors.[134]

Schuyler would have agreed with his aide, Richard Varick, had he read Varick's late August letters to Col. Joseph Ward. Gates was fortunate "to arrive at this Moment when Gen. Schuyler had just paved the way to Victory," Varick wrote. Months later the Yorker aptly referred to Gates's "luck of reaping harvests sown by others." Nathanael Greene certainly agreed. To him Gates was "a mere child of fortune. The foundation of all the Northern success was laid long before his arrival there." The victory would have been impossible without "Schuyler[']s direction ... General Gates came in just timely to reap the laurels and rewards."[135]

If time and fortune are the two most important determinants in military matters, as the seventeenth-century French commander Turenne said, Schuyler had been favored by both, although his superiors had failed to perceive them and impatiently interfered. Nothing that the Yorker had done or failed to do, however unpopular or misunderstood, had been beyond wise necessity. He had acted boldly and responsibly within the limitations of resources. He practiced most of the tactics and strategy that were as ancient as Fabius: when the enemy advances, retreat; when he camps, harass; if he tires, attack; when he retreats, pursue. For the right moment you must wait. Schuyler employed the few troops he had in devastating the countryside and blocking the invaders' path. If he benefited from Burgoyne's sluggishness, he also took advantage of his opportunities; "a vainer man and one of less stability" might have risked an encounter with the enemy and desperately tried to counteract the wildly circulated charges of treason, cowardice, and incompetence by taking some precipitant action. Considered professionally, Schuyler's "handling of the 1777 campaign rates as one of the finest strategic operations of the Revolution—only Washington's Trenton-Princeton-Morristown campaign and Greene's campaign in the South are in the same class."[136]

Because Schuyler was diligent in seeking aid from every possible source, careful in his movements, and prolific in his correspondence, critics like Congressman William Whipple sneered at him as "a certain letter writer"; alluding to Schuyler's ill health, which earlier removed him from activity in the field, Whipple also jeered at the prospects that he might "be seized with a fit of rheumatism or a certain eruptive disorder ... This would produce such a fit of letter writing," Whipple scoffed, "that much paper would be wasted as well as much precious time in a certain room reading those precious performances." It is sometimes "dangerous to tell the truth" as Schuyler did "to frightened politicians, especially when that truth may reflect unfavorably on the politicians' constituents." But if the general seemed too much inclined to report news—much of it pessimistic—to Washington, Congress, and other government bodies, it was only a part of his responsibility to tell the truth and to raise and maintain an army with all of its attendant necessities. Horatio Gates engaged in much the same kind of practice. But Gates also fell heir to two great assets: time and a good store of provisions that Schuyler had supplied—a sizable part of the groundwork that the Yorker laid for the victory at Saratoga and "the fruits of his efforts [that] remained and made possible the victory which changed the entire course of the Revolution."[137]

By his cautious retreat in measured stages, Schuyler ran no unnecessary risks but drew Burgoyne's lines to the breaking point while he kept his small and at times even dwindling army as the nucleus for a larger one that could eventually turn from the plodding toil of defense to the bolder thrusts of an offensive campaign. On the other hand he displayed a readiness to risk taking valiant action when the opportunity arose and the need was most pressing. So it was when he detached regulars from his ragged ranks and sent them flying under Arnold's daring leadership to relieve Fort Schuyler. He must have surmised that Burgoyne was unlikely to launch a mighty push until he was assured that Howe would move up the Hudson or that St. Leger had broken through the far-western defenses of the Mohawk valley. And the American victory there came only a few days after Horatio Gates had actually taken Schuyler's command. Three days before Gates arrived at Van Schaick's Island the victory at Bennington had jolted the British and heartened the fearful patriots whose morale had steadily declined since early July.

If many Yankees were reluctant to aid Schuyler's efforts, they did not require a Gates to rouse them, nor had all of them completely refused to help stem the tide of Burgoyne's invasion. Even so, John Stark continued to refuse anything but the most independent and indirect cooperation of his New Hampshire volunteers with any Continental commander. What he and Seth Warner accomplished at Bennington on 16 August was of vital assistance to the American army whether commanded by Schuyler or Gates. But Stark's brigade thereafter did nothing to harass Burgoyne or pursue the advantage they had won at Bennington. As of early September, neither Benjamin Lincoln nor Gates could persuade Stark to move even to the east bank of the Hudson, for his volunteers' term was soon to expire, and he claimed that with but eight hundred effective troops he was too weak to move! When indeed Stark's men finally joined Gates's army in mid-September, they declined to remain beyond the term of enlistment that ended on 19 September; they would show Horatio Gates no more favor than they had Philip Schuyler. Only in early October did Stark return with a thousand New Hampshire troops.[138]

Two weeks after the news of Gates's replacement of Schuyler was circulated, no New England militia had appeared in the Northern Army camp. They remained as tardy as ever they had been during Schuyler's command. By early September Gates's only reinforcements—regulars, not militia—came with the return of Arnold's twelve hundred men from the Mohawk valley and the arrival of Daniel Morgan's five hundred riflemen, whom Washington had sent on their way in mid-August. By 3 September the Northern Army numbered between six and seven thousand, of which "seventy percent were Continentals, and of these forty-five percent had been ordered forward by" Washington since the fall of Ticonderoga. "It was the Continental Line, not the militia that 'turned out' to face Burgoyne's invaders." And not until after the first battle of Saratoga (on 19 September) did many militia come flocking to Gates's army, emboldened finally by the increased chances of success. There is no adequate evidence that Gates more than Schuyler made the difference between victory and defeat.[139]

In short, Schuyler's removal was as unnecessary as it was unjust. And Col. James Wilkinson, once partial to Gates and later disgruntled, aptly summarized the reasons why the Yorker could have won the final victory that came two months later. The American victories at Bennington and Fort Schuyler disabled Burgoyne's army, restored a measure of safety to the countryside, and helped abate popular panic. Friends to the patriot cause were reanimated to make a "manly resistance," and even Loyalists of the neighborhood grew inactive and silent. Schuyler's "zeal, patriotism, perseverance, and salutary arrangements" gradually roused drooping spirits and vanquished prejudices against him, which were the damages wrought by "artifice, intrigue and detraction." The shift of circumstances enabled Schuyler—and then Gates—to concentrate the

Continental army against an enemy largely limited to the north. And "the same force which enabled General Gates to subdue the British Army would have produced a similar effect under the orders of General Schuyler." The latter might rightly have said sic vos non vobis! "Thus you labor, but not to your own benefit."[140]

Saratoga and Reconstruction

1

"Persevere then, Worthy Sir, in the Grand Conflict"

*D*eclining Congress's order to repair to headquarters, Schuyler wrote President Hancock that he would remain at Albany to give what aid he could in meeting the mounting danger. As soon as Congress made inquiry into his conduct before and after the fall of Ticonderoga, he would, he said, "put it out of the power of any Body on Earth, however respectable, to offer me further Indignities and shall therefore resign every office I hold under Congress." Schuyler's nephew-in-law, Walter Livingston, assured the general that "all honest men" were confident that his failure to report to Washington's headquarters was motivated by his honest concern for the public good; even his enemies knew this to be true.[1]

Meantime, parties of Iroquois (Oneida, Tuscarora, and Onondaga) appeared in Albany, and on 7 September Schuyler gave permission to five of their sachems to visit Gates's encampments in an effort to impress them with American strength before a general conference of tribesmen was held a week later at Albany. As president of the board of Indian commissioners Schuyler did persuade the conferees to accept the war belt and to send about a hundred and fifty warriors to assist the Northern Army. Although Gates had requested the Indians to scout, to harass stragglers in the enemy army, and to intimidate Burgoyne's own Indian allies, he did not otherwise see fit to take his predecessor into his confidence or accept his proffered counsels; his failure to do so marks the pettiness of his character.[2]

Schuyler's reluctance to visit Washington's headquarters or Congress until the campaign had been clearly won was understandable. He considered it possible that Gates might request his services, and he also was concerned for the fate of his property at Saratoga. British inroads had "so capitally affected" his landed interest that his private affairs must claim his attention before he could hope to settle his public business. Meantime, he suggested, Congress should specify charges for the inquiry to be made into his conduct so that he might prepare the papers and witnesses needed for the investigation.[3]

The loss of his command of the army clearly did not disgrace Schuyler in the eyes of his Albany neighbors. On 7 September a delegation presented a congratulatory address, indicating that the general was not without honor in his own country. They commended him for his able services and especially for his judicious disposition of troops by which the enemy had been repelled at Fort Schuyler and Bennington. Their encomium included a note of encouragement: "Persevere then, Worthy Sir, in the Grand Conflict, in a Cause that will reflect Honor on your Memory." The testimonial, Schuyler replied, gave him "a very sensible Satisfaction." And he was consoled by his own conviction that he had not failed to do his duty. "Perhaps," he said, "the Honorable Congress was under the disagreeable Necessity of sacraficing [sic] the Feelings of an innocent Individual to the General Weal of the whole. If so, Time will make it appear and I shall not repine at having once more unjustly suffered in the Cause of my Country."[4]

Schuyler's suspicion that Congress had used him as a scapegoat was perhaps prompted but certainly confirmed by letters from Gouverneur Morris and James Duane. His resolution to remain in Albany to assist the army was in Duane's opinion a clear testimony of his virtue, bravery, and patriotism. And the fact that New Hampshire had provided reinforcements would not be forgotten; this alone contradicted Yankee assertions that their militia would not serve while Schuyler remained in command.[5]

Walter Livingston added confirmation to Duane's views when he wrote Schuyler on 7 September. "You are," he insisted, "in high estimation with those members of that august body, by whom you would wish to be esteemed." The new governor of New York, however, commented to James Duane in a vein that was a trifle less complimentary. "Our friend Phil has good qualities," he wrote, "but he has contrived to make himself disagreable [sic] and suspected by the Yankees—prejudices not easily got over. His cursed attachment to the comforts of Albany and doing the fighting business by proxy for two campaigns has destroyed him."[6] The governor's latter statement was hardly fair, for Schuyler's frequent sojourns in Albany were justified by the need to conduct business there for both the army and the board of Indian commissioners.

Gouverneur Morris hoped that Congress would come to see that a successful northern campaign was based upon the judicious plans that Schuyler had made before he was removed. The victories at Bennington and Fort Schuyler were already indicative of what he had been able to accomplish. Schuyler thanked Morris for "sympathizing with me on my removal ... at a time when our affairs were at the worst and when no change could happen but what must be for the best." Although Congress had disliked his "painting In strong colours the Situation we were In," Schuyler was convinced that had he not done so "and any Capital misfortune had happened they would have asked me why they had not been truly Informed. But my Crime consists in not being a New England Man in principle, and unless they alter theirs I hope I never shall be. Gen. Gates Is their Idol because he is at their direction." Content now that Congress intended to inquire into his conduct, Schuyler was willing to postpone resigning his commission until his reputation had been cleared. Had this not been offered, the general would, he said, have resigned the moment Gates had relieved him on Van Schaick's Island. "I believe a certain set will wish that they had not urged for an Enquiry," he told Morris.[7]

Schuyler's jealous defense of his honor and his dogged determination to vindicate himself may suggest mere obsession, or pride and arrogance, and the ambitions of a pompous man. But men of the Age of Enlightenment (of which he is surely a reflection) followed the ideal of earned public honor. That ideal was sacred, and a love of fame or glory was not deemed ignoble. Honor was "a guard to virtue. It held men's opinion in high esteem, and felt shame to be caught in less than virtuous action before mankind." Unjustly accused of dishonorable acts or motives, such men could not be indifferent to calumny. Even the *appearance* of virtue was a precious part of one's good name.[8] No wonder, then, that Schuyler was outraged by slander, by misjudgment of his motives, and by the traducing of his competence and fidelity in the discharge of his duties. His sentiments were wholly in tune with much of the Revolutionary ideology that was focused on creating a republic of virtue—a political economy whose people could be truly free only if they were public spirited, honest and uncorrupt, and disciplined in their devotion to the common good.

Aside from Schuyler's own massive collection of papers through which he began to sift in preparation of his vindication, Richard Varick's report on musters to a congressional committee buttressed the general's case for exoneration. The deputy muster-master general's comprehensive review of the state of the army since the spring of 1777 ably argued that the loss of Ticonderoga could by no means be attributed to the general's neglect of duty. If anything, Horatio Gates had neglected his duty as Schuyler's surrogate. Chief Justice John Jay and James Duane were also sympathetic supporters of the general's efforts to seek vindication of his military record. "Truth must and will triumph," Jay insisted. "Permit me to hint that Care should be taken lest Posterity be influenced in their opinions of your Character & Conduct by the Tales and Prejudices of the present Day."9

Schuyler needed no prompting to make a careful preparation of his defense. He intended to present all of his correspondence with Washington, Congress, and every other public body with whom he had dealt, and also every order he had issued since the close of the 1776 campaign. Candid readers of this record would surely see that the "Misfortunes to the Northward" had not originated with him. For the moment Schuyler watched his successor's moves. Gates's choice of a position three miles above Stillwater to make a stand against Burgoyne was not, he thought, as advantageous as a spot to his rear, but perhaps Gates did not dare make the slightest hint of a retreat lest it dampen the spirits of his troops. Schuyler feared that Gates erred by detaching "so capital" a part of the army as Benjamin Lincoln's corps and sending them north to Skenesborough and Ticonderoga. Lincoln's men, he was convinced, were needed closer to Stillwater, where the major British offensive was expected to occur, and Schuyler guessed that Gates had finally recognized this when he summoned the Albany County militia to reinforce his own position. From the area about fourteen miles east of Saratoga Lincoln might better maneuver against the posts captured by Burgoyne or against the British flank and yet be within easy striking distance to assist in a "general engagement" with the main army once the British chose to attempt it. Praying that God would grant Gates success, Schuyler was convinced that he could "never Impute It to his [Gates's] Military Abilities, for altho he may have Courage I am sure he has nothing Else."10

From the last days of August until mid-October, as summer changed to autumn, Schuyler remained in Albany, anxiously watching Gates's and Burgoyne's armies and relying upon his former secretary, the deputy muster-master general Richard Varick, and a former aide, Maj. Henry Brockholst Livingston, to keep him abreast of their maneuvers. Hoping of course that the British could be forced to retreat before reaching Saratoga,

Fig. 6. Richard Varick, 1753–1831. Engraving by H. B. Hall and Sons for the *Magazine of American History*. Varick, Schuyler's trusted aide, kept him apprised of events and the byplay between Horatio Gates and Benedict Arnold during the battles of Saratoga. Courtesy, The New-York Historical Society, New York City.

if not to surrender, Schuyler was little less anxious about the state of his property when Burgoyne's army passed the Hudson River and encamped on the "plains of Saratoga" on 13 September. The first onslaught to Schuyler's estate was described by Thomas Anbury. Noting the "handsome and commodious dwelling-house, with out-houses, and exceedingly fine saw- and grist-mill, and at a small distance a very neat church, with several houses around it," the British officer remarked that

> This beautiful spot was quite deserted, not a living creature on it. On the grounds were great quantities of fine wheat, as also Indian corn; the former was instantly cut down, threshed, carried to the mill to be ground, and delivered to the men to save our provisions; the latter was cut for forage for the horses.
>
> Thus a plantation, with large crops of several sorts of grain, thriving and beautiful in the morning, was before night reduced to a scene of distress and poverty! What havoc and devastation is attendant on war![11]

While wishing that Gates's army might press north to Saratoga before Burgoyne's could reach his "plantation," Schuyler wrote Varick on 14 September, anxiously requesting confirmation of a report that none of his buildings had been burned. "If you get to Saratoga," he asked, "I wish you would hint to Gen: Gates that care ought to be taken that the troops do not damage any of the buildings, Nor destroy the fences. Mention It also If You please to Colo: Wilkinson, as from Yourself and desire Livingston & Lansingh to do the like." While the loss of some property like the crops could be expected, Schuyler mostly feared the ruin of more permanent fixtures on the estate.[12]

Varick of course obliged. On 16 September, in one of his frequent missives, he sent word that he had rescued a part of Mrs. Schuyler's roaming property—a cow taken from Gates's entourage. The cow had not been surrendered without some altercation. Varick continued to lament Schuyler's loss of command: "I wish to God we had a Commander who could see a little Distance before him without Spectacles and we would probably make as *Brilliant* a stroke as that of Bennington." But Schuyler was not in the best of health, and it was not particularly unfortunate for him not to be in the field. On 18 September after being bled by his doctor he felt much better, but he was obliged to let others conduct even routine business like pushing the Indian warriors out of Albany and on to the army north of Stillwater.[13]

2

"The Event ... makes the heavy loss ... sit quite Easy on me."

Between mid-September and early October the two great armies maneuvered. Like Varick, Schuyler's former aide, Henry B. Livingston, continued to keep Schuyler abreast of the activities of Gates's army. Gates, he noted, intended to advance only when he was assured that Burgoyne was moving south of Saratoga. Late in the evening on 19 September Schuyler obtained news of the fierce battle of Freeman's Farm, which had raged from noon until almost dark. The two armies fought each other to a standstill, but Gates refused to commit reserve forces that Benedict Arnold felt were necessary to win a decisive victory. Had Gates taken the risk Arnold wanted, he might have exploited a weak spot between Burgoyne's center and his right wing commanded by General Simon Fraser, and the British defenses might have been decisively crushed then and there.[14]

Arnold was furious that Gates had declined to take the offensive, chagrined to learn that he had been given no mention in Gates's dispatches to Congress, and annoyed by a variety of other grievances. After quarreling bitterly with Gates on 22 September, Arnold finally demanded a pass to visit Philadelphia. Although Gates quickly granted it, Arnold followed the urgings of fellow officers to stay, and he realized that were he to go he would lose a chance to be restored to a rank senior to that of officers like Benjamin Lincoln. But again on 1 October Gates and Arnold fell into further altercation when Arnold charged Gates with jealousy, timidity, and losing touch with the sentiments of his troops. Gates then removed Arnold from command of the left wing of his army—a step that did not, however, prevent Arnold from rushing onto the field in the second battle of Saratoga (7 October) and gallantly leading Ebenezer Learned's brigade to break through the enemy's lines.[15]

In Varick's account of the first battle on 19 September he had little to tell Schuyler about Gates except that he would rather see him drawn and quartered than to serve him. Since his work as muster-master had been completed, Varick had chosen to serve as supernumerary aide to Arnold. Varick also found that Gates had not yet drawn General Lincoln's corps toward the main army as Schuyler himself had proposed to do. With them, Gates's army could surely ruin Burgoyne's. Lamentably, the colonel noted, Lincoln remained "on some airy Scheme" to the northward.[16]

When Schuyler obtained Varick's battle report early on 20 September, he promised, as Varick had requested, to send wagons to carry the wounded from the field. Happy to hear of Americans' gallant behavior under fire, the general hoped the day would "crown them with never fading glory." Unfortunately, he had found that about sixty Iroquois warriors had not yet been persuaded to leave Albany because several of them had wanted to be made captains. But he hoped to push them out of the city yet that morning. Evidently he succeeded; about a hundred and fifty tribesmen had reached Gates's army before noon on 20 September.[17]

With an eye to the enemy's future maneuvers, Schuyler warned Varick of a swamp that would likely separate Burgoyne's left wing from the right when it reached a small bridge south of "old Dunham's house" near the Hudson River. Schuyler suggested that a "retrenchment" be thrown between the river and the swamp; a small body of troops might defend the position, giving Arnold time to augment his own division and thereby to rout Burgoyne's right wing before it could be relieved from the left. If Varick thought proper, he might, Schuyler suggested, show his letter to Arnold because Arnold may not have been present with the party that had reconnoitred the swamp earlier. "Destroy my letters," he warned the colonel, "lest an accident should throw them Into hands I do not wish they should fall Into I mean the person you mention."[18]

The person Varick mentioned of course was Gates. Like Henry B. Livingston, Varick sided with Arnold in his quarrel with Gates. And Schuyler, too, regarded Arnold as the abler of the two leaders. Gates's refusal to answer Arnold's repeated calls for reinforcements on 19 September had deprived the army of a complete victory over Burgoyne. Indeed, Varick alleged that Gates never intended to fight Burgoyne at all until Arnold urged and begged him to do so. "Nay, he meant by moving the Army to cast on Odium on" Schuyler's own reputation "in hopes that Burgoyne would be frightened by his Movement from the South & North." Varick also believed that Arnold had been so offended by Gates's treatment "that I make not the least doubt the latter will be called on [out?], as soon as the Service will admit, they are not on speaking terms."[19]

Henry B. Livingston wrote Schuyler of the Arnold-Gates dispute in a similar vein. Aside from their gossipy accounts to Schuyler both Livingston and Varick were able to glean snatches of news about the general's country house. On 24 September Varick announced that the interior of the house had been found ruined, with windows knocked out and wallpaper torn down by enemy occupants. Except for some demolished fences, however, the rest of the property remained "pretty safe." And but for Gates's refusal to furnish Arnold the troops he had called for on 19 September, Varick was certain that he might have been able to write Schuyler his report of 25 September at Saratoga instead of from the camp near Stillwater ten miles away.[20]

Little evidence of Schuyler's reaction to Varick's and Livingston's reports remains, but it is clear that he shared their sympathies for Benedict Arnold. Like Arnold, the general was beset by a variety of misfortunes, many of them the work of military rivals and hostile partisans. Schuyler quietly observed that he was certain of the reason for the quarrel between Arnold and Gates. Gates was a man of limited capabilities, at least as far as they were demonstrated in the campaign of 1777. And he would probably be indebted to Arnold "for the glory he may acquire by a victory; but perhaps he is so very sure of success that he does not wish the other to come in for a share of it." And whatever other sentiments he may have entertained of his successor, Schuyler's share in the Arnold affair was certainly recognized beyond the confines of the Northern Army. James Lovell of Massachusetts, for example, informed Gates that he feared "that sprightly gentleman [Arnold] will be duped by an artful senior now disgraced [Schuyler], so as to become a tool for base purposes."[21]

While the clash between Arnold and Gates unfolded after the first battle of Saratoga, Schuyler exchanged reports of military actions laced with a variety of political news and views with Gouverneur Morris. From Kingston, Morris had much to say not only of assembly business but of the behavior of Horatio Gates and the Continental Congress. Gates, he said, "may if he pleases neglect to ask or disdain to receive Advice, But those who know him will, I am sure, be convinced that he wants it." Morris was "confident" that Gates was not the man to take proper advantages of Burgoyne's situation, and he doubted his skills to manage a battle—the only "resource" the American army might have. "Congress have a good Right to be displeased with you," he teased, "for Painting your Situation in its native colors For it is impossible to be pleased with a Man who puts one in bodily Fear but in Revenge you will have the Applause of your own Mind and the pleasing Consideration that Posterity will do you the Justice which it is to little Purpose whether the present Age either grant[s] or refuse[s]." Morris was mistaken about posterity; nor would the general be content only with the "applause" of his own conscience. The Yorker coveted the fame and honor that he and so many of his contemporaries valued. The nobility of his motives, like the diligence of his labors, made this desire for renown something better than a sin.

Still, Morris endeavored to bolster Schuyler's spirits. Turning to the business of the legislature, Morris told him that the senate "is doing I know not what. In Assembly we wrangle long to little Purpose ... from nine in the Morning till Dusk in the Evening we were employed in appointing [John Morin] Scott, [Levi] Pauling [Abraham] Yates [Jr.] & [Alexander] Webster to be the Council of Appointment. I tremble for the Consequences but I smile and shall continue to do so if possible." The question of naming a new slate of delegates to Congress remained unresolved. In fact what Morris perhaps did not yet realize was that Schuyler was soon to lose his place as a congressman—the only one of five men chosen in May who was not reelected on 2 October. But Morris gave no hint that such an insult to the general was in the offing. "We are just about to think of a Militia Law," he said, "and I should be happy to be informed of your Sentiments, or rather Plans, upon that Subject. It is doubtless of Importance, and the Mode now to be adopted, whether Good or Evil, will have a very Distant Operation. It will become a principal Part of the Jurisprudence of the State, and, as such, shed an Influence upon the Constitution."[22]

Like Morris, other members of the legislature occasionally solicited Schuyler's views on legislative and constitutional matters. Several had invited him to comment on the features of the draft constitution in 1776. John Morin Scott now asked for a copy of a "balloting bill" that had formerly been submitted to the legislature, and the general was obliged to unpack his papers to find it.[23] Similarly, he found time to answer Morris's latest request on 21 September. "The draft of a miltia law," he wrote, "was sent to Convention. I have no Copy of It. It is imperfect as you will easily perceive when you see It."

As for Morris's account of legislative activity, Schuyler had less to say than he did on military affairs of the moment. He did not, he explained, find Morris's news distasteful, "not that I am fond of wrangling, but some good will come from It, and those who have merit & abilities will in the End Succeed." On occasion the general's perception of the realities of public life could be called that of an optimistic Stoic. Professing indifference to Yankee opinion of him, the Yorker decided that "If It was what they esteem a good one I should suspect that I had more of the villain In me than my Conscience will allow." Although the general thought "the Event of the campaign" still doubtful, the prospect of an American victory was "more agreeable" than it hitherto had been. News of the enemy in New Jersey suggested that they intended a diversion to support the northern invasion. Burgoyne must have expected this, he said, else he would never have ventured to bring his entire force so far south or to have failed to make the best provisions for a retreat.[24]

The Yorker correctly guessed that the British would attempt some diversion to assist Burgoyne. Early in October, Gen. Sir Henry Clinton broke through the defenses of the lower Hudson valley, taking Fort Clinton and Fort Montgomery. Gen. Sir John Vaughan and Sir James Wallace moved north to Kingston and burned the town, and on 17 October they sailed on to a point in Livingston Manor, within about forty miles of Albany. *"We are hellishly frightened,"* exclaimed Gouverneur Morris on 8 October, *"but don't say a word of that* for we shall get our spirits again."[25]

After Gates's army encountered Burgoyne's on 7 October, the British might have been finished off once and for all, but Gates failed to press forward. Deciding to rest and revictual his troops, he allowed Burgoyne, still hoping for assistance from Clinton, to fall back to still another position. Ironically, Gates has been praised for being wisely cautious, but critics have castigated Schuyler's caution as weakness and even cowardice.[26]

The British began their retreat to Saratoga on 8 October, and again Schuyler's mansion offered Burgoyne shelter from the heavy rains of 9–10 October. Aside from skirmishing, Gates's army did not follow until the afternoon of 10 October. Annoyed by Gates's dawdling, Schuyler thought that "If Arnold's advice had been pursued, the Enemy would have been routed on the 20th of last month and the Fortifications below would in all probability not have been attacked. The same want of vigour has taken place after the Action of the 7th Instant [October]." While fifteen thousand American troops sat looking at Burgoyne's dispirited five thousand, Schuyler admitted that Gates's own inactivity and failure to move "within Ken of the Enemy" might be prudent. But it was "not very gallant." Surely his successor knew that Burgoyne could not retreat; was this why Gates refused to risk an engagement? On 12 October Schuyler was convinced that if Sir Henry Clinton's forces managed to reach Albany, the tables would be turned on Gates. Already, he wrote Gouverneur Morris, Saratoga had been destroyed: "I expected it would be so!" It was hardly comforting to hear that Gates intended to remonstrate with Burgoyne regarding the devastation; Schuyler doubted that Gates's personal missives would be more successful than his official correspondence.[27]

As the American army forced their enemy north of the Fishkill on 10 October, Schuyler's house, together with other buildings, mills, and barracks were fired by Burgoyne's order to prevent them from serving as a cover for the Americans. Curiously there were rumors of conflagration well before it occurred. William Smith, Jr., for example, noted that as early as 6 October the Saratoga mills had been burned by order of Horatio Gates! "Poor Schuyler," Smith exclaimed in his diary, "Whither is he to fly—neither South nor North—If the West he is exposed to the Savages and in N England he has many Thousands of Enemies ... there is no Escape down the River as he is said to have intended by chartering a Sloop to remove them to New Windsor for whence he was to proceed by Land & winter in Jersey or Pensilvania."[28]

By 13 October, however, it was not Schuyler but Burgoyne who was obliged to consider the prospects of escaping the clutches of the enemy. Surrounded by a force three times larger than his own, Burgoyne asked for a cessation of hostilities. For the next three days he stalled for time, still hoping to be rescued from final surrender by General Vaughan's foray up the Hudson. Increasingly anxious about the enemy's threatening diversion from the south, Gates finally caved in to Burgoyne's demands for a "convention" instead of a forthright "capitulation." On the morning of 16 October Gates forced Burgoyne to accept his own officers' advice to yield. Even so, the American commander was unnecessarily generous with the terms of surrender, which "should have been an unqualified one."[29]

The first reports of the negotiations and surrender terms that Schuyler probably received came from Richard Varick. Congratulating Schuyler on the victory, Varick exclaimed, "I wish to God, I could say," it might have been "under Your Command." If the general wished to see Burgoyne, he must visit him at Saratoga. When Varick's letter reached Schuyler at 2:00 A.M. on 15 October, he responded briefly: "The Event that has taken place makes the heavy loss I have sustained sit quite Easy on me. Britain will probably see how fruitless her Attempt to Inslave us will be. I set out today [.]"[30] He must have reached the army on 15 or 16 October.

With the articles of surrender finally signed, on 17 October Gates's army drew up in "two lines, flags flying and fifes and drums shrilling 'Yankee Doodle,' while the enemy entered the meadow north of the Fishkill ... to lay down their arms." One native of the area, seeing a parade of light horse before the British entered the lines to surrender, recalled a report that one soldier threatened to "put a brace of balls through" General Schuyler if he dared show his face at the scene. John Becker dismissed the news as Yankee bravado and saw Schuyler approach the corps on his favorite white horse "in a very handsome style." The ex-commander gave them the passing review as military etiquette prescribed. But eager to catch a glimpse of Burgoyne, the observer did not stay to hear what Schuyler said as he began to address the troops.[31]

The field of surrender that autumn day swarmed with many friends and comrades with whom Schuyler could rejoice. Among the officers were also relatives and boyhood chums like Brig. Gen. Abraham Ten Broeck of the Albany County militia. Col. Stephen Schuyler, the general's brother, and Col. Robert Van Rensselaer, his brother-in-law, were also present. Schuyler's twelve-year-old son, John Bradstreet, also witnessed the surrender with his father; "placed on an eminence, at the foot of which stood General Gates and near which the American army was drawn up," the lad might have thrilled to watch the array of the ragged victors and the vanquished in their splendid uniforms.[32] But did he appreciate the position of his father who had contributed so much to the achievement of the day and who now confronted the devastation of a once-flourishing estate?

Another observer, British lieutenant William Digby, recorded the highlights of the day in his diary. "About 10 O'clock we marched out . . . with Drums beating & the honours of war; but the Drums seemed to have lost their former inspiring sounds, & though we beat the Grenadiers March . . . yet then it seemed by its last feeble effort, as if almost ashamed to be heard . . . I never shall forget the appearance of their Troops on our marching past them. A dead silence universally reigned thro' their numerous Columns, & even then they seemed struck with our situation, & dare scarce lift up their eyes to view British Troops in such a situation. I must say their decent behavior during the time (to us so greatly fallen) merited the utmost approbation & praise."[33]

The wife of Maj. Gen. Frederick Von Riedesel thought so, too. As she rode through the American camp in her calash, the baroness was gratified that the victors were not insolent, and that no one insulted her. "When I drew near the tents," she recelled, "a good looking man advanced towards me, and helped the children from the calash, and kissed and caressed them: he then offered me his arm, and tears trembled in his eyes." It was the squire of Saratoga, Burgoyne's "moral vanquisher—victor chiefest of all in magnanimity." And if we may believe John Trumbull's great painting of the surrender scene, he was no longer wearing the regimentals of rebellion, but the plain clothes of a private gentleman. One of Schuyler's grandsons remembered him as a man not quite six feet tall, a rather thin but well-proportioned figure with brown complexion and black eyes. His manners were warm and courtly, as Baroness Riedesel and many others have attested. His raspy voice was clear. The baroness was reassured by his benevolent countenance and the kind gestures to her children. Schuyler ushered her into Gates's tent, where he was conversing amiably with Burgoyne and Phillips.[34]

While the captured army filed by the American headquarters, the generals dined with Gates. The two principals exchanged toasts to Washington and the king. Baroness Riedesel was relieved to escape the "large

Fig. 7. The Surrender of General Burgoyne at Saratoga, 17 October 1777. Mural by John Trumbull in the United States Capitol Rotunda. Philip Schuyler (the fifth figure from the right) was present at the surrender of the British troops. His many contributions to the American victory included the sacrifice of his country estate at Saratoga. Courtesy, Architect of the Capitol.

company of gentlemen" and to dine in Schuyler's tent. She relished her host's hearty meal of smoked tongue, beefsteak, potatoes, fresh butter, and bread. Later in the afternoon, after consulting her husband, she accepted Schuyler's invitation to his house at Albany. The erstwhile commander then set her off on the first lap of the journey south. On 18 October she reached Albany, where she was overwhelmed by the friendly and courteous reception tendered by Mrs. Schuyler and her daughters. "We remained three days with that excellent family," she wrote, "and they seemed to regret our departure."[35]

3

"My hobby-horse has long been a country life"

While the baroness and others made their way south to Albany, Schuyler lingered amid the ruins of his beloved Saratoga. The task of reconstruction was doubtless formidable, but his forebears had faced similar circumstances, and the Yorker was no stranger to the labors of gentlemen farmers. Schuyler had inherited the property, added to it, and developed it so that by 1765 there were "two good Saw Mills and a very pretty little house. On this Land," Lord Adam Gordon reported, Schuyler produced "Hemp, from Six to Ten Feet high, and for two Crops running." Another contemporary, Mrs. Anne Grant, wrote that it was here that Schuyler's "political and economical genius had full scope. He had always the command of a great number of those workmen who were employed in public buildings, etc." These constructed "squares of buildings in the nature of barracks, for the purpose of lodging artisans and laborers of all kinds. . . . Schuyler built a spacious and convenient house [with] barracks at a distance, not only as a nursery for the arts which he meant to encourage, but as the materials of a future colony. . . . He had here a number of negroes well acquainted with felling of trees and managing sawmills; of which he erected several. And while these were employed in carrying on a very advantageous trade of deals and lumber, which were floated down on rafts to New York, they were at the same time clearing the ground for the Colony." Schuyler's "establishment was an asylum for every one who wanted bread and a home"; and "some hundreds of people . . . were employed at once." Tenants paid their rents in timber and grain and patronized Schuyler's country store. After a winter's work of cutting wood, employees busied themselves with fishing during summer. Flax was raised, dressed, spun, and made into linen. "It is inconceivable," Mrs. Grant observed, "what dexterity, address, and deep policy were exhibited in the management of this new settlement; the growth of which was repaid beyond belief." Her description, though general, is well borne out by Schuyler's account books and other papers.[36] But now practically everything lay in ruins.

Schuyler's estate did not occupy a position of safety until after the Revolution. It had long lain in the path of invaders—first the French and Indians and then the British. Then came the great invasion of 1777. The final calamity at Old Saratoga did not occur until the British were forced to retreat north of the Fishkill, the creek running east into the Hudson and just north of the house. On 10 October "As soon as Burgoyne was forced to leave his headquarters, General Schuyler's mansion, together with several other houses, were burned to the ground, set on fire," according to the Baron Von Riedesel's *Memoirs,* "by wicked hands." Two days later Richard Varick penned Schuyler the news. The enemy's retreat revealed their wanton barbarity. None of the buildings had escaped their malice "except the *Necessary* & your Saw Mill which is in the Same Situation we left It," he wrote. "Hardly a Vestage *[sic]* of the Fences is left except a few Rails of the Garden." In all Schuyler found that the "upper mill" was the only building "out of five and twenty" that had not been destroyed.[37]

While the Baroness Von Riedesel alluded to the destruction as being "without any necessity, as it was said," Burgoyne insisted otherwise. On 26 May 1778, the defeated general rose to address the House of Commons on a motion for an enquiry into the "Saratoga business." He said, "I positively assert there was no fire by order or countenance of myself, or any other officer, except at Saratoga," where large barracks built by Schuyler "took fire the day after the army arrived upon the ground in their retreat." The barracks were used as a British hospital, and their burning was an accident. Burgoyne estimated that Schuyler's "very good dwelling house, exceeding large storehouses, great saw mills, and other out-buildings," were worth about £10,000. He further explained that a few days before the negotiations with Gates, the Americans moved to attack. And as a large column of their troops approached to pass the Fishkill, they were protected by these buildings from the fire of the British artillery. Hence Burgoyne had ordered them burned. The diary of William Digby, lieutenant of the 53d Regiment, supports Burgoyne's allegations. And Burgoyne insisted that "to show that the person most deeply concerned in that calamity did not" construe the conflagration as proceeding from malice, "I must inform the House, that one of the first persons I saw, after the convention was signed, was General Scuyler *[sic].*" And when Burgoyne expressed his regret and the reasons for the destruction, Schuyler, he said, "desired me to think no more of it: said, that the occasion justified it according to the principles and rules of war, and he should have done the same upon the same occasion, or words to that effect." Moreover, Burgoyne's handsome reception at Albany indicated that Schuyler bore no grudge.[38]

By 12 October Schuyler must have already received word of the ruins, for he was sending "Tom and another servant" to salvage the iron work from the charred remains. Iron and nails were scarce, and he urged Varick to procure some help in gathering them up if he could. Intending to ride up in the next day or two if he were not "too indisposed," he wondered whether any turnips and potatoes remained. "Pray ask" Udny Hay, the deputy quartermaster general, he said, "to let as much of my forage be saved as possible as I intend Immediately to have my mills rebuilt and some house Erected." He would need fodder for his draft animals.[39]

It was not surprising that Schuyler should wish to concentrate upon private pursuits. The summer and early fall of 1777 had brought him to the nadir of his public career. Defeated in the first state elections for governor in June, dismissed from his command of the army in August, and unpopular because of the loss of Ticonderoga and the failure to turn the invaders back, he had also seen his eldest daughter, Angelica, elope with John Barker Church. The New York State Legislature added insult to injury by denying him a place on the state's delegation to Congress and electing Francis Lewis in his "place and stead." The legislature, fumed Gouverneur Morris, "like other of the Vulgar follow the Current of Opinion." The general, however, responded with equanimity. "The Step the Legislature has taken is not at all mortifying to me. I have been so unfortunate in public life and have met with so much Chagrin In It That I really do not wish to risque It any longer. I shall soon sit down a private citizen."[40]

Upon witnessing the surrender ceremonies on 17 October, Schuyler sent Colonel Varick to Albany to prepare Mrs. Schuyler to receive Burgoyne, the Riedesels, and their entourage. Varick found the general's wife and household well but much disconcerted over news of the enemy's recent approaches up the Hudson. And in order to feed Burgoyne's suite, Varick called upon the deputy quartermaster general Udny Hay for several barrels of pork and beef for Mrs. Schuyler's kitchen.[41]

Meantime, the general set to work rebuilding his property at Saratoga. One of his grandsons, Philip Church, later recalled that though in manners warm and gentlemanly, his grandfather seldom allowed guests to interfere with his duties.[42] In less than a fortnight he accumulated the materials and workmen for the erection of a new house. During that time Burgoyne lingered for more than a week at the mansion on the southern edge of Albany, and the exchanges between his host and Schuyler's aides in the city offer a curious commentary on the aftermath of the great campaign. It was ironic, too, that the vanquished general should tarry so comfortably in Schuyler's Albany mansion, while Schuyler, one of the victors, lived in a tent amid the ruins of Saratoga. The defeated army, however, began to march to Boston, and Gates's troops fell back to Albany before being scattered to new assignments.

At Saratoga Schuyler encountered difficulties in obtaining carpenters, masons, and building supplies. And there were other problems at Albany.

A number of Gates's riflemen and light infantry had camped on the hill behind Schuyler's house, and Mrs. Schuyler delayed sending some servants to the country to help her husband because she needed them to guard her potatoes from pilferers. In addition the soldiers took Schuyler's fencing to make shelters for themselves, and all their officers would promise was that the material would not be destroyed. Burgoyne's suite, said John Lansing, "have entirely discomposed the Oconomy [sic] of the Family and have given no small Degree of Trouble to Mrs. Schuyler." Thus the poor woman was harassed by conquerors and conquered alike. "God knows," Varick sputtered, why Gates's army was not sent south to deal with the "barbarians" on the Hudson. The nominal hero of Saratoga had informed Mrs. Schuyler that he had "put some things in" her husband's way and had left a company of carpenters to assist him at Saratoga. "We doubt It," Varick quipped.[43]

Finally, on 27 October Lansing wrote triumphantly, "General Burgoine & Train have at last decamped. They set off early this Morning. Mrs. Schuyler and Family are well." It was not necessary to add that she and they were also relieved to be rid of them.[44]

By 1 November Schuyler had gathered the means to begin his new house at Saratoga, but not without difficulty. On 23 October, for example, he found that a company of carpenters had been ordered to leave Saratoga, thus requiring the hiring of other workmen, including masons from Schenectady. So eager was he to get them that the general instructed John Lansing to hire them at extraordinary wages rather than do without them. Lansing engaged an Albany mason and his apprentice at 16 shillings and 12 shillings per day respectively—enormous wages, he thought, but absolutely necessary. Autumn rain hindered their departure from Albany as it did Schuyler's construction work farther nother. Henry Glen was asked to hire other men at Schenectady.[45]

Pausing from his construction work, Schuyler wrote President Hancock, reminding him of his promise to inform him whenever Congress determined the points on which their official inquiry would proceed. Noting that on 2 November two British officers had taken shelter from a violent rainstorm in his hut, Schuyler concluded from their conversation that British forces in Canada together with those still at Ticonderoga numbered about two thousand. Another fifteen hundred to two thousand were probably scattered among Oswegatchie, Niagara, and the "upper" posts. Schuyler therefore proposed a winter invasion of Canada; the enemy should be driven out of Ticonderoga and the northern province before the momentum of the Saratoga victory disappeared. In detail he suggested the necessary preparations if an expedition was to be ready when the lakes were frozen to permit crossing, probably in mid-February. Admitting the difficulties, he insisted that the project was not impossible if measures were promptly taken to collect provisions and the means of transportation.

No less particular were Schuyler's proposals for military operations. But if Congress decided to approve the winter campaign, he would give every aid at his disposal as a private genetleman without "fee or reward." Within three weeks he expected to bring near completion "a comfortable House" and then he would be happy to be ordered to headquarters for his trial.[46]

Schuyler's fresh proposals for yet another campaign suggest an inability to resist completely the habits that over two years of military life had thrust upon him. Although his immediate concerns remained focused upon his country project, the pull of public interests was also apparent, as he wrote Chief Justice John Jay on 6 November. The British devastation of Kingston and the fact that so many others had suffered property losses was no consolation to him. Jay's own need for better accommodations than he could find at Fishkill prompted the general to ask, "Can I be of any service?" Perhaps the chief justice might like to take one of the fine farms between Saratoga and Albany, which Schuyler's Tory tenants had lost. The frame of an entire house could be sawed and other construction materials procured at the cheapest rates. His new house, Schuyler explained, was begun on 1 November, and by midmonth he expected to have it under cover with two rooms finished, provided the weather turned not too wet; "it is only a frame house, sixty feet long, twenty-one broad, and two stories high, filled in with brick." But it would enable him to "be as far out of the noise and bustle of the great world as possible." Expecting to enjoy "true felicity" in this retreat, Schuyler mused, "My hobby-horse has long been a country life; I dismounted with reluctance, and now saddle him again with a very considerable share of satisfaction (for the injurious world has not been able to deprive me of the best source of happiness, the approbation of my own heart), and I hope to canter him gently on to the end of the journey of life." Perhaps he knew better. Despite his protestations, Philip Schuyler was never quite able to keep his hand out of public affairs, as his later years all too clearly show. Even now, he urged Jay to mention the necessity of several actions to his friends in the state legislature. If the enemy again tried an invasion up the Hudson and attacks on the eastern states, as Schuyler expected them to do, there would be a shortage of bread; it would therefore be prudent to store flour east of the Green Mountains and to obstruct the river against British penetration beyond the Highlands. Similarly, Schuyler hoped that care would be taken in army recruiting. Now was no time to grow negligent or to trust too much in good fortune. It was dangerous to slide into "too much confidence."[47]

Jay found himself unable to decide what to do or whether to leave Fishkill. The legislature had fled Kingston on the British approach in October, and the council of safety was obliged to conduct the government alone until January 1778. Agreeing with Schuyler's proposals to prepare for another campaign, he was happy the general's "Firmness [was] unimpaired, and your Attachment to your Country unabated by its Ingratitude. Justice will yet take Place," he insisted, "and I do not despair of seeing the Time when it will be confessed that the Foundation of our Success in the northern Department was lain by the present Commander's Predecessor." Jay hoped soon to consult Schuyler about how he might best publicize the record of his military career. "Evidence of the Propriety of your Conduct may be transmitted to Posterity as may contradict the many Lies which will be told them by writers under Impressions and under an Influence unfriendly to your Reputation." As for the general's thought that he had lost influence in the legislature, Jay deemed "it is less so than you may imagine. The virtuous & sensible still retain their former Sentiments. The Residue will ever be directed by accident & Circumstances."[48]

Meantime, by 5 November Mrs. Schuyler had joined her husband in his makeshift hut at Saratoga. Together they saw the frame of the new house raised three days later. By 19 November a room and the cellar kitchen were finished. A number of army mechanics had speeded the work. But their services were not a public expense. Evidently exchanging labor for some of Schuyler's lumber in November, General Gates asked him to have bateaumen at Saratoga raft joists from his sawmill down to Albany where an ordnance store was to be built, and where the hospital and garrison needed wood. If, however, the deputy quartermaster general furnished articles like nails and glass from army stores, this seems to have been an entirely appropriate compensation for the capital losses that Schuyler had sustained at Saratoga.[49]

During November, while the Schuylers were at Saratoga, their older children remained with servants or relatives at Albany; there John Lansing, Jr., and Richard Varick continued to superintend affairs as required. The aides' letters offer glimpses of family affairs and of household management so intimately affected by the recent military campaign. Mary Eggemont, the housekeeper, wished to know how to dispose of the cows, which some rascal milked each day before servants could be sent to do so. Lansing promised to send several guards to watch the cattle and try to detect the thieves. Charles, evidently a slave, had to be sent to Saratoga because his every look and action showed that he was too lazy to remain in Albany without a mistress to direct him. Mary refused to surrender her whitewash brush, broom, or a kettle for use in the country because she had need for them, so Colonel Varick searched in Albany for the articles. John Lansing wondered whether the hogs should be slaughtered. Dr. Treat would send up some medicine for young John Bradstreet Schuyler, who was with his parents. Schuyler's sloop, Varick wrote on 1 December, had just arrived with wood for the barracks master, for which it had been pressed into service. Some of the cargo would be sent to the Albany house for the winter fires.[50]

By 1 December Mrs. Schuyler returned to Albany, where a larger household demanded her attention. There, too, she might assist her consort in a thousand ways that can only be imagined from the few remaining scraps of evidence of her busy life. "Dear Caty," the general wrote tersely on 15 December, "please pay Captain Richard Warner £139.8.0 *for value received*." Was this perhaps for some of the construction work at Saratoga? On 19 December Mrs. Schuyler also paid John Bromly £12 for work he had done at Saratoga.[51]

The reconstruction of Saratoga kept Schuyler from returning to Albany until 21 December. Perhaps in keeping with the approaching holiday— but certainly with his lifelong record of dedication to the principles of mercy and humane justice—the general found occasion to intercede for several unfortunate individuals. With the conclusion of the campaign he asked General Gates to release Walter Butler from the Albany gaol where he had been confined such August. The young Mohawk valley Loyalist had deserved the treatment he had received as a spy, but Schuyler thought it was possible to prevent him from doing the public any "disservice" by granting him parole under proper bond for his good behavior. Butler's fellow prisoner, Peter Ten Broeck, might also be entitled to the same clemency, and he asked Gates "to confer it."[52]

About this same time Schuyler alerted the Albany committee to the behavior of a certain Philip Rogers and others who were plundering Loyalist property in the neighborhood of Saratoga and failing to differentiate between Tories who had joined the enemy and those who had returned peaceably to their homes. Because wives of men who had already been jailed for Loyalism would suffer without their husbands' protection, Schuyler advised the committee to release its prisoners on bail. Families of the latter would thereby not burden public charity.[53] The general's clemency, his sense of decency, and his eye for practicability were similarly displayed in the postwar years; as in 1777, he sought to ameliorate the harsh penal laws that the New York State legislature imposed upon those who failed to accept as patriotic the rebellion against Great Britain.

The Yorker's lenient views toward Loyalists were probably prompted by the freeing of the northern frontiers from any further danger. Early in November the remnant of British forces withdrew from Lake Champlain. After burning the buildings at Ticonderoga and Mount Independence, they evacuated these posts on 8 November. Consequently the last of Gates's forces at Albany could also be safely shifted to serve along the lower Hudson and with Washington's army in Pennsylvania.[54]

4

"a State prisoner, indulged with the Liberty of being so at large"

At the end of 1777 Schuyler discovered that his losses were "much more Capital" than he had first imagined. Many of his tenants were ruined, unable to pay arrears in rents or the money that he had advanced them when they began their settlements. Other neighbors around Saratoga were unable to pay for goods purchased from his store, and some, like his Tory tenants, had fled with the enemy. Still, as he told James Duane, he could bear all with great temper, consoled by the prospect of being undisturbed by either the enemy or further public business. "I long much to Smoak a Segar with you when you come up," he wrote. "Supply Yourself well If you can and I will do myself the pleasure to pay you a visit In whatever part of the State You may be, and I will do as much for [William] Duer altho the Idler will not favor me with a Line." While the general longed for letters from old comrades like Duane or hoped to visit them, he reiterated his determination to adhere to private pursuits. Yet he could not resist his penchant for proposing public policies. He wanted Duane's report of how Congress had reacted to his "hint ... about a Sudden Irruption Into Canada In the latter end of Winter." By the end of November he had confirmed reports that he had made to Congress earlier in the month on the size of British forces in Canada. Montreal would be worth seizing because it was the magazine for British goods shipped to the western Indian tribes, as well as a store of a variety of other merchandise and considerably large stocks of ammunition. Canadian merchants might be attached to the American interest if they were encouraged to divert their wares to Albany and were offered payment by bills drawn on France. Similarly, he urged that steps must be taken to secure the Hudson valley;

already Yorkers had "severely felt the calamity" of not having sufficiently done so. Practicable measures should be executed with spirit![55]

Although clearly interested in the state of public affairs, Schuyler found that circumstances afforded opportunities for certain private pursuits. Lumber was scarce and much in demand, and prices were high. Although wages had also risen, Schuyler intended to operate his mills throughout the coming year. And he suggested that he might be of assistance to William Duer by endeavoring to let Duer's mill to the public on shares. The army quartermaster might furnish the manpower to cut the timber and hand it in for sawing. Duer might expect a third of the lumber that was cut as his share—nearly the "Old Lay," Schuyler thought, but as the price of boards was high, "it will answer." Although he had not been idle, the general felt obliged to be more vigilant than ever if he was to recover his very heavy losses.[56]

Recognizing that Schuyler's personal affairs had greatly suffered "by the barbarous Ravages of the British Army," Congress voted him the liberty to tend them "until the Committee appointed to enquire into the Causes of the Loss of Ticonderoga and Mount Independence shall make their Report." It was James Duane who had moved the resolution on his behalf. Grateful for the gesture, Schuyler nevertheless wished that the committee would get on with its work. Sympathetically, Henry Laurens, the new president of Congress, meant to hasten Schuyler's case,[57] but the general was denied a court of inquiry until October 1778. In the latter weeks of 1777 Congress remained preoccupied with other business, including making appointments to a board of war in late November. The quartermaster general Thomas Mifflin supported both Schuyler and Gates as members and wanted Schuyler to be the board's president. Instead Congress chose Mifflin; Gates; Adj. Gen. Timothy Pickering; Richard Peters; and Schuyler's old critic, Col. Joseph Trumbull. And Mifflin then proposed Gates for the chairmanship—a position that Gates proceeded to use not only to his own advantage but to threaten Washington's control of the army.

By December rumors had begun that a cabal, which included Maj. Gen. Thomas Conway, whom Congress had made inspector general, intended to replace Washington with Gates. Recent military reverses like Howe's occupation of Philadelphia and Washington's losses at Brandywine (in September) and Germantown (in October) had roused critics of the Virginian; his authority was resented, and his arguments for a stronger regular army and for less reliance upon militia were resisted. Congressmen like James Lovell seemed to prefer Gates because of his apparent success in using militia at Saratoga. On 17 November Lovell wrote Gates that he might soon replace Washington. "In short this army," he argued, "is to be totally lost unless you come down & collect the virtuous band, who wish to fight under your banner, and with their aid save the southern hemisphere. Prepare yourself for a jaunt to this place— Congress must send for you—I have ten thousand things to tell."[58]

Congress did send for Gates, but it moved him from command on the Hudson to the board of war. If leaders like the Adamses, Richard Henry Lee, and Benjamin Rush did not intend to force Washington to resign, it nonetheless appears that they expected Gates and the new board of war to exert increased civilian control over the Virginian and the army.[59] The Schuyler-Gates factionalism of earlier months was now revived and the supporters of the maligned Yorker and the nominal hero of Saratoga continued to find themselves in similar company. Those who had been hostile to Schuyler were no less so to Washington. But happily for the erstwhile commander of the Northern Army the denouement of the cabal did not involve him except for the board of war's scheme to invade Canada in 1778—a proposal that was poorly made and too tardily planned, although Schuyler himself had made a similar one to Congress in early November 1777, insisting however that were it to be accepted it would require extensive preparations well in advance of its actual execution.

Content with the completion of a comfortable new country house, the general returned to his family at Albany on 21 December for the holidays. Preparations for their festivities were perhaps dampened by news of the death of John Cochran, the son of the general's sister Gertrude and Dr. John Cochran. The boy had fallen from a horse and fractured his skull. His death left his mother "most distressed," but as her son-in-law Walter Livingston proposed to invite her to visit him and his wife at Teviotdale, Schuyler was at least relieved of the anxiety that his only sister might otherwise lack the consolation of her family.[60] And as usual, the return to the comforts of his Albany fireside did not entirely free him from the cares of other business from which he could seldom escape for long.

Just before leaving Saratoga, Schuyler received James Duane's notice that Congress had directed him to meet with the Northern Department's Indian commissioners. A bit uncertain about the propriety of acting for the board, because he considered himself "a State prisoner, indulged with the Liberty of being so at large" until he could be cleared by a court of inquiry, the general nevertheless decided to oblige both Duane and the Congress. Summoning commissioners Oliver Wolcott and Timothy Edwards to Albany, Schuyler proposed that they assemble on 5 January. Congress had taken tentative steps on his proposals for a campaign against Canada. But although these included the reduction of Niagara, Congress had not seen fit to commit troops to the western enterprise; instead, it resolved to ask the Indian commissioners to engage the Iroquois, authorizing them to spend up to $15,000, and to draw a "reasonable amount" of ammunition for the tribesmen from the public stores.[61] Duane's mission was to meet with the board, negotiate suitable alterations in the western scheme, and then report to Congress.

Schuyler's willingness to discharge the duties of Indian commissioner, he decided, depended upon whether his fellow board members did or did not object. The general wondered whether it was wholly proper for him to act in view of Congress's delays in the investigation of his official conduct. But he did not wish to withhold his services entirely until he had been exonerated, or to resign all of his offices until he could properly do so as a vindicated patriot. "Altho deeply Injured by Congress," he told Chancellor Livingston, "unkindly treated by the Senate & house of Representatives of this State ... I thank God my affection for my Country is not diminished in a Single grain and [I] shall be ever ready to afford her my best Efforts in a private Station." Expecting soon to be freed of public office, he proposed "to retire to Saratoga and mount my Hobby horse which I shall not wish to quit until the End of the Journey of Life." Inviting Livingston to comment on Horatio Gates's "Convention" with John Burgoyne, Schuyler clearly was not so enamored of private hobbyhorses to forsake public ones. He had not, he said, ventured to publicize his own opinion because it would not be favorable to Gates; and being so, it would only have been discounted as evidence of the Yorker's resentment.[62]

Reluctant then to publicize many of his views, with his friend of prewar years, William Smith, Jr., Schuyler was even more hesitant to commit many opinions to paper. On Livingston Manor where he was confined by state authorities for his unwillingness to embrace the rebel cause, Smith spent his time reading until he had fairly got Col. Peter Livingston's small library by heart. He then turned to Schuyler, asking for something else to read in English or French, "provided it be neither Law, nor Mathematics, nor any thing in Favor of a Republican Form of Government." Sick of a government under which he had been deprived of property and liberty, too, Smith promised to return the books as soon as "our Friend George ... George the Governor," he sneered, would consent to make him a free man. Clinton had not answered Smith's request for permission to return to his house at Haverstraw, and the New York State Council of Safety refused his request to visit "the capital," where Smith thought he could contribute some "mite towards peace." The council, he said, feared that his influence would subvert the cause of independence. Now subject to a legislature instead of a king, Smith assured Schuyler that whatever his fate, "I shall never lose my Affection for my old Friends, by a Diversity of Sentiment about piddling Points of angry Politics."[63]

Not until Christmas day did Smith receive Schuyler's reply—the first, in fact, since he had written the general at the end of October to thank him for interposing to have Smith regain the use of his servants and to offer condolences for the destruction of Saratoga. In his letter of 30 October Smith had insinuated that men became soldiers out of fear of the masses. Had he offended the squire of Saratoga by hinting that Schuyler himself had been intimidated by the popular clamors raised against him? Or by asking whether Schuyler could keep Smith's letter from "the pimping Search of a Committeeman?" Perhaps he had gone too far by asking why the general was so long retarded in pursuit of the rebel assembly as it fled from Philadelphia. "Once we were all happy," Smith sighed. "When shall we be so again." Perhaps *When there are no more Soldiers thro' Cowardice,* and Men dare run Risks for Peace."[64]

However Schuyler answered Smith's two letters, nothing remains to suggest what he said beyond Smith's diary entry that he received the general's reply on Christmas day under cover of another letter sent to James Duane. Evidently Schuyler had not been offended as Smith feared; but his promise to visit Smith (which he kept later in January) was given as though for the purpose of discussing a purported offer by Smith to sell some land. The subterfuge Smith scorned as evidence of Schuyler's "dread of the multitude!" Instead of sympathetic recognition of his old friend's concern that forthright correspondence with a Loyalist might miscarry and be misinterpreted, Smith preferred to perceive Schuyler's missive in another light. How difficult it was, he thought, for officers of Congress to withdraw from support of the rebel cause since independence had been declared.[65]

Schuyler, like Smith, may have hoped for the return of peace in 1778 and a reconciliation with Britain, but the prospects for such were few, even with the notable American victory of 1777. As the fateful year drew to its close the general was content to be free of military responsibilities. And as Smith noted, "Schuyler does not meddle. He has no Command."[66]

Indeed, without the burdens of military jurisdiction, the Yorker gladly turned to pleasanter pursuits such as planning the restoration of productivity of his farms and mills, paying bills, and reckoning accounts. With Capt. Silas Sprague, for example, Schuyler settled the final payment due for the purchase of twenty oxen and the expense of driving and tending the cattle since the previous March. The tender of £24.14.4 completed payment of a bill totaling £426.1.0. Stanton Tefft's account was a bit more complicated because it included transactions dating from 1774–75 as well as the latter weeks of 1777. Tefft, who had been employed as early as 1771 to run a sawmill on the Battenkill near Saratoga, had sold sizable quantities of Schuyler's lumber. But Schuyler rejected his claim of £258.9.5 1/4 as the balance due him on the account. Carefully perusing the figures, the general detected "a Mistake in Casting up," £100 too much. If William Smith's assessment of Schuyler's mathematical prowess was true—that he could instruct Smith "as much in an hour, as I could learn [of the subject] in an Eternity alone"—Stanton Tefft also could have been no stranger to his employer's eye for accuracy and his ability to superintend with thoroughness and vigilance.[67]

The Long Wait for Exoneration

1

Again the Anxious Indians

*W*hile waiting for an official investigation of his military command, Schuyler followed Congress's directions to convene the Northern Department Indian commissioners in an effort to meet the ever-present danger of British influence upon the Iroquois. Increasingly the Six Nations threatened to divide over the question of maintaining a unified policy of peace and neutrality with the rebels. During much of 1778 the general's efforts were focused upon Indian affairs and upon the delays in Congress's investigation of his military service. Related to the latter situation were repeated proposals for invading either Indian territory in the west or British-held Canada.

The British occupation of New York City, together with threats from the north and west, kept Albany and the Hudson valley in a state of siege. And in January 1778 Admiral Lord Richard Howe attempted secret negotiations with Albany County and Tryon County Loyalists who asked whether the British peace commissioners could guarantee that a peace treaty could be made without first requiring unconditional submission. Perhaps such a promise would enable them to win coming elections of representatives and to instruct them to work for peace short of independence. When Howe responded later in February, he asserted that neither he nor his brother, Sir William, wanted an unconditional surrender. Nor did they wish to insist upon parliamentary taxation of Americans. Although Howe refused[1] Loyalists' requests for a publication of his views, their presence in upper New York State complicated the danger that Schuyler and the other Indian commissioners confronted when dealing with the tribes of the Mohawk valley.

335

By the time Timothy Edwards and Oliver Wolcott reached Albany on 4–5 January, Schuyler was obliged to prod James Duane to join the meeting that Congress had assigned him to attend. Late in arriving from Livingston Manor, where he had spent the holidays with his in-laws, Duane finally appeared for the commissioners' consultations on 9–10 January. He explained Congress's proposals regarding an attack on Niagara and its wish that the commissioners endeavor to persuade all of the Six Nations to observe their previous pact of neutrality. If this was not possible, they might enlist friendly tribes like the Oneida, Tuscarora, and Onondaga to ally openly against the increasingly hostile tribes, the Seneca and Cayuga.[2]

On 10 January the commissioners decided to invite the Six Nations to a conference at Johnstown in Tryon County in mid-February and to explain to Congress the inexpediency of executing its instructions. Accordingly, Schuyler wrote President Henry Laurens that the victory of 1777 had not proven generally advantageous to the American cause, particularly among the Seneca and Cayuga. The commissioners now feared that the tribesmen would disregard any engagements that they might be persuaded to make. Nor did they think that the Indians would agree to attack Niagara unless Congress adopted a "more vigorous mode of proceeding" and employed an army for the western enterprise. The Indian commissioners suggested that at the upcoming treaty the Iroquois be ordered to join the American cause or to suffer the consequences. Perhaps such a threat would persuade them to join an army assault upon Niagara. Asking for Congress's speedy determination of directions, Schuyler noted that friendship with the Oneida and Tuscarora and many of the Onondaga would make possible an attempt to destroy enemy vessels on Lake Ontario. But he also admitted that the British enjoyed a "capital advantage" because of their geographic position and their ability to satisfy the Indians' demands for trade. The department commissioners were as usual strapped for funds, and five to six thousand blankets were also needed. Finally, Schuyler warned, the board should be strengthened by the appointment of additional members. Frequently only he and Volkert Douw were on hand to conduct business because of the distance Wolcott and Edwards were forced to travel from their homes in Connecticut and Massachusetts. Wolcott now feared that he would be unable to attend the next conference, and Schuyler hoped soon to be called to Washington's headquarters for the inquiry into his military stewardship.[3]

About ten days after Schuyler dispatched his summons to the Iroquois to attend the Johnstown conference, he obtained a response from the Oneida and Tuscarora. Fearing that the British would persuade Seneca tribesmen to attack them, the two tribes requested protection. On 24 January Schuyler asked the Continental commander at Albany, Col. John Greaton, to send whatever troops he could spare to guard the Oneida and to equip them with tools for the construction of a stockaded fort.[4]

Again the general wrote Congress, pressing the urgent need for their directions to the Indian commissioners. If the Seneca succeeded in attacking Oneida and Tuscarora villages, Americans would be proven impotent in aiding their allies. Seven or eight heavy cannon, he suggested, should be ordered for Fort Schuyler; artillery pieces there were not only too light, but also too few for adequate defenses. Although anxious that Congress clear his reputation as a military leader, the general now seemed more intent upon the discharge of Indian department business and the unceasing work of military intelligence. Indeed, one of his greatest contributions to the Indian service and to the army was the organization of a network of scouts and spies that he maintained throughout much of the war. As he reviewed the latest news of Indian affairs for Congress on 26 January, he recommended a reward to Dominique Leglize for his long services in Canada. During the winter of 1776–77 Schuyler had sent the Frenchman to Canada to spy and to cultivate Canadian friendships.[5]

While waiting for Congress's response to the Indian commissioners' proposals, Schuyler obtained news confirming his earlier suspicions of the Seneca and the Cayuga; and now the Onondaga also seemed to be turning hostile. From Fort Schuyler the commissioners' agent, James Dean, wrote of Col. John Butler's council with the Iroquois and other tribes at Niagara. Schuyler's message to the Six Nations had been rebuffed by the Cayuga and the Seneca. There was "much reason," the general believed, to expect attacks along the western frontiers of Virginia and Pennsylvania as well as New York.[6]

The British-Indian raids on the Wyoming valley and Cherry Valley in July and November 1778 were but the most dramatic incidents in a series of forays begun by Butler's Loyalist rangers and Joseph Brant's Indians in May. Schuyler's predictions of early February proved all too true, but the advice he gave was not heeded until 1779.

Still hoping to meet friendly tribesmen at Johnstown in mid-February, the general, Volkert Douw, and James Duane decided to notify Congress and Governor Clinton of the growing crisis. In response to Schuyler's urgings of both defensive and offensive measures, the state legislature merely suggested that the commissioners pacify the Mahican west of Ulster County and negotiate a treaty with them! As for Congress, the general urged the delegates that unless war was carried directly into their homeland, where they might "feel the power and just resentment of" the United

States, there could be no safety from the sullen tribesmen. The friendly Oneida and Tuscarora must be protected, and without a proper contingent of regulars to wage war in the west, the inhabitants would flee and the loss of their grain crops would produce flour shortages for patriot armies in the east.[7]

The Seneca and Cayuga refusal to assemble at Johnstown on 15 February delayed Schuyler's conference with any of the tribesmen until March. But there were, perhaps, other causes for the postponement. The arrival of Gen. Thomas Conway and Lafayette in Albany with a view toward launching a winter campaign into Canada suggests that Schuyler's attention was diverted to that project and how it might relate to a conference with the Indians. Robert Yates's resignation as secretary to the board of Indian commissioners also suggests that Schuyler's secretary, John Lansing, needed time to assume Yates's responsibilities. Moreover, the commissioners waited until 14 February before receiving Congress's final instructions.

The instructions were framed in a series of resolutions passed on 2 February. First, the commissioners were ordered to speak to the tribes in a tone that would convince them of American self-confidence and sovereignty. If the Iroquois were not inclined to act openly as friends and allies, they should at least be encouraged to pledge neutrality. Congress could furnish no hard money because what was available in the military chest at Albany had already been appropriated for other purposes (doubtless a reference to the projected invasion of Canada). But the commissioners were authorized to purchase or obtain from public stores five or six hundred blankets for the Johnstown conferees. In answer to Schuyler's earlier pleas that the Indian board be enlarged, Congress promised that a new commissioner would be named, and that Governor Clinton would also be asked to appoint still another to attend the Johnstown conference. As for the general's earlier hint that he might not be on hand to conduct commission business, Congress brushed aside his expectation of a call to headquarters for the official inquiry into his activities as a department commander; the Yorker was directed to attend the treaty.[8]

Schuyler bridled. The resolution on the point of his attendance at the Johnstown conference might have been phrased more delicately, because whoever read it might believe that it had been prompted by his refusal to attend. Perhaps he was nettled by the implication of the congressional mode of communication. As he forwarded the instructions Congress had sent for the Indian commissioners to James Duane, it was apparent why he and Volkert Douw insisted that Duane join them for the Indian council. *Addressed* to the commissioners, they had nevertheless been *sent* to Duane.[9]

When Governor Clinton asked Schuyler to recommend the appointee Congress had authorized Clinton to name to the board, the general politely declined. Intending to resign from the board as soon as the treaty could be held, Schuyler thought that it might be considered improper for him to oblige the governor. For this and "other reasons"—perhaps his resentment of orders to conduct Indian negotiations while Congress dawdled over the question of clearing his military reputation—the general refused to interfere.[10]

Ever wary about appearances that might adversely reflect upon his obedience to orders and devotion to duty, Schuyler complained to Gouverneur Morris about the wording of Congress's 2 February resolution. His "Malevolent enemies," he thought, might conclude thereby that he had refused to attend the Indian treaty. On the other hand, commissioners Wolcott and Edwards had expressed "great uneasiness" lest Congress summon him for inquiry or trial before the Indian business had been concluded. But the general assured them that were such an order to arrive, he would risk disobeying it, provided that Edwards and Wolcott publicize their request that he do so rather than be absent from the treaty. The two men agreed to furnish safeguards against any accusation that Schuyler would shrink from the long-awaited examination of his conduct by pleading the necessity of completing other official business. Still, he wished Morris to persuade Congress to order its committee of inquiry to report. It was seven months since Ticonderoga had been evacuated, and there seemed to be no sign of a decision about Schuyler's culpability for the loss of the strategic outpost. Not only was the delay injurious to his reputation and nourishing to the "unjust conclusions" of his enemies, but it was also proving fatal to his "character."[11]

2

"to rise superior to resentment and pain"

Tormented by long delays in Congress's investigation of his military record, which left his reputation besmirched, Schuyler did not falter in his adherence to the American war effort. Whatever his thoughts may have been of establishing independence or of winning British recognition of claims to liberty without separation from the empire, the general's deeds speak louder than ever the words of some who thought that he "had never really accepted the idea of independence." Contemporaries like William Smith, Jr., and Peter Van Schaack claimed that Schuyler's loyalty to the patriot cause wavered when the war seemed to falter and Congress proved indifferent to his clamors for a speedy vindication of his honor. According to Smith, in January 1778 Schuyler was willing to "run every Risk to put down Independency if Great B[ritain] would cede the Taxing Power and he knew many who would join him." And Smith later recorded Peter Van Schaack's tale that Schuyler had expressed a similar idea to several of Burgoyne's officers after the surrender at Saratoga; the general would be content if taxation could be "explicitly given up" and Congress renounced independence. With Maj. John Ackland he had also proposed a toast to Anglo-American reconciliation upon constitutional principles.[12]

Smith's interpretation of Schuyler's views stemmed from a visit that the general paid him at Livingston Manor during 19–22 January 1778. Despite news of French preparations to aid the American war effort and of militia reinforcements for Washington's army, the Yorker seemed un-elated. "He and his Party," Smith thought, had "parted under Anxieties on Account of the Flatness of the Multitude under their increasing Distress," the inadequacy of Washington's army, and the withdrawal of many members from Congress. Although Schuyler expected Congress would discover nothing in his record with which to proceed against him, Smith noted that "he taxes them with Injustice for ruining his Character to humour the N England Mobility."[13]

Perhaps Schuyler did wish for the success of the Howe brothers' mission as peace commissioners. Or perhaps, as Smith admitted, he had simply turned his mind against Congress, with whom he was disobliged and against whom he sought a pretext to conceal his private resentment. But according to his old friend, the general thought that because of "motives of Ambition & Interest" Congress would not take hints of British overtures that Howe gave by "retarded operations." And Schuyler, he said, predicted that "the assembly" would be instructed to negotiate with the Howes on the basis of peace, liberty, and safety without independence. The Loyalist deduced that Schuyler also would not risk alarming the populace by openly advocating reconciliation with the mother country. "He could not bear to hear," Smith wrote, "that the War would be a predatory one next Year & with universal Desolation, & yet he appears to be strongly impressed with the Idea that the Multitude are tired of the War & the Country exhausted, & that the Leaders have more to fear from them than the Crown."[14]

Far different, however, were the views of patriot friends like John Jay and Robert R. Livingston, with their opinions that Schuyler's talents must be exercised in some public office. On 28 January, for example, a congressional committee assigned to confer with Washington on the need for supplies in the army, and including Gouverneur Morris, recommended that Schuyler be made quartermaster general. But too many congressmen still regarded him with suspicion or hostility, and Nathanael Greene was appointed instead. John Jay, however, insisted that Schuyler "seriously determine to serve your Country, at least in a legislative Capacity. Class yourself with those great men of Antiquity," he wrote, "who, unmoved by the Ingratitude of their Country, omitted no opportunities of promoting the public weal."[15]

Schuyler's reply to the chief justice's urgings in late February contained little of the tone of dismay or uncertainty mentioned by William Smith a month earlier. While declining a further public life, he was neither so depressed with adversity nor strongly attached to the comforts of a private life as to refuse to aid his country. And he agreed to venture again "into the world," confident that the time would come when his enemies would blush to find him innocent of any misconduct in his military office. He had, he thought, conquered his "strong resentment" of Congress for its ill usage of him.[16]

The question of Schuyler's reentry into public life remained unanswered in any specific way until late February. Chancellor Livingston then proposed to rectify the New York legislature's insult of the previous fall when it had refused to reelect Schuyler as a delegate to Congress. Citing Congress's recent puerility, fickleness, and inattention to business, Livingston insisted that Schuyler's service there would be a valuable curative. Letters from army officers like Alexander Hamilton also indicated that every man who could render service in the national legislature was "loudly called" to attend it. When Livingston sounded out members of the legislature about adding Schuyler to the state's congressional delegation, he found that many "relished" the idea. He would not, however, press it unless he could be certain that the "vile party spirit" would not prevent its accomplishment. And before proceeding Livingston wished to be certain that Schuyler would accept the appointment. Here was an opportunity for the general to overcome the prejudices of his enemies. "Your presence," he urged, " ... is the more necessary as a certain faction will omit no opportunity of calumniating you & of distressing the man who alone can support our cause. All our departments are in confusion [and] you alone can restore them to order [;] let me beg of you to do it."[17]

Schuyler responded to Livingston's suggestion on 5 March at Caughnawaga, en route to the board of Indian commissioners' meeting at Johnstown. In discharging Congress's orders to conduct negotiations with the Iroquois he continued to prove both his profession as a patriot and his willingness to discharge official responsibilities, duties that he had not resigned nor from which he had been removed. Congress's "unjustifiable Conduct," Schuyler found, had not affected him "in so high a degree as that which I Experienced from the Legislature of the State In which I drew the breath of life and for which I have suffered so much merely because I Sacrificed my own feelings In Its favor." After being passed over for election as a delegate, perhaps only because the legislature supposed him "no longer a favourite so greatly affected," the general "had determined never again to be their Servant." But he could not now resist Livingston's pleas. Being a delegate to Congress whether he attended or not might prod that body into action on his appeals for investigation of his military record. But Schuyler's motives were not ignoble. The "little philosophy" that he possessed, he said, had taught him "to rise superior to resentment and pain when they are put on one Scale and my Countrys good In Another. . . . Altho It is probable that I shall be able to do her but very Small Services yet these I cannot withhold." Livingston might act as he pleased upon the proposal to add Schuyler to New York's congressional delegation, but the general cautioned him not to attempt it without great probability of success. He wished "no farther opportunity be given to my enemies to Exult In a defeat."[18]

Livingston and other friends made certain that Schuyler was subject to no further rebuffs in the legislature. The proposal to elect an additional member of the congressional delegation was initiated in the assembly. By 25 March Schuyler was chosen, evidently without rivalry or altercation, to serve with the current delegation until the regular expiration of the members' terms in October. Other events, however, prevented his return to Congress until over a year later.[19]

3

The "Partizan Expedition"

On 5 March, when Schuyler assented to Robert R. Livingston's scheme for restoring him to a seat in Congress, he was on the verge of opening a treaty with the Indians at Johnstown. The prospects of war on the frontier were grim; but the general's reply to Livingston said less of the Iroquois than of a scheme of the invasion of Canada that had only just been aborted. Concocted by Horatio Gates and the board of war and approved by Congress on 22 January, the proposed expedition represented the efforts of a number of officers and congressmen to thwart or check the authority of Washington and to demonstrate that the Virginian was not the only man capable of directing the war. As the nominal victor of Saratoga, Gates was suspected of caballing with generals Thomas Conway and Thomas Mifflin and congressmen like R. H. Lee, Benjamin Rush, James Lovell, and the Adamses, to replace Washington. The so-called Conway Cabal seems to have been more rumored than real, but at least their efforts to launch an invasion of Canada reflected serious tensions between civil and military branches of the government. Such tensions are evident in the roles played both by Congress and the board of war— which was a creature of Congress—and in the fact that Washington was neither consulted nor did he approve of the Canadian project.[20]

In reviewing the events of February when Lafayette and Conway arrived in Albany, Schuyler aptly summarized for Chancellor Livingston how the enterprise had turned into a fiasco. Inspector General Conway, he said, had reached Albany only to find the troops that had been ordered for the invasion of Canada "vastly Less than what was promised, and not one earthly thing in readiness." When Conway applied to Schuyler for advice, the general suggested that he also invite generals Arnold and Lincoln, who were then in the city to offer theirs. All three submitted their views in writing, and Conway agreed with their common conclusion "that It was not advisable to prosecute the Enterprize [sic]." Schuyler's own letter to Conway calmly suggested that the idea of invading Canada was a good one, and he rejoiced that Congress had ordered it. Moreover, he advised that until Lafayette arrived in Albany and until it was certain that no "unexpected supply" of men, provisions, and carriages would turn up, Conway should not issue orders to abandon the plan. However, Schuyler made clear that "a competent Force" was indispensable. And it was very doubtful that enough troops—at least twenty-five hundred Continentals and fifteen hundred militia—could actually be assembled. By Conway's own report no more than a thousand were then available. And Gen. John Stark had raised no militia. Finally, Schuyler noted that no one should risk proceeding without clothing, provisions, sleds, and forage; lamentably, no such preparations had been made. But even if they had, a thousand troops would be no match for the enemy's army in Canada.[21]

Shortly thereafter, when Lafayette appeared, expecting to lead the expedition, "his surprize [sic] was extreamly [sic] great when he found how matters stood, and he could not help expressing the Greatest resentment." Complaining "that he had been greatly deceived and rendered ridiculous," the marquis told Schuyler that he had been urged to inform friends in France that the command of an army had been given him whereby he might "reap a plentiful harvest of Laurels." The viewpoint of William Smith, Jr., was rather different. Referring to the French aristocrat and to Conway's Irish origins, he noted, "What a Contempt of General Schuyler to interest the Northern Service to two foreign Officers! He and his Friends will certainly feel it." But it was too late to prepare for the "Partizan Expedition."[22]

Schuyler was convinced that much of the folly of the project could be attributed to the president of the board of war, Horatio Gates. In his first letter of instructions to Col. John Greaton, the commanding officer at Albany, to prepare for the expedition, Gates had announced that $200,000 would be sent—a sum "sufficient for discharging the public debts and for the Currant Expences [sic] of the service pointed out. When the Marquis arrived," Schuyler "advised him to call for a State of the public debts, and to transmitt It to Congress." Lafayette followed the suggestion and then informed Schuyler of his discovery that previously contracted debts exceeded $700,000, not including those involving the expedition. "The public money," Schuyler fumed, "has been Squandered with more profusion than words can Express. It is high time a Stop should be put to It."[23]

The idea of a winter invasion of Canada was no harebrained scheme; nor was it thought up only by Horatio Gates and his colleagues on the board of war. Had it been properly planned as soon as Philip Schuyler proposed it to Congress early in November 1777, and had his recommendations for the necessary manpower (five thousand), equipment, and supplies been executed, it might have succeeded in producing the "happy results" that he anticipated. Schuyler's proposal had also specified that one force be sent west to Oswego and Niagara while a second pushed north from Lake Champlain to St. John's, Montreal, and Quebec, which was the British campaign of 1777 in reverse. A month after Schuyler submitted his proposals, Congress asked him and the Indian commissioners to entice the Iroquois to attack Niagara. This proved to be impossible; it also was no adequate substitute for Schuyler's proposal to use regular troops. And neither Congress nor Gates and the board of war pursued more than a single-pronged attack on the north. Even so, it was decided too late in the season, and neither Gates nor anyone else displayed the ability to assemble adequate troops and supplies to make it work.[24]

When Schuyler got wind of the proposal to invade Canada, he explained to friends like John Jay and Gouverneur Morris exactly why it was not likely to succeed: there were insufficient manpower, provisions, and carriages. More sarcastically, he offered pointed criticisms of the plan and of its principal author. If reports of the rumored expedition were true, he said, "doubtless that Great Man has foreseen what was necessary, what obstacles were to be Surmounted and has made such provision as that no difficulties will arise. Others that do not think quite so favorable of his Abilities and foresight are under apprehension that our troops will be Scourged If they reach Canada and our Arms disgraced." Of course Gates had "the Art of drawing from Congress their public thanks, for Battles Fought & Seiges raised before he came to the Command of the Northern Army, and for taking an Army which he had the prudence not to approach nearer than to about two Miles whi[l]st they had Arms in their hands."

As in his letter to Jay, the general told Morris of his concerns for the waste of funds and the fiscal miscalculations of both Gates and Congress. Schuyler had heard that Congress had adopted a plan to raise continental currency to a value equal to that of gold and silver. Wishing "sincerely" that this news was true, he continued, "I have a mighty Inclination to see every utensil in a pe[a]sant's house Even that of the Bedchamber Included made of those precious Metals, and that will happen If gold & Silver can be bought for Bills and the same Generous diffusion of the public Money Continues which has prevailed In this dpeartment for some months past." The times were indeed out of joint. Reminding Morris again of his wish to end the everlasting delays with Congress's inquiry of the loss of Ticonderoga, Schuyler also complained of the state of local politics. Increasingly state and county government was slipping into the hands of unworthy men—men of the meaner sort—leaders whose judgment and ability were not to be trusted, and whose partisanship had been responsible for the legislature's refusal to reelect the general to Congress in the previous fall. "Abraham Yates, [Jr.]," he sneered, "I mean the Honorable Abraham Yates Esqr. one of the Senate of this State, A Member of the Council of appointment and of the Committee of the City & County of Albany, Recorder of the City of Albany, D: Postmaster General, late Cob[b]ler of Laws & old Shoes, is to be put In Nomination for Lieut Governor I Congratulate you on the Event."[25]

Despite the flicker of snobbery about Yates's youthful apprenticeship to a shoemaker, it is not altogether clear why Schuyler objected to him so pointedly. Perhaps it was because Yates had already switched his allegiance from the landed interest. Schuyler probably thought that neither Yates's rank nor fortune fitted him any better for the lieutenant governorship than George Clinton's suited him for the office of governor.[26] In 1777 Clinton had won both offices; his resignation of the second enabled the runner-up, Pierre Van Cortlandt, to fill it. As a Westchester landlord and Schuyler's cousin, Van Cortlandt was doubtless preferable to a candidate who depended on office holding for his income. And Schuyler may have been perspicacious, anticipating Yates's bent for Anti-Federalist or Clintonian populism, which was a doctrine that the proud general fought as harmful to both the state and the nation.

Reports on the Canada project, like Schuyler's letter of 3 February to Gouverneur Morris, duly reached the ears of Congress. Lafayette complained of the folly of Gates's ambition, which clearly outran his ability to organize a successful venture. On 24 February Congress asked the board of war to instruct the marquis to act as best he saw fit if his force was inadequate to begin the march to Canada. But on 2 March it decided to suspend the project altogether. Schuyler deduced that the lack of preparation and of funding stemmed from Gates's ignorance and his failure to give the board of war "the best information." This was inexcusable unless indeed ignorance could be deemed an excuse. Had he been able to direct the expedition himself, and had at least five thousand troops with adequate supplies been collected, the Yorker believed the venture probably would have succeeded. Referring to his own proposals of the previous November, Schuyler was outraged by William Duer's allegation that he could "be considered the father of this Expedition." Duer may have been jesting, but Schuyler was not altogether amused. "God In heaven," he told Morris, "forbid that I should be the parent of such an Ill shaped Monster. I have Sins enough to Answer for not to have those of others fastened upon me, besides I do not wish to rob Mr. Gates of one Iotta of honor, he has reaped no laurels that I would purchase at the price he has given, adulation and the Lowest Flattery. I shall never stoop to acquire popularity by such means." Schuyler also thought Gates's carelessness in drafting and executing the terms of his "Glorious convention" with General Burgoyne at Saratoga was partly responsible for Congress's later difficulties with the "convention army." Like Congress, he recognized that Gates had agreed to terms of surrender by which a victory of arms may have been forfeited by the pen.[27]

4

Spring Anxieties

While watching the disintegration of Horatio Gates's plans for an invasion of Canada and suffering with the repercussions of the campaign of the previous year, Schuyler faced the troublesome prospects of British and Indian threats to the New York and Pennsylvania frontiers. Obliged to delay a meeting scheduled with the Iroquois in February, the Indian commissioners finally assembled at Johnstown on 7 March 1778 for several days of talks. There Schuyler, Timothy Edwards, and Volkert P. Douw were accompanied by Congressman James Duane, Lafayette, Gen. Thomas Conway, and several other "officers and gentlemen" of New York and Massachusetts. Few of the Mohawk and Cayuga attended and none of the Seneca. The Six Nations were divided. Of the seven hundred-odd tribesmen present, most were Oneida, Tuscarora, and Onondaga.[28]

Schuyler and his colleagues agreed that short of chastisement the only means of persuading the tribesmen to observe strict neutrality was to threaten them with severe reprisals for future treacheries. In view of the absence of the wayward tribes, they deduced that many of the Mohawk and Onondaga, the Cayuga, and the Seneca would make war in the British interest. But they agreed to an Onondaga chieftain's request that another attempt be made to persuade the Seneca to reaffirm the policy of neutrality. Clearly the Iroquois league's structure of government had broken down as the council and sachems were unable to enforce their decisions except by persuasion. Privately, the Oneida and Tuscarora warned the commissioners not to rely upon Onondaga promises, and they requested both a resumption of trade and the protection of American troops for fear that other tribes would attack them. In response, Schuyler persuaded Lafayette to build a small picket fort at Oneida village, and he agreed to ask for a supply of trading goods to be stocked at Fort Schuyler. Because some of the Oneida and "Oriskas" lost their homes, stock, and food supplies in enemy attacks after supporting Nicholas Herkimer in the previous campaign, the general also ordered the commandant at Fort Schuyler to furnish them with food until Congress decided what further provision might be made for them.[29]

In further attempts to pacify the tribesmen Schuyler reacted to complaints that Tryon County inhabitants had incited certain tribesmen to attack settlers under the pretense that they were Tories. The county committee was urged to apprehend the instigators of such outrages lest further disorders create anarchy and confusion and threaten the property of even the "warmest friends of the Country." Moreover, Schuyler warned the committee to prevent the thefts of "sundry effects" of the Mohawk Indians at Canajoharie and to make restitution for what had already been pillaged. Stealing not only tended to destroy the Indians' affections, but, Schuyler insisted, it was unjust.[30]

While seeking means of encouraging the peaceful Iroquois to persuade the more truculant tribes to maintain neutrality, Schuyler was unwilling merely to wait for more than a month until the Six Nations might assembly at Onondaga to render a verdict. He was convinced that the enemy would instigate the Seneca and Cayuga and probably other tribes, the Mohawk and Onondaga, to attack the American frontiers. With news that the enemy had taken post at Oswego, he doubted that the tribes would remain neutral. Reporting to Congress after his return to Albany, he suggested that no more troops would be required to destroy the towns of the Iroquois than would be necessary to defend the entire frontier. Already communities in the Schoharie valley and Cherry Valley, and others along Charlotte Creek and the Delaware River were begging for help. Schuyler suspected that the British would follow the French plan of 1753, establishing forts along the frontiers from which to launch raids with their Indian allies. Immediate and vigorous measures should be adopted to send an army to seize Oswego and Niagara by the end of May.[31]

Schuyler's suggestion for a western campaign in 1778 was not adopted until 1779, but at about the very time he had proposed its beginning, the enemy began a series of raids against the New York and Pennsylvania frontiers. At the end of May Joseph Brant led a force of some three hundred Indians and Tories to Cobleskill. Between then and the more notable attacks in the Wyoming valley and Cherry Valley in July and November, events proved the accuracy of Schuyler's predictions and the wisdom of his proposals. In June, Congress did approve other steps designed to counter the Indian menace. An expedition was authorized to enter the area between Fort Pitt and Detroit, and General Gates was instructed to secure the Mohawk valley as a means of ensuring the success of the far western campaign. Preferring an assault on Canada to mere reprisals against the Seneca and Cayuga, Gates dawdled despite Congress's orders for him to proceed. In the end Gates entirely thwarted Congress's designs while concentrating upon defenses of the Hudson valley and New England. However, in late July, Congress decided to restrict Gen. Lachlan McIntosh's forces to Fort Pitt and to defer further movements toward Detroit. And with the subsequent approach of winter no preparations were made to follow Schuyler's proposal for an attack on Niagara.[32]

In the meantime, however, Schuyler was obliged to wait for Congress to respond to his plans and for the results of the promised Iroquois council at Onondaga. Because of James Duane's detention at Poughkeepsie, the general was unable to assemble the Indian commissioners at Albany again until mid-April. However, on 22 March he proceeded to test the sentiments of Oneida and Tuscarora tribesmen by posting a message to Col. Marinus Willett at Fort Schuyler. With the aid of an interpreter Willett was ordered to discover how several of the sachems and warriors might respond to the invitation to enlist in Washington's army. Schuyler also notified the Virginian of the recent negotiations at Johnstown. Of the Six Nations only the Oneida and Tuscarora seemed faithful to the pledge of friendly neutrality. The other four, he observed, would probably turn to fight for the British.[33]

During Schuyler's conference with the Iroquois at Johnstown, preparations were made to move his family to Saratoga. Anxiously awaiting his return to Albany, Mrs. Schuyler expected the general to escort her and the children to their newly built house on the banks of the Fishkill. With arrangements made for another meeting of the board of Indian commissioners in April, and reports of the Johnstown conference posted to Washington and Congress, the Yorker finally found freedom to direct some of his energies toward work on his country estate. The replacement of various buildings destroyed during the previous autumn required considerable supervision, while the planting of crops and gardens, like the management of his sawmill and the collection of new livestock, were diversions that were both pleasant and refreshing to a man who had been burdened for so long by the cares of public office.[34] Yet Schuyler was unable to escape such tasks entirely by fleeing into the country.

At Saratoga Schuyler was still obliged to answer various calls for advice from political and military leaders. After receiving James Duane's news that the legislature had named him to New York's congressional delegation, for example, Schuyler professed surprise that it had not occurred to any of the legislators to argue that he could not sit in Congress as long as he remained in the army. "If my Enemies In Congress learn that I am appointed," he observed, "they will Stave of[f] the Enquiry Into my conduct to deprive me of a Seat, for altho they have nothing to fear from me, their machinations will not leave me unpersecuted." At this same time the commissioners of accounts of the Northern Department asked for information about Col. Samuel Elmore's charges for services in 1775 and 1776. The general replied that if Elmore's charges were not in the accounts and vouchers that Schuyler had submitted for the public service up to 19 March 1777, he had not paid them. And in response to Thomas Conway's question of how to respond to the Cherry Valley committee's reports that a large body of Indians and Tories was assembling at Tunnidilla, Schuyler advised against drawing too many troops from the north and from western posts like Schenectady, Johnstown, and Fort Dayton for service elsewhere. To do so would only encourage the enemy to invade the frontiers at all points where defenses had been weakened.[35]

When Schuyler returned to Albany for the Indian commissioners' meeting of 15 April, he discovered that there was little he and his colleagues could do to alleviate the deterioration of Iroquois neutrality. They agreed to request General Conway to authorize the issue of provisions for the faithful Oneida and Tuscarora. But the two tribes had been denied the protection that they had requested at Johnstown in March; except for the Fort Schuyler and Albany garrisons, all Continentals had been drawn off for the defense of the Hudson valley, and no troops had been assigned to defend the tribesmen from their hostile neighbors. Nor were there enough local militia to guard them. Again they recommended that one or two companies of Continental troops be sent into the Oneida country. It was ironic to ask the Indians to volunteer for Washington's army while able-bodied warriors were wanted to defend their own families and homes. And it is not surprising that only fifty of the two friendly tribes finally responded to the commander in chief's call for two hundred of them. Except for this limited success, Schuyler and the commissioners accomplished little else at their April meeting.[36]

Immediately thereafter came Governor Clinton's notification of the legislature's request that Schuyler assume a seat in Congress. But for several reasons the general could not as yet set out for Pennsylvania. Because of the withdrawl of troops from the north he must now return his family to Albany. Without protection neither they nor other inhabitants of the Saratoga countryside could remain there in safety. Failure to post some troops in the lake country by 1 May, he thought, would be a certain invitation to the enemy to invade it. And Mrs. Schuyler, he explained, expected to "lay in" about the first week in May, and he would not leave her until she had safely been delivered.[37]

Despite his eagerness to return to Saratoga, Schuyler tarried long enough at Albany after the Indian commissioners' meeting to attend a political caucus. In an effort to thwart Abraham Yates, Jr.'s, electioneering, Walter Livingston assembled a number of prominent Albanians to nominate a slate of candidates for the legislature and lieutenant governorship. Unable to discover Yates's list of candidates, the cabal proposed Gen. Abraham Ten Broeck for lieutenant governor and Schuyler for senator. Nominees for the assembly included Livingston, Schuyler's brother Stephen, Leonard Gansevoort, James Gordon, Killian and Robert Van Rensselaer, John Taylor, Jacobus Teller, Peter Vrooman, and William B. Whiting. Although the caucusers did not manage to unseat Abraham Yates or to replace Lieutenant Governor Pierre Van Cortlandt, with few exceptions the nominees and those who attended the caucus represented an emerging "interest" of opposition to Governor George Clinton and his own adherents.[38]

5

"whenever I move the whole Country will follow the Example"

Schuyler rushed back to Saratoga on 18 April, intending to remain there with his family as long as they might stay with any degree of safety. He expected to put in crops of hemp and flax and otherwise to restore the productivity of his farms and mills. However, by the end of the month the increasing threats of enemy troops who had returned to Lake Champlain promised to force many inhabitants to abandon their homes and to flee southward. Although Schuyler did not fear a full-scale invasion until sizable reinforcements from Europe could reach Canada, the British presence at Ticonderoga and Crown Point could be expected to produce raids and scalping parties. And he warned Gen. Abraham Ten Broeck and both Washington and Gen. Thomas Conway that regulars as well as militia should be assigned to northern posts like Fort George and Fort Ann. On 25 April he notified Ten Broeck that unless troops were sent up within the following week, he could not continue to keep his family safely at Saratoga. Already inhabitants of Kingsbury, Queensbury, and Skenesborough were moving down, "and whenever I move," Schuyler warned, "the whole Country will follow the Example." The prospects grew more alarming as news spread that Castletown and Rutland had been destroyed, and that the enemy was advancing from Skenesborough to Fort Ann.[39]

Significantly, the escape of young Walter Butler from Albany on the night of 18–19 April coincided with Schuyler's first reports of danger on the frontiers both north and west of the city. The escape later proved to be portentous, indeed. Young Butler joined his father, Col. John Butler, at Kanadesaga, and after visits to Niagara and Quebec returned to New York to serve as a captain of Butler's Tory rangers. It was he who led "the notorious expedition against Cherry Valley" in November after his father's assaults on the Wyoming valley in early July. Meantime, as spring turned to summer, Schuyler endeavored to alert military and civil authorities to the necessity of timely action for meeting the frontier crisis. After first hoping to hold his ground and even to fortify his Saratoga house as an encouragement to other neighbors not to flee the countryside, the general retreated with his family to Albany.[40] It was perhaps also safer to move Mrs. Schuyler to more comfortable surroundings for her lying-in.

On 7 May, however, the general received news from Congress dispelling some of the gloom that had descended upon the American effort over the winter months. Now, in spite of all the prospects of another difficult year of campaigning, punctuated by Schuyler's own expectations of a predatory war on the frontiers, there were promises of hope. Treaties of alliance and commerce with France reached York, Pennsylvania on 2 May, and two days later Congress, meeting there, ratified them. About a week earlier it had also rejected Lord North's overtures of a negotiated peace with renunciation of taxation except for regulatory purposes.[41]

Schuyler promptly suggested that Congress spread the news of the French alliance as an effective way of persuading timid Americans to forsake ideas of ending the war short of independence. Would it not, Schuyler asked, be rewarding to have the papers translated into French and disseminated in Canada, together with as much of the French treaty as might be prudent to disclose? Frenchmen there might be encouraged to a less friendly disposition to the British. Schuyler's suggestions not only indicate that he was no trimmer in the patriot cause; they buttressed his case for exoneration after many months of being suspected of incompetence and disloyalty. And again he asked for Congress to get on with the public inquiry so long awaited because this must surely induce the people of other states to forsake their prejudices against him. The inquiry should be made before the general took his seat in Congress because he could otherwise be accused of using it unfairly as a weapon in the struggle for vindication.[42]

On 17 May Schuyler expressed his views on independence and Lord North's proposals for reconciliation even more forcefully to Gouverneur Morris. "I laboured under great apprehension that It might be deemed expedient to treat with Brita[i]n," Schuyler noted.

I foresaw a variety of destructive Consequences If we did, amongst others I feared a relaxation In our military operations, and that too much attention would be paid to what the Enemies Emissaries would not fail to propogate with Industry, the needlessness of any further opposition as Brit[a]in would grant us every thing short of Independency. I had Just expressed these apprehensions to Jay & Hobard [Judge John Sloss Hobart] and a wish that Congress would publish the Speech & Bills with Animadversions when the Express entered the room with the resolutions of Congress. Judge of the Joy with which I felt myself penetrated. ... Tho Injured by Congress I will do them the Justice to declare, that In My opinion the[ir] act of the 22d Ult: was the wisest and most desicive *[sic]* of any of theirs since the declaration of Independency.

Far different were William Smith's imaginings that Schuyler had been willing since January to bargain away independence for concessions on "the Point of Taxation."[43]

Buoyed by the news of the French alliance and still hopeful that he might soon pay a visit to Congress, Schuyler remained in Albany for both private and public reasons. Among the former was his concern for Mrs. Schuyler, who finally gave "Another Citizen to the State," Cortlandt Schuyler, on 14 May. Thereafter she suffered violent swelling in her legs and between late May and early July lameness continued to plague her. And about the time of his son Cortlandt's birth the general succumbed to his old illness, a vile ague, which he gradually put to flight by dosing it with "the bark." Even without this "troublesome companion" or the ailments of his wife, Schuyler was determined to manage the Indian commissioners' business and to lend what assistance he could to the defenses of the Hudson valley. Ready as ever with helpful advice, he dispatched an officer to Gen. Alexander McDougall with plans for constructing fireboats as part of the defenses of the Highlands. Still hoping for a favorable response from an Iroquois conference at Onondaga, he got wind of Oneida efforts to persuade their Seneca brethren and others of the desirability of joining the war against the British. Promptly he announced the news of the Franco-American alliance, hoping to strengthen the Oneidas' and Tuscaroras' arguments with the Seneca, Cayuga, Mohawk, and Onondaga and urging the two tribes to persevere in their attachment to the American cause.[44]

The general's hopes that hostile members of the Six Nations might be persuaded to accept an American alliance were wisely guarded. He considered the possibility of a further delay in plans to visit Congress. The Seneca seemed on the verge of quitting the British interest. A visit to Fort Schuyler might therefore be necessary to rally the Six Nations once again and to hasten the enlistment of some of their warriors for service in Washington's army.[45]

Until 17 May, however, Schuyler was obliged to wait for Congress's response to the Indian commissioners' recommendations of 14 March. A full two months elapsed between the date of his report of the Johnstown conference and the receipt of an answer. Finally he was able to act upon the recommendation that trade be opened for the Indians at Fort Schuyler. Although £2,500 worth of goods were sent to the Mohawk valley in June, the effort to woo most of the Six Nations from their hostile inclinations came too late to be effective.[46]

Similarly, although Congress agreed to the Indian commissioners' calls for army protection of the Oneida and Tuscarora, this did nothing to alleviate the Tory and Indian menace to the New York frontier. Washington informed Schuyler that the defensive posture of the British and the delay in opening the 1778 campaign had rendered the call for Indian reinforcements unnecessary. Accordingly, the Yorker canceled the invitation to the Iroquois to volunteer for army service.[47]

By the end of May Schuyler was also forced to admit that the savages' behavior had become quite mysterious. But he noted the immediate need for stationing troops at Cherry Valley. A thousand regular troops together with the garrison at Fort Schuyler, the Tryon County militia, and auxiliaries furnished by the Oneida and Tuscarora might be sufficient to burn the villages of hostile Cayuga and Seneca and to invade Canada. Such an expedition seemed all the more desirable not only because of British incitement of the Iroquois but because of their renewed activities at Isle aux Noix and the Lake Champlain forts. But preparations, he warned, must be adequate, and the decision to launch such a campaign must be made early enough for the stockpiling of provisions and other supplies and the arrangement of a proper system of transportation.[48]

While the board of war and Congress agreed to launch an expedition for the reduction of Detroit in June 1778 and a similar thrust from the Hudson valley into Seneca country by General Gates, no such enterprises were actually undertaken.[49] Not until the summer of 1779 were generals John Sullivan and James Clinton sent to chastise the Seneca and Cayuga for the havoc they wreaked in 1778.

During June, as both news and rumors of British-and-Indian activity filtered into Albany, Schuyler continued to watch for clues to the enemy's intention in their maneuvers into the northern and western regions of the state. Tories in the Albany environs, he noted, were heartened by hints that a British army would invade the Hudson valley; some were known to have moved west to join John Butler at Kanasedaga, while others collected near the northern branch of the Hudson to ally with British forces at Crown Point. The fresh signs of danger in the north country finally prompted Schuyler to send for his children, who had been at Saratoga since late March. Another enemy party of about two hundred, the general heard, had been formed at Sacandaga, and on the afternoon of 6 June word reached Albany of attacks at Stone Arabia and Cherry Valley. Others were expected at German Flats and Schoharie. The scattered appearances of the enemy in so many places created considerable consternation, and Schuyler urged Governor Clinton to visit Albany to inspire patriots' exertions and help arrange their defenses. There the citizenry was organized to mount night watches, and, according to William Smith, Schuyler himself slept with a loaded blunderbuss at his side.[50]

Indeed, the causes for alarm were real enough. On 18 June at German Flats a party of militia, en route to aid settlers against lurking parties of Indians, was ambushed. One American was killed and two were captured. Three days later Schuyler had confirmed reports from Col. Timothy Bedel that about fifteen hundred enemy reinforcements had already reached Canada. In fact, on 27 June Gen. Frederick Haldimand arrived at Quebec to replace Sir Guy Carleton as governor of Canada and commander of Canadian military forces. Bedel, who had been posted to watch British activities on Lake Champlain at Haver Hill, in Hampshire Grants territory, claimed that there were no signs that the enemy intended to take the offensive there; but Schuyler insisted that Bedel's judgment was contradicted by other information that he had gleaned from Crown Point. Still, by 21 June the general did not feel that local circumstances would compel him to remain at Albany much longer. Heartened by Henry Laurens's word that "the Tyonderoga affair is likely soon to be determined on," and at last relieved that Mrs. Schuyler's "very dangerous Illness" after childbirth had largely passed, the Yorker announced his intention to set out for Congress within the next few days.[51]

On 24 June the return of the general's daughters Elizabeth and Margaret from a visit to their sister Angelica Church at Boston, seemed also to be propitious. At the ages of nearly twenty-one and twenty, respectively, the young ladies could be expected to free their father from some of his anxieties about their invalid mother. Her recuperation from the birth of Cortlandt on 14 May was slow; the aftereffects, her swollen legs, were painful, and she remained more or less lame well into July. Within a few days of his daughters' homecoming, however, the general discovered that responsibilities of the board of Indian commissioners would again prevent him from taking his seat in Congress. Two days before his intended departure from Albany he received Timothy Pickering's message from the board of war. Congress had resolved to launch an attack on Detroit "if practicable," and orders were given for the assembling of three thousand troops at Fort Pitt together with the necessary supplies. And another expedition to support the Detroit enterprise was to move from the Hudson valley along the Mohawk to chastise the insolent Seneca and wrest Oswego from the British. Horatio Gates, who had been reassigned to the Northern Department after a few months on the board of war, was directed to take the "most expeditious" measures to execute this second prong of the attack, and the Indian commissioners of the Northern Department were ordered to cooperate with Gates and whomever he assigned to lead the invasion.[52]

Pickering's letter to the Yorker indicated that the board of war would soon consider Schuyler's "Hints relative to a future Expedition against Canada," but for the moment the general must bend his attention to the business of preparing for the western campaign. He would tarry in Albany until he and the Indian commissioners discharged Congress's orders for their cooperation with Gates and the officer he assigned to lead the expedition.[53]

Insisting that accounts from Oneida country warranted Gates's speedy action, Schuyler sought to hasten preparations by advising the quartermaster to adapt the construction of a number of unfinished bateaux to navigation of the Mohawk River. Fearful that Gates would not respond to Congress's directions with dispatch, Schuyler asked Governor Clinton press upon him the necessity for speed.[54] He recognized Gates's inability to move with alacrity, but Schuyler also discovered that he was wholly unenthusiastic in responding to Congress's orders for the Oswego expedition.

By 19 July Schuyler still had heard nothing from Gates; nor had he been able to discover that anyone in Albany had received the slightest order to prepare the expedition for the west. It was regrettable, he explained to Henry Laurens, that a party of Iroquois lately returned from Philadelphia had been told of Congress's intentions to send one army west of Fort Pitt and another into the Mohawk valley. Once Col. John Butler heard of these plans, he was certain to hasten attacks on Schoharie and German Flats before there were any American troops on the scene to resist them. And if plans for the New York expedition were actually laid aside, the Indians would likely believe that American troops could not be spared from the eastern theater of war; they might then be encouraged to continue their barbarism along the frontiers with impunity. Without word from Gates, or indeed the slightest signs of any preparations for such a campaign, Schuyler had largely wasted his time sitting in Albany. As president of the board of Indian commissioners he could do little but post scouts to watch for signs of John Butler's activities in the Schoharie valley and at German Flats. A party from Fort Schuyler did manage to destroy the old buildings at Oswego, thereby attempting to discourage the British from taking post there. Fortunately, after their return to the fort on 10 July, the garrison was threatened by no military action during the summer. The Indians and Tories circumvented the outpost, attacking frontier settlements from the south.[55]

Unlike Schuyler, who fully recognized the seriousness of the Indian and British menace to the west, Horatio Gates preferred to plan an invasion of Canada. Although he accomplished nothing beyond collecting information and advice about proceeding with such a scheme, Gates "intentionally refused to obey explicit orders of Congress" because he felt that an attack on the western Indians "would squander precious military stores that he wished to husband in preparation for an offensive against Canada." Repeatedly he contravened explicit orders by vacillating, once arguing that the country should "Steer clear of that hornet's nest, the Six Nations"; then insisting that there were insufficient provisions at Albany and Fort Schuyler; and finally, in August, maintaining that he thought "the entire plan had been 'laid aside' for the season."[56] In the end neither an "eruption into Canada" nor one into western New York was even attempted in 1778. Although ideas of the former lingered, it was the latter that was executed in 1779. The Sullivan-Clinton expedition was also as much a vindication of Schuyler's wise counsels in 1777–78 as it was a reprobation of Gates's willful frustration of the orders of his superiors.

With the best of motives for remaining in Albany to assist with the expedition that Congress had ordered but that Gates refused to launch, Schuyler jeopardized his political fortunes with the New York legislature. Increasingly impatient with the general's delays in taking his seat in Congress, the legislators began to consider naming Chancellor Livingston and members of the supreme court as delegates. The state, they thought, was underrepresented in the national assembly; since March, when he had been designated an additional delegate, Schuyler seemed unable or unwilling to serve. At one point his nephew-in-law, Walter Livingston, urged that he place the business of the Indian department in the best hands he could find and hurry to Congress. For the moment Livingston found that his colleagues were content to name no other congressman in the general's place, but he became dismayed when Schuyler indicated on 26 June that he had been forced to change his mind. The assembly's adjournment then saved Livingston the embarrassment of having to tell them that Schuyler could not yet take his congressional seat and that the state would remain underrepresented in the national council. But many "who voted for you last March," he warned "will not do so again unless you repair to Congress Speedily." Already they had vowed that if Schuyler was so busy with Indian affairs as to neglect his assignment as a congressman, he should not be a delegate at all.[57]

Meanwhile, however, the general refused to be intimidated by Livingston's insistence that he leave Albany and his duties as an Indian commissioner. The events of July did not change his mind. Although Gates failed to execute orders for the western campaign, Schuyler loyally stood ready to assist, collecting and relaying news from the frontiers to appropriate civil and military authorities as well. Finally his absence from Congress was justified by his presence at Arthur St. Clair's court-martial and by the conduct of the defense of his own trial at Quaker Hill.

6

Trial at Quaker Hill

For fourteen months after losing command of his army Schuyler waited for a congressional inquiry into his conduct of the campaign of 1777. Although a committee was selected to investigate the loss of Ticonderoga on 27 August 1777, little headway had been made. Would it find evidence of neglect or misconduct and recommend a court-martial? As weeks dragged into months the membership of the committee changed. Schuyler fumed and urged that the business be expedited, and friends endeavored to prod the committee to report. On 8 February 1778 the committee's evidence was sent to Washington, but the Virginian declined to order a court-martial unless charges were made. Moreover, he refused to make them because he did not know how Congress had instructed Schuyler to conduct the campaign of 1777.[58]

Congress again delayed; and because the old committee had been discharged, a new one was appointed to investigate the general's case. It, too, resisted promptings to specify charges against Schuyler. Unfortunately, even the general's friends caused more delay. On 28 March William Duer and Gouverneur Morris won postponement of the committee's report for "particular considerations respecting Genl. Schuyler."[59]

For a time Schuyler was willing not to press the "painful subject." He was content to remain at home to conduct the business of the Indian commissioners and to await Mrs. Schuyler's lying-in. By the end of April 1778 still another committee was directed to examine the evidence and to state charges as well. Gouverneur Morris's only complaint was that their instructions were framed in terms of doing *"Justice to an injured Country"* instead of *"Justice to these injured Gentlemen."*[60]

With Morris's report in hand John Jay observed that the proceedings in Congress seemed "calculated more to make a noise than decide: perhaps that was their object; if so, you have spoiled the plan," he told Morris. The Yorkers knew all too well that partisans of Horatio Gates and critics of Schuyler, St. Clair, and also Washington preferred to leave their enemies under a cloud of public odium and suspicion. Yet Jay perceived one danger in having specific charges leveled against the generals: the possible implication neither of neglect nor of criminality, which could be misleading. If one of the charges happened to be Schuyler's absence from Ticonderoga, it must be asked whether it was his business to have been there. Jay thought not; a commander placing himself for six to eight weeks "in salva et arca custodia" (a place of safety and confinement) was no way to extend his care and superintendence to an entire department.[61]

The formal charge that Congress finally voted on 12 June was neglect of duty—a monstrous accusation for a man whose entire career testifies to a conscientious pursuit of obligations in both his private life and public offices. More specifically, Schuyler was accused of failing to remain at Ticonderoga (after mid-June 1777) to expedite the fortification of Mount Independence until it was no longer possible to avoid retreat in order to save his troops and their supplies. However, by Congress's own instructions in May 1777, the general was permitted freedom of movement in his department, which was generally defined to include Albany, Ticonderoga, Fort Stanwix, and their dependencies, which was an entirely sensible order for any commander who had more than a single outpost to defend and duties such as those of the board of Indian commissioners to discharge.[62]

Washington's 22 July notice to Schuyler indicated that there would be further delays in the court of inquiry. Two other courts-martial, including Arthur St. Clair's, must be held first, he said, and Schuyler would be summoned later.[63] Either the subsequent summons reached Schuyler not long thereafter, or the Yorker decided to set out for White Plains early. Or perhaps St. Clair asked him to attend his own trial, where the general served as one of the principal defense witnesses. In any case, on 6 August or shortly thereafter Schuyler set out from Albany. By 16 August he was in Washington's camp at White Plains, where the Virginian had collected the largest body of regular troops yet assembled during the war. Of the main army of almost seventeen thousand between eleven and twelve thousand men were encamped in and around White Plains as Washington warily watched for signs of movement by Sir Henry Clinton. In November Washington finally settled his men into winter camps in a semicircle with a forty-mile radius about the city and the Hudson Highlands. Meantime, the lull in activities enabled the commander in chief to proceed with courts-martial.[64]

Arthur St. Clair's trial, which began on 23 August, proved to be a promising prelude to Schuyler's own ordeal. Both men were accused of neglect of duty, but the charges against St. Clair included "cowardice, and treachery, in abandoning" Ticonderoga and Mount Independence. Point by point St. Clair argued against them, summoning as principal witnesses Gen. Horatio Gates, Thaddeus Kosciuszko (who testified as an engineer that the fortifications were inadequate to withstand the British siege), Brig. Gen. Enoch Poor, and Schuyler. The testimony on St. Clair's behalf was no less beneficial to Schuyler's case.[65]

St. Clair's trial dragged on for a month. At the end of the second week, on the evening of 4 September, several of the participants dueled after becoming embroiled in an altercation of several months' standing. Col.

James Wilkinson accused his old commander, Horatio Gates, of derogatory remarks about his conduct at a previous duel in February, which was an incident that had stemmed from Wilkinson's allegations concerning Gates's ambitious caballing against George Washington. Wilkinson, now attached to St. Clair's cause, challenged Gates for casting aspersions upon his character and motives. Gates's second, Thaddeus Kosciuszko, and John Church, who served as Wilkinson's second, continued to fight after the duel was over. The principals satisfied the demands of honor without bloodshed, but their seconds quarreled about exchanging signed statements of Gates's apology to Wilkinson and of Wilkinson's admission that Gates was a gentleman.[66]

Until St. Clair's court-martial could be concluded, Schuyler found little to do but attend as a witness and prepare for his own trial. He did of course have time to consider whether to attend Congress before it acted on the verdict that he expected his military judges to render. Members of the New York legislature clearly expected him to resume service in Congress well before a court-martial had even been ordered, and Walter Livingston had warned him that "many who voted for you last March will not do so again unless you repair to Congress speedily." James Duane, however, doubted that such a step would be wise; although his enemies *might* not dispute it, Duane thought they *would* place "the worst construction" upon such an act and hinder the reestablishment of Schuyler's position and influence in the national assembly. The general agreed that the delegates must first act on the proceedings of his court-martial. Even then, he said, he might remain aloof "until the Close of the Campaign especially If any movement against the Enemy is In Contemplation." Nor did he seem responsive to Walter Livingston's suggestion that it might "be worth your while to accept of the Quart.R Master Generals place and Command the Army," because Washington was expected to visit Virginia during the winter.[67]

St. Clair's trial was finally concluded on 25 September. Acquitted of all charges "with the highest honor," St. Clair proved as helpful to Schuyler's defense as the Yorker had been to his subordinate's. On 30 September at Fredericksburgh, Washington ordered Schuyler's trial to commence. When assembled at Quaker Hill, the court included with but one exception all of the officers who had tried St. Clair; most had also served under Schuyler's command and therefore knew something of his military record and talents: Maj. Gen. Benjamin Lincoln, who was president; brigadier generals John Nixon, James Clinton, and Anthony Wayne; and Col. John Greaton. John Lawrence was judge advocate. Assisted by his ex-aide, Richard Varick, and by John Lansing, Jr., his secretary, Schuyler not only presented a voluminous array of papers with which to supplement Varick's and Lansing's testimonies, but he also called Arthur St. Clair as his principal witness. That St. Clair's case had already been heard perhaps made Schuyler's easier to cover, and the happy verdict in the former surely boded well for the latter.[68]

Before summoning St. Clair, the Yorker reviewed the history of his command of the Northern Army since 1775. Step by step he demonstrated his thorough attention to all of his responsibilities and how he could not have properly discharged them by residing only at Ticonderoga, as the charge against him specified that he should have done. A department commander must remain "at large to concert and execute measures for the relief of such posts," exactly as Schuyler had done. Furthermore, congressional orders in May 1777 had specifically authorized the general to exercise this freedom; without it he could not have dealt properly with the Indians and both northern and western prongs of the British invasion. With typical thoroughness Schuyler presented evidence of orders that "descended to minutiae, in a manner not usual for general officers, and which nothing but the most ardent zeal for the service could have prompted." When Schuyler asked St. Clair whether he had witnessed any neglect of duty in his commander's behavior, St. Clair answered simply, "the direct contrary." Similarly, when queried about the "probable consequences" had the Yorker restricted himself to Ticonderoga, St. Clair agreed that the remainder of the department must surely have been neglected. When the long stream of testimony ended, Schuyler requested the court to pardon his prolixity; only "Facts and plain narrative, not declamation, have made it so," he noted. Without any apparent hesitation the judges unanimously pronounced Schuyler not guilty of neglect of duty; "the Court therefore do acquit him," read the verdict, "with the highest honour." At long last the general was vindicated. Would Congress concur? Schuyler was satisfied that his defense consisted "chiefly In a detail of facts with very few remarks," and he proudly told James Duane that "not a Single angry word has Escaped me. If I have the happiness of Living a little longer with you," he added, "I shall become the meakest man of the Age, and I shall by no means Esteem that a Misfortune. . . . In Proportion as I conquer the unhappy propensity to Anger which Inslaved me I feel myself a happier and I hope a better man." Now if Congress would quickly approve the court's verdict, Schuyler was ready to resume the duties of his commission until the close of the campaign. Thereafter, he expected to enjoy "the Luxury of private life which becomes every day more Inviting."[69]

In prompting President Laurens to press Congress for a quick approval of the verdict, Schuyler suggested that further delays would be heartless. Nearly fourteen months had elapsed since the general's loss of his command. Had he forthrightly resigned or even been deprived of his commission, he might have been freer to pay proper attention to his private affairs. Surely, he pleaded, Congress would not suffer him to languish longer in a situation that was more painful than any other.[70]

In a far different tone the Yorker scribbled a message to his friend William Duer on 4 October. Exultant and playful, he chided Duer for a long lapse in his correspondence. Saluting him as "Late a delegate in Congress ... But now happily partaking of that Bliss which defunct patriots enjoy In the Elisian fields," Schuyler wondered whether he had died and crossed the Styx. "Dear Shade," he wrote, was Duer inhibited from communicating with the inhabitants of earth? Was Charon really the rough, surly, ill-natured fellow described by the poets? Were female spirits also permitted to cross the Styx? If Duer did not soon reply, Schuyler must conclude that Minos had condemned him to be chained down like Tartarus. Referring to his recent trial "for Supposed Crimes against the American States," Schuyler assured Duer, "Every body here believes that I am acquitted. ... But how long the Congress may take to determine on the propriety or Impropriety of the Sentence I know not. Pray Employ a Sylph or rather a host of them to Insinuate to the members that It will be vastly Cruel and terribly distressing to your poor old Friend to Continue any Longer In that Kind of Purgatory which he has Indured *[sic]* near fourteen months past."[71] Schuyler's purgatory, in fact, lasted two more months.

7

"you should resume that command"

Following his court-martial victory early in October, Schuyler tarried at Fredericksburgh (now Patterson), New York, for several weeks. Apparently Washington both solicited and obtained his advice about Hudson valley defenses and congressional orders to consider plans for a fresh assault upon Canada. Although the commander in chief resisted suggestions for diverting his army from its focus upon Manhattan, he at least heeded directives to consider the Canadian project. In November, for example, he asked for Schuyler's written advice on a winter campaign. Even after ruling it impossible because of inadequate provisions, the

Virginian urged him to continue to offer his reflections and inquiries about it.[72]

Meantime, at Poughkeepsie the New York legislature dealt with two questions that directly bore upon Schuyler's immediate political future. One concerned the disputed election returns of the previous spring. The other was the general's position as a delegate to Congress. The first was decided by the senate, the second by a vote of both houses.

The spring election of senators from the Western District (Albany and Tryon counties) had produced a victory for Abraham Yates, Jr., but the polls for a second seat had been so muddled that the senate could not be certain whether Schuyler or Jacob G. Klock should be declared the winner. Copies of poll lists suggested that several men surnamed Klock had received votes and that others had been cast variously for "Philip Schuyler" or "General Schuyler." Whom did the electors intend? On 13 October the senate ordered county sheriffs of the Western District to submit poll lists according to the proper legal form; but three days later, after Schuyler was relected to Congress and the senators had examined poll lists from the Mohawk District of Tryon County, Jacob Klock was given the senate seat by a vote of eight to six.[73]

The resolution of Schuyler's claim to a senate seat was perhaps influenced by the legislature's prior decision to reelect him to Congress. But because he had failed to attend the national assembly after his election as a special delegate in March, it appears that Schuyler lost support for reelection just as Walter Livingston had prophesied. Still, on 15 October, the day that both houses agreed to elect five delegates for regular annual terms, Assemblyman Leonard Gansevoort was certain that the choice would "be Genl. Schuyler Mssrs [James] Duane G.[ouveneur] Morris, [Francis] Lewis & [William] Floyd." Correct in his judgment about the final choice of delegates, Gansevoort discovered that while the senate nominated all five men, the assembly chose Senator John Morin Scott instead of the general but agreed to the other four. On 16 October the two houses met in joint session to compare their lists of nominees; obliged now to choose between Schuyler and Scott, the legislators balloted as one body, giving Schuyler the narrowest of victories, twenty-seven votes to twenty-six for Scott.[74]

The legislature, however, was anxious that their delegates be present in Congress and proceeded to consider the eligibility of the chancellor and supreme court judges for such service. Indeed, by 4 November both houses agreed that a "special occasion" now warranted the choice of such state officers; they also decided that an additional delegate be named for service until 1 March, and that Chief Justice Jay be sent.[75]

The choice of John Jay was probably a fortunate one, for Schuyler refused to appear in Congress without first having its approval of his court-martial verdict, but Jay accepted the task in the interests of assuring the state of proper representation. Seeking William Duer's advice on his line of conduct, the general professed an inability to attend Congress until it ruled on the trial verdict, and "perhaps not even then. I am appointed much Against my Inclination," he wrote. And he had "intreated friends" not to elect him.[76]

The Yorker's inclination to avoid Congress became more resolute. After three years of devotion to the patriot cause, two of them in military service, the destruction of much of his property, and the slump in the productivity of his farms and mills, Schuyler calculated that he had lost the equivalent of £20,000 in specie since the war began. His wife and family also deserved more of his attention. During his sojourn at Fredericksburgh his youngest son, Cortlandt, died on 17 October. The fourteenth of the Schuylers' children, he was an infant of five months. Whether news of the baby's death reached him soon thereafter is a question unanswered by the existing records. If so, the general made no extraordinary haste in returning to Albany; for several days he paused at Poughkeepsie where the state legislature was in the midst of its fall session, and not until 29 or 30 October did he reach the arms of his grieving "Caty." It was the second time Schuyler had not been at hand to bury his offspring; during 1761, while he had been in England settling John Bradstreet's quartermaster accounts, Mrs. Schuyler bore a set of twins, one of whom died even before he could be baptized and the other not long thereafter.[77]

The return to Albany now brought Schuyler back to the business of the board of Indian commissioners as well as to the management of his country estate. The former he quickly dispatched by notifying Congress that friendly Oneida and Tuscarora deserved relief from the high prices of goods that had been shipped to Fort Schuyler for the Indian trade. Arguing that their scouting services deserved consideration, he urged that they not be charged at all for clothing.[78]

While complaints from friendly Iroquois proved to be but a minor problem, the hostile tribes continued to pose more serious threats to the New York frontiers. Under Joseph Brant's leadership they and John Butler's Tory rangers moved from the Mohawk River, where attacks were made on Fort Dayton and Fort Herkimer in September, into Cherry Valley in early November. There Butler's inability to control his Seneca warriors resulted in an indiscriminate slaughter of women and children and ultimately the exaction of well-calculated revenge for the outrage.

When Schuyler heard of the Cherry Valley massacre of 11 November he was watching for signs of British and Indian maneuvering through the lake country north of Saratoga. Having taken his family to their country home, where they remained during much of November and December, he had been alerted by Indian scouts to expect attacks along the Schoharie Creek or the Cherry Valley Creek. With the onset of winter the enemy could attempt incursions south of Lake Champlain; ice-covered waters would then become a convenient highway for invaders.[79]

Between 15 and 23 November, however, the general discovered that the British contingent at Crown Point had retired the Canada. But they and their Indian allies had also ravaged settlements along the east side of Lake Champlain. Some of Schuyler's uneasiness was ameliorated when he also obtained intelligence from Canada that enemy forces actually feared an American invasion during the winter. Their numbers, he informed Congress, did not exceed four thousand, including Loyalists, and the garrisons were scattered.[80]

The idea of a winter assault upon Canada—proposed by Schuyler in November 1777 and then by Horatio Gates early in 1778—was considered by Washington again in the fall of 1778, partly upon the urgings of Congress. After apparently discussing the project with Schuyler at Fredericksburgh in October, Washington solicited the Yorker's advice again in November. Urging Schuyler to continue his collection of intelligence from Canada, he also asked him to advise deputy Q.M. Gen. Morgan Lewis about the operations of sawmills at Fort Edward and Fort Ann. Lumber would be needed for the construction of ships on Lake Champlain, but Washington later expressed doubts that plans for a fleet would succeed; too many men must be consulted to execute it with the necessary secrecy. Writing again on 20–21 November, the Virginian bombarded Schuyler with questions about the geography of possible invasion routes to Montreal and Quebec. If the enemy's forces on Lake Champlain could not be removed, and an overland route via "Co'os" could not be selected, what door might otherwise be open to an invasion of Canada? Perhaps a drive could be made via Oswego early in the spring. What were the prospects of using the Mohawk valley as an approach to Niagara?[81]

On 30 November Schuyler responded with a detailed commentary upon the pros and cons of pushing an army into Canada via the lake country and the Mohawk valley. While advocating a northern invasion, he also proposed an alternative venture—the expulsion of the British from Niagara. After two weeks Washington ruled out any winter campaign against Canada. Without adequate provisions it was simply impossible. Preparations, however, should be made for the spring; accordingly, the Virginian instructed commissary and quartermaster officers to consult Schuyler about stockpiling provisions for an army of ten thousand, collecting forage and acquiring building materials for boats, all with as much secrecy as possible! "No person I know," Washington wrote, "has it more in his power to judge of the measures proper to be taken"; and he trusted that Schuyler would assist in the work as much as the situation of his public and personal concerns permitted.[82]

On second thought, the Virginian decided, why not ask Schuyler to accept full command of the Northern Department. Although he suspected the general would decline, "it is very much my desire," he wrote, that "you should resume that command." If his trusted friend had no "material objections," he should "consider this as an order for the purpose."[83]

Washington's New Year's Eve offer was a substantial vote of confidence in Philip Schuyler's abilities, but on 27 December the Yorker had already posted his resignation as a major general to the president of Congress. However, he made no move to resign from Congress or to abandon his place on the board of Indian commissioners. His affection for his country undiminished, he again vowed to seize every opportunity as a private citizen to promote the public weal.[84]

Willing to justify Congress's removal of him from the Northern Army because "It was their duty to Sacrifice the feelings of an Individual to the Safety of the States when the people who only could defend the Country refused to Serve under him," Schuyler refused to excuse the delays in his trial and vindication or Congress's assignment of two lawyers to assist the judge advocate in prosecuting him—the attornies general of Pennsylvania and New Jersey. The latter suggested that his "Crime was of a heinous nature, and thousands have by that very resolution been made to believe so." This, too, he explained to John Jay, made him more than ever determined both to resign his commission and to reject further arguments or offers that he resume a military career. Schuyler also seemed indifferent to the efforts of friends to add still another measure of honor to the verdict of his court-martial. Even before acquittal had been voted in October, Gouverneur Morris thought that if Schuyler would take his seat on Congress, he "would be made President and certainly the best President Congress ever had. His Wife would be worth the Gold of Ophir Yea the purest Gold," he told Robert R. Livingston "—she would out intrigue Adams." Morris's scheme did not long remain a secret, especially after Congress had received word of Schuyler's acquittal "with the highest honor, of the charges exhibited against him." On 3 November Massachusetts congressman James Lovell scoffed at the idea: "We shall do great Things when we get *President Schuyler here,* he sneered, "—Tace—I think that is one of the next Manoeuvres."[85]

A month later the maneuvers were concluded after Congress voted to confirm the verdict of Schuyler's court-martial on 3 December. Jay assured him that friends would welcome him to Congress and that he might render essential services to the country within "this House." By no means should he think of resignation.[86]

When Henry Laurens resigned as president of Congress, Duane indicated that a majority of delegates wished one of the New York delegation to take a turn as presiding officer. "We held up General Schuyler," Duane wrote, "which seemed to be very agreeable. On account of his absence, Mr. Jay was prevailed on to take the chair with a resolution on his part to resign in favor of General Schuyler as soon as he attends."[87]

Schuyler, however, never exercised the office by which his political allies sought to honor him. Nor did the signal recompense for his previous sufferings at the hands of suspicious and hostile congressmen alter his decision in January to resign his seat on the New York delegation. Not until November 1779 did the proud patriot again accept an active role in the national legislature.

Public Demands upon the Private Man

1

"The times are pressing . . . you can't be spared"

*L*ike the very nature of a revolutionary culture that imposes heroic demands upon its participants, the winter of 1778–79 tested the endurance of the American army. It was a season more severe than the previous one at Valley Forge, but nothing compared to that of 1779–80. Divided principally among encampments at Redding, Connecticut, the New York Highlands, and Middlebrook, New Jersey, where Washington fixed his headquarters, the troops contended with heavier snowfalls, lower temperatures, and scantier food supplies than the year before. The political outlook of many citizen-soldiers shifted to increasing doubts about their ability to win the war and about their leaders' success in establishing independence and a republican society. Army officers soured as Congress and the states seemed unwilling or unable to support the military effort.[1]

As in 1778, Schuyler's public services in 1779 remained focused largely upon Indian affairs. While wishing to free himself from both his military commission and Northern Department's board of Indian commissioners, circumstances and conscience persuaded him to continue with the latter— a position that involved him in one of the major campaigns of the year and of the war. Apparently content not to seek the power of office, the Yorker allowed himself to be sought out and finally to accept, however reluctantly, the sacrifices that republican self-government thrust upon him.

After learning that Congress had approved the verdict of his court-martial in December 1778, Schuyler insisted upon resigning his commission as a major general. For reasons of poor health and of family and

Fig. 8. James Duane, 1733–1797. Oil on canvas by Robert Edge Pine. Duane, a delegate to the First Continental Congress, then to the New York Congress, and later mayor of New York City and U.S. district judge, was one of Schuyler's close friends. There is much evidence of Duane's support and encouragement in his correspondence with Schuyler. Courtesy, The New-York Historical Society, New York City.

business obligations, he resisted the urgings of Washington and other friends to resume military service or to take his seat in Congress and the president's chair. Early in January, James Duane begged the Yorker to continue as a major general rather than enter Congress: "It would be a bad exchange both in a public and a private View," he wrote. Schuyler's popularity in the "Southern Army" was great and he was much respected by the commander in chief. Duane also offered to persuade Mrs. Schuyler to abandon her prejudices against the general's continued service: "put your Family in Security & go to Business," he insisted. "The times are pressing & require Vigilence & Wisdom—you can't be spared—."[2]

On 5 January a congressional committee conferred with Washington on Schuyler's letter of resignation and decided to table it. But the Yorker notified the presiding officers of both houses of the state legislature that he was unable to attend Congress; Washington's order that he direct preparations "for a very important Enterprize [sic]"—a possible winter campaign against Canada—prevented his leaving Albany. The legislature might therefore deem it advisable to appoint another gentleman in his place.[3]

Neither Congress nor New York authorities were prompt to accept Schuyler's resignations, and after spending the holidays in Albany, Schuyler again visited his Saratoga estate. Now content with his freedom to reestablish his family fortunes, he was more than ever convinced that Congress's shabby treatment of his pleas for a speedy public vindication justified his retirement from office. Neither Washington's offer of a department command nor Congress's choice of the Yorker as its president seemed to be an adequate "reparation." Were his services to the public weal deemed necessary, however, Schuyler would "never decline giving them ... when reparation has been made, but w[h]ether that takes place or not, as a Citizen they shall never be with[h]eld."[4]

Like John Jay, Dr. John Cochran thought that Schuyler should not retire. Cochran asked his brother-in-law whether he might not lose the esteem of friends and damage the welfare of the country by resigning? He also warned that the Yorker's support of Washington was important in view of Gen. Charles Lee's malicious desire to replace the commander in chief.[5]

Although the Virginian, too, expressed regret that Schuyler refused to accept further military assignments, he was grateful for the Yorker's willingness to serve as a military advisor and to assist with preparations of other campaigns in other ways. In January, for example, Schuyler was invited to proceed with a plan to incite friendly tribesmen to attack enemy shipping on Lake Ontario. Would it be practicable to attempt a similar maneuver at St. John's? And what about carrying the war into Indian territory in the spring: How many troops would be needed? What should be their routes of deployment? How could they be properly supplied?[6]

In February and March 1779 Washington and Schuyler continued to correspond on what became the famous Sullivan-Clinton campaign. And James Duane persisted in his attempts to persuade Schuyler that he could do more for the army by not insisting upon resignation. As of late February there was still time to withdraw it, and Duane chided Schuyler for "breath[ing] the Spirit of our friend Mrs. Schuyler" who adamantly insisted that her husband be free of military duties. "You pant for Retirement and private Life," Duane sighed. "She takes the advantage of me." Signing his 20 February missive "with very great gloom," Duane perhaps realized the futility of his importunities.[7]

While some wished to retain Schuyler in the army, others urged him to take his seat in Congress. But by early March 1779 Schuyler decided that he must quit the army. "I am torn to pieces and reduced to a Skeleton by the Gout, and other disorders still more alarming," he told James Duane. And he was distressed by the very thought of leaving his "young family" during a "season of troubles."[8]

Although he could continue to assist Washington with advice and information and also discharge the business of the Indian commissioners of the Northern Department, Schuyler stiffened his resolve to resist the summons to public service because of the demands of his estate, his family, and other business responsibilities. Some of those responsibilities included the property of his sister Gertrude and her husband, John Cochran; the education of his two oldest sons; and the unsettled estate of his old friend and patron, Gen. John Bradstreet. Bradstreet had died in 1774, but the course of the war prevented the payment of legacies owed to his heirs. Now Schuyler asked President Jay for help in raising £1,000 (in bills of exchange in France) for Bradstreet's daughter Elizabeth. Congress did not respond to Schuyler's request, and two months later he repeated it after receiving two letters from Miss Bradstreet in which she complained of delays in the payment of her inheritance. Again in December she wrote, surprised and astonished that Schuyler had not taken some method to remit her the legacy with the interest due. She would have been more than chagrined had she known then that her father's estate would not be settled until 1794. But for the moment Schuyler's immediate concern for Bradstreet's business lapsed until 1783 and the reestablishment of peace with Britain.[9]

On 18 March Congress finally acted on Schuyler's request to resign his commission as major general. Insisting that his military knowledge be "kept alive" and his authority be left undiminished, the New York delegates led the move to reject the resignation. James Duane argued that Schuyler could better offer advice and military "superintendence" *with* a commission than without it; "why shou[l]d you wish to be a Silent Spectator where you have a Right & abilities to direct?" Duane asked. "At least let us first see our Frontiers protected, and proper Posts established for our future Security." Whenever the general might finally resign, it must not be until adverse impressions of his services, cruelly inculcated, had been effaced. There must be no room to conclude that Schuyler had been obliged to step aside by those who had persecuted him without a cause.[10]

As president of Congress, John Jay was obliged to inform Schuyler "that the situation of the army renders it inconvenient to accept his resignation and therefore Congress cannot comply with his request." New Englanders and Pennsylvanians were all too willing to let the Yorker have his way, but "from New York South you have fast friends," he wrote. And "the Commander in Chief wishes you to retain your Commission. The Propriety of your Resignation is now out of the Question ... You have Talents to render you conspicuous in the Field, and Address to conciliate the affections of those who may now wish you ill." The main army should be Schuyler's "proper Object." There he was best known and best regarded, and there he might best exert military influence. Jay was also overly sanguine, for he suggested that the campaign of 1779 would "in all probability" be decisive and the last of the war.[11]

Jay's blandishments did not alter Schuyler's determination to lay aside his commission. Momentarily, perhaps, he considered them with some care. Courteously but doggedly he entreated Congress to reconsider its 18 March resolution out of concern for his private affairs and ill health.

Schuyler was also annoyed by the language of the 18 March resolution: "inconvenient to accept his resignation" because of "the situation of the army." He insisted that the delegates remember that he had been deprived of a command in 1777 and throughout 1778, but there had never been "*any Complaint of Inconviency on the part of the public.*" Therefore Congress surely would not insist that he continue in service. And as a private citizen he would demonstrate, as he hitherto had hoped to do, that "the Weal of my Country is my first Wish."[12]

At last Congress relented. On the fourth anniversary of the battle of Lexington and Concord Samuel Adams moved to accept Schuyler's resignation, and it was quickly carried, without remark or dissent. Washington continued to wish for Schuyler's help in the army, and James Duane was tempted to expostulate with him; but knowing this was useless, he did nothing more than register his disappointment.[13] With news that his resignation had been accepted Schuyler quickly notified President Jay that he would continue his work as an Indian commissioner until a replacement could be appointed. Thereafter he would promote the country's welfare as a private citizen. For the moment Schuyler decided not to attend Congress lest the entire Indian department "run into confusion." Might James Duane be spared from his congressional duties to take charge of the board of Indian commissioners? Meantime, Schuyler would complete the business of managing "important matters" that had recently developed; there seemed to be no one more competent to deal with them. The need for a supply of trading goods was urgent lest the service of friendly tribesmen be lost to the patriot cause. "Who is the great Man that is who is the assistant Deputy Quarter Master at Boston[?]" he fumed; "he is extreamly [sic] tardy."[14]

2

"unremitted Exertions"

During the months of Schuyler's struggle to divest himself of a major general's commission, he neglected neither his duties as president of the board of Indian commissioners of the Northern Department, nor his promises to contribute to the war effort as Washington's advisor, informant, and unofficial commissary-quartermaster general. With the development of the Sullivan-Clinton expedition against Loyalists and Indians along the Pennsylvania-New York frontier, which was perhaps the major American campaign in 1779, Schuyler's role in Indian affairs and his efforts on behalf of Washington and the expeditionary forces proved how accurately John Jay had characterized his "unremitted Exertions" to promote the happiness of his country.

The campaign originated late in 1778 with proposals for a winter invasion of Canada. After soliciting Schuyler's advice and information Washington finally decided in December that it would be impossible to proceed for want of adequate provisions. But he urged the Yorker to continue to make inquiries and to submit his reflections upon such a campaign should it later prove feasible to launch it. From that point the idea of invading Canada evolved into the Sullivan-Clinton campaign against the enemy and their Indian and Loyalist allies in the west.[15]

Early in January 1779, before receiving word that a full-scale assault upon Niagara, which was the British base on Lake Ontario, could not be undertaken, Schuyler instructed the deputy commissary general Jacob Cuyler to proceed with preparations of provisions for a sizable army by April. And he confronted the problem of cultivating certain of the Six Nations who were friendly and others who remained hostile or neutral. He and the Indian commissioners decided not to distribute their full stock of blankets and other goods to friendly Iroquois tribesmen in the Mohawk valley lest it encourage the natives to become idle and to regard the Americans as "tributaries." A partial distribution of blankets and stores at Fort Schuyler was made to the Oneida and Tuscarora who were clearly allies of the rebels; the rest were to be reserved for later distribution. And Schuyler proposed that the Oneida be given no specific encouragement to invite the divided Onondaga to come and live with them; such a step might lead the tribesmen to overvalue their importance to the rebel cause. However, he decided to hint to the Oneida that those Indians who chose to reside with them would benefit by having American protection against the British and other hostile tribes. In February forty Onondaga surrendered British medals that they had received in token of their stance against the Americans, and a number of them moved to live among their Oneida brothers.[16]

Such cultivation of the western Indians was a part of Washington's own scheme to conduct "some operation in a smaller scale against the savages" rather than a full-blown march against Fort Niagara. Between 18 and 25 January he informed Schuyler to proceed only with plans to send Indian parties to destroy enemy shipping on Lake Ontario. Thinking of a similar maneuver against St. John's in the north, the commander in chief solicited Schuyler's and Gen. James Clinton's views on the practicability of the attempt. Clinton, now at Albany as commander of the Northern Department, hoped that Schuyler would accede to Washington's desire that he resume his old command.[17]

More than ever convinced that the war must be carried into Indian territory in the spring, Washington again requested Schuyler to suggest the number of troops that would be required, routes of their deployment, and other arrangements for provisioning and equipping them. During February the Virginian and the Yorker exchanged further correspondence, and gradually plans for a fresh campaign against the British and the Iroquois on the frontiers of Pennsylvania and New York emerged. Bombarding Schuyler with a series of questions, Washington clearly expected him to furnish all the information he needed to launch the campaign, and he pored over the Yorker's papers about western campaigns of the Great War of 1754–63 with interest. Weeks passed into months before Washington managed to collect the kind of information he wanted or before he could assemble the forces needed to chastise the western Indians for their raids of Cherry Valley and the Wyoming river valley. He approved Schuyler's proposals for the construction of bateaux, the collection of forage, and the establishment of a garrison at Fort George for defense of the north country as well as a post at Stone Arabia, about thirty-five miles west of Schenectady.[18]

On 19 February the New York delegation in Congress urged Governor George Clinton to support Schuyler and the preparations for the frontier campaign. The governor, like Washington and others, continued to hope that Schuyler might remain in the army and lead "in the intended Operations against the hostile Savage Tribes; for exclusive of his Abilities and Experience, his general Knowledge of the western Country and of the Manners of those people, would have given him great Advantages in the command of such an Expedition." But by early March, Washington was obliged to ask Horatio Gates to do so. Fully expecting that Gates would refuse, the Virginian asked him to pass the request to John Sullivan. After the idea of a winter incursion into Canada had been dropped, Gates showed no interest in leading one into the west, but John Sullivan accepted Washington's orders and joined the commander in chief at Middlebrook, New Jersey, where final plans were worked out in April and May. Sullivan accepted Washington's plan for the route of march after Schuyler warned that a main army moving along the Mohawk valley could not be adequately supplied. Washington also agreed with Schuyler's proposal that the main objective of the campaign should be the Seneca tribe. Accordingly, Sullivan was to lead three thousand men up the Susquehannah River from Easton, Pennsylvania, while a thousand auxiliary troops used the Mohawk route and another five hundred from Pittsburgh proceeded north into Seneca country. Before Sullivan had joined him, Washington had also approved Schuyler's plan to launch an early surprise attack from Fort Schuyler upon Onondaga.[19]

Schuyler directed arrangements for this initial assault led by Col. Goose Van Schaick into Onondaga territory during 19 through 25 April. Watching for British and Indian movement in the northern and western regions of the state, he also submitted estimates of the numbers of each tribe that the invading army would be likely to encounter.[20]

By the time Van Schaick left Fort Schuyler on 19 April, Washington was still undecided as to whether to allow Gen. James Clinton to move up the Mohawk or to order him southward via Otsego Lake to join

Sullivan's main army at some point on the upper Susquehannah River. In accordance with Schuyler's suggestions for the security of the northern frontier, Washington applied to Governor Clinton to assign militia to replace regular army detachments along the Hudson River because the latter were to be assigned to the western enterprise. Lacking sufficient Continentals, he also asked Pennsylvania authorities for six hundred militia to join Sullivan's main army.[21]

Toward the end of April a delegation of Oneida, Tuscarora, and Onondaga sachems visited Schuyler in Albany to confirm James Dean's earlier reports that the Cayuga were ready to sue for peace. The possibility that these or other hostile tribes might come to terms was welcome but also embarrassing in view of the decision to punish them for their depredations since 1778. Yet Schuyler thought that "little dependence" could be placed upon the mere word of these "savages," and he suggested that hostages be taken as a guarantee for any peace overtures. Both Congress and Washington, he thought, must instruct the Indian commissioners how to proceed. A month later the Virginian wrote that Congress had voted resolutions for negotiating peace and exchanging prisoners of war. If the Indian commissioners managed any exchange of prisoners, they must not agree to the exchange of soldiers for civilians.[22]

The Sullivan expedition remained bogged down in preparations until well into June before it moved beyond Easton, Pennsylvania. But in the latter part of April an initial attack was made on Onondaga, west of Fort Schuyler, a move that was Schuyler's own proposal to open the campaign by surprising the British and their Indian allies and striking fear and uncertainty into their ranks. The maneuver was also designed to reduce the hazards of later invading Seneca country while the Onondaga remained on the right flank of the army.[23]

Schuyler soon informed Washington of the success of Van Schaick's Onondaga raid and of Gen. James Clinton's complementary maneuvers. The former had been accomplished with speed and secrecy and without losses. A town of fifty houses and fields of corn and beans were destroyed, seventeen warriors killed, and thirty-two prisoners taken. Discovering no signs of enemy parties active elsewhere in Tryon County, General Clinton turned to Sacandaga on the west branch of the Hudson to erect a picket fort as a part of defenses for the northern frontier. And the commander in chief agreed with Schuyler's proposal to retain the captives taken by Van Schaick at Albany or Poughkeepsie for use in prisoner exchange.[24]

3

The Sullivan-Clinton Campaign

With much of his advisory work for Washington completed, and assurances that the western campaign had been opened auspiciously, Schuyler withdrew from Albany to the country, savoring the news that Congress had at last accepted the resignation of his major general's commission. At Saratoga during May he was able to manage his tenants and mills and to continue correspondence with Washington and with the Indian commissioner Volkert Douw. Washington backed his reliance upon Schuyler for information about enemy activities in the north country and Saint Lawrence valley with promises to support his expenses and any decisions with regard to "approaches" to the lakes. At the end of May, however, Schuyler was relieved to report that there were no signs of trouble with the enemy in Canada; no troops had been moved to Montreal, nor was there indication of preparations to do so.[25]

In May, Schuyler's former aide, Richard Varick, and his friend, James Duane, urged him to return to Congress. Varick reported that officers at Washington's headquarters wished he might at least support their interests in Congress; its neglect of the army they deemed contemptible. Only their respect for Washington prevented the officers from some full-blown eruption. Duane wrote in a similar vein. Schuyler answered that he would "repair to Congress" only if it was certain that he could serve more effectually there than he could by remaining at Albany. The Indian commissioners' business continually required attention, and there were few who seemed able to give it.[26]

Determined to run the Indian department lest it fall into confusion, Schuyler made no move to assume his seat in Congress. In June preliminary peace negotiations were begun with the Onondaga; Schuyler intended to proceed by assuring them that their prisoners would be released. He also finished the last of a series of reports to Washington on the area between Fort Schuyler and Oswegatchie. Seeking as much information as possible about even the northernmost territory into which Sullivan and Clinton's army might penetrate, the Virginian was grateful for pains that Schuyler took to procure it. He also left Schuyler to decide whether part of Col. Peter Gansevoort's Third New York Regiment should guard military stores or be sent on as a part of the brigade led by Gen. James Clinton. Informing Schuyler on 13 June that Clinton was now expected to be en route from Canajoharie to rendezvous with Sullivan's men at Tioga, Washington expected the Yorker to prod Clinton into action if need be—and to inform him that he was subordinate to Sullivan.[27]

After a trip to Albany in June, Schuyler returned to Saratoga, where he remained until almost mid-September. Volkert Douw handled routine Indian department affairs in Albany while the general collected and forwarded intelligence gleaned from Canada to Washington and to generals Clinton and Sullivan. In June and July, for example, there were signs of minor troop movements along the Saint Lawrence, and rumors that Joseph Brant was endeavoring to enlist a thousand Ottawa and Chippewa to join Seneca raids on the western frontiers. In late August he discovered enemy probes south of Lake Champlain. Neither an Indian attack on Fort George on 2 September nor the threats of a band of Tories and Indians to the area south of Saratoga proved especially alarming. But on 11 September the general did request Governor Clinton to take steps to force "those vermin" into the interior or to enemy lines. Following Schuyler's suggestion, the Governor asked the commissioners for detecting and defeating conspiracies at Albany to seize and hold disaffected frontiersmen to be exchanged for prisoners held in Canada.[28]

It was at Saratoga, too, at the end of June that Schuyler decided to heed James Duane's plea that he not resign as an Indian commissioner, at least not until matters took on a "more favorable aspect." And as soon as his health permitted, the Yorker intended to visit Washington to discuss the work of establishing peace with the various tribes.[29]

In mid-July, while John Sullivan's expedition against the Iroquois remained immobile at Wyoming, Pennsylvania, Brig. Gen. Anthony Wayne launched a counterattack at Stony Point, which the British had seized on 1 June. Wayne's success in bagging the garrison and dismantling the fort relieved the pressure placed on the Hudson valley by Sir Henry Clinton. While Clinton's attention was thus diverted, other American forces were able to push the British from Paulus Hook (now Jersey City), their last major stronghold in New Jersey. Schuyler promptly sent Wayne his congratulations. "Pray make, *not my compliments only*," he wrote, "*but my love, to General St. Clair,* and especially to that great and good man General Washington, to whom we are all so much indebted." Generous in acknowledging the services of his army comrades and political allies, Schuyler perhaps realized that the war effort depended more than ever upon men like Wayne and upon the perseverance of the Virginian.[30] Did the squire of Saratoga begin to realize the necessity of reentering the public arena, at least to the extent of ceasing to be a nonsitting Congressman? Perhaps.

For the moment, however, he found nothing more compelling than to counsel his fellow member of the Northern Department's board of Indian commissioners, Volkert Douw. Before Douw released Indian prisoners, he must determine which of them were Onondaga who could legitimately claim to have been living peaceably among the friendly Oneida. Others must be retained for later exchange.[31]

For Schuyler the issues of a general exchange of prisoners of war and of setting terms for a peace with the Indians were matters of considerable concern well before the campaign of 1779 had been concluded. Still, there seemed little to be settled until the long-delayed chastisement of the Iroquois had been executed. While the Yorker waited at Saratoga, Sullivan's and Clinton's troops did not join forces at Tioga until 22 August. After weeks of delay they finally began to slash through central New York, laying waste to forty Iroquois towns, including storehouses, fields, and orchards as far as the north ends of Cayuga and Seneca lakes.

In destruction and devastation the campaign fulfilled Washington's expectations admirably. Sullivan did not, however, succeed in capturing hostages as he had been instructed to do, nor did the campaign "accomplish its real purpose, the protection of the border settlements from further ravages," for the "Indian and Tory forces were not destroyed, nor even crippled." Driven from their towns, they fell "back upon the British at Niagara for shelter and food," and there they were "welded more firmly than ever to the King's cause." The frontiers had not been rendered permanently safe. However chastened, the Iroquois power had not yet been wholly broken. In 1780 they ravaged "the borders with even greater malignity than before."[32]

Almost two months before John Sullivan submitted his report to Congress of the foray against the Six Nations, Schuyler was asked to proceed with an exchange of prisoners with Col. John Butler at Niagara. Like the question of negotiating a general peace with the Indians, Schuyler found that prisoner exchange was not business to be quickly concluded, and his work with both dragged on into the following year. Although hopeful that a treaty with the Cayuga might induce the Seneca to make one, he could not proceed with negotiation without instructions from Congress and the commander in chief. And he recognized that unless a majority of each of the tribes wished to negotiate a peace, no compact made by a few would be considered binding upon the others. Accordingly, he informed the commander at Fort Schuyler and the Indian agent James Dean to encourage the Cayuga to make a formal application for peace with the understanding that they must not regard the grant of such a favor something to which they were entitled. To this Washington also agreed, but the Virginian insisted that only Congress could specify particular terms for treaty making with individual tribes and the entire Iroquois confederacy.[33]

The issue was not to be resolved soon. Late in October the New York legislature complicated the business by passing legislation to appoint state commissioners to assist in any negotiation between the United States and those Indians within the confines of the state. It was an indication of provincialism that long checked the progress of nationalist sentiment in the United States. After Schuyler finally assumed his seat in Congress in November 1779, he discovered that no decision had been reached concerning his earlier question because most of the Six Nations had given no indication of seeking a peace treaty. Despite his urging, Congress neither decided to seek an alliance with the tribes nor did it determine upon settling terms of general friendship and neutrality. Apparently the action of the New York legislature inhibited the delegates from dealing with such issues.[34] The failure to do so in the latter years of the war continued into the postwar era, illustrating to Schuyler and others the weakness of the government under the Articles of Confederation and the need for a stronger national union.

Aside from the Indian department Schuyler was "Most happily deprived" of the cares and anxieties of public business, and he found work at his Saratoga estate to be a welcome relief during the summer of 1779. Indeed, he had begun to recoup his property losses, and the resumption of his milling not only enabled him to make money but to supply the public with much-needed lumber for a variety of construction projects.[35]

The squire of Saratoga was not, however, wholly given to his business and family interests. In September, for example, he decided to visit Washington's headquarters, where he was assured by James Duane that his "many Friends in the Army . . . would be happy to see" him. Before leaving Albany Schuyler responded to Washington's need for a vast quantity of lumber with which to pursue the "work of reducing" New York City. Apart from the continued fortification of West Point, the commander in chief hoped that the arrival of the French fleet under the Comte d'Estaing would enable the Americans to drive the enemy from the lower reaches of the Hudson. Both Q.M. Morgan Lewis and Schuyler endeavored to meet Washington's call for lumber. Schuyler applied to teamsters of the neighborhood south of Saratoga to haul boards from the Battenkill to Stillwater, where they could be rafted down the Hudson, and he ordered the collection of lumber from the Saratoga neighborhood. Lewis subsequently insisted that Schuyler's own fences were not to be spared, for he expected they would produce least three thousand boards.[36]

4

Again a Congressman

When Schuyler left Albany for his visit to Washington at West Point he doubtless intended to offer the commander in chief whatever aid and information might be asked of him. As Indian commissioner he also wanted the Virginian's advice or instructions on the pending question of a pacification treaty. For whatever purposes Washington might have wished to see his loyal friend, it is clear enough that he anticipated the visit with pleasure. Between mid-October and mid-November the two men shared one another's counsels while waiting to discover whether d'Estaing's French fleet might appear. With its aid Washington might attempt "something important and interesting . . . against the Enemy."[37]

Little evidence of Schuyler's activities at West Point remains, but they doubtless included extensive deliberations with Washington and his military family. After the British abandoned their position at Stony Point and Verplanck's Point Schuyler found "everyone" at Washington's headquarters eager to repossess New York City. Willing to risk much to do so, he nevertheless deemed the obstacles too great; and "the Amicable man I am with," Schuyler noted, also recognized the difficulties with the limited forces at hand. At the end of October Schuyler still found it difficult to tear himself away from the army. By mid-November his wife was urging him to return to Albany, but perhaps he enjoyed being beyond her reach, as much as she might have realized his temptation to escape the political backwater where he had rested for almost a year. He must also have come to recognize that duty and interest required that he reassert a more active role in the revolutionary cause. At any rate, the general turned not toward Albany but south toward Philadelphia, and Mrs. Schuyler was not to see him again until 12 December. He had at last consented to be a congressman once more.[38]

When the New York legislature made its annual selection of delegates to the Continental Congress on 1 October it was not inclined to choose Schuyler because of his long-standing rejection of the office. Months earlier Chancellor Robert R. Livingston observed that Gouverneur Morris and Schuyler would "be left out [at] the first opportunity." And indeed they were, for on 1 October the delegation chosen by the legislature consisted of James Duane, William Floyd, John Jay, John Morin Scott, and Ezra L'Hommedieu. L'Hommedieu had been chosen instead of Morris. On 8 October after it was learned that Jay was to become minister to

Spain, friends in the senate nominated Schuyler. Determined to furnish as full a representation of the state in Congress as possible, they also nominated Chancellor Livingston and then quickly obtained the assembly's concurrence.[39]

After four weeks at West Point, Schuyler agreed to accept his reelection as a delegate. Any of a variety of reasons may have led him to go on to Philadelphia. It is likely that Washington and other officers persuaded him to accept the seat because they wanted an able spokesman for the army's interests. In the aftermath of the Sullivan campaign a visit to Congress might also serve to wring from it an answer to his request for terms under which the Indian commission could negotiate peace with the Iroquois. Knowing that he could rely upon John Lansing, Jr.'s, offer to manage the works at Saratoga and to attend the needs of Mrs. Schuyler and her family, the erstwhile general had no pressing need to return to Albany. And because John Jay had persuaded Congress to ask New York, New Hampshire, and Massachusetts for authority to deal with their mutual disputes over the Hampshire Grants territory, the New York legislature responded by passing an act empowering Congress to settle the boundary disputes. Thus it was important, as James Duane noted, that someone like Schuyler be in Congress to represent New York's interests. No one was more familiar with questions of land grants or boundary claims than he.[40]

Schuyler reached Philadelphia on the evening of 15 November and next morning promptly presented his credentials for admission to Congress. Although his stay lasted but a brief three weeks, his attendance was steady. And he was immediately immersed in Congress's business of finance, problems of currency depreciation and foreign policy, ways and means of supporting the army, arrangements for the quartermaster and commissary departments, and terms for negotiating peace with the northern Indians.

At the moment Congress's most serious challenge was fiscal. The treasury verged on exhaustion. The states had failed to contribute more than about $3,000,000 of quotas totaling $60,000,000. What was Congress to do in order to carry on the war in the face of inadequate revenue? On his first day in Philadelphia, Schuyler helped cast New York's vote refusing Massachusetts's request to retain $6,000,000 of its tax quota designed for the Continental treasury. Here at least was a hint that states should get on with paying their assessments. But for every question of raising funds there was one of spending them. On 16 November Schuyler was assigned to a committee charged to consider allowances for officers of the different departments of the army who had not otherwise been covered by Congress's 18 August provision.[41]

On 17 November Congress proceeded to vote the emission of more than $10,000,000 in bills of credit and then named a committee to devise further ways and means of supplying the treasury. The committee proposed to anticipate the negotiations of European loans by drawing £200,000 sterling in bills of exchange on John Jay and Henry Laurens, ministers to Spain and Holland. Although on 23 November he voted to approve the draft of bills on Jay and Laurens, Schuyler knew that such steps would not alleviate the problems of currency depreciation. Reacting to these measures and to a proposal to solicit loans by which creditors could receive £100 sterling with six percent interest at the end of ten years in exchange for $8,000 paid into the treasury, Schuyler commented that he feared the consequences of such financial disarray. Alarmed by rapid currency depreciation and the deepening debt of every department of government, he also found that there was no overall plan to remedy the evils.[42]

Although on 19 November Congress requested the states to pass strict laws against engrossing and withholding and to legislate wage and price controls so that rates would not exceed those of 1774 more than twentyfold, this seemed to be little more than a gesture, especially because salt and military stores were to be excepted from the price limits. On the same day Congress also considered asking the states to revise their laws making paper currency a tender in payment of debts so as to prevent injustices to creditors and debtors alike. When John Witherspoon moved to amend the request to include provision for also remedying past injustices "as far as may be practicable," there was immediate objection. Consideration of both the amendment and the question were postponed by a vote of five states to three, while three were divided. Schuyler's vote to postpone consideration probably indicated his wish for a comprehensive economic policy or plan instead of piecemeal measures. It was after all the lack of a *plan* for remedying fiscal evils that he emphasized to Washington. And on 29 November, after Congress voted still another emission of $10,000,000, he observed with dismay, "I wish I could say that there was one member of Congress adequate to the important business of Finance." The limit of $200 million, previously set as a "dead-line," had been reached, and the precarious state of the treasury was indicated by Congress's reservation of $4,000,000 of the latest issue to discharge warrants for the supply of various military chests.[43]

Schuyler's ties to Washington and his seat in Congress enabled him to serve both the interests of the army and the commander in chief—national interests. In considering allowances for military officers, the committee to which Schuyler was assigned was given a memorial of general officers to study on 18 November. Promising Washington that he would prod the body into speedy action, Schuyler noted that fellow delegates were not as attentive to business as the vast variety and importance of their responsibilities warranted.[44]

Within two weeks the Yorker's work on the committee on allowances for officers in the various army departments was ready for Congress's consideration. Well aware of the legitimate anxieties of soldiers whose pay was often in arrears and whose economic future was jeopardized by rampant inflation, Schuyler and his fellow committeemen sought to alleviate complaints, proposing to reward men who faithfully served the military cause rather than abandon the army for private pursuits. He considered Benedict Arnold's arguments that general officers were not so much desirous of more rations and subsistence money as they wanted their pay "made good." What Schuyler did not know of course was that Arnold some months earlier had "made his first offer to become a traitor." But Arnold's case illustrated the severity of the problem of disgruntled officers.[45]

As a result of the committee's report, submitted in Schuyler's own handwriting, on 1 December Congress passed a series of resolutions, promising land grants and adjustments in salaries necessitated by depreciated currency. Officers holding commissions from Congress were to have their pay (as it had hitherto been established) made good by a "liquidation" of different rates of depreciation. Those continuing to serve during the war were to be entitled to half-pay for life according to the schedule established before January 1777. Ten thousand acres of land were promised to Washington and to any subsequent commander in chief; major generals were to have three thousand acres and brigadiers two thousand. Other officers and men might claim a hundred acres of land for every $5 "of monthly pay reduced to real value at the rate of depreciation when their appointments and pay were respectively established." Moreover, the heirs of men entitled to land and who died before the war ended were to inherit the promise of lands; and widows of officers who died in service before the end of the war were assured of half the pay to which their husbands would have been entitled.[46]

Aside from meeting officers' demands for salaries, clothing, and subsistence money, Schuyler was concerned for the long-standing need to reform the quartermaster and commissary departments. After months of delay and a variety of congressional committees had grappled with complaints of abuses and frauds, nothing had been done to deal with the expensive practice "of rewarding purchase agents by commissions on purchases." Nathanael Greene, the quartermaster general, and Jeremiah

Wadsworth, the commissary general of purchases, repeatedly threatened to resign, and by 18 November Schuyler feared that Wadsworth's immanent retirement would soon leave his office vacant unless Congress was pushed to appoint a successor. On 25 November, in an effort to simplify superintendance of the quartermaster and commissary departments, which hitherto had been the responsibility of several committees, Congress assigned the two departments to the board of war. Four days later it finally agreed to accept Wadsworth's resignation, effective on 1 January, but it delayed the choice of a replacement until 2 December, when it elected Ephraim Blaine.[47]

Schuyler witnessed a considerable amount of parliamentary maneuvering not only over the question of congressional appointments but also with the issue of Indian policy. Forced to press for an answer to his 17 October request for instructions on negotiating peace with the New York tribes, he discovered that what Congress initially decided on 27 November was complicated rather than clarified by an ensuing debate and a variety of motions. At first Congress agreed to conditions for establishing peace with the savages: the tribes must initiate the request and surrender all Americans then in their custody; they must expel all British agents and emissaries and also agree to "deliver up" such as might thereafter come among them; they must agree never again to take up the hatchet under penalty of being driven from their country; and for a guarantee of strict adherence to these promises they must surrender hostages. To these six points Congress added the wish that the Indians "make considerable Offers of Territory" as marks of their contrition.[48] Members promptly began to jockey around this final point of land cessions.

Schuyler opposed the move to require the Iroquois to cede lands to the United States because it would divest New York of territory to which it had long held a rightful claim, and he thought it unlikely that the Indians would agree to it. The motion was rejected, but not without a fight. Later, in mid-December Schuyler explained to James Duane more fully the wrangle over Indian policy and the land issue, which ultimately delayed the ratification of the Articles of Confederation until 1781. The proposal that the Indians cede their lands, which Congress would dispose of for the benefit of the United States, had produced a "lively debate" before it was rejected. Happily, he thought, no congressman in favor of the proposal happened to remember the recent act of the New York legislature that made a similar demand in favor of that state. Had the resolution carried, Schuyler said, New Yorkers would surely encounter "much trouble" in the future. The idea was not yet dead, for he had seen a motion in Roger Sherman's hand to the effect that all lands heretofore grantable by the Crown and not already so granted should be the property of the United States and grantable by Congress for the benefit of the states. Connecticut and Maryland delegates had argued that such a move was equitable; if New Yorkers would agree to a reasonable western limit to their state, such an accommodation would "complete the Union" and afford general "satisfaction." To this Schuyler answered that he was curious to know their ideas of "a reasonable western extent, as they might widely differ from others. I was then Carried to the Map," he recounted, "and Mr. Sherman explained himself" by drawing a line from the northwest corner of Pennsylvania (on Lake Erie) through the strait leading to Lake Ontario and thence down the Saint Lawrence to the 45-degree latitude. For Virginia, the Carolinas, and Georgia, Sherman proposed a western boundary along the Allegheny Mountains, or at the farthest point, the Ohio River; land west of the boundary should be the joint property of all the states and subject to Congress's disposition. As North Carolina congressmen had requested instructions from their constituents, Schuyler now begged Duane to consider the matter in preparation for the next meeting of the New York legislature; for the present it would be "impolitic and injurious" to the state to insist upon any cession of territory from the Indians.[49]

Fearful of economic advantages that larger states might have if they retained jurisdiction over much of the American interior, smaller states insisted that the Confederation Congress must control the disposition of the west for the benefit of all the states. Schuyler recognized that New York authorities must be willing to adjust their western land claims in order to assure ratification of the Articles of Confederation by states like Maryland.

5

Mission to Morristown

When Schuyler left Washington's West Point headquarters in mid-November, the commander in chief had not yet moved his army into winter quarters at Morristown and other points in Connecticut and New Jersey. Instead, he waited to discover whether d'Estaing would bring the French fleet north from Georgia for a joint assault upon Sir Henry Clinton's forces in Manhattan. In communicating his anxiety about necessary military arrangements to Congress on 14 November—the day before he learned that d'Estaing had withdrawn to the West Indies—Washington raised the question of whether Congress should specifically instruct him to suspend preparations for further campaigning. Schuyler thought Congress might propose to send American reinforcements to Georgia under the Comte de Grasse's convoy if de Grasse followed d'Estaing south. But on 18 November Congress voted to suggest that the commander in chief act as he thought "most proper" upon the intelligence that he must have by then received.[50]

The failure of the Franco-American siege of Savannah in October placed matters in the South on a "delicate footing," and Washington did not see what more could be done there for the moment. His own army would now be moved into winter quarters; but were reinforcements from it to be assigned to the Southern Department? The commander in chief's report of its growing necessities was read to Congress on 26 November and promptly referred to a committee composed of John Mathews, Schuyler, Roger Sherman, Elbridge Gerry, and William Churchill Houston. Alerted to the Virginian's worries about the alarming state of congressional finances and currency depreciation and their effect on the army, Schuyler found his position on this committee to be especially useful in determining how Congress would also deal with the questions of further military operations in the South. By 29 November it was clear the reinforcements for Gen. Benjamin Lincoln had been ordered to move to Georgia; the action was timely, for the military initiative had passed to the British. D'Estaing's fleet withdrawal and Clinton's evacuation of Rhode Island in October would permit an increased enemy effort in the South. By the end of November reports of preparations for some "special embarkation" from New York City had reached Philadelphia. Sir Henry Clinton did not, however, leave the city with eight thousand British troops until almost a month later. His target was Charleston.[51]

Washington's questions about reinforcing the Southern Department commanded by Gen. Benjamin Lincoln was referred to the Mathews committee on 26 November. Four days after Schuyler's assignment to the committee, Congress responded to its report and its proposals, apparently without debate. Six resolves were passed with no sign of any attempt to amend or to demand any division of votes. One created a committee of two delegates to confer with Washington on the state of the Southern Department. They were to consider proposals recently presented by the French minister, the Chevalier de la Luzerne, and his Spanish counterpart, Don Juan de Miralles, for a joint campaign with the Americans against British Florida; but Congress cautiously directed Washington and the committee to recommend only such measures as might seem "most advisable to be taken." Finally, it named Schuyler and Henry Marchant as the Committee to Headquarters, ordering them to "have leave of absence" from Congress for the mission.[52]

Before the two men left Philadelphia a few days later, Schuyler fired a parting shot on behalf of the army with whose problems he had become so familiar. Characteristically displaying his concern for careful preparations well in advance of the yearly rounds of campaigning, his work on a committee report on quartermaster and commissary department affairs emerged in the form of a resolution. Submitted in his own handwriting, the resolve that Congress passed on 2 December directed the board of war to prepare estimates of provisions for the army for the ensuing year.[53]

Schuyler and Marchant lost little time in making their way to Morristown or in fulfilling their mission to consult with Washington about the new year's campaign in the Southern Department. By 7 December they had written their report, and four days later it was laid before Congress. The commander in chief and the two men agreed upon the "propriety" of sending Virginia Continentals to reinforce General Lincoln and suggested that a French fleet lingering in Chesapeake Bay be pressed into convoy service for the troops. Although Washington did send some fourteen hundred Virginia and North Carolina Continentals south from New York in December, they were obliged to march overland and did not reach South Carolina until March-April 1780. In view of the prospective shift of these troops, which constituted a loss that could rouse the enemy to take the offensive, and because of the need to maintain a variety of posts, Schuyler and Marchant "humbly recommended" that immediate, decisive measures be taken to draw quotas from the states and to complete those battalions already "on the establishment." Substituting militia was *not* proposed except as a last resort because they were deemed "a resource too precarious to be depended upon" at present. Having also consulted Washington on the French and Spanish proposals to attack the British in Florida, the two congressmen agreed with him that such an effort would be "highly imprudent" until the enemy was decisively beaten in Georgia or driven from that state. It should rather be proposed that French and Spanish naval power be concentrated upon the South Carolina coast, especially at Charleston, and that they furnish five thousand soldiers to help the Americans force the British out of Georgia. Once that was accomplished, the combined forces could move into east or west Florida. As to Don Juan de Miralles's request for provisions for Havanna and the island of Cuba, the committee and Washington also agreed that none should be promised until Congress was certain of having surplus supplies for its own army and navy. But as an inducement to the Spanish to cooperate with American troops in Georgia—especially if they could not do so without aid in the form of provisions—some risk might be taken: "extraordinary exertions" should be made to procure provisions for the American army, which might then have enough to share with allied troops.[54]

Instead of returning to Philadelphia, Schuyler made use of Congress's grant of a leave of absence to escape to Albany. After almost two months away from his wife and family he was again ready for the comforts of his own fireside. Meantime, between 11 and 16 December, Congress responded to his and Henry Marchant's report, voting requests to Virginia, Maryland, Pennsylvania, Delaware, New Jersey, and Connecticut for corn, wheat, flour, and more troops. The delegates decided to inform the French ambassador that few provisions could be sent to Cuba except for some rice that Spanish agents could procure in South Carolina; and they also followed the committee's proposals by insisting that the conquest of Florida depended upon removing the British from Georgia. Washington's dispatch of reinforcements to the Southern Department would enable the department commander to cooperate with the Spanish governor of Havanna and others in working toward those ends.[55]

Schuyler had evidently impressed many members of Congress with his talents for military organization and planning. Although they had refused Nathanael Greene's attempt to resign the quartermaster department, Robert R. Livingston told the Yorker that "all eyes are fixed upon you wd. to God you could be perswaded to take it with [y]our former rank [;] write to me on this subject as soon as possible."[56]

The general, however, had already decided against it. That he had been "much pressed" to take on the quartermaster or commissary departments—or both—was flattering, as was the idea of restoring his major general's commission. But because both offices were deemed to be lucrative, he declined them. Never again did he wish to be the subject of suspicions or charges of peculation or mismanagement in office. On the other hand, Schuyler was tempted by the proposition that he be made secretary at war. As the "objection" he had raised against the other appointment "did not hold here," he "desired time for Consideration." By 16 December he "concluded to Accept of It, If offered and If restored to my rank in the army. After what I have experienced In public life," he told James Duane, "you will be Surprized at this determination but the Considerations which Induced me I trust you will approve of [.] I defer giving them until I have the pleasure of a tete-a-tete with you."[57]

What inclined Schuyler to accept the notion of serving as secretary at war? Perhaps Washington's urgings at Morristown. Doubtless, the army's need of his talents and energy and his concern for the derangement of both Congress's finances and the "Ill-policied System" of the civil departments of the army, which he deemed a "fruitful Source of distress." The Yorker's recent if brief stint in Congress and his visits with Washington at West Point and Morristown had at least demonstrated how much he might yet contribute to the war effort. Already he had outlined a plan for remedying the evils of a depreciated currency. If it passed Duane's scrutiny, Schuyler was certain that it would be feasible.[58]

Other plans were also much on Schuyler's mind as he left Morristown for Albany and the impending holidays. The evils of which he and Washington spoken together at Morristown were "nigh" indeed, and how was the Virginian to "stem a torrent which seems ready to overwhelm us"? Might a sortie into Canada be attempted?[59]

For the moment, however, winter intervened; snowy blasts began to strike the coastal regions north from Virginia, creating "the most severe winter in the meteorological history of the United States." Between late December and early January three major snow storms ravaged the countryside north of Virginia. The harbors of New York City, Philadelphia, and Baltimore were closed until March. With snow often four feet deep not only was the army pierced and petrified by the cold, but it also nearly perished for want of food. Starvation now proved more threatening than any "military engagement of the American Revolution." Even the winter of 1777–78 at Valley Forge had not been so terrible. Despite food shortages created by drought in 1779, the interruptions of transportation, and the inadequacies of quartermaster and commissary systems, the army somehow endured. Washington forced reluctant sellers to part with food supplies, and his men foraged and confiscated when they could not otherwise obtain provisions from the governments of New Jersey and Maryland.[60]

In January 1780, as temperatures fell sixteen to twenty degrees below zero between New York City and Albany, Schuyler and his family hovered at their marble-faced fireplaces, happily warmer than the soldiers who shivered in tents and brushwood huts at Morristown. Winter devastations proved to be a hindrance to a revival of the military effort in the spring.[61] And with the turn of seasons Schuyler confronted fresh challenges when he returned to Congress.

That Great Circle of Politics

1

The Pleasures and Occupations of a Retreat

*F*or Schuyler, as for the course of the war, the events of 1780 were indeed momentous, perhaps as striking as those of 1777. The British capture of Charleston and a fifty-four-hundred-man garrison in May was the heaviest American defeat of the war. The arrival of Rochambeau's army in July might have enabled Washington to attack New York City but for the lack of suitable naval support. And Horatio Gates's failure to check Cornwallis at Camden, South Carolina, in August led to a British invasion of North Carolina in September, which was the month in which Arnold's treason was exposed. As the military theater of action shifted more and more to the South, Schuyler, too, shifted his political focus. After trying to reform the quartermaster and commissary departments, and three months' service on a congressional committee at headquarters, where he endeavored to raise reinforcements and supplies for Washington's army, the Yorker wearied of the national legislature. Once gone, he did not return to it while the confederation lasted but concentrated his political pursuits at the state level. Schuyler began the first of three four-year terms in the New York State Senate, to which he was elected in 1780, 1786, and 1792. Unlike others however, whose state interests reflected an antinational bias, his wartime experience convinced him of the necessity of a stronger national union—a cause that he came to share with Alexander Hamilton, who became his son-in-law in December 1780. Elizabeth Schuyler's marriage to Hamilton that year inaugurated a liaison that powerfully affected the course of New York State politics and the early development of the nation under the Constitution of 1787.

391

Schuyler's return to Albany in December 1779 afforded him a quiet prelude to yet another burst of activity when he resumed his seat in Congress in March. John Jay aptly surmised that the general could never long remain on the periphery of public affairs. Writing from Cadiz in February, the new American minister to Spain invited his old friend to resume a long-interrupted correspondence. "Your attention," he wrote, "is not I am persuaded so restrained to domestic objects, and the Pleasures or occupations of that Retreat, which you have too much Reason to prize, as to prevent your turning your Eyes toward every Part of that great Circle of Politics which envolves and affects us all."[1]

During the first two months of 1780, Schuyler did enjoy his prized retreats at Albany and Saratoga. As usual there were arrangements to make for his family and business matters that required his attention. In January, for example, his twenty-two-year-old daughter Elizabeth was sent off to visit her aunt, Mrs. John Cochran, at Morristown. Armed with her father's letters to Washington and Baron Steuben, Eliza was to be attracted to Alexander Hamilton. Only about two years her senior, he soon found her "most unmercifully handsome," good natured and sensible, vivacious without being frivolous, and not least of all she was neither vain nor ostentatious.[2]

Having launched his handsome daughter on the visit that in a few months was to lead to her nuptials, Schuyler concentrated upon various kinds of private and public business. He arranged the lease of one farm and collected a down payment for another. The Indian commissioners' business demanded attention; Washington wanted information and advice about the possibility of winter attacks on Niagara and Saint John's; the New York legislature meeting in Albany must consider the question of land cessions; and, alerted to Congress's decision to send a commission to Washington's headquarters, Schuyler finally responded to a summons that he join Col. Timothy Pickering and Gen. Thomas Mifflin in the commission's assignment to reform the civil departments of the army.

2

Commissioner "to arrange and regulate"

Schuyler's business for the Indian commissioners largely concerned correspondence with Col. Guy Johnson, royal superintendent of the Six Nations at Niagara. The arrangements for prisoner exchanges remained

tedious and only partially successful. And the Iroquois could not be neutralized because the terms for establishing peace with them remained to
be worked out.[3]

Like the army the civilian arm of the Revolution suffered the ravages
of the bitter winter. Delayed by the "deep Fall of Snow and inclement
Season," the New York legislature was unable to establish a quorum for
business for three weeks after the 4 January date of call. Two days after
it assembled in Albany on 27 January, Schuyler submitted a letter to Lt.
Gov. Pierre Van Cortlandt and Evert Bancker, speaker of the assembly,
urging their respective houses to instruct the state's congressional delegation to deal with the issues of peace negotiations with the Indians and
the state's western boundary. Schuyler's suggestion for peace negotiations
with all the tribes, he said, was based upon fears that an inadequate and
ill-supplied army would not be equal to renewed hostilities on an extensive and already weakened frontier. But certain congressmen proposed
terms for negotiations that included land cessions, and the latter, if made
to the United States, might be injurious to New York claims. Perhaps the
claims could be protected if New York congressmen were authorized to
accept a "reasonable Western Limitation" of their state.[4] Because small
states like Maryland refused to ratify the Articles of Confederation without guarantees of congressional jurisdiction over the American interior,
it was necessary to consider how to reconcile New York's territorial claims
with its support of the new confederation.

On 1 February the legislature created a joint committee to study Schuyler's letter, and a few days later the committee presented a bill "for facilitating the Completion of the Articles of Confederation." By 19 February
the bill was passed, empowering New York's delegates to Congress to
agree to a western boundary for the state. Instructed on the particulars
of the line to be drawn, they surrendered only a comparatively small area
for the common use of the new federal alliance.[5]

In other actions supportive of the war effort the legislature touched
upon a variety of problems that Philip Schuyler encountered upon his
return to Congress in March. Among them were measures for "the more
effectual" provision of the army with flour, limiting prices of merchandise
and produce, and preventing the engrossing and withholding of provisions, levying $5,000,000 in taxes, and raising a body of troops for the
defense of the frontiers. The legislature declined to furnish more than
eight hundred militia reinforcements for Washington's army, insisting
that Congress provide their pay and subsistence, which was a responsibility that Congress had been increasingly trying to shift to the states.[6]
Finally, in anticipation of a convention of states scheduled to meet at

Philadelphia on 4 April to consider the "expediency" of limiting prices of merchandise and produce, the legislature named James Duane, William Floyd, Robert R. Livingston, John Morin Scott, Ezra L'Hommedieu, and Philip Schuyler as "commissioners." The Yorkers were instructed to present their own state's new law on price limitation for the guidance of the convention. But the Philadelphia convention of states never assembled because of widespread doubts of the efficiency of price regulation and because Congress decided to try another remedy for inflation—the exchange of old depreciated currency for a new issue that would be redeemable in specie.[7] This scheme was, significantly, the work of a committee on which Schuyler played a principal role.

The Yorker, in fact, was well recognized as a man whose acquaintance with many subjects and whose powers of execution fitted him for many tasks. Added to his titles of Indian commissioner and prospective commissioner on price-fixing was that voted by Congress on 21 January as commissioner to "arrange and regulate" the civil departments of the army. Congress wanted reform and retrenchment in the hospital, quartermaster, and commissary services. Waste and inefficiency were to be rooted out. Accordingly, Schuyler, Col. Timothy Pickering of the board of war, and Gen. Thomas Mifflin were selected to "break up" unnecessary "posts" and to establish others as needed, to discharge supernumerary officers and unnecessary men, to stop rations and forage allowances wherever improperly drawn, to propose the cheapest and fastest means of transportation of supplies, and to report to Congress a general system of economy for the army together with an estimate of supplies required for the ensuing campaign. Although the three commissioners or any two of them were to make decisions in cooperation with the commander in chief, Schuyler objected to the proposal partly because of "subtle distinctions" he drew "between service as a member of Congress and acting in a capacity that" implied "that he was a servant of Congress."[8]

Schuyler was reluctant to accept appointment with Pickering and Mifflin because the two men were "not only . . . unfriendly to Washington but would probably attempt measures to injure him" and the army. Although the appointment was "extremely delicate" to a person in his "peculiar circumstances," Schuyler assured President Huntington that neither "the Strong Propensity which I feel to walk in the path of Domestic life, nor any consideration of personal Convenience will ever Induce me to withold any Services I may be deemed Capable of rendering a Country so dear to me and In the weal of which I am so eminently concerned." He was "most willing" to act in any line consistent with his principles.[9]

Schuyler elaborated on those principles with two points. He could not accept any assignment less honorable or important than that which he had once held as a major general. Yet he denied wanting a restoration of the rank and place he held in the army. Second, he admitted that "reform In the Civil departments of the Army is of the highest necessity," but he insisted that he could offer Congress his services only "as a member of their house on a Committee to Consult with the Commander In Chief and the head[s] of the several civil departments of the army." In short, it was a committee of Congress, not an inferior commission that included men unfriendly to Washington and not delegates, that should "complete the object" of department reforms. He did not trust the abilities of Pickering and Mifflin to plan the kind of reforms that would best serve the army or the commander in chief.[10]

3

"placed in a conspicuous Station"

Reappearing in Congress on 7 March, Schuyler promptly submitted his letter of explanation for refusing to serve on the commission for army reforms. Events, however, soon led him to accept a similar assignment that engaged most of his time away from Philadelphia. It would be a full five months before he could again return to Albany.

In rejecting the proceedings of the special commission the Yorker nevertheless managed to persuade Congress to adopt his idea for a committee at headquarters. And between late April and early August he directed the committee's efforts first at Morristown and during July at Totowa and Preakness, where Washington moved from his winter camp. Extensive absences from home by now had become commonplace for the Yorker. He could be content, however, knowing that Mrs. Schuyler could manage both the household at Albany and the farming and milling enterprises at Saratoga. And his reliable secretary, John Lansing, Jr., could also be trusted to meet the general's calls for a variety of information and to assist in work like superintending repairs of a broken gristmillrace.[11]

For three weeks after Schuyler returned to Congress he anguished over its failure to prepare for the season's military operations and "fruitlessly rang every change" on the critical state of affairs. Never had he seen "our councils ... weaker," and exertions less, or torpor greater. But he did not sit idle. Continuing to seek some alternative to the Pickering-Mifflin commission on reform and retrenchment, Schuyler hammered away at the problems of finances and depreciated currency until he had produced a solution. At least it was the first positive attempt at a remedy after months of congressional diversion and delay. "In its consequences the decision proved to be a momentous one," especially because by it Congress renounced "its plighted faith."[12]

Before Schuyler returned to Congress it had struggled with the question of finances in committee of the whole. Finding that it had made no progress, the Yorker thought it paradoxical that the whole should be more incompetent than a part; he would have the business referred to a small committee. Having "thrown together" his own ideas on the subject, he told Washington that only time would tell how they might be adopted.[13] On 9 March Congress not only accepted Schuyler's idea of a committee but assigned him to its membership. Also chosen were Thomas Burke of North Carolina, Oliver Ellsworth of Connecticut, Samuel Holten of Massachusetts, William C. Houston of New Jersey, and Robert R. Livingston. Two days later the Yorker predicted that a committee report would probably be ready by 13 March.

What the committee finally proposed was in fact largely Schuyler's handiwork. His object, he said, was to fix the present circulating medium at a given ratio, retire it, and destroy it in exchange for new notes whose value would depend upon each state having a share that it was to redeem. Should any state fail to provide specifically for funds, the faith of the United States would be pledged to redeem its proportion of bills. The amount of the new issue would be proportionate to the periodical destruction of bills currently in circulation. The new bills were to bear interest payable at the end of six years in specie or in bills on France (at the option of the holders). And according to Schuyler there "shall never be of old [bills] at 40 for 1 and new at par above ten Million in Circulation." Confident that the committee's report would substantially reflect his points—as indeed it did—he could not be certain what Congress might change or accept "as every Man wishes to be thought a Financier and must have his Ideas." The ultimate result, he surmised, might be like Joseph's coat, "a composition of patches partly coloured."[14]

Schuyler's committee submitted his scheme in its report on 18 March, and Congress also accepted it without material alterations. A nominal debt of $200,000,000 was reduced to an actual one of $5,000,000. The "new issues were to bear interest at five per cent, that interest likewise to be paid in specie upon the redemption of the bills, or (at the option of the holder) annually in sterling bills of exchange drawn by the United States on their commissioners in Europe." Although the public generally regarded the act "as downright repudiation, a confession of bankruptcy," Congress had convinced itself that because holders of the old currency "at least had received the money at a depreciated value, justice and fairness required that it be redeemed only on such a basis of depreciation as might appear equitable," which was one-fortieth of its face value. Significantly, too, the attempt to check the depreciation of a national currency represented nationalist sentiment for strengthening the national government. Men like Schuyler who entered Congress in 1780 were paving the way for further efforts to revise and strengthen the Articles of Confederation. And by early 1781, with Robert Morris's leadership, they had become a powerful force in Congress.[15]

Beyond the reform of finances in March, Schuyler also pressed to reverse the course of army retrenchment. To this end he sought to replace the commission assigned for that purpose with a committee at headquarters that could assist with the collection of reinforcements and supplies. And he resisted efforts to reform the civil departments of the army unless the commander in chief and department heads like Q.M. Gen. Nathanael Greene were invited to cooperate fully with the committee.[16]

While commissioners Pickering and Mifflin proceeded with their efforts at reform, Schuyler refused to serve with them, nor would he agree to join Roger Sherman and Allen Jones as a committee to cooperate with the two commissioners. This maneuver did not comport with the Yorker's "Ideas of propriety," and at least some "men of sentiment," he thought, approved his firmness and "delicacy." Others, however, were chagrined, but Schuyler imagined that they would not risk driving him into offering a more "pointed explanation." Having made clear that as a member of Congress he would not be a mere servant of it, Schuyler explained only to close friends that he would not work with Pickering and Mifflin or Sherman and Jones because their ideas were "not consonant to mine."[17]

As the time approached for Sherman and Jones to make some recommendation for reform of the quartermaster system, Schuyler feared that whatever they and the commission recommended would be inadequate to the army's needs and also "wound" the quartermaster general. He was resolved to try to "overturn" the proposed system; were it to be approved, he would endeavor to make it merely recommendatory. Accordingly, he begged Nathanael Greene not to resign in dismay. And he promised that his own proposed "line of Conduct" might yet atone for Congress's "indelicate" treatment of Greene, who had been attacked with the charge of profiteering in his office. The Yorker intended to fight to make Greene "perfectly free of every shackle." And Washington supported Schuyler by urging Congress that some plan "be adopted by which every thing relating to the Army could be conducted on a general principle under the direction of Congress."[18]

The plan, however, which Roger Sherman and Allen Jones presented to Congress on 27 March, satisfied neither Washington nor Schuyler. The latter denounced it as a "voluminous system" concocted mostly by "General Sherman." Indeed, its volume may be judged from the fact that the plan for the quartermaster department alone occupied "eighteen pages of text." Proposals for the commissariat of issues and the hospital had yet to be submitted. Schuyler fumed when he discovered that the commissariat of purchases was to be abolished, leaving the states to furnish all supplies to the commissary general of issues. Despite Sherman's boast that the scheme would eliminate waste by removing four thousand officers from the civil departments, Schuyler deemed "It . . . replete with absurdity and petitess," nor was he alone in thinking that it would starve the army in ten days. Both Schuyler and Greene were "convinced that there was also a design to embarrass Washington" in the committee's report. The Virginian suspected "that the plan had been devised partly to disgrace and injure" himself.[19]

Schuyler asked Greene to tarry in Philadelphia for further consultation, anxious to devise some means of dealing with the "consequences" should Greene be driven to resign. On 28 March the Rhode Islander had been threatened by a resolution of no confidence. Although a motion supportive of his administration had been introduced, it had roused heated debate. Maneuvers to amend it finally ended with adjournment so that the delegates could cool their tempers. Congress rejected the simple statement, affirming "a high sense of the abilities and fidelity of Major Genl Green[e] in the execution of the important Office of Quarter Master General." Although Schuyler thought that Washington's recent report of army conditions had persuaded many delegates to rely fully on him to manage department reforms, the Yorker remained determined to push for further action. One such step was his proposal on 28 March to circularize the states, urging them to greater exertions in furnishing supplies to the army. The action taken, Schuyler gladly accepted membership on a committee assigned to prepare the letter. While the Yorker found some delegates averse to the "decisive plainness" of a proposed draft, others suggested that it be made even more pointed. After more drafts were considered Congress finally agreed to the language for requesting the states to renew their efforts on behalf of the army on 24 April.[20]

Meantime, Schuyler's proddings and Washington's letter of 3 April persuaded Congress to establish a committee at headquarters on 6 April. It would confer with Washington on the reduction of the regiments and the plan for rearranging the army staff departments. The Sherman-Jones plan, which was actually the work of Sherman and the ex-quartermaster general Thomas Mifflin, might yet be circumvented if the right members

Fig. 9. John Jay, 1745–1829. Oil on canvas by Joseph Wright, 1786. Jay, president of Congress in 1779, tried unsuccessfully to dissuade Schuyler from resigning his military commission as a major general after Schuyler was exonerated at his court-martial. Courtesy, The New-York Historical Society, New York City.

were placed on the new committee and armed with appropriate instructions. If, however, "General Sherman" headed the committee, Washington
would surely be tormented with the thousand "little thesses [sic] which
Roger was thrown together and which he Entitles a System." Because
members deemed it improper to send a veteran with a probable bias in
the army's favor, Schuyler was convinced that Congress would not assign
him to the committee. Yet he was somewhat reassured by the determination to authorize the committee to act only in consultation with Washington—"a kind of dictatorial power"—and he trusted the good judgment of the three delegates who were assigned to prepare the instructions
for the committee.[21]

Waiting to see whom Congress would name to the committee to headquarters and how it would be instructed to act, Schuyler found a pleasanter topic to consider with Washington's dashing and able aide-de-camp,
Alexander Hamilton. Since at least February Hamilton had been courting
Elizabeth Schuyler at Morristown, where she was visiting her father's
sister, Mrs. John Cochran. Hamilton's correspondence with the black-
eyed "charmer" had quickly blossomed into a real love affair, and as early
as March they had asked Eliza's parents for permission to marry.[22]

As with his eldest daughter's marriage, Schuyler wanted assurances
that a prospective son-in-law enjoyed a respectable reputation. He had
objected to John Barker Church precisely because so little was known of
his origins and character. Hamilton was not as recent an emigré to the
mainland colonies as Church had been, but his West Indies antecedents
were not exactly comparable to those of the Hudson valley grandees. If
any question concerning Hamilton's background was posed, there is no
evidence of it or that Schuyler found reason to hesitate about permitting
his daughter to marry the "Creole bastard," as John and Abigail Adams
later referred to him. As to the West Indian's antecedents, it is unlikely
that Hamilton was anything but perfectly candid with the Schuylers. The
whole tenor of their relationship over the years was both deeply intimate
and invariably affectionate. Reinforced by mutual political views, Hamilton's connection with his father-in-law probably could not have flourished as it did or even have endured had it been rooted in the slightest
deception or indecorum. For that matter Schuyler may well have been
more than sympathetic toward his prospective son-in-law's situation; he
could not have forgotten that his first-born child was conceived out of
wedlock. And above all he recognized and understood ambition and
talent when he saw them. A connection by marriage with a man like
Hamilton was nothing to be scorned.[23]

As Schuyler discussed the couple's plea for approval of their marriage, he registered but one caveat: There must be no elopement! On 8 April he received a letter from Mrs. Schuyler consenting "to Comply with" Hamilton and Eliza's wishes. Hamilton could not, Schuyler assured him, "be more happy at the connection you have made with my family than I am. Until the child of a parent has made a judicious choice his heart is in continual anxiety; but this anxiety was removed the moment I discovered on whom she had placed her affections. I am pleased with every instance of delicacy in those who are dear to me, and I think I read your soul on that occasion you mention. I shall therefore only entreat you to consider me as one who wishes in every way to promote your happiness, and I shall." Remarkably, Catharine Schuyler had not yet met Hamilton, but her husband's approval of him had evidently satisfied her. "You will see the Impropriety," Schuyler continued, "of taking the dernier pas where you are. Mrs. Schuyler did not see her Eldest daughter married." Angelica's elopement "also gave me pain, and we wish not to Experience It a Second time. I shall probably be at Camp In a few days, when we will adjust all matters."[24]

The prospective bridegroom promptly followed the general's hint to cultivate Eliza's mother by thanking her for her consent to the marriage. As Eliza, too, had warned Hamilton of her mother's mettle, Hamilton wrote, "I am no stranger to the qualities which distinguish your character and these make the relation in which I shall stand to you, not one of the least pleasing circumstances of my union with your daughter. My heart anticipates the sentiments of that relation and wishes to give you proofs of the respectful and affectionate attachment, with which I have the honor to be Madam." These were words well suited to satisfy the proud Schuylers.[25] Remarkably, Hamilton's code of conduct and political philosophy matched those of his father-in-law almost exactly, certainly as well as any man's could. The bond of sympathy between them was even greater— though perhaps not as influential—than that which Hamilton shared with Washington. Cor ad cor loquitur.

Comforted as he was by Eliza's fortunate match, Schuyler found perhaps as much relief in Congress's 12 April instructions to the committee to be sent to headquarters. It was to reform the army staff departments, in consultation with the commander in chief, and was empowered to institute a variety of regulations and to supervise the execution of its own plans. Most significant of all was the agreement that Washington and the headquarters committee could adopt, amend, or alter the report of the Sherman-Allen committee as they thought advisable and execute any plan they wished for conducting the quartermaster and commissary departments. But they must adhere to the 25 February resolution assigning quotas of supplies to the various states; and they must report their actions to Congress, which was a reminder that civil authority was to remain supreme.[26]

Before proceeding with the balloting for members of the headquarters committee, Congress fell to wrangling over several proposals, which suggests that the fear of some was that members might be chosen by less than a proper majority. Or was it that certain candidates for the committee might be excluded, depending upon the size of the majority required? Schuyler and his fellow Yorkers, for example, helped defeat a motion to require election by seven of the ten states then represented in Congress. Following the procedural controversy Congress elected the committee to headquarters. In the balloting, however, there were no signs of altercation. Ranked first in the election was Philip Schuyler, who thereby became the chairman. Geographical balance was achieved by the choice of a southerner and a Yankee to complement the middle states' representation on the committee. John Mathews of South Carolina, who had helped draft the instructions for the committee, was elected, and so was Nathaniel Peabody of New Hampshire.[27]

Congress recognized that Schuyler's experience and talents made him especially well qualified for this new assignment, but there were relatively few men who appreciated them more than his close friends and associates. As James Duane observed, "you my dear Sir peculiarly are placed in a conspicuous Station: because it is a Station to which you are fully competent and on the Execution of the Duties of which much very much depends." John Jay and Henry Brockholst Livingston agreed.[28]

Within a week of its appointment Schuyler's committee set about its task by ordering reforms in local army staff offices. That of the commissary general of issues, for example, was instructed to abolish the office of magazine keeper at Philadelphia as of 1 May. Business conducted there in the future might be handled by the assistant commissary and a single clerk. The pruning of unnecessary personnel from various parts of the bureaucracy was perhaps one of the easiest steps for the committee to take. Dr. M. Treat assured Schuyler that like all departments, the medical division had more employees than were necessary for the public good.[29]

4

"There is no man who can be more useful"

After delays in making inquiries at several posts along the way and finding travel difficult in the rains, Schuyler's committee finally reached

Morristown on 28 April. Its mission soon took on a special urgency; on 10 May Lafayette brought news of the impending arrival of French naval and military reinforcements. "Preparation to cooperate with these forces therefore became at once of first importance."[30] As the committee strove to prepare Washington's army for an effective campaign with the allied forces, they discovered the need for more power to act if men and supplies were to be speedily drawn from the states.

In his letter to the state's congressional delegation the governor of New York had already given proof of the committee's need for greater authority. George Clinton warned that the state might not have the means to fill its quotas of provisions because of "former exertions" and current shortages. There was barely enough wheat and meal to tide New Yorkers over until harvest time, and threats of Indian raids on the frontiers made it unlikely that more troops could be raised for Washington's army.[31]

Clinton's warnings of the difficulties confronting the committee at headquarters, however, did not deter Schuyler, Mathews, and Peabody in their resolution to prepare the army for the expected campaign of 1780. Anticipating a lengthy stay at Morristown, Schuyler rented a house and called his wife down from Albany for a visit with her daughter Eliza and her sister-in-law Gertrude Schuyler Cochran. Her stay at Morristown was perhaps significant in two respects: there Mrs. Schuyler met Alexander Hamilton and there she conceived the last of her fifteen children, Catherine Van Rensselaer, who was born on 20 February 1781.[32]

On 10 May Schuyler's committee made their first report to Congress. They had not realized how difficult the problems at camp had been, and while promising to work at retrenchment and reform of staff departments, they decided first to grapple with the problem of supplies. In this they discovered that Congress's requisitions of 25 February had omitted any provision for the transportation of supplies from the states responsible for collecting them. Accordingly, they recommended that the states be asked to repeal legislation preventing Continental officers from making purchases, and they requested funds to cover the costs of moving provisions to the army and to redeem the public's working cattle; farmers tending the cattle expected payment for their winter subsistence before releasing them. Shortages of provisions, the committee noted, threatened "pernicious" results, for soldiers were hungry and discontented; meat supplies were due to run out on 12 May, and the commissary general of purchases feared there were no immediate prospects for relief. If such conditions persisted, some "violent convulsion" was sure to erupt, harming the war effort and discrediting the cause. Only Pennsylvania seemed in a position to help, and unless it did so at once, the committee warned, "We will not pretend to say whay may be the event!"[33]

Friendly delegates like James Duane and William Churchill Houston immediately promised Schuyler their help in pushing Congress to respond to his committee's 10 May appeal. Houston, for example, wrote him three days later that Pennsylvania authorities had been contacted and promised to furnish supplies of meat. Although Duane was certain that Congress would comply with Washington's requisitions to the extent of its powers, he also recognized the difficulties. The "Great National Council," he wrote, wanted power and decisiveness, and the public lacked active perseverance. "To a republican form of Government Jealousy in confering extensive authority is natural: and equally natural is it for Men to relax and become supine after long and violent Exertions." Yet experience proved that calamity could produce a suitable display of public confidence and private virtue, and together they would be enough to surmount the difficulties.[34]

A few days before his committee decided to ask Congress for an augmentation of their powers, Schuyler alerted Duane to the need for it. As Lafayette arrived at headquarters on 10 May with news of reinforcements already dispatched from France, the allied forces would require enormous efforts to assemble the supplies necessary for an effective cooperation. Congress must display resolution else the war effort would suffer. The country, he insisted, did not lack the supplies necessary for forcing the British to give up the contest. The means of obtaining provisions were available, "but not In the ordinary way. ... extraordinary cases require Extraordinary remedies and exertions." Inertia *must* be overcome; "popular bodies," Schuyler argued, were "unequal to that Celerity so requisite to the Effectual prosecution of Military Operations ... by Invariably holding up to the States that It had only a Recommendatory power, they have been taught to pay little attention to any decision of Congress," which "should resume, or even take new powers. The present Occasion will Justify It. ... " Only one resolution of Congress was needed, and that was to "lodge dictatorial powers either In the Commander In Chief, or In him, Conjointly with a Small Committee of Congress." Such a body must include able men, and Schuyler hinted that John Mathews and Nathaniel Peabody might better be replaced by one of the New York delegates—perhaps Duane himself—and Oliver Ellsworth of Connecticut. If possible, Joseph Jones of Virginia might be the third.[35]

Whether Schuyler was echoing Washington's thoughts or the Virginian those of the Yorker, it is clear that the commander in chief wanted a new committee with enlarged powers to manage the business of a Franco-American military campaign. To James Duane, however, he suggested a committee of three New Yorkers: Schuyler, Robert R. Livingston, and Duane himself. To his Virginia friend Joseph Jones, he was more general in urging the appointment of a new and powerful committee. Although

Washington asked Jones to keep his wishes private, he insisted that "There is no man who can be more useful as a member of the Committee than General Schuyler. His perfect knowledge of the resources of the Country, the activities of his temper, His fruitfulness of expedients and his sound Military sense make me wish above all things [that] he may be appointed."[36]

In view of the need to devise a plan of operations that would include Rochambeau's reinforcements, Washington and Schuyler's committee agreed on 15 May that it would not be expedient to fix upon arrangements until Congress responded. As they could not depend upon the states to furnish provisions according to the 25 February requisition, the committee suggested that officers of both commissary and quartermaster departments be enabled to purchase additional supplies. And they sent Mathews back to Philadelphia to present their ideas for a committee armed with "essentially dictatorial powers." Lafayette's visit to Philadelphia to confer with Luzerne was similarly designed to promote the idea of a more powerful committee, and the French minister promptly urged it upon Congress.[37]

Before sending Mathews off to Congress on 16 May, Schuyler rushed letters north to the governor of New York and south to James Duane at Philadelphia. Alerting Governor Clinton to the prospects of a Franco-American campaign, the general passed along Washington's request that the New York legislature not rise until Congress had responded to the committee's call for more assistance and additional power. And Robert R. Livingston was persuaded to return to Philadelphia to aid in the business instead of visiting the legislature. Despite his preoccupations with the committee's work, Schuyler offered to go to Kingston to meet the legislature if Clinton decided that he should explain the army's needs in person.[38]

Schuyler's letter to James Duane on 15 May touched upon another matter that Washington did not choose to present to Congress himself. This was the delegates' recent orders that reinforcements be sent to South Carolina under General DeKalb. Not wishing to risk arousing congressional hackles, Washington agreed that Schuyler should explain to Duane why the reinforcements should be remanded. Perhaps Congress could be persuaded to see the necessity of their recall. Because Sir Henry Clinton could be expected to return most of his Carolina troops to Manhattan, DeKalb's troops would likely prove to be more useful to Washington's campaign with Rochambeau if they were recalled to New York or at least to the Chesapeake Bay, where they could easily move north or south. Schuyler also suggested that Congress request all legislatures currently in session to continue sitting, and that others be called to meet to respond to applications for supplies that were to follow. Finally, the Yorker suggested that Congress reconsider the plan it had expected the committee at headquarters to follow; the system of state supplies would be far more expensive than a well-directed purchasing system.[39] In short, Schuyler armed Duane with arguments well suited to demonstrate the need for a committee with plenipotentiary authority, if not a dictatorial commander in chief.

With John Mathews on the road to Philadelphia, Schuyler and Peabody proceeded with committee business on 16 May. They decided to ask all states to forward recruits to complete Congress's 9 February quotas; militia should be used to do so with directions to serve until 31 December unless sooner discharged; Washington was to send each state executive returns of all other deficiencies in manpower caused by casualties. Although three New York regiments were to be reduced and annexed to others, Schuyler advised Governor Clinton that if the legislature insisted upon maintaining one of them, this could be accomplished at little extra expense to the state. Clearly, immediate and effective measures must be taken to augment the army, which was another reason for granting the committee at headquarters the power that was exercised only fitfully at best by Congress.[40]

Congress agreed that there should be no partial reduction of the army, and on 19 May, excepting Georgia and the Carolinas (where the enemy pressure was particularly noticeable), it called upon all the states for an additional contribution of $10,000,000 . Thereby the committee at headquarters won increased powers to bring an army into the field, to purchase supplies, and to pay for transportation—all deemed to be necessary additions to the requisition system. The powers added to the committee were useful but "not especially significant" and "certainly far short of what Washington had descried." The additional authority voted was mainly in the form of "instructions to expedite the drawing forth of supplies," and in the event that these "proved insufficient, then, with the advice of the commander-in-chief, to apply to the states or to civil magistrates for the purchase of other supplies at the expense of the United States." Supportive of the committee, too, was Congress's request that the states "invest their executive authority, or some other persons, with such powers as would enable them" to meet the committee's applications for supplies.[41]

It was difficult, however, to persuade Congress to comply with the wishes of the two generals. Robert R. Livingston failed to get the Maryland line recalled, and he dared not move the reversal of Congress's orders for dispatching reinforcements to South Carolina for fear the southern delegates might lose confidence in their New York brethren. Nor was he able to persuade Jones of Virginia or Mathews of South Carolina to move for the recall. At best, Livingston could promise only that the reinforcements could be ordered to return north if the siege of Charleston was raised before they reached the city. However, another corps might be prevented from moving south because they had not yet left Philadelphia. The New York delegation expected Congress soon to consider the Hampshire Grants issue, so Livingston urged Schuyler to persuade Nathaniel Peabody to return to Philadelphia at once. The New Hampshire delegate might better be spared from headquarters now than later, and his help was vital to the success of dealing with the New York legislature's "warm and pressing representations" against Vermonters' claims to statehood.[42]

Schuyler of course was disappointed, but he was too busy to be dismayed. On 21 May Washington posed a series of tactical and logistical questions about the intended campaign, and the Yorker was obliged to answer. While Schuyler prepared his responses in his customarily thorough way, his committee was also confronted by questions from Nathanael Greene: How, for example, might they function with Congress's directives of 19 May? Greene consulted Schuyler on the morning of 23 May, suspecting that the committee might not have adequate powers to act effectively. Indeed he deemed their powers "wholly incompetent" to the purposes and ends proposed. Urging Washington to ask the committee for a written statement of the powers that they lacked and to press Congress again to grant them, Greene warned that if the Virginian exercised powers beyond those allowed by the present scheme, he would be asked why he did not request more for the committee; and if the army failed for want of support, he would be rebuked for attempting to engage the enemy without adequate preparations.[43]

Following Greene's suggestion, Washington asked Schuyler's committee for "a written opinion respecting the competency of its powers," but the record shows no response save for evidence of the committee's actions.[44] On 25 May Schuyler and his colleagues issued the first of a series of calls to the states and to Congress. Instead of further efforts to obtain authority de jure, they dared to exercise it de facto.

The 25 May circular, entitled "To the Several States," explained the army's difficulties: its pay was five months in arrears; it was seldom without more than a week's provisions in store and now without meat, and some days on half- or quarter allowances; it suffered deficiencies in camp equipage, forage, hospital stores, carriages, and boats; it wanted several thousand horses; and it was attracting few recruits. Certain that the states had resources to relieve the army, the committee urged that drafting men to serve for the campaign would be preferable to relying upon volunteers to enlist for the duration of the war. To meet the gap in

Congress's 25 February levy of requisitions, the committee urged the legislatures to offer citizens six percent annual interest on unpaid debts and to empower their executives to furnish transportation of supplies to the Continental commissariat. State executives should be empowered to furnish supplies above the 25 February quotas whenever the committee or its appointed agents so requested. As additional requisitions were "indispensably necessary," the committee promised to make the "burden as equal in proportion to the ability of each State as their situation, and the nature of the service will admit." Patriots must be ready with the means to cooperate with French land and naval forces. Only this could make victory certain. The time for sacrifice was at hand. Shifting from their solemn tone of warning, Schuyler and his colleagues added a note of flattering encouragement; hoping for wise and virtuous responses from the states, they begged the executives to convene their legislatures and to present the application for speedy action.[45]

Washington heartily endorsed the committee's circular; its recommendations were full, just, and explicit, and the suggested consequences accurately stated. He wished, however, that they had elaborated upon the subject of drafting reinforcements. It was important that each regiment be filled to its full complement of 504 rank and file, and the Virginian wanted no less than 20,000 effective Continentals; yet if all regiments of the states from New Hampshire to Pennsylvania were completed, he calculated that they would fall short of the number.[46]

On 28 May the committee relayed a copy of its circular to the states to President Samuel Huntington, making "bold to thrust its admonitions into the very face of Congress itself." After warning Congress on 9 May of threatened mutiny, they now reported that two Connecticut regiments had paraded under arms on the evening of 25 May, threatening to march off because of impending famine. Although mollified, the troops remained discontented, and their officers argued the need for provisions with tears in their eyes. Again the committee pleaded that "something more is necessary than mere recommendation" for exigencies required "Growing powers to deviate from the strict lines of conduct which Regular Constitutions prescribe." Bold and decisive measures must surely now be taken. "The meaning of this admonition . . . is sufficiently clear: Do not wait for the states to grant you powers; take them."[47]

Challenged by the Schuyler committee's cries for aid to Washington's army and the necessity of providing defenses for their own borders, New York's governor and legislature labored throughout June to meet a variety of demands placed upon their resources. The governor himself led militia forces north to Lake George while the legislature carried on at Kingston. Although the senate expected to benefit from Schuyler's personal appearance and delayed the passage of a supply bill, it finally acted after despairing of his ability to leave Morristown. Happily, the general's presence at Kingston was not required to persuade the legislature to act as he hoped it would. It also followed the Schuyler committee recommendation to empower the governor to mobilize all of the state's resources between sessions of the legislature.[48]

Governor Clinton agreed, but upon his return to Kingston after chasing Sir John Johnson's British marauders north into the lake country, he warned Schuyler that the state's frontier defenses required the retention of levies for the Continental army. Some were needed at Fort Schuyler in the Mohawk valley as well as at Fort Edward and Fort George. Others, in Westchester and Orange counties, might be able to join Washington's troops when operations were commenced against British-held Manhattan. But New York State, he said, should be credited for these troops in the quotas that Schuyler's committee and Congress had assigned to it.[49]

Meantime, at Morristown, Schuyler and his colleagues pursued their duties with vigor. Hearing that the West Point garrison was reduced to a hand-to-mouth existence for want of provisions, the committee fired off a request to the governor of Connecticut to send speedy relief. If the enemy seized the post, American forces would be blocked from establishing an "easy cooperation" across the Hudson to the east. Should the British get control of the Highlands, the committee warned, the shipment of flour and other provisions from the Delaware River must be diverted around Sussex County, Pennsylvania, through Orange and Ulster counties, New York. The lack of wagons and forage would aggravate the delays of transportation overland, and "every prospect of making an impression on the enemy in this Campaign must vanish."[50]

5

"profoundly snoring amidst threatened ruin"

Beyond their concern for preventing enemy penetration along the Hudson, Schuyler's committee encountered Washington's proddings for other measures. Having revised his estimate of the size of the army he wanted, the Virginian suggested that it should be twice the size of the enemy's— 35,000 strong, including 5,000 French. If the committee's recommendation for drafts to fill the ranks of existing regiments worked, the army at Morristown would number only 22,680 at best. The other 17,320 must be militia raised in the states from New Hampshire to Maryland inclusive, and they should be assembled by 30 June. The commander in chief now urged Schuyler and his colleagues to be specific in their calls for a variety of provisions and to discover the number of men and supplies that each state would be able to furnish within a time certain. They should not, he said, be afraid to alarm the states by making large demands![51] The three men responded forthrightly.

On 2 June Schuyler, Mathews, and Peabody fired off another round of letters to the states, listing specific quantities of flour, meat, rum, forage, horses, oxen and wagons and other supplies to be furnished monthly by each state. The initial deliveries were requested by 1 July, and each state was urged to complete its regiments in the Continental line to their full complement of 504. Only Georgia and the Carolinas were excepted from this appeal. The volume of detail contained in the committee's letters reveals Philip Schuyler's penchant for thoroughness and explicit planning. Aside from determining quantities of provisions mentioned, his hand may be detected in the suggestions that horses and wagons be hired instead of purchased because their drivers would be more careful in the handling of their own property than they would with the public's. Contracts should be made payable in specie or its equivalent, and the value of livestock and carriages should be appraised under oath, certification of which should then be filed with the quartermaster general. Requisitions for militia should not be allowed to retard the completion of each state's Continental battalions.[52]

By calling for men and supplies in addition to those requisitioned earlier by Congress, Schuyler's committee was of course acting according to instructions of 19 May, but it was exercising a function ordinarily confined to Congress itself. Increasingly the real center of activities for the war effort seemed to be the committee at headquarters "rather than the floor of Congress." But the committee forthrightly explained that deficiencies in certain of the estimates must be supplied by purchase through the quartermaster general; and they entreated Congress to furnish him the funds as soon as possible.[53]

With the explanation of the committee's latest efforts posted, Schuyler turned his thoughts to a visit home. Having satisfied her family mission to Morristown, Mrs. Schuyler wished to return to Albany, and the general wished to accompany her. Would it be proper, he queried James Duane, to ask Congress to fill his place on the committee? He did not, he said, intend to be absent from the army long, but preferred to be with it as a volunteer "that I may not be confined as I am at present."[54] Then, pressed by Washington and the unceasing chores of the committee, the Yorker abandoned plans to return to Albany. The turn of events would not allow it. On 5 June Sir Henry Clinton left Charleston; Washington was convinced that he would soon return to New York with all or most of his forces. This and the long-expected arrival of the French fleet and army (which appeared at Newport on 11 July) were causes for increased anxiety. And despite military weakness and public lethargy Washington was determined to attempt a decisive blow at the enemy. Again, he thought, it was necessary to reiterate the army's needs to the states. "We must," the Virginian exhorted Schuyler's committee, "absolutely have a force of a different composition or we must relinquish the contest." His Continentals were inadequate. There *must* be a draft to fill up the battalions. It would not be as risky to "diffuse" knowledge of the circumstances as to conceal them.[55]

Schuyler, Mathews, and Peabody immediately issued a third round of letters on Washington's behalf. Urging the states to comply with the more particular requisitions of 2 June, they summoned their countrymen to display virtue by acting. News of the British victory at Charleston and the capture of the garrison compelled the committee to entreat "most earnestly" that no deductions be made in the troop quotas assigned to the various states. "Should our present application not be attended with the desired effect, the consequences must in all human probability be fatal."[56]

Explaining their actions to Congress on 12 June, the committee pointed out that if the enemy forced Washington's army to retire, it must move either beyond the Delaware River or to the Highlands. When Congress acted on 15 June, it chose to reinforce the committee's circular with an eloquent appeal of its own to the states. Yet the delegates pointedly altered Robert R. Livingston's draft, replacing the Yorker's "scorching criticism of the states for their negligence and failures" with a milder exhortation that they meet their obligations. Significantly, however, Congress dared to "intimate that the states should bestow upon their 'Common Council' a larger 'power of direction.' "[57]

Meantime, Schuyler and James Duane mused over the question of enlarged national power so much at the center of the Yorker's committee efforts to prepare the army for the 1780 campaign. Duane agreed that Congress lacked power and decisiveness while the public lacked active perseverance. However, experience had proved, Duane said, "and I trust it will prove again, and as often as may be necessary, that Distress and Calamity will rouse us to a suitable display of *publick* Confidence and *private* Virtue." Schuyler generally agreed. We have lingered on too long, he insisted, and now are "profoundly snoring amidst threatened ruin." Only when the house became "fairly on fire" would its inhabitants be roused. But then it might be too late to extinguish the conflagration.[58]

News of the British victory at Charleston spurred Philadelphia merchants to action. They offered the army three million rations and five hundred hogsheads of rum on their own credit, which was enough to provision forty thousand men for seventy-five days. This would give time for the states to collect and forward other supplies and for the harvest to be reaped. Duane assured Schuyler that the committee at headquarters had rendered "very essential" services to the cause, and that "you my dear Sir peculiarly are placed in a conspicuous Station ... a Station to which you are fully competent and on the Execution of the Duties of which much very much depends."[59]

Although Schuyler's committee won the support of Congress for most of the measures they recommended to the states, not all of their proposals were readily accepted. On the one hand Congress agreed that the states should report what steps had been taken to meet the committee's requisitions, and they sanctioned those appeals on 17 and 21 June; furthermore the states' executives had been urged to correspond weekly with Schuyler's committee. On the other hand, the delegates rejected proposals to increase the powers of Congress "to call forth ... the military resources of the said States" or to accept the Schuyler committee's own plan for the quartermaster department.[60] That plan emerged as the committee worked with Q.M. Gen. Nathanael Greene.

6

"all our zeal and all our exertion"

By mid-June the committee at headquarters had been prodded by Greene to rouse themselves to still bolder action. Unless the system proposed for his department's operation was amended to permit him to engage "suitable characters" for its work, Greene threatened to resign. Congress's resolutions, he told Schuyler, would alter neither the nature of men nor the realities of the quartermaster's business.[61] In consultation with Washington and the Rhode Islander the committee decided to send Schuyler to Congress with proposals that would satisfy the quartermaster general.

Characteristically, Congress responded to Schuyler's committee report on the quartermaster department by assigning it to another committee, and "at intervals during nearly a month, the new plan underwent discussion." The Yorker did not tarry in Philadelphia much longer than a week, but while there he did endeavor to persuade the president of Pennsylvania, Joseph Reed, that his state must respond to the pleas of the committee at headquarters. Although Reed promised to do what he could, Schuyler suspected that the state would not meet its requisitions. For the moment, the only hope for action lay with Philadelphia's merchant association headed by Robert Morris. Already, on 18 June, they had sent five hundred barrels of flour to the army.[62]

Toward the end of June, unable to wait longer for congressional action on the quartermaster department plans, Schuyler left Philadelphia. It was some days before he caught up with Washington's moving headquarters, for the army had been maneuvering against Knyphausen's British forces, which had crossed into New Jersey from Staten Island. In Schuyler's absence his fellow committeemen continued to bombard the states with exhortations to send reinforcements and supplies to meet the rising danger, and Washington requested their particular help in obtaining wagons from the governor of New Jersey and the president of Pennsylvania in order to move his stores beyond the enemy's reach. Both he and Schuyler were cheered to learn that Maryland had proposed to raise an extra Continental battalion in lieu of the militia that had been first requested.[63]

By 4 July Schuyler lay about eight miles from Preakness, where Hamilton wrote Eliza that her father was almost recovered from a "touch of the Quinsy." Next day the Yorker joined Washington at his Totowa headquarters, northeast of Morristown. As yet John Mathews and Nathaniel Peabody had not reached Washington's new headquarters, and notifying them of its position, Schuyler again urged them to join him at once. Washington, he said, had business that required their prompt attention.[64]

Once again Schuyler's committee endeavored to meet the commander in chief's demands for the army—this time calling for the formation of a magazine of "short forage" near the Hudson River as well as for flour and tents. On 10 July a circular was sent to Delaware, Pennsylvania, Maryland, and Virginia authorities, explaining the recent exhaustion of the Jersey countryside and the previous year's crop failure in New York State. The states south of the Delaware River must make up the deficiency, and Congress, too, was asked for help. And unless the quartermaster general was given discretion to manage the collection of supplies from a variety of sources and by way of different channels, the contingencies could not be effectively solved. The only alternative seemed to be that members of Congress must visit the various states in order to press for the shipment of supplies.[65]

Scarcely having posted these supplications to Congress and the states, Schuyler and Peabody were obliged to respond to another of Washington's urgent pleas. John Mathews had been obliged to leave them. On 13 July the Virginian announced the impending arrival of the French reinforcements. News had come on 9 July that the fleet was somewhere between the Virginia capes and Delaware. (Indeed, Rochambeau's army reached Newport on 11 July.) Preparations were lamentably lagging despite the news of "animation" among the states; not a thousand men had yet joined the army, and if the allied reinforcements discovered that Americans were unrepared to campaign for several more weeks, it would place Americans in a bad light as well as at a military disadvantage. It would be inexcusable not to employ "all our zeal and all our exertion."[66]

Had Congress and the states demonstrated as much zeal and exertion as Schuyler's committee, Washington's army would surely have been strengthened more promptly and extensively than in fact it was during the summer of 1780. Pennsylvania had "not even deigned to acknowledge the receipt of any" of the Schuyler committee's letters. Deeming Pennsylvania's silence an insult to both the committee and Congress, the committee made a further appeal to President Joseph Reed, scolding him for failing to acknowledge correspondence and warning him of Washington's latest request for men, provisions, and transportation. New Hampshire, too, was chided for failing to indicate what the committee might expect the army to receive from that quarter. And copies of Washington's 13 July letter were forwarded to all the states from New Hampshire to Maryland. Schuyler and Peabody warned them that the prospects of military success must be diminished in proportion to each state's failure to meet its quota of requisitions.[67]

A measure of the success of the committee at headquarters may be taken from its reports to Congress on 18, 21, and 23 July. After a full two months at their task, Schuyler and his colleagues were no less insistent upon the need for fuller support of the army. The arrival of French reinforcements in Rhode Island simply made the necessity more pressing than ever. By 18 July the various state executives had reported progress in their efforts to fill requisitions, but the committee was unable to determine "with precision" exactly how completely they would be met. Connecticut and New York, for example, pledged full compliance; but Governor Trumbull doubted that Connecticut could raise all of the flour and salt requested, while Governor Clinton feared that forage would be short until after harvest. New Jersey promised provisions, horses and wagons, and completion of three battalions, but no number had been specified. Delaware's agreement to comply had been general, while Maryland agreed to fill her battalions by raising 1,469 men for the duration of the war and to raise another in lieu of militia. Virginia would send everything possible beyond her first responsibility to supply the Southern Army. New Hampshire officials had been silent, although private news had come that they were exerting themselves. Pennsylvania authorities had reported nothing but sent a few horses, some beef, a few barrels of flour, but little rum and no bacon nor forage and no wagons. Apparently Pennsylvania did not intend to complete her regiments as requested, nor to furnish the 3,465 militia that had been asked for.

In sum, Congress must appreciate what Schuyler's committee was unable to determine and must realize how the commander in chief was reduced to distress at a time when all doubts should have been removed. The committee cited the alarming facts without exaggeration. Pennsylvania's noncompliance with the requisitions, for example, threatened to render Washington's plans impossible to prosecute, and it was not fair to expect other states to exert themselves while one remained inactive.

Staff officers of the quartermaster, adjutant general, judge advocate, and hospital departments were demanding land bounties such as Congress had promised to Continental line officers in April; and Schuyler's committee begged Congress to resolve the rising discontent and to spare them the labors of constant confrontation with so many complaints. Similarly, Schuyler and Peabody pressed Congress to respond to the French troops' need for forage; that which was required of the eastern states could not be assigned to the allied forces because there was not enough for the American army. Finally, they said, Congress should reconsider the restrictions placed upon the operations of the commander in chief; these should not be confined to the limits of the United States lest they impede his effective cooperation with the French land and naval forces.[68]

Three days later John Mathews rejoined Schuyler and Peabody at Preakness, bearing a letter from the governor of Maryland and news from the president of New Hampshire, Mesech Weare. Much satisfied by the promises of help from these states, the committee forwarded the information to Congress by express. By then the committee had also consulted William Livingston, governor of New Jersey, and found that he and his council were authorized to summon their militia whenever Congress or the commander in chief called for them.[69]

Toward the end of July Schuyler's committee discovered that Virginia and New Jersey had been remiss in furnishing the horses they had promised for the transportation of flour. The quartermaster general's application for teams in New Jersey had failed because Governor Livingston insisted that it was the business of the courts, not the executive branch, to deal with the neglect of local magistrates in providing the livestock and their forage. As for Virginia, the committee begged Gov. Thomas Jefferson to furnish horses and other supplies, especially grain, as soon as "impediments" to transportation between Virginia and Head of Elk, Maryland, could be removed.[70]

Thus far the Yorker and his colleagues seem to have labored conscientiously and with a measure of success. In the midst of general gloom the army's food supplies were improved, and many "other problems had been solved or were quiescent." Proceeding also with their assignment to rearrange army units, the committee faced failure in dealing with Nathanael Greene and the quartermaster general's department.[71]

Among the chief points of controversy between Congress and Greene was the question of "the degree of responsibility that he would assume." Schuyler's committee sided with Greene, who insisted upon sizable discretionary authority both in making appointments and adapting measures according to contingencies as they arose. Greene wanted authorization to purchase supplies and services directly from individuals, whereas Congress was determined to obtain them from state governments. And he did not agree that plans for one assistant quartermaster near Congress's place of sitting and one deputy for the main army were sufficient for the discharge of his work.[72] Other details of the congressional plan were also objectionable. Although, for example, they indicated where and how forage should be received, there were no specifications as to how transportation could be obtained effectively.

For about a month Congress delayed action on the Schuyler committee proposals. On 15 July it enacted its own plan, and on 24 July the delegates further declined to accede to Greene's and the committee's wishes. Although insisting that "all officers entrusted with the disbursement of public monies . . . should be responsible for such disbursement," Congress promised only to "determine on circumstances as they arise, and make such favorable allowances as justice may require."[73]

Greene balked, and on 26 July he resigned. On 28 July Schuyler's committee "most earnestly" entreated him to "continue to direct the department" until Congress could consider their 27 July request that Greene not be "permitted to leave it in this advanced stage of the campaign." In taking up cudgels for Greene, Schuyler and his fellows as well as Washington also dared to recommend that Congress suspend its plans for the quartermaster department. On 30 July they explained that enemy maneuvers had obliged the Virginian to begin moving his army toward the Hudson. They had persuaded Greene to offer to withdraw his resignation, suggested that Congress accept Greene's gesture, and urged that Washington be empowered to arrange the quartermaster's department so as to expedite the work of the campaign. Congress might "let the business slide on under the orders of the General" subject to the committee's approval; repeal of the act of 15 July might be avoided, they said, except that Greene could not continue to function without the assistance of several of his subordinates, and they were determined to resign. The alternative was for Congress to repeal the act, increase the powers of

Washington or the committee—or both—to act, and to request Greene's able assistants, John Cox and Charles Pettit, to stay on. Cox was a Philadelphia merchant, and Pettit the secretary of New Jersey. Well aware of the "delicacy" of what they were recommending, Schuyler's committee remained convinced that in the face of the opening of the campaign a change of quartermaster officers "must be absolutely productive of ruin." Accordingly they urged a suspension of the new plans and a speedy determination of the issue. To clinch their arguments they stressed that the movement of Washington's troops to the Hudson required uninterrupted services from the quartermaster general and funds for the purchase of forage and transportation. Fresh dispatches from Rhode Island indicated the arrival of a British fleet "in such force as to give us great pain for the event, should an attack be made on ours."[74]

Schuyler and John Mathews followed Washington from Paramus to the Highlands on 30 July, struggling to meet the army's need for transportation and forage. Nathaniel Peabody remained at Morristown, too ill to accompany them. While aided by Robert Morris's work in collecting and shipping provisions from Philadelphia—and Morris's promise of "segars" from Havana—the two committeemen felt obliged to urge the use of impressment in order to obtain the wagons, horses, and forage that were so desperately needed by the moving army. From Peekskill on 3 August they also posted to Congress a reminder of unfinished plans for the inspector general's and muster-master general's departments. Although fresh troops were appearing daily at Peekskill, there were no proper officers to muster them. "Abuses" were certain to arise, and it was otherwise impossible to discover whether the states were meeting their quotas of militia and regulars.[75]

At Peekskill neither Schuyler nor his colleagues were aware of Congress's icy response to their quartermaster proposals when the Yorker struck out for Albany. Leaving Mathews to manage the committee's work on Washington's behalf, the general found his relative proximity to home inviting, and there were demands for his attention to Indian department business as well. For the moment, perhaps, there was little that he and the committee could do for Washington in the field that the Virginian could not do for himself. Mathews could of course maintain the liaison with Congress until Schuyler returned to camp. And the delegates might not be particularly prompt in resolving the Greene affair if they "penelopized" as usual.[76]

7

Answering Alarms from the North and West

Since early spring when Schuyler returned to Congress it had become increasingly evident that the Iroquois, with British aid, meant to take revenge for the Sullivan-Clinton expedition of 1779. Sir John Johnson and his cousin Guy launched British regulars and Indian allies under Joseph Brant east along the Mohawk, raiding settlements and devastating fields and crops. Oneida, Onondaga, and Tuscarora tribesmen were similarly threatened by their Iroquois brethren, who urged them to return to the king's service, and by early July a number of their warriors succumbed to this intimidation. Others, however, withstood the danger, and Schuyler endeavored to provide protection, clothing, and provisions to faithful tribesmen, especially the Oneida, by moving them to places of safety. In this, however, he was obliged to rely heavily upon Volkert Douw in Albany, because his duties in Congress and at Washington's headquarters kept him far from home for almost five months.[77]

Away from Albany, Schuyler found his secretary John Lansing, Jr.; James Dean, the agent of the Indian Commissioners; and others like Douw and Governor Clinton able to keep him informed of the rising danger to the northern and western frontiers. In response to Johnson's attacks Governor Clinton left Kingston on 25 May to rally militia at Albany and to chase the marauders out of the country. Schuyler, too, lent his aid to meet the danger, suggesting that recent requisitions for levies to complete New York's Continental line units could be diverted for defense of the northern frontiers. The Yorker also persuaded Washington to send James Clinton's brigade of Continentals north for the relief of the frontiers. On 30 May the New York legislature responded readily to the call for subsistence and transportation of the brigade to Albany. The governor, meanwhile, tried to cut off Johnson's retreat by rushing to Lake Champlain. Crossing Lake George on 31 May with some seven hundred men, he pressed forward to Crown Point, but Johnson's raiders had fled six hours before Clinton's troops reached that outpost.[78]

During June and July the New York frontiers were further endangered by the efforts of hostile Iroquois to force Oneida, Tuscarora, and Onondaga tribesmen to move west to Niagara and join the king's friends. Some were persuaded to do so, but many, especially the Oneida, refused. Subjected to further attacks, some four hundred loyal tribesmen fled to Fort Schuyler for protection. Consequently, the arrival of Gen. James Clinton's brigade at Albany early in June was especially welcome; his troops were needed to reinforce militia defenses at both northern and western outposts.[79]

In the west at Fort Schuyler, there was also considerable disaffection among the troops. Thirty-four men had deserted and thirteen were killed in the ensuing effort to capture them. Perhaps more than the overall danger to northern New York, it was the particular problem of retaining the Oneidas' friendship that finally propelled Schuyler to leave Washington's headquarters and return to Albany in August. Wishing to flee from their western homes to the safer regions of Canajoharie, Fort Hunter, or Schenectady, they correctly apprehended that the enemy would resume attacks from Niagara. Their pleas for support were duly passed to Schuyler from Samuel Kirkland, the missionary at Fort Schuyler, and Commissioner Volkert Douw at Albany. On 24 June Douw also warned the general that unless the sachems' cries for provisions could be answered, they would surely turn to the enemy to save themselves and their crops from devastation.[80]

The attacks renewed in July came principally in the west. In response to Schuyler's promptings, John Lansing, Jr., also investigated the state of affairs in the north country, and by the end of July he had discovered that Ethan Allen had been making mysterious trips to Connecticut, ostensibly in search of powder, and to Lake George. Whether his Vermont supporters intended to prepare against enemy incursions from Lake Champlain or to collaborate with them in an effort to win recognition for a jurisdiction independent of New York State was all conjectural. Lansing discovered that some of Allen's followers were violently opposed to New York's claims of jurisdiction over their territory, while others were willing to accede to it provided they were guaranteed titles to their lands. Thus, the unsettled dispute between Yorkers and Yankees afforded another dimension to the state's frontier dangers and another reason for Schuyler's August visit to Albany.[81]

By the time the harried general and Volkert Douw encountered Oneida tribesmen with some of their Tuscarora and Caughnawaga brethren at Schenectady on 16 August, there had been still more Indian and Loyalist attacks in the Canajoharie district and the Schoharie valley. The Oneida and their friends had good cause to want the protection and aid of the commissioners for Indian affairs. Schuyler observed that it was indeed unfortunate that the Sullivan campaign had not brought all of the Six Nations to their senses. Since the Oneida had already moved from their homes and crops, they might now remain at Fort Hunter where provisions would be supplied to them. In their proximity to white settlers, he warned, they must avoid clashes by refraining from drink and the theft of their new neighbors' vegetables. Grasshopper, the Oneida chieftain, promised to heed these admonitions, and Schuyler proposed that his men send representatives with James Dean to visit Rochambeau's army in Rhode Island. The appearance of the French allied forces might encourage the miserable tribesmen to hold fast to their American friends if not to persuade their faithless fellows to abjure allegiance to the British cause.[82]

Alerting Lafayette to expect the visitors, Schuyler wrote to explain that the tribesmen would be able to counteract British allegations that there was no Franco-American alliance. Five Caughnawaga might be especially helpful in this for they were men of influence in their nation and could spread the word among their people near Montreal. Well aware of the effectiveness of both flattery and reproof, Schuyler also urged that Rochambeau and the chevalier de Ternay address the delegation. To convince them of the French king's "favor to us," the Yorker continued, "I most earnestly wish" that they be "forcibly impressed" with the king's support of the American cause. They should see the force of the French arms. Let them be warned, he said, that their continued hostilities would incur the king's resentment and bring chastisement upon them. Lafayette might also invite other Canadian Indians to visit Rochambeau's army, and if any gifts had been sent from France for the Indians, they should be forwarded for distribution at Schenectady upon Dean's return.[83]

The general's diplomacy with the Indians in August was perhaps a desperate diversion, but it was not ill conceived or wholly useless. Dean and the delegation were duly received by Rochambeau on 30 August, and they could not have failed to be impressed by his army's display of Franco-American unity. Meantime, Schuyler concluded arrangements to furnish supplies to the tribesmen who were to live at Fort Hunter. Volkert Douw was obliged to borrow $2,000 to purchase provisions because the Indian commissioners' funds were exhausted.[84]

8

Discharged by the "Grand Multiform'd Sanhedrin"

By 27 August Schuyler had returned to Washington's moving headquarters, which were then located at Liberty Pole, New Jersey. When he had left Peekskill earlier in the month he could not have known of Congress's response to the committee at headquarter's pleas on behalf of

Washington's army and Q.M. Gen. Nathanael Greene's department. In only one particular was that response favorable. Restrictions on the commander in chief limiting his operations to United States territory had been removed in the interest of allowing him a freer hand to cooperate with the French reinforcements. But on 2 August Congress icily voted that the committee "ought not to have interfered" in Greene's questions about his responsibilities as quartermaster general. As for officers' applications for adjustments in their salaries and relief for Col. Moses Hazen's suffering Canadians, Congress declared that the committee had given too much time and attention to matters beyond their concern; and petitions "should have been made directly to Congress, and the committee should thus have informed the applicants." Moreover, Schuyler and his colleagues should have consulted the Pennsylvania delegation in Congress about the issue of their state's deficiency in meeting requisitions.[85]

John Mathews did not meekly accept these reprimands in silence. Instead, during Schuyler's absence he displayed the Yorker's own spirit in lecturing Congress about general military conditions and the particular case of Nathanael Greene. Mathews insisted that no other competent officer was available to replace the quartermaster general, and that it was a duty Congress owed "to their constituents, not to suffer punctilio, to militate against their essential interests ... Remember the Gentleman at the head of your Army ... For God's sake! have some regard to his feelings."[86]

Congress, however, had already ended the Greene affair. On 5 August they elected a new quartermaster general, Timothy Pickering, the very man whose complicated plans had been so objectionable to Greene and the Schuyler committee. Greene continued to function as quartermaster general until the end of September. His successor's administration proved to be frugal and careful, but it did not particularly improve the army's condition, and the troops were obliged largely to continue living off the countryside.[87]

No sooner did Congress hear John Mathews's pleas for Greene than it ordered the committee at headquarters to "be discharged from further attendance there, and that they report their proceedings to Congress." The vote on 11 August was ten ayes, two nays (Mathews's South Carolina and Schuyler's New York), and one state divided (Virginia). Ezekiel Cornell of Rhode Island explained that the decision was made in the interest of congressional harmony because some delegates had opposed the appointment of the Schuyler committee from the beginning. Writing to General Greene on 15 August, Cornell claimed that no particular charge had been made against the committee; "some of their letters were in a stile rather warm but that I imputed to Schuyler's zeal and the warm Climate of Mathews Nativity [South Carolina]." Congressmen, he noted, were not "apt to be angry at any thing we can evade." Evasion was, of course, Congress's besetting sin. Not long after Cornell had mentioned it to Greene, Alexander Hamilton observed the need for the appointment of chief ministers of state, which was a task Congress did not complete until 1781.[88]

While such decisions were months in the making, Congress remained tardy even in the dispatch of news of more immediate activities. Not until 22 August, for example, did Mathews receive its orders for the committee to disband and to report. Meantime, in response to Washington's call for "more competent" means of answering "the public expectation," the South Carolinian issued circular letters on behalf of the army, again urging the states to meet their quotas of troops and supplies. When Mathews finally notified Schuyler of the Congress's rebuke to their committee, he properly questioned the order for them to "report their proceedings," which was an insult implying that they had been remiss in fulfilling a duty that had been carefully observed. As for the "complexion of things" in Philadelphia, he wrote, "we stand on delicate ground," and prudence dictated that they be prepared "to meet them on whatever ground they Please to take." With "sincere esteem" the South Carolinian urged the Yorker to return to Congress, "for it is not in my power to stand bluff to the whole Phalanx."[89]

Again the object of high-handed congressional critics, Schuyler refused to return to Philadelphia. In fact, he never again set foot in Congress until the Confederation had been replaced and he became a United States senator in 1789. Disinclined to serve longer in a body that repeatedly had caused him so much harm and anguish, Schuyler was dismayed that it had infrequently been able to accomplish much of any good for the army and the country; even when it had, the results too often came too little and too late. Like Schuyler, Nathaniel Peabody did not return to Congress. The Yorker apparently remained stonily silent, and the New Hampshire Yankee displayed an "amused aloofness." Peabody wryly observed, "I once read of a people who were at times led by a cloud; And I have known a people whose *Grand Multiform'd Sanhedrin* were often times in the midst of a Fog."[90]

Although Schuyler refused to return to the "multiform'd Sanhedrin," he did not hesitate to hasten back to Washington's army. The commander in chief must be apprised of the circumstances threatening the northern and western reaches of New York. By the evening of 27 August he rejoined the Virginian at the Liberty Pole Tavern in New Jersey, just northwest of Fort Lee. Perhaps it was there that he discovered that the committee at headquarters had been dismissed—a step that Washington much regretted, for he readily informed Congress of his gratitude for the committee's "cheerful and vigorous exertions." Their duties must now fall more heavily on his own shoulders.[91]

Within the next few days Schuyler had the opportunity to consult with Mathews and Peabody at nearby Morristown about preparing their final report to Congress. Without further committee responsibilities there and no desire to return to Congress, Schuyler set out for home. He might, it seemed, serve the best interests of both his state and the embryo nation by taking his seat in the state senate. Moreover, Washington's efforts to field a properly provisioned army for the campaign of 1780 finally ground to a halt. With news that the second French squadron had been blocked up in Brest and was not likely to reach America in time for the allied armies to accomplish much more before winter, Washington "gave up all idea of an effective campaign" for the season "and decided to dismiss the greater part of the militia."[92]

9

"I made great Interest to be left Out"

Delayed in his departure from Liberty Pole because of a violent storm on 3 September, Schuyler reached Poughkeepsie in time for the convening of the senate on 7 September. The general had won his first four-year term in the New York State Senate in the annual spring elections of 1780.[93]

Gradually, the impact of the Revolution was altering the complexion of politics and the composition of the state's government. Fewer of the old political elite came to sit in the legislature, whose very size made more seats available to men of the "lower orders." Although this was more noticeable in the assembly than in the senate, Schuyler had few social peers in the upper house save for his cousin, Lt. Gov. Pierre Van Cortlandt; and a handful of associates like Isaac Roosevelt and Lewis Morris; or men with experience, such as provincial assemblymen like Morris and Henry Wisner. Similarly, among the ten Albany County assemblymen there were only two Van Rensselaers (Robert and John) and one Livingston (Peter R.). The others were "new-comers" like John Taylor and young John Lansing. The newer element in the legislature, more reflective of the power of the people than of the old elite class, also began to contribute to the formation of distinct party lines. But as of 1780 that clarity was still lacking, for there were few signs of strict party continuity and cohesion: formal organization, permanent membership, systematic electioneering, written platforms, or faithful adherents among the electorate. Only at the end of the war did the lines harden between the supporters and critics of Gov. George Clinton; it was the gubernatorial elections of 1783 that marked the dissolution of a general coalition of Whigs and Patriots when Schuyler finally stood against Clinton as he first had in 1777.

In September and October 1780, however, there were few indications of legislative partisanship in New York. Ringing with notes of common concern for the wartime effort, Governor Clinton's opening address enumerated the major points of business to be conducted. The disputed boundary with the New Hampshire Grants, expected to be considered soon by Congress, would demand the special attention of the state's delegates who were soon to be chosen. Provision must be made to meet the devastations of the enemy on the frontiers. A variety of general embarrassments, Clinton noted, were the result of a defect of power in those who ought to exercise a supreme direction of the war. And he proposed the need to consider further means "for accelerating the proposed Confederation"—vesting Congress with authority to deal effectively with the war effort. To this end the governor submitted the proceedings of a convention held at Boston during the previous month by delegates of Massachusetts, Connecticut, and New Hampshire.

Schuyler was immediately named to committees to draft the senate's reply to Clinton's address and to plan for "more effectually" procuring supplies for the army. On 8 September the senate appointed him to a joint committee with assemblymen to consider a response to the Boston convention and to the senate's committee on means of raising revenue for the state treasury. It was clear that his colleagues recognized Schuyler's abilities and far-ranging knowledge of a variety of business. And as a member of the committee at Washington's headquarters he could be expected to be particularly effective in shaping the legislators' response to the needs of the Continental army.[94]

In their reply to the governor's message, the product of Schuyler's first committee assignment, the senate enthusiastically promised to expedite the various business that Clinton had urged to be done. Between 13 and 18 September the general was named to four other joint committees of the house and senate, two of which dealt with national issues: a congressional recommendation to compensate soldiers for their loss in pay due to depreciated currency, and Congress's act of 26 August respecting the circulation of new bills of credit and the payment of public debts. The other two committees were assigned to consider whether to continue or postpone an act for the sales of forfeited estates and to determine ways and means to increase the revenue of the state treasury. In addition Schuyler introduced a bill to raise a sum in specie to redeem one-sixth of the bills emitted on New York's credit by act of Congress (18 March), with the latter providing for a discharge of interest to be paid on the bills. The bill was enacted after illness obliged Schuyler to leave the senate, which was a testimony to his ability to persuade the legislators to accept a proposal in the national interest without further need for his presence to marshal supporters against any notable opposition.

Indeed by the time Schuyler left Poughkeepsie, about a fortnight before the session adjourned on 10 October, much of the work he had helped to begin had either been accomplished or was well on its way to enactment. Significantly, the senate journals reveal practically no divisions of votes—no indications of distinctive blocs or discordant interest groups. Only on the issue of compensating soldiers for pay in depreciated currency did the general encounter particular hesitation to respond to a problem of national significance. Rather than establish specific allowances for the depreciated pay schedules, the legislature decided to wait for a uniform system adopted by all of the states or discovery of what the others provided. Meantime, the New York delegates were to move Congress to determine what soldiers should be provided by each state exclusive of its Continental line units; and it was likewise urged that Congress establish the values and amounts of allowances for veterans' widows and children.[95]

On 12 September the senate made its annual choice of delegates to Congress. James Duane, William Floyd, John Morin Scott, Alexander McDougall, and Philip Schuyler were named. However, when the senate compared its list with the assembly's slate, there was a single notable difference. Instead of Schuyler the assembly had proposed Ezra L'Hommedieu, and a joint ballot was then taken to resolve the issue. L'Hommedieu was chosen. The outcome, according to Schuyler, was due to his own efforts: "I made great Interest to be left out of the delegation," he told Hamilton; and he had succeeded "altho not without much difficulty."[96]

Schuyler had no wish to return to Congress after his long struggle on behalf of Washington's army and Q.M. Gen. Nathanael Greene and the curt dismissal of his committee to headquarters. If aught could be done for the commander in chief and the infant nation itself, perhaps the Yorker could accomplish it by his seat in the New York Senate and by attending the Hartford Convention. Although the legislature did not name the convention delegates until the day following Schuyler's departure from Poughkeepsie, he was correct in suspecting that he would be sent to Hartford with orders to propose the appointment of a dictator.

On 26 September the senate approved the assembly's appointment of Schuyler, Judge John Sloss Hobart, and Atty. Gen. Egbert Benson as delegates to Hartford. Schuyler deemed the others "as deeply Impressed as men can be with the necessity of more power in directing the council or what would be better in our present Situation." "What would be better" he did not specify, but he undoubtedly meant some degree of dictatorial power for Washington, which was a subject that he did mention in writing to Hamilton on 10 September and again on 16 September. The Yorker's prediction that the legislature would instruct the delegates to propose dictatorship at Hartford was also as accurate as that of the choice of representatives.[97]

Like Hamilton, who wished some improvement in the as yet unratified Articles of Confederation, Schuyler saw the needs of both the miserable army and the nascent union of states; they might be met only by a stronger centralized power. The senator's hand may be seen in the very language of the resolution that as a member of the joint committee he had helped to write and that the senate approved on 23 September. New York's commissioners to Hartford were "to propose and agree to ... all such Measures as shall appear calculated to give a Vigor to the governing Powers, equal to the present Crisis: *Provided,* That nothing to which they may agree, shall be binding upon this State, unless the same shall be approved and confirmed to the Legislature."[98]

The "present Crisis" of October 1780 was the product of a series of military reverses as well as the lack of effective national government. Charleston was taken by the British in May, Horatio Gates defeated at Camden in August, the French squadron unable to reach American waters to support the allied army efforts to recapture New York City—and in late September came the revelation of Arnold's treason. All were sharp blows to popular expectations that 1780 would bring final victory to the rebel cause. Schuyler's musings indicated the widespread concern for the patriot struggle. And as he anticipated the immediate future, his sentiments were decidedly mixed.

After learning from Alexander Hamilton of the 16 August disaster at Camden, for example, Schuyler feared the consequences of Horatio Gates's defeat. But, he noted, "it will ... be attended with one good, the adherents in Congress to the Gallant comander—[a snide reference to Gates] will not have it any longer in their power to play him off against the General [Washington]." Foolishly committing an army of some fifteen hundred Continentals against twenty-three hundred British regulars, Gates proved conclusively that he was not only inexperienced in actual battle but also that he had learned nothing from the campaign of 1777. Or perhaps he forgot what Schuyler had rightly calculated three years earlier: that an opposing army might be defeated after it had first been whittled down by strategic retreats, a scorched-earth policy, and timely auxiliary blows such as had been struck at Bennington and in the Mohawk valley. This time "there was no Schuyler to save American troops for later use on other fields by giving up a Ticonderoga; Lincoln had lost them all at Charleston."[99]

With pointed reference to the Conway cabal, Schuyler no less than Washington had long been leery of Gates. "Gracious God!" he exclaimed to Hamilton, "that any rational being should put two men in compe[ti]tion, one of which has *commanded* an army the other only been at the head of one, for I aver that when he [Gates] was to the northward he never made a disposition of his troops. Indeed he was incapable, he never saw an Enemy except at a good distance—and from places of perfect security. Indeed! Indeed, he has not lost a unit in my estimation by this last stroke of his." Later, when Gates was deprived of his command, Schuyler rejoiced, hoping that "he may never command, at any Important Post."[100] In that, too, Schuyler was to find satisfaction, for Gates never won a court of inquiry to clear himself as he requested, and he was left idle for the remainder of the war. Only after Congress reinstated him in the summer of 1782 did Washington call Gates to the army posted at New Windsor, New York. Neither there nor elsewhere did he ever contribute anything solid to match the extensive services of Philip Schuyler, whether as a general or a congressman and senator or as a private citizen.

While Schuyler noted his views on the Southern Army for Hamilton, he was, in September 1780, more concerned for the prospects of the Hartford Convention, which was scheduled to begin on 8 November. Might it initiate reforms of the yet unfinished Confederation and an enlargement of congressional power? Encouraged that both houses of the legislature seemed animated by a renewed spirit for the cause and were talking of a dictator, he expected to go to Hartford and push for such a scheme. He also wished to rejoin Washington, who was then about to visit Connecticut for consultations with Rochambeau.[101]

Unfortunately for the Yorker, just as recurrent gout had forced his return to Albany on 26 September, a fortnight before the legislature adjourned, both illness and the renewal of enemy threats to the northern frontier prevented Schuyler from seeing the allied commanders or from attending the Hartford Convention. After reaching his Saratoga country house in early October, he maintained a watch for enemy maneuvers in the lake country until the Indian summer dangers subsided.

10

Again a Northern Invasion

From Canada in September 1780 the British launched another two-pronged invasion of New York, one from Niagara toward the Schoharie valley, and the other along Lake Champlain toward the upper reaches of the Hudson. The first, comprised of some eight hundred to a thousand men, was led by Sir John Johnson, Col. John Butler, and Joseph Brant. The second, also about a thousand strong (regulars, Loyalists, and Indians), was led by Maj. Christopher Carleton. Coming as they did after the spring incursions into the Mohawk valley and the north country and at about the time that Arnold's treason was uncovered on 25 September, Americans suspected that they were designed to facilitate Arnold's plans. Frontier threats might force a diversion of American troops from West Point. And at the same time, the Canadian governor-general Frederick Haldimand began negotiations with the leaders of the Hampshire Grants. Ethan Allen and his colleagues "were bent on delivering Vermont to the enemy," although they later alleged that they intended only to force New York State and the Confederation government to recognize Vermont as the fourteenth state of the union. Their intrigue with Haldimand began in earnest in August, and early in October over a thousand British forces crossed Lake Champlain to occupy positions at Ticonderoga and Skenesborough.[102]

While Johnson's western forces menaced Fort Schuyler and other points like Schoharie, Carleton's struck at the feeble garrisons at Lake George and Fort Ann. Other northern settlements in Charlotte County were burned, as were parts of the Saratoga district and Ballston. An estimated hundred and fifty thousand bushels of grain and two hundred dwellings were ruined in this final campaign of the season. In all, the British-Indian damages to the New York frontiers in 1780 included the burning of seven hundred houses and barns, three hundred and thirty people killed or captured, and nearly seven hundred head of cattle driven off by the enemy.[103]

At first confined to his Albany house by gout, Schuyler was able to do little but relay information to Governor Clinton and military officers, advising them of the need for regular troops and militia to check the enemy's approaches. Unable to leave Poughkeepsie because of rheumatism, Clinton later in October managed to pursue Sir John Johnson's western marauders and to stop their depredations. Meantime, the governor's brother, Brig. Gen. James Clinton, was dispatched to command troops at Albany and to direct the deployment of Gen. Abraham Ten Broeck and Gen. Robert Van Rensselaer's militia forces. From the Highlands Maj. Gen. William Heath sent several New York and New Hampshire regiments and an artillery detachment; and he, like the governor, urged Schuyler to furnish news by a chain of express messengers who were assigned to ride between Albany and the Highlands. Suspicious of Ethan Allen and his Vermonters, Clinton also asked Schuyler to continue a surveillance of the Hampshire Grants people.[104]

Friendly Oneida and Tuscarora also demanded Schuyler's attention in October because of complaints that they lacked the provisions that he and Volkert Douw had promised them in August. Their well-being was in some respect important to maintain in light of renewed hostilities on the frontiers. Unable to inspect their situation west of Schenectady because of his illness, the Yorker begged Congress to remember the Indians' pitiful poverty and their lack of clothing. While urging Clinton to alleviate the shortage of provisions, he asked Henry Glen of Schenectady to house the wretched tribesmen in barracks. Meantime, Col. William Malcolm, commander of the Second Regiment of New York militia, consulted Schuyler about enlisting some of the Indians against the enemy and obtained his agreement to employ them in forays west to Lake Otsego and along the Schoharie frontier.[105]

By mid-October, despite lingering illness, Schuyler managed to reach Saratoga, a closer vantage point from which to watch the enemy's northern maneuvers. Alerted to their arson at White Creek on 17 October, he quickly asked General Ten Broeck for militia. Arriving at Albany on 16 October, Governor Clinton learned of Schuyler's plea and ordered his brother, Col. Stephen Schuyler, to march his regiment to Saratoga. Clinton promised more reinforcements as soon as they could be called out, and he asked Washington to hasten additional troops up the Hudson; the militia service time would soon expire, and without the commander in chief's aid, the New York frontiers could be pushed back to Albany and Schenectady. The governor's major concern for the moment, however, was to remove the enemy's threats to the Mohawk and Schoharie valleys. On 26 October when he returned to Albany, Clinton was able to tell Schuyler that Sir John Johnson had been forced to flee, and that the devastation was halted.[106]

The threats from the north lingered. At first Schuyler feared that Carleton's forces would range as far south as his country estate. By 19 October they had come to within five miles of his Saratoga house after taking Fort George and Fort Ann and burning Kingsborough and Queensborough townships. Many "Inhabitants [were] flying down the Country. I believe," he wrote Hamilton, "my turn will be in a few days unless troops are sent up." With eight hundred regulars and about two hundred Tories and an equal number of Indians, Carleton was waiting at Ticonderoga for reinforcements before venturing to raid settlements as far south as the Mohawk River.[107]

Schuyler of course welcomed Governor Clinton's news that Sir John Johnson had been routed at Caughnawaga, but he warned both Clinton and Washington that more troops were needed to repel the menace of Christopher Carleton and to persuade settlers not to flee their homes. The Yorker also found reports of activities of Hampshire Grants people both mysterious and alarming. "A flag under pretext of setting a cartel with Vermont has been on the Grants," he announced on 31 October. Ethan Allen had disbanded his militia and over sixteen hundred of the enemy were rapidly moving south from Lake Champlain. The governor, Schuyler urged, should himself lead reinforcements north from Albany, and Washington must likewise furnish aid.[108]

The governor, however, decided to return to Poughkeepsie to discharge the business of the legislature, but he assured Schuyler on 2 November that Brig. Gen. James Clinton was en route to command the army at Albany and that orders had been issued to call up fresh militia levies. Washington, too, finally responded to the Yorker's cries for troops; on 6 November he ordered Gen. William Heath to send three New York regiments up from the Hudson Highlands if he could "conveniently spare" them. Disturbed by accounts of Ethan Allen and his Vermonters' activities, Washington instructed Schuyler to "concert" with General Clinton about seizing Allen and his papers if there were "palpable proofs" of his connivance with the enemy. The business was admittedly delicate, but the Virginian trusted Schuyler's prudence to decide how to proceed.[109]

North country people remained uneasy early in November as Carleton's British forces moved from Lake Champlain to Lake George. Schuyler himself was agitated when a number of militia ordered to remain at Fort Edward abandoned it instead. Col. Peter Gansevoort, he feared, would be unable to hold the position without reinforcements, and Saratoga militiamen could not be expected to assist him after they began to remove their families for fear of other enemy maneuvers on the Hampshire Grants. Schuyler's efforts to allay their alarm proved wholly useless, but he urged Governor Clinton that it would be prudent to make "the suspicions of the Grant business as little public as possible."[110]

Although Christopher Carleton's bands did not again range far south of Lake George, Schuyler sensed their threat until about mid-November. The turn of the season proved to be perhaps a better defense against Carleton's raiders than all of Schuyler's efforts to assemble an adequate force to oppose them. With Sir John Johnson's flight back into Canada, and winter closing in, Carleton also withdrew. The severity of the season, however, did not halt Haldimand's negotiations with Ethan Allen and his Vermonters. But Schuyler hoped to draw them from temptation by inducing the New York legislature to surrender the state's jurisdiction and to create a commission to settle disputed land titles. In the meantime he knew that there would be only a respite in the enemy's assaults on the frontiers.[111]

11

"a Character . . . debased beyond description"

Before Carleton's withdrawal from Ticonderoga for the winter Schuyler found occasion to inform the British commander of the Arnold-André affair—a poignant reminder of the gentleman's code that prevailed throughout even the horrors of the war. The general may also have decided that publicizing the failure of Arnold's treason might discourage further incursions on the frontiers and British dickerings with those "bent on delivering Vermont to the enemy." And he could not have been unmindful of the link between Arnold's intention to surrender West Point and the raids out of Canada that appeared to be ploys to divert American military strength from the lower Hudson.[112]

It was probably Hamilton who supplied Schuyler with accounts of Arnold's miscarried treason and Maj. John André's exemplary behavior before he was hanged as a spy. But it was not until 10 November that the general revealed his knowledge of the West Point episode when he offered his account of it to Maj. Christopher Carleton. "Altho I believed your curiosity would prompt you to wish for the particulars relative to your unfortunate Acquaintance with Major Andre," Schuyler began, "I had my doubts on the Propriety of sending You the Inclosed papers as they

Contain Intelligence which cannot be agreeable to your side of the question, but finding myself Incapable to offer, what might by some be deemed an Insult, I easily concluded that a man of honor and Liberal Sentiments would not consider this as one."[113]

Schuyler's reaction to Arnold's treason, like that of the general public, was one of outrage; Arnold's effort represented a violation of the very heart of the Revolution, which was public virtue, and the ideals of honor, integrity, valor, industry, and generosity.[114] Certainly, the general's letter to Carleton reveals his own devotion to virtue and honor and the qualities of character for which the proud patriot justly deserves to be remembered.

While Schuyler sent Carleton copies of André's letters to Washington and Sir Henry Clinton, he recounted the substance of the "whole transaction," relying only upon his memory of a written narrative, which he did not then have at hand to copy. Arnold, he explained, had approached the British and "agreed to deliver up the fortifications of which he had the command and which he had most earnestly solicited." Schuyler did not, however, explain to Carleton that his own sympathy for Arnold, who had not been accorded the recognition due him for his abilities and services, had led him and others to endorse Arnold's application for the West Point command or some other significant military assignment.[115]

Months later, in October, Washington recalled that the suggestion that Arnold might be assigned to West Point had made "little impression on me." Schuyler, he said, "seemed to have no other view in communicating the thing than because he was requested to do it." The Virginian clearly held Schuyler in high regard. His confidence in the Yorker's judgment and proven abilities, his intimate knowledge of military affairs, candor, "personal civilities," and warm friendship, Washington maintained was the result of a pretty long acquaintanceship. The villainous perfidy of Arnold could not besmirch Schuyler's reputation and record of devoted service to the army.[116]

Schuyler had of course been duped, and Arnold was deeply involved with his British coconspirators at the very time that he solicited the Yorker's aid in efforts to return to active military service. After he arrived at West Point, Arnold arranged his conference with Sir Henry Clinton's agents, Beverly Robinson and John André. After meeting with Arnold, André was persuaded "much against his Inclination, to change his dress, and . . . In this disguise and with a pass from Arnold . . . he past [sic] the posts at Stoney point, and the Guards below, and had reached Tarrytown." There, on 23 September, he was accosted by three lads; he asked, Schuyler explained, "If they were Cow Boys (an appelation given to a set of Mara[u]ders on both sides, ours being called *upper* and the British *lower*

Cow Boys) they answered in the affirmative," and when André "enquired wether *upper* or *lower*" they misled him by answering *"lower."* André then requested that they "conduct him to the british lines, on which they seized him, and on examination found a number of papers" proving that he was a spy. On 25 September Washington announced that "Treason of the blackest dye was yesterday discovered."[117]

Although Schuyler was grieved by the baseness of Arnold's scheme, he was, like many others, sympathetic to his accomplice, André. His dignity, Schuyler said, "drew the admiration of his Judges and acquired him the Esteem of our whole Army, whose resentment rested w[h]ere every man of sentiment will place It on Arnold, and most Chearfully *[sic]* would Every officer in the army have Interceded for his life If Arnold could have been Substituted ... Just before his exit," Schuyler noted, André "Observed to a Gentleman that his sentiments In this unhappy Conflict had always been liberal, but If any prejudices had remained, the Candor and affection he had experienced would have erazed *[sic]* them for ever; he certainly was an Ornament to the profession he had adopted, of such strict honor that when It was Intimated that If Arnold was given up his life would probably be saved, he declined hinting It to Sir Henry Clinton. Indeed If he had," Schuyler vowed, "I should have from that moment siezed *[sic]* to esteem him, for altho his life was worth a thousand of Arnolds, It would have been bought at too high a price." Schuyler's final pronouncement on Benedict Arnold agreed very well with another officer's judgment that the ball that hit Arnold in the leg at Saratoga should have struck his heart: "He then would have finished his career in Glory." That Arnold should now be "made a Brigadier In the british line," Schuyler found to be even more offensive. "If he was a mere deserter," he told Carleton, "I should think It probable, but I cannot believe that men of honor can so far sacrifice their feelings as to serve under such a Character, which is debased beyond description."[118]

Arnold's sordid deed touched others with whom he had been associated, and because of it Schuyler was obliged to intervene on behalf of his former aide-de-camp, Lt. Col. Richard Varick. As Arnold's aide Varick, too, was suspected of treason; he was also charged with misuse of government supplies, and Washington ordered his arrest on 25 September. By mid-October when Schuyler received Varick's request to attend a court of inquiry and to testify on his behalf, the Yorker begged to be excused. Only a very ill state of health, he said, prevented his travel to West Point where the court sat on 2–5 November. But Schuyler did not hesitate to file written testimony of Varick's exemplary character and attachment to the "glorious cause," thereby demonstrating his own standards of public virtue and personal honor. Happily, Varick persuaded the court to acquit him of all suspicion.[119]

Schuyler decided not to attend the Hartford Convention, scheduled to begin on 8 November, because of his illness and also the enemy's military threat on Lake Champlain and British diplomatic maneuvers with the Hampshire Grants people, who appeared ready to accept the status of a British colony if they could not obtain recognition as an independent state from New York or the Continental Congress. The general evidently regarded his role of watchdog for his and New York's landed interests and for the military authorities as more important than going to Hartford. Judge Egbert Benson could be trusted to represent Schuyler's views at the convention, and before Benson set out for Connecticut he had consulted him on the business at hand.[120]

As for the Hampshire Grants problem, Schuyler advised Governor Clinton to summon the legislature into early session to reach some settlement with Vermonters in order to gain their support for the army and for the defense of American frontiers. Unfortunately, however, after Schuyler persuaded the state senate to relinquish New York's jurisdiction over the Grants and to establish a commission to settle certain property claims in 1781, Clinton opposed these ideas, threatened prorogation, and prevented the assembly from proceeding with the business. Congress might wrestle with the problem. Although it procrastinated until 1791, Schuyler's stand on the Vermont question was clear as early as 1780; selfish provincial interests must give way to those of the union—a union with enlarged national powers such as Hamilton himself advocated.[121]

Before leaving his countryside retreat early in December and returning to Albany to witness preparations for Elizabeth's wedding and the ensuing holidays, Schuyler reckoned accounts for Morgan Lewis, deputy quartermaster general, who had used his Saratoga sawmill. The net sum owed to the squire of Saratoga on 1 December 1780 was £1,062.19.2, in all an indication of a sizable enterprise. However profitable or unproductive the remainder of his farms and forests may have been during this gloomy period of the war, there was something to show for it beyond mere subsistence.[122]

12

"a new graft on an old stock"

For Philip Schuyler and his family the December 1780 holidays were indeed notable, and they began early with the festivities of Elizabeth's marriage to Alexander Hamilton on 14 December. In keeping with the Dutch custom of home weddings, their vows were exchanged in the drawing room of the bride's parents and in the presence of only a few relatives and friends. Marriage records of the Reformed Dutch Church of Albany carry the simple entry: "1780, Dec. 14. Colonel Alex. Hamilton and Elisabeth Schuyler," and no particular reference to the local minister, Dominie Eilardus Westerlo. A graduate of the University of Utrecht, Westerlo used Dutch in the conduct of church services until he died in 1790, but it is not likely that he solemnized the marriage in other than English.[123]

The nuptials were doubtless a relief to Elizabeth's mother and her grandparents, the John Van Rensselaers. There had been no repetition of Angelica's elopement with John Barker Church. Although the Churches were not able to come to Albany in December, Elizabeth's aunt Gertrude and her second husband Dr. John Cochran were present to witness the culmination of the suit begun at their Morristown house only ten months earlier. Cochran, who had become chief physician and surgeon of the Middle Department of the army in October, was soon to be appointed director general of military hospitals by Congress. Other members of the wedding party included Eliza's sisters, Margarita, who was twenty-two; five-year-old Cornelia; and her brothers, John Bradstreet, fifteen; Philip Jeremiah, almost thirteen; and Rensselaer, not quite eight. Attended by his friend James McHenry, who was also one of Washington's aides, Hamilton had no kinsman to share the occasion. But the taking of vows with Eliza made him the member of an important family network. If Hamilton intended to gain status by such a connection, Schuyler also profited. "His satisfaction in Hamilton's achievements, to which he notably contributed, was a sufficient compensation. Here was a new graft on an old stock, which bore even better fruit."[124]

Before the newlyweds' departure from Albany, four French officers from Rochambeau's army joined their family circle at Schuyler's fireside. The vicomte de Noailles, comte de Damas, and chevalier de Mauduit arrived at the city on 23 December. The chevalier (later marquis) de Chastellux appeared on Christmas Eve in time to be invited to dinner. Chastellux's account of his reception offers a tantalizing picture of an animated household and the Schuylers' generous hospitality. Grateful to find several

Fig. 10. Alexander Hamilton, 1755–1804. Oil on canvas by John Trumbull. Philip Schuyler heartily approved of the match between his daughter Elizabeth and Alexander Hamilton, Washington's aide-de-camp. Their political philosophies and outlook were compatible, and each viewed the alliance as a beneficial one. Courtesy, Museum of Fine Arts, Boston. Bequest of Robert C. Winthrop.

of his countrymen present to enjoy the warm welcome and good food and drink, he admired the general's fine Madeira and his attractive family. The young ladies and their three brothers, he thought, were "the handsomest children you can see." In the 1781 edition of his travels Chastellux observed that "Mrs. Hamilton . . . lacks none of the attributes of a pretty woman . . . Miss Peggy . . . lacks only teeth to be as pretty as her sister." Wishing for another invitation to dinner, Chastellux had misgivings about Mrs. Schuyler, "une grosse hollandoise," he observed, "a big Dutchwoman, with a rather serious disposition [who] appeared to be the mistress of the house." He decided "it best not to treat her in too cavalier a fashion," and when no invitation was forthcoming, Chastellux decided simply "to call on the General during the evening" of 26 December. Schuyler was in the drawing room with Hamilton and Elizabeth when Chastellux arrived. Informed that Mrs. Schuyler "was indisposed," the visitor "took this at face value." In discussing the military campaigns of 1775–77 Schuyler decided to show Chastellux and the comte de Noailles his maps and papers. As they entered another room the guests "found Mrs. and Miss Schuyler by the fireside, appearing to be in rather good health." Chastellux was miffed, if not chagrined, that the general's wife was in no mood to entertain him, but her announced indisposition was no mere subterfuge. Well advanced in pregnancy, she gave birth to the last of fifteen children, Catherine Van Rensselaer, on 20 February 1781.

After an abortive attempt to reach the Cohoes Falls through the Christmas snows (25 December) and a visit to Schenectady (27 December), Chastellux again called on Schuyler on the evening of 28 December to plan a trip to Saratoga. The general had hesitated to go because he had had a touch of the gout, but at sunrise on 29 December he and his visitors set out for Saratoga in five sleighs. Crossing the frozen Mohawk, the party paused at Stillwater to view the redoubts and sites of the armies' maneuvers in 1777, and Schuyler pushed ahead to prepare accommodations at his country house. On 30 December he sent Chastellux and the others with two officers to inspect Fort Edward, and next day the general guided the Frenchman's party over the Saratoga battlefield, pausing at Bemis's Heights and Halfmoon on their way back to Albany.

Chastellux found that he "could not have [had] a better guide," and that "no person but the proprietor of the ground himself was able to conduct us safely through the woods; the fences and entrenchments being covered a foot deep with snow." Schuyler's indisposition prevented him from overexposing himself to the winter air, but he evidently did not spare the effort to make Chastellux's party comfortable in the "temporary apartments" the Frenchman said he had fitted up until happier times would allow him to build another house. Whether Schuyler intended to build a more substantial dwelling than he had in 1777—the house that Chastellux saw and that still stands—or whether he was merely being apologetic and modest about the unfinished quarters the Frenchmen visited is not clear. But the 1777 house was not replaced, although Schuyler added a back room, a veranda, and a cookhouse to replace the cellar kitchen. The house was of course not as handsome or elegant as the mansion in Albany, but Chastellux appreciated the good rooms, which were well warmed, and an excellent supper prepared for him the evening of his arrival there. The conversation was gay and agreeable, too, "for General Schuyler, like many European husbands," he found, "is still more amiable when he is absent from his wife."[125]

More than a year later, in February 1782, Chastellux found occasion to recall his Albany visit with considerable pleasure. It had been perhaps a happy ending for another difficult year for his host. Responding to Schuyler's praise of the Frenchman's book, *De la Félicité Publique,* Chastellux lauded the Yorker's service to humanity and urged him to rely upon his own experience and judgment for guidance in politics; a reasonable constitution must be based upon more than the abstract ideas of either the ancients or modern thinkers like Locke and Montesquieu. Both local customs and habits must be consulted, and Americans, he said, would do well to look not only to the Greeks and Romans and more recent philosophers, but also to the maxims of Franklin, Adams, and to those of Schuyler himself![126]

The advice was timely. The preponderance of the general's public activities had increasingly shifted from the military arena to the political one. And when he received Chastellux's flattering encomium he happened to be sitting in the New York State Senate at Poughkeepsie. Although the state's constitution and the Confederation were already fixed, they were not unalterable. Then, as before, Schuyler was confronting constitutional issues with legislation and resolutions in an attempt to settle New York's relations with Vermont and to enlarge the powers of the Confederation government.

Leading and Misleading the Enemy

1

A System "totally inadequate to its object"

*P*rospects for the patriot cause in 1781 were dim until Washington first threatened British-held New York City and then moved to corner the enemy at Yorktown. Horatio Gates's defeat at Camden in August 1780 and then news of Arnold's betrayal had cast a pall over patriot morale. Indeed, 1780 had passed largely in stalemate or reverse for Congress, the Continental army, and New York. Currency reforms did not prevent the continued devaluation of Continental money, which became practically worthless by February 1781. Yet there were several encouraging signs on the horizon: a sizable new loan from France; the prospects of finally establishing the Articles of Confederation, which went into effect in March 1781; the organization of new executive departments, and especially the vigorous efforts of Robert Morris as superintendent of finance; and the support of French army and naval reinforcements for another campaign against the British.[1] It was the arrival of the latter that most clearly demonstrated the turning of the tide in 1781, and it was in this context that Philip Schuyler continued to play a significant role in the war from his vantage point on the New York frontier. One measure of his importance to the patriot cause is the British attempt to kidnap him in 1781. Potentially valuable to the enemy in prisoner exchanges, Schuyler was evidently regarded as a mischief-maker whose power and effectiveness in supporting the revolutionary effort were sufficiently noteworthy to make him a target for removal.

Perceiving that the root of American difficulties lay in the ineffectiveness of the government, Schuyler was convinced that the states had been

439

left with too much power under the proposed Confederation government. The crisis of the army, he thought, should prove to the states "the necessity of parting with so much of their sovereignty, respectively, as would enable the governing power to draw forth the strength and resources of the country." If, however, the alarm passed "and no adequate means are pursued for the future subsistence and pay of the army," Schuyler believed "our cause is lost, unless another system of government is adopted," and "competent powers" were lodged "somewhere" to prosecute the war with vigor and success. Only in the last session of the senate, he told Washington, he had moved to request the eastern states to hold a convention for adjusting differences on boundaries and forming a "perpetual league of incorporation, subservient, however, to the common interest of all the States." The motion was testimony to the growing despair that the Articles of Confederation might never become operative. And Schuyler wanted "to create a new State in this quarter, on conditions to be stipulated in such Convention," and the Vermont question might be resolved for the benefit of a united war effort. But realizing that the problem of power was fiscal, he proposed "to devise a fund for the redemption of common debts; to form a permanent and uniform system for drawing out the resources of the country"; and "to invest Congress with powers so extensive as to oblige each State to do its duty." Unhappily, however, the general's motion had not been brought to a decision beyond New York's agreement in 1780 to send delegates to the Hartford Convention.[2] And in little more than a month, Maryland's ratification at last brought the Confederation into existence. It was a union that Schuyler and others knew to be weak even before its birth, and the course of its short life quickly proved to them the necessity of its replacement.

However, just before the Confederation was inaugurated on 1 March, Schuyler did succeed in persuading the New York legislature to address Congress on the subject of improving powers of the union. Despite recurrent illness Schuyler was able to attend the senate throughout February and March because the session was conveniently held at Albany. There he set to work on a joint committee that was assigned to prepare an address to Congress on the pressing state of public affairs.[3]

The joint committee was directed to consider the proceedings of the Hartford Convention, held in November 1780, and on the afternoon of 2 February the senate took up the committee's report, which was a draft of a letter to be sent to Congress in support of "a solid confederation to give sufficient powers ... for calling forth the resources of the country." After the senate passed it the assembly swiftly concurred. Jubilantly, Schuyler wrote Hamilton of his success in urging the enlargement of

Congressional powers, the establishment of adequate funding for the war effort by taxing imports, and the relinquishment of land claims that would facilitate recognition of Vermont's statehood.[4]

But Schuyler's enthusiastic nationalism did not persuade Congress or other states to act accordingly. The New York legislature's address, which was read in Congress on 14 February, was shelved, and a fortnight later the Articles of Confederation went into effect. New York's governor himself squelched assembly action on Schuyler's subsequent proposal to recognize Vermont statehood. Six years later, the general described what had happened. "I beheld with Chagrin," he wrote Henry Van Schaack, "that the politicians of this state seldom if ever drew with those of the eastern states. I wished to eradicate the injurious jealously which prevailed between them and us ... But my plan was too bold to meet with success from timid politicians and such as still regarded with jealous suspicion the people of New England. In short, I failed." Almost a decade passed before leaders of the nation agreed to act upon what Schuyler "attentively considered" as soon as the Confederation "was promulgated." The system, he said "struck me as totally inadequate to its object."[5]

Meantime, as Schuyler grappled with problems of supplying the army, he also found that the Tuscarora and Oneida continued to be worrisome. On 17 January several of the tribesmen called upon him, pathetically begging for relief of their nakedness and hunger. The public stores were empty, and the general's private stock of provisions had been expended, but he promised to use his personal credit to help them. And again he begged Congress for funds, clothing, and provisions, warning that if the Oneida were driven to desperation they might join enemy parties that even then were raiding the Tryon County countryside. Happily, the aid of the assistant commissary general at Newburgh was of some help. Schuyler's senatorial office proved to be an effective instrument for obtaining assistance for the tribesmen. The legislature complied with his and Volckert Douw's petition on 24 February for clothing.[6]

Occupied with efforts to relieve the needs of both the army and the Indians and with plans for government reform, Schuyler was singularly perturbed when his new son-in-law suddenly announced his resignation as Washington's aide-de-camp. Hamilton's famous tiff with the commander in chief on 16 February was the result of youthful impatience with onerous duties and the strains of war. He wanted a post at which he might win a measure of military renown, unshadowed by his commander's stature—perhaps in the artillery or light infantry. And apparently the young man's new marital alliance brought him the kind of family security that hitherto his association with Washington had afforded. With a father-in-law who so sympathetically read his soul and had urged him "to consider me as one who wishes in every way to promote your happiness," Hamilton probably sensed a new freedom from the commander in chief. In short, Schuyler had replaced the Virginian in the role of father, mentor, and patron.[7]

Conscious that Schuyler's respect for Washington was deep and strong, Hamilton sensed the need to justify himself. His long letter to the Yorker was written freely and with full "assurance of the interest you take in all that concerns me," as he told Eliza's father. Finding no impropriety in Hamilton's conduct, Schuyler nevertheless urged reconciliation. He feared that the resignation might have harmful effects on the war effort and on the country "I love, which I affectionately love," and he urged Hamilton to reconsider. Hamilton alone had the qualifications so necessary for one serving a commanding general. Moreover, Schuyler argued, the appearances of such divisions among the patriot leaders might have ill effects on the French court and the allied officers collaborating with Washington's army. "Your services are wanted," he wrote, "in that particular station which you have ... filled so beneficially to the public, and with such extensive reputation." Let Washington's own display of anger be imputed to human frailty, the Yorker urged; drop a tear, and blot it on the page of life. The Virginian had not breathed a syllable about the quarrel, and Schuyler was certain that he must have quickly repented of his outburst. Hamilton, however, remained obdurate.[8]

For a moment in February, just before he received Hamilton's disturbing news of his resignation, Schuyler's personal affairs were brightened by his wife's safe delivery after her twelfth pregnancy. The last of their children, Catherine Van Rensselaer, was born on 20 February, and that both daughter and mother were well and strong the general gratefully deemed "beyond what is usual." The babe was the fifteenth of the Schuyler children, only eight of whom survived childbirth or infancy. Had she been a son, Schuyler intended to name the child after George Washington—his "amiable chief." Baptized on Sunday, 4 March, by the Reverend Eilardus Westerlo, the infant had as sponsors her sister Margarita; an uncle, James Van Rensselaer; and General and Mrs. Washington. Although Washington did not write his acceptance of Schuyler's request to be Catherine's godfather until 23 March, the Yorker had confidently registered the Virginian as such by proxy.[9]

Doubtless relieved for his wife's and daughter's well-being but distressed that Hamilton wished to sever ties with Washington's headquarters, Schuyler found little in the early months of 1781 that boded well for the country. The governor's handling of the Vermont question and the assembly's acquiescence were disappointing. Despite Schuyler's proposal for a settlement of the boundary dispute in 1780, nothing had been accomplished. Recognition of statehood for the Hampshire Grants, provided that New Yorkers' land titles could be adjusted, he believed was vital for strengthening the military effort and enlisting Vermonters in the defense of the frontiers. After the legislature convened on 31 January, however, he had encountered more frustration.[10]

On 21 February, at Schuyler's prompting, the senate passed three resolutions by an all but unanimous vote: that commissioners be appointed and empowered to deal with the Hampshire Grants people and their demand for statehood, and that a joint committee prepare the commissioners' instructions and the terms on which New York would cede jurisdiction; that Vermonters be invited to do likewise, defining the extent of their claims and offering proposals for settlement; and that Thomas Chittendon be requested to circulate copies of the New York offer to the people of the Hampshire Grants. On 1 March, however, Governor Clinton informed the senate that their resolutions were directly opposed to his own views of the sentiments of the New York citizenry. Referring the controversy to Congress as the proper tribunal, the governor threatened to prorogue the legislature if the assembly passed the senate resolutions.

Schuyler and the senate fought back on 12 March by considering a response to Clinton's diatribe. Two weeks later the general grumbled that "If the milky disposition of some" men saved his proposed answer to the governor from material alterations, his excellency might "wish he had not ventured on his Message." But the maneuver was evidently dropped, and the issue was simply left in the hands of Congress. Schuyler's hopes that the Vermonters might be persuaded to support the common cause went a-glimmering, and their statehood was delayed for as long as the Confederation lasted. Time would prove whether Schuyler's proposal for Vermont's statehood deserved Clinton's harsh censure and whether he or Clinton had been right in the stands that each had taken.[11] More and more the two men were slipping into political rivalry and were at loggerheads on both state issues and the wider question of national and state sovereignty.

In the matter of strengthening the newly emerging Confederation government, Schuyler managed to some extent to offset his frustration over the Hampshire Grants issue. He and Egbert Benson persuaded the New York legislature to declare its willingness to confer adequate powers on Congress; and when the national assembly requested authority to lay a five percent impost, the legislature granted it on 19 March 1781, which was the very day on which they received the governor's announcement that the Confederation had at last been established.[12]

There were of course other measures that Schuyler supported in the state senate and that revealed both his commitment to the war effort and the legislature's willingness to support it. Because the Hartford Convention had recommended price-fixing legislation and "strict laws against engrossing and withholding" in 1780, the New York legislature finally decided to approve the convention proceedings, deeming them favorable to the interests of the United States. However, senators fell into debate on an assembly resolution stating that it was unnecessary to send commissioners to another convention of states then scheduled to meet at Providence on 12 April. Schuyler opposed the resolution and its argument that New York need not name the commissioners because French authorities had already contracted with individuals in the state to supply their fleet and army. But only two of his fellow senators, Abraham Yates, Jr., and Abraham Ten Broeck agreed with him; others seemed content to wait for the Confederation to function under the newly ratified Articles.[13]

Despite the legislature's favorable action respecting the fiscal powers of Congress, Schuyler felt that it had not gone far enough. The effort to expel the enemy could not be effective, he thought, unless Congress was vested with more powers by "Additional articles of confederation." Schuyler was pleased, however, that Congress had decided to create "great officers" of state instead of relying on a committee system for executive action. If the proper persons were chosen as ministers of war, finance, foreign affairs, and the navy, order and economy might yet prevail.[14]

The question of the moment was "Who were the proper persons to choose" as great officers of state? Washington, for one, thought Schuyler had the qualifications to serve; on 20 February he wrote the Yorker of his "infinite pleasure (though no nomination has yet taken place) that you are generally spoken of for the department of War. At the same time I learn with pain," the Virginian added, "from Colo. Hamilton that your acceptance of it is doubtful if the Choice should fall on you. I am perfectly aware of all your objections ... but they ought not to prevail."[15]

Congress, however, moved with characteristic speed. Having named Robert Morris superintendent of finance and Alexander MacDougall secretary of marine in February, it delayed the choosing of a foreign secretary (Robert R. Livingston) until August and a secretary at war (Benjamin Lincoln) until October. Concerning the latter position Gouverneur Morris observed on 14 March that he doubted "whether Schuyler will be nominated, I think Greene will be the man." Morris of course misjudged Nathanael Greene's chances, but he was correct about Schuyler's. By April the motives of Congress for delay had leaked out: Horatio Gates was a prime candidate. In light of imputations of misconduct after Gates's flight from the British at Camden in 1780, Schuyler believed that partisans were disregarding the public interest; Gates's inabilities would prove a disgrace, and "the inveterate enmity" Gates bore Washington would "lead him, without hesitation, to reject or thwart the most salutary measures" that the commander in chief might propose. "Gracious God!" Schuyler erupted, "How much it is to be lamented that rulers charged with the affairs of an empire, will sacrifice the best interests of their constituents to little, narrow-minded prejudices and local politics, favorable only to their unworthy sycophants!" The Yorker also feared that Gates would embarrass the superintendent of finance, for "he has not the least idea of public economy ... nor do I believe that they entertain much esteem for each other."[16]

Fortunately Schuyler's excitement was unnecessary because Benjamin Lincoln finally received the office. The episode was however yet another example of the perilous state of American affairs in government and military organization in 1781. More than two years later Samuel Osgood, congressman from Massachusetts, observed that had "Genl. Schuyler, who nearly carried the Choice, been plac'd in that Office, It is a great Question in my Mind, whether it would have been practicable for Congress to have disbanded their Army! The Financier only wanted a Person in that Office who would go any Lengths with him."[17]

In the meantime Robert R. Livingston again urged Schuyler to accept a place on New York's delegation to Congress, which was a responsibility the general steadfastly refused. Clearly he was not interested in the war department either. For the moment his public services would be focused largely on the state of New York. In spite of his increasing disagreement with Governor Clinton over issues like that of the Hampshire Grants, no clear partisan breach had yet been made between them. On 30 March Clinton and the council of appointment named Schuyler state surveyor general, which was an old colonial office that had been renewed by act of the legislature ten days earlier. Accepting the post with no apparent hesitation, the general decided that he must do so partly to prevent an "improper" person from being named instead. Anticipating the legislature's recess, he professed himself "that Happy man whose wish and care, a few paternal acres bound, Content to breathe his native air, on his own ground." James Duane might think his friend on the point "of departing for that country from which none ever returns" when Schuyler told him he could not "take more than one, or two Glasses of Madeira at most; my Disorders indeed increase but my spirits are good and I am determined as the saying goes, to live all the days of my life, that is cheerfully and gayly without suffering myself to be tormented with fruitlessly repining at what heaven has decreed."[18]

But Schuyler was incapable of living as cheerfully and gaily as he said he wished. Even when his aid and advice were not solicited for the war effort, he was ever attentive to the opportunities to offer them. Thus, for example, he assisted Brig. Gen. James Clinton in procuring flour for the Albany garrison and advising him of the need for erecting fortifications. As May lengthened into June, Schuyler returned to Albany to carry on the work with which he had been so engrossed at Saratoga. Soon he must attend another meeting of the legislature, but he and Mrs. Schuyler were also expecting the arrival of their daughter Angelica, who was sent home by her husband John Church before "her Situation" made the journey from Newport, Rhode Island "too fatiguing." With her came Schuyler's first grandchildren, Philip, John, and Catherine, aged three, two, and one respectively. And in July Elizabeth Hamilton also returned to Albany, making the family circle of five sisters and three brothers once more complete.[19]

The particular timing of Schuyler's departure from Saratoga in May, however, seems to have been decided by the onset of a quinsey attack. Severely stricken by fever and swelling of the throat just after he reached Albany on the evening of 27 May, he was bled twice in an attempt to prevent suffocation. Three days later he reported to James Duane that the enemy was assembled "in force" at Crown Point; to Alexander Hamilton he wrote that their numbers might be as great as two thousand. The frontiers were undefended, and Schuyler expected that the area south to Halfmoon and Schenectady soon would be ravaged. He had not yet, however, taken his "Servants & Effects" from Saratoga lest, as he said, "the whole country ... follow my example." But the Yorker was determined that if the Saratoga garrison were removed, he would "order all my people & Stock down, persuaded that in less than six days after the removal of the troops the Enemy will be down."[20]

Schuyler himself was already a marked man. In early May Sir John Johnson was preparing another foray into the Mohawk valley from Montreal. On 3 May he informed Gen. Frederick Haldimand that he intended to send Philip Lansing with about sixteen men to destroy the mills and other buildings at Saratoga and "to bring off Mr. Schuyler, if there." Lansing, a Loyalist, had fled to the enemy in July 1780 and was well acquainted with Schuyler's property; he assured Johnson that he could accomplish both of these errands in one stroke.[21] It was well, then, that the Yorker returned to Albany at the end of May for the sake of both his safety and his health.

2

Senator, Supplier, Spy

Momentarily, the range of Schuyler's activities once more widened when Robert Morris, agent of Pennsylvania and Congress's "Financier," called upon him for assistance in supporting Washington's army. For years the squire of Saratoga had furnished supplies to the army, some of which were sold from his farms and mills, and others provided by the extension of his personal credit.[22] And he had repeatedly promised to aid the war effort in whatever way he could as a private citizen after refusing to accept further official military duties. Now he was to aid in collecting flour, contracting supplies for the peaceful Indians, and building bateaux for the main army poised on the lower Hudson.

When Morris appealed to Schuyler for help on 29 May, the army needed flour, but the treasury was empty and without credit. As he knew of no "Gent[lema]n of Such Resource as Genl. Schuyler," Morris applied to him as "the most likely of all men to give assistance under the present Circumstances." Specifically, that meant collecting a thousand barrels of flour on the most reasonable terms practicable and without delay. Until there was time to raise the hard money to pay for it, Morris assumed that Schuyler could extend his personal credit either to "borrow the Money for a few months ... or ... make the purchases on Such Credit without giving higher prices." For his reimbursement, Schuyler might take Morris "as a Public or a private Man for I pledge my Self to repay you with hard Money wholly if required or part hard part paper if so you transact the business."[23]

Although Morris was obliged to wait for some weeks for an answer, he was not disappointed; Schuyler found the flour and also offered his advice on the business of contracting. His expenditures in obtaining flour for Morris in August 1781 amounted to £2,133.17.3. Calculated at eight shillings to the dollar, the total was reckoned at $5,334.48/90.[24]

Whether at the national or state level of politics and government, Schuyler could not escape confrontation of economic and fiscal problems. Such were among the major items of business of the New York legislature when it met again in June 1781. As ever, ways and means must be devised to support the war effort. And some kind of action must be taken to deal with the people on the Hampshire Grants.

Almost immediately Schuyler was assigned to three committees charged with responding to business that had been announced by the governor; all were of considerable importance: supplies for the army, the

Fig. 11. Gouverneur and Robert Morris, 1752–1816, 1734–1806. Oil on canvas by Charles Willson Peale. Schuyler was able to assist Robert Morris by purchasing over £2,000 of flour for the army when the young nation's treasury was depleted. Courtesy, The Pennsylvania Academy of the Fine Arts. Bequest of Richard Ashhurst.

Hampshire Grants, and general finance.[25] The Yorker's particular knowledge of these subjects and his active interest in them were applied effectively, and he pressed for actions that were taken before he was obliged to leave the senate after 28 June, although several were not completed until 1 July, when the legislature adjourned.

At Schuyler's urgings the laws prohibiting the shipment of provisions outside the state were repealed, and a new act was passed for obtaining flour for the army along the lines he had sketched for Robert Morris, which stipulated that troops be ordered to assist farmers in harvesting and threshing their grain. The senate's response to the issue of the Hampshire Grants was not made until 30 June, several days after Schuyler had left Poughkeepsie. However, this did not result in the kind of settlement the general advocated. By resolution on that day Congress must "cause" Vermonters "to desist" from all attempts to extend a "usurped jurisdiction" over New York inhabitants who as of 24 September 1779 had claimed to be "subjects of this state." Alluding to New York and congressional legislation passed in 1779–80, the resolution insisted that Congress had been authorized to settle boundary disputes, equitably determining the claims of grantees of Massachusetts, New Hampshire, and New York.[26]

But the business was not speedily concluded. Although Congress offered on 20 August to recognize the new state if she would relinquish claims to New Hampshire lands east of the Connecticut River, Vermonters balked. After further efforts to reach a solution in 1782 the stalemate lingered until a new Congress under a new constitution resolved it in 1791.[27]

More urgent perhaps, and no less difficult a matter, was the problem of finance. It was the most complicated of the issues with which Schuyler and both senate and assembly dealt in June 1781. Without a seaport (which was occupied by enemy forces), it was impossible to obtain specie through ordinary commercial activity or to levy taxes in specie. The use of paper currency, however, raised the question of checking depreciation. On the other hand, New York was obliged to act in accord with Congress's March 1781 directions, and interest due on Continental emissions remaining in the state loan office must be paid in specie. Schuyler's finance committee recommended that the state treasurer be authorized to exchange up to $8,225,000 in old Continental bills for new ones bearing interest in specie, and that all references in state legislation (passed before or after 4 July 1776) to paper currency as legal tender be repealed.[28]

The senate quickly agreed to bills repealing legal tender laws and enabling the treasurer to exchange old Continental currency for new bills in the state loan office. And the assembly and council of revision concurred. But a proposal to levy taxes in specie and in paper currency raised considerable disputation.[29]

On 27 June Sen. Abraham Yates, Jr., proposed that instead of assessing real estate at its value over and above the debts or liabilities of the owner's personal estate, the assessments should be made according to the estate and "other circumstances and abilities" of the owner to pay taxes. Schuyler resisted this scheme unsuccessfully, the senate dividing eight to seven in favor of Yates's motion. Another division arose on the specie amount to be assessed on each $100 of property valuation according to old Continental currency. Schuyler agreed with William Floyd's move to set it at four shillings instead of 8/6, as proposed by a committee of the whole. This time his vote fell with the majority, which passed Floyd's motion ten to six. The votes on these two questions suggest the existence of two senatorial blocks whose members tended to vote together although they came from all four senatorial districts of the state: Abraham Yates, Jr., and five supporters, and Schuyler with five. A third group fluctuated between them.[30]

The Senate was obliged to give way to the assembly's objections to several amendments it made to the tax bill, but after Schuyler's departure the council of revision vetoed the measure. The council explained the veto by arguing that the bill perpetuated inequalities in the distribution of taxes among the various towns and other units of the state; and it failed to afford the latter a means of redressing grievances. The veto apparently vindicated Schuyler's opposition to the earlier Yates motion that assessments be made according to the estate and "other circumstances and abilities" of the owners to pay taxes. But the legislature promptly overrode the veto and repassed the act to raise a tax in both specie and paper currency.[31]

Meantime, however, Schuyler had obtained leave from the senate in order to undertake yet another assignment from the commander in chief. The Virginian's plans for cooperation with Rochambeau's army to recover Manhattan from the British required bateaux with which to maneuver troops on the lower Hudson. Having corresponded with the Yorker, he also visited Poughkeepsie to discuss the boat-building project. Congress would be asked to pay for it. In an interview with Governor Clinton, Lt. Gov. Pierre Van Cortlandt, Sen. Abraham Ten Broeck, and Schuyler on 25 June, Washington also explained that he must summon Continental regiments from Albany and the posts above the city, and he pressed for speedy recruitment of more New York troops. To replace the regulars drawn from the north Washington agreed to order up six hundred militia from Berkshire and Hampshire counties in Massachusetts. And he discussed the prospects of Schuyler's success in filling Robert Morris' pleas for flour. Later he referred Brig. Gen. John Stark to the Yorker for advice on redistribution of troops along the frontiers and for help in obtaining supplies. These, then, were the pressing reasons for Schuyler's early departure from the legislative session.[32]

Characteristically, the senator fell to work energetically, using his interest and credit to push the repair and building of boats for the projected campaign along the lower Hudson. The work proved onerous, for there were delays in hiring carpenters and providing nails, oakum, and other materials. As usual Schuyler also had to satisfy wage demands with his own pledges. Still, by 21 July he was able to report to Washington that the bateaux were completed and were being sent down river. By that time the French and American armies had assembled above Manhattan. Nor was this the only service Schuyler rendered to Washington during this period. Avidly collecting and distributing information about British movements from Canada into upper New York State, he also intercepted communications between generals Frederick Haldimand at Quebec and Henry Clinton in New York City. Since his establishment of connections in Canada during his active command of the Northern Army from 1775 to 1777, he had continued a secret correspondence.[33]

Because of his efforts, Schuyler's safety was frequently threatened; in May 1781 he was again assigned a guard at Saratoga and at Albany. Again in January 1782, when Washington issued orders for the guard, Schuyler wrote him that "It is now a notorious fact, that three parties have been expressly sent from Canada to take or put me to death." Several persons returning to New York from Canada agreed in their reports that the British were determined to capture him, and after a major attempt to do so, the general urged Washington not to leave him without adequate protection. As late as the spring of 1782 the commander in chief was still issuing instructions for guarding his New York friend.[34]

Perhaps the principal reason for enemy attempts to kidnap Schuyler was his effectiveness as an intelligencer. One of his spies was a Monsieur L'Eglise, and some of the links in Schuyler's intelligence network were doubtless forged as a part of his involvement with prisoner exchange. In addition, as a member of the Board of Indian Commissioners of the Northern Department and as a man familiar with the country north and west of Albany, the general was particularly knowledgeable of the territory and its inhabitants. And of course, there was another side to the gathering of intelligence; Schuyler occasionally found himself interrogating disaffected Americans and spies who were intercepted in their operations out of Canada.[35]

In May 1781 the general continued his surveillance of British forces, which were poised at Crown Point, providing Washington and Governor Clinton with reports of the enemy's attempts to loosen Vermonters' tenuous ties to the revolutionary cause. Although he did not reproach Clinton for his short-sighted refusal to negotiate with the Vermonters, Schuyler must have seen the irony of the governor's reliance upon him for information on how to deal with these troublesome neighbors. At Saratoga he insisted that troops were needed on the northern frontiers.[36]

As the days slipped by, the dangers mounted. By 21 May as Washington and Rochambeau conferred at Wethersfield, Connecticut, on the impending campaign, Schuyler had received a warning from Ethan Allen that the British were seeking his capture. This caution was a puzzling gesture in light of Ira Allen's dickerings with the British at Isle aux Noix for a cessation of hostilities and an exchange of prisoners, and reports that the Vermonters neither wanted assistance from New York State nor would they give any. Schuyler lingered at Saratoga until the end of May, partly because he feared his departure would spark a general flight of the inhabitants, and partly because the danger might be surmounted if the enemy did not press their advantage and if American troops arrived in time. Meanwhile, he tried to rally forces to resist the expected British invasion, sending out scouts and relaying news of each new development to Washington, Governor Clinton, and local military commanders. The enemy was expected to attack in the Mohawk valley as well as along the Lake Champlain basin.[37]

With the evacuation of Fort Schuyler in the Mohawk valley in May, the Yorker's fears were aggravated from still another direction. The move would inspire the enemy and their "savage" allies in the west with a "belief that our cause is becoming desperate." A small hostile party was hovering around Saratoga, and Schuyler hoped to capture them under cover of darkness. The enemy's strength was uncertain, but their campfires indicated a large force, later estimated two thousand.[38] But not until June did Washington order Gen. John Stark to Saratoga, and not until July did Stark begin his assignment there, comfortably quartered in Schuyler's house.

3

"Calculated to Mislead the Enemy"

Of all Schuyler's efforts at operating a private intelligence system none was more curious than his endeavor in July to mislead the British by furnishing them with deceptive "information" about movements intended by Rochambeau's and Washington's armies. While they with the bulk of the revolutionary forces had concentrated their efforts on the liberation of New York City, active operations had generally shifted to the South, where Nathanael Greene, commander of the Southern Department, and his subordinates, Daniel Morgan and Henry Lee, used guerrila tactics to

wear down Cornwallis in the Carolinas. After his Pyhrric victory at Guil-
ford Courthouse on 15 March 1781, Cornwallis moved into Virginia in an
effort to end the use of that area as a training ground and supply depot
for the patriot army, choosing Yorktown as a base from which to establish
communications by sea with Sir Henry Clinton in New York.

In March 1781 Washington had decided that the most powerful diversion possible in favor of the South would be a strong force pressing on
New York City; this might prevent Clinton from aiding Cornwallis and
enable the allies to strike a decisive blow at Sir Henry. While proceeding
with these arrangements, the Virginian received news that the Comte
de Grasse would lead his fleet from the West Indies to the North American
coast for a limited time beginning about mid-July. On 25 June Washington
met New York State authorities at Poughkeepsie, explaining his plans to
recall regiments from Albany and other western posts for support of the
main army and requesting speedy recruitment of new state levies. The
best that could be managed for the frontier was the dispatch of six
hundred Berkshire and Hampshire militiamen to Albany. Washington
ordered Gen. John Stark to seek Schuyler's advice on matters of supply
and the disposition of troops along the frontiers. Unfortunately, by the
end of July, Washington's request to John Hancock for the Massachusetts
militia had not yet been answered, and he was obliged to repeat it.[39]

At mid-July Schuyler attempted what must be the least well known
hoax of the war. It was a simple design to plant "information" in British
hands—a letter to the commander in chief "Calculated to Mislead the
Enemy with respect to Gen: Washington's Intentions." Although "Directed to the Genl," the missive was "carried to the Enemy." In it Schuyler
discussed what appeared to be plans for the French fleet to attack Quebec
while one American force penetrated Canada from Cohoes and another
made a feinting movement against Manhattan to keep the British
occupied there.[40]

Evidence of the effect of this letter upon the British high command is
lacking, but the missive did reach enemy lines and finally came to rest in
the papers of Gen. Frederick Haldimand. And it indicates Schuyler's activities on behalf of the American cause, his close cooperation with Washington, and a reason for the enemy's interest in plucking this nettle out
of their path. It is not altogether certain what Schuyler meant by endorsing his own copy of the letter "carried to the Enemy," for it is not
clear to which quarter it was really directed. That it was "Calculated to
Mislead" the British with respect to Washington's intentions is obvious
enough. Perhaps he and Schuyler had arranged the scheme when the two
had conferred at Poughkeepsie with Governor Clinton and others late in

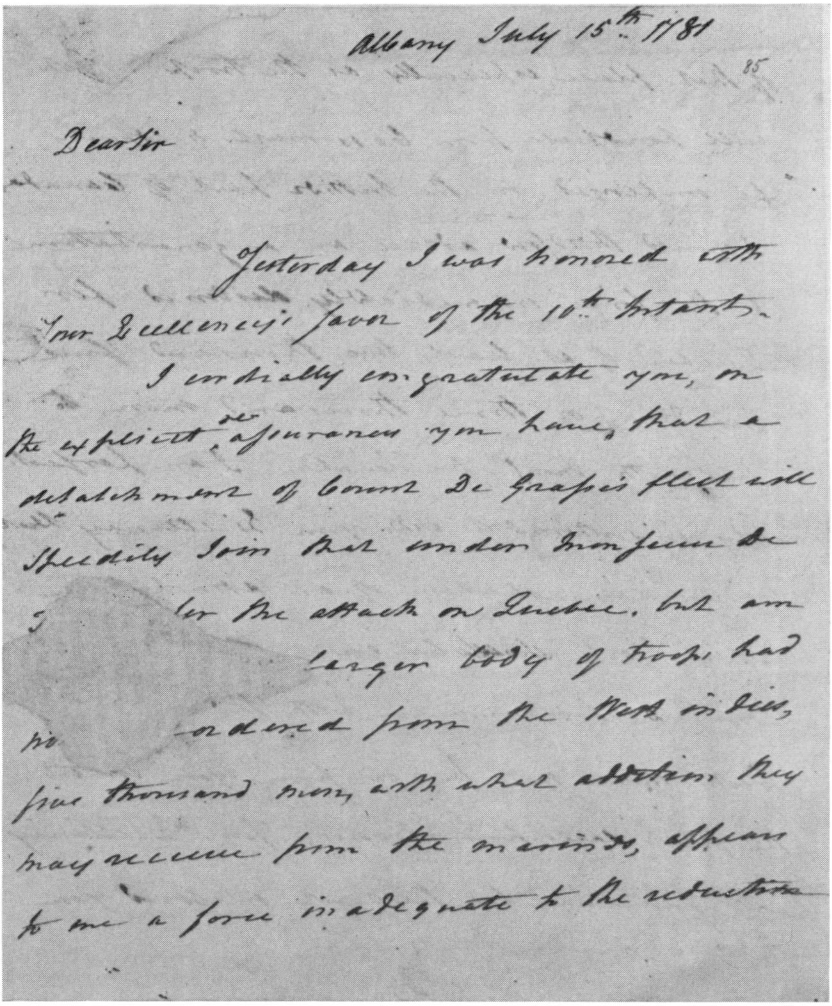

Fig. 12. Schuyler's letter, July 15, 1781. Albany, New York. Schuyler's letter to mislead the British on the 1781 Campaign. By permission of the British Library, Add. Man. 21794 ff 85–86v.

June. Perhaps Schuyler's plan was to get British troops in upper New York State withdrawn to Canada, thus relieving the northern frontier of pressures that also inhibited Washington's maneuvers on the lower Hudson, or it may have been simply an attempt to sow confusion at enemy headquarters.

Washington and Rochambeau continued to prepare an assault on New York City, but late in July a reconnaissance of the British lines found them to be discouragingly strong. The Virginian's best chances still lay with de Grasse's bringing up his fleet from the West Indies. As July turned to August, part of the Second New York Regiment (carried by the bateaux that Schuyler had constructed at Albany) arrived at Washington's head-quarters, and at about the same time the Albany County Commissioners for Detecting and Defeating Conspiracies received information that a raiding party had been sent to kidnap or assassinate Philip Schuyler.[41]

4

A "happy escape"

Although evidence of British designs on Schuyler dates from the spring of 1781, it is difficult to trace the origins of these schemes with much precision. The earliest document tying them to official British sources appears to be Sir John Johnson's 3 May letter to the British commander in chief in Canada, Frederick Haldimand, proposing to raid Saratoga and capture the prominent Yorker. On 15 May Ethan Allen wrote Schuyler that British forces at Crown Point, who had threatened several times "to Captivate your person, said that it had been in their power to have taken some of your family [during] the last campaign, but that they had an Eye to your self." Although Allen thought the remarks indicative more of "flummery than real premeditated design," the Yankee deemed the Yorker worthy of the warning.[42]

By May 29 May Schuyler was assured that he was marked for capture. Soon after he returned to Albany, on 27 May, the general took precautions to defend his house, which lay at the south edge of the city. By early July he had also been assigned a guard from the Second New York Regiment stationed at Albany. Then, on 29 July the Albany County Commissioners for Detecting and Defeating Conspiracies discovered that a party from Canada led by a Captain Myers of Rogers's Rangers was lurking in the wilds near Albany, intending to capture or assassinate their fellow citizen. The news agreed with intelligence received by Gen. James Clinton that the government in Canada had placed a price of two hundred guineas on Schuyler's head. On 5 August Maj. John McKinstry, commander of troops at Saratoga, wrote him by "express" that another party, captained by one John Jones, was also after him. Expecting Schuyler to return to Saratoga, the enemy was ready to intercept him. McKinstry surmised that "their intention is to Make prisoner of a Number of the Principle [*sic*] inhabitanc [*sic*] Near this place as a proof of which they have taken Esqr. Blaker [John Bleecker] of Tomhanock last Friday."[43] The general, however, did not expose himself by leaving the safety of his Albany home, and it was there that a violent assault was launched on 7 August.

A considerable legend arose in the aftermath of this attack, most of it recorded in the reminiscences of the general's youngest daughter, Catherine, who was not six months old at the time of the raid.[44] Schuyler's own accounts of the affair form the solid core of evidence of what happened. The first of these, written in the excitement of the hour, reveals the bare outline of the episode; others sent to Washington and Governor

Clinton provide details that could be set down only in calmer moments on 8 and 9 August. Finally, on the British side, Col. Barry St. Leger's record contains several points that corroborate the major outlines of the miscarried coup.

At 9:00 o'clock on Tuesday evening, 7 August, Schuyler penned an alarm to Henry Glen of Schenectady. Sent by "express," his message announced,

> An hour ago I was attacked by [John] Waltemyer and a party of about twenty, one of my people bravely defended a door which gave time for me to gain my room, where I remained without their attempting me [.] by Firing I allarmed the town which turn[ed] out with alacrity and expedition. The villains carried of[f] one of my men, wounded another, and took some of my plate. I have to Intreat you to request the Oneidas[,] Tuscarroras, and Cajhnwajas to turn out. I wish them to divide Into parties one towards the Wellsbergh [Hellsbergh? Helderberg?] another towards Canistighenna and a third to Cross the river towards balls town [Ballston]. They must take up every suspected person. [P.S.] Please to make my compliments to Colo. Wimple, and request him to send a few militia out with the Indians.[45]

The bare bones of this message can be appreciated only by imagining the reactions of Schuyler's family and household retainers who were confronted by the attackers. Aside from the four guards and perhaps at least a half-dozen servants, the domestic circle included the general and his wife and probably all of their children, because their two married daughters, Angelica and Elizabeth, had recently arrived for a visit. Margarita, as yet unwed, and Cornelia, almost six, were present, as was the infant Catherine. Angelica and Elizabeth were both pregnant; the former's children, Philip, age three, John, two, and Catherine Church, one, were also at hand. The general's three sons, John B., age sixteen; Philip Jeremiah, age thirteen, and Rensselaer, age eight, were probably present too, although the eldest may have been visiting relatives. In all, some two dozen souls were a part of the uproar, terrorized and shaken.

The next day Schuyler wrote Washington for authorization to continue a guard provided earlier by Brig. Gen. Clinton and telling him of the events of the previous evening. "Myers" and about twenty men forced the backyard gate and then the kitchen door. Four white servants "flew to their arms" and resisted the invaders at the door. This gave Schuyler the opportunity "to retire out" of the hall on the main floor, where he had been at supper, and into an upstairs bedroom where he kept his arms.

Two of the general's retainers were captured, a third was wounded, and one was forced to flee into the cellar with Schuyler's Negro slaves. Evidently some of the attackers surrounded the house while others ventured indoors. Schuyler gave the alarm from an upstairs window, and those exposed to his fire drew back, while others who "got into the saloon [upper hallway] to attempt as I suppose the room I was in retreated with precipitation as soon as they heard me call [']come on my lads Surround the house the villains are in it.['] This I did to make them believe that succour was at hand and It had the desired effects." As the raiders retreated, they carried off two of Schuyler's men and plundered some of his silver. Militia from the town soon appeared to take up the chase but were too late to catch the culprits.[46]

On 9 August the general recounted the story to Governor Clinton and also informed him of John Bleecker's kidnapping. Vermonters, however, captured the "Bleecker party" and discovered that it was following orders from Col. Barry St. Leger at St. John's. Schuyler looked to his own defenses; with a guard supplied by Brig. Gen. James Clinton, he vowed that if "these kidnapping Gentry" made another attempt, "they will not be able to retire with impunity." Governor Clinton responded on 14 August, congratulating Schuyler on his escape and announcing that he had been warned that a party had been sent from New York City to seize him also. Taken together, these projects suggest a concerted attempt on the enemy's part to demoralize the New York revolutionary effort. Simultaneously, a party of 300 Indians and 90 Tories was launched from Niagara, striking as far east and south as Ulster County. The attempt, however, failed, and the governor directed Birg. Gen. Peter Gansevoort to send part of his militia brigade to Schoharie until it became certain that the raiders had left the frontiers.[47]

On 17 August Col. Barry St. Leger wrote a slightly different version of what had happened in the Albany venture. "Myers" reached St. Leger's post at St. John's that morning, explaining that his party had been "too small to Effect his Purpose, Sch[u]ylers House being too large to be invested by a few Men by which Means he Escaped by a back Window." "Myers" was evidently confused about the Yorker's movements, or was inventing excuses for his failure to achieve his ends. "The Attack and defense of the House was bloody and obstinate, on both sides, when the doors were forced the Servants fought till they were all wounded or disarm[e]d. The uproar of Mrs. Schuyler And the cries of the children obliged them to retire with their two prisoners being the only persons that cou[l]d be mov[e]d on Account of their Wounds; two Men of the 34th were slightly wounded."[48]

Fig. 13. Schuyler's Albany residence was the scene of an attempt by Tory rangers to capture him on 7 August 1781. Today the house is a museum, located at 32 Catherine Street.

When Hamilton heard of his father-in-law's "happy escape," he wrote Eliza that her father had shown "an admirable presence of mind, and has given his friends a double pleasure arising from the manner of saving himself and his safety." Hamilton was "glad this unsuccessful attempt has been made." Perhaps it would prevent Schuyler "hazarding himself here-after as he has been accustomed to do. He is a character too valuable to be trifled with, and owes it to his country and to his family to be upon his guard."[49]

The attack on Schuyler's house, when combined with other develop-ments in August, occasioned further alarm. The inhabitants of Albany feared that their city would soon suffer a similar danger, and there were rumors of a design to burn it. The county commissioners for defeating conspiracies investigated these allegations and discovered they were related to the assault on Schuyler. Thus Mayor Abraham Ten Broeck, one of the general's oldest friends, finally asked him to intercede with Washington in an effort to have Gen. John Stark leave a company of levies in the city. Although raised for duty on the frontier, the men were wanted to guard public buildings and protect a variety of stores and stocks of arms.[50] Albany, however, reamined unharmed, and autumn fell before there were any more significant enemy forays on the New York frontiers.

5

A Critical Crisis on the Frontiers

Despite his concern for expelling the enemy from New York City, Washington was forced to seize the initiative elsewhere and to leave Schuyler and the northern frontier to their small defenses. Although the bateaux constructed at Albany were ready for the crossing on the lower Hudson, Washington's army was deficient in numbers because the states had failed to furnish their quotas, and he could not attack. Then by mid-August the Virginian and Rochambeau learned that de Grasse was leaving the West Indies with almost thirty warships and three thousand troops but would proceed only as far as Chesapeake Bay. As he also knew that Sir Henry Clinton's army in New York City was being reinforced, Washington decided to leave twenty-five hundred men to guard the Hudson Highlands and to throw the rest of his strength against Cornwallis. By mid-September the American forces joined their French allies in Virginia to begin the struggle. The French army and navy units, vastly superior to the Americans in both manpower and equipment, decided the campaign, and before Clinton's British reinforcements could reach Yorktown by sea, Cornwallis surrendered on 19 October.[51]

Although the decisive victory was being won, events in New York State and elsewhere during and immediately after the Yorktown campaign indicated that the war was far from ended. Minor military operations might yet have a serious impact on the terms of peacemaking. Philip Schuyler not only contributed to the general effort but also demonstrated an awareness that circumstances could still alter the victory of the moment.

On 18 August the general hastily set out from Albany for Washington's headquarters, which was then still on the lower Hudson. At King's Ferry he witnessed the allied armies' crossing of the North River from 23 to 25 August. Happy to see his father-in-law before moving south with the army, Hamilton had hoped his wife would accompany Schuyler on the jaunt down the Hudson. "Your father," he wrote, "has been as usual kind. He has offered me an order for money on Mr. [Robert] Morris, and has given me liberty to draw on him, though I shall probably not make use of it."[52]

Schuyler missed seeing the superintendent of finance, which had been one of the particular purposes of his trip from Albany. With Morris he had hoped to make further arrangements for the purchase of flour for the army and the needy Indians at Schenectady. After returning to Albany, Schuyler submitted accounts to Morris by messenger, requested him to honor a draft for $220 in specie, and continued his efforts to feed the Oneida and Tuscarora Indians as well as to settle accounts of the workmen who had built the bateaux for Washington. Similarly, the general remained attentive to his intelligence network.[53]

As the allied forces began to close in on Yorktown during September, an uneasy quiet prevailed on the New York frontier. Schuyler informed General Heath, commanding in the Highlands; Governor Clinton; and Brig. Gen. John Stark, who was then at Saratoga; that it appeared the British intended to attack Vermonters for having duped them in negotiations. The arrival at St. John's of a brigade from Quebec suggested the likelihood of fresh attacks along the Mohawk and Hudson valleys. The Yorker proposed that General Fellows's militia be called into readiness. Thinking that "something is on the wing," John Stark relayed the warnings to Governor Chittendon of Vermont, asking him to direct the frontier troops to watch the enemy. Thus Schuyler's secret service work continued, and by helping to guard the north country, he contributed to the substance of the southern victory when it was won in October.[54]

"No one should underestimate the terrific strain" that Schuyler, Governor Clinton, Col. Marinus Willett, and Maj. Gen. William Heath were under in the late summer and early fall of 1781. Enemy forces at New York City were over sixteen thousand strong and ready to move. It is difficult to say what kept Sir Henry Clinton in the city (except for his attempt to relieve Cornwallis), when he might have offset the Yorktown disaster by seizing West Point from Heath's twenty-five hundred Continentals, or even Albany. Perhaps too irresolute, except for his determination to hold New York City at all costs, he was preoccupied with the events in Virginia. Then Yorktown "brought Clinton's distress of mind to a climax," and he worried over who would be blamed for it.[55] Haldimand made good a promised diversion by launching forces south into New York from Canada, but the British in the southern reaches of the state made no effort to take advantage of this maneuver.

In mid-September 1781 alarm again spread in Albany that enemy parties were lurking about, intending to burn the city. Schuyler persuaded General Stark to leave new militia reinforcements in Albany until it was absolutely certain that they were needed at Saratoga. Noting that "all here is quiet except small parties on the frontiers," Schuyler thought that if the southern campaign could be expedited, Rochambeau and an American-French army might still launch an invasion of Canada. Rochambeau's former "fellow-citizens" might thus be freed "from the british government, most truly tyrannical."[56] It is clear that the Yorker had not surrendered his conviction that the persistent frontier threat warranted a major campaign in the north.

Schuyler was concerned not only for the outcome of the war. The convening of the legislature in October, he observed, would enable friends to propose Hamilton for election as a delegate to Congress. If Cornwallis could be beaten, peace was probable, and Schuyler "earnestly" wished to see Hamilton seated in the national council. Without an American victory, however, he was certain that his son-in-law should remain in the army. But the Yorker's political ambition for Hamilton proved a trifle premature. The legislature's choice of congressmen fell upon James Duane, William Floyd, John Morin Scott, Ezra L'Hommedieu, and Egbert Benson. Although the assembly nominated Schuyler instead of Benson, who was the senate's choice, Benson was finally elected by a joint ballot.[57]

Meantime, as the general shared his military and political views with Hamilton, there was family news to pass along. Schuyler's other son-in-law, John Barker Church, whom he continued to call by his alias, "Carter," might be relieved to know that he had become the father of a "fine boy" on 15 September. Church and Jeremiah Wadsworth, like Hamilton, were then with Rochambeau's army. But while Hamilton led a corps of artillery, they were making a fortune, contracting for provisions. Mrs. Church had not only presented her parents with their latest grandson but with all four of their first grandchildren. Now, at 48, Schuyler was looking forward to another grandson, this time from Hamilton's Eliza. And he was soon to be satisfied. The Hamilton's first child, a son, was born in January 1782, and like the Churches' firstborn he was named Philip after his maternal grandfather.[58]

Coincidentally, it seems, Schuyler's attention to family affairs and the prospects for enlarging his brood of grandchildren extended to yet another of his famous sons-in-law. Young Stephen Van Rensselaer, the last patroon, was about to leave for Boston in September 1781, and the general armed him with letters of recommendation to several gentlemen of his acquaintance there. Van Rensselaer was to graduate from Harvard College in 1782, and in June 1783 he married the Schuylers' third daughter, Margarita, when she was nearly twenty-five and he not yet twenty. Stephen's sister Elizabeth in turn married their son, John Bradstreet in 1787. Although this liaison could hardly have been imagined in 1781 (when he was sixteen and she only thirteen), Schuyler was perhaps already aware of the seventeen-year-old manor lord's attractions to a twenty-three-year-old spinster, and he offered him some appropriate fatherly advice. His 18 September letter tells us perhaps as much about himself as it does about the scion of a notable and ancient Albany family.

"An unbecoming forwardness in a young Gentlemen," Schuyler began,

> altho more odious is hardly more prejudicial, than in Improper backwardness. Of the first I am persuaded you are incapable of being guilty. The latter may proceed from virtuous motives, but must still be considered as a misfortune. If you labour under it, you ought to take measures to conquer it, and none will be more likely than to Associate with men [of] reputation and virtue. The contrary characters I believe you abhor. I am sure you and every young Gentleman ought to detest them, for they can, and will inspire you with sentiments Inevitably destructive to your peace and happiness, and tending to bring yourself into Contempt And anguish to your friends, amongst whom I wish to be considered. Pardon this liberty. It proceeds from a heart that wishes you honor & happiness.[59]

It was sound counsel, and Schuyler may well have given it fully expecting the lad to join the ranks of his other sons-in-law. Without clear vision of the particulars of Van Rensselaer's career, he might well have contemplated the outlines of opportunity and privilege that made the patroon a member of the legislature, lieutenant governor of New York, and United States congressman. But for the moment, there were more pressing matters with which the general must be concerned.

As September waned, further news of enemy activities at St. John's and of raiding parties along the Mohawk and Lake Champlain served as a prelude to the last significant enemy threat to upper New York State. Anxious to provide permanently established forces on the frontiers instead of making do with levies from year to year, Col. Marinus Willett begged Schuyler to plan a proper military system for enactment by the legislature, which was soon to convene in October. Schuyler, however, had his attention focused too much on the threats of the moment to be able even to think of attending the legislature. And he continued to collect and pass along information and warnings of frontier marauders and enemy threats to generals John Stark and William Heath. British forces in Canada were preparing new maneuvers. It was from Oswego and Oneida that Maj. John Ross and Walter Butler were to launch the war's last significant Indian raid into the Mohawk valley.[60]

On 9 October Stark asked Schuyler to come up to Saratoga, his health permitting, to offer advice on meeting the "critical" and "interesting" crisis. Mrs. Schuyler, he said, and two of her daughters (Margarita and perhaps Elizabeth) had safely reached their country house, evidently to inspect Stark's occupancy and to arrange the removal of family possessions if the enemy pushed too far south of Lake George. Well aware of Barry St. Leger's presence on Lake Champlain, Schuyler suspected that another party was moving into the country from the west. Accordingly, he directed Indian agents at Schenectady to see that scouts were posted to detect the invaders and sound the alarm.[61]

At eight in the morning of 12 October, having received an "express" message from General Stark at Saratoga, Schuyler relayed word to Governor Clinton that the invaders were marching south from Lake George. Complaing of the lack of regulars at Albany, he urged Clinton to get reinforcements from General Heath and to hasten up to the city himself. Already he had requested General Rossiter of Massachusetts and generals Fellows and Gansevoort of New York to raise their militia, and he had hurried "expresses" to every quarter of the country to summon men northward. Once again Albany was threatened with destruction, and the Yorker refused to leave it and go to Saratoga until militia reinforcements appeared. Without his efforts to organize local defenses he feared that the consequences would be "disagreeable."[62]

Pleading that ill health prevented him from leaving Poughkeepsie, Governor Clinton responded to Schuyler's alarm with reassurances that troops had been sent north. By 14 October John Stark learned that reports of the enemy reaching south of Lake George had been false. As the militia moved spiritedly from "all quarters," Schuyler could be reassured also that Marinus Willett had given no alarms in Tryon County, where the countryside remained quiet. William Alexander, Lord Stirling, reached Albany on 22 October to assume command of the Northern Department, and news from Virginia certainly encouraged Schuyler; before the end of the month, he was relieved and pleased to hear unofficial accounts of Cornwallis's surrender.[63]

Not even reports of the uncertain behavior of Vermonters in the face of enemy invaders seemed to unsettle the Yorker. General Stark and his son, Maj. Caleb Stark, kept Schuyler informed of Yankees' visits to Saratoga to inspect fortifications and to "fish out" the minds of the patriot forces there. Young Stark found their conduct very ambiguous and suspected the "veracity" of their intentions. When he asked Schuyler for his opinion of their rash threats in asserting jurisdiction over New York territory, the general obliged with a lengthy statement of his views on the entire dispute.[64]

What would happen, Schuyler asked, if he claimed a neighbor's estate, which that neighbor and his ancestors had long possessed in peace and quiet? If Stark presumed to exercise authority over property Schuyler had claimed, the Yorker would of course use force to stop him. "I have been too Long," Schuyler insisted, "and am too much the friend of Vermont to wish that so odious conduct should be justly chargeable to them." The Yankees' jurisdictional pretension he regarded as a "mere political maneuver" to force a settlement of the controversy. He could not believe that Vermonters would openly join the enemy. "Why Sir if the people of New England believed the Vermonters capable of such conduct," he exclaimed, "they would extirpate them [as] a people so little worthy of Liberty." Surely the virtue of Vermonters would save them from such misfortune; joining the enemy would ruin them, for it would not alter the independence of the United States. The solution to the problem, Schuyler thought, was that Congress should persuade New York, Massachusetts, and New Hampshire to pass acts of indemnity for illegal behavior of the claimants. Thereafter, the cultivation of "good understanding" among neighbors might induce support of the common cause: "This sir is the language I would hold and it would convey the undisguised sentiments of my heart."[65]

During November, however, the New York legislature warned Congress not to venture the establishment of an "arbitrary boundary" between Vermont and New York or to erect an independent state. Under the Articles of Confederation no state could be deprived of its territory without its consent, and the Yorkers insisted that Congress must limit its role in the dispute to other means of negotiation between the contending parties.[66]

The legislature's resolution of protest generally agreed with draft proposals that Schuyler evidently prepared in anticipation of attending the senate. Except for the argument that Congress had no right to deprive the state of territory without its consent, Schuyler's draft differed in one significant particular from the legislature's statement. He would have warned that New York would be justified in withholding troops and supplies requisitioned for the confederation government in order to protect itself from Vermonters' attempts to dismember the state. But Schuyler's nationalism was too strong for him to press execution of the threat. New York, he wrote, was unwilling to give the enemy any occasion to exult in the prospect of American disunity; therefore, one more application should be made to Congress to settle the matter in accordance with New York's act of submission in October 1779 and Congress's 1779 pledge to negotiate the question of boundaries and jurisdictions.[67]

Schuyler's busy days of correspondence in meeting the frontier dangers of October were affected not only by the anxiety of the circumstances, but also by his ill health. Aside from growing fatigue, a "fit of the gravel" unsettled him until midmonth and then again a week later, preventing him from visiting Saratoga until early November. Illness and the autumn crisis also kept him from attending the legislature, which had been summoned to meet at Poughkeepsie on 1 October. Meantime he had arranged for troops to march north should the enemy venture south of the lakes, and he ordered Indian allies to ready themselves to help and to scout the area between Schoharie and Batts's Hill. The militia's response to the emergency so heartened him that he characterized as ridiculous the enemy's idea of conquering a country whose inhabitants turned out so readily to defend it. If the enemy intended a permanent occupation of Ticonderoga, the post might serve as a "cage" for trapping them. In the Mohawk valley their advance under Maj. John Ross was repelled by New York and Massachusetts militia.[68]

On 1 November Schuyler received Hamilton's word of the victory at Yorktown, which was an event that moved him to send Washington congratulations with "every sentiment of affection esteem and gratitude." Before setting out for Saratoga, he seized the advantage of using the good news to post a request to Col. Barry St. Leger, then British commander on Lake Champlain. Would St. Leger favor him with the liberation of his overseer John Tubbs and Pvt. John Cockley, who had been carried off by the men who attacked his house in August. Lord Stirling, the new commander of the Northern Department, authorized the promise of two British prisoners in exchange. Referring to Cornwallis's "gallant defense" and surrender, the Yorker insisted, however, that his "only motive to communicate" this news arose "from a conviction that you must be anxious to know it, for Indeed, Sir I am incapable of those insulting petitesses which disgrace humanity, and mark a little ungenerous mind." The men were eventually freed, and Schuyler rewarded them with lands in the Saratoga patent. But the general evidently had some difficulty in arranging their return, not to mention the recovery of the silver that the raiders had stolen from him.[69]

The Yorktown victory did not mark the end of the war, but only the decision of it. The New York frontier remained in danger, and Schuyler was quick to renew his arguments for launching another campaign against Canada. The British were strengthening Ticonderoga, and the prospects that some Vermonters might yet be "gained by the enemy" worried him. Cornwallis's defeat might induce Britain to listen to terms, but she could not be moved to surrender Canada and the west without the Americans' successful invasion of Canada. (The events of the next several decades proved how correctly the Yorker had assessed the problem of having the British at the doorstep of the Republic.) Accordingly, he wrote Washington early in November 1781 from Saratoga that if the Virginian had the means to make the attempt, "averse as I am to public life, I will most cheerfully afford any services I am capable of rendering in collecting and preparing what every [sic] may be necessary, and attainable in this quarter, and accompany the troops on the Expedition." Again at midmonth he warned that although the British were retiring from Lake Champlain, the states should not think that the war was ended.[70]

Word of Schuyler's proposals for an attack on Canada later reached the ears of Gen. Frederick Haldimand. Through William Smith, Jr.'s, agency Sir Henry Clinton alerted Haldimand in February 1782 to the possibility of a Franco-American assault, and Haldimand postponed plans for an invasion of Vermont. By the time that it became clear that the rebel forces would not attempt an invasion, it was too late for Haldimand to act against Vermont, because all British forces on the continent were ordered to stand on the defensive.[71]

While the war raged in other parts of the world, in America it ebbed away. As the new year approached, Schuyler was freer to turn his attention more toward politics than the army. Having exchanged the warrior's mantle for a senator's, he should have been justly proud of his part in the American triumph. The problems of peacetime, however, were perhaps no less pressing than those of the war with which he had grappled so unwearedly. And he faced them with no less trepidation or determination.

The victory at Yorktown and the relief of the pressure on New York's northern and western frontiers enabled Schuyler's daughter Angelica Church and her children to leave Albany on 17 November. Bound for Virginia to rejoin her husband, a provisioner of Rochambeau's army, she was accompanied by her sister Margaret. And armed with her father's letter of request to Maj. Gen. William Heath, she was aided in her descent from the Highlands and the river crossing at King's Ferry. Heath obligingly assigned an assistant quartermaster general to accompany the two women and Schuyler's grandchildren and promptly informed him of their safe passage. With the departure of Admiral Thomas Graves and most of the British fleet, the British troops and their adherents were essentially constrained to the immediate area of New York City.[72]

While his army enveloped New York City, however, Washington wintered in more sophisticated surroundings; "military affairs were now so obviously in a less grievous state than the civil that Congress held him in Philadelphia." If Schuyler hoped for the commander in chief's proximity and for a convenient exchange of visits, he was disappointed. But at year's end, unlike Washington, he was at least able to savor the comforts of his own fireside. And sharing it was Alexander Hamilton, whose return from Yorktown began several months of agreeable comradeship.[73] Within a few short months Schuyler proudly witnessed his son-in-law's admission as an attorney by the supreme court and then his licensing as a counselor-at-law.

As defenses on the lower reaches of the Hudson were reasonably secure, so Schuyler felt no pressures from the north after mid-November. Mrs. Schuyler and her sons, seven-year-old "Master Rensselaer" and John Bradstreet, who was sixteen, inspected Saratoga where John Stark's troops had built blockhouses as a part of the fortifications and barracks around the family's house and outbuildings. Schuyler and Hamilton apparently followed the boys and their mother to look at the works. Military operations there were a mixed blessing, for the construction of defenses provided protection for the Schuylers but also meant the destruction of fences and other property and the inconvenience of having strangers in their midst. In December, for example, the assistant deputy quartermaster general Christopher Yates certified the troops' use and destruction of hundreds of boards, fence rails, and logs, not to mention the planks and timbers pulled up from a raceway of one of the mill dams. In addition, one of the sentinels, perhaps accidentally, shot and killed one of the general's horses, a nine-year-old half-blooded bay mare.[74] Schuyler was entitled to more than gratitude for his services to the revolutionary cause; the squire of Saratoga knew precisely the meaning of the rebels' pledge to win it with their fortunes as well as their lives and sacred honor.

Preliminaries of Peace

1

"various and essential services"

*F*or Schuyler as for the nation the American victory at Yorktown inaugurated a period of watchful waiting until an end to hostilities could be proclaimed and terms of peace could be negotiated. On the verge of postwar reconstruction, he and his countrymen faced the last problems of the wartime effort and the first steps toward peacetime recovery. The war did not altogether cease with Washington's defeat of Cornwallis. In the spring of 1782, for example, the Spanish captured New Providence in the Bahamas, and throughout that year "a ferocious struggle was fought for the empire of India." There were also American skirmishes; the last notable land action of the war along the seaboard came in August at Cambahee River, South Carolina. American casualties for the year included 277 killed, 124 wounded, and 80 captured. On the New York frontier the final campaign came in early February 1782. Col. Marinus Willett led forces west of Fort Herkimer in an effort to capture Fort Oswego. After stumbling through snow-filled woods they missed their chance for a surprise attack, gave up, and turned home again.[1]

Yet the end of the Yorktown campaign had enabled Alexander Hamilton to rejoin Schuyler and his family at Albany in November 1781. Except for service in Congress at Philadelphia and Princeton in 1782, he and Eliza made their home with the Schuylers for the next two years. There, on 22 January 1782, their first child was born. With a wife and child to support Hamilton fell diligently to work to prepare for admission to the bar, using the private law library of Schuyler's good friend James Duane. Other students also gained access to Duane's books. Schuyler's old secretary,

John Lansing, Jr., and Hamilton's friend, Robert Troup, were able to "coach him on the kinds of questions asked at the bar examinations after they passed them in April" 1782.[2]

It is one of the ironies of history that the beginning of Hamilton's legal career—and even his marriage—almost exactly coincided with that of his political nemesis and murderer. About the time of the Yorktown victory Aaron Burr appeared on the Schuylers' Albany doorstep with a letter of introduction from Maj. Gen. Alexander McDougall. Burr may have met Schuyler in 1776 after the army's retreat from Canada, but McDougall now assured Schuyler that as an officer commanding with "uncommon vigilence" in the sourthern part of the state in the winter of 1779, Burr was a good soldier and worthy citizen who merited every attention that the general might think proper to show him. With characteristic noblesse oblige Schuyler evidently commended Burr to Chief Justice Richard Morris.[3]

Like Hamilton, Burr both studied and practiced law in Albany during 1782–83. But in the law Burr was faster; he qualified as a barrister or counselor in April 1782. His domestic life also began in Albany after his marriage to Theodosia Prevost in July of that year, but in this he trailed Hamilton by a year and a half. And in Albany, like the Hamiltons', the Burrs' first child was born in June 1783. Ironically, too, both Burr and Hamilton moved to New York City in November 1783 in anticipation of lucrative law practices after the British evacuation.[4]

It is also curious that these two men who later played such sizable roles in the formation of the Republic entered public life almost simultaneously, Hamilton as a congressman in 1782 and Burr as a state assemblyman in 1784. But aside from their similar professions and their ambitious pursuit of power there was little they held in common. Burr did not have a powerful father-in-law, and each man espoused a different view of the national interest. In the end their rivalry was also peculiarly focused upon Hamilton's father-in-law. Burr replaced Schuyler as United States senator in 1791 only to be ousted by Schuyler six years later. And from that day until Burr murdered Hamilton in 1804 their political enmity repeatedly involved the famous Albanian at whose very house both men had found succor in 1781.

In the early months of 1782 while Hamilton undertook the study of law, Schuyler remained attentive to possible dangers from Canada and Vermont and to the need for providing the friendly Oneida and Tuscarora at Schenectady with supplies. His earlier proposal for an overland attack on Canada in conjunction with French forces, although accepted by Washington, had by now been laid aside. Rochambeau "had verbal instructions to evade any such proposal, for it was no part of French policy that the Americans should establish themselves without a rival on the Atlantic seaboard." And without the "French troops the Continental army could not mount a serious offensive anywhere." Sensing the danger of British forces in Canada, however, Schuyler insisted upon maintaining a personal bodyguard and upon sending scouting parties to the northern frontier to watch for possible enemy incursions. Appealing to Washington for orders to restore cuts made in a thirteen-man guard, he insisted that he must otherwise remove himself and his family to a place of greater security. "It is now a notorious fact," he wrote, "that three parties have been expressly sent from Canada to take or put me to death." Convinced that the Yorker's "various and essential services" had rendered him "extremely obnoxious to the Enemy," Washington ordered a new guard for him from John Stark's New Hampshire regiment stationed at Saratoga.[5]

Ever alert to dealing with threats to the security of the state, Schuyler discovered a potentially dangerous state of affairs at Claverack, which he visited early in February. Just south of Kinderhook, Claverack was the "lower manor" of Rensselaerwyck, which was owned by Mrs. Schuyler's father. There the general found a large stand of arms stored on the eastern banks of the frozen Hudson. Thinking that people on the opposite shore, who were notorious for their "most immoderate" Tory views, might easily cross the ice and capture the weapons, Schuyler quickly arranged for a militia guard to protect them and urged General Heath to reimburse the expense of the guard.[6]

As for the problem of Vermonters' persistent claims to New York territory and their rumored willingness to cooperate with the British in Canada, Schuyler continued to believe that an amicable settlement might yet be reached. In mid-January he learned that a number of town meetings on the Hampshire Grants had recently voted to give way on the extravagant claims of their leaders to territory both in the east and also as far west as the Hudson. He thought that Washington's correspondence with Thomas Chittenden, governor of Vermont, might help persuade the Vermont legislature not to forsake their American connections. To the Virginian Schuyler's efforts to heal the "unhappy disturbances" in the north proved his "ardent desire to put an period to internal contention, and unite all the separate and jarring interests in prosecuting the great common cause of America." Upon arriving at Poughkeepsie in February, Schuyler was however unable even to guess at how the legislature might respond to the Vermont question. But he was determined that nothing would be wanting on his part to promote "an amicable adjustment of a business" otherwise fraught with much distress to all parties concerned.[7]

2

A State Senator with National Views

Two days before the legislature finally convened on 23 February Schuyler was alerted to developments in Congress on the Vermont business. The foreign secretary Robert R. Livingston had discovered that a congressional committee had been alarmed by evidence of the Yankees' intercourse with the enemy. Vermont agents had tried to explain away their behavior by claiming that they had temporized with the British in order to prevent the "distress" of their country. It was doubtful that the Vermonters would withdraw their extravagant claims to New York territory and to lands east of the Connecticut River, as Congress had requested in August 1781. But the committee decided that Congress should repeat the request, threatening that unless Vermonters complied within a month, the Green Mountains would be regarded as the boundary between New York and New Hampshire.[8]

In his opening address to the legislature on 23 February, Governor Clinton presented papers proving a "treasonable and dangerous Intercourse and Connection" between the enemy and rebel leaders in the northeast corner of the state. Prudence dictated that their names (Gen. Frederick Haldimand and Ethan and Ira Allen) not be divulged. It was probably William Smith, Jr., who had furnished the papers because he feared for the security of his own titles to land in the Hampshire Grants. Inviting the senate and assembly to respond, Clinton also drew their attention to calls from Congress and Washington for requisitions and troop support.[9]

Despite the urgency of the Vermont issue the legislature did not proceed to act upon it for almost a month. Meantime, Congress considered a resolution calling for compliance with its August 1781 appeal to Vermonters. On 1 March it voted seven to four against deleting the time limit proposed for Vermont's retraction of boundary claims. New York delegates failed to defeat the entire resolution outright but succeeded in returning it to committee. So the issue was stalemated. Southerners opposed adding another northern state to the Union, and it was generally recognized that congressional dismemberment of New York State might be a dangerous precedent for settling the pretensions of other states to western lands.[10]

Between 28 February and 6 March both Ezra L'Hommedieu and Schuyler detected a defiant sentiment in the assembly, a threat to the nation's military strength. For daring to offer a settlement with Vermont in August 1781, contrary to New York's own terms of submission (including the state's participation in negotiations) Congress might be deprived of requisitions only recently levied to maintain the war effort. New York's resources, including manpower, might be withheld in order to pressure Congress and also to facilitate the state's defense of its own frontiers. Indeed, at the end of March, when the legislature authorized the completion of New York's Continental line, it was with the stipulation that two regiments be raised for the further defense of its own frontiers. Despite Schuyler's efforts, it would not furnish the aid requested by both Washington and Congress for the Continental cause.[11]

The legislature's further response to the Hampshire Grants issue came in the form of two measures, one for pardoning "certain offenses" committed in the northeastern parts of the state, and another for quieting the minds of the inhabitants of that quarter. The pardon bill apparently passed without controversy. But Schuyler and several other senators found the bill for quieting the inhabitants with regard to their land titles to be objectionable. Without success, however, they voted against limiting the security of land titles to grantees and their heirs who were then actual residents of the territory. The limitation offered nothing to nonresident title claimants. Similarly, Schuyler failed to retain several other provisions of the bill. One would have confirmed title to actual occupants of land who received grants from New Hampshire before New York grants had been issued. Another would have "provided a Compensation" to those grantees whose lands were decided to be the property of rival claimants. Accordingly, the general finally voted against passage of the bill that the council of revision approved as law on 14 April.[12]

There were, however, several significant enactments in the February-April session of the legislature for which Schuyler may be in part particularly credited. These included laws regulating the state militia, establishing the Bank of North America, and qualifying the prohibition of British imports to the state.

On 28 February the general and Sen. Henry Oothoudt were ordered to prepare a militia bill, which was then introduced on 1 March. Familiar with military affairs, Schuyler was the obvious choice of the senate to draft such a measure. This time his handiwork apparently roused no controversy. The senate readily accepted minor assembly amendments on 28 March. One merely reduced the sum imposed on Quakers in lieu of military service from £15 to £10, and another authorized the governor to call out the militia for up to three months' service upon requsition by the Continental commander in chief. On 4 April the council of revision registered its approval of the measure, which then became law.[13]

Similarly, Schuyler found no difficulty in introducing and winning passage of an act to incorporate the Bank of North America, which had begun operations in January. Part of Robert Morris's national fiscal program, the bank had been chartered by Congress in December 1781; but because congressmen raised questions about their own power of incorporation, the states were requested to give the bank "all the necessary validity within their respective jurisdictions."[14]

Undoubtedly Morris's connection with Schuyler as a supplier of flour and bateaux for Washington's army led the Yorker to act on behalf of the financier and his bank; the senator introduced the bank bill on 26 February, only a day after he was ordered to do so. The bill must have been drafted earlier. Apparently the only notable change made in the measure was to add to its title a specific reference to preventing the establishment of any bank in the state other than the Bank of North America. Both recommendations of Congress were thus accepted by New York. Although Schuyler's son-in-law John Church and Church's partner in the business of contracting for army supplies, Jeremiah Wadsworth, were the two largest stockholders in the bank, the Yorker's principal interest in the enterprise seems to have been a general one, not a personal one as an investor. Even so, he and others alike might benefit by promoting sound national fiscal policy and facilitating the payment of creditors with undepreciated currency, which were expected of the bank.[15]

National interests were at stake in still other issues before the legislature in 1782. While some of its members were bent upon blocking the importation of British commercial goods to New York, Schuyler managed to attach a qualification to the prohibitory bill, indicating his own perception that peace would soon make desirable the resumption of trade with the mother country. In the meantime, however, it seemed necessary to prevent certain trade with the enemy and to demonstrate American interest in a peace treaty whose terms might encourage the resumption of lawful commerce. On 11 March the senate rejected (seven to five) his first proposal, which was the addition of a clause to suspend operation of nonimportation until the governor publicly declared that all the states "east of Maryland" had enacted similar restrictive legislation. However, Schuyler's second proposal, a more complicated one, passed by a vote of ten to two. This one was a stipulation that the governor must suspend the act up to twenty days after the legislature's next meeting whenever he had been informed that any state "east of Maryland" had neglected to prohibit such trade or had passed such a law and then repealed it or that Congress had recommended the repeal of such laws by newspaper proclamation. In short, the nonimportation act was to be regarded as a wartime measure that must be lifted as soon as peace terms had been settled or as soon as other states failed to cooperate with the nonimportation policy. A month later the measure had also passed the assembly, and on 13 April the council of revision certified it as law.[16]

Amidst the welter of much other legislative business, including the levying of taxes and appointment of an auditor for the settlement of state accounts, Schuyler endeavored to institute regulations for surveyors of land in an effort to promote accuracy of surveys and to reduce the chances of lawsuits needed for the correction of errors. As state surveyor general he was particularly interested in initiating a licensing system to encourage professionalism in surveyors' work. Accordingly he proposed that a commissioner be named for each county to examine applicants for licenses. Appointed for his own abilities in the art of surveying, the commissioner would be bound by oath to administer effective tests and to issue licenses only to the competent. Licensed surveyors must themselves swear to perform their work carefully and impartially and to report with accuracy. Practice without a license would be punishable by a fine of £5 and the assessment of costs as determined by county justices of the peace.

Schuyler's proposal seems to have proceeded no further than a second reading in the senate, which referred it to a committee of the whole. Similarly, his bill to "facilitate the settlement of all controversies" arising from the jurisdictional dispute between New York and New Hampshire seems never to have advanced beyond its introduction to the senate on 23 March. The surveying bill perhaps was less controversial and less pressing. The Vermont issue, as has been noted, was managed in another way. Whatever his influence, Schuyler was of course not omnipotent. No single individual, as Alexander Hamilton later observed in August, had a "decided influence" in the state government at the moment. And although the budding attorney thought Schuyler had "more weight in the Legislature than the Governor," it was "not so much as not to be exposed to the mortification of seeing important measures patronised by him frequently miscarry."[17]

3

State Surveyor General

Without the benefit of a licensing system, Schuyler perforce executed his duties as New York surveyor general guided chiefly by his own knowledge of surveying and his personal familiarity with the abilities of others to delineate boundaries. Applicants for new lands and for corrected measurements of old grants had somehow to be satisfied. On 1 May the general appointed Christopher Yates, former major in the First New York Regiment (1776–78) and lieutenant colonel and deputy quartermaster general of the New York militia (1779–81), his deputy. Within a fortnight of Schuyler's return from Poughkeepsie following the legislature's April adjournment, the Albany City Council appealed to him for confirmation of a ruling made by the old provincial council and lieutenant governor in 1764. At issue was the Albany corporation's title to certain lands exempted from the royal patent for Rensselaerwyck; the city council was determined to prevent the filing of "location certificates" for tracts they believed were corporation property. Admittedly sympathetic to the council's effort to head off claimants to municipal territory, Schuyler insisted that he be given cogent and conclusive reasons for accepting the city's assertion of ownership.[18] However the business was resolved, it may be safely presumed that Schuyler did so with a strict regard for the impartial discharge of his duty.

Acting under legislation passed in March and in July 1782, the Yorker soon received dozens of petitions for thousands of acres, which were bounties promised to enlistees to fill the New York Continental line and to complete two regiments raised for defense of the state's frontiers. For the next several months—and indeed until he resigned his office in 1784—Schuyler's land office business diverted a considerable amount of his attention from his private affairs as a landlord and estate manager. The enormity of his task of registering the applications may be glimpsed by noting the restrictions stipulated by the legislature in July and the extent of his surveyor general's papers. The July law imposed prohibitions on locating certain lands in western Tryon County to any but New York officers and enlisted men. Except for the loyal Oneida and Tuscarora, the surveyor general was permitted to pass certificates for lands occupied by the Six Nations. Land titles in King's District of Albany County were specifically confined to those grantees holding them under royal auspices, provided that no one else claimed the same land by royal warrant.[19]

Free of senate duties from mid-April until June, when the governor summoned a newly elected legislature for a brief session at Poughkeepsie, Schuyler found a variety of business awaiting him at Albany. In addition to the growing volume of work as state surveyor general he met Washington's request to establish contracts for supplying frontier posts with provisions. He intervened on behalf of Oneida and Tuscarora tribesmen accused of murder, issuing a warning to Tryon countians against the injustice and imprudence of threatening to kill all Indians on sight. Lawless retaliation might lead the Indians to join the enemy, causing serious "distress" on the frontiers. "Most earnestly" Schuyler entreated the settlers to injure no person or his property but to allow him to bring accused delinquents to justice.[20]

Other official or public and private business demanded much of Schuyler's attention. In June, for example, he collected £15 from Jacob Cuyler to pay a tuition bill for "three Scholars" at the Albany Academy. The sum probably represented the charges for instruction of the general's three sons, John Bradstreet, Philip Jeremiah, and Rensselaer between 20 November 1781 and the following 20 May. In another June transaction he obtained Dirk Swart's lease of two lots in the Saratoga patent for five shillings and the nominal rent of one peppercorn.[21]

During the last days of June Washington finally paid a visit to Albany and his trusted colleague, which was a welcome respite from the tedium of maintaining the army's last stand at Newburgh. The Virginian may have also wished to inspect the terrain over which another invasion of Canada might be launched and to obtain Schuyler's advice for such an undertaking. As early as May the commander in chief had devised plans for such a campaign, thinking that a September launching along the Richelieu River might be too late for Gen. Frederick Haldimand to obtain reinforcements for a successful resistance. It was also feared that Haldimand might renew the war in the north and that Sir Guy Carleton, the new commander in New York City, was trying to lull Americans into a false sense of security. The continued presence of enemy troops, like the possibility of their renewal of the war, was also regarded as a threat to American hopes for the most advantageous peace terms.[22]

Although Carleton had instructions to capitulate if necessary, Haldimand's anxiety continued because of rumors that Americans were concentrating forces at Albany, that the French would attack Halifax, and that they would arm Canadians against the British forces in the north. Such rumors were evidence of the work of American agents and their Canadian sympathizers, but in August Haldimand received instructions from the British secretary of state to refrain from further offensive actions. Parliament had in March resolved to make peace, and formal negotiations finally produced preliminary peace terms in November.[23]

In June, however, Washington, like Schuyler, could not be certain that upper New York would not again be ravaged by British regulars, Loyalists, and Indian allies. Their consultation in Albany began on the evening of 27 June with a thirteen-gun salute, two hours of bell ringing, and a ceremonial address from the city council. Next day a civic banquet was accorded to the distinguished visitor and his entourage, Lafayette, Steuben, Henry Knox, and Nathanael Greene. The Virginian received the freedom of the city in a gold box and was welcomed by an illumination of the inhabitants' houses. During the next few days Schuyler escorted him and Governor Clinton to Schenectady. "What their business was I canot [*sic*] learn," wrote an anonymous informant to General Haldimand, but "Washington was over heard [to] Say in Albany fort this is a strong fort," and "Schuyler [replied] this and the lik[e] of this will do for us."[24]

Little else is known of Washington's business at Albany or of Schuyler's involvement in it. By 2 July the Virginian had returned to Newburgh to await the New York legislature's response to the continuing needs of the army and the war effort. On 11 June Governor Clinton had summoned the legislators to assemble on 3 July and to respond to a congressional committee's call for "competent Means for a vigorous Prosecution of the War." Citing also the need to revise the state's tax system, Clinton argued that sizable arrearages in collections were proof that it was seriously defective. The persistence of a state of war and of enemy efforts to detach Americans from their French allies demanded the legislators' serious consideration.[25]

4

"putting the common Cause out of the Reach of Contingencies"

The legislature did not make a quorum until 11 July, and in the brief session that ended on 25 July Schuyler and Alexander Hamilton worked hand in hand to "convert the New York lawmakers to the necessity of supplying funds to Congress" and to take a significant "step that conducted to the conventions at Annapolis and Philadelphia and the establishment of the new federal government." Hamilton appealed to the legislature in person as Robert Morris's appointee to the office of receiver of Continental taxes in New York. Both houses obligingly named a committee to confer with him, and within a few days the two bodies fell to work on bills to raise £18,000 in specie and bank notes whose appropriation might be made by order of the superintendent of finance and to authorize Congress to adjust the proportion of New York's share of war expenses in a mode different from that prescribed by the Articles of Confederation. Whether he regarded the sum as too little or too much, Schuyler voted unsuccessfully against establishing Albany County's quota of the £18,000 tax bill at $7,920. But he did not oppose the bill when the senate passed it on 20 July. By the time Hamilton was obliged to leave

Poughkeepsie to resume preparations for his bar examination, these measures had been enacted into law, together with a bill to meet Washington's request for forage for the army at Newburgh.[26]

The problem of arrearages in tax collections was not, however, to be so quickly solved. Hamilton's "undoubted agency" in pressing for a bill to compel the payment of arrearages resulted in a slight diversion. Although the bill was enacted into law, both senate and house "at his instance" appointed a joint committee on 22 July to prepare a report for the next session of the legislature. Schuyler and two of his colleagues were named to serve with six assemblymen. Charged with devising a system for providing funds adequate for the state as well as for the United States, the committee was to confer with Hamilton and to plan more effectual means of taxation; payment must "be truly compulsory and collection economical."[27]

Amidst the welter of these activities the legislature responded to the ferment of Hamilton's energies and to his father-in-law's influence by electing the promising law student to Congress and calling for a convention of states to revise the Articles of Confederation. The first of these actions launched Hamilton upon the political career that Schuyler had envisioned at least a year earlier. The call for an interstate convention began half a decade of efforts that finally produced the Constitution of 1787.

Hamilton's election actually followed in the wake of the senate and assembly's passage of a series of resolutions on the state of the nation on 20–21 July. These resolutions, like his efforts on behalf of Robert Morris's national fiscal program, were doubtless Hamilton's handiwork, at least in part, but the influence of Philip Schuyler is equally unmistakable. The senate's election of congressmen, however, seems not to have involved any particular maneuvers by Schuyler to push Hamilton into office. Indeed, the senate nominated Schuyler himself, together with incumbent congressmen James Duane, William Floyd, John Morin Scott, and Ezra L'Hommedieu; but the assembly proposed Hamilton instead of his father-in-law. In the ensuing joint ballot cast by the two houses in the assembly chamber Hamilton's candidacy prevailed. Had Schuyler imagined the popularity of his son-in-law in the assembly perhaps he would have moved his senatorial colleagues to nominate Hamilton in the first place. Now he was happy to make way for him. Although the election removed Hamilton from the office of continental receiver, it "gave him a superior opportunity to urge the political reforms which were the conditions of satisfactory revenue."[28] It was the very sort of opportunity for which Schuyler had also been waiting.

Another opportunity exploited by the general and his son-in-law was the legislature's concern for the state of the nation. Caught between the last gasps of war and the first breaths of the newborn Confederation and the promise of peace, it appeared to be in a precarious balance. On 19 July Schuyler moved the senate to go into committee of the whole to consider the whole range of state and national problems looming before them. In part the effort was an answer to Governor Clinton's address at the opening of the legislative session. On 20 July they resolved to deal with signs of enemy forces assembling at Oswego, which were hints of a possible renewal of attacks in the west and perhaps as far east as Schenectady and Albany. Because Tryon County's militia were debilitated and regular troops available there were few, the governor should be requested to repeat his calls upon Washington for more Continental troops.[29]

After still another session in committee of the whole on 20 July the senate agreed to a series of eight resolutions that won the speedy and unanimous concurrence of the assembly on the following day. In sum, the resolves reflected unmistakably the sentiments of men who could only be considered to be nationalists. Evidence from the secretary for foreign affairs and the superintendent of finance revealed "That the Situation of these States is in a peculiar Manner critical" and that a "Continuance of the present Constitution of the Continental Government" would subvert not only public credit but the very safety and independence of the states. Failure of Congress's sound financial plan because of "Want of the Support which the States are able to give, would be productive of Evils too pernicious to be hazarded." Britain's diplomatic efforts to conciliate in Europe while seducing America with a defensive war and augmenting their navy could be productive of consequences ultimately dangerous to the United States. Beleaguered by problems both domestic and foreign, the Confederation left Americans "at the mercy of events" that they could not influence. The country must exert itself and unite upon "some System more effectual, for producing Energy, Harmony and Consistency of Measures, than that which now exists, and more capable of putting the common Cause out of the Reach of Contingencies." As most of the nation's embarrassments were rooted in Congress's powerlessness to obtain the states' cooperation and especially to provide a revenue, these defects should be quickly remedied. And as the annual income of the states promised to fall short of yearly expenditures, the deficiency must be supplied on credit; if not the credit of the states, then that of individuals whose loans must be secured by adequate interest. Debts already incurred must be paid, and "competent Means provided for future Credit, and for supplying the current Demands of the War."

Finally, these ends were not to be "attained by partial deliberations of the States separately," which was an expedient that had already been tried and found wanting. Congress should summon all the states to a "general Convention . . . especially authorized to revise and amend the Confederation, reserving a Right to the respective Legislatures to ratify their Determinations."[30]

Whether Hamilton was the author of these resolutions or advised the person who did compose them is a question to which there is no clear answer. But both his and Schuyler's influence had been brought to bear; both men had advocated a revision of the Articles of Confederation even before they had become operative in 1781. No other New Yorkers were more prominent in the nationalist cause. For Schuyler this was not the first effort to move a public body to call for reform. But he had at last succeeded in registering "the first demand by a public body" that led to Congress's proposals to strengthen the Confederation in 1786 and to the interstate conventions of 1786 and 1787.[31]

The legislature adjourned on 25 July, leaving Congress to respond to its call for an interstate convention and the joint committee to prepare a report on improved taxation and finances for its next meeting in January. In the meantime Schuyler and Hamilton were not idle. By the end of the summer they had found still other ways to reinforce the legislature's proposal for reforming the Confederation, strengthening the union, and establishing sounder public credit.

On 30 September at the Albany city hall a meeting of public creditors convened for the purpose of publicizing their claims for interest due on loan office certificates. Hamilton and Schuyler were surely as responsible for calling the meeting as they were for what it proceeded to do. Chaired by the general, the creditors at Albany approved an address to their fellows throughout the state, arguing that both the nation and the state owed them justice for having violated "public engagements." In June Philadelphia creditors had also met, and in August a committee representing their interests had issued a similar address to the public. Reduced from affluence to indigence after depositing much of their fortunes in public funds, the creditors admitted that breaches of the nation's obligations might be justified by necessity, but they were also caused by want of a proper system of finances. Taxes alone would not pay the public debt, nor would they suffice for ordinary expenses of government. And although credit must still be employed, it must be restored to a healthy state by punctual payments of interest. It was further proposed that creditors throughout the counties of New York should send deputies to a convention at Poughkeepsie on 19 November; there an effort might be made to apply to both Congress and the legislature "for a redress of . . . grievances."[32]

Although it does not appear that the Poughkeepsie convention ever assembled, the Albany creditors continued their efforts to publicize their case. Schuyler promptly responded to their orders to sign and circulate copies of their address throughout the state, asking others to hold similar meetings and to establish committees of correspondence—a network that included the creditors' committee at Philadelphia. Nor was it surprising that the creditors named the general to their local committee, together with friends like Abraham Ten Broeck, Leonard Gansevoort, and John N. Bleecker. Such was the grassroots movement that worked for years to promote a reform in the national government. By 4 October Schuyler had ordered the Albany address printed in the local newspaper and began to circulate two hundred copies of it throughout the state. Doubtless the product, in part, of Hamilton's mind and pen, it was also much the result of Schuyler's own labors. Both men were determined to advance the efforts they had begun with the legislature in July.[33] The impact of these efforts finally extended to officers of the army camped at Newburgh. As creditors made common cause with military leaders there and with Hamilton and Robert and Gouverneur Morris at Philadelphia in the waning weeks of 1782 and early part of 1783, they pressed Congress for responsible fiscal measures even to the point of raising the specter of an army mutiny.

5

Guarded, but "perfectly at Ease"

About to leave Poughkeepsie at the end of July, Schuyler was again stricken by his old illness, and he returned to Albany, grateful for the comforts of home and the chance for a respite from public activity. His concern for the general disarray of state and national finances, however, was hardly interrupted, and it was obviously more than that of a disinterested theoretician. Apparently his personal finances were pinched, for he was obliged to raise some cash by parting with a few of his far-flung properties. On 30 July the general sold a 265-acre farm to Sampson Dyckman for £795.10.0 and obtained a down payment of £500.[34] As much as any holder of Continental securities he knew the importance of creating fiscal stability and monetary security for the state and for the entire nation. And he recognized in the interests of public creditors the larger interests of the public as a whole.

As ever, attentive to his personal business and to that of the New York government, Schuyler never lost sight of the national welfare nor did he fail to use every opportunity to act in its support. Friends like James Duane continued to inform him of the state of the nation as they viewed it from Philadelphia. In mid-August, for example, Duane reported that Congress had agreed to supply new troop levies from New York so as to place them on equal footing with Continental battalions, and that the needs of the loyal Oneida Indians would be met. Although there had been no news regarding preparations for peace, Duane thought that the British ministry's determination to end the war was no justification for a relaxation of American efforts to compel the enemy to leave the country. Debates in Parliament suggested that Englishmen thought the rebels might yet be induced "to accept an Irish instead of an absolute Independence," which was an absurd delusion. While Duane wished Schuyler had been elected to Congress, he looked forward to working with the "ingenious and worthy" Hamilton, and pledged "every effort" within his power to press for "the particular subject you mention"—the reform of the Confederation.[35]

The maintenance of the army throughout the period of peace negotiations repeatedly involved Schuyler in work on behalf of the quartermaster general; and interest in prisoner exchanges and the collection of Canadian intelligence prompted more correspondence with General Haldimand as well as continuous contact with informants beyond the Saint Lawrence in the fall of 1782. As of September, the Yorker's prominence because of such services still entitled him to a twelve-man bodyguard. In preparation for the coming winter Schuyler was asked for his assistance in obtaining lumber for sheltering troops at West Point. The place was so stripped of wood that quartermaster general Timothy Pickering found it necessary to order seven thousand boards from Albany. Fearing that the local deputy quartermaster might be unable to manage contracts for the lumber on three months' credit because of "common suspicions of public faith," Pickering asked Schuyler to lend his aid.[36]

The task was both time-consuming and a bit difficult, and when Schuyler turned to Schenectady in his efforts to fill Pickering's requisition, he found through Henry Glen that charges for lumber were exorbitant—one to one-and-a-half shillings for one to one-and-a-half-inch boards. Neighborhood mills at Saratoga were more reasonable, and Schuyler decided to contract with local owners there for the lumber.[37]

Although Schuyler's intelligence gathering in September revealed that Governor-General Haldimand had been inhibited from launching Indian attacks from Canada along the New York frontier, the Yorker was not altogether easy about news that reinforcements had been ordered from England to the northern province, or that several hundred Iroquois,

Chippewa, and Ottawa were moving up the Saint Lawrence and that flour and military stores were being shipped for British outposts in the west. Suggesting that Congress instruct the Indian commissioners how to proceed should the hostile Iroquois request "accommodation" with the United States, the general warned the president of Congress that it was time to attempt a general peace treaty with the Six Nations. But what were Congress's wishes about how to proceed?[38] These were not settled for months, and in mid-1783 Schuyler at last felt obliged to make overtures to the tribesmen without them.

In October the presence of British forces on Lake Champlain remained disquieting, but Schuyler was confident that the arrival of a Continental regiment at Albany (ordered up by Maj. Gen. William Heath) would suffice to prevent any enemy attempt to move southward. By 22 October when General Stirling arrived in the city, the Yorker felt "perfectly at Ease" about the defenses of the north country. Should General Von Riedesel, again in Canada at Isle aux Noix, venture to press south of Lake George, Schuyler imagined that the German officer would "probably afford me the satisfaction of seeing him once again at my house"—as in 1777 when he was a prisoner of war.[39]

The general did not hesitate to contact Von Riedesel and Frederick Haldimand when Governor Clinton asked that he forward proposals for freeing New Yorkers who were prisoners of war in Canada. There were those, however, who were disturbed by the "notorious" activities of Schuyler's intelligencers in Canada. George Smyth and his son Terence at St. John's advised that "for the Safety of . . . friends in the Country that his Servants may not be Sent out either for Exchange nor upon Parole." The elder Smyth happened to have some of Schuyler's silver spoons and plate, which had been stolen in the raid on Albany in 1781. He promised in September to return these to the Yorker "by the first Public and Safe Opportunity" but continued to urge that certain captives including "Schuylers Two Servants" not be released for the sake of "the Preservation of the few distressed friends we have in the Colonies."[40]

Schuyler's "two servants" were actually soldiers who had been kidnapped in the 1781 raid that had been designed for the capture of the Yorker himself. These and a number of other prisoners were the objects of both his and Governor Clinton's solicitude. Through Baron Von Riedesel at Isle aux Noix, Schuyler's appeal to Governor-General Haldimand was answered in early November. Haldimand promised "every Occasion of gratifying the Feelings of Humanity . . . consistent with my duty." He had released prisoners, but by mistake Schuyler's two guards had been put aboard a vessel bound for New York City instead of being escorted south to the lake country. Soliciting Schuyler's influence in freeing some of his Brunswickers who had been captured at Bennington in 1777, the Baron remembered the days of their captivity at Saratoga and Albany and politely acknowledged his wife's gratitude for Mrs. Schuyler's kind reception and courtesies six years earlier.[41]

The hardships of warfare would not erase pleasant memories of those whom rebellion had made determined enemies. Nor did the years of struggle, tedium, and savage bloodshed obliterate the practice of civility and generosity among gentlemen-soldiers. Those bound to codes of honor and noble standards of grace and virtue did not wholly succumb to the barbarisms of war.

Sentiments of Reconciliation
and Affection

1

For the Sword, a Toga

*B*y the onset of winter 1782 the country awaited news of a treaty with Britain, hoping for the enemy's evacuation of New York City and other principal American posts and suffering the disorders of an unstable economy, which was due in part to the inadequacies of the Articles of Confederation. Not until April 1783 could Congress proclaim a cessation of hostilities or ratify the terms of a provisional peace treaty that had reached them on 23 March. Also needing money to pay arrearages in army salaries and interest on the public debt, Congress had proposed a tax on imports in 1781, but unanimous ratification of the impost amendment had been withheld. Efforts to settle the arrearages with state governments had likewise failed, and army officers grew apprehensive and desperate. Were their long years of service to go unrewarded, their return to civilian life to be impoverished? Not all were as fortunate as Col. Alexander Hamilton, whose future was ensured by the security of his Schuyler marriage alliance and by the beginnings of legal and political careers as barrister and congressman.

Hamilton observed what Schuyler could also see—the challenge of peace, of "a new scene ... The object ... to make our independence a blessing."[1] In seeking allies for his political projects, Hamilton found none more solid nor closer than his father-in-law, and it was more than a happy fortuity that Schuyler quickly followed him to Philadelphia in November 1782. Apart from plans to escort his daughter Margaret and her sister Angelica Church back to Albany, the jaunt down the Hudson certainly served to introduce Hamilton to Schuyler's political allies, New Yorkers like James Duane and others like John Rutledge and Ralph Izard of South Carolina. During his beleaguered career as a department commander, Schuyler had often found an almost natural axis of support between leaders of his native state and those of the South, which was an alliance that Jeffersonian Republicans cultivated twenty years later with telling success against Federalists of Schuyler's stripe.

The journey to Philadelphia was made overland, down the east bank of the Hudson, where Schuyler could inspect his father-in-law's property at Claverack, and on through Kingston and Poughkeepsie. From the west side of the river at New Windsor the roads became very bad, which was especially fatiguing for Mrs. Schuyler and little Caty, who was not yet two years old, but they endured the jolting carriage ride "much beyond" Schuyler's expectations. His son, seventeen-year-old Johnny, like his father and Hamilton who preceded them, probably traveled on horseback. On the eighth day out of Albany the party finally reached Philadelphia, where Schuyler announced their safe arrival. Greeted by Mrs. "Carter" (John and Angelica Church had not yet dropped the alias) and another of Schuyler's daughters, Peggy, the family settled down to what became almost a seven-week stay.[2]

The general did not intend to tarry in Philadelphia longer than a fortnight before returning to Albany, which was enough time for Angelica and Margaret to recover fully from recent illness. But he and the family failed to stir until mid-January.[3] Both the reasons for the Yorker's extended sojourn and his activities during this interlude remain concealed because of lacunae in the record. Angelica's recuperation or perhaps her relapse may have delayed him, or simply the necessity of avoiding bad weather or the difficulties of arranging suitable transportation. It may also have been Hamilton's initiation to Congress and the business of urging proper support of the army or of determining a peace policy for the board of Indian commissioners that turned Schuyler's attention to lobbying the delegates and other officers of government. Or perhaps he found nomination as secretary for foreign affairs, an office that Robert R. Livingston had decided to resign, to be a subject for exploration and negotiation. Whatever initial inclination the Yorker may have had to consider such an appointment, by June he obliged the New York delegates to withdraw his name. But Congress's choice of Livingston's successor was not made until May 1784! John Jay was the man, and because he was then absent in Europe, he could not assume the office until the beginning of 1785.[4]

Of all of Congress's business or Alexander Hamilton's involvements as a freshman delegate, nothing may have held Schuyler for so long in Philadelphia as the joint concern of Washington's officers, the public creditors, and leaders like Robert Morris, who had been trying to enlarge the powers of national government since 1780. The government was indebted to soldiers and civilians alike, but would it be able to pay without an effective fiscal program, including an amendment to the Articles of Confederation, empowering Congress to tax imports? Although Maj. Gen. Alexander McDougall did not arrive in Philadelphia until 29 December with the army's petition for arrearages in salaries and for the commutation of half-pay pensions, promised by Congress in 1780, to some lump sum payment, the groundwork for his presentation had been laid more than a month before. Just after Schuyler and Hamilton reached Philadelphia, Henry Knox, who had written the address, appealed to secretary at war Benjamin Lincoln; and Lincoln proceeded to press the case with members of Congress. Hamilton and Schuyler must certainly have been privy to these maneuvers, for they sympathized with them and their makers. On Christmas Eve "Congress was shocked to learn that Virginia had repealed her ratification of the impost of 1781. Since Rhode Island had refused earlier to ratify, the measure was now dead." But nationalists were encouraged that McDougall's petition could be used to pressure Congress to find new sources of money—a new funding system.[5]

"Within twenty-four hours of arrival, McDougall ... conferred with Robert Morris" and "within another week, the nationalist leadership had convinced McDougall and his colleagues that the Army's only hope for payment lay in a new funding system." They must either cooperate or face opposition to referring any claims to the states until "all prospect of obtaining Continental funds was at an end." In this the financier consulted with only a few others like Hamilton and Gouverneur Morris.[6] It is impossible to believe that these men did not share their deliberations with Schuyler.

Until mid-January, when he left Philadelphia, the general had every opportunity to observe developments of the Newburgh conspiracy. After Congress referred the army memorial to committee on 6 January, Robert Morris met with the group to explain that he had no money to advance the army, nor could he promise any "until certain funds should be previously established." A week later McDougall and his companions, colonels John Brooks and Matthias Ogden, added to the pressure by warning committee members that failure to act could lead to a mutiny. In response the committee appointed Hamilton, James Madison, and John Rutledge of South Carolina to consult with Morris and prepare a report on the army's claims.[7]

While the report was in preparation the superintendent of finance resisted "congressional efforts to refurbish the old Confederation taxing system and turned aside initiatives to seek new foreign loans." Morris then threatened to resign by the end of May unless Congress made "permanent provision for the public debts of every kind." The momentum of the previous month's events prompted Congress to grant Morris discretion to settle the "first two claims of the Army—present pay and the settlement of unpaid salaries." And it promised to attempt "every effort ... to obtain from the respective states substantial funds, adequate to the object of funding the whole debt of the United States." The question of commuting half-pay for the officers into an outright grant remained unanswered until late March, and that of proposing a new impost until April. Meantime during February and early March, in an effort to settle these points, Morris and his cohorts fomented rebellion at Washington's Newburgh headquarters, taking care that after the officers had been incited to utter more serious threats, such as a refusal to disband, their mutiny should be quickly snuffed out.[8] Against the background of these developments, Schuyler's work in the New York senate may be seen as complementary to that of the Newburgh conspirators. And it illuminates the predicaments of both the Confederation and New York State as they stood on the threshold of an uncertain peace. The question was no longer one of freedom or independence so much as one of happiness, which entailed setting the security of both the states and the union upon solid foundations.

2

Business at Kingston and the Affair at Newburgh

Summoned by Governor Clinton to its second meeting, the sixth session of the New York legislature failed to reach a quorum from 7 January until three weeks later. Obliged first to escort his wife and daughters to Albany, Schuyler was unable to take his senate seat at Kingston until 28 January. Except for a three-week absence between 8 February and 2 March, when he was called home because of the fatal illness of his father-in-law, the Yorker worked diligently if not always successfully on a variety of issues that were crucial to the welfare of both the state and the Confederation. Appointed to fill a vacancy in the senate, Congressman James Duane was on hand to offer companionship and support much as that afforded by Schuyler's boyhood friend, Abraham Ten Broeck.[9]

Duane's friendship was as ever valuable to Schuyler for the support he sought on general policy issues, but Duane was also helpful in matters of a more personal nature. He kindly managed, for example, the petition of the general's brother-in-law, Dr. John Cochran, for two thousand acres of Mohawk valley land. Less immediately successful were Schuyler's efforts with another measure, which nevertheless had far-reaching implications when it was finally passed in 1786. In response to Noah Webster's request for copyright protection for a spelling book he had written in 1782 when he was a schoolteacher in Goshen, New York, Schuyler introduced a bill to vest authors of books and pamphlets with the sole right of printing and vending their writings. The senate's passage was perhaps too late for assembly action before the legislature adjourned on 28 March, and the bill did not become law until April 1786. Reasons for the three-year delay are unknown, but Webster worked to obtain copyright laws from other states, which is a significant commentary on the nature of the Confederation and the subsequent provision for national copyright legislation under the Constitution of 1787. Schuyler's efforts on Webster's behalf, however, finally bore fruit; and they were but the first of a series of measures he supported to encourage a variety of educational advances such as the "promotion of literature," the establishment of the Regents of the University of the State of New York, the founding of academies and colleges, and the provision of libraries and scientific apparatus for their use.[10]

The joint committee assigned in July 1782 to report ways and means of revising the state's system of taxation and of improving revenue collection seems to have been dilatory in performing its duty—a surprising fact in view of Schuyler's assignment as a member of it. If he could not move the committee to act, who would do so? Could he have deliberately avoided the task, hoping that the state's failure to act would strengthen the nationalists' case for a more powerful central government, armed with adequate fiscal powers? After ordering that the joint committee report by 7 February, the senate agreed to extend the time to a "farther day." And on 27 February, during Schuyler's absence, Abraham Yates indicated that the committee needed still more time to complete its work. Thereafter its labors petered out or were otherwise replaced by other efforts, like Schuyler's introduction of a bill "to sink the Bills of Credit issued by this State, and for the Payment of the public Debt." On 22 March, despite Schuyler's efforts, the senate postponed the bill by a vote of nine to seven.[11]

On Schuyler's motion, however, the senate did declare its sentiments on a restoration of public credit. On 24 March the house resolved that at its next meeting, circumstances permitting, the legislature would place all forfeited estates not then within the enemy's power into a "train of speedy sale." Because of the depreciation of securities issued by both Congress and the state and held by citizens who had loaned funds, sold supplies, and performed a variety of services, the state must provide means of redeeming them. All securities, the resolution stated, whether state or national and whether specified in specie value or reducible to specie by the Continental scale of depreciation, must be received in payment for forfeited lands.[12]

The assembly, however, was either uninterested in the senate's views or did not find time to act upon them in the rush of other business during the final days of the session. This only illustrated why men like Schuyler found the state and confederation system so inadequate to serve the needs of the citizenry at all levels. Although the legislature considered congressional requisitions to meet current expenses and payments on the domestic portion of the national debt and also grappled with the old question of empowering Congress to levy a tax on imports, its actions, like those of Congress, were a mixture of advance and delay. On 4 February the senate referred the requisitions issue to a committee comprised of Ephraim Paine, Schuyler, and John Haring, but during Schuyler's subsequent three-week absence nothing was done, and by the time he returned to his seat on 3 March the legislature had been confronted by a congressional resolution that complicated the issue of assessments.[13]

The Articles of Confederation required state contributions to the national treasury in proportion to all granted or surveyed lands within their respective jurisdictions, "valued in such mode as Congress should point out." While Congress assessed quotas to the states, each "laid what taxes [it] chose to make up requisitions." On 17 February, amidst the rumblings about the army's unpaid claims, Congress asked the states to submit "an accurate account of lands and buildings and of white and black inhabitants" by 1 March 1784. It would then estimate "the value of all lands in each of the United States," thereby furnishing "the rule for adjusting all accounts with the individual states" and for apportioning requisitions. The New York legislature responded by passing a law to execute the 17 February act of Congress. It also levied a fresh round of taxes, assigning quotas to the counties in an effort to raise funds to meet the requisitions.[14]

The impost also received favorable action in New York, but the legislature's disposition of the subject *preceded* Congress's 18 April recommendations and involved some tangled parliamentary dickering over the details. Congress asked for a tax of five percent to be used only to pay interest and principal on the national debt; the import duties would stop in twenty-five years, and the states were to appoint the collectors, although Congress would have the power to regulate and remove them. What the New York legislature provided, however, followed on the heels of Rhode Island's and Virginia's rejection of the impost in December 1782 and did not anticipate the later proposals that the impost should last twenty-five years or that collectors named by the states would be regulated and removable by Congress. Instead the Yorkers voted to approve the 5 percent ad valorem duty on imports and also a duty on prizes and prize goods condemned in the state admiralty court, stipulating that such would not continue longer than necessary to pay the principal and interest of the wartime debt.

In the senate there was little evidence of wrangling on the issue except for the question of amending or repealing the previous authorization of the impost. Because Congress's impost proposal of 1783 was not made until after the New York legislature adjourned, no action could be taken upon it until the 1784 session. Opponents like Abraham Yates, Jr., then staved off agreement until the spring of 1786 when New York approved the five percent duties but without permitting exclusive congressional control over the collectors and the method of collection.[15]

Meantime, the legislature hung the fate of both the impost duties and requisitions upon the outcome of still other measures. New York's future compliance with requisitions, for example, would depend upon effective execution of an act appointing a commissioner to collect information from county supervisors and assessors about real estate and population of the entire state. Yet the Confederation government never completed such an inventory or accounting, and under the Constitution of 1787 the secretary of the treasury was obliged to propose other measures for an effective fiscal system. As for the impost, neither the senate nor the assembly hesitated to agree to the Massachusetts legislature's call for another Hartford Convention, this one to consider a uniform system of customs duties and other taxes. Schuyler, James Duane, and three of their colleagues were assigned to prepare a response. They recommended both the measure for complying with Congress's 17 February requisitions and the appointment of a delegation to Hartford. Senator Ephraim Paine and assemblymen Ezra L'Hommedieu and John Lansing, Jr., were chosen to go to Hartford, but as did the step for assessing land valuation as the basis for congressional requisitions, the convention idea fizzled out, perhaps because of developments of subsequent measures like the new impost proposal of April.[16]

The inability of the Confederation to solve other problems whether because of inertia, irresolution, or want of jurisdiction was also demonstrated by the resumption of efforts to settle a long-standing boundary dispute with Massachusetts. Involved in the controversy since the period from 1764 to 1767, Schuyler found himself again drawn into the business, no doubt in part because he was state surveyor general. Land business and surveying, however, were matters with which he had long become familiar because of personal interest; and his father-in-law's Claverack land claims abutted western Massachusetts. Col. John Van Rensselaer's death on 21 February now made the general an executor of his estate, and he was naturally concerned with the protection of Mrs. Schuyler's share in it.[17] A bill for naming boundary commissioners to complete the unsettled New York-Massachusetts line was introduced to the senate on 5 March shortly after Schuyler returned to Kingston from Van Rensselaer's deathbed and obsequies. Passage of the measure made Robert Yates, Schuyler, and Gerard Bancker the commissioners, any two of whom were empowered to settle the line with Massachusetts counterparts. The business dragged on for years. Delays arose over practical problems like assembling the commissioners and their surveyors in the field. As in 1773 they ran into trouble because of variations in the magnetic needle. After the two states referred the matter to Congress in 1785, surveyors were appointed in December, but there were still more delays. Not until 1788 was the line actually run. The long process was but one of many reasons that Schuyler found to justify his growing nationalism.[18]

On the Ides of March 1783, however, a more serious question of national interest came to a head at Washington's Newburgh headquarters. Nationalism was the overall theme of the conspiracy that the Virginian defused on 15 March, the very day on which New York's act to authorize the impost in revised form became law. On that fateful March Saturday forenoon Washington confronted his impatient officers to discuss their demands for back pay and commutation of half-pay pensions "to some equivalent lump sum payment." Reminding them that refusing to disband the army and openly threatening to defy the civil authority would sully their record of courage and patriotism, he urged them to reject "attempts to open the flood-gates of civil discord" and "deluge our rising empire in blood." The Virginia congressman Joseph Jones had written of Congress's good intentions, and as Washington read Jones's letter he donned spectacles, referring as he did so to having grown both gray and blind in the service of the country. The unaffected but dramatic gesture stunned the assemblage, and with memories of their chief's unswerving patriotism the officers recoiled. Some wept. And when Washington left, a committee headed by Henry Knox quickly drafted resolutions to affirm the army's "attachment to the rights and liberties of human nature" and its "unshaken confidence" in Congress and to denounce "secret attempts of some unknown persons to" act "in a manner totally subversive of all discipline and good order."[19]

Schuyler evidently witnessed the denouement of the Newburgh meeting, although it is problematical whether he could have arrived in time to attend the entire proceedings. The senate journal of 15 March indicates that he was present for at least part of its morning session at Kingston, but the thirty-mile ride to Newburgh was not impossible to make within four hours or less.[20] Interested as he was in the efforts of Robert Morris, Hamilton, and others at Philadelphis to manipulate the army in order to force Congress to commute half-pay pensions and to propose a new impost amendment to the Articles of Confederation, it is impossible to believe that the Yorker was not informed of developments in Philadelphia and Newburgh before 15 March. One may reasonably suspect that he was ready to rush to Newburgh to support Washington's efforts to squelch the threatening movement whose leaders included Horatio Gates, the man who for years had caused the Yorker and the Virginian so much discomfort.[21] At the very least Gates's role in organizing the movement was designed to pressure Congress to pay the army; but something else was afoot. Gates "was susceptible to passion and delusion," and to grasp "the fame that had eluded him" he gambled on his chances to replace Washington by catering to men who had grown impatient with the Virginian's moderate leadership. He "encouraged an American army—in wartime—to refuse to fight, or if hostilities ceased, to march armed on Congress." What he did not reckon perhaps was the ability of civilian and military officers to manipulate such a conspiracy without permitting it to run amok.[22]

Schuyler's own views of the Newburgh affair and the only evidence of his presence there were but briefly recorded in a letter he wrote to young Stephen Van Rensselaer, who was soon to become his son-in-law. "Never, through all the war," he observed, had Washington achieved "a greater victory than on this occasion—a victory over jealousy, just discontent and great opportunities." In citing jealousy the Yorker unmistakably pointed to Gates, and he correctly noted the army's legitimate claims to justice. The "great opportunities" surely referred to the power of the army to have caused more serious distress for the country. "The whole assembly," he went on, "were in tears at the conclusion of his address. I rode wtih General Knox to his quarters in absolute silence, because of the solemn impression on our minds. I have no doubt that posterity will repeat the closing words of his Excellency's address—'Had this day been wanting, the world had never seen the last stage of perfection to which human nature is capable of attaining.' "[23]

After the weekend jaunt to Newburgh, Schuyler resumed his senate seat at Kingston on Monday, 17 March. Significantly, the final two weeks of the session brought the legislators to adopt measures that revealed a mixture of national and localistic attitudes. Perhaps the governor's announcement on 24 March of the arrival of a provisional peace treaty affected the display of these sentiments. On the one hand the senate and assembly repealed the wartime authorization of commissioners for the detection and defeat of conspiracies, abolished the offices of state agent and commissary of provisions, and resolved to offer appropriate land bounties to New Yorkers for their military service. The latter gesture was an appropriate response to the Newburgh incident. On the other hand they pushed aside Schuyler's bill for sinking the state's bills of credit and paying the public debt, called upon Congress for five hundred men to garrison the northern and western posts of the state, and created a state board of Indian commissioners to assist in treaty making between the native tribesmen and the United States. The land bounties were voted in addition to those that had been recommended by Congress in September 1776 and August 1780, and they represented a true bonus. New York officers and men who were presently serving in the United States Army were promised tracts ranging from fifty-five hundred acres for major generals to five hundred acres for privates. As Schuyler had long since surrendered his commission, his support of this measure could in no way be regarded as even partially self-serving. When the land was actually allocated in 1784, and surveys ordered for sixty thousand-acre townships in west-central New York, however, Schuyler resigned as state surveyor general, thereby escaping the enormous chore of executing the bounty enactments.[24]

3

"anxious to maintain, and deserve an honest reputation"

For the moment, however, Schuyler's return to Albany at the end of March brought him face to face with a variety of land business, some as surveyor general and some more strictly that of an individual landholder and as an executor of his father-in-law's estate. His executorship nevertheless was related both to his office as senator and to his prospects as a gubernatorial candidate in the spring elections.

The Yorker's personal dealings were for the moment few and relatively minor. Aside from paying a grain tax, Schuyler executed a lease with Increase Green for a 192-acre farm in the old Saratoga patent on 9 April. Interestingly enough, the terms of the indenture indicated only one notable change from prewar years. There was no stipulation of "riding" service: the tenant's obligation to ride with team and wagon several days each year, hauling his landlord's grain or lumber, which smacked of a semifeudal relationship. But in other respects Schuyler's lease terms continued to show few signs of liberalization, which some have thought accompanied the ferment of revolutionary ideology. The Yorker's agreement with Green was drawn as he made most indentures during the next two decades, with specification of rent payable in cash or kind (usually deferred, as Green's was until 1 January 1784), the landlord's rights of quarter sale and distraint and reentry, and the tenure set at three lives.[25]

As for his public involvement in land matters, Schuyler found that the combination of his roles as a legislator and estate executor invariably subjected him to political suspicions and criticisms. Accused of "odious and injurious" conduct and sinister motives in promoting passage of a land law in July 1782, the general prepared an address to the inhabitants of King's District and filed an official deposition before Judge Abraham Ten Broeck on 4 April. Referring the papers to his senatorial colleague, Col. William Whiting, with the request that he communicate them to his "fellow citizens" near Kinderhook, Schuyler explained his involvement in John Van Rensselaer's affairs for the past ten years. The "man who is not anxious to maintain, and deserve an honest reputation," he admitted, "is little deserving of any regard."[26]

The charges as rumored were that Schuyler had obtained a grant from the colony for lands surrendered in 1773 by John Van Rensselaer, who had thereby obtained royal confirmation of title to the remainder of his Claverack estate; and that Schuyler's support of a statute passed in July 1782 was only a subterfuge. Although the law favored the occupants of the land, who were squatters, he must have known that it could not prejudice his prior rights, and therefore he must have had some sinister intention to regain the lands that his father-in-law had previously surrendered. Schuyler answered that his support of the law was rooted in principles that were both equitable and just: occupants of land not otherwise clearly granted might invariably be preferred to others in making good their claims. This he also insisted was his longheld position on the New Hampshire Grants dispute as well. Had Schuyler or his late father-in-law in fact obtained such a grant, he would not have sought passage of a law that would militate against his interests or place him in the "most odious and contemptible situation imaginable." Since Van Rensselaer's 1773 surrender neither he nor his son-in-law had directly or indirectly petitioned for or obtained a grant for any part of the relinquished territory.

Schuyler's disclaimer to the King's District people, requesting them to publicize his proof of rectitude, was signed "Your affectionate fellow citizen," which was an obvious pitch to an electorate about to choose members of both executive and legislative branches of the state government. There is, however, little other evidence that Schuyler campaigned vigorously to unseat Gov. George Clinton, although his candidacy marks both his opposition to Clinton and the dissolution of the wartime coalition of New York Patriots. More conservative Whigs, principally the landed families with commercial allies and public creditors, were now seeking a stronger national government. Provincial-minded "men of the 'middling classes,' who were cemented to Clinton by the perquisites" of his office, proved victorious over half-hearted opposition. Although friends took "infinite pains for him," Schuyler garnered only 643 votes, all from Albany County. "Robert R. Livingston's family backed Clinton, the upper manor Livingstons were indifferent, and New York City was still in enemy hands." Sen. Ephraim Paine, whom Hamilton regarded as a fiery and primitive radical, "received 520 votes, all very likely from his home county of Dutchess and conceivably a protest against Clinton's moderation on" the issue of confiscating Loyalists' lands. "With about 1,100 more votes cast than in 1780, Clinton got 3,584, almost his previous total and still 'a very disproportionate vote,' "as Margaret Beekman Livingston observed to her son, the chancellor.[27]

The election of 1783 did not, however, yet reveal an altogether clear-cut partisan cleavage or that the emerging parties represented a simple split in ideology or even of old landed families and their moderately well-to-do rivals. Some of the Livingstons were after all pro-Clinton, and Schuyler's cousin, Pierre Van Cortlandt, of another manorial family, was Clinton's running mate as lieutenant governor. Mrs. Schuyler's cousin Philip Van Rensselaer readily congratulated Clinton for "the Great Election in your favor" and wished that he might "with more satisfaction Enjoy that office than you have done for several years past."[28] Moreover, if there were signs of any democratic rumblings against so-called aristocratic politics, they were somewhat obscured in the maunderings of wartime patriotism. The resolves of a general committee meeting in Fredericksburgh Precinct, Dutchess County, on 12 April indicated a lingering animus against the provincial elite, which Schuyler personified. But they also reveal a more positive vote in support of Clinton, which was increasingly related to institutional changes of power, a broader franchise, easier access to government, and a wider participation of ordinary folk in both the polls and public office. According to the resolves a governor "should have as few Family Connections as possible," be thoroughly versed in civil and military matters, and have "uniformly taken an Active and decisive Part in favor of the United States" from the earliest period of the recent contest with Britain. Clinton, it was asserted, met all these qualifications. Whether he had bested Schuyler in active support of the United States might be seriously questioned; but his propriety of conduct, his participation in battle, and his gallant defense of Fort Montgomery were evidently regarded as superior to Schuyler's greater but less sparkling record. And it was also argued by the Fredericksburgh leaders that it would be the height of "ingratitude, cruelty and baseness" to displace him at the very moment that Clinton had safely steered New Yorkers through the war and landed them in a haven of peace, liberty, and independence.[29] So much for the popular perception of Philip Schuyler's sacrificial efforts and enormous contributions to the state and nation.

If the general was at all diverted by electioneering in the spring of 1783 or even hoped to become governor, as he most certainly deserved to, he nevertheless found a myriad of activities with which to console himself after Clinton's victory. Still a senator and state surveyor general, he continued to process applications for land, busied himself with his property and family affairs, and soberly considered the opportunities of the future. There were the challenges of an impending peace to meet, the provisional terms of which Congress had ratified in April, and still the occasional duties of the board of Indian commissioners to perform.[30]

From the prewar years other business also lingered. In July 1783 John Morin Scott proposed to sell his share of lands purchased with Schuyler, John Bradstreet, and Rutger Bleecker in 1772 in the Mohawk valley. The vast acreage was a part of Cosby's Manor, which had been acquired by the partners' payment of arrears in quitrents. Wishing to take advantage of the "continual applications" by prospective purchasers and to concentrate his business affairs in New York City, Scott offered to sell his portion to Schuyler and his friends. Although he estimated the value of some sixty-eight thousand acres at forty shillings per acre, Scott offered to sell at the rate of twenty-five shillings. Willing to wait three years for most of his money, he wanted £3,000 at once and the balance payable at three percent interest. It is not clear whether Schuyler obtained any of Scott's land or whether he otherwise disposed of it for his partner.[31] But it is apparent that the end of the war had reopened vast opportunities for land speculation and agricultural development. And those who held tracts in the Mohawk valley would be particularly fortunate as peace increasingly lured Yorkers and Yankees alike into the vast area west of Albany.

4

"to render the reconciliation cordial and compleat"

Albanians cheered the news of a provisional peace treaty on 27 March but did not celebrate their relief from the wartime siege until after Congress had approved the treaty. On 22 April a civic program of rejoicing included a procession from city hall to the hilltop fortification, which is now the site of the state capitol, and cannon fire and bells resounded across the Hudson. Banqueting and thirteen victory toasts were followed by an evening bonfire and the illumination of houses until almost midnight, the streets having been filled with people for most of the day.[32]

Philip Schuyler's participation in the festivities is unrecorded. Indeed, he may have remained quietly in the country. From mid-April until September much of his time was spent at Saratoga; during the time from October through December he also seemed content to follow rural pursuits, for he and Mrs. Schuyler did not return to Albany with their family until after Christmas.

The hectic pace of the past few years gave way to more leisurely moments. Although Schuyler seldom found chances to be idle, official duties were fewer or at least seemed to come only in occasional spurts. And there was more time for work on his lands and other personal affairs, for his family, and miscellaneous interests. With the establishment of peace, however, there would come a host of new opportunities, a variety of problems and pleasures, and the resumption of interrupted business. The still unsettled estate of his old friend and patron, John Bradstreet, for example, was to involve the Yorker in many years of effort. Largely stalled by the war, his executorship required fresh attention with the return of peace. In May 1783 Schuyler assured Johannes Ball that Bradstreet's agreements with Ball and others would surely be confirmed as soon as the Bradstreet heirs could legally give title to lands conveyed by the deceased general. Since Bradstreet had not obtained a government patent for some of his own purchases from the Indians, his heirs, Schuyler thought, would probably apply to the legislature to confirm both Bradstreet's acquisitions and his subsequent conveyances.[33]

In April 1783 Sir Charles Gould of London posted word of the death of Bradstreet's widow and one of his daughters, Martha. As executor and devisee in trust of the two women's estate, Gould sent Schuyler copies of their wills and requested accounts of Bradstreet's possessions in America. Since duplicates mentioned in the Yorker's previous correspondence had evidently miscarried, Gould begged for another transcript, hoping that

peacetime resumption of packet boat service would spare Schuyler a repetition of further difficulties in communication. The general could now
expect to deal with Bradstreet's heirs at less of a distance since one, Agatha
Evans, proposed to settle in America, and another, Elizabeth Bradstreet,
was espoused to Peter Livius, who was formerly of New York and now
chief justice of Quebec.[34]

When Mrs. Evans finally reached New York early in November with
her husband and family, she promptly notified Schuyler of her arrival,
chiding him for failing to meet her at landing. With the departure of
British troops she imagined that her father's old protégé must necessarily
be on hand to participate in the affairs of state! Now she wished to meet
Schuyler and to obtain an inventory of Bradstreet's affairs. But it was not
until 1784 that the general was able to proceed to deal with the Bradstreet
heirs. Perhaps neither he nor they fully realized how the business would
drag on for another decade, finally involving Alexander Hamilton as
legal counsel.[35]

Another curious result of the establishment of the Anglo-American
peace came in December 1783 when a Mr. St. John requested Schuyler's
aid in obtaining specimens for King George's gardens. Upon inquiry of
the British minister of marine affairs, Benjamin Franklin had recommended that the Yorker be asked to provide a sizable quantity of cones
of white pine and Balm of Gilead and seeds of sugar and curled maple;
of white, black, and prickly ash; and the swamp elm. St. John offered not
only to pay for the shipment of the cones and seeds but promised whatever
seeds of curious plants or shrubs in the royal gardens as Schuyler might
choose. Whether the general responded to St. John's application may only
be conjectured. It is likely, however, that he did so gladly, for he was an
avid horticulturist. During the next two decades the grounds of his Albany house included gardens, orchards, and vineyards, and he carefully
developed a variety of plum, called the Schuyler gage. This tree, however,
he refused to share with others who coveted seedlings from his stock.
The pride of ownership evidently tempted him into an uncharacteristic
lack of generosity.[36]

With the dawn of peace Schuyler's display of liberality during the years
of war remained evident in his longing for full reconciliation with the
mother country. From Saratoga in mid-April he again wrote to Gen.
Frederick Haldimand at Quebec, interceding for the release of two young
men captured as prisoners of war but known to have enlisted in either
the corps of Sir John Johnson or Col. John Butler. The reestablishment
of peace suggested that those who wished "that the political seperation
[sic] should be as little prejudicial as possible, and who are attentive to

the future weal of both Countrys" must "seek occassion [*sic*], to render the reconciliation cordial and compleat." Accordingly, Schuyler proposed that permission be "given to such persons who were Made prisoners of war, and afterwards inlisted in the British corps, and who incline to return to their families . . . to do so."[37]

When the Canadian governor general replied on 30 June, he acceded to Schuyler's requests. Haldimand happily agreed "to adopt every Measure that can tend to bury in oblivion the fatal distractions which have so long subsisted between the Mother Country and America." Yet there were disquieting signs of trouble to come. Haldimand had seen certain "inflammatory papers" emanating from Saratoga and designed to counteract articles of the peace treaty that had been designed to protect Loyalists.[38]

Postwar anti-Loyalist sentiment indeed became rampant in New York, but Schuyler misjudged the prospects for preventing it after 1783. The general promised to publicize Haldimand's tokens of British goodwill in an effort to promote "unequivocal reconciliation, and the restoration of perfect harmony." Although wartime exigencies had "rendered it justifiable in districts of this state, to assume and exercise powers unknown to the constitution," Schuyler recognized that it would be difficult to eradicate widespread disrespect for law and popular habits of hatred and vengeance. When the New York legislature again met he was "fully persuaded" that it would establish "effectual regulations . . . to prevent any infraction of the treaty."[39] Unfortunately, the legislature, like that of other states, pursued a contrary policy, rejecting petitions of Loyalists who wished to return from exile and refusing until 1788 to repeal laws inconsistent with New York's compliance with the treaty of 1783. For years, then, Schuyler worked to remove anti-Loyalist strictures from the statute books and pressed for state compliance with the nation's treaty obligations.

"Sincerely satisfied" that preliminary peace terms had been signed, Schuyler like Hamilton had dreaded the likelihood that France and her allies might insist upon terms that would have "thrown the game" into Lord Shelburne's hands. Ardently nationalistic, Schuyler also did not relish the invitation to Russia and Austria to serve as mediators between Britain and France lest European powers meddle with or complicate American interests. Although he found that some people were dissatisfied with the national boundaries, he deemed these to be "more favorable to us" than those which the American commissioners had been instructed to insist upon. Happy that the New York legislature seemed inclined to confer powers on Congress "Adequate to the proper discharge of the great duties of the Sovereign Council of these states," Schuyler remained uneasy. I "perceive with pain," he wrote, that some men were trying to inculcate a contrary principle. Should this gain too deep a root, it would not be eradicated until enough "confusion" made men feel the necessity of the states surrendering more sovereignty. Widespread sentiment against pardoning Loyalists whose lands were confiscated was also so strong at the recent session of the legislature that their warmest sympathizers would not attempt to introduce a bill to relieve them. Schuyler believed however that in conformity with the provisional peace treaty no molestation would be made to other citizens of the state who had been within enemy lines and whose conduct may have been equivocal or even more clearly opposed to the patriot cause.[40]

5

"Thoughts Respecting peace with the Indians"

Unlike the Loyalists, the Indians were by the Treaty of Paris wholly abandoned to the mercies of the United States. Schuyler was troubled for the Iroquois as well as for the others, and as head of the Commissioners for Indian Affairs of the Northern Department he endeavored to promote a formal peace settlement for them. Long unable to obtain directions from Congress about the policy the commissioners were expected to pursue, the general managed the business according to his own best lights. In May, for example, he was able to answer the request of a number of faithful Oneida and Tuscarora near Schenectady who wished to return to their lands to plant corn. At Saratoga with Mrs. Schuyler and his daughter Margaret, he promptly ordered the contractors for army and Indian supplies in the Northern Department to furnish up to two months' supply of provisions and a quantity of corn according to Henry Glen's certification of the amount they might need for planting.[41]

In June rumors spread among the tribes in western New York that those who had warred against the United States were to be deprived of their lands and forced to remove to Canada; Schuyler, it was alleged, would demand satisfaction at an Indian conference or humble the proud Iroquois with military force. Meantime, secretary at war Benjamin Lincoln had sent Ephraim Douglass into Indian country to announce Congress's favorable intentions toward them. Douglass reached Fort Niagara on 11 June, but the British commander there, Gen. Allan Maclean, would permit him to talk only with Col. John Butler and Joseph Brant. Both Butler and Maclean quieted the Indians' fears on 2 July at a council at Onondaga. Maclean's written assurances to Douglass that he wished to promote the peace between Britain and the United States were then sent to Schuyler. Maclean, however, was obliged to wait for authorization to proceed with negotiations.[42]

After hearing allegations that he had sent a threatening message to the Iroquois, Schuyler prepared a letter to Joseph Brant and an address to the western tribes. Dated 29 July, the letter announced that Schuyler was determined to pursue peace without military force and denied the idle stories that had been circulating to the contrary. "Your Grandfather and mine," he wrote to Brant, "were strictly united in friendship, and It will be your fault if you and I are not so too." Perhaps some of the Indians did not wish to establish peace, else why had they spread falsehoods about the Yorker's intentions? Congress had not yet decided what terms could be offered, but Schuyler suggested that a deputation of sachems and warriors from each nation be sent to the board of Indian commissioners to petition for a settlement. They must prove their sincerity by bringing along all of their prisoners. Meantime, Schuyler promised to request more particular directions from Congress.[43]

Like his letter and address to Brant and the Iroquois, the Yorker's "Thoughts Respecting peace with the Indians" were dispatched to the president of Congress on 29 July. Without instructions for policy, Schuyler explained that he had notified the tribes of terms that should neither wound the dignity of Congress nor drive the Indians to despair. At a moderate expense the Iroquois might be obliged to leave the United States, but Schuyler saw no advantage in that. Their residence in New York would not prevent settlement of the country between the region already occupied and what lands the Indians might be permitted to retain. As white settlements inched westward the Indians could naturally be expected to move on, seeking better hunting ground and gradually surrendering more of their lands. On the other hand, to expel them would make them allies of the British and more troublesome to the United States; continual harassment of the frontiers would create expenses for defense and difficulties in subduing the hostiles. Moreover, expulsion would arrest the American fur trade. A settled peace would also be cheaper than maintaining "respectable" garrisons at Oswego, Niagara, Detroit, and Michilmackinac and on the Miami and Illinois rivers. Urging Congress to give the Indian commissioners its directions, Schuyler suggested that an Indian deputation could be expected to arrive between five and fourteen weeks "at farthest." Already the New York legislature had assigned Onondaga and much of the Cayuga territory for veterans' bounty lands, so the Indians could not simply return to their former homes. Congress must consider this fact and also the unlikelihood that the legislature could be induced to permit the Indians to reside just anywhere within the state. Finally, Schuyler urged that when the definitive peace treaty had been received, the faithful Oneida and Tuscarora should be returned to their homes with gifts of food, ammunition, a hundred axes, and a like number of hoes and camp kettles.[44] Congress, it seems, had fallen once again into lethargy or paralysis. For months it did not respond to the Yorker's pleas for the establishment of a national Indian policy.

6

An "unhappy business"

The spring and summer of 1783 passed almost pleasantly for Schuyler as his thoughts focused mainly upon his estate and family. Diverted only briefly by distinguished visitors (Washington, Governor Clinton, and Count dal Verme) he spent much of his time at Saratoga, busy with overseeing his mills and fields and sales of lumber. His bucolic pleasures were marred however by a touch of scandal. On 3 June the general paid one Derby Lendsay fifty-five "french Guineas" on condition that Lendsay and a certain Mary Carpenter move at once to Canada. Lendsay's receipt acknowledged Schuyler's previous payment of thirty-four guineas for the same purpose, which was a sizable sum that was supplemented by an annual pension of £10 for Mary until such time as she married. At that point the pension was to cease, and she was to be paid £50 outright, provided that she remained in Quebec province with her husband.[45]

The affair of Mary Carpenter remains largely a mystery. Except for Lendsay's receipt for Schuyler's payoff and a copy of a 1787 account statement of Edward Aubery and Mary Carpenter, who was then his wife, there is little to explain who she was and why she was forced to leave the country. Perhaps she was the Mary who was the Albany housekeeper or servant mentioned by Schuyler's aides, John Lansing and Richard Varick, in November 1777. Between 24 May and 3 June 1783 Lansing, now a lawyer, exchanged correspondence with the general who was then at Saratoga. These letters perhaps suggest the reasons for Mary's removal from the Albany environs.[46]

Managing Schuyler's affairs in Albany, Lansing wrote of some in cryptic fashion. His letters are more tantalizing for what they hint at than they are illuminating. Reading between the lines, one can but guess at the story that both he and Schuyler knew in full. Lansing examined witnesses to what he termed an "unhappy business" involving Schuyler's son, probably John Bradstreet, who was almost eighteen; his brothers Philip Jeremiah and Rensselaer were but fifteen and ten, respectively, and therefore unlikely subjects of their elders' anxiety. Accusations had been made, but Lansing found that certain testimony could not affect the boy if the principal witness did not appear for the prosecution. If the girl could be induced to go to Canada, Lansing thought, there would not be sufficient proof for an indictment. The son of one Hans Van Der Werken might also be conveniently removed as an eyewitness to the undesignated offense if Schuyler agreed to pay for his board and tuition at some school in another state. On further investigation Lansing discovered that Van Der Werken's statement of evidence proved that he knew nothing of the "Farce" except that he had heard "the girl shriek" from a distance and had not seen her "make any resistance." Informed on 3 June that the girl, "Lindsey and McGowen" were "gone off," Lansing wrote Schuyler that if that was not already the case, measures should be taken at once to send her off, because only her evidence could "fix the Charge." Evidently Albany townsmen had come to think that malice had "painted the affair in its worst colors," and Lansing imagined that it would blow over "without judicial notice." Expecting, however, that a grand jury would summon "the girl" on the following morning, Lansing insisted that "she must be concealed at all events" if she had not already disappeared.[47]

Was Schuyler's son guilty of some serious assault, or perhaps only an embarrassing peccadillo? Would a man of his father's rectitude countenance even his own son's escape from his just deserts under the law? Apparently the squire of Saratoga was willing to avoid notoriety or disgrace, willing to squelch proceedings that could be more damaging than mere gossip or rumored misdeeds. Before receiving Lansing's last missive, the general had acted as the lawyer advised. With eighty-nine guineas in his pocket Derby Lendsay had probably set out with Mary Carpenter on their long trek to Canada through the wilds of the north country beyond Saratoga. With the wedding of his third daughter impending, Schuyler perhaps deemed it imperative to be quickly rid of the threat to both her nuptial festivities and the settled reputation of the entire family.

On 6 June, only three days after Derby Lendsay's payoff, Schuyler's daughter Margaret followed her father's example and married a Van Rensselaer—this one the scion of the major branch of the patroonal clan (the general had chosen his bride from the Claverack or lesser side of the family). The *New-York Gazetter or, Northern Intelligencer* announced on 9 June that the "Lord of the Manor of Rensselaerwyck" had wed "Miss Peggy Schuyler, third daughter to General Schuyler of this city; a most amiable young Lady, possessed of every qualification necessary to render the married state completely happy." Hints that the couple married against the wishes of the bride's parents and even eloped, as had her sister, are tenuous. The only objection the Schuylers might have had was to Van Rensselaer's age: he was not yet nineteen; his bride was almost twenty-five. Unlike Angelica's choice of John Barker Church, Stephen Van Rensselaer was no unknown adventurer, and the Schuylers were of course well acquainted with the patroonal family as well as allied to its collateral line. Like Schuyler's other sons-in-law, the young patroon proved to be a man of considerable ability; like the general, he found public office to be as much a duty as an opportunity and served successfully in the state assembly and senate as lieutenant governor and congressman. Fifth in direct descent from Kilean Van Rensselaer, the first patroon, his social credentials were impeccable, and he was a Harvard graduate as well.[48]

Her third daughter safely married, Mrs. Schuyler set out for Philadelphia early in July to bid farewell to the eldest, whose elopement in 1777 had caused her so much annoyance. Angelica and John Church were to sail for Europe at the end of the month with Jeremiah Wadsworth. Partners in the work of supplying Rochambeau's army, Church and Wadsworth found it necessary to visit France to solicit payment of bills drawn in their favor by the army's intendant.

Fearing that his wife might be detained in her passage through New York City, Schuyler armed her with a letter to Sir Guy Carleton, the British commander in chief in America. In requesting Carleton's "intervention for expediting her," the Yorker registered his desire for Anglo-American harmony by thanking Carleton "for that conspicuous humanity, which has marked your Conduct in the late war, [and] for those generous exertions to eradicate that national animosity, which has arisen in the course of a civil contest between the contending people." Carleton gladly met the request and politely acknowledged it by indicating that the gesture was no more than a testimony of "a desire to repay an obligation; for the polite attentions I experienced many years ago at your house are fresh in my rememberance." Like Schuyler he hoped that Englishmen and Americans would forget the "mischiefs of civil contention" and cultivate "sentiments of reconciliation and affection." These alone might bring the blessings of peace and open the future prosperity of both countries.[49]

Similarly, both Schuyler and Hamilton endeavored to pave the way for the Churches' reception in France with letters of introduction to John Jay and Benjamin Franklin.⁵⁰ The transatlantic voyage was but the first of several for Church and his wife, who established a residence in England. And Schuyler's wishes for a rapprochement with the mother country were gratified in part when his successful son-in-law became a member of Parliament for Wendover, Berkshire, from 1790 to 1796.

Meantime, during July and August 1783, while Schuyler resumed work at Saratoga, it is clear that his newest son-in-law and his bride had begun their marriage without any of the strains experienced by John and Angelica Church and her parents. Following their honeymoon, Stephen and Margaret Van Rensselaer took charge of the Schuyler brood at Albany. Two-year-old Caty had accompanied her father to Saratoga, but the other children, Cornelia, her brothers Philip Jeremiah and Rensselaer, and her sister Elizabeth with the Hamiltons' infant son, Philip, remained behind.

Schuyler of course relied upon Van Rensselaer to discharge a variety of chores, but he worried about the young man's recurrent fits of fever. The elder's letters afford but glimpses of the family's life, but even from afar the paterfamilias seemed to dominate. Would the young bridegroom send up three pounds of tobacco for Uncle John Livingston? Rensselaer must "not neglect the school" and should "adhere . . . closely to his books." Would Mrs. Hamilton send her father a pound of cotton? As soon as Mr. Tubbs had done with the hay of the Albany meadow he must send all the fallow cows to Saratoga. Was Dick likely soon to be better of the rupture that troubled him? Were Cornelia's feet improved, her father asked. He hoped so, and also that she was able to go to school. "Kiss her for me," he wrote. Eager to see all of his dear ones, the general wrote on 10 July that "my avocations are so many and so pressing that I must deny myself the pleasure for the next fortnight." With the beginning of harvest, he could not leave Saratoga. By early August he had grown uneasy about Mrs. Schuyler's long absence. "My anxiety about your Mama," he wrote Mrs. Van Rensselaer, would be much relieved "if I could learn where she" was en route from Philadelphia and "when we might probably expect her." The Van Rensselaers' constant attention, Schuyler noted, "affords me the most agreeable sensation." There had been some contretemps with a certain "Jenkins and his pretended wife"—tenants perhaps—and Schuyler was disgusted by the man's insolence. Jenkins "certainly deserved to have been kicked out of the house." Whether the general meant that he or Mrs. Jenkins should have done the kicking is not clear. Wishing he could visit Albany even for a few days, Schuyler found that his carpenters "so incessantly want my directions" that he dared not leave the country. "Kiss the little ones for me," he wrote; "God bless you. I am ever affectionately yours."⁵¹

7

Comrades of the Cincinnati

Only three days after the general witnessed the marriage of the Van Renssealers in June 1783, officers of Washington's army organized the New York Society of the Cincinnati at New Windsor. The state president general chosen there was Alexander McDougall; the vice president, secretary, and treasurer were George Clinton, Benjamin Walker, and Philip Van Cortlandt. The general association had been formed a month earlier in anticipation that the army would soon disband and in hopes that its officers might maintain in peacetime the comradeship and interests that had bound them together during the war. Henry Knox had drafted the society's general constitution, and Washington served as its national president until his death in 1799. Although an original member of the state chapter of the society, Schuyler probably was not present for its inaugural meeting. Whereas practically no evidence remains of his activities as a member, the aims of the society were certainly such as he could heartily endorse, especially the perpetuation of officers' friendship, together with their rights and liberties, and the promotion of national honor.[52] In July 1783 Schuyler readily demonstrated his devotion to his wartime comrades by pausing to entertain a number of them instead of adhering to his plans to remain at Saratoga for the overseeing of his harvest.

None of Schuyler's military friendships was more enduring and notable than Washington's. And before the Virginian finally left Newburgh (on 18 August) he wanted to see the northern part of the state on which so much of his colleague's work and interests were centered. His short visit to Albany in June 1782 had not enabled him to travel much farther than Schenectady. "The present irksome Interval," he wrote on 15 July, "while we are waiting for the definitive Treaty, affords an opportunity of gratifying this inclination." It was also an opportunity for renewing comradeship, and Washington did not hesitate to ask for Schuyler's help in preparing the necessary arrangements. Governor Clinton, he announced, would accompany the tour of those places made famous by the campaign of 1777. And Washington also wanted to inspect the Mohawk valley, celebrated for its fertile soil, "beautiful situation," and attraction for speculators.[53]

Washington and Clinton set out from Newburgh on Friday, 18 July, only three days after the Virginian sent Schuyler his request to assist the quartermaster in providing boats for lake travel and other transportation. After a night at Kinderhook, the party, which included several field officers and Count Francesco dal Verme, arrived at Albany. A few miles beyond the city a canoeist delivered the town officials' invitation for refreshments, and by noon a crowd had gathered to greet the visitors at the wharf with a show of flags. A thirteen-gun salute roared from the local fort, followed by a tavern dinner for thirty-two. After smoking and wine drinking the guests moved to Mayor John Jacob Beekman's house for afternoon tea. Count dal Verme recorded that they then "Lodged with General Schuyler, a very rich man, whose home is as magnificent as it is well situated on a hill a quarter of a mile from the city and the same distance from the River, of which it enjoys a panoramic view."[54]

Despite his earlier expectation to oversee the harvest at Saratoga, Schuyler evidently rushed to Albany immediately after receiving Washington's 15 July request. For his Saturday night guests he paid £1.8.0 for three-and-a-half gallons of spirits furnished that day by James Caldwell. Dal Verme mentioned nothing of Schuyler's fare, only that the company "Ate supper here with two of his married daughters [Elizabeth and Margaret] and an Indian colonel from Canada who spoke French and English fluently in addition to five Indian languages." This was probably Louis Atyataghronghta, a Caughnawaga who was one of Schuyler's wartime agents in the quest for Canadian Indian support of the American cause.[55]

On Sunday morning after breakfast Schuyler and Mayor Beekman led Washington and his companions out of Albany to the Mohawk River. Transferring from horseback to a boat, they crossed to see the Cohoes Falls and then moved on toward Saratoga. Dal Verme found the woodland road generally good but said little of his host's country house, where they arrived at six o'clock for dinner and lodgings. "Saratoga consists of a few houses and many sawmills," he observed, evidence of Schuyler's extensive restoration since 1777.[56]

On Monday Washington's entourage proceeded to Fort Edward and then to Fort George. En route they encountered over two hundred people returning to their homes from Indian captivity. On Lake George the party, which, according to Dal Verme, numbered thirty-nine, embarked in three bateaux, each rowed by six armed soldiers. Schuyler, however, seems not to have accompanied them into the wilds beyond Saratoga. Although no one could have been a better guide for a visit to Ticonderoga and Crown Point, the general probably remained behind to resume his supervision of the harvest and other work until the visitors returned on 26 July. Dal Verme then inspected one of Schuyler's mills. Particularly noteworthy he thought was the fact that it had fifteen saws that simultaneously cut a log into sixteen boards.[57]

Next day the density of the fog evidently slowed the journey of Washington's party to the mineral springs about a dozen miles west of Saratoga. Dal Verme's journal does not specify whether Schuyler accompanied them on their ride up the Mohawk, but his report that they got lost in the woods in spite of having a guide does not suggest that Yorker was with them. It is difficult to believe that Schuyler could have stumbled about in territory with which he was so long familiar. After stops at Schenectady and Fort Rensselaer (Canajoharie), where the garrison gave Washington a thirteen-gun salute and a parade of maneuvers, the tourists moved on to Fort Herkimer and Fort Dayton and then to Fort Schuyler, which had been totally destroyed by fire and flood in 1781. Their circuitous return to Albany led them south into the Cherry Valley and to Lake Otsego and then back to Canajoharie. At Schenectady the city fathers laid on a dinner of thirty-two covers, and two hundred Indians presented honors to the commander in chief on 3 August. By that evening he and his companions again rode into Albany. "Lodged with General Schuyler," Count Dal Verme concluded; "Warm."[58]

On 4 August, when Washington parted with his New York friend, neither could have expected that they would not meet again until 1789, almost exactly six years later. Nor could they have dreamed that the one would then be president of the United States and the other a United States senator. Washington's boat slipped away from an Albany dock amidst a farewell cannonade. Armed with a passport and letters of introduction from the commander in chief, Count Dal Verme tarried with Schuyler, inspecting horses that the merchant John Taylor helped him purchase for his tour to Boston. His Albany host furnished dinner, tea, and supper on 4 August, and lodgings from a "Terrible storm," but the count was entertained by Taylor and Col. Morgan Lewis on the following day when Schuyler probably returned to his work at Saratoga. The nobleman himself left Albany on 6 August.[59]

Mrs. Schuyler may have been grateful to have missed the round of visitors. When she returned to Albany on 11 August from her visit to Philadelphia, where she had made her farewells to the Churches, the general's weary wife was certainly happy to be home. After more than a month's absence she found a happy reunion awaiting her. With her came Congressman Alexander Hamilton, who had been parted from Eliza and their infant son for almost nine months. Hamilton had been more than anxious to hasten the journey with his mother-in-law, yet he deferred to her determination to tend "some business" at New York City. "Being in company with Mrs. Schuyler," he explained to Chancellor Livingston, "I was induced, in complaisance to her, to pass through New York." The stop afforded him an opportunity to inquire about the arrival of a definitive peace treaty, but he discovered none.[60]

For the next several months Hamilton remained in the bosom of his family at Albany. More than a "physical haven," the Schuyler home offered him "mental and emotional comfort." His father-in-law relished their companionship, and the young lawyer doubtless divided his time between the city and the Saratoga country house. "If he and the Schuyler household ever differed in domestic relations or in public desires, the evidence does not exist in the long record we have of their affectionate mutual reliance." Both the years of war and the next two decades of Hamilton's short life revealed his and Washington's "identity of purposes, and similarity of solutions for particular problems; with Schuyler the concidence was even more cordial." Father and son "were more alike in temperament, and their teamwork was promoted, of course, by the family bond. The balance of practical obligation was of the younger man to the older, partly because Schuyler had fewer public responsibilities, and found enough reward in Hamilton's accomplishments. No account of the latter can be just," however, that does not show the general's frequent official activities in the next two decades and that "does not point to the prompting and resourceful support which Schuyler constantly afforded to his brilliant friend."[61]

At Albany Hamilton began his legal practice, some of it for Isaac Sears of Manhattan, some for the Livingstons, and a memorial from Renssealer Manor to the legislature. "As his mind continued to run on public issues, so did his pen. His 'Vindication of Congress' probably belongs to October 1783."[62] Similarly, his father-in-law returned from time to time to public issues to tend to business both national and parochial in scope.

8

A "disagreeable dilemma"

As a senator and especially as an Indian commissioner Schuyler, too, was obliged to turn occasionally from rural pursuits to the conduct of public business. Like Hamilton's recent work in Congress, the general's responsibilities were doubtless topics for the two men to discuss when they were not otherwise inspecting the fields and mills of Saratoga or the orchards and gardens of the Albany household. From late summer until well into the autumn of 1783 the question of an Iroquois peace settlement persisted, and Schuyler continued to wait for Congress to act.

At the end of July he had shared his thoughts of peace with both the Iroquois and the delegates at Philadelphia, but the Indians were the first to respond. From Niagara chiefs and warriors of the Six Nations dispatched a belt of wampum in confirmation of an accompanying letter, dated 8 September. Expressing great surprise at Schuyler's earlier announcement that Congress had "not yet signified its pleasure to the Commissioners for Indian Affairs on a peace with the Indians," the message acknowledged that Ephraim Douglass had already promised Congress's peaceful intentions. The Iroquois stolidly assured the general "that we are hearty and sincere in our desire of Peace and Friendship with Congress."[63]

Before Schuyler received the Indians' message of 8 September, James Dean notified him that an Iroquois deputation had set out to meet with him and the board of Indian commissioners. But would they be permitted to approach the eastern settlements? Without the general's order, it seemed "very unsafe" for them to do so. On 25 September, Schuyler passed Dean's message on to Congress, noting that the tribesmen's arrival would greatly embarrass the commissioners unless they obtained Congress's instructions for the terms on which a peace could be negotiated. Begging for a speedy answer from President Elias Boudinot, the Yorker promised to employ some excuse to detain the delegation should they reach him before instructions could be sent from Princeton.[64]

Meantime, except for a proclamation on 22 September prohibiting settlement on lands claimed by the Indians, Congress waited for a committee to agree upon the terms that Schuyler had proposed. On 25 September the committee seems to have settled upon the necessity of a surrender of prisoners and an assertion of United States ownership of Indian lands. The tribesmen might be offered the clemency of a boundary settlement; the friendly Oneidas' and Tuscaroras' claims must be respected, and it would be "advantageous" if the tribes could be persuaded to exchange their lands for others "more remote." The commissioners of both northern and western Indian departments might unite for a general conference with the tribes. However, a counterproposal, perhaps made by James Duane, was offered that the national commissioners should arrange an Indian cession in conjunction with those recently authorized by the New York legislature.[65]

Such were the issues that aggravated the long delay in determining a course of action for Schuyler. To him a speedy decision about Indian policy had seemed imperative earlier in 1783; should the British evacuate the Great Lakes posts—a course in fact that they proved to be in no hurry to follow—Americans should move in to establish their own protection against the tribes and against the British presence in Canada.

When Schuyler finally received the Iroquois message from Niagara, he was surprised to read its allegations that Congress had offered terms through Ephraim Douglass and that the tribes had accepted. The general also found it lamentable that he had not been informed that the commissioners were to be replaced by other negotiators. Might the Indians grow suspicious of such divided counsels in the American government and thereby be easily exploited by the British? Resenting, moreover, his exposure to such a "disagreeable dilemma," Schuyler notified Congress how "forcibly" he felt the propriety of telling the Indians that they need negotiate no further with him if they had established a peace with other commissioners. However, he also recognized that such a step would "be consonant to British wishes." Being "incapable of sacrificing my Country's interest to a *just* resentment," he wrote, he would endeavor instead to "explain away" the sentiments of his 29 July message to the Iroquois in some manner "least injurious" to the interests of the United States.[66]

The general then proceeded to carry forward the work of furnishing a variety of supplies to the friendly Oneida and Tuscarora and to collect others in preparation for a conference with all the tribes. Meantime, he and the other Iroquois remained puzzled by the contradiction between what Ephraim Douglass had informed them at Niagara in June and what Schuyler had announced late in July. On 22–23 October, for example, Joseph Brant addressed a solemn exhortation to "Korah Thanyendakayea, alias Gen'l. Schuyler." Congress, he said, must declare unequivocally with whom the Iroquois were to negotiate. Brant also complained "that the messages delivered to us, immediately from Congress, differs [sic] amazingly in Language from that of yours. Therefore at present [we] are at a loss to know who Congress have appointed for this business." And there were complaints of people surveying land in contravention to the 1768 Treaty of Fort Stanwix. Had Congress authorized such activity? Still determined upon peace, Brant vowed, the Iroquois could not now attend Schuyler's proposed conference because of the lateness of the season and other business.[67]

By now it had been months since Ephraim Douglass had reported his mission into the Ohio country and western New York to the secretary at war.[68] Sent by Secretary Lincoln in May to announce the peace settlement between Britain and the United States, Douglass was instructed to attempt to head off efforts of British agents like Sir John Johnson to persuade tribesmen to continue the war. Douglass visited Sandusky, Detroit, and Niagara in June and July, and British commandants there agreed to encourage peace but could not engage in the negotiation of specific terms without orders from their superiors. And at Niagara, Col. John Butler and Joseph Brant warned Douglass that unless Americans respected tribal land claims, peace could not be ensured. Brant wanted United States promises to recognize those claims before any treaty was made. Schuyler evidently did not receive a copy of Douglass's 18 August report until after President Elias Boudinot answered the Yorker's 11 October letter on 29 October.

Boudinot explained to Schuyler that Congress had merely instructed Secretary Lincoln to inform the Indian tribes of the Treaty of Paris's promise of peace and its provisions for national boundaries. Lacking a quorum, it had been unable to take further action, but Boudinot assured the general that his fears were groundless. The information given to him of Congress's willingness to negotiate through channels other than the Indian commissioners was probably part of a scheme of "our late enemies" or other western interests. Boudinot was sorry that the scheme had produced confusion and the appearance that Schuyler was being bypassed. Congress had not yet decided whether to proceed with the wartime board of Indian commissioners or to name others to negotiate a general Indian peace. The press of other business had simply delayed a settlement of the Indian question.[69]

Schuyler remained unable to satisfy the Iroquois as long as Congress failed to act. And he feared the possibility of renewed hostilities. Soured by loss of their Mohawk valley lands, Sir John Johnson and Guy Johnson might very well incite the Iroquois to resume hostilities. And if garrisons were established for the western posts, the movement of troops along the Mohawk should be expedited by the collection of munitions and the construction of bateaux by no later than March.[70]

By the end of 1783 and the opening of the new year the incredible delays with Indian negotiations may be explained as the result of the New York government's interests and of the waning power of nationalists in Congress to press for vigorous Indian and defense policies. Earlier in the year the state had authorized its own Indian commissioners to negotiate with the New York tribes. In Congress the force of local interests clashed with that of the nationalists who wanted the central government to exercise its rightful powers to make treaties and regulate Indian affairs. Opening the west to settlement required not only land cessions by the tribes, but also the garrisoning of troops to support peace negotiations, police the settlers, and occupy the strategic forts like Oswego, Niagara, Detroit, and Mackinac. Hence Schuyler's recommendation of 16 December for negotiations during the winter and preparations to move troops up the Mohawk by spring at the latest.[71]

But by 8 January 1784, when Schuyler and Volckert Douw finally met the Iroquois deputation, they had still obtained no instructions. The two commissioners could do no more than promise a future treaty conference and to answer charges that Americans were already trespassing on Indian lands. United States citizens, Schuyler said, had a right to explore their territory confirmed to them by the Treaty of Paris unless expressly for-bidden to do so. As yet they had no right to settle that territory. Meantime, prisoners held by the Indians must be returned before any treaty would be made.[72]

Still Congress did not move with any sense of urgency. Not until March 1784 did the delegates vote instructions for negotiations and advice on the desirable boundaries for Indian land cessions. Although agreeing with Schuyler's overall philosophy and his particular proposals of July 1783, it did not include him among the commissioners who were named to con-duct the treaties with the formerly hostile tribes. Only as an afterthought was the Yorker chosen on 8 April. After a creditable career as Indian commissioner since 1775, Schuyler resented the slight and refused to serve.[73]

Peace with the Six Nations was finally negotiated by United States commissioners in October at Fort Schuyler. The appalling delay was still another instance by which Philip Schuyler was convinced that the Articles of Confederation were an imperfect framework for the new nation. The establishment of independence might not endure unless so frail a structure could be strengthened—or replaced by one capable of guaranteeing Americans prosperity and happiness as well as their liberty and security.

9

"the din of War no longer disturbs our Ears"

Anno domini 1783—not the year of Yorktown—marks the end of American War of Independence, for although Congress did not ratify the definitive treaty of peace until 14 January 1784, the preliminaries had been solidly accepted, and the British evacuation of New York signaled clearly the expectations of a final peace. Washington's farewell to his officers at Fraunces's Travern on 4 December and the resignation of his commission to Congress at Annapolis on 23 December were also final testimonies that the years of conflict were no to give way to peaceful experimentation with the fruits of independence.

For Philip Schuyler, too, the last months of 1783 pointed to a decided shift of pace as he increasingly settled into the life of a country squire.

Like Washington's return to Mount Vernon, the Yorker's full resumption of peaceful pursuits was satisfying. He welcomed the work of managing his mills and farms at Saratoga and the prospects of developing his holdings in the Mohawk valley much as Washington undertook the improvement of his own estate and looked westward with an eye to the development of the interior. The Yorker, however, unlike the Virginian, remained much closer in touch with political life by the retention of state office.

"The change of times and circumstances," wrote Barry St. Leger, Schuyler's secondary foe in the campaign of 1777, "naturally produce a change in the complexion of our sentiments and expressions; as the din of War no longer disturbs our Ears, our business, as Christians, is to speak the words, and to do the actions of Peace." The sentiment was one that Schuyler understood perfectly, and he agreed. As St. Leger applied to him on behalf of a Colonel Edmiston, who wished to return to his property, Schuyler was already committed to the policy of reconciliation. He would do what he could to relieve those who for their loyalty to King George or because of their equivocal stand on independence would fall under the "designation of proscription or confiscation."[74]

From far-off Passy, John Jay lamented that Schuyler had largely withdrawn from public life. Had his reasons for retiring been less urgent than one of ill health, Jay would have thought his friend had acted prematurely. He might well have said "selfishly." Men of talents, weight, and influence should exert themselves for the establishment and maintenance of proper constitutional authority and subordination. Jay wrote what Schuyler already knew—that their countrymen stood in great need of wisdom and perseverance to save and secure what they had gained. Well-ordered government, Jay told Schuyler, would be needed for "the duration and enjoyment of the tranquillity and leisure you promise yourself at Saratoga." The general must therefore be willing to "attend to those subjects" as much as his health permitted. Expecting to return to New York the following summer, Jay promised to do what he exhorted the general to practice: to devote his time to the public's health as duty might require.[75]

In the next two decades Schuyler indeed answered the call of duty to promote the public weal. Repeatedly elected to the state and the United States senates, he also promoted the spread of schools and colleges as a regent of the University of the State of New York, supported prison and penal law reform, and fostered internal improvements as president of two inland lock and navigation companies. For the moment, however, little beyond his efforts to settle a treaty with the Iroquois or the occasional applications for surveys from land-hungry petitioners disturbed the Yorker's celebration of peace or managing his family and business.[76]

The Hamiltons' move to New York City in November deprived Schuyler of some of the immediate comforts he relished as paterfamilias, and he anxiously protested when Mrs. Schuyler told him that Margaret and Stephen Van Rensselaer intended to set up housekeeping in "the parsonage house" in Albany. "Such a measure will give room for censorious conjectures," he wrote his youngest son-in-law, who had not yet reached his majority. Evidently not relishing the departure of both young couples, the general willingly stayed in the country to give the remaining one as much privacy as possible at the Albany manse. While much of their time was spent at Saratoga, Schuyler and his wife also depended upon their daughter and the young patroon to manage their Albany household and the younger children.[77]

Acknowledging Van Rensselaer's "affectionate letter" on 4 December, Schuyler was apparently content with his son-in-law's response, perhaps an acquiescence to the family patriarch's wishes or a satisfactory explanation of the couple's determination to move. The general and his wife, however, remained at Saratoga until the end of the month, delayed in part by efforts to complete the construction of a new gristmill and then by the weather. Signs of a long, hard winter had already blasted along the Atlantic seaboard from New Jersey to Maine, and snow had been widespread during 12–13 November and again at the end of that month. Anticipating a grim season, Schuyler urged Van Rensselaer to expedite a servant's collection of sundry supplies before travel became obstructed and their shipment delayed. Similarly, he ordered the purchase of five "large and good" deerskins, ready dressed for making moccasins for several of his Negroes.[78]

Far down the Hudson the last military operation of the war on the Atlantic seaboard—the British evacuation of New York City—was followed by the city's first postwar elections. But the prospects for an end to all hostilities were slim. The politics of peacetime promised to be turbulent and rancorous. John Lansing, Jr., warned Schuyler on the day after Christmas that from the most recent news of the electoral campaign "violent Commotions are to be apprehended." Although many Loyalists had moved with the British forces in late November and early December, the election of assemblymen and senators had sparked an ugly movement against others who remained. The cry had gone up that "no *Tories* notoriously so shall be permitted to reside amongst us." And voters otherwise willing to wait for appropriate action from the legislature had threatened to deal with Loyalists in their own way should the government not establish legal reprisals.[79] The tide of animosity was such that Schuyler subsequently found that it was difficult to check or to reverse. But as a state senator he stubbornly fought to uphold the principles of the treaty of peace that had promised Loyalists the cessation of confiscations and prosecutions.

Far different was the comradely sentiment surrounding Washington's farewell to his officers at Fraunces's Tavern on 4 December. Marking in its own way the advent of peace and the joyous completion of independence, the parting was as emotional a scene as the Virginian's dramatic quelling of the Newburgh conspiracy in March. In mid-December, Schuyler, too, was the focus of a minor farewell address presented by seven officers of the Rhode Island Continental line. About to leave Saratoga, where their military service had ended as part of a frontier garrison, the handful of men saluted the Yorker for whom so many fellow Yankees had held the deepest suspicion and mistrust. Congratulating the general upon the achievement of victory and peace, they thanked him for his favors and generosity, for his attentiveness and services during their residence at Saratoga. "Such, Sir, has been your conduct towards us. The tenderness of a father, the solicitude of a guardian, & the beneficience of a friend, have been constinuous [sic] thro' the whole of it." Cordially, they offered warm wishes for Schuyler's future prosperity, his honor, and his happiness.[80]

Treasured among Schuyler's papers, the simple accolade was altogether unlike those perfunctory courtesies so often bestowed by military or civilian superiors. Well deserved, it and similar scraps of evidence did not, however, gain the general a particular place in the pantheon of the Revolution—a position to which he was certainly entitled for all of his labors since 1775. But it aptly summarized Philip Schuyler's signal attributes and his contributions to the American War of Independence. Resolutely faithful, meticulously careful, daring, and resourceful as circumstances warranted, and ever generous though frequently misjudged and misunderstood, he, like his "amiable chief," had persevered. Dutifully he had served despite adversity, resenting the insults to his honor, but proving above all else that he was a man of virtue—a proud patriot.

Abbreviations

AAS	American Antiquarian Society, Worcester, Massachusetts
AA4	*American Archives, Fourth Series,* ed. Peter Force, 6 vols. (Washington, D.C., 1837–46).
AA5	*American Archives, Fifth Series,* ed. Peter Force, 3 vols. (Washington, D.C., 1848–53).
Add. MSS.	Additional Manuscripts, British Museum, London
AIHA	Albany Institute of History and Art, Albany, New York
GCP	*Public Papers of George Clinton, First Governor of New York, 1777–1795, 1801–1804,* ed. Hugh Hastings, 10 vols. (N.Y. & Albany, 1899–1914).
HL	Henry E. Huntington Library, San Marino, California
JCC	*The Journals of the Continental Congress, 1774–89,* ed. Worthing C. Ford, *et al.,* 34 vols. (Washington, D.C., 1904–37).
JPCCNY	*Journals of the Provincial Congress, Provincial Convention, Committee of Safety and Council of Safety of the State of New-York, 1775–1776–1777,* 2 vols. (Albany, N.Y., 1842).
LMCC	*Letters of Members of the Continental Congress,* ed. Edmund C. Burnett, 8 vols. (Washington, D.C., 1921–36).

521

MNHP	Morristown National Historical Park, Morristown, New Jersey (LWS Coll., Lloyd W. Smith Collection).
NYHS	New-York Historical Society, New York City, New York
NYPL	New York Public Library, New York City, New York
NYSJ	New York State Senate Journals (titled *Votes and Proceedings of the Senate of the State of New-York* and *Journal of the Senate of the State of New-York, 1777–1805*) in the New York State Library, Albany, N.Y.
NYSL, MSS. Div.	New York State Library, Manuscripts and Special Collections Division, Albany, New York
PAC	Public Archives of Canada
PAH	*The Papers of Alexander Hamilton,* ed. Harold C. Syrett *et al.,* 26 vols. (New York, 1961–79).
PCC, NAR	*Papers of the Continental Congress,* National Archives Reel (microfilm).
PNG	*The Papers of Nathanael Greene,* ed. Richard K. Showman, vols. I– (Chapel Hill, N.C., 1976–).
PRM	*The Papers of Robert Morris, 1781–1784,* ed. E. James Ferguson, vols. I– (Pittsburgh, 1973–).
S Lbk.	Schuyler Letterbooks, I–V, New York Public Library, New York, N.Y. I—22 June 1775–16 June 1778 II—28 June 1775–24 Feb. 1776 III—25 Feb. 1776–19 Nov. 1776 IV—18 Apr. 1776–29 June 1777 V—19 Nov. 1776–1 June 1778 Continuation of IV (29 June 1777–18 Aug. 1777) is held by the American Antiquarian Society, Worcester, Mass., and is cited AAS, S Lbk IV.
S Papers	Schuyler Papers (general collection with particular parts indicated where catalogued as miscellaneous military, land, surveyor general, Indian papers, personal and household accounts).

Smith Memoirs	*Historical Memoris from 16 March 1763 to 9 July 1776 of William Smith* [I] and *Historical Memoirs from 12 July 1776 to 25 July 1778 of William Smith* [II], ed. William H. W. Sabine, 2 vols. (New York, 1956–1958).
WGW	*The Writings of George Washington, 1745–1799*, ed. John C. Fitzpatrick, 37 vols. (Washington, D.C., 1931–40).

In the interest of brevity and economy, letters and other references from printed sources and from the Schuyler letterbooks in the New York Public Library and the American Antiquarian Society are cited only by volume and page number with abbreviated titles (e.g., *WGW* 10: 255). Citations from unpublished manuscript collections are of course more fully identified (e.g., S. Fay to Schuyler, 13 July 1775, NYPL, S Papers).

Notes

INTRODUCTION

1. Robert Livingston Schuyler, "Philip Schuyler," *New York History* 18 (April 1937): 132. Dr. Eugene F. Kramer, senior historian in the New York State Office of History, once observed that a single volume could not adequately portray Schuyler's life from 1775 to 1804. Aware of the nature of the sources and sensible of the Yorker's significance, he was probably correct in this assessment.

2. Ibid., 131.

3. Ved Mehta, *Fly and the Fly-Bottle* (Baltimore, Md., 1965), 183.

4. George Dangerfield, review of *Philip Schuyler and the American Revolution in New York, 1733–1777,* by Don R. Gerlach, *The New-York Historical Society Quarterly* 49 (Jan. 1965): 90.

5. Erik Erikson, "On the Nature of Psychohistorical Evidence: In Search of Gandhi," *Daedalus* 97 (Summer 1968): 713.

6. Richard B. Morris, ed., *John Jay: The Making of a Revolutionary, Unpublished Papers, 1745–1780* (New York, 1975), 1:452–54. Hereafter cited as Morris, *Jay Papers*.

7. John Brooke, *King George III* (New York, 1972), xvii. Alfred E. Young, *The Democratic Republicans of New York: The Origins, 1763–1797* (Chapel Hill, N.C., 1967), x.

8. George M. Trevelyan, "Clio, a Muse" in *The Varieties of History,* ed. Fritz Stern (Cleveland and New York, 1956), 234.

CHAPTER I

1. *JCC*, 2: 76, 80, 86, 90, 93, 99. Edmund C. Burnett, *The Continental Congress* (New York, 1941), 77–79. Hereafter cited as Burnett, *Congress*.

2. *LMCC*, 1: 110–11. P. V. B. Livingston to N.Y. delegates in Continental Congress, 7 June 1775, NYSL. *Journals of the Provincial Congress, Provincial Convention, Committee of Safety and Council of Safety of the State of New York, 1775–1776–1777,* 2 vols. (Albany, N.Y., 1842), 1: 33.

3. *Collections of the Connecticut Historical Society* (Hartford, Conn., 1870), 2: 251–52, 266–68. *LMCC*, 1: 168 n. Deane to Schuyler, 3 July 1775, NYPL, S Papers.

4. *LMCC*, 1: 150. Sung Bok Kim, *Landlord and Tenant in Colonial New York: Manorial Society, 1664–1775* (Chapel Hill, N.C., 1978) 107 and passim, 409–12. Don R. Gerlach, *Philip Schuyler and the American Revolution in New York, 1733–1777* (Lincoln, Nebr., 1964), 49 n, 85,

319–22. Jackson Turner Main, *The Social Structure of Revolutionary America* (Princeton, N.J., 1965), 9–10.

5. Schuyler helped his father-in-law defend the Claverack property from squatters and speculators, but Van Rensselaer surrendered part of his claims in order to secure the rest in 1772–73. Kim, *Landlord and Tenant*, 181, 200, 409–12, 421–22; the total sales revenue was £6,314, not counting about thirty-eight hundred other acres, which, if they were sold at the same average of £1 per acre, would mean an additional £3,800. For other evidences of the sales value of land see Main, *Social Structure*, 9–10; in 1774 James Duane sold land at the rate of £80 per hundred acres.

6. Kim, *Landlord and Tenant*, 200, 209–10. Mrs. Philip Verplanck was General Schuyler's cousin.

7. J. Graham to Schuyler, 19 Dec. 1775, NYPL, S Papers. Lewis A. Leonard, *Life of Charles Carroll of Carrollton* (New York, 1918), 284. NYPL, S Lbk., 4: 36–37 also mentions Schuyler's overseer Graham. Ludlow, Shaw and Ludlow to Schuyler, 1 Jan. 1775, Daniel Hale to Schuyler, 23 Dec. 1775, and Cornelius Wendell's receipt for £14.14.0, 4 Jan. 1776, NYPL, S Papers. Schuyler to Walter Livingston, 12 July 1775 refers to "Mr. Hale my Clerk," HL, Schuyler Orderbook, no. 150.

8. Mrs. Schuyler's hardy constitution withstood twelve pregnancies. Twins born in 1761, triplets in 1770, and the first John Bradstreet in 1763 were stillborn or died in infancy. And of fifteen only eight of the children lived to maturity. Remarkably enough, Elizabeth, who married Alexander Hamilton, lived to the ripe age of 97 (9 Aug. 1757–9 Nov. 1854). All the children save the first were conceived in wedlock. Gerlach, *Philip Schuyler*, 17–18. See also Catherine M. Scholten, " 'On the Importance of the Obstetrick Art': Changing Customs of Childbirth in America, 1760 to 1825," *The William and Mary Quarterly: Third Series* 34 (July 1977): 427. The records of Schuyler's slaveholding are fragmentary. The slaves are mentioned in scattered receipts, correspondence, household accounts for shoemaking, census figures, and a record of executors' manumission as follows: 1761, Harry (purchased for £100); 1767, Jupiter, Tom, Har (Harry?), Libea, Pol and Peter; 1768, Tom and Harre (Harry?); 1769, Bob, Juba and the six of 1767; 1776, Cato, Dinah, Prince, Adam, Moll, Lively, Jenny, Peter, Tom, and Lisbon; 1787, fourteen including Jacob, Peter, Cuff, and Bett, ten others at Saratoga (and thirteen at Albany?); 1790, thirteen at Albany and fourteen at Saratoga; 1797, four purchased in July: Silvia and her two children for £80; and Tom (or Tone?) for £115; 1801, eleven at Albany and mention of Toby and Anthony; 1804, Tone, Stephen, Phoebe, Silvia and three children: Tom, Talleyho and Hanover.

9. Main, *Social Structure*, 123, 161. For more about the house and Schuyler's property valuation see Gerlach, *Philip Schuyler*, 33 n, 38–41; NYPL, S Papers, Box 2; The Division for Historic Preservation Bureau of Historic Sites, *Schuyler Mansion: A Historic Structure Report* (State of New York, Office of Parks and Recreation, 1979). L. Clarkson's receipt, 21 Sept. 1789, and W. C. Hulett's receipt, 2 Feb. 1775, and Jacob Hendrick's receipt, 30 Jan. 1776, NYPL, S Papers, Personal and Household Accounts.

10. Schuyler Ledger (1774–96) f. 259, James Ponpard's receipt, 1 Feb. 1776, and Jacob Wendell's receipt, 16 Feb. 1776, NYPL, S Papers, Personal and Household Accounts. The Harmanus Ten Eyck and Wendell Co. freighted a variety of goods for Schuyler in Nov. 1775: drygoods, apples, pots, nails, cider, wine, rope, a barrel of tobacco, glass, chocolate, earthenware, soap, codfish, potatoes, etc. For Burgoyne's estimate see *The Parliamentary Register; or, History of the Proceedings and Debates of the House of Commons: Series One*, 17 vols. (London, 1802), 8: 311–12. For comparative figures on the purchasing power of the pound see W. Jackson Bate, *Samuel Johnson* (New York and London, 1975), 145.

11. Don Higginbotham, *The War of American Independence: Military Attitudes, Policies, and Practice, 1763–1789* (New York, 1971), 414.

12. Forrest McDonald, *Alexander Hamilton: A Biography* (New York, 1979), 74–75. The DeLanceys, who led one faction in the New York Assembly and who seemed to prevail as spokesmen for local interests to the royal government, were Schuyler's cousins. James and Oliver DeLancey and their brothers Stephen and Peter were the sons of Anne Van Cortlandt DeLancey, sister to Schuyler's mother Cornelia. Gerlach, *Philip Schuyler,* 244–73. For the Bradstreet-Gage problems see William G. Godfrey, *Pursuit of Profit and Preferment in Colonial North America: John Bradstreet's Quest* (Waterloo, Ontario, Canada, 1982), 233–40.

13. Kim, *Landlord and Tenant,* 409–515 et passim.

14. Schuyler's commission, NYSL, MSS. Div.

15. Jacob Ten Eyck and Philip Schuyler to the Mayor, Recorder, Aldermen and Commonality of the City of Albany, 10 Mar. 1775, NYSL, MSS. Div. See also NYPL S Lbk., 2: 78–80; *AA4,* 2, 1762, gives different spelling, punctuation, and capitalization. Where printed sources differ from manuscripts I have tended to use the latter in all quotations and to prefer the manuscripts for citation; printed sources contain lacunae because of editorial omissions. Both manuscript and printed sources are given to allow the reader to refer to the latter because they are obviously easier to consult. Kenneth S. Lynn, *A Divided People* (Westport, Conn., 1977) offers another possible reason for Schuyler's choice between rebel and loyalist positions. Lynn argues that a man's relation to his father may determine his politics, and that loyalists lacked the parental guidance of fathers who died young or had unsatisfying relations with fathers who were "uncompromising patriarchs," men who were too possessive and restrictive. Rebels he says experienced happier relationships and consequently were more childlike in self-confidence, optimism, and willingness to take risks. Schuyler was deprived of a father early in life, but his upbringing seems to have been the work of his mother and paternal grandfather. One can only speculate where Schuyler fits into such a theory of motivation.

16. NYPL, S Lbk., 2: 195–96.

17. *AA4,* 3: 1595 and NYPL, S Lbk., 2, 238–39; ibid., 237–38.

18. *LMCC,* 1: 110–11; 5: 358 n.

19. R. Duncan's Receipt, 23 June 1775, NYPL, S Papers, Personal and Household Accounts; David Hawke, *A Transaction of Free Men* (New York, 1964), 75.

20. James Thomas Flexner, *George Washington,* 4 vols. (Boston, 1965–72), 2: 22, 24. Flexner's description is at variance with the miniature portrait of Schuyler painted by John Trumbull in 1792 (Yale University Art Gallery) and with Philip Church's Answers to Mr. [Benson] Lossing's questions respecting General Schuyler, 6 June 1859, NYSL, MSS. Div. (Church was Schuyler's grandson.) See also Christopher Ward, *The War of the Revolution,* ed. John Richard Alden, 2 vols. (New York, 1952), 1: 140, for a description somewhat at variance with Flexner's; DeAlva Stanwood Alexander, *A Political History of the State of New York,* 3 vols. (New York, 1906–9), 1: 18.

21. Paul David Nelson, *General Horatio Gates: A Biography* (Baton Rouge, La., 1976), 18–20, 40; Morris H. Saffron, *Surgeon to Washington: Dr. John Cochran, 1730–1807* (New York, 1977), 22. John Cochran was born in Chester County, Pa., and met Schuyler's sister Gertrude (1724–1813) in 1758 while on duty in the war. Relict of Peter Schuyler, she married him on 4 Dec. 1760. Gertrude and Peter Schuyler had two children, Peter (1745–92), who studied law with William Smith, Jr., and later served as major in the U.S. army, and Cornelia (1746–1822), who married Walter Livingston, son of the third Lord of Livingston Manor. Gertrude and John Cochran had five children of whom only James (1769–1848) and Walter (1773–1867) survived infancy or youth. Dr. Cochran practiced medicine in Albany in 1760–62 and then in New Brunswick, New Jersey. James Cochran, who was Schuyler's nephew, also became his son-in-law as the second husband of Schuyler's daughter Catharine Van Rensselaer, who first married Samuel Malcolm.

22. *AA4*, 2: 1078.
23. NYPL, S Lbk., 1: 14–15. Flexner, *Washington*, 2: 27. *WGW*, 3: 302–4; Schuyler had these orders copied into his own letterbook, NYPL, S Lbk., 1: 15–17. In August 1777 Congress responded to Washington's question about his relation to the Northern Department by resolving that it had "never intended . . . by the Establishment of any Department whatever to Supersede *[sic]* or Circumscribe the powers of General Washington as the Commander in Chief of all the Continental Land Forces." John S. Pancake, *1777: The Year of the Hangman* (University, Ala., 1977), 198.
24. Schuyler et al. to the Albany Committee of Correspondence, 6 June 1775, NYPL, MSS. Div. NYPL, S Lbk., 1: 17 and *JCC*, 2: 109–10.
25. David Richard Palmer, *The Way of the Fox: American Strategy in the War for America, 1775–1783* (Westport, Conn., 1975), 59, 95. Gustave Lanctot, *Canada and the American Revolution, 1774–1783* (Cambridge, Mass., 1967), 26–39.
26. Palmer, *Way of the Fox*, 20.
27. E.g. Flexner, *Washington*, 2: 52, says Washington's approval of the Arnold expedition to Quebec "was, in effect, a pitchfork in the reluctant conservative's back." George F. G. Stanely, *Canada Invaded, 1775–1776* (Toronto, 1973), 28, says Schuyler "lacked Arnold's dynamism" and "was at his age [a mere forty-one] better qualified to lead a quadrille than an undisciplined mob of men." Other caustic and ill-advised assessments may be seen in Higginbotham, *War of American Independence*, 108–10; and Jonathan Gregory Rossie, *The Politics of Command in the American Revolution* (Syracuse, N.Y., 1975), 41–44 and passim.
28. Alexander Flick, ed., *The American Revolution in New York: Its Political, Social and Economic Significance* (Albany, N.Y., 1926), 133–34. *JPCCNY*, 1: 268–69. *AA4*, 2: 1134, 1139, 1530–31. Schuyler to Continental Congress, 28, 29 June 1775, *PCC*, NAR 172 #1–4, #5–6, NYPL, S Lbk., 2: 6. Schuyler to Hinman, 28 June 1775, *PCC*, NAR 172 #7–9.
29. *AA4*, 2: 1138–39. HL, Schuyler Orderbook, 13–14. (Son of the third lord, Robert, Jr., of Livingston Manor, Walter married Schuyler's niece Cornelia in 1767.) NYPL, S Lbk., 2: 13–14.
30. *LMCC*, 1: 150 and NYPL, S Lbk., 1: 18–20, 62. *JCC*, 2: 123.
31. HL, Schuyler Orderbook, 10–13, 15. *AA4*, 2: 1530–31, comments on the vigor of Connecticut troops and their need for regimentals.
32. *AA4*, 2: 1667 cf. Schuyler's General Monthly Return, 14 July 1775, *PCC*, NAR 172. Schuyler to Varick, 1 July 1775, Albany Institute of History and Art, S Papers. In Sept. 1776 Varick became deputy muster-master general of the Northern Army. Promoted to lieutenant colonel in 1777, he became an aide to Benedict Arnold. In the 1780s he served as recorder of New York City, state assemblyman, and speaker of the house; he was mayor of New York from 1789 to 1801. Like Schuyler, he was an anti-Clintonian and a Federalist. John G. Rommel, Jr., "Richard Varick: New York Aristocrat," (Ph.D. dissertation, Columbia University, 1966). Franklin B. Hough, comp., *The New-York Civil List from 1777 to 1855* (Albany, N.Y., 1855), 170–71.
33. *AA4*, 2: 1525–26.
34. Ibid., 1530–31.
35. *LMCC*, 1: 168 n, cf. *Collections of the Connecticut Historical Society*, (Hartford, 1870), 2: 251–52.
36. Broadus Mitchell, *The Price of Independence: A Realistic View of the American Revolution* (New York, 1974), 4–5; and Higginbotham, *War of American Independence*, 110.
37. Duer to Schuyler 19 July, 10 Aug. 1775, NYPL, S Papers, cf. Benson J. Lossing, *The Life and Times of Philip Schuyler*, 2 vols. (New York, 1872–73), 1: 384. Duer declined for fear his brothers in Dominica should lose their fortunes because of his involvement in rebel politics. *LMCC*, 1: 168 n. *AA4*, 2: 1731, 1803, 1804 and 3: 139, 531, 548. *JCC*, 2: 186.

38. Flick, *American Revolution in New York*, 133–34. *JPCCNY*, 1: 268–69. Roger J. Champagne, *Alexander McDougall and the American Revolution in New York* (Schenectady, N.Y., 1975), 82. McDougall to Schuyler, 9 Aug. 1775, NYPL, S Papers.

39. N.Y. Provincial Congress Orders, 4 July 1775 and Stephen Fay to Schuyler, 13 July 1775, NYPL, S Papers. NYPL, S Lbk., 2: 47. *AA4*, 2: 1535–36. Charles A. Jellison, *Ethan Allen, Frontier Rebel* (Syracuse, N.Y., 1969), 139–42.

40. *JPCCNY*, 2: 11.

41. P. Curtenius to Schuyler, 10 July 1775, NYPL, S Papers. Curtenius was to be paid a commission of 1.5 percent for using his own funds, and 1 percent of the purchases made with congressional funds; the New York merchant employed an agent, three deputies, seventeen subcommissaries, and a variety of storekeepers and clerks. Flick, *American Revolution in New York*, 101. *JPCCNY*, 1: 27–28.

42. NYPL, S Lbk., 2: 24–25. *Colls. Conn. Historical Soceity*, 2: 278–80.

43. B. Hinman to Peter V. B. Livingston, 3 July 1775, NYPL, S Papers. *AA4*, 2: 1605–6.

44. *AA4*, 2: 1535–36. Return of Troops, 7 July 1775, NYPL, S Papers.

45. Patricia U. Bonomi, *A Factious People: Politics and Society in Colonial New York* (New York, 1971), 18. Cornelius Wendell's Receipt, 11 July 1775 (£5 for cabin hire, £2.13 for 2 "clubs"), NYPL, S Papers: Personal & Household Accounts. Schuyler's Account with Richard Varick, 11 Aug. 1775, ibid. Misc. Military Accounts. "Clubs" refers to sharing drinking costs for bowls of punch, etc.

46. W. Livingston to Schuyler, 6 July (two letters), 18 July 1775, NYPL, S Papers. *AA4*, 2: 1594–96, 1621–22.

47. Richard H. Kohn, review of *The Toll of Independence*, *William and Mary Quarterly* 32 (April, 1975): 340. Stanley, *Canada Invaded*, 28.

48. *AA4*, 2: 1615. Rommel, "Richard Varick," 6.

49. *AA4*, 2: 1615. Alice P. Kenney, *Albany: Crossroads of Liberty* (Albany, N.Y., 1976), 23.

50. Higginbotham, *War of American Independence*, 109–12.

51. Palmer, *Way of the Fox*, 8, 32–33, 50, 53–55.

52. Kenney, *Albany: Crossroads of Liberty*, 6–16.

53. Ibid., 2–5. The Committee of Safety, Protection, and Correspondence of the City and County of Albany will hereinafter be referred to simply as the Albany committee. Ten Broeck's boyhood friendship with Schuyler was further cemented by family ties. Mrs. (Elizabeth) Ten Broeck (1734–1813) was the sister of the patroon Stephen Van Rensselaer II (1742–69) and the aunt of the patroon Stephen III (1764–1839). The latter married Schuyler's daughter Margaret (1758–1801) in 1783. Also, Schuyler's son Rensselaer (1773–1847) married the Ten Broecks' daughter Elizabeth (1772–1848).

54. Schuyler et al. to Albany Committee, 3, 6, 24 June 1775, NYSL, MSS. Div., Albany Committee of Correspondence Papers. NYPL, S Lbk., 1: 17–18. For Albany politics see Kenney, Albany: *Crossroads of Liberty*, 23–24 and Division of Archives and History, University of the State of New York, *Minutes of the Albany Committee of Correspondence*, 2 vols. (Albany, N.Y., 1923–25), 1: 156–59. Hereafter cited as *Minutes of Albany Committee*.

55. When Schuyler assumed command of the New York Department, it included 2,857 troops (1 July: 1,505 at New York City under Wooster and 1,352 at the northern posts under Hinman.) Washington's command at Cambridge and Boston contained 13,743 fit and present for duty, although there were 16,770 enrolled. *AA4*, 2: 1667. Ward, *War of the Revolution*, 1: 105.

56. Kenney, *Albany: Crossroads of Liberty*, 24. NYPL, S Lbk., 2: 33–34. *AA4*, 2: 1645–46. See also Return of Stores Received, Forwarded and Delivered to Elisha Phelps by John N. Bleecker, 3 July 1775, NYPL, S Papers, Box 48.

57. HL, Schuyler Orderbook, pp. 17, 67. *AA4*, 2: 1621–22, 1647.

58. HL, Schuyler Orderbook, pp. 18–19, 66. NYPL, S Lbk., 2: 35.

59. *AA4,* 2: 1123–24, 1645–46. If all of Hinman's troops numbered no more than 1,400 (1,383 as of the 7 July return), for example, forty days' rations for each would total 56,000. Yet Schuyler's report showed that 75,400 rations of flour and 65,000 rations of pork had disappeared, although only 56,000 should have been appropriately consumed. Even allowing for ten percent spoilage, he was right to suspect waste and embezzlement.

60. S. Chase to Schuyler, 10, 18 July 1775, G. Bedford to Schuyler, 18 July 1775, NYPL, S Papers. *JCC,* 2: 186. HL, Schuyler Orderbook, p. 50. The question of a muster-master general was the subject of Schuyler's exchanges with Congressman Samuel Chase of Maryland. Chase favored the naming of a *deputy* by Schuyler himself—not "the Principal," that is the *general,* and he recommended Gunning Bedford for the New York Department. The provision of officers like Campbell, who was made deputy quartermaster general only for New York's Continental troops, shows how fragmentary the initial arrangements of the army were.

CHAPTER 2

1. NYPL, S Lbk., 1: 21–22; *AA4,* 2: 1165–66, 1645–46, 1702–4. Schuyler to Albany Committee, 13 July 1775, NYSL, Albany Committee Papers. HL, Schuyler Orderbook, pp. 19–21. NYPL, S Lbk., 2: 36–37. Schuyler to C. Van Dyke, 14 July 1775, *PCC,* NAR 172.

2. *AA4,* 2: 1666–67.

3. A. Yates, Jr., to Schuyler and Examination of G. Roseboom, 15 July 1775, NYPL, S Papers. NYPL, S Lbk., 2: 39, 41–42. *AA4,* 2: 1668.

4. Barbara Graymont, *The Iroquois in the American Revolution* (Syracuse, N.Y., 1972), 66–67. Hereafter cited as Graymont, *Iroquois.* NYPL, S Lbk., 2: 97–98. R. Montgomery to Schuyler, 23 July 1775, NYPL, S Papers. *AA4,* 2: 1730–31. HL, Schuyler Orderbook, pp. 43, 97. W. Gilliland to Schuyler, 6 Aug. 1775, NYPL, S Papers. NYPL, S Lbk., 2: 94–95, 106–7, 129.

5. *AA4,* 2: 1730. *JPCCNY,* 2: 12.

6. HL, Schuyler Orderbook, pp. 21–22, 35–36.

7. HL, Schuyler Orderbook, pp. 51, 62. Continental Army Courts-Martial Proceedings, 24 July 1775–5 Aug. 1777, NYPL, S Papers.

8. HL, Schuyler Orderbook, p. 118. J. Visscher to Schuyler, 23 July 1775 and Schuyler to J. Visscher, 25 July 1775, NYPL, S Papers; HL, Schuyler Orderbook, p. 45.

9. R. Montgomery to R. R. Livingston, 3 June 1775, NYHS, R. R. Livingston Papers.

10. HL, Schuyler Orderbook, pp. 19, 79–80, 86–87; and NYPL, S Lbk., 2: 59–60. R. Montgomery to Schuyler, 17, 27, 29 July; 2, 5, Aug. 1775, NYPL, S Papers.

11. *AA4,* 2: 1685–86.

12. Higginbotham, *War of American Independence,* 7. Washington appreciated the Yorker's difficulties because they were similar to his own—"a Portrait at full length," he wrote, "of what you have had in Miniature." *WGW,* 3: 373–376.

13. Schuyler et al. to Albany Committee, 6 June 1775, NYSL, MSS. Div. Albany Committee Papers. Schuyler's return of troops, 7 July 1775, NYPL, S Papers. Schuyler's General Monthly Return, 14 July 1775, *PCC,* NAR 172. *AA4,* 2: 1702–4 cites 200 fewer than the previous return, which listed 535 at Ticonderoga, 412 at Crown Point, 102 at the Landing, and 334 at Ft. George. Lanctot, *Canada,* 21, 50, 55, 57, 60. Ward, *War of the Revolution,* 1: 148 refers to 470 at Saint John's, 110 at Chambly, 80 at Quebec, and 20 at Montreal as of 3 Aug.

14. *AA4,* 2: 1685–86.

15. HL, Schuyler Orderbook, pp. 24–26.

16. Schuyler's orders to various officers and general orders, 20 July 1775, ibid., 26–30.

17. *AA4*, 2: 1702–4.

18. John Pierce, Jr., to Andrew Adams, 24 Aug. 1775, NYSL, MSS. Div.

19. *AA4*, 2: 1702–4. HL, Schuyler Orderbook, p. 24, 26–27. NYPL, S Lbk., 2: 46. As late as Dec. 1775 Langan presented Schuyler with charges for the loss of Skene's property. These included Langan's estimates for items like sails, a crane and French canoe, a burned barn, and a broken scow. But he requested Schuyler to establish the compensation for two missing bateaux and two houses that had been burned at Crown Point. P. Langan to Schuyler, 21 July; 10, 26 Dec. 1775, NYPL, S Papers. NYPL, S Lbk., 2: 56–58. For Schuyler's orders to several officers, 22, 25, 29 July; 5 Aug. 1775, see HL, Schuyler Orderbook, pp. 33–35, 45, 62, 85.

20. L. Mackintosh to Schuyler, 6 Aug. 1775, NYPL, S Papers.

21. *AA4*, 2: 1702–4.

22. S. Fay to Schuyler, 13 July 1775, W. Marsh to Schuyler, 16 July 1775, NYPL, S Papers. NYPL, S Lbk., 2: 46.

23. NYPL, S Lbk., 2: 47.

24. *AA4*, 2: 1702–4.

25. N. Clark to Schuyler, 28 July 1775; N. H. Grants Return of Officers (marked received 30 July 1775), NYPL, S Papers. Herman Allen was named a captain and the list of lieutenants included Ebenezer and Ira Allen. *AA4*, 2: 1760–61.

26. HL, Schuyler Orderbook, 86–87.

27. Orders of N.Y. Provincial Congress, 15 Aug. 1775, P. V. B. Livingston to Schuyler, 17 Aug. 1775, NYPL, S Papers. *JPCCNY*, 2: 14. HL, Schuyler Orderbook, p. 117. *AA4*, 3: 469.

28. R. Montgomery to Schuyler, 24 Aug. 1775, NYPL, S Papers. Jellison, *Ethan Allen,* 146, 152.

29. *LMCC,* 2: 187–88.

30. J. Trumbull, Jr., to Schuyler, 14 Aug. 1775, NYPL, S Papers. Schuyler to J. Trumbull, Jr., 14, 23 Aug. 1775, Connecticut Hist. Soc., Trumbull Papers: Paymaster General, vol. 1.

31. W. Livingston to Schuyler, 8 Sept. 1775, NYPL, S Papers.

32. N. Buell to Schuyler, 16 Sept. 1775, ibid.

33. NYPL, S Lbk., 2: 154. J. Trumbull, Jr., to Schuyler, 14, 23 Nov. 1775, NYPL, S Papers. Schuyler to J. Trumbull, Jr., 26 Oct. 1775, Conn. Hist. Soc., Trumbull Papers: Paymaster General, vol. 1. J. Trumbull, Jr., to Schuyler, 23 Nov. 1775 with Abstract of Cash, 21 Nov. 1775, NYPL, S Papers.

34. *AA4*, 3: 48–49.

35. *AA4*, 3: 987; NYPL, S Lbk., 1: 32–33.

36. S. Stringer to Schuyler, 6, 8 Oct. 1775, NYPL, S Papers. Robert W. Chambers, *The Maid-At-Arms* (New York and London, 1902), v.

37. *AA4*, 2: 1734–35; 3: 242–43. Daniel B. Reibel, "The British Navy on the Upper Great Lakes, 1760–1789," *Niagara Frontier* 20 (Autumn 1973): 67.

38. *AA4*, 2: 1702–4, 1762–63; 3: 17.

39. W. Gilliland to Schuyler, 14 Aug. 1775, NYPL, S Papers.

40. HL, Schuyler Orderbook, 24, 31.

41. *AA4*, 2: 1734–35.

42. HL, Schuyler Orderbook, 59, 70, 72, 85. *AA4*, 3: 49. *AA4*, 3: 11, 14. J. Smith to Schuyler, 5 Aug. 1775, NYPL, S Papers.

43. *AA4*, 3: 11–14, 50–51.

44. *AA4*, 3: 17, 468.

45. Troop Return, 29 Aug. 1775, NYPL, S Papers. *AA4*, 2: 1685, 1704−5, 1721; 3: 17, 19, 70−71, 97. HL, Schuyler Orderbook, 94.

46. *AA4*, 2: 1729−30, cf. 1711. HL, Schuyler Orderbook, 41−42. Schuyler to Albany Committee, 22 July 1775, NYSL, MSS. Div., Albany Comm. of Correspondence Papers. *AA4*, 2: 1731, 1735.

47. *AA4*, 2: 1729−30, 1735. *WGW*, 3: 370−71, 373−76. HL, Schuyler Orderbook, 76, 78.

48. R. Montgomery to Schuyler, 5 Aug. 1775, NYPL, S Papers. HL, Schuyler Orderbook, 86−87.

49. HL, Schuyler Orderbook, 86−87. Cf. Christopher P. Yates to Schuyler, 25 July 1775, NYPL, S Papers.

50. HL, Schuyler Orderbook, 77−78, 80. NYPL, S Lbk., 2: 53−54; *JPCCNY*, 2: 12. *AA4*, 2: 1731.

51. Abraham Yates, Jr., to Schuyler, 18 July 1775, NYPL, S Papers. HL, Schuyler Orderbook, 41−42, 44. NYPL, S Lbk., 2: 67.

52. HL, Schuyler Orderbook, 27, 31, 45, 68.

53. W. Livingston to Schuyler, 18 July 1775, NYPL, S Papers.

54. W. Livingston, to Schuyler, 26 July 1775, NYPL, S Papers.

55. HL, Schuyler Orderbook, 53−54. W. Livingston to Schuyler, 27 July 1775, NYPL, S Papers.

56. W. Livingston to Schuyler, 27 July 1775, NYPL, S Papers. E. Phelps to Schuyler, 28 July 1775, Benson J. Lossing, *The Life and Times of Philip Schuyler*, 2 vols., Da Capo Press edition (New York, 1973), 1: 372−73.

57. W. Livingston to Schuyler, 29 July 1775, NYPL, S Papers. *AA4*, 2: 1760. J. Cuyler to Schuyler, 5 Aug. 1775, NYPL, S Papers.

58. HL, Schuyler Orderbook, 67; NYPL, S Lbk., 2: 77−78.

59. E. Phelps to Schuyler, 17 July 1775, NYPL, S Papers. HL, Schuyler Orderbook, 66. Lossing, *Schuyler*, 1: 373−74.

60. NYPL, S Lbk., 2: 74−76.

61. J. Strong to Schuyler, 15 Jan. 1776, NYPL, S Papers. *AA4*, 3: 1520−27, 1529. Victor L. Johnson, *The Administration of the American Commissariat during the Revolutionary War* (Philadelphia, 1941), 132.

62. *AA4*, 2: 1760. W. Livingston to Schuyler, 31 July; 1, 2 Aug. 1775, NYPL, S Papers. HL, Schuyler Orderbook, 74−75.

63. W. Livingston to Schuyler, 2 Aug. 1775, NYPL, S Papers. Bernard Mason, "Entrepreneurial Activity in New York during the American Revolution," *Business History Review* 40 (Summer 1966): 194. Mason shows that between August 1775 and June 1777 three New England commissaries (Elisha Phelps, Elisha Avery, and James Yancey) disposed of £210,436 in New York, most of which (£187,400) was spent between June 1776 and June 1777. Elisha Phelps's account of Provisions, etc., purchased for Schuyler's army, 20 June−8 Aug. 1775, totaled £5,535.3.5 1/2. "Accot of Provisions & Necessarys Purchased by Elisha Phelps," 11 Sept. 1775, NYPL, S Papers.

64. J. Bleecker's Return of Provisions at Crown Point, 5 Aug. 1775; J. Bleecker to Schuyler, 10 Aug. 1775; W. Livingston to Schuyler, 6, 10, 13, 16 Aug. 1775, NYPL, S Papers.

65. Ward, *War of the Revolution*, 1: 146. See also HL, Schuyler Orderbook, 108; *JPCCNY*, 2: 13−14.

66. *AA4*, 3: 1066.

67. S. Deane to Schuyler, 20 Aug. 1775, NYPL, S Papers.

68. Ward, *War of the Revolution*, 1: 145. Cf. fn. 12 above.

69. P. V. B. Livingston to Schuyler, 8 Aug. 1775; A. McDougall to Schuyler, 9 Aug. 1775; W. Livingston to Schuyler, 10 Aug. 1775, NYPL, S Papers. *JPCCNY*, 2: 13−14.

70. HL, Schuyler Orderbook, 101, 117. G. Van Schaick to Schuyler, 18 Aug. 1775, NYPL, S Papers.

71. Ward, *War of the Revolution*, 1: 146. Jacob Judd, ed., *The Van Cortlandt Family Papers*, 4 vols. (Tarrytown, N.Y., 1976–1980), 1: 110. Hereafter cited as Judd, *Van Cortlandt Papers*. NYPL, S Lbk., 2: 59–60; HL, Schuyler Orderbook, 52, 79–80. W. Livingston to Schuyler, 27, 29 July 1775; R. Montgomery to Schuyler, 29 July, 2 Aug. 1775; and D. Wooster to Schuyler, 29 July 1775, NYPL, S Papers. HL, Schuyler Orderbook, 88–89, 96–97. Chaplain Benjamin Trumbull's Journal, *Collections Conn. Hist. Soc.,* 7 (1899): 139.

72. J. Sullivan to Schuyler, 5 Aug. 1775 and R. Montgomery to Schuyler, 24 Aug. 1775, NYPL, S Papers. HL, Schuyler Orderbook, 98, 107. Ward, *War of the Revolution*, 1: 152.

73. NYPL, S Lbk., 2: 97–98.

74. *LMCC,* 1: 110–11 and NYSL, MSS. Div., Albany Comm. Papers.

75. *JCC,* 2: 123; 4: 394–96. Graymont, *Iroquois,* 34–39, 65. Ralph T. Pastore, "Congress and the Six Nations, 1775–1778," *Niagara Frontier* 20 (Winter 1973): 82. James F. and Jean H. Vivian, "Congressional Indian Policy During the War for Independence: The Northern Department," *Maryland Historical Magazine* 63 (Sept. 1968): 243. NYPL, S Lbk., 1: 21–22.

76. Pastore, "Congress and the Six Nations," 82–83. J. Hawley to Schuyler, 23 Aug. 1775, NYSL, MSS. Div.

77. NYPL, S Lbk., 1: 21–22; 2: 64–65.

78. *AA4,* 2: 1746. *JPCCNY,* 2: 12. *AA4,* 2: 1729–30, 1745–46. Schuyler to Albany Comm., 28 July, 1 Aug. 1775, NYSL, MSS. Div., Albany Comm. Papers.

79. A. Yates, Jr., to Schuyler, 31 July 1775, NYPL, S Papers. G. Morgan's receipt to Col. T. Francis, 29 July 1775 and Thomas and Isaac Wharton's receipt to T. Francis, 31 July 1775, ibid. (Indian Papers).

80. A. Yates, Jr., to Schuyler, 4 Aug. 1775, NYPL, S Papers. Albany Comm. to Schuyler, 5[4] Aug. 1775, NYSL, MSS. Div., Albany Comm. Papers. E. Wheelock to Schuyler, 6 Aug. 1775, Dartmouth College Library, Wheelock Collection.

81. Schuyler to Albany Comm., 12 Aug. 1775, NYSL, MSS. Div., Albany Comm. Papers. V. Douw and T. Francis to Schuyler, 10 Aug. 1775, NYPL, S Papers.

82. NYPL, S Lbk., 2: 97–98.

83. Stanley, *Canada Invaded,* 33–36. Graymont, *Iroquois,* 74–75. *AA4,* 3: 442–43 cites 350 to 400 at Saint John's (in fact ca. 420), 150 to 200 at Chambly (114 infantry and a few artillerymen), 50 at Montreal (actually 111) and a single company (61) at Quebec.

84. *JPCCNY,* 2: 13–14. NYPL, S Lbk., 2: 97–98, 128.

85. A. Yates, Jr., to Schuyler, 18 Aug. 1775, NYPL, S Papers. V. Douw, Schuyler, and T. Francis to Albany Comm., 23 Aug. 1775 (with answer), NYSL, MSS. Div., Albany Comm. Papers. Cf. *AA4,* 3: 475–82 and Graymont, *Iroquois,* 70–74. *JPCCNY,* 2: 14. J. Pierce, Jr. to A. Adams, 24/26 Aug. 1775, NYSL, MSS. Div.

86. Marquis De Chastellux, *Travels in North America in the Years 1780, 1781 and 1782,* ed. Howard C. Rice, Jr., 2 vols. (Chapel Hill, N.C., 1963), 1: 202. Hereafter cited as Rice, *Chastellux Travels. AA4,* 5: 1100–1104. The name Dean mentioned should perhaps have been Thoniondakayon. The author is indebted to Charles Gehring (in a letter dated 4 Oct. 1976) for inquiry about the name at a 1976 conference of Iroquois scholars. Also Barbara Graymont reported (in a letter dated 16 April 1973) variants of Schuyler's Indian name as Thanyeada-kayough, Thanyendakayea, and Thoniyoudakayon; Graymont also reported that the Canadian linguist Gunther Michelson, who is a compiler of a Mohawk dictionary, and two Mohawks could not translate the name; they agreed that the suffix comes from *agayough,* meaning "old," that the prefix is typical of male names, and that the root, *ganyeade* or *onyeade,* is from an unknown and possibly obsolete word. We may trust that the references to "old" denote wisdom and not senility. Sarah B. Wister and Agnes Irwin, eds., *Worthy*

Women of Our First Century (Philadelphia, 1877), 89, cite the name as "Tho-ra-thau-yea-da-kayer" but give no meaning. Maunsell Van Rensselaer, *Annals of the Van Rensselaers in the United States* (Albany, N.Y., 1888), 56 n, alleges that the name was "Ta-ha-ne-ye-a-ta-káu-ye," meaning "ancient his legs," which suggests that Schuyler was not very nimble in movement—odd for a man so active, enterprising, and at times impatient; but then it could refer to his occasional lameness from rheumatic gout.

87. Copy of Congress's address, 18 July 1775, endorsed as delivered on 25 Aug., NYPL, S (Indian) Papers. Proceedings of the Commissioners, 15 Aug.–2 Sept. 1775, *AA4,* 3: 473–93 indicate that it was given on 26 Aug.

88. L. Gansevoort to P. Gansevoort, 28 Aug. 1775, NYPL, Peter Gansevoort Military Papers: Gansevoort-Lansing Collection. Cf. Kenney, *Albany: Crossroads of Liberty,* 25.

89. Vivian and Vivian, "Congressional Indian Policy," 246.

90. Kenney, *Albany: Crossroads of Liberty,* 26–27. John Albert Scott, "Joseph Brant at Fort Stanwix and Oriskany," *New York History* 19 (Oct. 1938): 403. Graymont, *Iroquois,* 65.

91. Allan S. Everest, *Moses Hazen and the Canadian Refugees in the American Revolution* (Syracuse, N.Y., 1976), 3–14. Members of the Anglo-American community included Moses Hazen, Edward Antill, James Livingston, Udny Hay, Thomas Walker, and James Price. *WGW,* 3: 302–4. NYPL, S Lbk., 1: 17.

92. Higginbotham, *War of American Independence,* 109. Jellison, *Ethan Allen,* 147. Palmer, *Way of the Fox,* 99. Rossie, *Politics of Command,* 42–43. Ward, *War of the Revolution,* 1: 149.

93. HL, Schuyler Orderbook, 98, 110–11, 113. *AA4,* 3: 135, 442–43, 670–71. R. Montgomery to Schuyler, 29 Aug. 1775, NYPL, S Papers.

94. *JPCCNY,* 2: 14. HL, Schuyler Orderbook, 31, 38–39. Cf. Lossing, *Schuyler,* 1: 368. Ward, *War of the Revolution,* 1: 147–48. Schuyler to [J. Price], 21 July 1775, HL, Schuyler Orderbook, 63–65. Washington's army at Boston had swollen to 23,000; Pennsylvania and New Jersey had mustered another 8,000, and Schuyler's Northern Army would shortly number almost 8,000, including David Wooster's 2,000 Connecticut men, 3,000 New Yorkers, 600 Pennsylvania riflemen, and 500 Green Mountain Boys. Ward, *War of the Revolution,* 1: 105, summarizes Washington's rolls as 16,770, of whom 13,743 were present and fit for duty. *AA4,* 3: 135–36 and 2: 1734–35. *AA4,* 2: 1734–35, 1762; 3: 135. HL, Schuyler Orderbook, 57–58, 105. W. Gilliland to Schuyler, 24 July, 1775, NYPL, S Papers. NYPL, S Lbk., 2: 73. R. Montgomery to J. Livingston, 18 Aug. 1775, NYPL, S Papers. R. Montgomery to Schuyler, 10, 18 Aug. 1775, NYPL, S Papers. *AA4,* 3: 442–43. Lanctot, *Canada,* 63. J. Livingston to Schuyler, [24] Aug. 1775, *AA4,* 3: 468–69 and NYPL, S Papers. R. Montgomery to Schuyler, 30 Aug. 1775, NYPL, S Papers, indicates that Livingston's August letter should be dated 24 Aug.

95. Jellison, *Ethan Allen,* 147–48. R. Montgomery to Schuyler, 29 Aug. 1775, NYPL, S Papers. S. Chase to Schuyler, 10 Aug. 1775, *LMCC,* 1: 189, but the full text is given in the original, NYPL, S Papers.

96. Jellison, *Ethan Allen,* 148. HL, Schuyler Orderbook, 101–2.

97. *AA4,* 3: 48–51.

98. B. Franklin to Schuyler, 10 Aug. 1775 and B. Franklin to Albany Comm., 10 Aug. 1775, NYPL, S Papers. Cf. *WGW,* 3: 436 n. *AA4,* 3: 242–43.

99. NYPL, S Lbk., 2: 99–100. Cf. *AA4,* 3: 50–51. NYPL, S Lbk., 2: 102–3. *AA4,* 3: 442–43.

100. *AA4,* 3: 442–43. Cf. NYPL, S Lbk., 1: 25 and *WGW,* 3: 436–37.

CHAPTER 3

1. R. Montgomery to Schuyler, 29 Aug. 1775, weekly return from Crown Point and Ticonderoga, 29 Aug. 1775, NYPL, S Papers.

2. R. Montgomery to Schuyler, 30 Aug. 1775, ibid. *AA4*, 3: 467–69, 669–70.

3. HL, Schuyler Orderbook, 120. NYPL, S Lbk., 2: 122–23.

4. *AA4*, 3: 671. HL, Schuyler Orderbook, 121–22. *AA4*, 3: 669–70. E. Allen to Schuyler, 8 Sept. 1775, NYPL, S Papers. Lanctot, *Canada*, 65–66, 96–97.

5. *AA4*, 3: 442–43, 467–68, 669–70. HL, Schuyler Orderbook, 113–14, 119–21.

6. Howard H. Peckham, ed., *The Toll of Independence: Engagements and Battle Casualties of the American Revolution* (Chicago, 1974), 7. Everest, *Moses Hazen*, 3–14, 17, 31. *AA4*, 3: 669–70, 672.

7. S. Mott to Schuyler, 5 Sept. 1775, D. Campbell to Schuyler, 7 Sept. 1775, NYPL, S Papers. NYPL, S Lbk., 2: 120–21.

8. HL, Schuyler Orderbook, 122–23. *AA4*, 3: 669–70. R. Ritzema to A. McDougall, 8 Sept. 1775, NYHS, McDougall Papers.

9. Higginbotham, *War of American Independence*, 110–11. Cf. Graymont, *Iroquois*, 78–79; NYPL, S Lbk., 2: 120–21.

10. *AA4*, 3: 749.

11. William B. Willcox, *Portrait of a General: Sir Henry Clinton in the War of Independence* (New York, 1964), viii.

12. *AA4*, 3: 669–70. J. Livingston to Schuyler, 8 Sept. 1775; E. Allen to Schuyler, 8 Sept. 1775, NYPL, S Papers. Lanctot, *Canada*, 64, 71–72, 76–80, 86–89.

13. *AA4*, 3: 738–40. NYPL, S Lbk., 2: 120–21. HL, Schuyler Orderbook, 126–27.

14. *AA4*, 3: 741–42. See also Graymont, *Iroquois*, 78; Peckham, *Toll of Independence*, 7; Allen Bowman, *The Morale of the American Revolutionary Army* (Port Washington, N.Y., 1964), 29.

15. HL, Schuyler Orderbook, 127, 129. NYPL, S Lbk., 2: 121.

16. HL, Schuyler Orderbook, 128. *AA4*, 3: 738–40. One soldier, mindful of impending danger, filed a personal request with Schuyler. A poignant reminder of the uncertainties of life for men at war, Walter Barrit's petition is also a testimonial of the regard that some men had for their commanding officer. Barrit would be glad, he said, if "[y]our Honor would take the Trouble . . . to Equally Divide my Effects among" his son at Stillwater and two daughters at Schenectady. W. Barrit to Schuyler, 14 Sept. 1775, NYSL, MSS. Div.

17. *AA4*, 3: 738–40, 743–44. Journal of Benjamin Trumbull, *Colls. Conn. Hist. Soc.*, 7: 143.

18. R. Montgomery to Schuyler, 19 Sept. 1775, NYPL, S Papers.

19. HL, Schuyler Orderbook, 125, 131. *AA4*, 3: 738–40. NYPL, S Lbk., 2: 122.

20. NYPL, S Lbk., 2: 122–23. *AA4*, 3: 751. HL, Schuyler Orderbook, 132. Kenney, *Albany: Crossroads of Liberty,* 28–29.

21. Montgomery to Schuyler, 19 Sept. 1775, NYPL, S Papers. *AA4*, 3: 738–40. *WGW*, 3: 485–86. *AA4*, 3: 751–54.

22. HL, Schuyler Orderbook, 131. NYPL, S Lbk., 2: 169–70.

23. *AA4*, 3: 826–27, 952, 954–55, 1095–96.

24. NYPL, S Lbk., 2: 169–70.

25. R. Montgomery to Schuyler, 20, 23 Oct. 1775; *AA4*, 3: 1132–33, NYPL, S Papers.

26. *AA4*, 3: 1392–93, 1602–3, 1633, 1682–84, 1694–95; 4: 188–90, 309–10, 464–65, and NYPL, S Papers.

27. *AA4*, 3: 1602–3, 1633.

28. Ibid.

29. *AA4,* 4: 188−90. Stanley, *Canada Invaded,* 78, 87.

30. Stanley, *Canada Invaded,* 78, 87.

31. *AA4,* 4: 464−65.

32. NYPL, S Lbk., 2: 269−71, 278−79. *JCC,* 3: 389, 418. *AA4,* 3: 1520−23. Peckham, *Toll of Independence,* 11. NYPL, S Lbk., 2: 281−82 cf. *AA4,* 4: 666−67.

33. B. Arnold to D. Wooster, 2 Jan. 1776, NYPL, S Papers.

34. *AA4,* 4: 668−70, 852−54.

35. Ibid., 880.

36. *JCC,* 2: 99, 103.

37. Rossie, *Politics of Command,* 46−51.

38. *AA4,* 3: 749, 1033−35, 1054.

39. T. Lynch to Schuyler, 20 Sept. 1775, NYPL, S Papers.

40. *WGW,* 4: 18−19. *AA4,* 3: 1066.

41. Rossie, *Politics of Command,* 56. NYPL, S Lbk., 2: 151−54. *AA4,* 3: 951−52, 1093−95, cf. 952, 954−55.

42. *AA4,* 3: 951−52. NYPL, S Lbk., 2: 172−73.

43. G. Bedford to Schuyler, 15 Oct. 1775, W. Livingston to Schuyler, 16 Oct. 1775, NYPL, S Papers. Rossie, *Politics of Command,* 54, says Schuyler and Walter Livingston had created "a barely adequate system which funneled supplies from central New York to the army before St. John's," but in fact the system became more than adequate. And Montgomery's army also captured and bought provisions in Canada, the latter with funds relayed by Schuyler as fast as he could raise them. Montgomery's major needs in Canada seem to have been rum, hard cash, and manpower. *AA4,* 3: 1132−33, 1392−93.

44. G. Bedford to Schuyler, 15 Oct. 1775, NYPL, S Papers.

45. *AA4,* 3: 1107.

46. *AA4,* 3: 1107−8.

47. Rossie, *Politics of Command,* 52. Cf. *AA4,* 3: 1065−66, misdated as 14 Oct., cf. NYPL, S Lbk., 2: 178−81; *AA4,* 3: 1195, NYPL, S Lbk., 2: 184−85.

48. *AA4,* 3: 1130−32, cf. NYPL, S Lbk., 2: 185−89.

49. Schuyler to D. Wooster, 23 Oct. 1775, enclosed in Schuyler to R. Montgomery, 24 Oct. 1775, *AA4,* 4: 1008 and NYPL, S Lbk., 2: 190.

50. R. Montgomery to Schuyler, 31 Oct., 5 Dec. 1775, NYPL, S Papers and *AA4,* 4: 188−90. D. Wooster to Schuyler, 18 Dec. 1775, 11 Feb. 1776, ibid., 4: 310, 1007. Rossie, *Politics of Command,* 51−56, explains the Wooster-Schuyler contretemps with an utterly wrongheaded outlook, blasting Schuyler for "a flaw in his personality which had serious consequences" and showing no sympathy for the general's character, his illness, or the full circumstances of his problems and responsibilities. Rossie's account is also factually flawed. For example, he suggests that Schuyler orally challenged Wooster (to his face) to march into Saint John's (upon Wooster's departure from Ticonderoga); in fact, the challenge was later sent in writing to Montgomery, who was asked to use his discretion in delivering it or withholding it.

51. NYPL, S Lbk., 2: 216. *WGW,* 4: 65−67.

52. G. Bedford to Schuyler, 9 Nov. 1775, NYPL, S Papers.

CHAPTER 4

1. *AA4,* 3: 11.
2. Ibid., 738–40, 840–41.
3. Ibid., 796–97, 839–40. NYPL, S Lbk., 2: 149–50.
4. *AA4,* 3: 1093–95.
5. Ibid., 1011–13, 1130–32.
6. W. Livingston to Schuyler, 24 Sept. 1775, NYPL, S Papers.
7. NYPL, S Lbk., 2: 184–85. *AA4,* 3: 1130–32.
8. *WGW,* 4: 45–47, *AA4,* 3: 1373–75.
9. *JCC,* 3: 339; *AA4,* 3: 1392, 1520–23.
10. Burnett, *Congress,* 108. G. Bedford to Schuyler, 9 Nov. 1775, NYPL, S Papers.
11. *JCC,* 3: 340–41.
12. Ibid. Cf. NYPL, S Lbk., 1: 39, 62–65.
13. For details of Schuyler's recommendations see J. Adams's Notes of Debates, 7 Oct. 1775, L. H. Butterfield, ed., *Diary and Autobiography of John Adams,* 4 vols. (Cambridge, Mass., 1961), 2: 199–200; NYPL, S Lbk., 1: 30–32; *AA4,* 3: 1108; NYPL, S Lbk., 2: 178–81; *AA4,* 4: 442–46. Cf. NYPL, S Lbk., 1: 67, and R. R. Livingston's Minutes of Conference, 30 Nov. 1775, NYSL, MSS. Div.
14. *AA4,* 3: 1602–3; *AA4,* 3: 1595–96; NYPL, S Lbk., 2: 239–40; *AA4,* 4: 442–46, cf. ibid., 3: 1681–82, 1692–93.
15. NYPL, S Lbk., 2: 242. S. Stringer to Schuyler, 27 Nov. 1775, NYPL, S Papers.
16. *AA4,* 4: 445–46, and 3: 1681–82, 1692–93. Congress ordered Prescott retained in gaol at Philadelphia on 26 Jan. 1776, and the following September he was exchanged for John Sullivan.
17. *JCC,* 3: 446.
18. Ibid., 446–51; *AA4,* 4: 442–46. R. R. Livingston's Minutes of a Conference, 30 Nov. 1775, NYSL, MSS. Div.
19. *AA4,* 3: 1681–82; 4: 219–20.
20. *WGW,* 4: 147–48.
21. *LMCC,* 1: 263–64; N. Woodhull to Schuyler, 9 Dec. 1775, NYPL, S Papers.
22. *JCC,* 3: 450; 4: 38–40, 109–110, 152, 213, 236, 297, 304, 375–78, and passim. See also Burnett, *Congress,* 111; *AAs,* 1: 1115.
23. *AA4,* 4: 219–20, 225–26. Cf. NYPL, S Lbk., 2: 255–59.
24. Graymont, *Iroquois,* 73; *AA4,* 4: 259–60; *LMCC,* 1: 325–26. See 325 n. for explanation of the Conn.-Pa. dispute over the Susquehanna lands.
25. *AA4,* 4: 260–61, 282; NYPL, S Lbk., 2: 262–63.
26. *AA4,* 4: 375–76; NYPL, S Lbk., 2: 279–81. Copy of a Minute of a Treaty, 3–6 Jan. 1776, NYPL, S (Indian) Papers.
27. *AA4,* 4: 580–82. James F. and Jean H. Vivian, "Congressional Indian Policy During the War for Independence: The Northern Department," *Maryland Historical Magazine* 63 (Sept. 1968): 248–49, 252–53.
28. *WGW,* 4: 92–93.
29. *AA4,* 3: 1692–93. Report of the Committee [28–30 Nov. 1775], ibid., 4: 442–46. R. R. Livingston's Minute of Conference with Schuyler, 30 Nov. 1775, NYSL, MSS. Div. Col. J. Holmes's Orders, 5–12 Dec. 1775 and H. Browne to Schuyler, 9 Dec. 1775, NYPL, S Papers.
30. North Callahan, *Henry Knox: General Washington's General* (New York, 1958), 39, cf. Callahan's "Henry Knox: General Washington's General," *The New-York Historical Society Quarterly* 44 (April 1960): 153; *AA4,* 4: 219–20, 225–26.

31. H. Browne to Schuyler, 9 Dec. 1775; J. Holmes to Schuyler, 12, 25, 28 Dec. 1775, and Holmes's Orders, 5–12 Dec. 1775; J. Holmes to T. Bedel, 16 Dec. 1775, NYPL, S Papers. Callahan, *Henry Knox*, 40–41.

32. *AA4*, 4: 282.

33. H. Knox to Schuyler, 17 Dec. 1775, Ft. Ticonderoga Museum MSS.

34. NYPL, S Lbk., 2: 264.

35. Callahan, *Henry Knox*, 47. "General Henry Knox's Diary During His Ticonderoga Expedition," *New England Historical and Genealogical Record* 30 (July 1876): 323. David M. Ludlum, *Early American Winters, 1604–1820* (Boston, 1966), 96, 147.

36. Callahan, *Henry Knox*, 47–48. "General Knox's Diary," 323–324; NYPL, S Lbk., 2: 271–73; *AA4*, 4: 580–82.

37. "General Knox's Diary," 324–325. E. Curtis to Schuyler, 10 Mar. 1776, NYPL, S Papers.

38. NYPL, S Lbk., 2: 279–81. Callahan, *Henry Knox*, 44–45, 48–49, 97.

39. Peckham, *Toll of Independence*, 3–11, shows total American losses. cf. Schuyler's army:

	Totals	*Schuyler's*
Killed	323	73
Wounded	436	61
Captured	519	436
Missing	5	0
Deserted	57	55

40. Ibid., 7, 9–11.

41. Montgomery and Arnold's forces together contained perhaps 1,000 effective fighting men. The Quebec garrison numbered about 1,100. Its fortifications were able to withstand the little damage done by a few American twelve- and nine-pounders, and the city was well enough provisioned to withstand a siege until May. Stanley, *Canada Invaded*, 84–89.

42. G. Morris to R. R. Livingston, 13 Oct. 1775, cited in Max M. Mintz, *Gouverneur Morris and the American Revolution* (Norman, Okla., 1970), 55; *WGW*, 4: 127–28.

43. *AA4*, 4: 906–7, 1483. Asserting that he could not take twenty-four- and twelve-pounders or an eight-inch howitzer to Quebec unless shot and shell were available, Wooster asked whether there were any such supplies at Ticonderoga and Crown Point that could be sent. Schuyler to J. Hancock, 1 Feb. 1776, ibid., 906–7; NYPL, S Lbk., 2: 314–20; *AA4*, 4: 1146, 1514–15.

CHAPTER 5

1. Eric Robson, *The American Revolution In its Political and Military Aspects, 1763–1784* (New York, 1966), 102, 108.

2. Marshall Smelser, *The Winning of Independence* (Chicago, 1972), 371. Willcox, *Sir Henry Clinton*, 95.

3. Smelser, *Winning of Independence*, 374, 376.

4. *JCC*, 3: 443 (Dec. 23); *AA4*, 3: 1520–23; 4: 219–20.

5. *AA4*, 4: 219–20, 260–61.

6. *JCC*, 3: 447–51; *AA4*, 4: 442–46; R. R. Livingston's Minutes of a Conference, 30 Nov. 1775, NYSL, MSS. Div.; *AA4*, 3: 1694–93 refers to about nineteen hundred men in Canada including Arnold's corps and suggests that they be increased to three thousand during the winter while other reinforcements were collected at Ticonderoga in readiness for movement in the spring.

7. *AA4*, 4: 188–90; B. Arnold to D. Wooster, 2 Jan. 1776; D. Wooster to Schuyler, 5 Jan. 1776, NYPL, S Papers.

8. *AA4*, 4: 226, 463–64, 480. NYPL, S Lbk., 2: 271–73.

9. *JCC*, 3: 446; R. R. Livingston to Schuyler, 11 Jan. 1776, cf. Schuyler to R. R. Livingston, 7 Jan. 1776, Franklin D. Roosevelt Library, Livingston Redmond Papers.

10. *AA4*, 4: 580–82.

11. *JCC*, 3: 450; 4: 109; *AA5*, 1: 1115; *AA4*, 4: 619–20.

12. Bull was subsequently succeeded by Col. John P. De Haas. On 8 Feb. Congress changed its mind about the shipwrights and instructed Schuyler to hire such artificers and boatmen as he could find within his immediate neighborhood. He had already suggested obtaining shipwrights from Albany. *JCC*, 4: 110–11; *AA4*, 4: 803–5. However, on 6 Jan. Schuyler signed a contract with Jacob Hilton of Albany to raise a company of men to construct boats, other vessels and buildings; *AA4*, 6: 1074.

13. *AA4*, 4: 802–5.

14. Ibid. Schuyler to J. Trumbull, 6 Jan. 1776, cf. Schuyler to J. Hancock, 10 Jan. 1776, NYPL, S Lbk., 2: 273–74, 279–81.

15. *AA4*, 4: 666–67. Schuyler to R. R. Livingston, 13[?] [15?] Jan. 1776, F. D. Roosevelt Library: Livingston-Redmond Papers. NYPL, S Lbk., 2: 281–82.

16. *AA4*, 4: 666–67.

17. Ibid., 880. NYPL, S Lbk., 2: 284–85.

18. *WGW*, 4: 254–57; *AA4*, 4: 671.

19. O. Belding to Schuyler, 15 Jan. 1776; C. Goodrich to Schuyler, 15 Jan. 1776; B. Simonds to Schuyler, 16 Jan. 1776, NYPL, S Papers; NYPL, S Lbk., 2: 287–88.

20. Lanctot, *Canada*, 111–12.

21. Ibid., 111–26. Everest, *Moses Hazen*, 36–42.

22. J. Hancock to N.Y. Convention, 20–21 Jan. 1776, NYPL, S Papers; *AA4*, 4: 790; P. Van Cortlandt to Schuyler, 17 Jan. 1776, NYPL, S Papers; *JPCCNY*, 2: 134–35; *AA4*, 4: 852–54, 1002–3; NYPL, S Lbk., 2: 321–24; *AA4*, 4: 880–81, 906–7.

23. Pancake, *1777*, 117.

24. *AA4*, 4: 818–29. Thomas Jones, *History of New York During the Revolutionary War*, ed. Edward Floyd de Lancey, 2 vols. (New York, 1879), 1: 71 and n. xxx; John W. De Peyster, *Life and Misfortunes of Sir John Johnson* (New York, 1882), cited in Justin Winsor, *Narrative and Critical History of America* 6 (1887): 624–25.

25. *JCC* (30 Dec. 1775), 3: 466; NYPL, S Lbk., 1: 46.

26. T. Lynch to Schuyler, 20 Jan. 1776, NYPL, S Papers, cf. *LMCC*, 1: 322–23. See also E. B. O'Callaghan, Berthold Fernow, eds., *Documents Relative to the Colonial History of the State of New York*, 15 vols. (Albany, 1853–87), 8: 663. James Sullivan, ed., *Minutes of the Albany Committee of Correspondence, 1775–1778 and Minutes of the Schenectady Committee, 1775–1779*, 2 vols. (Albany, 1923–25), 1: 310 indicates an Albany committee meeting at Schuyler's house on 11 Jan. but no reference to the business then conducted. NYPL, S Lbk., 2: 281 refers to his receipt of Isaac Paris's 11 Jan. letter on 12 Jan.: *AA4*, 4: 667–68.

27. *AA4*, 4: 666–67, 880. Schuyler's message to the Mohawk (copy), 15 Jan. 1776, PCC, NAR 172.

28. The Mohawks' answer to Schuyler's 15 Jan. 1776 message (copy), ibid.

29. *AA4*, 4: 818–29; Graymont, *Iroquois*, 81–82.

30. *AA4*, 4: 818–29.

31. Ibid., 823–24; NYPL, S Lbk., 2: 350–51.

32. N. 29, above.

33. NYPL, S Lbk., 2: 351, 352.

34. *AA4*, 4: 26 gives 8:00 P.M. as part of the date, but NYPL, S Lbk., 2: 352, cites 5:00 P.M.

35. *AA4*, 4: 827–28 and n. 29, above.

36. N. 29 above and *AA4*, 4: 805.

37. G. Marselis et al. to Schuyler, 19 Jan. 1776, NYPL, S Papers.

38. NYPL, S Lbk., 2: 288. Champagne, *Alexander McDougall,* 96–97. Bernard Mason, *The Road to Independence: The Revolutionary Movement in New York, 1773–1777* (Lexington, Ky., 1966), 121, 129–33.

39. NYPL, S Lbk., 2: 354–55; *AA4*, 4: 818–29.

40. *AA4*, 4: 818–29. Schuyler to the Six Nations, 21 Jan. 1776, *PCC*, NAR 172, enclosed in Schuyler to Hancock, 23 Jan. 1776.

41. *AA4*, 4: 947–48. Graymont, *Iroquois,* 84–85.

42. Schuyler to R. T. Paine, 29 Jan. 1776, Mass. Historical Society; NYPL, S Lbk., 2: 329–32.

43. T. Lynch to Schuyler, 20 Jan. 1776, *LMCC*, 1: 322–23, cf. NYPL, S Papers.

44. *AA4*, 4: 802–5, 829–30.

45. Ibid., *JPCCNY,* 2: 134–35; *AA4*, 4: 1481–83.

46. *AA4*, 4: 829–930. Schuyler to J. Trumbull, Jr., 26 Jan. 1776, Conn. Hist. Soc. J. Trumbull, Jr., Papers: Paymaster Gen. vol. 1. An Account of Arms and Accoutrements received by P. Van Rensselaer, 27 Jan. 1776, NYSL, MSS. Div. Van Rensselaer Family Papers. J. Trumbull, Jr.'s, State of the Military Chest to Schuyler, 28 Jan. 1776, and Schuyler to J. Hancock, 1 Feb. 1776, *AA4*, 4: 906–7. J. Trumbull, Jr., Estimate of pay due . . . 17 Feb. 1776 in Schuyler to J. Hancock, 20 Feb. 1776, *PCC*, NAR 172.

47. *AA4*, 4: 881–82.

48. Ibid., 882.

49. Ibid., 852–54, 1002–3.

50. Ibid., 851–52.

51. NYPL, S Lbk., 2: 321–24.

52. Ibid., 324–25, 336. This regimental reorganization proved to be another point on which the two generals disagreed.

53. Ibid., 315–20.

54. *AA4*, 4: 1007.

55. D. Wooster to Continental Congress, 11 Feb. 1776 (copy), NYPL, S Papers.

56. D. Wooster to R. Sherman, 11 Feb. 1776, ibid.

57. *AA4*, 4: 1218–19.

58. NYPL, S Lbk., 2: 369–71.

59. *AA4*, 4: 1214–16.

60. Ibid.

61. *AA4*, 4: 1483, 1499.

62. Ibid., 5: 868–69.

63. NYPL, S Lbk., 2: 377–79.

64. *AA4*, 5: 91. A variety of Schuyler's notes to twenty-eight persons, dated 26 Feb. 1776, covered amounts between £4 and £300. They account for £1,645.16.0 of the sum sent to Wooster on 28 Feb. NYSL, MSS. Div., Misc. MSS.; NYPL, S Lbk., 3: 22–23; *JCC*, 4: 157: resolves of Feb. 17; *LMCC*, 1: 357–58.

65. *AA4*, 4: 1510–11.

66. Ibid., 5: 355–57.

67. L. Gansevoort to Schuyler, 3 Mar. 1776, NYPL, S Papers; NYPL, S Lbk., 3: 41; *AA4*, 5: 452.

68. *AA4*, 5: 99–100.

69. *WGW*, 4: 278–81, 301–2; *AA4*, 4: 990–91, 1131–32.

70. *AA4*, 4: 990–91, 1131–32, 1156–57; NYPL, S Lbk., 2: 358. (The Indian name remains a puzzle because of the variations: the g above may be a y, and in other places the name is given as Thoniyoudakayon and Thorathauyeadakayer.) Graymont, *Iroquois*, 95.

71. *WGW*, 4: 278–81; *AA4*, 4: 1146.

72. *AA4*, 4: 1481–83; NYPL, S Lbk., 2: 372; *AA4*, 4: 1499–1500. A. Allen to Schuyler, 19 Mar. 1776, NYPL, S Papers (misdated as 17 Mar. in *LMCC*, 1: 397–98).

73. NYPL, S Lbk., 2: 372. *AA4*, 5: 91, 194–95. 6 April Resolve, NYPL, S Lbk., 1: 92.

74. NYPL, S Lbk., 1: 92; *AA4*, 5: 194–95, 415–16, 772–73; NYPL, S Lbk., 3: 72–73; NYPL, S Lbk., 3: 68. R. Van Yereren et al. to Schuyler, 9 April 1776 and R. Varick to Schuyler, 11 April 1776, NYPL, S Papers.

75. *AA4*, 4: 906–7.

76. W. Duer to Schuyler, 1 Feb. 1776, J. Graham to Schuyler, 19 Mar. 1776, NYPL, S Papers.

77. *AA4*, 4: 938–39. Harmanus Schuyler to Schuyler, 8, 12, 16, 22 Feb., 5, 16, 21, 27 Mar., 5, 24 April, 12, 20, 28 June 1776, Cornell University Library Collection of Regional History and University Archives: Harmanus Schuyler Papers.

78. *AA4*, 5: 375, 389. (The sloop was the *Enterprise*, taken at Ticonderoga in 1775; the schooners, *Royal Savage* and *Liberty*, had been seized from the British at Saint John's and Skenesborough, respectively.) Martin H. Bush, *Revolutionary Enigma: A Re-appraisal of General Philip Schuyler of New York* (Port Washington, N.Y.; 1969), 65 et passim, suggests incorrectly that Arnold was more responsible than Schuyler for the fleet.

79. *AA4*, 4: 938–39, 990–91; NYPL, S Lbk., 2: 339; ibid., 344–45. John Knickerbacker, Jr.'s, receipt (to Schuyler), 2 Mar. 1776, NYPL, S Papers: Public and Household Accounts.

80. NYPL, S Lbk., 2: 357–58. Schenectady Comm. to Schuyler, 24 Feb., 4 Mar. 1776, Sullivan, *Minutes of Albany Committee . . . and . . . Schenectady Comm.*, 2: 1050, 1054; NYPL, S Lbk., 3: 36–37, 42; H. Glen to Schuyler, 19, 24 Mar. 1776, NYPL, S Papers; *AA4*, 5: 415–16; NYPL, S Lbk., 3: 18, 27. Memorandum of Agreement by Gen. Philip Schuyler and A. Marselis and J. Vrooman, 1 Mar. 1776, N.Y. Genealogical and Biographical Society, and Union College Library.

81. *AA4*, 5: 147 refers to roads, etc.; NYPL, S Lbk., 3: 42.

82. *AA4*, 5: 91, 194–95, 415–16. H. Van Rensselaer to Schuyler, 1 Mar. 1776, NYPL, S Papers. NYPL, S Lbk., 3: 43; C. Wharton to Schuyler, 2, 27 Mar. 1776, NYPL, S Papers; NYPL, S Lbk., 3: 28.

83. *AA4*, 4: 906–7. This inventory appears to be at variance with Capt. J. McCracken to Schuyler, 13 Mar. 1776, NYPL, S Papers. McCracken's list of artillery and shot at Ticonderoga is

Artillery		Shot
19	four-pounders	49
15	six-pounders	1,356
5	nine-pounders	2,304
6	twelve-pounders	56
1	eighteen-pounder	1,293

84. *AA4*, 4: 1481–83; NYPL, S Lbk., 3: 30–31; *WGW*, 4: 346–47, 356–58.

85. *AA4*, 5: 103–4, 147–48.

86. Ibid. E. Curtis to Schuyler, 10 Mar. 1776, NYPL, S Papers.

87. Champagne, *Alexander McDougall*, 108–9. Schuyler to A. McDougall, 14 Mar. 1776, NYHS, McDougall Papers.

88. *AA4*, 4: 938–39, 5: 415–16; NYPL, S Lbk., 3: 41, 48–49; *AA4*, 5: 250, 868–69.

89. Richard Buel, Jr., review of Charles Royster, *A Revolutionary People at War,* in *The William and Mary Quarterly,* 3d Ser., 38 (Jan., 1981): 122.

90. NYPL, S Lbk., 2: 329–32.

91. *AA4,* 4: 1156–57; *AA4,* ibid., 1147–48, ibid., 5: 39–40; ibid., 4: 1201–2.

92. NYPL, S Lbk., 1: 92. J. Trumbull to Schuyler, 25, 31 Jan. 1776, Conn. Hist. Soc., J. Trumbull, Sr., Papers and *AA4,* 4: 898–99; NYPL, S Lbk., 2: 329–32; *AA4,* 4: 955–56, 1156–57.

93. *AA4,* 4: 955–56; ibid., 5: 251–52.

94. Ibid., 4: 1131–32, 1146; ibid., 5: 415–16.

95. N. 93, above.

96. *AA4,* 4: 1146, 1481–83, 1499; NYPL, S Lbk., 3: 25, 30–31; *AA4,* 5: 91, 194–95, 147–58.

97. *AA4,* 5: 91, 194–95, 147–58, 415–16.

98. Ibid., 250.

99. Ibid., 436–37, 174–75; NYPL, S Lbk., 3: 45–47. Schuyler's message to the Six Nations, [?] Mar. 1776, enclosed in Schuyler to J. Hancock, 2 April 1776, *AA4,* 5: 767–68. Graymont, *Iroquois,* 97 n. See also NYPL, S Lbk., 3: 52. Schuyler to N. Herkimer, 28 Mar. 1776, NYPL, S Papers.

100. *AA4,* 5: 519–20. And see Charles Royster, *A Revolutionary People at War: The Continental Army and American Character, 1775–1783* (Chapel Hill, N.C., 1979).

101. W. Thompson to Schuyler, 28 Mar. 1776, NYPL, S Papers; *AA4,* 5: 452; NYPL, S Lbk., 3: 51; *AA4,* 5: 520, 535–36.

102. *WGW,* 4: 406–8; NYPL, S Lbk., 3: 49–50; *AA4,* 5: 519–20; NYPL S Lbk., 3: 60–61. J. McCracken to Schuyler, 25 Mar. 1776, NYPL, S Papers.

103. NYPL, S Lbk., 3: 56; *AA4,* 5: 767–68.

104. Ibid.; ibid., 5: 812–13; *WGW* 4: 481–82.

105. NYPL, S Lbk., 3: 84–85; *AA4,* 6: 414–15; NYPL, S Lbk., 3: 96–97; *AA4,* 5: 1086.

106. *AA4,* 5: 1086, 751–53. See also Stanley, *Canada Invaded,* 118; Lanctot, *Canada,* 133–34.

107. Kenney, *Albany: Crossroads of Liberty,* 29–30; Ward, *War of the Revolution,* 1: 196–97. Cf. Lanctot, *Canada,* 133–34.

108. *AA4,* 5: 767–68; NYPL, S Lbk., 3: 58–60.

109. *AA4,* 5: 767–68; NYPL, S Lbk., 3: 59–61.

CHAPTER 6

1. *JCC,* 3: 451; *AA4,* 4: 666–67; *LMCC,* 1: 322–23.

2. For the Schuyler-Wooster clash see chapt. 4. Stanley, *Canada Invaded,* 110–12.

3. Ibid., 111–13. Lanctot, *Canada,* 127–28. M. Hazen to Schuyler, 8 April 1776, NYPL, S Papers.

4. Burnett, *Congress,* 112, 114. *JCC,* 4: 151–52. *LMCC,* 1: 354.

5. *JCC,* 4: 215–18, 233.

6. B. Franklin to Schuyler, 11 Mar. 1776; Stirling to Schuyler, 2 April 1776, NYPL, S Papers; *AA4,* 5: 99–100.

7. Stanley, *Canada Invaded,* 114–115. Stirling to Schuyler, 2–4 April 1776, NYPL, S Papers. Leonard, *Charles Carroll,* 282; NYPL, S Lbk., 3: 85–86.

8. Gerlach, *Philip Schuyler,* 61. Leonard, *Charles Carroll,* 282–84.

9. Leonard, *Charles Carroll,* 282–85.

10. *AA4,* 5: 868, 871–72.

11. Ibid.; *WGW,* 4: 459–60, 511–12. Schuyler's "scorbutick eruption" was an attack of scurvy, which meant that his diet lacked green vegetables. Reference to the "more disagreeable disorder" may have been to his ancient malady, rheumatic gout.

12. Schuyler to J. Hancock, 12 April 1776 (with four enclosures), *PCC,* NAR 172; *AA4,* 5: 1086.

13. *AA4,* 5: 1086, 927; NYPL, S Lbk., 3: 65–67. Leonard, *Charles Carroll,* 285–86. Carl Van Doren, *Benjamin Franklin* (London, 1939), 544–45; *AA4,* 5: 1097–98.

14. R. Varick to Schuyler, 15 April 1776 and V. Douw to Schuyler, 15 April 1776, NYPL, S Papers; NYPL, S Lbk., 3: 67–68; 4: 4.

15. NYPL, S Lbk., 4: 5–6. R. Varick to Schuyler, 15, 18, 22 April 1776, NYPL, S Papers.

16. Leonard, *Charles Carroll,* 289, 291, 293.

17. Ibid., 297; NYPL, S Lbk., 4: 8, 11–12. Schuyler to J. Thomas, 23, 25 April 1776, NYPL, S Papers, and S Lbk., 3: 86–87. W. Livingston to Schuyler, 21, 25 April 1776, NYPL, S Papers.

18. NYPL, S Lbk., 4: 8–10, 14–15; 3: 69.

19. Ibid., 4: 16–18, 19, 21.

20. *AA4,* 5: 1097–98, 1182–83; *WGW,* 4: 495–97; NYPL, S Lbk., 4: 18. Schuyler to R. Varick, 30 April 1776, Pierpont Morgan Library.

21. B. Arnold to Schuyler, 20 April 1776 (copy enclosed in Schuyler to G. Washington, 27 April 1776), NYPL, S Papers (*AA4,* 5: 1097–98); NYPL, S Lbk., 4: 24–26.

22. Schuyler to J. Hancock, 28 April 1776, with M. Ryan's testimony of 23 April, *AA4,* 5: 1114–15 and *PCC,* NAR 172; NYPL, S Lbk., 1: 91, 93.

23. *AA4,* 5: 1155, 1182–1883.

24. Charles Henry Jones, *History of the Campaign for the Conquest of Canada in 1776* (Philadelphia, 1882), 40. Hereafter cited Jones, *Campaign for Canada.* D. Wooster to L. Vincent, 2 May 1776; Baron F. W. von Woedtke to C. O. at Chamblee, 10 May 1776; and J. Thomas to Congressional Commissioners, 7 May 1776, NYPL, S Papers.

25. NYPL, S Lbk., 3: 75–76.

26. W. Livingston to Schuyler, 30 April, 1 May 1776, NYPL, S Papers. NYPL, S Lbk., 3: 81–83; 4: 22–23.

27. *AA4,* 6: 417. Otis G. Hammond, *Letters and Papers of Major-General John Sullivan; Continental Army,* 3 vols. (Concord, N.H., 1930–39) 1: 197–98. Hereafter cited Hammond, *Sullivan Papers.* R. Yates to Schuyler, 4 May 1776, NYPL, S Papers.

28. NYPL, S Lbk., 4: 29–30.

29. Minutes [Indian] Commissioners for the Northern Dept., 29 April–21 May 1776, NYPL, S (Indian) Papers; Hammond, *Sullivan Papers,* 1: 197–98; *AA4,* 6: 417, 428–29.

30. NYPL, S Lbk., 4: 30–32.

31. *AA4,* 6: 449–50; and see 5: 1116, 1214; NYPL, S Lbk., 3: 95 ([misdated?] 13 May in *AA4,* 6: 449); NYPL, S Lbk., 3: 96–97, 99–100.

32. Lanctot, *Canada,* 135; *AA4,* 6: 481; NYPL, S Lbk., 3: 125. B. Franklin to Schuyler, 27 May 1776, NYSL, MSS. Div. (italics added).

33. *AA4,* 6: 480–81.

34. R. R. Livingston to Schuyler, 6 May 1776, NYPL, S Papers. Schuyler to R. R. Livingston, 12 May 1776, NYSL, MSS. Div.

35. NYPL, S Lbk., 3: 99–100. W. Thompson to Schuyler, 19 May 1776, NYPL, S Papers.

36. NYPL, S Lbk., 4: 35–38; ibid., 3: 104–5. Schuyler's general orders, 17 May 1776, NYSL, Hanson Collection; NYPL, S Lbk., 4: 38; ibid., 3: 105; *AA4,* 6: 537–38; ibid., 479–480; cf. NYPL, S Lbk., 3: 102–4; NYPL, S Lbk., 4: 38.

37. NYPL, S Lbk., 4: 38, 43. Schuyler's general orders specified seventeen bateaux for Stark's regiment, each loaded with 10 barrels of pork as well as baggage, men, and their own food supplies. Ibid., 43–44; *AA4,* 6: 537–38; ibid., 564–65. Since 13 May Schuyler had shipped about 300 barrels of flour and 1,191 of pork; he calculated that 115 barrels of meal should have reached Saint John's on 17 May and a like amount on each of four succeeding days.

38. NYPL, S Lbk., 3: 125; 4: 54; *AA4,* 6: 578, 581–82; NYPL, S Lbk., 4: 56–58; Judd, *Van Cortlandt Papers,* 1: 111–12; NYPL, S Lbk., 4: 56–58, 76–78.

39. NYPL, S Lbk., 4: 52–53, 56–58, 76–78.

40. *AA4,* 6: 537–38.

41. *WGW,* 5: 65–67; J. Trumbull, Jr., to Schuyler, [?] May 1776, W. Livingston to Schuyler, 20 May 1776 and P. McEahron's deposition, 2 June 1776, NYPL, S Papers.

42. *AA4,* 6: 608–9, 639–41.

43. A. McDougall to Schuyler, 11 June 1776, NYPL, S Papers; NYPL, S Lbk., 3: 102–4, 135–36; Gerlach, *Philip Schuyler,* 67–73.

44. *WGW,* 5: 115–19.

45. *AA4,* 6: 910–13. E. Bennett to Schuyler, 18 June 1776, NYPL, S Papers.

46. NYPL, S Lbk., 3: 136–37; *AA4,* 6: 639–41; NYPL, S Lbk., 1: 107–9. Ibid., 3: 138–39; *AA4,* 6: 639–40. Lanctot, *Canada,* 107–9.

47. Julian P. Boyd, ed., *The Papers of Thomas Jefferson,* vols. 1–; (Princeton, N.J., 1950–   ), 1: 295. Lanctot, *Canada,* 140; *AA4,* 6: 558–59, 639–40.

48. *AA4,* 6: 559, but NYPL, S Lbk., 1: 109–10 copy reads, "I shall leave it to your determination." *AA4,* 6: 639–40.

49. *AA4,* 6: 639–40, 677–79.

50. R. Varick to Schuyler, 1, 2 June 1776, and W. Livingston to Schuyler, 1, 2 June 1776, NYPL, S Papers; NYPL, S Lbk., 4: 76–80.

51. Leonard, *Charles Carroll,* 311. *AA4,* 6: 711.

52. C. Carroll to Schuyler, 7 June 1776, NYPL, S Papers; R. Varick to Schuyler, 1 June 1776, NYPL, S Papers. Leonard, *Charles Carroll,* 313.

53. *JCC,* 4: 376–78, 388, 397.

54. *JCC,* 5: 474, 617–18.

55. NYPL, S Lbk., 4: 83, 85–86. Schuyler to I. Putnam, 8 June 1776, *PCC,* NAR 172; *AA4,* 6: 762–63.

56. *AA4,* 6: 762–63, 83–85. H. Schuyler to Schuyler, 12, 28 June; 4, 9, 24, 26 July; 1, 4, 10, 16, 25 Aug.; 2 Sept. 1776, Cornell Univ. Library Collection of Regional History: Harmanus Schuyler Papers.

57. *AA4,* 6: 762–64.

58. NYPL, S Lbk., 3: 152–53; 4: 88–90.

59. Ibid., 3: 155–156.

60. *AA4,* 6: 794–96, *AA5,* 1: 816–17; cf. *WGW,* 5: 101–3. Graymont, *Iroquois,* 100–1. Wallace, *Death and Rebirth of the Seneca,* 131. *JCC,* 4: 394–96.

61. *AA4,* 6: 819–20, 974–76.

62. NYPL, S Lbk., 3: 192–93; 4: 97–98; *AA4,* 6: 939–41.

63. B. Arnold to Schuyler, 6 June 1776; and J. Sullivan to G. Washington, 5–6 June 1776, enclosed in Schuyler to G. Washington, 12 June 1776, *AA4,* 6: 925–26; cf. NYPL, S Papers and S Lbk., 3: 159–60.

64. NYPL, S Lbk., 3: 159–60, 163–64.

65. *AA4,* 6: 914–16, 943.

66. Resolve of Congress, 24 June, NYPL, S Lbk., 1: 125; *WGW,* 5: 185–86; *AA4,* 6: 1126, 1203. Schuyler to T. Edwards, 1 July 1776, Boston Public Library.

67. NYPL, S Lbk., 4: 93–94. Resolve of Congress, 17 June, ibid., 1: 122–23. *JCC*, 5: 448–52; cf. Boyd, *Jefferson Papers*, 1: 392–96; *WGW*, 5: 115–19; *AA4*, 6: 910–13.

68. *WGW*, 5: 137–38; *AA4*, 6: 943, 969–70. Stanley, *Canada Invaded*, 119–23. Lanctot, *Canada*, 141–42; *WGW*, 5: 115–19, 129–32; *AA4*, 6: 939–41, 943–44. Hammond, *Sullivan Papers*, 1: 257–59.

69. NYPL, S Lbk., 1: 115 and *WGW*, 5: 162–63; *AA4*, 6: 910–13; NYPL, S Lbk., 3: 189–90. Mason, *Road to Independence*, 213, 246–47.

70. *AA4*, 6: 939–41, 977–79.

71. Jones, *Campaign for Canada*, 82–97. Schuyler to G. Washington, 19–20 June 1776, *AA4*, 6: 974–76. One of Schuyler's most interesting letters, this reveals a progression of events from 19 June until the next day when additions were made at 8:00 and 11:00 A.M. *AA4*, 6: 917–18, 1057–58. NYPL, S Lbk., 3: 200–1. Schuyler to J. Sullivan, 20 June 1776, and J. Sullivan to G. Washington, 8–12 June 1776, NYPL, S Papers, indicate that *AA4*, 6: 1036–38 mistakenly cites the 8–12 June letter as Sullivan to Schuyler. Schuyler received the dispatch and forwarded it to Washington on 19–20 June 1776, *AA4*, 6: 974–76.

72. NYPL, S Lbk., 3: 205; 4: 103–4.

73. *WGW*, 5: 162–63. Rewards were offered for each British commissioned officer captured ($100) and for every private ($30). NYPL, S Lbk., 1: 122–23; *AA4*, 6: 1057–58.

74. *AA4*, 6: 1057–58, 1103–04. Lanctot, *Canada*, 145–46. Stanley, *Canada Invaded*, 129–31.

75. *AA4*, 6: 1102–03. Hammond, *Sullivan Papers*, 1: 264–65.

76. James Wilkinson, *Memoirs of My Own Times*, 3 vols. (Philadelphia, 1816), 1: 60. Hereafter cited as Wilkinson, *Memoirs*.

77. *AA4*, 6: 1071–72, 1074. List of Tories from Tryon Co., 25 June 1776, NYPL, S Papers; *AA4*, 6: 1222; *AA5*, 1: 237; NYPL, S Lbk., 4: 107–8. H. Glen to Schuyler, 28 June 1776, NYPL, S Papers.

78. Schuyler and V. Douw to J. Frey, 26 June 1776, HL MSS.; NYPL, S Lbk., 4: 105.

79. E. Dayton to Schuyler, 27 June 1776 and J. Caldwell to Schuyler, 27 June 1776, NYPL, S Papers; NYPL, S Lbk., 3: 217; 4: 109–12. E. Dayton to Schuyler, 3 July 1776, NYPL, S Papers.

80. A. Yates, Jr., to Schuyler, 26 June 1776, ibid.

81. NYPL, S Lbk., 3: 218–19.

82. S. Stringer to Schuyler, 22 June 1776, NYPL, S Papers.

83. NYPL, S Lbk., 3: 216–17.

84. *AA4*, 6: 1071. *JCC*, 5: 448; NYPL, S Lbk., 3: 216–17.

85. Nelson, *Gates*, 52, 58.

86. Ibid., 61. Flexner, *Washington*, 2: 99–100.

87. Samuel White Patterson, *Horatio Gates: Defender of American Liberties* (New York, 1966), 83–84. Hereafter cited as Patterson, *Gates*.

88. Butterfield, *John Adams Diary and Autobiography*, 3: 386–87.

89. Ibid., 385–86, 390–91. Patterson, *Gates*, 66–67, cf. Nelson, *Gates*, 50–52, 54–56; Ward, *War of the Revolution*, 1: 384; *JCC*, 5: 448.

90. Memorandum, "In a Conversation with General Gates," 30 June 1776, HL; NYPL, S Lbk., 4: 117.

91. *AA4*, 6: 1199–1201, 1266–68.

92. J. Trumbull to E. Gerry, 5 July 1776, Library of Congress, Gerry Papers. Jedediah Huntington to Jabez Huntington, 7 July 1776, *Colls. Conn. Hist. Soc.*, 20: 308–10.

93. July 8 Resolves, *JCC*, 5: 526–27; *AA5*, 1: 115–16.

94. Katharine Schuyler Baxter, *A Godchild of Washington* (New York, 1897), 182–83. Hereafter cited as Baxter, *Godchild*. *AA5*, 1: 394, 396.

95. *AA4*, 6: 1199–1201, 1217, 1266–68; NYPL, S Lbk. 3: 221–22; 4: 113; *AA4*, 6: 1199–1201, 1203–4, 1266–68. E. Dayton to Schuyler, 2 July 1776, NYPL, S Papers.

96. *AA4*, 6: 1217, cf. 1121–23.

97. T. Jefferson to W. Fleming, 1–2 July 1776, Boyd, *Jefferson Papers*, 1: 411–13. J. Trumbull, Jr., to [J. Trumbull, Sr.], 12 July 1776, MNHP, LWS Coll. cites the lake fleet as composed of a large schooner (12 guns), two small ones (4–6 guns each), a sloop (8 guns), and three gondolas. Jones, *Campaign for Canada*, 97, cites fifty-two hundred effectives and twenty-eight hundred sick. D. Campbell to Schuyler, 28 June 1776, NYPL, S Papers, cites three thousand sick.

98. Hammond, *Sullivan Papers*, 1: 271–74.

99. Everest, *Moses Hazen*, 47.

100. Palmer, *Way of the Fox*, 115, 117, 125.

101. NYPL, S Lbk., 4: 115–16.

102. H. Schuyler to Schuyler, 12 June; 24, 26 July; 1, 4, 10, 16, 25 Aug.; 2 Sept. 1776; Cornell Univ. Library Collection of Regional History: Harmanus Schuyler Papers. J. Trumbull, Jr., to [J. Trumbull, Sr.], 12 July 1776, MNHP, LWS Coll. List of Vessels on Lake Champlain, 10 Oct. 1776, NYPL, S Papers.

103. NYPL, S Lbk., 4: 117. David B. Davis, ed., "Medicine in the Canadian Campaign of the Revolutionary War: The Journal of Doctor Samuel Fisk Merrick," *Bulletin of the History of Medicine* 44 (Sept.–Oct., 1970): 468. Jones, *Campaign for Canada*, 100; *AAs*, 1: 235.

104. *AAs*, 1: 235.

105. Ibid., 223. NYPL, S Lbk., 4: 119–20; *AAs*, 1: 145, indicates that Connecticut militia not only feared smallpox and begged to be protected from infection, but also that, more than anything, they quaked at the prospect of being forced into hospitals.

106. *AAs*, 1: 233–34, 650–51.

107. Ibid., 234–35, 390–91. Nelson, *Gates*, 67.

108. John A. Williams, "Mount Independence in Time of War, 1776–1783," *Vermont History* 35 (April, 1967): 93–95. Irma B. Jaffe, *John Trumbull: Patriot-Artist of the American Revolution* (Boston, 1975), 25. *AAs*, 1: 232–33, 237, 260–61. J. Trumbull, Jr. to [J. Trumbull, Sr.], 12 July 1776, MNHP, LWS Coll. Trumbull agreed with Schuyler's view of the army, "void of every Idea of Discipline or subordination." He noted that the wretched situation had induced the decision to evacuate Crown Point. H. Gates to M. Morse, 12 July 1776, *AAs*, 1: 237–38 also recounts the miserable circumstances leading to the abandonment of Crown Point. NYPL, S Lbk., 3: 250; *AAs*, 1: 699.

109. *AAs*, 1: 699, 206–7, 857; NYPL, S Lbk., 4: 124. R. Varick to Schuyler, 8 July 1776; C. Wynkoop to Schuyler, 15 July 1776, NYPL, S Papers.

110. Angelica Schuyler to Schuyler, 12 July [1776], NYSL, MSS. Div.; *AAs*, 1: 206, 237.

111. NYPL, S Lbk., 3: 247–48.

112. *AAs*, 1: 338; NYPL, S Lbk., 4: 125–27.

113 *AAs*, 1: 193–94, 237, 259–61, 423.

114. *AAs*, 1: 232–33, 390–91.

CHAPTER 7

1. NYPL, S Lbk., 3: 247–48, 308–14; *AAs*, 1: 394–95.

2. R. Varick to Schuyler, 22 July 1776, NYPL, S Papers. Schuyler to R. Yates and the Secret Comm., 25 July 1776; cf. R. Yates and the Secret Comm. to Schuyler, 21 [20?] July 1776, Washington's Headquarters Museum, Newburgh, N.Y.

3. Richard J. Koke, "The Struggle for the Hudson: The British Naval Expedition under

Captain Hyde Parker and Captain James Wallace, July 12–August 18, 1776," *The New-York Historical Society Quarterly* 40 (April 1956): 115–75.

4. Vivian and Vivian, "Congressional Indian Policy," 255. NYPL, S Lbk., 4: 126; *AAs*, 1: 394, 396; *WGW*, 5: 357–60.

5. H. Glen to Schuyler, 8 July 1776, NYPL, S Papers (misdated 10 July in *AAs*, 1: 176).

6. NYPL, S Lbk., 4: 126–29. E. Dayton to Schuyler, 18 July 1776, NYPL, S Papers.

7. *AAs*, 1: 472–73; cf. NYPL, S Lbk., 3: 265–68; ibid., 1: 133–35.

8. *AAs*, 1: 716, 815–16. E. Dayton to Schuyler, 5 Aug. 1776, NYPL, S Papers; NYPL, S Lbk., 4: 160–62; NYPL, S Lbk., 4: 127–29, 143. Court-Martial Proceedings, 30 July 1776, NYPL, S Papers; S Lbk., 4: 146–47.

9. NYPL, S Lbk., 4: 146–48. T. Paterson and J. Ross to Schuyler, 5 Aug. 1776, NYPL, S Papers.

10. NYPL, S Lbk., 4: 162–63.

11. J. Ross, T. Paterson to Schuyler, 8, 10 Aug. 1776; A. White to Schuyler, 9, 10 Aug. 1776; Examination of Sundry Officers Touching the Plunder Taken from Johnson Hall, 1776, NYPL, S Papers; Schuyler to G. Washington, 18 Aug. 1776, NYSL, MSS. Div.

12. *WGW*, 5: 482–85; NYPL, S Lbk., 4: 167. J. Bloomfield to Schuyler, 20 Aug. 1776, NYSL, MSS. Div. Proceedings of Court of Inquiry at Fort Schuyler, 13–17 Sept. 1776; Proceedings of General Court-Martial at Albany, 1–7 Oct. 1776; E. Dayton to Schuyler, 11, 14, 22–24 Sept., 5 Oct. 1776; Receipts of the Johnstown plunder include: H. Glen to W. White, 17 Aug. 1776; Copy of Inventory of Sundries Delivered . . . to H. Glen, 17 Aug. 1776; J. Lansing Memorandum, 14 Aug. 1776, NYPL, S Papers. NYPL, S Lbk., 4: 179, 196–97.

13. *AAs*, 1: 193–94, 394.

14. NYPL, S Lbk., 1: 131–32; *AAs*, 1: 399–400, 423. R. Varick to Schuyler, 20 July 1776 and N. Cooke to Schuyler, 24 July 1776, NYPL, S Papers. *AAs*, 1: 511–12, 580–81.

15. *AAs*, 1: 511–12, 580–81, 629, 648–49; NYPL, S Lbk., 3: 296.

16. NYPL, S Lbk., 3: 296; 4: 130–31, 133. R. Varick to Schuyler, 20, 22 July 1776, NYPL, S Papers; NYPL, S Lbk., 3: 268; 4: 138–40; *AAs*, 1: 680.

17. NYPL, S Lbk., 4: 144–45, 150–51. R. Varick to Schuyler, 2 Aug. 1776, NYPL, S Papers; NYPL, S Lbk., 3: 297–98, 314. C. Wynkoop to Schuyler, 1 Aug. 1776, NYPL, S Papers. R. Varick to Schuyler, 27 July, 29 July (2 letters) 1776; List of Skippers in Albany, 29 July 1776, NYPL, S Papers; NYPL, S Lbk., 3: 291–93; ibid., 4: 144–45; ibid., 3: 324–27. R. Varick to Schuyler, 7, 9 Aug. 1776, NYPL, S Papers. J. Van Zandt to R. Varick, 31 July 1776, ibid. S. Tuder's account with Schuyler, 3 Aug. 1776–2 July 1777, NYSL, MSS. Div., Philip Van Rensselaer Papers. As of 19 July 1777 over £1,859 of the bill remained unpaid. See also NYPL, S Lbk., 3: 346–47. Ibid., 339–42.

18. NYPL, S Lbk., 3: 339–42, 323–24. B. Arnold to Schuyler, 8, 10 Aug. 1776 and R. Varick to Schuyler, 9, 10 Aug. 1776, NYPL, S Papers. NYPL, S Lbk., 3: 319–22, 338, 347–48. J. Porter to R. Varick, 5 Aug. 1776, and J. Porter to Schuyler, 19 Aug. 1776, NYPL, S Papers. R. Livingston to J. Jay, 12 Aug. 1776, Washington's Hqs. Museum, Newburgh, N.Y. J. Porter to Schuyler, 2 Sept. 1776, HL.

19. List of Continental Armed Vessels, 5 Aug. 1776; cf. B. Arnold's Return of the Ordnance . . . , 31 July 1776, *AAs*, 1: 681, 797; ibid., 826–27, 1033. List of Vessels on Lake Champlain, 10 Oct. 1776, NYPL, S Papers; NYPL, S Lbk., 3: 298–99, 301–2; *AAs*, 1: 714–16.

20. *WGW*, 5: 302–3; *AAs*, 1: 559–63. N. Greene to N. Cooke, 22 July 1776, W. Clements Library, Greene Papers. R. Morris to H. Gates, 25 July 1776, NYHS, Gates Papers. *AAs*, 1: 559–63; ibid., 650–51; ibid., 730, 747. Schuyler to G. Washington, 6 Aug. 1776, Schuyler to J. Hancock, 7 Aug. (misdated 8 Aug.) 1776, ibid., 793–95, 856–57; cf. NYPL, S Lbk., 3: 336–38. Schuyler to J. Trumbull, Jr., 7 Aug. 1776, Conn. Hist. Soc., J. Trumbull, Jr., Papers: Paymaster Gen. vol. 1; *AAs*, 1: 932–33.

21. *AAs*, 1: 932–33, 559–63. W. Livingston to Schuyler, 22 July 1776, NYPL, S Papers.

22. NYPL, S Lbk., 4: 136–38; *WGW*, 5: 356–60.

23. *WGW*, 5: 356–60. *AAs*, 1: 793–95. W. Livingston to Schuyler, 5 Aug. 1776, NYPL, S Papers.

24. NYPL, S Lbk., 4: 158.

25. *LMCC*, 2: 35–36.

26. Ibid., 41; *AAs*, 1: 555–56 and NYPL, S Lbk., 1: 146. J. Trumbull to S. Adams, 12 Aug. 1776, NYPL, S Adams Papers.

27. Sullivan, *Minutes of Albany Committee* 1: 510–11. S. Chase to Schuyler, 19 July 1776, NYPL, S Papers. David Freeman Hawke, *Benjamin Rush: Revolutionary Gadfly* (Indianapolis and New York, 1971), 164.

28. NYPL, S Lbk., 3: 308–14.

29. Ibid. Schuyler to J. Trumbull, Jr., 24 July 1776, Conn. Hist. Soc., J. Trumbull, Jr. Papers: Paymaster Gen. vol. 1; *AAs*, 1: 559–63.

30. NYPL, 'S Lbk., 3: 290–91; *AAs*, 1: 714–15, 825. (Schuyler told Hancock that twelve hundred Indians consumed as much as an army of three thousand.)

31. *AAs*, 1: 714–15, 825. The threats Schuyler mentions as the curses of "Ernulphuses," evidently a reference from Sterne's *Tristram Shandy*, are to Ernulf, Bishop of Rochester (1040–1124) who devised a curse for persons he excommunicated. Ibid., 714–16.

32. Ibid., 825. Schuyler to J. Hancock, 7 Aug. 1776, misdated 8 Aug. ibid., 856–57; cf. NYPL, S Lbk., 3: 336. Graymont, *Iroquois*, 107–8.

33. German Flatts Treaty: Proceedings of the Commissioners, Aug. 1776, NYPL, S Papers; cf. *AAs*, 1: 1035–49. Schuyler's 8 Aug. 1776 speech, HL. J. Pierce, Jr., to A. Adams, 28 Aug. 1776, NYSL, MSS. Div.

34. *AAI*, 1038–45.

35. Ibid., 1045–49.

36. Ibid., 983–85, 1030–31. Vivian and Vivian, "Congressional Indian Policy," 255–58. Graymont, *Iroquois*, 108, 112. Wallace, *Death and Rebirth of the Seneca*, 131–32. *AAs*, 3: 1495–97 and NYPL, S Lbk., 5: 58–62.

37. See note 18 above. *AAs*, 1: 924; NYPL, S Lbk., 3: 346–47. R. Livingston to R. Varick, 18 Aug. 1776 and J. Porter to Schuyler, 19 Aug. 1776, NYPL, S Papers; *AAs*, 1: 1083–84; NYPL, S Lbk., 3: 433–34. H. Glen to Schuyler, 26 Aug. 1776, NYSL, MSS. Div. Hanson Collection. NYPL, S Lbk., 4: 177–78; *AAs*, 1: 1165–66; 2: 185–86, 203, 353, 481, 619–620; ibid. 2: 110–11, 249–50, 264, 294–95, 469–70, 555; ibid. 1: 1115–16, 2: 279–80; ibid. 2: 126–27, 469.

38. *AAs*, 2: 343, 530–31, 619–20; ibid., 374. In addition to three cables, Gates requested eighty-one fathoms of rope and twenty coils of rope of varying sizes. Schuyler to J. Hancock, 3 Oct. 1776, ibid., 847, reported that the cables had reached Ticonderoga.

39. *AAs*, 2: 555, 833, 922–23. Pancake, *1777*, 74, 78–79. The Pa. and N.J. regiments were led by John P. De Haas, William Maxwell, and William Wind; fortunately their terms ran through October, and only Wind's refused to tarry after early November while the army waited to see whether the enemy would retire for the winter or attempt a further penetration. Jones, *Campaign for Canada*, 155.

40. Jones, *Campaign for Canada*, 155, 163. List of Vessels on Lake Champlain, 10 Oct. 1776, NYPL, S Papers; *AAs*, 2: 617–18; see also 555, 885, 999–1000.

41. *AAs*, 1: 1220–21, 1264–65; 2: 248–49, 352–53, 922–23; NYPL, S Lbk., 3: 433; 4: 195–96, 205; ibid. 4: 201–3. Schuyler to Lt. Van Vechten, 21 Sept. 1776; and J. Van Rensselaer to Schuyler, 22 Sept. 1776, NYPL, S Papers.

42. *AAs*, 2: 469–70 mentions the 160,000. Ibid., 922–23; *WGW*, 6: 192–94; NYPL, S Lbk., 3: 482, 485.

43. NYPL, S Lbk., 3: 482, 485, 345–46; *AAs*, 1: 999–1001; ibid., 1115–16, 1204–5. Hawke, *Benjamin Rush*, 29.

44. *AAs*, 1: 1050–51, 1218. Cf. B. Arnold to J. Wynkoop, 17 Aug. 1776 (two letters); J. Wynkoop to B. Arnold, to H. Gates, 17 Aug. 1776; B. Arnold to H. Gates, 17, 18 Aug. 1776, NYPL, S Papers. J. Wynkoop Memorial to Congress, 27 Aug. 1776, ibid.; *AAs*, 1: 1083, 1217–18, 1221–22.

45. *AAs*, 1: 651–53, 1083, 1217–18, 1221–22. S. Stringer to Schuyler, 31 July 1776, NYPL, S Papers.

46. Broadus Mitchell, *The Price of Independence: A Realistic View of the American Revolution* (New York, 1974), 152–53. Patterson, *Gates*, 81. Hawke, *Benjamin Rush*, 170.

47. *AAs*, 2: 125–26.

48. NYPL, S Lbk., 3: 384–85.

49. The Public In Account with M: Gen: Schuyler, 16 July 1776, NYPL, S Papers: Misc. Military Accounts. The 8,441 white pine boards charged at £316.10.9 amount to nine pence each; the 4,218 planks were one shilling each, which came to exactly £210.18.0.

50. NYPL, S Lbk., 3: 432–33. Schuyler acknowledged Morgan's 6 Sept. letter. It has not been found, but its contents are deduced from Schuyler's reply.

51. *AAs*, 2: 263.

52. *AAs*, 1: 1083. Schuyler to Joseph Trumbull, 31 Aug. 1776, Conn. State Library, Gov. Joseph Trumbull Collection, 3: 237 a-c. E. Avery to Schuyler, 25 Aug. 1776, NYPL, S Papers; *AAs*, 2: 110–11. E. Avery to Schuyler, 5 Sept. 1776, NYPL, S Papers; *AAs*, 2: 213–14; *JCC*, 5: 753. Victor L. Johnson, *The Administration of the American Commissariat during the Revolutionary War* (Philadelphia, 1941), 123–25. Hereafter cited as Johnson, *American Commissariat*. NYPL, S Lbk., 3: 397–99; *AAs*, 2: 249–50.

53. *AAs*, 2: 249–50, 294–95.

54. NYPL, S Lbk., 4: 185–87.

55. *LMCC*, 2: 84. J. Trumbull to Schuyler, 20 Sept. 1776, NYPL, S Papers; *AAs*, 2: 469–70; NYPL, S Lbk., 4: 206.

56. NYPL, S Lbk., 4: 206; 3: 442–43.

57. Schuyler to B. Arnold, 17 Aug. 1776 and Arnold to Schuyler, 23 Aug. 1776, NYPL, S Lbk., 3: 344–45 and S Papers; *AAs*, 1: 1204–5; 2: 125–27.

58. *Smith Memoirs*, 2: 2–3. R. R. Livingston to Schuyler, 2 Oct. 1776 and L. Gansevoort to Schuyler, 17 Nov. 1776, NYPL, S Papers; *AAs*, 3: 1101. Gerlach, *Philip Schuyler*, 296–97.

59. *JCC*, 5: 664–65. Butterfield, *John Adams Diary and Autobiography*, 3: 408–9.

60. *AAs*, 1: 1031–33, 1083–84, 1153–54, 1204–5; 2: 125–27.

61. Ibid., 2: 220; cf. Patterson, *Gates*, 90–91.

62. *AAs*, 2: 245–47; NYPL, S Lbk., 3: 457 (requesting a duplicate receipt for £6,364 in specie, which had been sent to R. Montgomery but had never been received by Wooster). Some sense of Schuyler's accounting of expenditures may be gleaned from Schuyler's account with Richard Varick, 27 Aug. 1776, NYPL, S Papers; Misc. Military Accts. (runs from 6 June 1776 to date and shows credits and debits balanced at £141,487.16.7 1/2; payments are shown for the hire of carpenters and bateaumen, the purchase of lumber, £792.8.8 etc.); Account of the Public with Schuyler for Sundries from Saratoga Store, 23 Aug. 1776 (signed by Schuyler's clerk, Daniel Hale), ibid. This account shows that between July 1775 and June 1776 Schuyler sold £444.18.1 worth of goods to the army and Indian commissioners. The army obtained glass, door hinges and locks, nails, etc. (969 pounds of nails charged at

£64.12.0), and the Indian commissioners got blankets (£133). See also NYPL, S Lbk., 3: 390; J. Lansing, Jr.'s, receipts, 2 Sept. 1776, NYPL, S Papers: Personal and Household Accounts and Misc. Military Accts. NYPL, S Lbk., 4: 210 indicates that Schuyler had advanced £48,071.1.4 for the public service, including the maintenance for prisoners of war. J. Carter to Schuyler, 28 Oct., 29 Nov. 1776, NYPL, S Papers and Lbk., 5: 8–9.

63. *AAs,* 1: 983–85; 2: 245–47.

64. Ibid. 2: 263–64, 293–94, 685.

65. Ibid., 619–20, 859–60.

66. Ibid., 333–34.

67. Ibid., 707–9. *Smith Memoirs,* 2: 17. J. Pierce, Jr., to A. Adams, 26 Sept. 1776, NYSL, MSS. Div.

68. NYPL, S Lbk., 3: 435–38. The review of funds that he had forwarded to Canada contained, in addition to payments of £469 and £725, the following: Oct. 1775, £6,364 and £575.16.6; Jan. 1776, £7,829.9.0 and £200; Feb. 1776, £2,139.18.10; May 1776, £685.4.0 and £1,662.1.3; June 1776, £2,400.

69. J. Porter to Schuyler, 7 Oct. 1776, NYPL, S Papers.

70. *AAs,* 2: 341–42, 535–36, 846.

71. Ibid., 525–26. Hancock did not write Schuyler of the 14 Sept. resolves, etc., until 27 Sept.; ibid., 560–61, 3: 236 and NYPL, S Lbk., 1: 174–80; *AAs,* 2: 525.

72. *AAs,* 2: 525, 609, 922–23.

73. P. R. Livingston to Schuyler, 2 Oct. 1776, NYPL, S Papers refers to the New York influence in Congress; *LMCC,* 2: 105, 107.

74. *AAs,* 2: 864 and NYPL, S Lbk., 1: 183–84; *LMCC,* 2: 114, n.

75. *AAs,* 2: 560–61, 847, 1078–79; 3: 236, cf. NYPL, S Lbk., 1: 174–80. Congress approved Schuyler's recommendations that J. Trumbull, Jr., be made deputy adjutant general and R. Varick deputy muster-master general; favorable actions were also taken to send medical supplies and artillery to the Northern Army.

76. *AAs,* 2: 922–23. The 25 Sept. resolves included reference to clothing shipped to Gates as addressed to "General Schuyler or the Commanding Officer at Albany," as if to say Schuyler was no longer in command. Also, Clymer and Stockton's instructions referred to their conferring with Gates at Ticonderoga. Ibid., 921–22, 932–33, 999–1000. Schuyler to R. R. Livingston, 7 Oct. 1776, NYSL, MSS. Div.; NYPL, S Lbk., 3: 464–65.

77. *AAs,* 2: 999–1000, 1016–17.

78. Schuyler to R. R. Livingston, 13 Oct. 1776, NYSL, MSS. Div.

79. NYPL, S Lbk., 4: 219–20; *AAs,* 2: 1039–40.

80. Ibid.; NYPL, S Lbk., 3: 476–77.

81. *AAs,* 2: 1079–80, 1131–32, 1138. Carleton claimed (ibid., 1040) that he had captured two of Arnold's vessels and burned ten so that only three of fifteen sail escaped. Arnold claimed to have saved six of his vessels.

82. *AAs,* 2: 847, 1078–79. Schuyler to Berkshire, Mass. Comm., 16 Oct. 1776, NYSL, MSS. Div. Schuyler to A. Ten Broeck, 16 Oct. 1776, MNHP, LWS Coll.

83. *AAs,* 2: 1125, 1169.

84. Ibid., 1067, 1142, 1197 and NYPL, S Lbk., 1: 195–202. See also *JPCCNY,* 1: 684, 693–95, 700, 910–11; Mason, *Road to Independence,* 202–3; *AAs,* 2: 1067, 1190–91, cf. *JPCCNY,* 1: 179; *AAs,* 2: 1297–98.

85. R. Yates to Schuyler, 24, 28 Oct. 1776; *AAs,* 3: 578 and NYPL, S Papers; *AAs,* 2: 1258, 3: 575, 577, 581.

86. *AAs,* 3: 1206; ibid., 582–83; NYPL, S Lbk., 3: 492–94. A. Ten Broeck to Schuyler, 25 Oct. 1776, NYPL, S Papers.

87. NYPL, S Lbk., 1: 187–88, 3: 497–98; *AAs*, 2: 1257.

88. Ibid., 1258. A. Ten Broeck to Schuyler, 26, 28 Oct., 3, 4 Nov. 1776; Col. D. Ten Broeck to Brig. Gen. A. Ten Broeck, 29 Oct. 1776, NYPL, S Papers; NYPL, S Lbk., 3: 502–4; *AAs*, 2: 1274, 1286–87, 1299.

89. Ibid., 1186–87, 1286–87, 1299; NYPL, S Lbk., 4: 246–47.

90. L. Allen to Schuyler, 21 Oct. 1776, *Calendar Historical MSS re. War of Revolution*, 1: 520. R. Varick to Schuyler, 27 Oct. 1776, NYPL, S Papers; *AAs*, 2: 1287.

91. *AAs*, 2: 577. Schuyler to N. Herkimer, to E. Dayton, 27 Oct. 1776, NYSL, MSS. Div.; NYPL, S Lbk., 3: 502–4; 4: 239; *AAs*, 2: 1274, 1287.

92. *AAs*, 2: 1206; NYPL, S Lbk., 4: 223.

93. NYPL, S Lbk., 4: 224–26; ibid., 3: 489–92; ibid., 4: 235, 254–55. H. Schuyler to Schuyler, 28 Oct.; 3, 4, 6, 7, 9, 16, 19, 23 Nov.; 7 Dec. 1776, Cornell University Library: Harmanus Schuyler Papers.

94. R. Varick to Schuyler, 19, 27 Oct. 1776, NYPL, S Papers; NYPL, S Lbk., 4: 236–37; *AAs*, 3: 490.

95. *AAs*, 2: 1296–97. R. Varick to Schuyler, 29 Oct. 1776 (two letters), NYPL, S Papers. Schuyler to Varick, 2, 3, 6 Nov. 1776, MNHP, LWS Coll.; NYPL, S Lbk., 4: 249–50; NYSL, MSS. Div. R. Varick to Schuyler 3, 4, 6 Nov. 1776, NYPL, S Papers; NYPL, S Lbk., 4: 248–49, 255–58.

96. R. Varick to Schuyler, 19 Oct. 1776, NYPL, S Papers; NYPL, S Lbk., 4: 261; Ibid., 3: 496–97, 526–27.

97. Ira D. Gruber, *The Howe Brothers and the American Revolution* (New York, 1972), 125. J. Barclay to Schuyler, 25 Oct. 1776, NYPL, S Papers; NYPL, S Lbk., 3: 499–500; ibid., 508–9. Joseph Young to Schuyler 24 Oct. 1776, NYSL, MSS. Div.; NYPL, S Lbk., 3: 501–3, 506–7; 4: 240–41; ibid., 3: 508–9, 511–412, 518–519; ibid., 4: 240–45; *AAs*, 2: 1299.

98. W. B. Whiting to Schuyler, 2 Nov. 1776, NYPL, S Papers; NYPL, S Lbk., 3: 527–28.

99. *AAs*, 3: 581–83, 585–86; NYPL, S Lbk., 3: 511–12, 518–19.

100. *AAs*, 2: 1314–15, 3: 502–3.

101. *AAs*, 3: 502–03, 489–90. J. Hoisington to H. Gates, 12 Oct. 1776, NYPL, S Papers; NYPL, S Lbk., 4: 250–51.

102. NYPL, S Lbk., 4: 250–51 and 3: 524–26.

103. Ibid., 4: 261. G. Van Schaick to Schuyler, 3, 7 Nov. 1776, NYPL, S Papers. James Lunt, *John Burgoyne of Saratoga*, (New York and London, 1975), 110. Arthur Granville Bradley, *Sir Guy Carleton (Lord Dorchester)*, (Toronto, 1966), 157–58.

CHAPTER 8

1. Hoffman Nickerson, *The Turning Point of the Revolution, or Burgoyne in America*, 2 vols. (Port Washington, N.Y., 1967), 1: 39, 48. Hereafter cited as Nickerson, *Turning Point*. Gates's Reasons for Thinking the British would invade the North, 29 April 1777, NYHS, Gates Papers.

2. Pancake, *1777*, 31–48; "Dress Rehearsal: 1776," 86; *AAs*, 2: 1040, cf. 1079–80.

3. Rossie, *Politics of Command*, 42–44, 60 and passim.

4. *AAs*, 3: 1477–78, 1495–97. NYPL, S Lbk., 1: 222–31.

5. Trumbull's commission as deputy adjutant general was first a temporary appointment made on 28 June 1776. It was finally approved by Congress on 12 Sept. after Schuyler had

recommended it on 8 Sept. *AAs*, 2: 245–47; *JCC*, 5: 753; *AAs*, 3: 1495–97; NYPL, S Lbk., 5: 58–62, included a copy of Joseph Trumbull to W. Williams, 18 Nov. 1776 (*AAs*, 3: 1497–98). Schuyler objected to "such injurious treatment" and demanded justice; Congress, he said, "can put us on a par by dismissing one or the other [of us] from the Service." See also Schuyler to J. Hancock, 4–5 Feb. 1777 (which is misdated as 4–5 Jan. in *PCC*, NAR 172) NYPL, S Lbk., 5: 68–72.

6. NYPL, S Lbk., 5: 47–51, 68–72. Gruber, *Howe Brothers*, 174, 179. S. Kirkland to Schuyler, 5 Jan. 1777, *PCC*, NAR 172.

7. Schuyler's speech (draft) to the Six Nations, 5 Jan. 1777, HL; NYPL, S Lbk., 4: 352–54, cf. Gruber, *Howe Brothers*, 193, who says Sir William Howe ordered Indian agents on the northern frontier to alert the tribes to help Burgoyne's invasion.

8. Schuyler cited $25,000 or £10,000. NYPL, S Lbk., 4: 47–53.

9. *Smith Memoirs*, 2: 62–64, 70.

10. Schuyler's 23 Jan. letters to the presidents of Mass. and N.H. requested two to three tons of steel, two thousand blankets, cannon and ammunition, and troops for Ticonderoga. NYPL, S Lbk., 4: 363–68; 5: 45–46, 55–56. E. Avery's Return, 23 Jan. 1777, NYPL, S Papers.

11. NYPL, S Lbk., 5: 162; *JPCCNY*, 1: 793.

12. A. Wayne to Schuyler, N. Buel to Schuyler, 22 Jan. 1777; Schuyler to J. Hancock, 25–26 Jan. 1777, *PCC*, NAR, 173; NYPL, S Lbk., 5: 63–65.

13. *WGW*, 7: 69–70; NYPL, S Lbk., 5: 63–65.

14. Gruber, *Howe Brothers*, 180. NYPL, S Lbk., 5: 66–68, 73–76. A. Wayne to Schuyler, 2 Feb. 1777, *PCC*, NAR, 173. A. Wayne to Schuyler, 4 Feb. 1777, Fort Ticonderoga Museum.

15. The letter to Hancock in *PCC*, NAR, 173, is misdated 4–5 Jan. Cf., NYPL, S Lbk., 5: 68–72, 73–74.

16. A. Wayne to Schuyler, 13 Feb. 1777, *Calendar Historical MSS re. War of Revolution*, 1: 633–34. NYPL, S Lbk., 4: 401–4, 406–8; ibid., 5: 81–82, and see 4: 396–99, 404–5.

17. R. Varick to Schuyler, 16 Feb. 1777, NYPL, S Papers; *WGW*, 7: 161–63.

18. *WGW*, 7: 161–63, 196–97; *LMCC*, 2: 269.

19. NYPL, S Lbk., 5: 102–3. Schuyler to A. Wayne, to Col. Bedel, 5 Mar. 1777 (mentions the spies, "Formonty & Traversie"), ibid., 4: 439–41.

20. *WGW*, 7: 272–78.

21. Schuyler to R. R. Livingston, 17 Mar. 1777, NYHS, R. R. Livingston Collection. Palmer, *Way of the Fox*, 137 and passim.

22. NYPL, S Lbk., 5: 113–15.

23. See n. 1 above, Gates's Reasons.

24. *JCC*, 7: 202 (25 Mar.).

25. A. Wayne to [Schuyler?], 23 [24?] Mar. 1777, William Henry Smith, ed., *The St. Clair Papers: The Life and Public Services of Arthur St. Clair ... with his Correspondence and other Papers*, 2 vols. (Cincinnati, 1882), 1: 387–88. Hereafter cited as Smith, *St. Clair Papers*. Cf. NYPL, S Lbk., 4: 464; 5: 116–17.

26. J. Pierce, Jr., to A. Adams, 25 Mar. 1777, NYSL, MSS. Div. Schuyler to R. Varick, 26 April 1777, MNHP, LWS Coll.

27. *JPCCNY*, 1: 931, Hough; *Civil List* (1885), 61, indicates that the first twelve New York delegates chosen on 21 April 1775 were not replaced until 13 May 1777 when Schuyler was again elected (except that William Duer had been added to the delegation on 29 Mar. 1777). *JCC*, 7: 230, indicates that Schuyler "attended, and took his seat" on 7 April 1777 with William Duer, who made his first appearance since his March appointment. Duane, Philip Livingston, and Schuyler were the only three of the original twelve N.Y. delegates chosen in 1775 who were reelected in 1777.

28. Nelson, *Gates*, 77; Joseph B. Mitchell, *Discipline and Bayonets: The Armies and Leaders in the War of the American Revolution* (New York, 1967), 140.

29. NYPL, S Lbk., 2: 89–91, 92–93. P. V. B. Livingston to Schuyler, 17 Aug. 1775, NYPL, S Papers; *JPCCNY*, 2: 14; *AA4*, 3: 443; NYPL, S Lbk., 1: 32–33; 2: 178–81. Congress's 20 Aug. 1776 resolve, Hawke, *Banjamin Rush*, 170. S. Stringer to Schuyler, 22 June 1776, NYPL, S Papers; NYPL, S Lbk., 3: 216–17.

30. S. Stringer to Schuyler, 31 July 1776, NYPL, S Papers. Broadus Mitchell, *The Price of Independence: A Realistic View of the American Revolution* (New York, 1974), 153; NYPL, S Lbk., 3: 384–85.

31. Hawke, *Benjamin Rush*, 182; *LMCC*, 2: 210. Francis B. Heitman, *Historical Register of Officers of the Continental Army during the War of the Revolution, April, 1775, to December, 1783*, (Washington, 1914), 525. Hereafter cited as Heitman, *Register*.

32. NYPL, S Lbk., 1: 232–35; 5: 68–72; cf. *AA5*, 3: 1495–97. John Trumbull did not receive his colonel's commission (dated 12 Sept. 1776) until 22 Feb. 1777. By then he was so furious over the delay and the fact that two lieutenant colonels had been promoted ahead of him that he refused the commission and returned to civilian status. Jaffe, *John Trumbull*, 29. NYPL, S Lbk., 5: 104–6, and see J. Cochran to Schuyler, 21 Jan. 1777, NYPL, S Papers; *WGW*, 7: 69–70.

33. *JCC*, 7: 180–81; *LMCC*, 2: 304; cf. NYPL, S Lbk., 1: 257–60.

34. NYPL, S Lbk., 1: 257–60, 302, and *JCC*, 7: 202. Indicative, too, that Schuyler retained command of the department is the fact that during Gates's service subordinates like colonels A. Wayne and S. Elmore continued to report to Schuyler; e.g., Wayne to Schuyler, 14 April 1777, Elmore to Schuyler, 22 April 1777, PCC, NAR, 173.

35. W. Duer to Schuyler, J. Duane to Schuyler, 19 June 1777, NYPL, S Papers; cf. *LMCC*, 2: 382–86. See also Nelson, *Gates*, 80, which indicates that Gates overstepped his authority by presuming to be department commander, although the command of Ticonderoga "seriously curtailed" Schuyler's overall authority in the Northern Department.

36. *LMCC*, 2: 304 n.

37. NYPL, S Lbk., 5: 91–94. J. Milligan, J. Carter, J. Welles, Commissioners for auditing Accounts in the Northern Dept. Statement, 20 Mar. 1777, NYPL, S Papers.

38. Schuyler to R. R. Livingston, 17 Mar. 1777, NYHS, R. R. Livingston Collection. *JCC* (7 April), 7: 230. Schuyler to R. Varick, 30 Mar. 1777, MNHP, LWS Coll.

39. Schuyler to R. Varick, 30 Mar. 1777, MNHP, LWS Coll.

40. R. Varick to Schuyler, 1, 2, 7 April 1777, NYPL, S Papers.

41. *PAH*, 1: 219–22. Schuyler at Morristown is also mentioned in R. Varick to Schuyler, 16 April 1777, and J. Lansing, Jr.'s, account, 26 Jan. 1778 in NYPL, S Papers. At Morristown £2.8.0 was paid for lodging, 4–5 April. According to Lansing's account Schuyler and his aides evidently traveled by sulky and wagon. See also R. Varick to Schuyler, 2 April 1777, ibid., for reference to Van Rensselaer and Lansing. NYPL, S Lbk., vol. 5, shows Van Rensselaer and H. B. Livingston as Schuyler's aides at Philadelphia. His account for food and lodgings refers to seven weeks for Schuyler and suite, three servants, an orderly, and aides. Sarah Clarke's receipt, 27 May 1777, and Schuyler's Account of Money Paid . . . at Mrs. Brock's, 14 April–27 May 1777, NYPL, S Papers, Personal and Household Accts.

42. *JCC*, 7: 230. Resolutions of 7, 12, 22, April 1777 in Schuyler's letterbook, vol. 1 (NYPL) indicate his careful notation of congressional arrangements applicable to his department.

43. John R. Elting, *The Battles of Saratoga* (Monmouth Beach, N.J., 1977), 12. Hereafter cited Elting, *Battles*. NYPL, S Lbk., 1: 278; 5: 465–92. Schuyler to Wharton, 10 April 1777, ibid., 118. Orders of Pa. Board of War, 14 April 1777, NYPL, S Papers. Historians have missed Schuyler's special Pennsylvania command. No one since Lossing, *Schuyler*, 2: 170–

78 himself omitted mention of this has remarked upon it. Yet the combination of civil and military offices that Schuyler simultaneously held is a remarkable commentary on his position and influence as well as indicative of the nature of revolutionary war and politics.

44. NYPL, S Lbk., 1: 283. Examination of J. Brown, 15 May 1777, NYPL, S Papers (Military Information). NYPL, S Lbk., 4: 487–88; 5: 136.

45. NYPL, S Lbk., 5: 136–38, 140–41; ibid., 4: 489–91; *WGW*, 8: 105–6.

46. *JCC* (April 17), 7: 279. Morris, *Jay Papers*, 1: 386–88; *LMCC*, 2: 337. Schuyler's failure to write his wife is indicated in R. Varick to Schuyler, 16, 21 April 1777 (NYPL, S Papers), and the only news of him that had reached Albany had been brought by travelers like John Van Cortlandt and Col. James Wilkinson until Varick reported on April 26 that Schuyler's April 16 letters had reached Albany.

47. NYPL, S Lbk., 5: 122. J. Lansing to R. Varick, 26 April 1777, Pierpont Morgan Library.

48. NYPL, S Lbk., 5: 123–24. Patterson, *Gates*, 127; *WGW*, 8: 11–12.

49. NYPL, S Lbk., 5: 125–34.

50. Ibid., 1: 291.

51. Ibid., 292, 301. *JPCCNY*, 1: 931. Hough, *Civil List* (1855), 61. *Smith Memoirs* (14 May), 2: 137–38.

52. *JCC*, 7: 364 ff.

53. NYPL, S Lbk., 5: 138; *LMCC*, 2: 364 n. *Smith Memoirs*, 2: 142.

54. *JCC*, 7: 364; 8: 375; cf. NYPL, S Lbk., 1: 302.

55. J. Lovell to H. Gates, 22 May 1777, NYHS, Gates Papers. R. Varick to a Comm. of Congress, 10 Oct. 1777 (draft), NYHS, Varick Papers. Varick noted that Gates did not leave Albany once he arrived there in April and alleged that during his tenure only a small amount of provisions had been "thrown into" Ticonderoga.

56. R. Sherman to J. Trumbull, 26 May 1777, Mass. Historical Society *Collections*, 7th Ser., 1: 51–52. Cf. W. Duer to R. R. Livingston, 28 May 1777, NYHS, R. R. Livingston Collection.

57. W. Duer to R. R. Livingston, 28 May 1777, NYHS, R. R. Livingston Collection. P. Livingston and J. Duane to N.Y. Convention, 23 May 1777, NYHS, Duane Papers. Morris, *Jay Papers*, 1: 406. Most probably helpful in Schuyler's case were Robert Morris and James Wilson of Pennsylvania; George Walton of Georgia; Mann Page, Jr., of Virginia; Arthur Middleton and Thomas Burke of South Carolina and North Carolina; and Marylanders Charles Carroll and William Paca. The general specifically sent greetings to these men when he thanked Philip Livingston, James Duane, and William Duer for their maneuvers to affect his resuming command. NYPL, S Lbk., 5: 156–58.

58. NYPL, S Lbk., 5: 142–44. Resolutions, 27 May, ibid., 1: 302–4. R. Arthur Bowler, *Logistics and the Failure of the British Army in America, 1775–1783* (Princeton, 1975), 225.

59. Morris, *Jay Papers*, 1: 411 n.

60. *Smith Memoirs*, 2: 153–57; NYPL, S Lbk., 5: 145–46; ibid., 155–58. Morris, *Jay Papers*, 1: 410–11.

61. Morris, *Jay Papers*, 1: 412.

62. R. R. Livingston to W. Duer, 12 June 1777, NYHS, R. R. Livingston Coll.; NYPL, S Lbk., 5: 156–58.

63. *Smith Memoirs*, 2: 157. R. R. Livingston to W. Duer, 12 June 1777, NYHS, R. R. Livingston Coll.

64. *Smith Memoirs*, 2: 159–60, 326. Schuyler to W. Duer, 3–5 July 1777; cf. W. Duer to Schuyler, 19 June 1777, NYPL, S Papers. Staughton Lynd, "The Tenant Rising at Livingston Manor, May 1777," *The New-York Historical Society Quarterly* 48 (April, 1964): 163–77. See

NOTES   555

also Bush, *Revolutionary Enigma*, 97–104; George Dangerfield, *Chancellor Robert R. Livingston of New York, 1746–1813* (New York, 1960), 94–95 (hereafter cited as Dangerfield, *Chancellor Livingston*); Alfred F. Young, *The Democratic Republicans of New York: The Origins, 1763–1797* (Chapel Hill, N.C.; 1967), 23–25 (hereafter cited as Young, *Democratic Republicans*).

65. Johnston, *Jay Papers*, 1: 142–43. *Smith Memoirs*, 2: 165, 170.

66. Morris, *Jay Papers*, 1: 416. NYPL, S Lbk., 5: 311–12. Judd, *Van Cortlandt Papers*, 2: 211. Returns by Counties:

	Clinton	Schuyler
Charlotte	2	35
Tryon	0	237
Albany	125	589
Ulster	464	12
Orange	223	1
Dutchess	206	132
Westchester	68	7
	1,088	1,013

67. Schuyler to W. Duer, 3–5 July 1777, NYPL, S Papers, Misc. Military.

68. Patterson, *Gates*, 122 cf. Elting, *Battles*, 11. R. Varick to Comm. of Congress, 10 Oct. 1777, NYHS, Varick Papers.

69. Numbers are difficult to compile. C. H. Lesser, ed., *The Sinews of Independence* (Chicago, 1976), includes monthly troop reports of the Continental Army, but none for the army under Schuyler or Gates, Nov. 1776–Oct. 1777. NYPL, S Lbk., 5: 113–15, reports the figure to be around 700. Smith, *St. Clair Papers*, 1: 387–88, refers to 1,200 at Ticonderoga, including militia and the sick. St. Clair, 13 June 1777, ibid., 1: 396–400, cited 1,576 Continentals fit for duty and a variety of other units, including artificers and militia; see footnotes re. Gates's success in calling troops; St. Clair reported only 250 Massachusetts militia out for two months with three weeks of their service already elapsed. R. Varick to Schuyler, 13 June 1777, NYPL, S Papers, mentioned 2,300 Continentals. Nelson, *Gates*, 81.

70. R. Varick to Schuyler, 21 April 1777; John Welles to Schuyler, 21 April, 13 May 1777, NYPL, S Papers. Cf. Lynd, "Tenant Rising at Livingston Manor," 170; Nelson, *Gates*, 81–83.

71. H. Gates to J. Hancock, 2 May 1777, NYHS, Gates Papers. Sydney Jackman, ed., *With Burgoyne from Quebec* [Thomas Anbury's *Travels Through the Interior Parts of North America*], (Toronto, 1963), 1: 3. Hereafter cited as Jackman, *With Burgoyne*.

72. R. Varick to Schuyler, 12 May 1777, NYPL, S Papers; cf. Patterson, *Gates*, 128–30. NYPL, S Lbk., 5: 150–54.

73. NYPL, S Lbk., 4: 493–95.

74. Ibid., 5: 146–47, 150–54.

75. Nickerson, *Turning Point*, 1: 133–34. R. Varick to Schuyler, 13 June 1777, NYPL, S Papers.

76. Smith, *St. Clair Papers*, 1: 396–400.

77. Ibid., 413–14. Returns of 28 June 1777, Wilkinson, *Memoirs*, appendix A. Jackman, *With Burgoyne*, 4–5. Nickerson, *Turning Point*, 1: 105–6.

78. NYPL, S Lbk., 5: 186–87, 195–204; 3: 530–31; Morris, *Jay Papers*, 1: 416. Nelson, *Gates*, 81.

79. NYPL, S Lbk., 4: 493–94, 496–501, 507; ibid., 5: 154–55; cf. *WGW*, 8: 253–55, shows Schuyler was forced to wait for artillery as Knox sent thirty-two cannon to Washington.

80. NYPL, S Lbk., 4: 497, 507–8; ibid., 5: 156–58, 170–71.

81. Ibid., 5: 161; ibid., 4: 502, 504–5.

82. Ibid., 509–10; ibid., 5: 162–67. Schuyler reported languor, want of attention, and confusion prevailing in the quartermaster's affairs. Ibid., 4: 510–11, 513–14.

83. *JPCCNY*, 1: 980. J. Duane to Schuyler, W. Duer to Schuyler, 19 June 1777, *LMCC*, 2: 382–86; cf. full text of letters in NYPL, S Papers. Mason, "Entrepreneurial Activity," 193–94.

84. NYPL, S Lbk., 5: 154–55; 195–204; 3: 530–31; 4: 527–28.

85. Ibid., 5: 154–55; ibid., 1: 323–25, 328; ibid., 4: 500, 502–3, 505, 509. Extract from J. Dean to Schuyler, 25 June 1777, *PCC*, NAR, 173.

86. G. Van Schaick to Schuyler, 12 June 1777, NYPL, S Papers; S Lbk., 4: 506–7, 5: 162–71; Smith, *St. Clair Papers*, 1: 396–400. Schuyler to J. Hancock, 14 June 1777, *PCC*, NAR, 173.

87. Smith, *St. Clair Papers*, 1: 401–2.

88. J. Wilkinson to H. Gates, 9 June 1777, NYPL, S Papers. Wilkinson, *Memoirs*, 1: 173–74.

89. Williams, "Mount Independence," 97. Smith, *St. Clair Papers*, 1: 404–5. R. Varick to Comm. of Congress, 10 Oct. 1777, NYHS, Varick Papers contains a review of Schuyler's council of war.

90. R. Varick to Comm. of Congress, 10 Oct. 1777, NYHS, Varick Papers. See also Wilkinson, *Memoirs*, 1: 176; Nickerson, *Turning Point*, 1: 138–40.

91. E. Stevens and Schuyler Agreement, 20 June 1777, Fort Ticonderoga Museum. NYPL, S Lbk., 4: 516–18. Schuyler to J. Potts, 21 June 1777, Fort Ticonderoga Museum and NYPL, S Lbk., 4: 518–20. H. B. Livingston's Orderly Book, *AAS*, 27–31. Memorial of Battalions' Commanding Officers at Ticonderoga to Schuyler, 21 June 1777, *PCC*, NAR, 173; NYPL, S Lbk., 4: 520–22.

92. NYPL, S Lbk., 4: 522–24; ibid., 5: 174–82.

93. Ibid., and 288–89.

94. Smith, *St. Clair Papers*, 1: 406–7, 409–10. St. Clair's general orders, 24 June 1777, *AAS*, H. B. Livingston orderly book, 25–27; Judd, *Van Cortlandt Papers*, 2: 203–4; NYPL, S Lbk., 5: 175–82, 288–89.

95. NYPL, S Lbk., 4: 524–25. J. Carter to W. Livingston, 3 July 1777, NYHS, R. R. Livingston Coll.

96. NYPL, S Lbk., 4: 525–26; 5: 190–94.

97. Ibid., 4: 526–27; ibid., 5: 187–89.

98. Higginbotham, *War of Independence*, 189. Like other historians who are not familiar with the general and who have not read the Schuyler papers in their entirety, Higginbotham admits that Schuyler was a "generous, selfless patriot" but deems him "pompous and overbearing." Rossie, *Politics of Command*, 59–60 and passim is even less generous and more wrongheaded. Wilkinson, *Memoirs*, 1: 207, 215.

99. NYPL, S Lbk., 5: 154–55, 159–60.

100. *WGW*, 8: 253–55.

101. NYPL, S Lbk., 5: 167–68, 172–73.

102. Ibid., 168–69.

103. Ibid., 162–67. Elting, *Battles*, 29.

104. *WGW*, 8: 273–76.

105. The distance from Peekskill to Ticonderoga is about 180 miles. Standard infantry march of 25 to 30 miles per day (St. Clair's record in fleeing Ticonderoga), when considered with moving troops by river transport between Peekskill and Albany, means that reinforcements might have reasonably traversed the 180 miles in about a week. NYPL, S Lbk., 5: 186–94.

106. *PAH*, 1: 283 n.

107. *WGW,* 8: 331–33.

108. A. St. Clair to Schuyler, 25 June 1777, HL; cf. *JPCCNY,* 2: 463, and Smith, *St. Clair Papers,* 1: 410–12.

109. Wilkinson, *Memoirs,* 1: Appendix A; cf. Elting, *Battles,* 28–29.

110. NYPL, S Lbk., 4: 525; ibid., 528–29; 5: 204–5.

111. Ibid., 4: 511–12; 5: 206–7. Morris, *Jay Papers,* 1: 416; NYPL, S Lbk., 5: 206. Elting, *Battles,* 30.

112. *Smith Memoirs,* 2: 170; e.g., Rossie, *Politics of Command,* 131 and passim.

113. J. Carter [Church] to W. Livingston, 3 July 1777, NYHS, R. R. Livingston Coll.

114. Schuyler to W. Duer, 3–5 July 1777, NYPL, S Papers: Misc. Military. A draft biography of John Barker Church (1748–1818) by D. R. Fisher in the files of the History of Parliament Trust was graciously supplied by E. L. C. Mullins, 19 Dec. 1973. Church evidently came to America in 1774 to escape his creditors after going bankrupt from stock speculation and gambling. See also *PAH,* 3: 417, 433 n, 459, 477, 620 n, 621, 627 n, 651 n, 658; 4: 280 n; 6: 274 n, 279, 308, 329–30, 332, 347–49; 8: 181, 279–80, 320; 9: 5 n.

115. Jackman, *With Burgoyne,* 131–32.

116. Smith, *St. Clair Papers,* 1: 413–16. H. B. Livingston to Schuyler, 30 June 1777, NYPL, S Papers. St. Clair's general orders, 30 June 1777, AAS, H. B. Livingston Orderly Book, 38–39. St. Clair to colonels Williams, Robinson, Warner, 2 July 1777, NYSL, MSS. Div. Williams Papers. Cf. Jackman, *With Burgoyne,* 4–5; Bowler, *Logistics and Failure,* 225–27, 229; Nickerson, *Turning Point,* 1: 105–6; Higginbotham, *War of American Independence,* 188.

117. Schuyler to R. Varick, 1 July 1777, NYSL, MSS. Div.

118. NYPL, S Lbk., 5: 208–10; AAS, S Lbk., 4: 7, 10–11. Schuyler to W. Duer, 3–5 July 1777, NYPL, S Papers: Misc. Military. NYPL, S Lbk., 5: 215. See also Schuyler to Ebenezer Learned, to Jacob Bailey [Bayley], 2 July 1777, ibid., 210–11. Learned's Continental brigade consisted of Col. James Livingston's N.Y. Regiment, Col. John Bailey's 2d Mass. Regiment, Col. Ichabod Alden's 7th Mass. Regiment, Col. Michael Jackson's 8th Mass. Regiment, and Col. James Wesson's 9th Mass. Regiment—all of whom served under Gates in the Saratoga campaign. Brig. Gen. Jacob Bayley led a Hampshire Grants (Vt.) militia brigade and also served under Gates (not to be confused with Col. John Bailey who led a regiment in Learned's or John Nixon's Continental brigades. AAS, S Lbk., 4: 8–9. Smith, *St. Clair Papers,* 1: 419–20. Elting, *Battles,* 30. NYPL, S Lbk., 5: 211–13; AAS, S Lbk., 4: 910. Memorandum of Articles . . . to purchase for the Indian Dept., 3 July 1777, NYPL, S (Indian) Papers. Schuyler to W. Duer, 3–5 July 1777, ibid., Misc. Military Papers.

119. Jane Clark, "The Responsibility for the Failure of the Burgoyne Campaign," *American Historical Review,* 35 (April 1930): 550–54; Gruber, *Howe Brothers,* 230–32.

120. Smith, *St. Clair Papers,* 1: 404–5. NYPL, S Lbk., 5: 317–23. Wilkinson, *Memoirs,* 1: 198. James Thatcher, *A Military Journal during the American Revolutionary War,* 2d ed. (Boston, 1827), 86.

121. Lunt, *Burgoyne,* 155–56. Nelson, *Gates,* 91–92. Miecislaus Haiman, *Kosciuszko in the American Revolution* (Boston, 1972), 16–17.

122. Jaffe, *John Trumbull,* 28.

123. Wilkinson, *Memoirs,* 1: 174, 176. Williams, "Mount Independence," 100–1. John Luzader, *Decision on the Hudson: The Saratoga Campaign of 1777* (Washington, D.C., 1975), 21. Bayard Tuckerman, *Life of General Philip Schuyler, 1733–1804* (New York, 1903), 189–92 recounts Col. John Trumbull's observations after experimenting with a cannon shot from Fort Ticonderoga to Mount Defiance. The experiment proved that the fort was vulnerable to cannon fire from the summit. But Gates had insisted that it "was inaccessible to the enemy" even after Trumbull, Benedict Arnold, and Anthony Wayne climbed Mount Defiance and

pronounced the assent "difficult and laborious, but not impracticable" for "driving up a loaded carriage."

124. Wilkinson, *Memoirs*, 1: 85. Williams, "Mount Independence," 100–2. George F. Scheer and Hugh F. Rankin, *Rebels and Redcoats* (New York, 1957), 254–55. Willard M. Wallace, *Appeal to Arms: A Military History of the American Revolution* (Chicago, 1964), 148.

125. Higginbotham, *War of American Independence*, 190. Elting, *Battles*, 34. Burgoyne's reasons for moving overland instead were to avoid the appearance of a retreat and to force the Americans out of Fort George; otherwise they might remain there to delay an approach via the lake and also have time to destroy the road between Fort George and Fort Edward. Moreover, Burgoyne wished to continue to threaten Connecticut "as a cover plan." Lunt, *Burgoyne*, 169. See also Luzader, *Decision on the Hudson*, 21–22.

126. AAS, S Lbk., 4: 15–17; NYPL, S Lbk., 5: 224; *WGW*, 8: 357, 358.

CHAPTER 9

1. NYPL, S Lbk., 5: 228–29. Schuyler to R. Varick, 7 July 1777, MNHP, LWS Coll.

2. NYPL, S Lbk., 5: 225–27, 229–30: *JPCCNY*, 2: 514.

3. J. Graham to Schuyler, 6 July 1777, NYPL, S Papers; NYPL, S Lbk., 5: 228; AAS, S Lbk., 4: 18–19.

4. NYPL, S Lbk., 5: 225–27.

5. *WGW*, 8: 378–79.

6. Ibid., 380–92 cf. *PAH*, 1: 285, which includes Washington's orders that Glover be ready to march and that the remainder of Nixon's brigade and some artillery should be sent to Schuyler.

7. AAS, S Lbk., 4: 18. Nickerson, *Turning Point*, 1: 173; NYPL, S Lbk., 5: 235–37.

8. NYPL, S Lbk., 5: 244–47. Schuyler to W. Heath, 14 July 1777, NYPL, S Papers. Return of Troops at Fort Edward, 20 July 1777, Wilkinson, *Memoirs*, 1: Appendix B; NYPL, S Lbk., 1: 327.

9. NYPL, S Lbk., 5: 292–95.

10. H. M. Muller and David A. Donath, " 'The Road Not Taken': A Reassessment of Burgoyne's Campaign," *The Bulletin of the Fort Ticonderoga Museum* 13 (1973): 284–85.

11. AAS, S Lbk., 4: 22–25. Nickerson, *Turning Point*, 1: 83–89, 158, 174–78. Joseph B. Mitchell, *Discipline and Bayonets: The Armies and Leaders in the War of the American Revolution* (New York, 1967), 50.

12. Nickerson, *Turning Point*, 1: 158. Although Nickerson praises Schuyler and notes that he did not despair (p. 172), he does not think him a great soldier. But the weight of the evidence suggests that the general was more than a great man, disinterested patriot, and worthy character; he *could* despair and succumb to impatience and exasperation, and he did much fuming and complaining. While his energies never flagged except when illness took its toll, his dogged determination and strict attention to duty accomplished much and were no less laudable than such virtues exemplified by other leaders such as Washington.

13. NYPL, S Lbk., 5: 230–32, 234, 240.

14. AAS, S Lbk., 4: 19–22, 25–26. Schuyler to Maj. [Christopher P.] Yates, 8, 9 July 1777, NYSL, MSS. Div., cf. AAS, S Lbk., 4: 21, 24.

15. AAS, S Lbk., 4: 23, 25–26, 28–29; NYPL, S Lbk., 5: 235, 239–40.

16. NYPL, S Lbk., 5: 232–33.

17. Caleb Stark, ed., *Memoir and Official Correspondence of General John Stark* (Concord,

N.H., 1860), 119–21, hereafter cited as Stark, *Memoir.* Cf. Schuyler's "Manifesto," 13 July 1777, Fort Ticonderoga Museum. AAS, S Lbk., 4: 30–31.

18. *WGW,* 8: 380–82, 392–93.

19. AAS, S Lbk., 4: 26–27; 5: 231, 234, 237, 240. Schuyler's 10 July 1777 letters to N. Herkimer and Tryon Co. Comm., ibid., 238–39; to P. Gansevoort and Major Badlam, AAS, S Lbk., 4: 27, 29. Cf. [P. Gansevoort] to [Schuyler?], 4 July 1777, NYPL, Peter Gansevoort Military Papers, which is a report on the state of Fort Schuyler, the need for three hundred reinforcements, and of the appearance of increasing numbers of hostile Indians. See also NYPL, S Lbk., 5: 235–38, for mention of only twenty pieces of artillery from Lake George. AAS, S Lbk., 4: 31–32.

20. NYPL, S Lbk., 5: 235–37, 240.

21. *WGW,* 8: 407–9.

22. *PNG,* 2: 119, cf. *PAH,* 1: 285–86.

23. Morris, *Jay Papers,* 1: 419, cf. Judd, *Van Cortlandt Papers,* 2: 212, 218–19.

24. AAS, S Lbk., 4: 35–37. R. Varick to Schuyler, 11, 12 July 1777, NYPL, S Papers.

25. NYPL, S Lbk., 5: 240–43.

26. AAS, S Lbk., 4: 38–39; NYPL, S Lbk., 5: 242–43.

27. Anbury's journal, 14, 17 July, Jackman, *With Burgoyne,* 147, 152. Lunt, *Burgoyne,* 174.

28. Schuyler to W. Heath, 14, 15 July 1777, NYPL, S Papers and Lbk., 5: 247–48.

29. AAS, S Lbk., 4: 42–43.

30. Ibid., 45; re. cattle, etc., see 44–46; NYPL, S Lbk., 5: 249–50; Johnston, *Jay Papers,* 1: 146–47.

31. NYPL, S Lbk., 5: 249–50.

32. Max M. Mintz, *Gouverneur Morris and the American Revolution* (Norman, Okla., 1970), 79–80; hereafter cited as Mintz, *G. Morris.* G. Morris to N.Y. Provincial Convention, 14 July 1777, NYPL, S Papers. Morris had been substituted for R. R. Livingston when the latter's father died and he could not serve. NYPL, S Lbk., 1: 345–46.

33. R. Varick to Schuyler, 14 July 1777, NYPL, S Papers.

34. Schuyler to R. Varick, 15 July 1777, NYSL, MSS. Div.

35. J. Van Rensselaer to Schuyler, 19 July 1777; Schuyler to R. Varick, 29 July 1777; H. B. Livingston to Schuyler, 30 July 1777, NYPL, S Papers.

36. NYPL, S Lbk., 5: 244–47.

37. *WGW,* 8: 426–28. Jared Sparks, ed., *Correspondence of the American Revolution,* 4 vols. (Boston, 1853), 1: 400–1, hereafter cited as Sparks, *Correspondence.*

38. *JPCCNY,* 2: 512; AAS, S Lbk., 4: 43–44, 49–50.

39. AAS, S Lbk., 4: 51. Nickerson, *Turning Point,* 2: 230.

40. "Nicholas Herchhiemer" to Schuyler, 15 July 1777, NYSL, MSS. Div.

41. NYPL, S Lbk., 5: 256–57; *JPCCNY,* 1: 997; 2: 511.

42. NYPL, S Lbk., 5: 257–64; AAS, S Lbk., 4: 57–58.

43. Graymont, *Iroquois,* 117–18.

44. Mintz, *G. Morris,* 80–81. NYPL, S Lbk., 5: 252. Jackman, *With Burgoyne,* 143. Haiman, *Kosciuszko,* 13–42. AAS, S Lbk., 4: 49, 51–53, 56–57; NYPL, S Lbk., 5: 252–54.

45. AAS, S Lbk., 4: 55–56.

46. Schuyler to G. Washington, 18 July 1777, HL and NYPL, S Lbk., 5: 257–62.

47. *WGW,* 8: 447–50.

48. *LMCC,* 2: 415, cf. NYPL, S Lbk., 1: 350–51.

49. Nickerson, *Turning Point,* 2: 227–29.

50. NYPL, S Lbk., 5: 267–68, 271; AAS, S Lbk., 4: 60–61, 63, 65.

51. AAS, S Lbk., 4: 58–59.

52. AAS, H. B. Livingston Orderly Book, 48–53.

53. *Smith Memoirs*, 2: 179. General Return of Continentals and Militia at and around Fort Edward, 20 July 1777, Wilkinson, *Memoirs*, 1: Appendix B. Cf. *JPCCNY*, 2: 505, Schuyler's claim to have fewer than three thousand Continentals.

54. P. Skene to Schuyler, 19 July 1777; Schuyler to P. Skene, 20 July 1777, W. Clements Library: Germain Papers.

55. Mintz, *G. Morris*, 81–82. Johnston, *Jay Papers*, 1: 148–51. *JPCCNY*, 2: 501–2, explains the seizure of carpenters' tools; Schuyler had none other for construction of bridges and gun carriages.

56. NYPL, S Lbk., 5: 267–72. Schuyler notified Douw, one of the Northern Department Indian commissioners, to detain the Indians at Albany if they arrived and to summon him if necessary for a conference.

57. Willcox, *Sir Henry Clinton*, 164–69; NYPL, S Lbk., 5: 274.

58. AAS, H. B. Livingston Orderly Book, 55–57; NYPL, S Lbk., 5: 272–74.

59. AAS, H. B. Livingston Orderly Book, 54–55, S Lbk., 4: 66. J. Barclay to Schuyler, 22 July 1777, NYSL, MSS. Div.; NYPL, S Lbk., 5: 276–77; *PAH*, 1: 289–90. Harry Alonzo Cushing, ed., *The Writings of Samuel Adams*, 4 vols. (New York, 1904–1908), 3: 387–88, 395, hereafter cited as Cushing, *Writings S. Adams*.

60. Mintz, *G. Morris*, 82–83. Morris, *Jay Papers*, 1: 429–31.

61. *LMCC*, 2: 433–35. J. Chester to J. Huntington, 23 July 1777, *Colls. Conn. Hist. Society*, 20: 65–66.

62. AAS, S Lbk., 4: 66–67.

63. NYPL, S Lbk., 5: 275–76.

64. Jane Clark, "The Responsibility for the Failure of the Burgoyne Campaign," *American Historical Review* 35 (April, 1930): 555–56, hereafter cited as Clark, "Responsibility for Failure." William B. Willcox, ed., *The American Rebellion: Sir Henry Clinton's Narrative of His Campaigns, 1775–1782, with an Appendix of Original Documents* (New Haven, 1954), 65–66, hereafter cited as Willcox, *American Rebellion; WGW*, 8: 484–86.

65. *WGW*, 8: 456–60. M. Willett to Schuyler, 24 July 1777, NYPL, S Papers. Lunt, *Burgoyne*, 183.

66. Lunt, *Burgoyne*, 182–83. Elting, *Battles*, 37–39. Graymont, *Iroquois*, 125–28. Pancake, *1777*, 141.

67. Nickerson, *Turning Point*, 1: 179. Schuyler to N.Y. Council of Safety, 24 July 1777, Union College Library (Schenectady). NYPL, S Lbk., 5: 283–84.

68. Schuyler to J. Jay, 26 [?] July 1777, Columbia Univ. Library, Jay Papers; cf. NYPL, S Lbk., 5: 284–87 (dating it 24 July) cf.; Morris, *Jay Papers*, 1: 429–31, refers to Schuyler's 24 letter. Ibid.; NYPL, S Lbk., 5: 287–88. Morris, *Jay Papers*, 1: 428–29.

69. AAS, H. B. Livingston Orderly Book, 57–64.

70. AAS, S Lbk., 4: 67–68. Baxter, *Godchild*, 385. The canvas is part of the collections of the Los Angeles, California, County Museum of Art. Los Angeles County Museum of Art *Bulletin 1977* 23: 26–33.

71. *Smith Memoirs*, 2: 183–84, 187. R. Varick to Schuyler, 14 July 1777, NYPL, S Papers.

72. AAS, S Lbk., 4: 68.

73. *Smith Memoirs*, 2: 194. Jackman, *With Burgoyne*, 170.

74. Schuyler to R. Varick, 29 July 1777; H. B. Livingston to Schuyler, 30 July 1777, NYPL, S Papers: Misc. Military.

75. J. Lansing to Schuyler, 27 July 1777, NYPL, S Papers: Misc. Military. AAS, H. B. Livingston Orderly Book, 64–68.

76. NYPL, S Lbk., 5: 289–92.

77. Higginbotham, *War of American Independence,* 191. Graymont, *Iroquois,* 151–54.

78. Brian Burns, "Bloody Burgoyne and the Patriot Martyr, or A Most Regrettable Fortune of War: British Indian Policy During the Northern Campaign of 1777," (M.A. thesis, University of Vermont, 1973), 98–104, 114. See also Elting, *Battles,* 40–41.

79. NYPL, S Lbk., 5: 289–92. Schuyler's papers reveal nothing more to suggest that the incident was particularly noteworthy. See also Jackman, *With Burgoyne,* 156–57.

80. *LMCC,* 2: 424–26.

81. AAS, H. B. Livingston Orderly Book, 69, 71–72. NYPL, S Lbk., 5: 295–98, 300–301.

82. NYPL, S Lbk., 5: 295–98, 300–01.

83. Nelson, *Gates,* 102. *LMCC,* 2: 429, and see 427–28 and *JCC,* 8: 585.

84. *LMCC,* 2: 428–29. *JCC,* 8: 596, 600–601, 603–4. N. Folsom to J. Bartlett, 12 Aug. 1777, Dartmouth College Library: Bartlett Collection.

85. J. Hancock to Schuyler, 5 Aug. 1777, cf. Schuyler to Hancock, 10 Aug. 1777, NYPL, S Lbk., 1: 364–65, where the resolutions were carefully copied, and 5: 333–34. Schuyler to J. Duane, 14, 15 Aug. 1777, NYPL, S Papers: Misc. Military.

86. NYPL, S Lbk., 5: 335–36. (Schuyler's earlier estimate of Burgoyne's forces was ten thousand, whereas he had six to seven thousand.) *PAH,* 1: 294–97.

87. Report of Militia at Fort Miller, *Smith Memoirs,* 2: 188. "Nicolas Herckheimer" to P. Gansevoort, 29 July 1777, NYPL: Gansevoort-Lansing Coll., P. Gansevoort Mili. Papers, vol. 3.

88. AAS, S Lbk., 4: 69–70; NYPL, S Lbk., 5: 302–6.

89. AAS, H. B. Livingston Orderly Book, 15–16; AAS, S Lbk., 4: 70–71.

90. Nickerson, *Turning Point,* 1: 189.

91. H. B. Livingston to R. Varick, 3, 4 Aug. 1777, cited by John G. Rommel, Jr., "Richard Varick: New Aristocrat," (Ph.D. diss., Columbia University, 1966), 26, hereafter cited Rommel, "Richard Varick."

92. NYPL, S Lbk., 5: 305–6, 309–10. Nickerson, *Turning Point,* 1: 186. Decker, *Arnold,* 234–237.

93. NYPL, S Lbk., 5: 307–10.

94. Ibid., 311–12.

95. Ibid., 312–14.

96. B. Lincoln to Gen. [Washington?], 4 Aug. 1777, Mass. Hist. Soc., B. Lincoln Papers.

97. Elting, *Battles,* 42. Nelson, *Gates,* 101. J. Sergeant to E. Wheelock, 6 Aug. 1777, Dartmouth College Library: Wheelock Coll. Sergeant's reference to the enemy attack probably was to the skirmishing of Glover's brigade, 2–5 August. But there is no evidence that Schuyler burned his own mills.

98. Morris, *Jay Papers,* 1: 434–35; NYPL, S Lbk., 5: 317–23; Columbia University: Butler Library, Jay Collection. Schenectady Comm. to Schuyler, 5 Aug. 1777, NYSL, MSS. Div.; NYPL, S Lbk., 5: 323–24.

99. NYPL, S Lbk., 5: 315–16.

100. Elting, *Battles,* 39. Graymont, *Iroquois,* 129–46. Nickerson, *Turning Point,* 1: 194–210. Ralph T. Pastore, "Congress and the Six Nations, 1775–1778," *Niagara Frontier* 20 (Winter 1973): 92. Jonathan G. Rossie, "The Northern Indian Department and the American Revolution," *Niagara Frontier* 20 (Autumn 1973): 60–61. Jack M. Sosin, *The Revolutionary Frontier, 1763–1783* (New York, 1967), 112. Peckham, *Toll of Independence,* 38, gives American losses at Oriskany: 72 killed and perhaps 75 wounded; but Nickerson, *Turning Point,* 1: 209, suggests 160 to 200 dead and 50 wounded. Elting, *Battles,* 38, notes the disagreement on losses: "possibly 250 to 300 Americans and 150 British and Indians." See also John Albert

Scott, "Joseph Brant at Fort Stanwix and Oriskany," *New York History* 19 (October 1938): 400–402; C. P. Yates to H. Gates (List of Prisoners Taken by the Enemy), 6 Aug. 1777, NYHS, Gates Papers.

101. NYPL, S Lbk., 5: 324; *PAH*, 1: 306–9.

102. Peckham, *Toll of Independence*, 38. Nickerson, *Turning Point*, 2: 231–40.

103. Pancake, *1777*, 228. Clark, "Responsibility for Failure," 556.

104. Schuyler to W. Duer, 8 Aug. 1777, NYPL, S Papers: Misc. Military.

105. NYPL, S Lbk., 5: 324–27.

106. Ibid., 328, 330, 331; AAS, S Lbk., 4: 34–35.

107. B. Lincoln to Schuyler, 8 Aug. 1777, Dartmouth College Library: Bartlett Collection. NYPL, S Lbk., 5: 329–31.

108. NYPL, S Lbk., 5: 332–33.

109. Ibid., 332.

110. Ibid., 333–34. The original in *PCC*, NAR 173 seems to be written in Schuyler's hand, not a secretary's.

111. AAS, S Lbk., 4: 32.

112. NYPL, S Lbk., 5: 334–35.

113. Hawke, *Benjamin Rush*, 188.

114. Ibid., 207. J. Hancock to Pennsylvania Assembly, 6 Aug. 1777, MNHP, LWS Coll. In May when Schuyler returned to his command from Philadelphia his journey to Albany took less than a week (28 May–3 June).

115. Nickerson, *Turning Point*, 1: 215–16.

116. Schuyler to Tryon Co. Comm., 10 Aug. 1777, NYPL, S Papers: Misc. Military; NYPL, S Lbk., 5: 335, 338–39. Schuyler asserted that his general officers had unanimously advised him to send Van Schaick's, Bailey's, and Jackson's regiments to relieve Fort Schuyler. Cf. Pancake, *1777*, 144, which says, "The officers, with one exception, adamantly opposed the relief" of the fort. Pancake repeats a time-worn allegation that other historians have made, citing Isaac N. Arnold's *The Life of Benedict Arnold* (Chicago, 1880), 153–54; see for example, Ward, *War of the Revolution*, 2: 489. Flexner, *Traitor and the Spy*, 164, does not fall into this error although Scheer and Rankin, *Rebels and Redcoats*, 307, and Elting, *Battles*, 45, do so.

117. AAS, S Lbk., 4: 77–79. Schuyler to General Herkimer and Tryon County committee, 12 Aug. 1777, MNHP, LWS Coll.; NYPL, S Lbk., 5: 335, 342–44. Lunt, *Burgoyne*, 185. When exactly the decision to send Arnold was made is not altogether clear. Nickerson, *Turning Point*, 1: 212, suggests 8 Aug., but it is apparent that Schuyler's council was held at Stillwater sometime before his orders to Arnold dated 13 Aug. but *after* Schuyler returned there from Albany (where on 8 Aug. he received news of Herkimer) on 10 Aug. Schuyler to G. Van Schaick (cited above) 12 Aug. 1777, indicates that Learned's brigade was set in motion on 12 Aug., and Arnold must have followed it on 13 Aug. Pancake, *1777*, 144, and Mitchell, *Discipline and Bayonets*, 81–83, indicate that Schuyler reached his decision to send Arnold on 12 Aug. Elting, *Battles*, 45, says 11 Aug. Nickerson, *Turning Point*, 2: 276 says that the decision to send relief to Fort Stanwix was "the last taken by Schuyler during the campaign." But this is hardly true unless one argues that it was the last *major* one of particular significance.

118. NYPL, S Lbk., 5: 335–36, 338–42; AAS, S Lbk., 4: 77–78, 82.

119. AAS, S Lbk., 4: 79; NYPL, S Lbk., 5: 335–36. Nickerson, *Turning Point*, 1: 213. Jackman, *With Burgoyne*, 159.

120. AAS, S Lbk., 4: 82–83. Court-Martial orders, 12 Aug. 1777, AAS, H. B. Livingston Orderly Book, 101–3. General Officers to Schuyler, 12 Aug. 1777, Mass. Hist. Soc. Schuyler to J. Duane, 14 Aug. 1777, NYPL, S Papers: Misc. Military.

121. NYPL, S Lbk., 5: 337.

122. AAS, H. B. Livingston Orderly Book, 104–5.

123. 14 Aug. orders, AAS, S Lbk., 4: 83–85.

124. NYPL, S Lbk., 5: 346–47, 351–52, 358–60.

125. Jackman, *With Burgoyne,* 166–67.

126. Schuyler to J. Duane, 14, 15 Aug. 1777, NYPL, S Papers: Misc. Military.

127. NYPL, S Lbk., 5: 352–54.

128. Clark, "Responsibility for Failure," 549–50.

129. Nickerson, *Turning Point,* 265, 443. Higginbotham, *War of American Independence,* 192. Elting, *Battles,* 43–44; NYPL, S Lbk., 5: 360–65.

130. AAS, H. B. Livingston Orderly Book, 107–9.

131. Patterson, *Gates,* 144, cf. Elting, *Battles,* 46. Judd, *Van Cortlandt Papers,* 2: 232–33.

132. NYPL, S Lbk., 5: 365–66.

133. Ibid., 367–68. (The Schuylers' fourteenth child was probably conceived in August 1777; Cortlandt Schuyler was born 14 May 1778.) Nelson, *Gates,* 106–7.

134. Nelson, *Gates,* 296–97. Schuyler to G. Morris, 7 Sept. 1777, Columbia University: Butler Library, Gouverneur Morris Collection.

135. Ibid. See also Rommel, "Richard Varick," 28. Theodore Thayer, *Nathanael Greene: Strategist of the American Revolution* (New York, 1960), 214. *PNG,* 2: 195. Schuyler to R. Varick, 3 May 1778, NYHS, Varick Papers.

136. Nickerson, *Turning Point,* 2: 276–77. Col. John R. Elting to author, 29 June 1977.

137. W. Whipple to J. Lovell, 25 Aug. 1777, Library of Congress, Whipple Papers. Elting, *Battles,* 46. Nelson, *Gates,* 81–83, 115. Pancake, *1777,* 183. Johnson, *Administration of American Commissariat,* 132.

138. Nickerson, *Turning Point,* 2: 286–87. Lunt, *Burgoyne,* 218. Elting, *Battles,* 50. Pancake, *1777,* 182.

139. Nickerson, *Turning Point,* 2: 284. Nelson, *Gates,* 111–12. Lunt, *Burgoyne,* 211, 215. Pancake, *1777,* 154.

140. Wilkinson, *Memoirs,* 1: 214–15, 222. The Latin fragment refers to insects (like bees) and animals that labor while others reap the benefits. I am indebted to Dr. R. E. Gaebel for identifying the line from Augustus Reifferscheid (ed.), *C. Suetoni Tranquilli Praeter Caesarum Libros Reliquiae* (Lipsiae: B. G. Teubner, 1860), 66–67. Nelson, *Gates,* 107, disagrees that Schuyler's exertions practically assured Gates's army of victory. Without denigrating Schuyler's important contributions to the ultimate victory in October, Nelson argues that Burgoyne's defeat "was not a foregone conclusion in late August." Nelson rightly avoids any assumption of inevitability and properly notes Gates's own contributions to the leadership of the army. But in a larger sense Schuyler's effective actions, combined with Burgoyne's own misfortunes and mistakes, were more crucially important in determining the outcome than anything else. See also Lunt, *Burgoyne,* 131, 166–70, 178, 185, 330. While Gates, Arnold, Morgan, and Stark must share the credit for the victories on the field of battle, Schuyler must not be excluded, for his previous efforts were also broadly responsible in the overall strategy, logistics, and tactics for the defeat of Burgoyne's invasion. See Elting, *Battles,* 69–70, for a succinct and apt assessment of Gates, including a commentary on his career after 1777.

CHAPTER 10

1. NYPL, S Lbk., 5: 347–49; *LMCC*, 2: 460–62. W. Livingston to Schuyler, 7 Sept. 1777, MNHP, LWS Coll.

2. NYPL, S Lbk., 5: 368, 371–73. Schuyler to J. Jay, 17 Aug. 1777, Columbia University Library, Jay Coll. Schuyler to G. Morris, 21 Sept. 1777, ibid., Morris Coll. H. Gates to Schuyler, 14 Sept. 1777, NYHS, Gates Papers. And see Higginbotham, *War of American Independence*, 202; Graymont, *Iroquois*, 149; Elting *Battles*, 56.

3. *WGW*, 9: 105–6. *LMCC*, 2: 508 n; NYPL, S Lbk., 5: 371–73.

4. An Address from Citizens of Albany, 7 Aug. *[sic]* 1777, NYPL, S Papers. The August date is obviously erroneous, cf. NYPL, S Lbk., 5: 369–70 (wherein he refers to the address presented to him "today," 7 Sept.).

5. *LMCC*, 2: 465–66. G. Morris to Schuyler, 27 Aug. 1777, Columbia Univ. Library: Morris Coll.

6. W. Livingston to Schuyler, 7 Sept. 1777, MNHP, LWS Coll. G. Clinton to J. Duane, 27 Aug. 1777, cited in Bernard Knollenberg, *Washington and the Revolution* (New York, 1940), 20.

7. G. Morris to Schuyler, 27 Aug. 1777; Schuyler to Morris, 7 Sept. 1777, Columbia Univ. Library, Morris Coll.

8. Garry Wills, *Inventing America: Jefferson's Declaration of Independence* (Garden City, N.Y.; 1978), 317.

9. R. Varick to Comm. of Congress, 10 Oct. 1777 (draft), NYHS, Varick Papers. J. Jay to Schuyler, 12 Sept. 1777, Columbia Univ. Library: Jay Coll. Morris, *Jay Papers*, 1: 444–45 misstates the word "Posterity" as "Prosperity." J. Duane to Schuyler, 5 Oct. 1777, NYPL, S Papers.

10. Schuyler to J. Jay, 17 Aug. [Sept.] 1777, Columbia Univ. Library: Jay Coll. Misdated in the original as "17 August," the letter shows (as does Jay's to Schuyler, shows (as does Jay's to Schuyler, 12 Sept.) that it should have been dated 17 Sept. Cf. Morris, *Jay Papers*, 1: 435–37, 444–45.

11. R. Varick to Schuyler, 12 Sept. 1777 (misdated as 12 Aug.), 13, 15, 16 Sept. 1777; H. B. Livingston to Schuyler, 15, 16 Sept. 1777, NYPL, S Papers. Schuyler to R. Varick, 13 Sept. 1777, NYSL, MSS. Div. Anbury's journal, Jackman, *With Burgoyne*, 170.

12. Schuyler to R. Varick, 13, 14 Sept. 1777, NYSL, MSS. Div.

13. R. Varick to Schuyler, 12, 15, 16 Sept. 1777 (the 12 Sept. letter is misdated "12 August"), NYPL, S Papers. Schuyler to R. Varick, 18 Sept. 1777, *Proceedings of the New Jersey Historical Society* 62 (April 1944): 100.

14. Ibid. M. Lewis to Schuyler, H. B. Livingston to Schuyler, R. Varick to Schuyler, 17 Sept. 1777, NYPL, S Papers. Lunt, *Burgoyne*, 220–27. Nickerson, *Turning Point*, 2: 473–77. Paul David Nelson, "Legacy of Controversy: Gates, Schuyler, and Arnold at Saratoga, 1777," *Military Affairs* 37 (April 1973): 43–44.

15. Paul David Nelson, "The Gates-Arnold Quarrel, September 1777," *The New-York Historical Society Quarterly* 55 (July 1971): 235–52, cf. Nelson, *Gates*, 122–32.

16. R. Varick to Schuyler, 19 Sept. 1777 (2 letters), NYPL, S Papers.

17. NYPL, S Lbk., 5: 371–73.

18. Schuyler to [R. Varick], 20 Sept. 1777 (dated 6 A.M.) MNHP, LWS Coll.

19. R. Varick to Schuyler 22, 22–23 Sept. 1777 (2 letters), NYPL, S Papers. Varick to Schuyler, 24 Sept. 1777 (typed copy), ibid., in box of land papers.

20. H. B. Livingston to Schuyler, 23 Sept. 1777 (2 letters), 24, 25, 26 Sept. 1777; R. Varick to Schuyler, 24 Sept. 1777 (2 letters), 25, 26, 27 Sept. 1777, NYPL, S Papers.

21. Schuyler to R. Varick, 25 Sept. 1777 cited in Nelson, "Arnold-Gates Quarrel," 246. J. Lovell to H. Gates, 5 Oct. 1777, NYHS, Gates Papers.

22. G. Morris to Schuyler, 18 Sept. 1777, Columbia Univ. Library: Morris Coll. *New York Senate Journal,* 1st Sess. (20 Oct. 1777), NYSL. Reelected were Philip Livingston, James Duane, William Duer, and Gouverneur Morris. Schuyler was replaced by Francis Lewis. Hough, *Civil List* (1855), 61.

23. Schuyler to Gen. Scott (copy), 2 Oct. 1777, NYPL, S (land) Papers.

24. Schuyler to G. Morris, 21 Sept. 1777, Columbia Univ. Library: Morris Coll.

25. G. Morris to R. R. Livingston, 8 Oct. 1777, NYHS, R. R. Livingston Coll.; Lunt, *Burgoyne,* 236–37. Nickerson, *Turning Point,* 2: 405. Mason, *Road to Independence,* 176–77.

26. Lunt, *Burgoyne,* 251–52; Nelson, *Gates,* 43–45, cf. Rossie, *Politics of Command,* 60 et passim. While crediting Gates for the Saratoga victory, Nelson uses arguments that may be equally applicable to credit Schuyler, i.e., chance, avoiding unnecessary pitched battles, timing, the terrain that favored a defensive stance, etc.

27. Nickerson, *Turning Point,* 2: 375–77. Lunt, *Burgoyne,* 253–57. Jackman, *With Burgoyne,* 189–90. Schuyler to G. Morris, 12 Oct. 1777, Columbia Univ. Library: Morris Coll.

28. *Smith Memoirs,* 2: 228.

29. Alexander J. Wall, "The Story of the Convention Army, 1777–1783," *Collections N-Y Hist. Soc.* 85 (1975): 184. Permitted to march out of camp with the honors of war, the British were also promised free passage home to England under condition that they not fight again in the war, and their baggage was exempted from search. See also Lunt, *Burgoyne,* 261–67; Nickerson, *Turning Point,* 2: 394–98; Nelson, "Legacy of Controversy," 45.

30. R. Varick to Schuyler, 13 Oct. 1777, NYPL, S Papers. Schuyler to Varick, 15 Oct. 1777, Fort Ticonderoga Museum.

31. Scheer and Rankin, *Rebels and Redcoats,* 326. [John P. Becker], *The Sexagenary, or Reminiscences of the American Revolution* (Albany, 1833), 113–14.

32. William L. Stone, *Visits to the Saratoga Battle-Grounds, 1780–1880* (1895; reprint, Port Washington, N.Y., 1970), 82, 104.

33. William Digby, "Some Account of the American War between Great Britain and her Colonies," British Museum: Additional MSS 32413/95-96. Lieutenant-General Burgoyne, *A State of the Expedition from Canada . . .* (London, 1780), Appendix 16 gives a different total of 18,624 for the U.S. army. Nelson, *Gates,* 142, cites 11,939 Americans, not including troops at other posts like Fort Edward, and 5,791 British and German forces. Lunt, *Burgoyne,* 270, cites 3,499 British and Germans and 13,216 Americans. An undated "Return of Gen. Burgoyne's Army after the surrender" (NYSL, MSS. Div.) lists 9,513, including 900 killed between 17 Sept. and 18 Oct., some deserters and men in Canada.

34. Stone, *Visits to Saratoga,* 82. Philip Church, "Answers to Mr. [Benson] Lossing's questions respecting General Philip Schuyler," 6 June 1859, NYPL, MSS. Div. See also Madame De Riedesel, *Letters and Memoirs Relating to the War of American Independence and the Capture of the German Troops at Saratoga* (New York, 1827), 187–89, hereafter cited as Baroness Riedesel, *Memoirs.*

35. Baroness Riedesel, *Memoirs,* 189–93. Ebenezer Mattoon's recollection is in Stone, *Visits to Saratoga,* 253. Lunt, *Burgoyne,* 269–70.

36. John Henry Brandow, *The Story of Old Saratoga,* 2d ed. (Albany, 1919), 309–11. "Journal of an Officer [Lord Adam Gordon] Who Travelled in America and the West Indies in 1764 and 1765," in Newton P. Mereness, ed., *Travels in the American Colonies* (New York, 1961), 446. Schuyler's Saratoga became the village of Schuylerville. Anne Grant, *Memoirs of an American Lady,* 2 vols. (New York, 1901), 2: 114–16, cf. Schuyler's Saratoga Daybook, 1764–70, NYHS.

37. H. B. Livingston to Schuyler, 23 Sept. 1777; R. Varick to Schuyler, 24 Sept. 1777, NYPL, S Papers. William L. Stone, trans., *Memoirs and Letters and Journals, of Major General Riedesel during his Residence in America*, 3 vols. (Albany, 1868), 1: 171. R. Varick to Schuyler, 12 Oct. 1777; Schuyler to [James Duane, 23 Nov.?] 1777 (fragment), NYPL, S Papers.

38. Baroness Riedesel, *Memoirs*, 191. See also *The Parliamentary Register; or, History of the Proceedings and Debates of the House of Commons: Series One*, 17 vols. (London, 1802), 8: 308, 311. Baroness Riedesel's account of Burgoyne's apology to Schuyler and the latter's reply agrees with the Britisher's story. Digby Diary, British Museum: Add. MSS. 32413/84.

39. Schuyler to R. Varick, 12 Oct. 1777, MNHP, LWS Coll. Schuyler to G. Morris, 12 Oct. 1777, Columbia Univ. Library: Morris Coll. and NYSL, MSS. Div.

40. Schuyler to G. Morris, 12 Oct. 1777, Columbia Univ. Library: Morris Coll. and NYSL, MSS. Div. G. Morris to Schuyler, 8 Oct. 1777, NYPL, S Papers.

41. R. Varick to Schuyler, 18 Oct. 1777, NYPL, S Papers.

42. Philip Church, "Answers to Mr. Lossing's questions . . . ," NYSL, MSS. Div.

43. M. Lewis to Schuyler, 20 Oct. 1777, NYPL, S Papers. Schuyler to Varick, 20 Oct. 1777, MNHP, LWS Coll. R. Varick to Schuyler, John Lansing to Schuyler, 21 Oct. 1777, NYPL, S Papers. For a fuller account of this period, see Don R. Gerlach, "After Saratoga: The General, His Lady, and 'Gentleman Johnny' Burgoyne," *New York History* 52 (Jan. 1971): 17–24.

44. J. Lansing to Schuyler, 25, 27 Oct. 1777; R. Varick to Schuyler, 29 Oct. 1777, NYPL, S Papers.

45. Schuyler to J. Lansing, 23 Oct. 1777, NYSL, MSS. Div. J. Lansing to Schuyler, 25 Oct. 1777, NYPL, S Papers. Schuyler to R. Varick, 25 Oct. 1777, MNHP, LWS Coll. R. Varick to H. Gates, 28 Oct. 1777, NYHS, Gates Papers, and copy in NYPL, S Papers. R. Varick to Schuyler, 30 Oct., 1 Nov. 1777, NYPL, S Papers.

46. NYPL, S Lbk., 5: 373–80, cf. 1: 367–68.

47. Johnston, *Jay Papers*, 1: 167–72.

48. J. Jay to Schuyler, 11 Dec. 1777, Columbia Univ. Library: Jay Coll., cf. Morris, *Jay Papers*, 1: 452–54. Jay finally declined Schuyler's offer of a farm in Feb. 1778, explaining that his duties with the state legislature and obligations to care for his father must deprive him of being Schuyler's neighbor at Saratoga. Johnston, *Jay Papers*, 1: 175–76.

49. R. Varick to Schuyler, 5 Nov. 1777, NYPL, S Papers. There seems to be some uncertainty about where the Schuylers' new house was built in relation to its predecessor, which Lt. W. C. Wilkinson's map of Burgoyne's Saratoga encampment suggests was a more pretentious establishment, replete with wings or closely attached buildings at two ends. Archaeological investigation suggests that the 1777 structure was raised on the very site of the earlier one. Commonsensical speculation supports this notion. On the other hand, in the reminiscences of Schuyler's youngest daughter (which is admittedly none too reliable in all points), reference is made to the house standing "almost on the site of the former mansion." Baxter, *Godchild*, 191. Brandow's *Story of Old Saratoga*, 311, says the older house stood about twelve rods southeast of the present one. And the account of Dr. Benjamin Waterhouse of Boston who visited the place in 1794 suggests that the new house was not built on the exact site of the old one; he went to "look at the spot where stood General Schuyler's large house and fine range of mills that were burnt by Burgoyne." Barbara Simison, ed., "Dr. Benjamin Waterhouse's Journey to Saratoga Springs in the Summer of 1794," *Yale University Library Gazette* 40 (July 1965): 30. A fragment dated only 1777 (in Schuyler's hand), NYPL, S Papers, Box 41, but probably part of Schuyler's letter to J. Duane, 23 Nov. 1777, NYPL, S Papers, indicates that Schuyler built the new house on the old site. Explaining the speed of his construction, he said that the timber was already available in his upper mill dam and that

he had a "cellar ready to my hand." The dimensions of the rooms that he described in this fragment vary somewhat from his description to John Jay on Nov. 6: three of 20' by 22' "in the clear," one of 16' by 20' and one of 18' by 10' etc., and a cellar kitchen of 20' by 18'. See also Brandow, *Story of Old Saratoga,* 324; and M. Lewis to Schuyler, 6 Nov. 1777; J. Lansing to Schuyler, 8 Nov. 1777; H. Gates to Schuyler, 9 Nov. 1777, in NYPL, S Papers. For work done on the house Schuyler paid £73 to Nicholas Veeder and his carpenters, Col. Yates's Receipt, Dec. 1777, NYPL, S Papers: Personal and Household Accounts.

50. J. Lansing to Schuyler, 7, 12, 16, 22 Nov. 1777; R. Varick to Schuyler, 8, 9, 12, 13, 16, 26 Nov., 1 Dec. 1777, NYPL, S Papers. Aurey La Grange's receipt from Schuyler, 13 Nov. 1777 (endorsed and received at Saratoga, 15 Nov.), NYPL, S Papers: Box 49: vouchers, receipts. Patrick McGraw and Mary Eggemont are named in J. Lansing's Account, 26 Jan. 1778, NYPL, S Papers: Personal & Household Accounts.

51. Schuyler to Mrs. Catharine Schuyler, 15 Dec. 1777, NYPL, S Papers: Misc. Military Papers. See also Col. Yates's Receipt, Dec. 1777, NYPL, S Papers: Personal & Household Accounts; John Bromley's Receipt, 19 Dec. 1777 and Schuyler to Mrs. Schuyler, 18 Dec. 1777, Rockefeller Archive Center: Schuyler Coll.

52. Although Gates referred the question to the Tryon County Committee of Safety, Butler was not released from prison until February 1778, when he was confined in an Albany house. Howard Swiggett, *War Out of Niagara: Walter Butler and the Tory Rangers* (Port Washington, N.Y.; 1963), 105–7. Butler then penned his thanks for Schuyler's "generous assistance," professing that "the obligation is the more binding on me, as it flow'd from a Principle of Humanity." W. Butler to Schuyler, 27 Feb. 1778, HL.

53. NYPL, S Lbk., 5: 380–81.

54. R. Varick to Schuyler, 5 Nov. 1777, NYPL, S Papers; *PAH,* 1: 347–49.

55. Schuyler to J. Duane, 28 Nov. 1777, MNHP, LWS Coll. See also fragment of a letter Schuyler to Duane, 23 Nov. 1777, NYPL, S Papers; Mason, "Entrepreneurial Activity," 193; NYPL, S Lbk., 5: 373–80.

56. Schuyler to W. Duer, 18 Nov. 1777, NYPL, S Papers.

57. NYPL, S Lbk., 5: 380. Ibid., 1: 368–70. J. Duane to Schuyler, 19–22 Nov. 1777, NYPL, S Papers.

58. J. Lovell to H. Gates, 17 Nov. 1777, NYHS, Gates Papers.

59. Flexner, *Washington,* 2: 271–77, 375. Nelson, *Gates,* 154–63.

60. W. Livingston to Schuyler, 3 Dec. 1777, NYPL, S Papers. Saffron, *Surgeon to Washington,* 43. The Cochrans' Morristown house was the site of Hamilton's courtship of Elizabeth Schuyler. The Cochrans had three sons: John, James, and Walter. James married his cousin, Catherine Van Rensselaer Schuyler, the general's youngest daughter, after her first husband, Samuel Bayard Malcolm, died. Saffron, *Surgeon to Washington,* 12, 15–16, 43, 221, 296, 299. *PAH,* 26: 96 fn. Alice Curtis Desmond, *Alexander Hamilton's Wife: A Romance of the Hudson* (New York, 1952), 85, 267. Hereafter cited Desmond, *Hamilton's Wife.*

61. *LMCC,* 2: 590–91; NYPL, S Lbk., 5: 382–84. Resolves of Congress, 4 Dec. 1777, ibid., 1: 373–74.

62. NYPL, S Lbk., 5: 383–84. Schuyler to R. R. Livingston, 22 Dec. 1777, NYHS, R. R. Livingston Coll.

63. W. Smith to Schuyler, 6 Dec. 1777, NYPL, S Papers.

64. W. Smith to Schuyler, 30 Oct. 1777, ibid. And see *Smith Memoirs,* 2: 248–49.

65. W. Smith to Schuyler, 12 Jan. 1778, NYPL, S Papers, cf. *Smith Memoirs,* 2: 278–79, 285.

66. Smith, *Memoirs,* 2: 281.

67. Capt. S. Sprague's Receipt, 31 Dec. 1777; G. Ludlow to Schuyler, 6 Jan. 1778, NYPL,

S Papers. Col. Yates's Receipt, Dec. 1777, ibid., Personal and Household Accounts. W. Smith to Schuyler, 6 Dec. 1777, NYPL, S Papers. Stanton Tefft's Account, 25 Dec. 1777, ibid., Misc. Military Accounts. And see Gerlach, *Philip Schuyler*, 57.

CHAPTER 11

1. Gruber, *Howe Brothers*, 290−91.

2. Schuyler to J. Duane, 6 Jan. 1778, MNHP, LWS Coll. Minute of N. Dept. Indian Commissioners, 9−10 Jan. 1778, NYPL, S (Indian) Papers. Vivian, "Congressional Indian Policy," 261. *JCC*, 9: 994−99, 1002−3.

3. NYPL, S Lbk., 5: 384−88.

4. Ibid., 388−89.

5. Ibid., 389−91. For other payments for secret services see J. Lansing, Jr.'s, Account with Schuyler, 26 Jan. 1778, NYPL, S Papers: Personal and Household Accts. H. Laurens to Schuyler, 20 Dec. 1777, *LMCC*, 2: 592, and 5 Jan. 1778, NYPL, S Lbk., 1: 369−70.

6. J. Dean to Indian Commissioners, 5 Feb. 1778; Schuyler to Pres. of Congress, 8 Feb. 1778, *PCC*, NAR 173. See also Graymont, *Iroquois*, 161; Swiggett, *War Out of Niagara*, 113.

7. NYPL, S Lbk., 5: 393−94. NYSJ (14 Feb. 1778). Schuyler to Pres. of Congress, 8 Feb. 1778 (with extract of minutes of Indian commissioners and copy of J. Dean to Schuyler, 5 Feb. 1778), *PCC*, NAR 173.

8. R. Yates to Schuyler, 11 Feb. 1778, NYPL, S Papers. Schuyler to J. Duane, 14 Feb. 1778, NYHS, Duane Papers. NYPL, S Lbk., 1: 374−75.

9. Schuyler to J. Duane, 14 Feb. 1778, NYHS, Duane Papers.

10. NYPL, S Lbk., 5: 394−95.

11. Ibid., 4: 37.

12. *Smith Memoirs*, 2: 287, 406. Bush, *Revolutionary Enigma*, 135−36, argues that between the fall of 1777 and early 1778 Schuyler "had given up completely on America's chances of defeating British arms," and that like other Americans he maintained a "safe course, that of judicious silence" in order to assure acquittal in his court-martial. This interpretation is unacceptable, for it runs counter to much evidence to the contrary. Bush's study does not adequately explore Schuyler's many contributions to the war effort before 1778, nor does it fully account for those he made after 1777.

13. *Smith Memoirs*, 2: 290. The Smiths had moved to Livingston Manor in Oct. 1776 to live with Mrs. Smith's sister and brother-in-law, Peter R. Livingston. Ibid., vii−viii.

14. Ibid., 287−288.

15. *LMCC*, 3: 62. Mintz, *G. Morris*, 94−95; *PAH*, 1: 425−28. Morris, *Jay Papers*, 1: 466.

16. Schuyler to J. Jay, 25 Feb. 1778, Columbia Univ. Library, Jay Coll.

17. [R. R. Livingston] to Schuyler, 27 Feb. 1778 (fragment), NYPL, S Papers.

18. Schuyler to R. R. Livingston, 5 Mar. 1778, NYHS, R. R. Livingston Coll., cf. Bush, *Revolutionary Enigma*, 137

19. NYSJ, 25 Mar. 1778. Schuyler's certificate of appointment from Gov. Clinton was not dated until 13 Aug. G. Clinton to Schuyler, 13 Aug. 1778, NYSL, MSS. Div. NYPL, S Lbk., 5: 433−36. Schuyler to R. Varick, 8 July 1778, MNHP, LWS Coll. Bush, *Revolutionary Enigma*, 137, alleges that "Schuyler probably did not want to attend Congress or even serve the public any longer;" but Bush ignores the evidence cited above. Apparently Schuyler did want to serve, but whether or not he wanted to return to Congress, he did continue to work as an Indian commissioner.

20. Nelson, *Gates,* 154–76. Flexner, *Washington,* 2: 271–77, 375. Mitchell, *Price of Independence,* 77–79. Palmer, *Way of the Fox,* 69–71.

21. Schuyler to R. R. Livingston, 5 Mar. 1778, NYHS, R. R. Livingston Coll. Schuyler to T. Conway, 17 Feb. 1778, NYPL, S Lbk., 5: 395–98; a copy of this letter attributed as one to H. Laurens and misdated 17 July 1778 is in the H. Laurens Papers, S.C. Historical Society.

22. *Smith Memoirs,* 2: 300–1. Schuyler to R. R. Livingston, 5 Mar. 1778, NYHS, R. R. Livingston Coll.

23. Schuyler to R. R. Livingston, 5 Mar. 1778, NYHS, R. R. Livingston Coll.

24. NYPL, S Lbk., 5: 373–80. Resolves of Congress, 4 Dec. 1777, ibid., 1: 373–74. H. Gates to J. Stark, to J. Greaton, 24 Jan. 1778, NYHS, Gates Papers. See also Lanctot, *Canada,* 168–69; Nelson, *Gates,* 175; Kenney, *Albany: Crossroads of Liberty,* 68; NYSJ, 9–10 Feb. 1778.

25. Schuyler to J. Jay, 1 Feb. [1778, misdated 1777]; Jay to Schuyler, 6 Feb. 1778, Morris, *Jay Papers,* 1: 463–66, cf. originals. Schuyler to G. Morris, 3 Feb. 1778, Columbia Univ. Library: Morris Coll.

26. Young, *Democratic Republicans,* 22–24, 44–45.

27. Saffron, *Surgeon to Washington,* 50, 52. Schuyler to G. Morris, 18 Feb. 1778, Columbia Univ. Library: Morris Coll. Burnett, *Congress,* 261–67.

28. Minutes: Indian Commissioners, N. Dept. with Six Nations, 7–10 Mar. 1778, NYPL, S Papers.

29. NYPL, S Lbk., 5: 399–404. Graymont, *Iroquois,* 163–64.

30. Schuyler to Tryon Co. Comm. Chrm., 11 Mar. 1778, NYSL, MSS. Div.

31. NYPL, S Lbk., 5: 399–404. Schuyler to J. Duane, 15 Mar. 1778, Baxter, *Godchild,* 189–90, cf. Colyer Meriwether, ed., "The Duane Letters," *Publications of the Southern Historical Association* 8: (Washington, D.C.: 1904): 378.

32. Vivian, "Congressional Indian Policy," 264–65. Nelson, *Gates,*188–200.

33. NYPL, S Lbk., 5: 405–6. Resolves of Congress, 4 Mar. 1778, ibid., 1: 375. T. Edwards to Schuyler, 25 Mar. 1778, NYPL, S Papers. Schuyler to J. Duane, 21 Mar. 1778, NYHS, Duane Papers. *WGW,* 11: 76–77. Schuyler to T. Edwards, 1 April 1778, Yale Univ. Library. Minutes of Indian Commissioners, N. Dept., 15 April 1778, NYPL, S Papers; NYPL, S Lbk., 5: 405–6.

34. R. Varick to Schuyler, 10 Mar. 1778; J. Lansing, Jr., to Schuyler, 27 Mar. 1778, NYPL, S Papers. Schuyler paid $13 to move his family and baggage from Albany to Stillwater; John Jackson's receipt, 27 Mar. 1778, ibid., Personal and Household Accts. Thomas L. Wilbeck's receipt, 3 April 1778 (for $2,000 to purchase cattle), ibid., Misc. Military Accts.

35. Schuyler to T. Edwards, 1 April 1778, Yale Univ. Library. Schuyler to J. Duane, 1 April 1778, NYHS, Duane Papers. NYPL, S Lbk., 5: 405–8.

36. Graymont, *Iroquois,* 165. Minutes of Indian Commissioners, 15 April 1778, NYPL, S Papers. Schuyler to H. Laurens, 16 April 1778 (with extract of minutes), PCC, NAR 173.

37. NYPL, S Lbk., 5: 410–11.

38. *Smith Memoirs,* 2: 353–54. Most notable of Smith's list of caucus members was Jeremiah Van Rensselaer, Schuyler's brother-in-law, who later became a Clintonian. He was the only member of the family who turned Anti-Federalist. Young, *Democratic Republicans,* 45 and 26–58, does not note this early hint of party division. Those on Smith's list who became Federalists included Schuyler, James Duane, Walter Livingston, Abraham Ten Broeck, Leonard Gansevoort, John Taylor, and James Van Rensselaer.

39. J. Lansing to Schuyler, 19 April 1778, NYPL, S Papers. Schuyler to A. Ten Broeck, 25 April 1778, Fort Ticonderoga Museum. Schuyler to J. Duane, 26 April 1778, NYHS, Duane Papers. NYPL, S Lbk., 5: 411–14.

40. J. Lansing to Schuyler, 19 April 1778; Schuyler to J. Duane, 26 April 1778, no. 39

above. Graymont, *Iroquois*, 164–65. Schuyler to R. Varick, 3 May 1778; Baxter, *Godchild*, 212, indicates his intention to return to Albany on 6 May.

41. Burnett, *Congress*, 324–25, 328–29. Gruber, *Howe Brothers*, 279.

42. Schuyler to H. Laurens, 9 May 1778, S.C. Hist. Soc., H. Laurens Papers. NYPL, S Lbk., 5: 414–15.

43. Schuyler to G. Morris, 17 May 1778, Columbia Univ. Library: Morris Coll. *Smith Memoirs*, 2: 368, 373, 402.

44. NYPL, S Lbk., 5: 416–17. Schuyler to G. Morris, 17 May 1778, Columbia Univ. Library, Morris Coll., announced the birth of his son Cortlandt on 15 May, but the entry in the family Bible cites 14 May. Schuyler's address to the Oneida, 11 May 1778 (copy in Schuyler to H. Laurens, 17 May 1778), *PCC*, NAR 173. NYPL, S Lbk., 5: 418–19. M. Willett to Sachems & Warriors of Oneida & Tuscarora Nations (copy), 12 May 1778, NYPL, S (Indian) Papers.

45. M. Willett to Schuyler, 29 April 1778 in Jack M. Sosin, "The Use of Indians in the War of the American Revolution: A Re-Assessment of Responsibility," *The Canadian Historical Review* 46 (June, 1965): 121. NYPL, S Lbk., 5: 418–19. Schuyler to G. Morris, 17 May 1778, Columbia Univ. Library: Morris Coll.

46. Schuyler to H. Laurens, 11 May 1778, S.C. Hist. Soc., H. Laurens Papers. NYPL, S Lbk., 5: 419–20. T. Edwards to Schuyler, 18 May 1778; Inventory of Goods Bought by T. Edwards, 16 Sept. 1778, NYPL, S Papers; NYPL, S Lbk., 1: 377–78.

47. *WGW*, 11: 389–92; NYPL, S Lbk., 5: 420–24.

48. NYPL, S Lbk., 5: 424–27. Stark, *Memoir*, 145, 151–53. S. Kirkland to Schuyler, 23 May 1778, *PCC*, NAR 173

49. Graymont, *Iroquois*, 167.

50. NYPL, S Lbk., 5: 427–30. T. Bedel to Schuyler, 25 May 1778, NYPL, S Papers. *Smith Memoirs*, 2: 402.

51. Peckham, *Toll of Independence*, 52. T. Bedel to Schuyler, 25 May 1778, NYPL, S Papers; NYPL, S Lbk., 5: 432–33.

52. *Smith Memoirs*, 2: 407, mentions the return of Schuyler's two youngest daughters. As the youngest was in fact only two and a half, Smith must have meant the second and third daughters, Elizabeth and Margaret. NYPL, S Lbk., 1: 380–83; 5: 433–35.

53. Bush, *Revolutionary Enigma*, 137. Bush's interpretation of Schuyler's attitude and in-activity (134–37) depends heavily upon the testimony of William Smith. Bush accuses Schuyler of refusing to attend Congress, but in fact the general fluctuated in his determination or willingness to do so. Bush claims that he probably did not wish to serve the public any longer, but Schuyler repeatedly offered to do so in a private capacity while intending to resign his military commission. And he was as good as his word. Bush's study simply does not explore in detail what the general said and did after 1777. See also *Smith Memoirs*, 2: 407.

54. NYPL, S Lbk., 1: 382–83; 5: 433–36. Schuyler to J. Duane, 27 June 1778, NYHS, Duane Papers.

55. Schuyler to R. Varick, 8 July 1778, MNHP, LWS Coll. *WGW*, 12: 200–201. Schuyler to H. Laurens, 19 July 1778, *PCC*, NAR 173. Graymont, *Iroquois*, 174–77.

56. Nelson, *Gates*, 197–202.

57. W. Livingston to Schuyler, 4 July 1778, NYPL, S Papers.

58. *JCC*, 8: 684–86; 10: 66; *WGW*, 10: 518–19. For a fuller account of Schuyler's trial see Don R. Gerlach, "Trial at Quaker Hill," *The Bulletin of the Fort Ticonderoga Museum* 14 (Fall 1983): 250–59.

59. *LMCC*, 3: 159–60. Morris, *Jay Papers*, 1: 468–69.

60. NYPL, S Lbk., 5: 409. Morris, *Jay Papers*, 1: 471–73, cf. *LMCC*, 3: 199; *JCC*, 8: 688, 10: 403.

61. Morris, *Jay Papers*, 1: 482–84.

62. *JCC*, 8: 375, cf. 7: 364; 10: 601–2.

63. W. Livingston to Schuyler, 18 July 1778, NYPL, S Papers; *WGW*, 12: 200–201.

64. Harmanus Schuyler's Receipt, 6 Aug. 1778, NYPL, S Papers: Personal and Household Accts. Dated at Albany, the paper (in Schuyler's hand) suggests that he was still at Albany. Morris, *Jay Papers*, 1: 489–90, indicates his presence at White Plains. See also Ward, *War of the Revolution*, 2: 594.

65. Smith, *St. Clair Papers*, 1: 447–57.

66. The Wilkinson-Church imbroglio with Gates and Kosciuszko is treated in some detail, although without precise dating, in Haiman, *Kosciuszko*, 56–68; Patterson, *Gates*, 280–81, 284; Nelson, *Gates*, 195–96; and Thomas Robson Hay and M. R. Werner, *The Admirable Trumpeter: A Biography of General James Wilkinson* (Garden City, New York, 1941), 44–45.

67. W. Livingston to Schuyler, 4 July, 30 Sept. 1778, NYPL, S Papers; Schuyler to J. Duane, 6 Sept. 1778, NYHS, Duane Papers. Morris, *Jay Papers*, 1: 491–96.

68. Smith, *St. Clair Papers*, 1: 457. See also "The Trial of Major General St. Clair, August, 1778," *Colls. N-Y Hist. Soc.* (New York, 1881), 1–72. Schuyler's comment about the delay in St. Clair's trial is in Schuyler to H. Laurens, 6 Oct. 1778, *PCC*, NAR 173. *Proceedings of a General Court Martial . . . Oct. 1 [–3], 1778 . . .* (Philadelphia, 1778) in *Colls. N-Y Hist. Soc.* (New York, 1880), 7–24.

69. Schuyler to J. Duane, 4 Oct. 1778, NYHS, Duane Papers.

70. Schuyler to H. Laurens, 6 Oct. 1778, *PCC*, NAR 173.

71. Schuyler to W. Duer, 4 Oct. 1778, NYPL, S Papers: Misc. Military.

72. Thomas Menzie's Receipt, 26 Oct. 1778, ibid., Box 49, indicates payment for Schuyler's horses at Fredericksburgh 15 Sept.–27 Oct. 1778. *WGW*, 13: 297–305 refers to Schuyler's earlier advice on routes of invasion; ibid., 264–66, 429–33; Nelson, *Gates*, 201; Everest, *Moses Hazen*, 62–63.

73. NYSJ, 13, 16 Oct. 1778. Two senators from the Western District (Abraham Yates, Jr., and Rinier Mynderse) voted for Klock, but one (Dirck Ten Broeck) voted against him, which is an indication of Schuyler's candidacy as part of the anti-Yates cabal at Albany.

74. Ibid., 15, 16 Oct. 1778. W. Livingston to Schuyler, 4 July 1778, NYPL, S Papers. L. Gansevoort to J. Ten Broeck, 15 Oct. 1778, NYSL, MSS. Div.

75. W. Livingston to Schuyler, 16 Oct. 1778, NYPL, S Papers. NYSJ, 4 Nov. 1778.

76. Schuyler to W. Duer, 18 Oct. 1778, NYPL, S Papers.

77. Schuyler to J. Duane, 19 Dec. 1778, ibid. See the family Bible at the Schuyler mansion, Albany, N.Y., and Montgomery Schuyler, "The Schuyler Family," Publication No. 16 of the Order of Colonial Lords of Manors in America (New York, 1926), 35. See also, Gerlach, *Philip Schuyler*, 38. Thomas Menzie's Receipt, 26 Oct. 1778, NYPL, S Papers Box 49; Jonas Kiley's Receipts, 25, 29 Oct. 1778, NYPL, S Papers: Personal and Household Accts., show costs of stabling Schuyler's horses at Fredericksburgh, 15 Sept.–27 Oct. 1778 and Poughkeepsie for five nights. Schuyler to H. Laurens, 30 Oct. 1778, *PCC*, NAR 173, written from Albany mentions that Schuyler was en route to Albany on 29 Oct.

78. Schuyler to H. Laurens, 30 Oct. 1778, *PCC*, NAR 173.

79. Schuyler to Brig. Gen. Edward Hand, 15 Nov. 1778, Pierpont Morgan Library.

80. Schuyler to H. Laurens, 23 Nov. 1778, *PCC*, NAR 173. Ida H. Washington and Paul A. Washington, *Carleton's Raid* (Canaan, N.H.; 1977).

81. *WGW*, 13: 264–66, 297–305. Cf. Rice, *Chastellux Travels*, 1: 204–5.

82. *WGW*, 13: 429–33. For discussion of Niagara see also Schuyler to J. Duane, 19 Dec. 1778, NYPL, S Papers.

83. *WGW*, 13: 469–70.

84. Schuyler to H. Laurens, 27 Dec. 1778, *PCC*, NAR 173. See also *JCC*, 12: 1186 and *LMCC*, 3: 515, 517. Schuyler to J. Duane, 19 Dec. 1778, NYPL, S Papers.

85. Morris, *Jay Papers*, 1: 534–36; *LMCC*, 3: 421, 477.

86. J. Jay to Schuyler, 8 Dec. 1778, NYSL, MSS. Div.

87. *LMCC*, 3: 529–30. J. Duane to Schuyler, 3 Jan. 1779 NYPL, S Papers.

CHAPTER 12

1. Champagne, *Alexander McDougall*, 143–48. B. Arnold to Schuyler, 8 Feb. 1779, NYPL, S Papers.

2. J. Duane to Schuyler, 3 Jan. 1779, *LMCC*, 4: 3–4, cf. original for full text, NYPL, S Papers.

3. *LMCC*, 4: 10. Schuyler to Pres. N.Y. Senate, to Speaker N.Y. House of Reprs., 12 Jan. 1779, NYPL, S Papers. NYSJ, 29 Jan. 1779.

4. Morris, *Jay Papers*, 1: 534–536.

5. J. Cochran to Schuyler, 19 Jan. 1779, NYPL, S Papers.

6. *WGW*, 14: 18–19, 44–46.

7. Ibid., 94–98, 121–23, 149–51. Schuyler to Washington, 1–7 Mar. 1779, Library of Congress: Washington Papers. J. Duane to Schuyler, 20 Feb. 1779, *LMCC*, 4: 79, but full text is in NYPL, S Papers.

8. S. Deane to Schuyler, 2 Feb. 1779, *Colls. N-Y Hist. Soc.*, 21: 342–45. Mintz, *G. Morris*, 118–24. Burnett, *Congress*, 360–69. *LMCC*, 3: 529–30, cf. Burnett, *Congress*, 364–65. J. Cochran to Schuyler, 28 Feb. 1779; A. McDougall to Schuyler, 2 Mar. 1779, NYPL, S Papers. Schuyler to J. Duane, 7 Mar. 1779, NYHS, Duane Papers. Schuyler to J. Jay, 5–8 Mar. 1779, NYSL, MSS. Div.

9. Schuyler to J. Jay, 5–8 Mar. 1779, NYSL, MSS. Div. cf. Morris, *Jay Papers*, 1: 573–74. Schuyler to J. Jay, 7 June 1779; Elizabeth Bradstreet to Schuyler, 5 Jan., 3 Feb. 1779, *PCC*, NAR 173. Elizabeth Bradstreet to Schuyler, 2 Dec. 1779; Charles Gould to Schuyler, 28 April 1783, NYPL, S Papers.

10. J. Duane to Schuyler, 20 Mar. 1779, *LMCC*, 4: 108–9, cf. original in NYPL, S Papers for what Burnett omitted. See also *JCC*, 13: 27–28, 332–33.

11. *JCC*, 13: 332–33. Morris, *Jay Papers*, 1: 579–80.

12. Schuyler to J. Jay, 2 April 1779, *PCC*, NAR 173.

13. *JCC*, 13: 473. *LMCC*, 4: 188; *WGW*, 14: 407–9. J. Duane to Schuyler, 1 May 1779, *LMCC*, 4: 188, cf. original, complete text, NYPL, S Papers.

14. Morris, *Jay Papers*, 1: 589. Schuyler to J. Duane, 5 June 1779, W. L. Clements Library: Misc. MSS.

15. *WGW*, 13: 297–305, 429–33, 469–70. Evidence of Schuyler's collection of intelligence from Canada and of his efforts to organize Indian support for an invasion from Lake Champlain is in Schuyler to J. Jay, 26 Jan. 1779, *PCC*, NAR 173 and T. Bedel to Schuyler, 3 Feb. 1779, NYPL, S Papers.

16. J. Lansing to Schuyler, 14 Jan. 1779, NYPL, S Papers. Schuyler to J. Cuyler, 5 Jan. 1779, Conn. Hist. Soc. Wadsworth Papers. Extract: Minutes of Indian Commissioners, 4 Jan. 1779; T. Edwards to V. P. Douw, 2 Jan. 1779, NYPL, S Papers. J. Dean to Schuyler, 18

Jan. 1779; Schuyler to J. Jay, 27 Jan. 1779, *PCC*, NAR 173. Graymont, *Iroquois*, 193. Morris, *Jay Papers*, 1: 573–74.

17. J. Clinton to G. Washington, 27 Jan. 1779, MNHP, LWS Coll.

18. *WGW*, 14: 18–19, 44–46, 94–98, 121–22, 149–51. Unfortunately many of Schuyler's letters to Washington about the plans for 1779 have not been located, although Washington's repeatedly refer to receipt of Schuyler's by date. It is possible to deduce some of Schuyler's advice and information from the content of Washington's replies. See also J. Lansing to Schuyler, 3 Feb. 1779, NYPL, S Papers.

19. *LMCC*, 4: 76. G. Clinton to J. Duane, 15 May 1779, MNHP, LWS Coll. J. Carter [Church] to Schuyler, 29 Jan. 1779, NYPL, S Papers: *WGW*, 14: 198–201, 268–73, 407–9. Hammond, *Sullivan Papers*, 3: 5. Graymont, *Iroquois*, 193–94. George S. Conover (Comp.), *Journals of the Military Expedition of Major General John Sullivan Against the Six Nations of Indians in 1779 With Records of Centennial Celebrations* (Auburn, N.Y.; 1887), 340. Hereafter cited Conover, *Journals Sullivan Expedition*. This letter indicates that Schuyler was preferred for the command but that Washington could not appoint him because he "was so uncertain of continuing in the army."

20. *LMCC*, 4: 108–9. Capt. A. Aarson to Schuyler, 23 Mar. 1779, NYPL, S Papers. J. Dean to Schuyler, 29 Mar. 1779; extract Schuyler to [Washington], 15, 24 April 1779, *PCC*, NAR 173. *WGW*, 14: 446–48. Hammond, *Sullivan Papers*, 3: 1.

21. *WGW*, 14: 407–9.

22. J. Dean to Schuyler (extract), 1, 10 April 1779; Schuyler to [Washington] (extract), 24 April 1779; Schuyler to J. Jay, 25 April 1779, *PCC*, NAR 173; *WGW*, 14: 496–97, 15: 168–70.

23. Donald R. McAdams, "The Sullivan Expedition: Success or Failure," *The New-York Historical Society Quarterly* 59 (Jan. 1970): 53–81.

24. Ibid. Morris, *Jay Papers*, 1: 589. See also Graymont, *Iroquois*, 196; Peckham, *Toll of Independence*, 59; *WGW*, 15: 30–31; Alexander C. Flick, "New Sources on the Sullivan-Clinton Campaign in 1779," *Quarterly Journal of the New York State Historical Association* 10 (July, Oct. 1929): 301–2.

25. *WGW*, 15: 31–32, 113–16. J. Lansing to Schuyler, 18, 24 May 1779; Schuyler to V. P. Douw, 26 May 1779, NYPL, S Papers. Hammond, *Sullivan Papers*, 3: 40–41. Schuyler to J. Jay, 30 May 1779, *PCC*, NAR 173.

26. R. Varick to Schuyler, 18 May 1779; J. Duane to Schuyler, 1 May 1779, NYPL, S Papers (only partially given in *LMCC*, 4: 188). Schuyler to J. Duane, 5 June 1779, W. L. Clements Library: Misc. MSS.

27. Minutes, Indian Commissioners, 5 June 1779, NYPL, S Papers. Schuyler to J. Jay, 7 June 1779, *PCC*, NAR 173: *WGW*, 15: 242–43, 267–69.

28. Minutes, Commissioner V. P. Douw meeting with the Oneida et al., 21 July 1779; Schuyler to V. P. Douw, 10, 26 Aug. 1779, NYPL, S Papers. Schuyler to J. Duane, 30 June 1779, MNHP, LWS Coll. For Schuyler's correspondence with J. Sullivan, G. Washington, and J. Clinton see Hammond, *Sullivan Papers*, 3: 63–64, 74–75, 84, 87–88; *WGW*, 15: 404–6, 468–70; Schuyler to Clinton, 21 (?) 24 (?) July 1779, N.J. Hist. Soc. *GCP*, 5: 273–74, 276. Peckham, *Toll of Independence*, 64.

29. J. Duane to Schuyler, 15 June 1779, NYPL, S Papers (*LMCC*, 4: 269–70 incomplete). Schuyler to J. Duane, 30 June 1779, MNHP, LWS Coll.

30. Smith, *St. Clair Papers*, 1: 478.

31. Minutes of Commissioner V. P. Douw's meeting with the Oneida et al., 21 July 1779; Schuyler to V. P. Douw, 10 Aug. 1779, NYPL, S Papers.

32. Ward, *War of the Revolution*, 2: 638–45. See also Higginbotham, *War of American*

Independence, 328–29; Flick, "New Sources on Sullivan-Clinton Campaign"; McAdams, "Sullivan Expedition"; Conover, *Journals Sullivan Expedition;* Graymont, *Iroquois,* 206–20; R. W. G. Vail, ed., "The Western Campaign of 1779: The Diary of Quartermaster Sergeant Moses Sproule . . . ," *The New-York Historical Society Quarterly* 41 (Jan. 1957): 35–69.

33. *WGW,* 15: 468–70. *GCP,* 5: 218, 269–70, 273–74, 276. Schuyler to J. Butler, 13 Sept. 1779, PAC, Haldimand Papers B, vol. 100 (M. G. 21). Conover, *Journals Sullivan Expedition,* 372. Hammond, *Sullivan Papers,* 3: 145–46. V. P. Douw to Schuyler, 22 Oct. 1779, NYPL, S Papers; *WGW,* 16: 460–61. Schuyler to G. Washington, 6 Oct. 1779 and copies of Lt. Col. Van Dyke to Schuyler, J. Dean to Schuyler, 10 Oct. 1779; Schuyler to Van Dyke, to J. Dean, 7 Oct. 1779, *PCC,* NAR 173.

34. NYSJ, 22, 23 Oct. 1779   Schuyler to S.' Huntington, 30 Oct. 1779, *PCC,* NAR 173. *LMCC,* 4: 528–29. Vivian, "Congressional Indian Policy," 271–74.

35. J. Duane to Schuyler, 24 Sept. 1779, NYPL, S Papers, cf. Schuyler to Duane, 11 Sept. 1779, NYHS, Duane Papers. Public Account to Ph. Schuyler, 30 Sept. 1779; Mr. Ensign to Schuyler, 30 Sept. 1779, NYPL, S Papers: Misc. Mili. Accts.

36. J. Cochran to Schuyler, 12 Sept. 1779, NYPL, S Papers. Schuyler to J. Duane, 11 Sept. 1779, NYHS, Duane Papers. Schuyler to Col. Yates, 8 Oct. 1779; M. Lewis to Col. Yates, 19 Oct. 1779, NYSL, MSS. Div. See also Ward, *War of the Revolution,* 2: 610–11; Flexner, *Washington,* 2: 352–53.

37. *WGW,* 16: 460–61; *PAH,* 26: 374–76. Ward, *War of the Revolution,* 2: 611. Schuyler's stay at West Point is shown in his claims to the treasury board, 3 Oct. 1786 (NYPL, S Papers) for expenses as Indian commissioner.

38. Schuyler to J. Duane, 22 Oct. 1779, NYHS, Duane Papers. Schuyler to Pres. S. Huntington, 30 Oct. 1779, *PCC,* NAR 173. J. Lansing to Schuyler, 14 Nov. 1779, NYPL, S Papers.

39. Morris, *Jay Papers,* 1: 583. NYSJ, 18 Oct. 1779; *LMCC,* 4: lix, 46 fn., 520.

40. J. Duane to Schuyler, 30 Oct. 1779; J. Lansing to Schuyler, 14 Nov. 1779, NYPL, S Papers. Marshall Smelser, *The Winning of Independence* (Chicago, 1972), 303; NYSJ, 2, 19, 20 Oct. 1779. And for evidence of Washington's and other officers' desire for Schuyler's presence in Congress see *PAH,* 2: 220–22 and R. Varick to Schuyler, 18 May 1779, NYPL, S Papers.

41. *JCC,* 15: 1272–74.

42. Ibid., 1286, 1288, 1299–1300; *LMCC,* 4: 522.

43. *JCC,* 15: 1290, 1292–93, 1324–25. Burnett, *Congress,* 419. *LMCC,* 4: 522, 528–29.

44. *JCC,* 15: 1286; *LMCC,* 4: 522.

45. B. Arnold to Schuyler, 24 Nov. 1779, NYPL, S Papers. Flexner, *Traitor and the Spy,* 307.

46. *JCC,* 15: 1336–37.

47. Burnett, *Congress,* 395–99. *JCC,* 15: 1312, 1326, 1343: *LMCC,* 4: 522, cf. *WGW,* 17: 176.

48. *JCC,* 15: 1320–22. See also *LMCC,* 5: 20–22.

49. *LMCC,* 4: 528–29. Schuyler to J. Duane, 16 Dec. 1779, NYHS, Duane Papers.

50. *JCC,* 15: 1286; *LMCC,* 4: 522. Flexner, *Washington,* 2: 353.

51. *JCC,* 15: 1312; *WGW,* 17: 176. Schuyler to G. Clington, 29 Nov. 1779, MNHP, LWS Coll. (only part in *LMCC,* 4: 528–29).

52. *JCC,* 15: 1301–02, 1331–32.

53. Ibid., 1343.

54. Ibid., 1368–70.

55. Ibid., 1371–72, 1376–77, 1386–89.

56. R. R. Livingston to Schuyler, 20 Dec. 1779, NYPL, S Papers, cf. *LMCC,* 4: 543, where "security" is mistaken for "fixture."

57. Schuyler to J. Duane, 16 Dec. 1779, NYHS, Duane Papers.

58. Ibid. What precisely this plan might have been is a puzzle, but it is interesting to note that it coincides with one devised by Alexander Hamilton. Sometime between December 1779 and March 1780 Hamilton prepared a long letter, proposing the creation of a stable currency by means of a national bank. For whom his letter was intended is not known. Perhaps it was for Schuyler, for except for him there were few members of Congress who showed as much familiarity with finance or who would have considered so drastic a scheme. Hamilton also had ample opportunity to discuss such matters with Schuyler as both were at Morristown in early December. The plan proposed that half the bank's capital be raised by a foreign loan and half from private subscribers who could buy stock with Continental bills of credit at a depreciated ratio. This might breathe new life into the bills as merchants would find it profitable to accept them. Owning half the bank's stock, Congress could use it to finance the government by means of loans and to facilitate taxation (through the increase of money in circulation). See *PAH*, 2: 234–51; McDonald, *Hamilton*, 39–40, 375; John C. Miller, *Alexander Hamilton: Portrait in Paradox* (New York, 1959), 52, 236.

59. *WGW*, 17: 314–16.

60. Smelser, *Winning Independence*, 270. Ludlum, *Early American Winters*, 112–15. S. Sydney Bradford, "Hunger Menaces the Revolution, December, 1779–January, 1780," *Maryland Historical Magazine* 61 (March 1966): 1–23.

61. Bradford, "Hunger Menaces the Revolution," *Maryland Historical Magazine* 61: 1–23. Ludlum, *Early American Winters*, 79.

CHAPTER 13

1. Morris, *Jay Papers*, 1: 733–34.

2. Schuyler to Baron Steuben, 10 Jan. 1780 (Copy from Steuben Papers), Union College Library, Schenectady, *WGW*, 17: 464–68; *PAH*, 2: 269–71.

3. G. Johnson to Schuyler, 7 Dec. 1779, British Museum Add. MSS. 21779/79, Haldimand Papers. Schuyler to G. Johnson, 23 Jan. 1780, ibid., ff. 81–82 (misdated as 7 Jan. in *PCC*, NAR 173, copy with Schuyler to S. Huntington, 24 Jan. 1780). Brig. Gen. H. W. Powell to Col. G. Van Schaick, 13 Feb. 1780, PAC, Haldimand Papers, B, vol. 175 (M. G. 21). Graymont, *Iroquois*, 225–29. Higginbotham, *War of American Independence*, 329. Proceedings of a Meeting, "Four Rebel Indians with Chiefs of the Six Nations at Niagara," 12 Feb. 1780, British Museum Add. MSS. 21779/78, Haldimand Papers. Minutes, Indian Commissioners, N. Dept., 3, 9 (?) Feb. 1780, NYPL, S Papers. Schuyler to S. Huntington, 5 Feb. 1780, *PCC*, NAR 173; *WGW*, 17: 464–68.

4. NYSJ, 27 Jan. 1780; *LMCC*, 5: 20–22.

5. NYSJ, 1, 5, 9, 19 Feb. 1780. *Report of the Regents of the University on the Boundaries of the State of New York*, (Albany, 1884): 181–84.

6. *JCC*, 16: 327–28.

7. NYSJ, 8, 10, 11, 12, 14, 29 Feb.; 2, 3, 8, 9 Mar. 1780. Burnett, *Congress*, 426–27.

8. Burnett, *Congress*, 400. *JCC*, 16: 73, 75–77, 79. R. R. Livingston to Schuyler, 27 Jan. 1780, NYPL, S Papers. Cf. *LMCC*, 5: 18–19.

9. Burnett, *Congress*, 400. Schuyler to S. Huntington, 15 Feb. 1780, *PCC*, NAR 173.

10. *LMCC*, 5: 60–61. Schuyler to J. Duane, 6 Mar. 1780 (dated at Morristown), NYHS, Duane Papers. Either the date or place may be in error, for Schuyler claimed to have reached Philadelphia on 5 Mar. (Sunday); on 7 Mar. (Tuesday) he was seated in Congress. Schuyler

to S. Huntington, 6 Mar. 1780 is also dated at Philadelphia (*LMCC*, 5: 60–61); that he was at Morristown on 6 Mar. is doubtful, especially because the distance from Philadelphia is about seventy-five miles. Cf. *LMCC*, 5: ix, 62; Schuyler to U.S. Treasury Board, 3 Oct. 1786 (draft), NYPL, S Papers, which states that he left Albany about 1 Mar. 1780.

11. J. Lansing to Schuyler, 11, 19, 26 Mar., 16 May, 5, 10 June, 7, 26 July 1780, NYPL, S Papers.

12. Schuyler to N. Greene, 22 Mar. 1780, *LMCC*, 5: 90–91, cf. W. L. Clements Library: Greene Papers. Burnett, *Congress*, 426.

13. *LMCC*, 5: 62.

14. Schuyler to G. Washington 13 [12(?)] Mar. 1780, cf. Schuyler to [G. Clinton], 11 Mar. 1780, *LMCC*, 5: 66–67, 71, 117–18 and *GCP*, 5: 642. See also Burnett, *Congress*, 426–27.

15. *LMCC*, 5: 80. Burnett, *Congress*, 426–27. Merrill Jensen, *The American Revolution Within America* (New York, 1974), 142; *LMCC*, 5: 87–89.

16. Schuyler to G. Washington, 7 Mar. 1780, cf. Schuyler to N. Greene, 22 Mar. 1780, *LMCC*, 5: 62, 90–91.

17. *LMCC*, 5: 66–67, 71, 80, 117–118.

18. *LMCC*, 5: 90–92; *WGW*, 18: 137–38. Flexner, *Washington*, 2: 368; *LMCC*, 5: 91–92; *WGW*, 18: 185–87. Burnett, *Congress*, 445.

19. Burnett, *Congress*, 400–401. *JCC*, 16: 293–311; *LMCC*, 5: 107–9. See also *WGW*, 18: 185–87.

20. *JCC*, 16: 312–13, 326–28; *LMCC*, 5: 107–9, 109 n; *WGW*, 18: 185–87.

21. *PAH*, 2: 305–7, cf. 1: 306, which mistakenly identifies this as Hamilton to Schuyler. Christopher Collier, *Roger Sherman's Connecticut: Yankee Politics and the American Revolution* (Middletown, Conn., 1971), 184–86 notes Mifflin's role as Sherman's coauthor and his notorious enmity towards Washington. See also *JCC*, 16: 332–33.

22. *PAH*, 2: 285–87, cf. 350; 347–49. McDonald, *Hamilton*, 16.

23. Page Smith, *John Adams*, 2 vols. (New York, 1962): 2: 908, 1043. Gertrude F. H. Atherton, *The Conqueror* (Philadelphia and New York, 1943), 191–92, suggests a fanciful notion of Elizabeth Schuyler's reaction to the subject of Hamilton's origins: "I am sure that it will make no difference with my dear father who is the most just and sensible of men. ... But if he should object—why, we'll run away." Schuyler was indeed just and sensible, but also sensitive; and the suggestion of elopement was the very thing that both he and Mrs. Schuyler were determined should not happen!

24. *PAH*, 2: 305–7.

25. Ibid., 309–10.

26. *JCC*, 16: 196–201, 354–57. Burnett, *Congress*, 446–47. Palmer, *Way of the Fox*, 72–73. Louis C. Hatch, *The Administration of the American Revolutionary Army* (New York, 1904), 20. Schuyler to J. Duane, 13 May 1780, NYHS, Duane Papers; *PAH*, 2: 322; *WGW*, 18: 356–58.

27. *JCC*, 16: 359–62.

28. J. Duane to Schuyler, 16 June 1780; H. B. Livingston to Schuyler, 1 Sept. 1780, NYPL, S Papers. J. Jay to Schuyler, 25 Nov. 1780, Jay Papers, Columbia Univ. Library.

29. *LMCC*, 5: 117–18, 120–21. Dr. M. Treat to Schuyler, 26 April 1780, NYPL, S Papers.

30. Burnett, *Congress*, 447; *LMCC*, 5: 132–34.

31. G. Clinton to N.Y. Delegates in Congress, 27 April 1780, NYHS, Duane Papers.

32. Saffron, *Surgeon to Washington*, 59. That Mrs. Schuyler was at Morristown as early as April is suggested in J. Duane to Schuyler, 6 May 1780, NYPL, S Papers.

33. *LMCC*, 5: 132–34.

34. J. Duane to Schuyler, 6 May 1780, NYPL, S Papers; *LMCC*, 5: 134–35, 136–39.

35. Schuyler to J. Duane, 13 May 1780, NYHS, Duane Papers.

36. *PAH*, 2: 322; *WGW*, 18: 356–58.

37. *LMCC*, 5: 141–42. Burnett, *Congress*, 447–48.

38. *LMCC*, 5: 142–43.

39. Schuyler to J. Duane, 15 May 1780, MNHP, Park Coll.

40. *LMCC*, 5: 145–48, 157–58.

41. *LMCC*, 5: 147 n, cf. Burnett, *Congress*, 448–50.

42. R. R. Livingston to Schuyler, 21 May 1780, NYPL, S Papers, cf. *LMCC*, 5: 158–59.

43. *WGW*, 18: 398–400; *LMCC*, 5: 170 n; Sparks, *Correspondence*, 2: 453.

44. Burnett, *Congress*, 450. *WGW*, 18: 408–9.

45. *LMCC*, 5: 164–69. And see Boyd, *Jefferson Papers*, 3: 391–96; Schuyler to J. Trumbull, 25 May 1780, Conn. State Library: Trumbull Papers.

46. *WGW*, 18: 416–19.

47. Burnett, *Congress*, 452. *LMCC*, 5: 173–75; *GCP*, 5: 764, 758, 760–61.

48. R. Benson to Schuyler, 7 June 1780, NYPL, S Papers. E. L'Hommedieu to Schuyler, 7 June 1780, MNHP, LWS Coll. The legislature's actions on Congress's financial recommendations of 18 May and the requisitions for the Continental army were as follows: ordered provision of transportation and subsistence of Brig. Gen. James Clinton's brigade, which was sent to Albany; approved Congress's act of 18 March respecting the issue of new currency and provided redemption of a share of the old bills of credit; passed bills to raise reinforcements for the Continental army and to complete New York's regiments in the Continental line; passed a bill for raising supplies for the army. NYSJ, 23 May–2 July 1780. See also G. Clinton to the N.Y. Delegates in Congress, 23 June 1780, NYHS, Duane Papers.

49. G. Clinton to Schuyler, 14 June 1780, NYPL, S Papers.

50. *LMCC*, 5: 179–80.

51. *WGW*, 18: 455–59.

52. *LMCC*, 5: 183–89 cf. 2 June Comm. letters to Joseph Reed of Pa. (N.J. Hist. Soc.), to Pres. of Council of State of Mass. (Mass. State House Archives Div.). List of Supplies requested from the States, 2 June 1780, NYPL, S Papers.

53. Burnett, *Congress*, 454; *LMCC*, 5: 194–95.

54. Schuyler to J. Duane, 5 June 1780, NYHS, Duane Papers.

55. *WGW*, 18: 504–6. Palmer, *Way of the Fox*, 163–65. Boyd, *Jefferson Papers*, 3: 436 n. Comm. of Congress to Gov. of Mass., 12 June 1780, Mass. State House Archives Div.

56. *LMCC*, 5: 207–8, 211–13. Schuyler to Gov. W. Livingston, 12 June 1780, Div. of State Library, N.J. Dept. of Education, Statehouse Annex (Trenton, N.J.).

57. *LMCC*, 5: 208–9. Burnett, *Congress*, 454–55.

58. J. Duane to Schuyler, 6 May [June] 1780, *LMCC*, 5: 198. Schuyler to Duane, 12 June 1780, MNHP, LWS Coll.

59. J. Duane to Schuyler, 16 June 1780; R. R. Livingston to Schuyler, 16 June 1780, NYPL, S Papers (only part of R. R. L. letter is in *LMCC*, 5: 220).

60. Burnett, *Congress*, 457, 461–62.

61. N. Greene to Schuyler, 14 June 1780, NYPL, S Papers; *LMCC*, 5: 221–22.

62. Burnett, *Congress*, 461; *LMCC*, 5: 224.

63. *LMCC*, 5: 229–30, cf. copy in Mass. State House Archives Div.; *WGW*, 19: 38, 57–58, 76–77; *LMCC*, 5: 240–42.

64. *PAH*, 2: 350–52; *LMCC*, 5: 248–49.

65. *LMCC*, 5: 253–56.

66. *WGW*, 19: 165–66.

67. *LMCC*, 5: 261–63.

68. Ibid., 271–78.

69. Ibid., 282, 288–90. Champagne, *Alexander McDougall*, 161–63.

70. *LMCC*, 5: 291–92.

71. Ibid., 290–91 n; *WGW*, 19: 205–6, 241–43. Burnett, *Congress*, 460.

72. Burnett, *Congress*, 461. *LMCC*, 5: 266–68, 282–84. Thomas L. Wells, "An Inquiry into the Resignation of Quartermaster General Nathanael Greene in 1780," *Rhode Island History* 24 (April, 1965): 44–45.

73. Burnett, *Congress*, 462.

74. *LMCC*, 5: 297, 299–304; *WGW*, 19: 234–36, 280 n.

75. *LMCC*, 5: 304, 308–9. R. Morris to Schuyler, 1 Aug. 1780, NYPL, S Papers.

76. For Schuyler's departure from Peekskill, see *LMCC*, 5: 309 and *PAH*, 2: 374–75. Schuyler accused Congress of "penelopizing" (*LMCC*, 5: 224), i.e., unravelling each night the web woven during the day like Penelope, who put off suitors whose offers she promised to consider when the web was finished.

77. Graymont, *Iroquois*, 223–35. Schuyler to J. Duane, 6 Mar. 1780, NYHS, Duane Papers.

78. J. Lansing to Schuyler, 11, 19, 26 Mar. 1780; J. Dean to Schuyler, 4 April 1780, NYPL, S Papers. Peckham, *Toll of Independence*, 69–70. G. Clinton to N.Y. Delegates in Congress, 9 May 1780, NYHS, Duane Papers. J. Lansing to Schuyler, 16 May 1780; M. Lewis to Schuyler, 17 May 1780; J. Tayler to Schuyler, 17 May 1780, NYPL, S Papers; NYSJ, 30 May 1780. E. L'Hommedieu to Schuyler, 7 June 1780, MNHP, LWS Coll. Judd, *Van Cortlandt Papers*, 2: 365–66; *GCP*, 5: 758. J. Lansing to Schuyler, 5 June 1780, cf. M. Lewis to Schuyler, 9 June 1780, NYPL, S Papers. G. Clinton to N.Y. Delegates in Congress, 14 June 1780, NYHS, Duane Papers.

79. Graymont, *Iroquois*, 233–36. J. Dean to Schuyler, 21 June 1780, Union College Library (Schenectady). J. Lansing to Schuyler, 10 June 1780, NYPL, S Papers.

80. J. Taylor to Schuyler, 19 June 1780; G. Clinton to Schuyler, 14 June 1780, NYPL, S Papers. G. Clinton to N.Y. Delegates in Congress, 14 June 1780, NYHS, Duane Papers. V. P. Douw to Schuyler, 24 June 1780; S. Kirkland to V. Douw, 3 July 1780; Dr. M. Treat to Schuyler, 25 June 1780, NYPL, S Papers.

81. Peckham, *Toll of Independence*, 73. Graymont, *Iroquois*, 235. J. Lansing to Schuyler, 26 July 1780 (two letters), NYPL, S Papers.

82. Minutes N. Dept. Indian Commissioners, 16 Aug. 1780, NYPL, S Papers (Indian Papers). Graymont, *Iroquois*, 236–237.

83. Schuyler to Quartermasters, Commissaries, 20 July 1780, NYPL, S Papers. Schuyler to Lafayette, 18 Aug. 1780, Library of Congress: Washington Papers. See also Howard C. Rice, Jr., and Anne S. K. Brown, trans., eds., *The American Campaigns of Rochambeau's Army, 1780, 1781, 1782, 1783*, 2 vols. (Princeton, 1972), 1: 121 n; Lafayette to Schuyler, 7 Sept. 1780 (so faint as to be practically illegible), NYPL, S Papers.

84. *PAH*, 26: 392. Schuyler to Gov. J. Trumbull, 18 Aug. 1780, Conn. State Library: Trumbull Papers, 12: 234b. *WGW*, 19: 416. V. P. Douw's Receipt to J. Cuyler, 19 Aug. 1780; Acct. of Monies Received by V. P. Douw, 23 Aug. 1776–1 Aug. 1780; the U.S. to V. P. Douw, Aug. 1780; V. P. Douw to Schuyler, 8 Aug. 1780, NYPL, S (Indian) Papers. A statement of the Indian Commissioners' account with the estate of Hugh Denniston, 2 Sept. 1780 (NYPL, S [Indian] Papers) shows expenses other than those for victualling the Indians. Between 21 May 1777 and 2 Sept. 1780 Denniston was credited for £1,631.8.11. Items include sums for meals, tobacco, pipes, wine, rum, bowls of toddy, and "Nips" of other drink.

85. Burnett, *Congress*, 464. Extract from Journals of Congress, 2 Aug. 1780 (signed by Charles Thomson), NYPL, S Papers.

86. *LMCC*, 5: 309–11.

87. Hatch, *Administration of American Revolutionary Army*, 111.

88. Extract of Journals of Congress, 11 Aug. 1780, NYPL, S Papers, cf. *LMCC*, 5: 322 n; 329–30. *PAH*, 2: 408–9.

89. *WGW*, 19: 391–94; *LMCC*, 5: 332–33, 336–38, 343.

90. Burnett, *Congress*, 465; *LMCC*, 5: 322 n.

91. Schuyler to G. Clinton, 28 Aug. 1780, NYPL, S Papers; *WGW*, 19: 449–51.

92. *PAH*, 2: 383, 387–89; *LMCC*, 5: 358. Schuyler to G. Clinton, 28 Aug. 1780, NYPL, S Papers. Burnett, *Congress*, 468.

93. *PAH*, 2: 418–20, cites the storm delaying Schuyler's departure. J. Lansing to Schuyler, 16 May, 5 June 1780, NYPL, S Papers.

94. NYSJ, 7, 8, 9 Sept. 1780.

95. NYSJ, 15, 19, 21, 23, 25, 27, 30 Sept., 7, 9 Oct. 1780.

96. *PAH*, 2: 425–26. Matthew L. Davis, *Memoirs of Aaron Burr*, 2 vols. (1836; reprint, Freeport, N.Y., 1970) 2: 6 erroneously alleges that "For some reason not then explained, there was a sudden and extraordinary change of opinion in the legislature in relation to General Schuyler." The change is "explained" by speculation that Governor Clinton, L'Hommedieu, and others opposed Schuyler's suggestion that the Hartford Convention propose making Washington a dictator. If that were true Schuyler should not have been made a delegate to the convention. Moreover, his letters to Hamilton on 10 and 16 Sept. (*PAH*, 2: 425–26, 432–34) indicate widespread legislative support for the idea of a dictator and vice dictators in the states, and that Schuyler expected to be sent to Hartford with orders to propose the idea!

97. NYSJ, 26 Sept. 1780. *PAH*, 2: 425–26, 432–34, 447–48. The editors of Hamilton's papers were mistaken to date Schuyler's letter to Hamilton, [20–25 (?)] Sept. 1780 from Saratoga as Schuyler mentioned that he must leave Poughkeepsie before the legislature adjourned because of illness. The senate journals indicate that he was present on 25 Sept. but absent thereafter. The letter *was* probably written between 20 and 25 Sept. while he was at Poughkeepsie. NYSJ, 10 Oct. 1780.

98. NYSJ, 23 Sept. 1780.

99. Nelson, *Gates*, 234–39. Mitchell, *Discipline and Bayonets*, 141–43. Higginbotham, *War of American Independence*, 359–60 and Don Higginbotham, *Daniel Morgan: Revolutionary Rifleman* (Chapel Hill, N.C.; 1961), 106.

100. *PAH*, 2: 425–26, 498–500.

101. Ibid., 425–26, 432–34.

102. Franklin B. Hough, ed., *The Northern Invasion of October 1780* (New York, 1866), 42–47, 63–64. Jellison, *Ethan Allen*, 247–50, 254. Hamilton Vaughan Bail, "A Letter to Lord Germain About Vermont," *Vermont History* 34 (October, 1966): 233.

103. Graymont, *Iroquois*, 237–38, 240. Peckham, *Toll of Independence*, 76–77.

104. *GCP*, 6: 275–76, 325–26. *PAH*, 2: 457–58. W. Heath to Schuyler, 12 Oct. 1780, NYPL, S Papers.

105. Schuyler to S. Huntington, 10 Oct. 1780, *PCC*, NAR 173. *GCP*, 6: 343–44. Graymont, *Iroquois*, 322, 342. Baxter, *Godchild*, 446.

106. Hough, *Northern Invasion*, 108–10. *GCP*, 6: 304–5, 325–26. E. Benson to Schuyler, 19 Oct. 1780, NYPL, S Papers.

107. *PAH*, 2: 480–81.

108. *GCP*, 6: 324–25, 343–44, 358; *WGW*, 20: 305 n.

109. *WGW*, 20: 304–6; *GCP*, 6: 368–69.

110. *GCP*, 6: 364–65, 376–77, 377–78.

111. Schuyler to J. Clinton, 5 Nov. 1780, NYPL, S (land) Papers. Schuyler to J. Duane, 6 Nov. 1780, NYSL, MSS. Div.

112. Jellison, *Ethan Allen*, 248, 250, 254. Hough, *Northern Invasion*, 63–64.

113. *PAH,* 2: 441–42, 448–49, 455–56. Schuyler to Maj. C. Carleton, 10 Nov. 1780, Haldimand Papers, British Museum Add. MSS. 21835/42.

114. Charles Royster, " 'The Nature of Treason': Revolutionary Virtue and American Reactions to Benedict Arnold," *The William and Mary Quarterly* 3d Ser., 36 (April, 1979): 163–93.

115. B. Arnold to Schuyler, 25 May 1780, NYPL, S Papers. Schuyler to B. Arnold, 2 June 1780, NYHS, Joseph Reed Papers, 7, cf. Decker, *Arnold,* 358; Flexner, *Washington,* 2: 381.

116. *WGW,* 20: 213–15.

117. Ibid., 94.

118. E. Oswald to J. Lamb, 11 Dec. 1780, NYHS, Lamb Papers. Schuyler to Maj. C. Carleton, 10 Nov. 1780, n. 112, above.

119. Schuyler to pres. of court for inquiring into the conduct of Lt. Col. Varick, 15 Oct. 1780, HL. See also R. Varick to Schuyler, 31 Oct. 1780, NYPL, S Papers; *PAH,* 26: 395–99; Albert B. Hart, ed., *The Varick Court of Inquiry to Investigate the Implication of Colonel Varick (Arnold's Private Secretary) in the Arnold Treason* (Boston, 1907), 46–48. M. Willett to J. Lamb, 12 Nov. 1780, NYHS, Lamb Papers; *PAH,* 2: 490–500.

120. *PAH,* 2: 498–500, cf. Smelser, *Winning Independence,* 304–5. Mitchell, *Hamilton,* 1: 206.

121. *PAH,* 2: 498–500.

122. M. Lewis (account) to Schuyler, 1 Dec. 1780, NYPL, S Papers: Misc. Mili. Accts.

123. *Year Book of the Holland Society of New York, 1924 and 1925* (New York, 1925), 2, cf. *PAH,* 2: 521.

124. Broadus Mitchell, *Alexander Hamilton,* 2 vols. (New York, 1957–1962), 1: 207. Saffron, *Surgeon to Washington,* 64–66. Little evidence remains of Schuyler's children except for scattered references as in Jared Root's Receipt, 20 Dec. 1780, NYPL, S Papers, Personal & Household Accts. The receipt shows that Schuyler paid Root £1.8.5 for four months and one week of Rensselaer's schooling, and other bills (not specified) of £2.8.0. Root evidently pressed for a settlement of accounts because he did not intend to continue his school "longer than next week." *PAH,* 2: 524–25, 526–27, 542–43.

125. Rice, *Chastellux Travels,* 1: 197, 200–201, 209–14, 217–23, 345–47, cf. Chastellux, *Travels* (1787), 1: 416, 425.

126. Chastellux to Schuyler, 18 Feb. 1782, NYPL, S Papers. Rice, *Chastellux Travels,* 2: 530.

CHAPTER 14

1. Douglas Southall Freeman, *George Washington: A Biography,* 7 vols. (New York, 1948–1957), 5: 263, 266–68, and passim. Hawke, *Benjamin Rush,* 248, gives an apt summary of conditions in 1781. Schuyler's connections with the Albany committee are noted in Victor Hugo Paltsits, ed., *Minutes of the Commissioners for Detecting and Defeating Conspiracies in the State of New York: Albany County Sessions, 1778–1781,* 3 vols. (Albany, N.Y., 1909–1910), 1: 86, 102, 303, and passim; 2: 552, and passim, hereafter cited Paltsits, *Minutes.* Freeman's meticulous and monumental biography of Washington does not explore in any detail his connections with Schuyler, although Freeman does indicate that the two men were intimates in military counsel and enjoyed each other's respect and support. Schuyler's role in the 1781 campaign and his efforts to deal with conditions on the New York frontier are scarcely mentioned, much less delineated, in other works like Francis Whiting Halsey, *The Old New York Frontier* (New York, 1901); Harold A. Larrabee, *Decision at the Chesapeake* (New York, 1964); Sosin, *The Revolutionary Frontier;* or Swiggett, *War Out of Niagara.*

2. Sparks, *Correspondence*, 3: 212–14.

3. NYSJ, 31 Jan. 1781.

4. NYSJ, 1, 2, 3, 5 Feb. 1781. *PAH*, 2: 549, 553.

5. Henry Van Schaack, *Memoirs of the Life of Henry Van Schaack* (Chicago, 1892), 152–53.

6. G. Washington to Schuyler, 10 Jan. 1781, John C. Fitzpatrick, ed., *Calendar of the Correspondence of George Washington with the Officers*, 4 vols. (Washington, D.C., 1915), 3: 1672. Schuyler to S. Huntington, 18 Jan. 1781, PCC, NAR 173. *PAH*, 2: 542–43, 551–53. J. Moylan to Schuyler, 29 Jan. 1781, NYPL, S Papers. Schuyler to J. Duane, 5 Feb. 1781, *Pubs. Southern Historical Ass'n.*, 8: 384–85. Schuyler and V. P. Douw to Senate and Assembly of State of N.Y., 24 Feb. 1781, HL. NYSJ, 24 Feb., 5, 8 Mar. 1781.

7. Mitchell, *Hamilton*, 2: 230; *PAH*, 2: 542–53.

8. *PAH*, 2: 563–68, 575–77. Mitchell, *Hamilton*, 1: 228–33.

9. *PAH*, 2: 575–77 mentions Catherine's birth. Schuyler family Bible, Schuyler Mansion, Albany, N.Y. Baxter, *Godchild*, frontispiece, 40. *WGW*, 21: 360.

10. *PAH*, 2: 498–500; NYSJ, 6 Feb. 1781.

11. Sparks, *Correspondence*, 3: 212–14. NYSJ, 21 Feb., 1 Mar. 1781. Copy of 21 Feb. 1781 senate resolve, NYPL, S Papers Misc. E. Wilder Spaulding, *His Excellency George Clinton: Critic of the Constitution* (New York, 1938), 146–47. See also Schuyler to J. Wadsworth, 25 Mar. 178, Wadsworth Papers, Conn. Hist. Soc.; Schuyler to J. Duane, 29 Mar. 1781, NYHS, Duane Papers; *WGW*, 22: 82 n. Confirmation of Schuyler's suspicions that Vermonters were dickering with Gen. Frederick Haldimand is in George Germain to Sir Henry Clinton, 7 Feb. 1781 (copy), NYPL, S Papers. How and when Schuyler got this copy are not indicated.

12. Clarence E. Miner, *The Ratification of the Federal Constitution by the State of New York* (New York, 1921), 15–17. NYSJ, 26 Feb., 19, 20, 29 Mar. 1781.

13. NYSJ, 20, 24, 27 Feb.; 6, 9–10, 12, 13, 29 Mar. 1781. Burnett, *Congress*, 423, 484–88.

14. Schuyler to J. Duane, 29 Mar. 1781, NYHS, Duane Papers.

15. *WGW*, 21: 261–62, 360.

16. *LMCC*, 6: 26 n. Sparks, *Correspondence*, 3: 280–82.

17. *LMCC*, 7: 379–400, cf. Burnett, *Congress*, 602.

18. R. R. Livingston to Schuyler, 28 Mar. 1781, NYPL, S Papers. Schuyler to J. Duane, 29 Mar., 30 May 1781, NYHS, Duane Papers. Hough, *Civil List* (1855), 37–38.

19. Schuyler to J. Clinton, 23 April 1781, Buffalo and Erie Co. Historical Soc.; *PAH*, 2: 603–4, 640–42, 646–47, 652–54. Schuyler to J. Clinton, 29 April, 8 May 1781, NYSL, MSS. Div.

20. *PAH*, 2: 646–47. Schuyler to J. Duane, 30 May 1781, NYHS, Duane Papers.

21. Sir John Johnson to General Haldimand, 3 May 1781, PAC, Haldimand Papers, B. vol. 158 (M. G. 21). J. Lansing to Schuyler, 16 May, 7 July 1780, NYPL, S Papers gives information on Philip Lansing.

22. East, *Business Enterprise*, 103–6, 113, 146–47, 212, 288–89. Statement of "The United States Account with Philip Schuyler," 25 Sept. 1781 and "The Public In Account with Philip Schuyler," 7 July 1779, NYPL, S Papers: Misc. Military Accts. These papers include items for wheat (2,040 bushels), peas, oats, potatoes, corn, and hay furnished to the army according to prices prevailing in 1777, and £3,599.10.0 "To Sundries furnished for the public Service" between July 1775 and July 1777. As of July 1779 Schuyler noted that unpaid bills meant that he had "not only lost the Interest" he might have obtained on his money "but shall Suffer by the Subsequent depreciation unless It should be thought Equitable to make Compensation for It."

23. R. Morris to Schuyler, 29 May 1781, NYPL, S Papers, cf. *PRM*, 1: 92–93, 128.

24. Schuyler to R. Morris, 23 June 1781 (draft), NYHS, Misc. MSS. Philip Schuyler, cf. *PRM*, 1: 174. *PRM*, 1: 235. Schuyler Ledger, 1774–96, ff. 171, 272; R. Morris to Schuyler, 25

June, 21 July 1781, NYPL, S Papers, cf. *PRM*, 1: 176–78. East, *Business Enterprise*, 288–89. Clarence L. Ver Steeg, *Robert Morris: Revolutionary Financier* (Philadelphia, 1954), 70, 73, 108. Schuyler to R. Morris, 9 June 1781 (letter not found), *PRM*, 1: 128, 154, 159, 161. See also Jacob Cuyler's and Philip Schuyler's Receipts, 24 Sept. 1781; R. Morris's Account with Schuyler, 24 Sept. 1781, NYPL, S Papers: Personal & Household Accts. Schuyler to Washington, 8 June 1781, Fitzpatrick, *Calendar*, 3: 1855.

    25. NYSJ, 18 June 1781.

    26. NYSJ, 21, 23, 28, 30 June 1781; *PRM*, 1: 174.

    27. Larry R. Gerlach, "Connecticut, the Continental Congress, and the Independence of Vermont, 1777–1782," *Vermont History* 34 (July, 1966): 188–93.

    28. NYSJ, 19 June 1781.

    29. NYSJ, 26, 28, 29 June, 1 July 1781.

    30. NYSJ, 27 June 1781. A third senate vote on 27 June confirms this division but also shows that Schuyler's cohorts tended to outnumber Yates's and that in all three votes the alliances were as follows: Yates, Wisner, Parks, Pawling, and Webster versus Schuyler, Stoutenburgh, Ten Broeck, Fonda, Lawrence, and Scott. In two out of three votes Klock and Floyd voted with Yates; and Woodhull, Roosevelt, and Ward voted with Schuyler.

    31. NYSJ, 30 June 1781, cf. Alfred B. Street, *The Council of Revision of the State of New York* (Albany, 1859), 241.

    32. Fitzpatrick, *Calendar*, 3: 1864, 1866, 1871, 1877. *PRM*, 1: 188–89. See also *WGW*, 22: 288; and John C. Fitzpatrick, ed., *The Diaries of George Washington*, 4 vols. (Boston, New York, 1925): 12: 229, hereafter cited Fitzpatrick, *Washington Diaries*.

    33. Fitzpatrick, *Calendar*, 3: 1864, 1866, 1871, 1877, 1881, 1884, 1886, 1887, 1889, 1893, 1902; *PRM*, 1: 367–68, 372–74. For further dealings with Morris, see Schuyler to Pres. Congress, 9 Aug. 1781, *PCC*, NAR 173; Thomas Russell to Schuyler, 5 Oct. 1781, NYPL, S Papers; Schuyler to R. Morris, 1 Dec. 1781, NYSL, MSS. Div.; Schuyler to William Heath, 10 Sept. 1781, Massachusetts Institute of Technology, Heath Papers; John Stark to Schuyler, 11 Sept. 1781, Dartmouth College Library: Wheelock Collection; Stark, *Memoir* 250; Benson J. Lossing, *The Pictorial Field-Book of The Revolution*, 2 vols. (New York, 1860), 1: 222.

    34. Sparks, *Correspondence*, 3: 462–63; *WGW*, 23: 467, 471 n; 24: 103. For the guard see *Collections of N-Y Hist. Soc. for 1915*, 68: 362–67: Corporal John Hanky, Privates Benjamin Goodale, Thomas Haynes, John Wyatt of Capt. John C. Ten Broeck's Company, First N.Y. Line Regiment. For records of other guards in Oct.-Nov. 1777 and Mar.-May, Nov.-Dec. 1778, ibid., 378–81, 388–89, 398–99; *WGW*, 22: 375.

    35. *JCC*, 15: 1341. Paltsits, *Minutes*, 1: 86, 303–4, 405; 2: 552, 554–55, 558, 567, 568, 595.

    36. Schuyler to J. Duane, 29 April 1781, NYHS, Duane Papers. *GCP*, 6: 770–71, 840–43. Fitzpatrick, *Calendar*, 3: 1813 and *WGW*, 22: 82 n. *GCP*, 6: 859–60, 890–91.

    37. Fitzpatrick, *Calendar*, 3: 1821, 1830, 1838, 1840. John Pell, *Ethan Allen* (London, 1930), 215–16. *GCP*, 6: 880–81, 890–91, 898–99. Schuyler to J. Clinton, 24 May 1781, NYSL, MSS. Div.

    38. Schuyler to J. Clinton, 24 May 1781, NYSL, MSS. Div.; *PAH*, 2: 646–47.

    39. Freeman, *Washington*, 5: 255–58, 263, 270, 276, 285–300. Piers Mackesy, *The War for America, 1775–1783* (Cambridge, Mass. 1964), 410–11, 413. Larrabee, *Decision at the Chesapeake*, 240–41, 251–52. Henry Steele Commager and Richard B. Morris, ed., *The Spirit of 'Seventy-Six*, 2 vols. (Indianapolis, Ind., 1958), 2: 1209–13. Fitzpatrick, *Washington Diaries*, 2: 223, 229. Fitzpatrick, *Calendar*, 3: 1840 *WGW*, 22: 288. Washington to G. Clinton (copy), 30 July 1781, NYPL, S Papers.

    40. Schuyler to Washington, 15 July 1781, (original) British Museum, Add. MSS., Haldimand Papers, 21794/85-86; copies in HL and PAC, Haldimand Papers, B vol. 134 (M. G.

21). The Huntington Library copy was evidently Schuyler's and carries an endorsement in his hand: "Copy of a Letter Calculated to Mislead the Enemy with respect to Gen: Washington's Intentions July 15 1781 Directed to the General but carried to the Enemy etc." The full text and another version of this story is Don R. Gerlach, "Philip Schuyler and the New York Frontier in 1781," *The New-York Historical Society Quarterly* 53 (April, 1969): 148–81.

41. Mackesy, *War for America*, 413. Fitzpatrick, *Washington Diaries*, 2: 246. Schuyler to Washington, 8 Aug. 1781 (draft), NYPL, S Papers, cf. Paltsits, *Minutes*, 2: 754–55.

42. Sir John Johnson to Gen. F. Haldimand, 3 May 1781, PAC, Haldimand Papers, B vol. 158 (M. G. 21). Fitzpatrick, *Calendar*, 3: 1830, cf. Pell, *Ethan Allen*, 215–16.

43. Schuyler to J. Clinton, 24 May 1781, NYSL, MSS. Div.; *GCP*, 7: 184–86. [Becker], *The Sexagenary*, 126, 174, says that Schuyler not only kept a twenty-four-man "life guard" during the winter of 1777–78, but also for the remainder of the war. Schuyler to Washington, 8 Aug. 1781 (draft), NYSL, MSS. Div., cf. Paltsits, *Minutes*, 2: 754–55, which do not mention the particulars Schuyler cited; the 30 July entry refers only to "some Scheme against the welfare of the State." J. McKinstry to Schuyler, 5 Aug. 1781, NYPL, S Papers.

44. The legend includes the following details for which there is little or no documentation, or for which the extant evidence is actually at variance: that the family was "in the front hall, with the doors wide open," taking the air; that three guards were asleep in the basement and three others stationed in the garden; that a servant announced there was a stranger at the back gate who wished to see Schuyler and that Schuyler took alarm, ordered the house closed up, and hurried his family upstairs as the assailants attacked the house; that Schuyler fired a pistol from the attic to alarm the guards or "arouse the city"; that Mrs. Schuyler suddenly discovered that they had left the six-month-old baby (Catherine) downstairs and that the general refused to let her go below; that his daughter Margaret (Mrs. Stephen Van Rensselaer) ran down to fetch the infant, and as she reached the "upper hall by a private way," the leader of the raiders, "Walter Meyer," accosted her, thinking she was a servant, and asked where her master was; that she replied he had gone to alarm the town, whereupon Meyer collected his men and fled; that as Margaret fled up the stairs, an Indian hurled a tomahawk that lodged in the banister and left a mark that is still claimed to have been caused by the blow; that (after Meyer had collected his men) "At this moment the General threw open the door and cried out in a loud voice, 'Come on, my brave fellows! Surround the damned rascals!' " (Another version is that Schuyler called from a third-floor window as if to rally men around the house; Schuyler's own version was that he did so from a second-floor window; reference to his throwing open a door might be a variation of opening a shuttered window.) The story includes the point that when the marauders fled, they carried off three of the guards, who were captured for want of arms, their weapons having been put out of reach of her little son by Schuyler's daughter Angelica (Mrs. John B. Church). Lossing, *Schuyler*, 2: 419–20; Georgina Schuyler, *The Schuyler Mansion* (New York, 1911), 34–35; Schuyler *Colonial New York*, 2: 275–77; Baxter, *Godchild*, 201–3. The "tomahawk story" is very curious. Schuyler did not mention anything about it in his versions of the affair that remain. The character of the mark in the banister is none too convincing a gash for such an instrument to make. Catherine Van Rensselaer Schuyler's reminiscences (in Baxter, *Godchild*) are not reliable in every detail, and they are inconsistent. If, for example, Margaret Schuyler Van Rensselaer fled up the main stairs, whose banister bears the mark allegedly caused by a tomahawk that was thrown at her, it is curious that Catherine mentioned that her sister reached the upper hall by "a private way," which probably means the small stairs linking the upper and lower halls and that are closed off by doors above and below. Her allegation that three guards were kidnapped by the raiders does not square with Schuyler's request for the return of only two men in Schuyler to Barry St. Leger, 1 Nov.

1781, British Museum, Add. MSS., Haldimand Papers, 21835/121. See also Victor Hugo Palt-sits, "The Attempt to Capture General Philip Schuyler During the American Revolution As told by an eye witness," *The Quarterly Journal of the New York State Historical Association* 10 (October, 1929): 351–53. This account, like an anonymously drafted manuscript (signed "Clio") in the Van Rensselaer Family Papers, NYSL, MSS. Div., contains a curious mixture of fact and fiction.

45. Schuyler to H. Glen, [7 Aug. 1781] "Tuesday eveng. 9 oClock," NYSL, MSS. Div.

46. Schuyler to Washington, 8 Aug. 1781 (draft), ibid. Cf. Schuyler to G. Clinton, 9 Aug. 1781, *GCP,* 7: 184–86. John Van Zandt (1767–1858), then a boy of about fourteen, later remembered hearing the signal gun from the Schuyler house when the raiders surprised the general. Joel Munsell, *The Annals of Albany,* 10 vols. (Albany, 1850–59) 10: 413.

47. *GCP,* 7: 184–86, 193–95; *WGW,* 12: 491–92. Paltsits, *Minutes,* 2: 758–66. J. Mc-Kinstry to Schuyler, 8, 9 Aug. 1781, NYPL, S Papers. For an account of one of the raiding parties against Stillwater see "Lt. Jones' Declaration, 14 Aug 1781," PAC, Haldimand Papers, B. Vol. 176 (M. G. 21), Jones reported rumors that Washington had written Schuyler, inti-mating that a French fleet was destined for the mouth of the Saint Lawrence, and that "Schuyler was falling off daily, from the Rebels, & would [have] come in long ago, were he not apprehensive of an ill reception on Acct. of his forward behavior at Johnstown." Mention of Johnstown probably refers to Schuyler's disarming Tryon County Loyalists in January 1776 and placing Sir John Johnson under parole. There were repeated rumors of his Loyalist sympathies.

48. Col. B. St. Leger to Capt. Mathews, 17 Aug. 1781 (copy) endorsed received 19 Aug. 1781, PAC, Haldimand Papers, B. Vol. 134 (M. G. 21).

49. *PAH,* 2: 666; *WGW,* 23: 2.

50. Paltsits, *Minutes,* 2: 758–66; A. Ten Broeck to Schuyler, 22 Aug. 1781, NYPL, S Papers.

51. Fitzpatrick, *Washington Diaries,* 2: 248–50. Mackesy, *War for America,* 415. Larrabee, *Decision at the Chesapeake,* 250–53, 270, 280–81. Rice and Brown, *American Campaigns of Rochambeau's Army,* 1: 41–42, 255.

52. Joseph Lewis's Receipt, 24 Aug. 1781; Francis Marshall's Receipt, 19 Sept. 1781, NYPL, S Papers: Personal-Household Accts. Schuyler paid fifty-five shillings "procn." in specie for five-and-a-half weeks' rent of the house at Morristown. *PAH,* 2: 668–69. R. Morris to Schuyler, 29 Aug. 1781, Library of Congress: Robert Morris Official Letterbook A.

53. Schuyler to R. Morris, 30–31 Aug. 1781, NYSL, MSS. Div. Hanson Coll.; R. Morris to Schuyler, 4, 14 Sept. 1781; T. Russell to Schuyler, 5 Oct. 1781; R. Peters to Commissioners for Indian Affairs in N. Dept., 14 Sept. 1781; W. Heath to Schuyler, 2 Sept. 1781, NYPL, S Papers. Schuyler to W. Heath, 29 Aug. 1781, Mass. Institute Technology, Heath Papers.

54. *GCP,* 7: 318–319. Schuyler to W. Heath, 10 Sept. 1781, Mass. Institute Technology, Heath Papers. J. Stark to Schuyler, 11 Sept. 1781, Dartmouth College Library, Wheelock Coll.; Stark, *Memoir,* 250. J. Stark to Schuyler, 13 Sept. 1781, NYPL, S Papers.

55. Swiggett, *War Out of Niagara,* 237. Willcox, *Sir Henry Clinton,* 418–19, 436–37, 446.

56. Stark, *Memoir,* 252–53. J. Stark to Schuyler, 16 Sept. 1781, NYPL, S Papers; *PAH,* 2: 676–77.

57. NYSJ, 26 Oct. 1781.

58. *PAH,* 2: 676–77, 679 n.

59. Schuyler to S. Van Rensselaer, 18 Sept. 1781, NYSL, MSS. Div.

60. M. Willett to Schuyler, 22 Sept. 1781; J. Stark to Schuyler, 23, 25 Sept. 1781, NYPL, S Papers. Stark, *Memoir,* 261. Schuyler to W. Heath, 4 Oct. 1781, Mass. Institute Technology, Heath Papers. Sosin, *Revolutionary Frontier,* 134. Graymont, *Iroquois,* 246–50. Peckham, *Toll of Independence,* 91.

61. C. Stark to Schuyler, 8 Oct. 1781; J. Stark to Schuyler, 9 Oct. 1781; M. Willett to Schuyler, 11 Oct. 1781, NYPL, S Papers. Schuyler to J. Dean, 9 Oct. 1781, NYSL, MSS. Div. Schuyler to H. Glen, 10 Oct. 1781, U.S. Naval Academy Museum.

62. *GCP,* 7: 395–96; Stark, *Memoir,* 271. Schuyler to [generals Rossiter and Fellows(?)] 12 Oct. 1781 (copy), Henry Ford Museum, Dearborn, Mich.

63. *GCP,* 7: 398–99, 404. J. Stark to Schuyler, 13, 14, 15 Oct. 1781; W. Heath to Schuyler, 12 Oct. 1781; Schuyler to W. Heath, 15 Oct. 1781, NYPL, S Papers. Stark, *Memoir,* 274–75, 283.

64. J. Stark to Schuyler, 13, 21 Oct. 1781; C. Stark to Schuyler, 18 Oct. 1781, NYPL, S Papers.

65. Schuyler to C. Stark, 22 Oct. 1781, ibid. Misc. Mili. Papers. Stark, *Memoir,* 276.

66. NYSJ, 15, 19 Nov. 1781.

67. Schuyler's draft resolutions 1780(?) 1781(?), NYPL, S Papers, cf. NYSJ, 15 Nov. 1781.

68. Judd, *Van Cortlandt Papers,* 2: 445–47. Stark, *Memoir,* 272, 274–75, 281–83. J. Stark to Schuyler, 21, 25 Oct. 1781; C. Stark to Schuyler, 29 Oct. 1781, NYPL, S Papers. Schuyler to Pres. Congress, 29 Oct. 1781, PCC, NAR 173. Peckham, *Toll of Independence,* 93; *GCP,* 7: 404.

69. Schuyler to B. St. Leger, 1 Nov. 1781, British Museum Add. MSS., Haldimand Papers 21835/121. Schuyler to Washington, 2 Nov. 1781, HL. Baxter, *Godchild,* 203, says a third guard named Nanse Corlies was carried off by the marauders with John Tubbs and John Ward, and that these three were later rewarded by Schuyler with gifts of farms in Saratoga County. However, Schuyler's letter specified only two guards, and the third was the one wounded in the defense of the house. Brandow, *Story of Old Saratoga,* 364, is most nearly accurate in stating that the three men were John Ward, John Tubbs, and John Cokely [Cockley], and that Schuyler gave them 275 acres, which they divided by drawing lots. This agrees with the land records, which show Schuyler's grant of 270 acres in the Saratoga patent to Ward, Tubbs, "and others" on 18 June 1784. *Index to the Public Records of the County of Albany, State of New York, 1630–1894: Grantors,* 14 vols. (Albany, 1902–1907), 11: 6520–21. Correspondence concerning the return of the captives and silver is in: R. Mathews to Dr. Smyth at St. John's, 4 Oct. 1781, PAC, Haldimand Papers, B. Vol. 134 (M. G. 21); St. Leger to Schuyler, 7 Nov. 1781, NYPL, S Papers; G. Smyth to Capt. Mathews, 21 Sept., 30 Oct. 1782; Terence Smyth to Capt. Mathews, 26 Oct. 1782; F. Haldimand to Schuyler, 8 Nov. 1782, British Museum, Add MSS., Haldimand Papers 21837/456/401/389 and 21835/134.

70. Schuyler to Washington, 2 Nov. 1781, HL, cf. Schuyler to Washington (undated) MNHP, LWS Coll. Schuyler to Washington, 15 Nov. 1781, Library of Congress, Washington Papers.

71. Upton, *The Loyal Whig,* 134–35.

72. Schuyler to W. Heath, 17 Nov. 1781, Mass. Institute Technology: Heath Papers. Heath to Schuyler, 21 Nov. 1781, NYPL, S Papers.

73. Flexner, *Washington,* 2: 472. Reference to Hamilton's arrival and trip to Saratoga is in *PAH,* 26: 419–20. Schuyler to J. Duane, 6 Dec. 1781, NYHS, Duane Papers.

74. Schuyler to J. Duane, 6 Dec. 1781, NYHS, Duane Papers. C. Stark to Schuyler, 24 Nov. 1781, NYPL, S Papers. C. Yates's certificates, 1 Dec. (two), 30 Dec. 1781, ibid., Misc. Military Accts.

CHAPTER 15

1. Mackesy, *War for America*, 490, 494. Graymont, *Iroquois*, 256–58. Peckham, *Toll of Independence*, 98–99. Peckham's tallies (130–31) for the entire war include 1,331 military and 215 naval engagements; an estimated 10,000 Americans died in camp, and 8,500 prisoners died in captivity. Numbers killed in action were 6,824 (probably 1,000 more), 8,445 wounded, 18,152 captured, 1,426 missing, and 100 desertions. These figures do not, however, include counts for men in state regiments and militia units or soldiers on Schuyler's Canadian expedition of 1775–76.

2. McDonald, *Hamilton*, 51–52.

3. A. McDougall to Schuyler, 12 Oct. 1781, NYPL, S Papers. Davis, *Burr Memoirs*, 1: 231. Herbert S. Parmet and Marie B. Hecht, *Aaron Burr: Portrait of an Ambitious Man* (New York, 1967), 19–22, 55.

4. *PAH*, 26: 450. Milton Lomask, *Aaron Burr: The Years from Princeton to Vice President, 1756–1805* (New York, 1979), 78–79, 81–82.

5. Schuyler to J. Lawrence and M. Smith, 10 Jan. 1782, Mass. Institute Technology: William Heath Papers. Schuyler to J. Cuyler, 14 Jan. 1782, NYPL, S (Indian) Papers. Mackesy, *War for America*, 489. Schuyler to Washington, 2 Nov. 1781, HL. Sparks, *Correspondence*, 3: 462–63. *WGW*, 23: 471 n, 467. Schuyler to Washington, 16 Feb. 1782 (draft), NYSL, MSS. Div., and Fitzpatrick, *Calendar,* 3: 2039; 2050. J. Dean to Schuyler, 12, 20 Feb., 4 Mar. 1782, NYPL, S Papers.

6. Schuyler to W. Heath, 9 Feb. 1782, Mass. Institute Technology: Heath Papers. W. Heath, to Schuyler, 26 Feb. 1782, NYPL, S Papers.

7. Sparks, *Correspondence*, 3: 462–63; *WGW*, 23: 487. Schuyler to Washington, 16 Feb. 1782, NYSL, MSS. Div.

8. R. R. Livingston to Schuyler, 13 Feb. 1782 (marked received 21 Feb.), *LMCC*, VI 306 n–307 n, but full text in NYPL, S Papers.

9. NYSJ, 23 Feb. 1782. Upton, *Loyal Whig*, 133–34, notes that Smith explained to Sir Henry Clinton that leaking copies of the clandestine negotiation would prompt Loyalists to move to Vermont and encourage Governor Clinton and other leaders to steer New York back to the Crown in order to prevent the losses of Vermont territory.

10. L. R. Gerlach, "Connecticut, Congress, and Vermont."

11. E. L'Hommedieu to J. Taylor, 28 Feb. 1782, NYSL, MSS. Div. L'Hommedieu Papers. Fitzpatrick, *Calendar,* 3: 2053. NYSJ, 25, 26 Feb., 4, 13, 20, 25 Mar., 1, 13 April 1782. Mitchell, *Hamilton,* 1: 264.

12. NYSJ, 20, 23, 26 Mar., 1, 2, 14 April 1782.

13. NYSJ, 28 Feb., 1, 19, 28 Mar., 4 April 1782.

14. Burnett, *Congress,* 515–16.

15. NYSJ, 25, 26 Feb., 21, 22 Mar., 10, 11 April 1782. *PAH*, 3: 477; Hamilton later handled Church and Wadsworth's legal affairs and bank business.

16. NYSJ, 28 Feb. 5, 11, 12 Mar., 12, 13 April 1782.

17. Schuyler's draft of an act to regulate surveyors of lands, 1782 (endorsed read in Senate, 1 and 4 Mar. and then referred to committee of the whole), NYPL, S Papers. NYSJ, 1, 23 Mar. 1782. *PAH*, 3: 138.

18. Schuyler to C. Yates, 1 May 1782 (copy), NYPL, S Papers: surveyor gen. Schuyler to M. Visscher, Albany City Clerk, 26 April 1782 (draft), NYSL, MSS. Div., cf. M. Vischer to Schuyler, 25 April 1782 and Albany Common Council Resolutions, 4 May 1782 (copy), NYPL, S Papers: surveyor gen.

19. NYPL, S Papers: surveyor gen. include: J. Sanders and W. Schemerhorn to Schuyler,

3 May 1782; Locations of Jacob Ford et al., 14 May 1782; P. Schuyler, atty. for E. L'Hommedieu and N. Platt to P. Schuyler, Surveyor Gen., 17 May 1782; undated list of certificates
delivered by Judge Z. Platt; undated list of nineteen tracts of land totaling 21,400 acres;
certificates and transfers filed by Col. Waterman, 29 May 1782; copy of act to prevent grants
or locations of lands, 25 July 1782; description of a tract of land (draft), 3 Aug. 1782; Schuyler's
certificate to Wheeler Douglass, 6 Sept. 1782; a variety of petitions for land dated 17, 20
May, 3, 14, 26 June, 31 July, 13 Sept., 7 Oct., 20 Nov., 7, 16 Dec., 1782. See also NYSL, MSS.
Div. for Peter W. Yates to Schuyler, 14 May 1782.

20. Schuyler to Washington, 3 May 1782 (unsigned draft), HL; *PAH*, 3: 83; *WGW*, 24:
119. Schuyler to Inhabitants of Tryon Co., 1 May 1782, NYSL, MSS. Div. Abbott Coll.

21. Cornet Cuyler's receipt, 10 June 1782, NYPL, S Papers: Personal-Household Accts.
Dirk Swart's lease, 28 June 1782, NYPL, S Papers. Schuyler to Col. Read, 20 June 1782,
NYSL MSS. Div. R. Morris to Schuyler 13 June 1782, Library of Congress: R. Morris's
Official Letterbook C. Schuyler to R. Morris, 28 June 1782 (copy), Mass. Institute Tech-
nology: T. Pickering Papers, cf. draft in NYPL, S Papers.

22. Palmer, *Way of the Fox*, 187, 191. Lanctot, *Canada*, 207. *WGW*, 9: 497–505. R. R.
Livingston to Schuyler, 11 June 1782 (marked answered June 22), NYPL, S Papers.

23. Lanctot, *Canada*, 207, 208. Palmer, *Way of the Fox*, 184.

24. Kenney, *Albany: Crossroads of Liberty,* 73. Alexander Flick, ed., *History of the State of
New York*, 10 vols. (New York, 1933–37), 5: 72. Freeman, *Washington*, 5: 416–17. Baxter,
Godchild, 256. Anon. letter, 26 July 1782, British Museum Add MSS.: Haldimand Papers
21837 f. 279 and G. Smyth to Capt. Mathews, 3 Aug. 1782, ibid. f. 292 remarks "Washington's
business at Albany is not yet made known."

25. NYSJ, 8–11 July 1782.

26. Mitchell, *Hamilton*, 1: 266. NYSJ, 16, 18, 20, 23, 24, 25 July 1782; *PAH*, 3: 114–17.

27. *PAH*, 3: 114–17. Mitchell, *Hamilton*, 1: 265. NYSJ, 22, 23 July 1782.

28. Mitchell, *Hamilton*, 1: 268. Contrary to what Mitchell alleges, there is no evidence
that Schuyler *withdrew* (in Hamilton's favor) from candidacy as a congressman. NYSJ, 22
July 1782.

29. NYSJ, 19, 20 July 1782.

30. NYSJ, 20, 22 July 1782.

31. Mitchell, *Hamilton*, 1: 266, argues that the resolutions were "unmistakably written
by Hamilton," but they are as certainly redolent of Schuyler's own thought and style. And
see *PAH*, 3: 110–13; and Hamilton to R. Morris, 22 July 1782 (114–17) refers to the resolutions
with no hint that he had written them although he did claim to have been active in work
on "solid" financial arrangements.

32. *PAH*, 3: 171–77.

33. Ibid., 176 n–177 n. Receipt of Balentine and Webster, 4 Oct. 1782 (for £9), NYPL, S
Papers: Personal-Household Accts. See also Young, *Democratic Republicans,* 76, and E. James
Ferguson, *The Power of the Purse: A History of American Public Finance, 1776–1790* (Chapel Hill,
N.C.; 1961), 142–43, 150–51.

34. J. Duane to Schuyler, 16 Aug. 1782, NYPL, S Papers (mentions Schuyler's letter to
him of July 25—not found—in which the illness was cited). Statement of Sampson Dyckman's Account with Schuyler, 4 Feb. 1788, ibid., Personal-Household Accts. The 265.5 acres
were sold for £3 per acre, and by 4 Feb. 1788 the unpaid balance due on 15 May 1783 was
£268.19.0 plus £88.18.0 interest, a total of £357.17.0.

35. J. Duane to Schuyler, 16 Aug. 1782, NYPL, S Papers (version in *LMCC*, 6: 445–46
incomplete). See also Duane to Schuyler, 18 July 1782, NYPL, S Papers, (*LMCC*, 5: 386).

36. Schuyler to Earl Stirling, 20 Sept. 1782, Boston Public Library. Schuyler to W. Heath,

15 Oct. 1782, Mass. Institute Technology: Heath Papers. T. Pickering to Schuyler, 17 Sept. 1782 (marked answered 25 Sept., letter not found), NYPL, S Papers.

37. H. Glen to Schuyler, 10 Nov. 1782, NYPL, S Papers. Schuyler to H. Glen, 12 Nov. 1782, Mass. Institute Technology: Sedgwick Papers.

38. Schuyler to Washington, 20, 21 Sept. 1782, Fitzpatrick, *Calendar,* 3: 2237, 2239, and NYPL, S Papers. Schuyler to Pres. J. Hanson, 21 Sept. 1782 with extract of 3 Sept. 1782 letter to Schuyler, *PCC,* NAR 173.

39. Schuyler to W. Heath, 15, 23 Oct. 1782, Mass. Institute Technology: Heath Papers.

40. G. Smyth to Capt. Mathews, 8, 21 Sept. 1782; T. Smyth to Capt. Mathews, 26 Oct. 1782, British Museum Add MSS.: Haldimand Papers, 21837/337/356/389. G. Clinton to Schuyler, 14 Oct. 1782, NYPL, S Papers. Ironically, a year later George Smyth requested Schuyler's aid in obtaining some books and papers he had left in Albany. Asking that his son not be insulted while on a business errand, Smyth also begged Schuyler's "notice" of a former ensign who was en route to New York City to take passage to Europe. G. Smith to Schuyler, 4 Nov. 1783, NYPL, S Papers.

41. Von Riedesel to F. Haldimand, 29 Oct., 2, 7, Nov. 1782, PAC: Haldimand Papers, B. Vol. 137 ff. 308, 322, 330)M. G. 21). F. Haldimand to Schuyler, 8 Nov. 1782 (copy), British Museum, Add MSS. Haldimand Papers, 21835/134. Von Riedesel to Schuyler, 10 Nov. 1782, NYPL, S Papers.

CHAPTER 16

1. Mitchell, *Hamilton,* 1: 279–290.

2. Schuyler to Elizabeth Hamilton, 2 Dec. 1782, NYSL, MSS. Div.

3. Fitzpatrick, *Calendar,* 3: 2287, 2291; *WGW,* 25: 403. Schuyler to Treasury Board, 3 Oct. 1786, NYPL, S (Indian) Papers, gives his departure from Albany as 20 Nov. 1782 and his return from Philadelphia as Jan. 15, 1783.

4. *LMCC,* 6: 567–68; 7: 23, 190, 190 n. See also Burnett, *Congress,* 583–84, and Jennings B. Sanders, *Evolution of Executive Departments of the Continental Congress, 1774–1789* (Durham, N.C.; 1935), 119–20.

5. Richard H. Kohn, "The Inside History of the Newburgh Conspiracy: America and the Coup d'Etat," *The William and Mary Quarterly:,* 3d Ser. (April 1970) 27: 190–92. Hereafter cited as Kohn, "Newburgh Conspiracy." See also Champagne, *Alexander McDougall,* 185–87.

6. Kohn, "Newburgh Conspiracy," 192–93.

7. Ibid., 194.

8. Ibid., 194–95 and passim.

9. NYSJ, 27 Jan., 3 Mar. 1783.

10. NYSJ, 13, 26, 27 Feb.; 1, 3, 6, 8 Mar. 1783. J. Cochran to Schuyler, 9 Mar. 1783, NYPL, S Papers. Saffron, *Surgeon to Washington,* 248. NYSJ, 4 Feb., 24, 25 Mar. 1783. Harry R. Warfel, ed., *Letters of Noah Webster* (New York, 1953), 5–7, 55–58, 527. Don R. Gerlach, *Twenty Years of the "Promotion of Literature": The Regents of the University of the State of New York, 1784–1804* (Albany, N.Y.; 1974), 2–3 and passim.

11. NYSJ, 27, 28 Jan., 7, 27, Feb., 4, 6, 12, 22, Mar. 1783

12. NYSJ, 24 Mar. 1783.

13. NYSJ, 27 Jan., 4 Feb. 1783.

14. NYSJ, 10, 14, 22, 26 Mar. 1783.

15. NYSJ, 11, 15 Feb., 1, 4, 15 Mar. 1783. Linda Grant DePauw, *The Eleventh Pillar: New York State and the Federal Constitution* (Ithaca, N.Y.; 1966), 33–36.

16. NYSJ, 8, 10, 12, 22 Mar. 1783.

17. Gerlach, *Philip Schuyler*, 70, 72, 136, 210; *PAH*, 3: 257–59, 266–67. Gertrude Van Rensselaer's receipt, 10 Feb. 1784, NYPL, S Papers: Personal-Household Accts., indicates that Van Rensselaer's widow received a £250 annuity in lieu of her dower rights, etc.

18. NYSJ, 5, 14, 17 Mar. 1783. *Laws of the State of N.Y.*, 6th Sess., 1783, c.28; 8th Sess., 1785, c.28. Julius Goebel, Jr., et al., eds., *The Law Practice of Alexander Hamilton: Documents and Commentary*, 5 vols. (New York, 1964–1981), 1: 546 n. *Report of the Regents of the University on the Boundaries of the State of New York*, 2 vols. (Albany, 1884), 2: 153, 156, 182–84, 189, 191, 194, 205, 210, 216.

19. Kohn, "Newburgh Conspiracy," 189, 207, 209–11.

20. *AAs*, 1: 237, and 2: 1039–40, indicate that he had ridden the thirty to thirty-five miles between Albany and Saratoga in about four hours.

21. Although full documentary evidence of this is not available, it is clear that Hamilton wrote Schuyler in February. Mention of such correspondence and of other letters not found (Mar. 18, 25, April 2, 23) is made in *PAH*, 3: 255, 293, 305, 314, 348–51.

22. Paul David Nelson, "Horatio Gates at Newburgh, 1783: A Misunderstood Role," with a rebuttal by Richard H. Kohn, *The William and Mary Quarterly*: 3d Ser. (January 1972) 29: 152–53, 156–58. See also Nelson, *Gates*, 267–76; Champagne, *Alexander McDougall*, 195–96; Richard H. Kohn, *Eagle and Sword: The Federalists and the Creation of the Military Establishment in America, 1783–1802* (New York, 1975), 18–21, 25–27.

23. Lossing, *Schuyler*, 2: 427, citing an autographed letter, 17 Mar. 1783. Like a few other documents cited by Lossing, this one has evidently disappeared or has been lost, for I have not discovered it in archival collections such as the NYPL or NYSL.

24. NYSJ, 17, 22, 24, 27, 28 Mar. 1783. Franklin B. Hough, ed., *Proceedings of the Commissioners of Indian Affairs, Appointed by Law for the Extinguishment of Indian Titles in the State of New York [1784–1790]*, 2 vols. (Albany, 1861), 1: 9 n–10 n. Paul V. Lutz, "Land Grants for Service in the Revolution," *The New-York Historical Society Quarterly* (July 1964) 48: 227–30.

25. J. N. Bleecker to A. I. Truax, 2 April 1783; Schuyler's lease to I. Green, 9 April 1783, NYPL, S (land) Papers. J. Franklin Jameson, *The American Revolution Considered as a Social Movement* (Princeton, 1926), 36–46, suggests "overthrowing . . . old-fashioned features which still continued to exist in the land laws." Commenting mostly on entail, primogeniture, and franchise requirements, Jameson argued too much from the limited evidence presented for democratizing land ownership, and he completely overlooked other evidence that indicates the continuation of old usages.

26. Schuyler's deposition, 4 April 1783, NYSL, MSS. Div. Schuyler to Inhabitants of King's District, 4 April 1783, NYPL, S (land) Papers. Schuyler to Col. [William] Whiting, 4 April 1783, Haverford College Library, Haverford, Pa.

27. Young, *Democratic Republicans*, 31, 33–34. See also Goebel, *Law Practice of Alexander Hamilton*, 3: 330–31.

28. P. Van Rensselaer to G. Clinton, 7 June 1783, NYSL, MSS. Div., Van Rensselaer Family Papers. Philip (1747–98) was the son of Kiliaen Van Rensselaer; Kiliaen and Mrs. Schuyler's father, John, were brothers.

29. Extract from Resolves of a General Committee held in Fredericksburgh Precinct, 12 April 1783, PAC, Haldimand Papers, B, Vol. 142, f.316 (M. G. 21). See also Jackson Turner Main, *Political Parties before the Constitution* (Chapel Hill, N.C.; 1973), 15–16, 126–27.

30. J. Cochran to Schuyler, 4–9 April 1783, NYPL, S Papers (marked answered May 1; Schuyler's reply not found). For examples of Schuyler's surveyor general work see NYPL,

S (surveyor general) Papers: petitions of 4 Jan., 22 Feb., 1 April, 13, 21 June, 9 July, 5 Aug., 15 Dec. 1783; Schuyler's receipt for John Taylor et al., 26 Feb. 1783; Schuyler's receipt for Ezra L'Hommedieu, 10 Mar. 1783; Schuyler's receipt for Zepheniah Platt, 20 Mar. 1783; Schuyler's receipt for Eleazer West and David Pixley, 16 Aug. 1783; Wheeler Douglass to Schuyler, 22 June 1783.

31. J. M. Scott to Schuyler, 9 July 1783, NYPL, S (land) Papers. Scott's calculation of unsold tracts included acreages of 21,850, 19,500, 10,850 and 16,950. At twenty-five to forty shillings per acre the land might be sold for about £85,000 to £136,000! See also Gerlach, *Philip Schuyler*, 218–19.

32. Kenney, *Albany: Crossroads of Liberty*, 73–74.

33. Schuyler to Johannes Ball, 13 May 1783, Mass. Institute Technology: Norcross Papers.

34. C[harles] G.[ould] to Schuyler, 28 April 1783, Yale Univ. Library, cf. copy NYPL, S Papers. No trace of any answer to Gould in 1783 or 1784 has been found.

35. Agatha Evans to Schuyler, 9 Nov. 1783, 14 Jan. 1784, NYPL, S Papers, and other correspondence and papers on the Bradstreet estate, ibid.

36. Mr. St. John to Schuyler, 23 Dec. 1783, ibid. N.Y. Bureau of Historic Sites, *Schuyler Mansion: A Historic Structure Report* (1979), 34–37. For other evidence of Schuyler's gardening see Conradt Ruby's bill, 1787–92 and Mott Sullivan's receipt, 30 Aug. 1790, NYPL, S Papers; Philip Schuyler Account Book, AIHA.

37. Schuyler to F. Haldimand, 17 April, 18 June 1783, British Museum, Add. MSS. (Haldimand Papers), 21835/151, 166. F. Haldimand to Schuyler, 8 July 1783, NYPL, S Papers.

38. F. Haldimand to Schuyler, 30 June 1783, NYPL, S Papers.

39. Schuyler to F. Haldimand, 16 July 1783, British Museum, Add. MSS. (Haldimand Papers) 21835/176.

40. *PAH*, 3: 348–51.

41. J. Lansing to Schuyler, 8 May 1783, NYPL, S Papers. Schuyler to Contractors [John N. Bleecker] for furnishing the Army and Indians, 11 May 1783, NYSL, MSS. Div.

42. Minutes of Council at Onondago (copy), 2 July 1783; A. Maclean to E. Douglass (copy), 16 July 1783, NYPL, S (Indian) Papers. Graymont, *Iroquois*, 265–66.

43. Schuyler to Capt. Brant, 29 July 1783; Schuyler's Speech [address] to the Indians (draft), 29 July 1783, NYPL, S (Indian) Papers.

44. Schuyler to Pres. Congress (draft), 29 July 1783, ibid.; Graymont, *Iroquois*, 264.

45. For example of Schuyler's lumber sales see Charles Robinson's receipts, 17 May 1783; copy of Account of Edward Aubery and Mary Carpenter with Jacob Jordan and Schuyler, 7 July 1787, NYPL, S Papers: Personal-Household Accts. Derby Lendsay's receipt, 3 June 1783, Rockefeller Archive Center: Schuyler Coll.

46. J. Lansing to Schuyler, 7 Nov. 1777; R. Varick to Schuyler, 12 Nov. 1777, NYPL, S Papers.

47. J. Lansing to Schuyler, 24 May, 3 June 1783, ibid.

48. Desmond, *Hamilton's Wife*, 81, 89, 127–28 says Peggy eloped because her father refused to forgive Van Rensselaer for introducing John Church to Angelica. This is a dubious possibility because when Church met Schuyler's daughter (1776–77) the patroon was only twelve or thirteen. Maunsell Van Rensselaer, *Annals of the Van Rensselaers in the United States* (Albany, 1888), 54–55. For pictures of Margaret and Stephen Van Rensselaer see *The Van Rensselaers of the Manor of Rensselaerwyck* (1888), limited edition of fifty copies, copyright by Mary King Van Rensselaer).

49. Schuyler to Sir Guy Carleton, 1 July 1783; Carleton to Schuyler (copy), 8 Aug. 1783, Public Record Office (London), Sir Guy Carleton Papers.

50. Schuyler to B. Franklin, 1 July 1783, American Philosophical Society. *PAH,* 3: 416–17, and see 26: 434.

51. Schuyler to S. Van Rensselaer, 17 July 1783; Schuyler to Mr. and Mrs. S. Van Rensselaer, [7(?) 14(?)] Aug. (marked Thursday), 1783, N.J. Historical Society. Schuyler to S. Van Rensselaer, 10 July 1783, NYSL, MSS. Div. Schuyler to S. Van Rensselaer, 13 July 1783, Campus Martius Museum, Marietta, Ohio, Slack Coll. Schuyler to S. Van Rensselaer, 17 July 1783, AIHA. Schuyler to Mrs. [Margaret] Van Rensselaer, 8 Aug. 1783, held by C. E. Rugg, Schuylerville, N.Y.

52. Callahan, *Henry Knox,* 211–12. Frederick R. Stevens, "New York in the Society of the Cincinnati," *New York History* (January 1944), 25: 18–31.

53. Washington to Schuyler, 15 July 1783, NYSL, MSS. Div.

54. Elizabeth Cometti, ed., trans., *Seeing America and Its Great Men: The Journal and Letters of Count Francesco dal Verme, 1783–1784* (Charlottesville, Va.; 1969), 11–13, 106 n.

55. Ibid., 13, 106 n–107 n; Louis Atyataghronghta is here mistaken for an Oneida, perhaps because he lived among the Oneida before settling among the Saint Regis Indians. Schuyler to S. Van Rensselaer, 17 July 1783, AIHA. Schuyler's account with James Caldwell, 1783–84, NYSL, MSS. Div.

56. Cometti, *Seeing America,* 13.

57. Ibid., 13–15. Curtis Hodge to Schuyler, 22 July 1783, NYPL, S (surveyor general) Papers. The letter, dated at Cambridge, is in Schuyler's hand, which suggests that Hodge could not write and that Schuyler was at Cambridge (southeast of Saratoga) on the day after Washington left Saratoga.

58. Cometti, *Seeing America,* 15–19.

59. Ibid., 19.

60. *PAH,* 3: 430–43.

61. Mitchell, *Hamilton,* 1: 330–31.

62. Ibid., 331–32, cf. *PAH,* 3: 417, 433 n.

63. The Six Nations to Schuyler, 8 Sept. 1783, British Museum, Add. MSS. (Haldimand Papers), 21779/121. See also Schuyler to Elias Boudinot, 11 Oct. 1783, *PCC, NAR* 173.

64. J. Dean to Schuyler, 18 Sept. 1783, NYPL, S Papers. Schuyler to Elias Boudinot, 25 Sept. 1783, *PCC,* NAR 173.

65. A Proclamation by the U.S. in Congress, 22 Sept. 1783, NYPL, S (Indian) Papers: Rare Books Div. Copy of Congressional Committee Reports on Indian Affairs and the Western Country, 25 Sept. 1783, NYPL, S (Indian) Papers.

66. Schuyler to Elias Boudinot, 11 Oct. 1783, *PCC, NAR* 173.

67. Answer to Gen. Schuyler's 29 July 1783 speech, from the Six Nations meeting at Loyal Village, 22 Oct. 1783, British Museum, Add. MSS. (Haldimand Papers), 21779/147-148. J. Brant to Schuyler, 19 Oct. 1783, HL. J. Brant to Schuyler, 23 Oct. 1783 (copies in Mohawk and English); B. Lincoln to Schuyler, 14 Oct. 1783; T. Pickering to Schuyler, 18 Nov. 1783, NYPL, S Papers. Schuyler to H. Knox, 5(?) 6(?) Nov. 1783, Mass Institute Technology: Knox Papers.

68. E. Douglass to Secretary at War, B. Lincoln (copy), 18 Aug. 1783, NYPL, S (Indian) Papers.

69. E. Boudinot to Schuyler, 29 Oct. 1783, Hist. Soc. of Pa. Boudinot Papers. *LMCC,* 7: 359–60, does not present the entire letter.

70. Schuyler to Pres. Congress, 16 Dec. 1783, *PCC,* NAR 173.

71. Kohn, *Eagle and Sword,* 55–56. Graymont, *Iroquois,* 267–69.

72. Schuyler's address to the Six Nations, [11] Jan. 1784, British Museum, Add MSS.

(Haldimand Papers), 21779/149–154 and PAC, B Vol. 119 (M. G. 21). Draft of speech, 11 Jan. 1784, NYPL, S (Indian) Papers.

73. Congress's Proclamation (copy), 8 April 1784; T. Mifflin to Schuyler, 8 April 1784, NYPL, S (Indian) Papers. Graymont, *Iroquois,* 264–66.

74. B. St. Leger to Schuyler, (?) Sept. 1783, NYPL, S Papers. For evidence of Schuyler's opposition to disfranchising Loyalists and otherwise depriving them of the rights of citizens see Johnston, *Jay Papers,* 3: 112–14.

75. Johnston, *Jay Papers,* 3: 81–82.

76. Thomas Palmer to Schuyler, 19 Nov. 1783, NYPL, S (surveyor gen.) Papers. Palmer, a fellow state senator, introduced a friend seeking to locate a tract west of the Susquehannah River. Explaining the efforts of other men of Westchester, Orange, and Ulster counties to make a settlement in the Susquehannah valley, Palmer assured Schuyler that this was no "Land Job[b]ing Scheme made up by a few" nor was it their intent "Meerly to Skim of[f] the Low Lands Along the River." They wanted a township seven miles square including rough land as well as smooth, and Palmer assured him that his intercession on their behalf was partly to prevent any "jealousy" from arising "Even [in] Your breast." Schuyler to Peter Colt, 26 Sept., 16 Oct. 1783, Conn. Hist. Soc., Wadsworth Papers. John Flansburgh's receipt, 27 Oct. 1783 and Killian Winney's receipt, 13 Oct. 1783, NYPL, S Papers: Personal-Household Accts.

77. Schuyler to S. Van Rensselaer, 17 Nov. 1783, NYSL, MSS. Div.

78. Schuyler to S. Van Rensselaer, 4, 10 Dec. 1783, ibid. Ludlum, *Early American Winters,* 65.

79. J. Lansing to Schuyler, 26 Dec. 1783, NYPL, S Papers. Champagne, *Alexander McDougall,* 204. Staughton Lynd, "The Mechanics in New York Politics, 1774–1788," *Labor History* (Fall 1964), 5: 235.

80. W. Allen, et al. to Schuyler, 15 Dec. 1783, NYPL, S Papers.

Bibliography

Manuscripts

Albany Institute of History and Art, Albany, New York
    Miscellaneous Schuyler Papers
American Antiquarian Society, Worcester, Massachusetts
    Bradstreet Papers
    U.S. Revolution Papers
    Henry B. Livingston's Orderly Book, 13 June–19 August 1777
    Philip Schuyler's Orderly Book, 29 June–18 August 1777
Boston Public Library, Boston, Massachusetts
    Miscellaneous Manuscripts
British Museum, London: Additional Manuscripts
    Auckland Papers
    Haldimand Papers
    Stevens Transcripts

Buffalo and Erie County Historical Society, Buffalo, New York
    Miscellaneous Manuscripts
Columbia University Libraries, New York City
    John Jay Papers, Butler Library
    Gouverneur Morris Papers, Butler Library
    Peter Van Schaack Papers, Columbiana
Connecticut Historical Society, Hartford
    Jonathan Trumbull, Sr., and Jonathan Trumbull, Jr., Papers
Connecticut State Library, Hartford
    Gov. Joseph Trumbull Collection
    Trumbull Papers
Cornell University Library, Ithaca, New York
    Harmanus Schuyler Papers
Dartmouth College Library, Hanover, New Hampshire
    Bartlett Collection
    Wheelock Collection
Detroit Public Library, Detroit, Michigan
    Burton Historical Collection
Fort Ticonderoga Museum, Fort Ticonderoga, New York
    Miscellaneous Manuscripts
Haverford College Library, Haverford, Pennsylvania
    Miscellaneous Manuscripts
Historical Society of Pennsylvania, Philadelphia
    Elias Boudinot Papers
Henry E. Huntington Library and Art Gallery, San Marino, California
    Schuyler Orderbook and Miscellaneous Papers
John Carter Brown Library, Providence, Rhode Island
    Madison Papers
Library Company of Philadelphia, Philadelphia, Pennsylvania
    Miscellaneous Manuscripts
Library of Congress
    Hamilton Papers
    Schuyler's Memorandum Book, 1776–1779
Maine Historical Society, Portland
    Fogg Collection
Manuscripts in Possession of Private Persons
    B. N. Huntington
    A. J. Morino
    Mrs. H. M. Sage
Marietta College Library, Marietta, Ohio
    Miscellaneous Manuscripts
Massachusetts Historical Society, Boston
    Lincoln Papers
    Miscellaneous Manuscripts

Massachusetts Institute of Technology Library, Cambridge
  Bowdoin-Temple Papers
  Heath Papers
  Jefferson Papers
  Knox Papers
  Pickering Papers
  Sedgwick Papers
  Weare Papers
Morristown National Historical Park, Morristown, New Jersey
  Lloyd W. Smith Collection
  Park Collection
National Archives Microfilm Publications
  Microscopy No. 247, "Papers of the Continental Congress, 1774–1789"
    (The National Archives and Records Service, General Services
    Administration, Washington, 1959)
    Items 63, 153, 154, 166, 170
National Library of Scotland: Edinburgh
  Miscellaneous Manuscripts
New Jersey Historical Society, Newark
  Miscellaneous Manuscripts
New York Genealogical and Biographical Society, New York City
  Miscellaneous Manuscripts
New-York Historical Society, New York City
  De Lancey Papers
  James Duane Papers
  William Duer Papers
  John Lamb Papers
  Robert R. Livingston Collection
  Alexander McDougal Papers
  Miscellaneous Manuscripts: Nicholas Bayard, Grove Bend, John
    Bradstreet, George Clinton, John W. Francis ("Old New York"
    bound volumes of manuscripts), Philip Schuyler
  Philip Schuyler's Saratoga Day Book
New York Public Library, New York City
  Bancroft Collections (Transcripts)
  Bleecker Papers
  Chalmers Manuscripts
  Emmett Collection
  Schuyler Papers
New York State Library, Albany, New York
  Abbott Collection
  Hanson Collection
    Miscellaneous Papers: Schuyler, Lansing, Livingston, L'Hommedieu,
    Van Vechten, John Williams, Melancthon Smith.

Manuscript Diary (copy) of Dr. Alexander Coventry, 1781–1783
Henry Stevens Collection
Records of the Reformed Protestant Dutch Church of Saratoga at
    Schuylerville, Saratoga County, New York (Typewritten
    transcription by the New York Genealogical and Biographical
    Society, December 1913)
Van Rensselaer Family Papers
Elkanah Watson Papers
Pierepont Morgan Library, New York City
    Miscellaneous Manuscripts
Princeton University Library, Princeton, New Jersey
    Andre de Coppet Collection
Public Archives of Canada, Ottawa
    Haldimand Papers
Rhode Island Historical Society, Providence
    Jeremiah Olney Papers
Rockefeller Archive Center, Tarrytown, New York
    Schuyler Family Collection
Franklin D. Roosevelt Library, Hyde Park, New York
    Livingston-Redmond Papers
Rutgers University Library, New Brunswick, New Jersey
    Miscellaneous Manuscripts
Schuyler Mansion, Albany, New York
    Schuyler Family Bible
    Miscellaneous Library
Senate House Museum, Kingston, New York
    Peter Van Gaasbeck Papers
South Carolina Historical Society, Charleston
    Henry Laurens Papers
Union College Library, Schenectady, New York
    Miscellaneous Schuyler Papers
Washington's Headquarters Museum, Newburgh, New York
    Miscellaneous Manuscripts
William L. Clements Library, Ann Arbor, Michigan
    Clinton Papers
    Gage Papers
    Germain Papers
    Greene Papers
    Members of Congress Collection
    Miscellaneous Manuscripts
    James S. Schoff Collection
Yale University Library, New Haven, Connecticut
    Miscellaneous Manuscripts

Government Publications, National

Fitzpatrick, John C., ed., *Calendar of the Correspondence of George Washington with the Officers.* 4 vols. Washington: Government Printing Office, 1915.

————— . *The Writings of George Washington, 1754–1799.* 37 vols. Washington: Government Printing Office, 1931–40.

Force, Peter, ed., *American Archives,* 4th ser., 6 vols. Washington: M. St. Clair Clarke & Peter Force, 1837–46; and 5th ser., 3 vols. Washington: M. St. Clair Clarke & Peter Force, 1848–53.

Ford, Worthington C. et al., eds. *The Journals of the Continental Congress, 1774–1789.* 34 vols. Washington: Government Printing Office, 1904–37.

Hodge, Frederick Webb, ed. *Handbook of American Indians North of Mexico.* 2 vols. Washington: Government Printing Office, 1907–10).

Wold, Ansel, comp. *Biographical Dictionary of the American Congress, 1774–1927.* Washington: Government Printing Office, 1928.

Government Publications, State

Calendar of Historical Manuscripts relating to the War of the Revolution in the Office of the Secretary of State, Albany, N.Y. 2 vols. Albany: Weed, Parsons & Co., 1868.

Catalogue of Maps and Surveys, in the Offices of the Secretary of State, State Engineer and Surveyor, and Comptroller, and the New York State Library. rev. ed. Albany: Charles Van Benthuysen, 1859.

Division of Archives and History, University of the State of New York, James Sullivan, ed. *Minutes of the Albany Committee of Correspondence, 1775–78, and Minutes of the Schenectady Committee, 1775–79.* 2 vols. Albany: J. B. Lyon Co., 1923–25.

Hastings, Hugh (supervisor of pub.) *Ecclesiastical Records: State of New York.* (6 vols.; Albany: J. B. Lyon Co., 1901–5).

————— , comp. & ed. *Military Minutes of the Council of Appointment of the State of New York, 1783–1821.* 4 vols. Albany: James B. Lyon State Printer, 1901–2).

Journals of Provincial Congress, Provincial Convention, Committee of Safety and Council of Safety of the State of New York, 1775–1776–1777. 2 vols. Albany: Thurlow Weed, 1842.

Laws of the State of New York passed at the Sessions of the Legislature Held in Years 1777–1801, inclusive, republished by the Secretary of State. 5 vols. Albany: Weed & Pàrsons & Co., 1886–87.

Lincoln, Charles Z., ed. *State of New York: Messages from the Governors.* 11 vols. Albany: J. B. Lyon Co., 1909.

New York [State] Bureau of Historic Sites, Division for Historic Preservation, *Schuyler Mansion: A Historic Structure Report.* State of New York: Office of Parks & Recreation, 1979.

O'Callaghan, Edmund B. and Berthold Fernow, eds. *Documents Relative to the Colonial History of the State of New York.* 15 vols. Albany: Weed, Parsons & Co., 1853–87.

Paltsits, Victor Hugo, ed. *Minutes of the Commissioners for detecting and defeating Conspiracies in the State of New York: Albany County Sessions, 1778–1781.* 3 vols. Albany: State of New York, 1909–10.

Vermont, State Papers of. Published by Authority, Secretary of State. Vol. 5, *Petitions for Grants of Land, 1778–1811* (1939). Vol. 7, *New York Land Patents, 1688– 1786* (1947). Vol. 8, *General Petitions, 1778–87.* 1952.

Votes and Proceedings of the Assembly of the State of New York: First Meeting of the Fourth Session, September 7, 1780. Albany: Munsell & Rowland, 1859.

Votes and Proceedings of the Senate of the State of New-York, at Their First Session, Held at Kingston, in Ulster County. Commencing, September 9th, 1777 [together with minutes of] *the Second Session, Commencing June 19, 1778* [without title page or publication date]. Kingston: John Holt, 1777. New York State Library.

Votes and Proceedings of the Senate of the State of New-York; at Their Third Session, In Ulster County. Commencing, August 24, 1779. Fishkill: Samuel Loudon, 1779. New York State Library.

Votes and Proceedings of the Senate of the State of New-York; At their Fourth Session, Held at Poughkeepsie. In Dutchess County. Commencing, September 7, 1780 (no publication data [1780?]). New York State Library.

Votes and Proceedings of the Senate of the State of New-York; at their Fifth Session, Held at Poughkeepsie. In Dutchess County. Commencing, October 10 1781 (no publication data; [1781?]). New York State Library.

Journal of the Senate of the State of New-York [Sixth Session: First Meeting, 8–25 July 1782; Second Meeting, 27 Jan.–28 Mar. 1783] (no publication data; ?), New York State Library.

Report of the Regents' Boundary Commission upon the New York and Pennsylvania Boundary. Albany: Weed, Parsons & Co., 1886.

Report of the Regents of the University on the Boundaries of the State of New York. Vol. 2. Albany: The Argus Co., 1894.

Memoirs and Writings of Public Figures

Boyd, Julian P. ed. *The Papers of Thomas Jefferson.* Vols. 1–. Princeton: Princeton University Press, 1950–.

Burnett, Edmund C., ed. *Letters of Members of the Continental Congress.* 8 vols. Washington: The Carnegie Institution of Washington, 1921–36.

Butterfield, L. H., ed. *Diary and Autobiography of John Adams.* 4 vols. Cambridge: The Belknap Press of Harvard University Press, 1961.

Carter, Clarence Edwin, comp. & ed. *The Correspondence of General Thomas Gage,* 2 vols. New Haven: Yale University Press, 1931–33.

Cometti, Elizabeth, trans. & ed. *Seeing America and Its Great Men: The Journal and Letters of Count Francesco dal Verme, 1783–1784.* Charlottesville: University Press of Virginia, 1969.

Conover, George S., comp. *Journals of the Military Expedition of Major General John Sullivan Against the Six Nations of Indians in 1779 With Records of Centennial Celebrations.* Auburn, New York: Knapp, Peck & Thomson, Printers, 1887.

Cushing, Harry Alonzo, ed. *The Writings of Samuel Adams.* 4 vols. New York: G. P. Putnam's Sons, 1904–8.

Davis, Matthew L. *Memoirs of Aaron Burr.* 2 vols. 1836. Reprint. Freeport, New York: Books for Libraries Press, 1970.

De Chastellux, Marquis. *Voyages De M. Le Marquis De Chastellux Dans L'Amerique Septentrionale Dans les années 1780, 1781 and 1782.* 2 vols. Paris, 1786.

De Riedesel, Madame, *Letters and Memoirs Relating to the War of American Independence and the Capture of the German Troops at Saratoga.* English trans. New York: G. & C. Carvill, 1827.

Ferguson, E. James, ed., *The Papers of Robert Morris, 1781–1784.* Vols. 1–. Pittsburgh: University of Pittsburgh Press, 1973–.

Fitzpatrick, John C., ed. *The Diaries of George Washington.* 4 vols. Boston and New York: Houghton Mifflin Co., 1925.

Goebel, Julius, Jr. et al., eds., *The Law Practice of Alexander Hamilton: Documents and Commentary.* 5 vols. New York and London: Columbia University Press, 1964–81.

Hammond, Otis G., *Letters and Papers of Major-General John Sullivan [of the] Continental Army.* 3 vols. Concord: New Hampshire Historical Society, 1930–39.

Hastings, Hugh and J. A. Holden, eds. *Public Papers of George Clinton, First Governor of New York, 1777–1795, 1801–1804.* 10 vols. New York, 1899–1914.

Johnston, Henry P., ed. *The Correspondence and Public Papers of John Jay.* 4 vols. New York: G. P. Putnam's Sons, 1890–1893.

Judd, Jacob, ed. *The Van Cortlandt Family Papers.* 4 vols.; Tarrytown, New York: Sleepy Hollow Restorations, 1976–80.

Kent, William, ed. *Memoirs and Letters of James Kent, LL.D.* Boston: Little, Brown and Co., 1898.

Mays, David John, ed. *The Letters and Papers of Edmund Pendleton, 1734–1803.* 2 vols. Charlottesville: University Press of Virginia, 1967.

Morris, Richard B., ed. *John Jay: The Making of a Revolutionary, Unpublished Papers, 1745–1780.* Vols. 1–. New York: Harper & Row, 1975–.

Rice, Howard C., Jr., and Anne S. K. Brown, trans. & eds. *The American Campaigns of Rochambeau's Army, 1780, 1781, 1782, 1783.* 2 vols. Princeton and Providence: Princeton University Press and Brown University Press, 1972.

Rice, Howard C., Jr., ed. *Travels In North America in the Years 1780, 1781 and 1782 by the Marquis De Chastellux.* 2 vols. Chapel Hill: University of North Carolina Press, 1963.

Sabine, William H. W., ed. *Historical Memoirs from 16 March 1763 to 9 July 1776 of William Smith.* New York: Colburn & Tegg, 1956.

_____ . *Historical Memoirs from 12 July 1776 to 25 July 1778 of William Smith.* New York: Colburn & Tegg, 1958.

Showman, Richard K., ed. *The Papers of General Nathanael Greene.* Vols. 1–. Chapel Hill: University of North Carolina Press, 1976–.

Smith, William Henry [ed.] *The St. Clair Papers: The Life and Public Services of Arthur St. Clair . . . with his Correspondence and other Papers.* 2 vols. Cincinnati: Robert Clarke & Co., 1882.

Stark, Caleb, [ed.] *Memoir and Official Correspondence of General John Stark, . . .* Concord, New Hampshire, 1860.

Stone, William L., trans. *Memoirs, and Letters and Journals, of Major General Riedesel during his Residence in America.* 3 vols.; Albany: J. Munsell, 1868.

Syrett, Harold C. et al., eds. *The Papers of Alexander Hamilton.* 26 vols. New York: Columbia University Press, 1961–1979.

Warfel, Harry R., ed. *Letters of Noah Webster.* New York: Library Publishers, Inc., 1953.

Watson, Winslow C., ed. *Men and Times of the Revolution or Memoirs of Elkanah Watson.* 2d ed. New York: Dana & Co., 1856.

Wilkinson, James. *Memoirs of My Own Times.* 3 vols. Philadelphia: Abraham Small, 1816.

Willcox, William B., ed. *The American Rebellion: Sir Henry Clinton's Narrative of His Campaigns, 1775–1782, with an Appendix of Original Documents.* New Haven: Yale University Press, 1954.

Other Primary Sources

Baxter, Katharine Schuyler. *A Godchild of Washington.* New York: F. Tennyson Neely, 1897.

[Becker, John P.] *The Sexagenary, or Reminiscences of the American Revolution.* Albany: W. C. Little & O. Steele, 1833.

Bonney, Mrs. Catharine V. R., comp. *A Legacy of Historical Gleanings.* 2d ed. 2 vols. Albany: J. Munsell, 1875.

Collections of the Connecticut Historical Society. Vols. 2, 7, 22. Hartford: 1870, 1899, 1923.

Collections of the New-York Historical Society. 38 vols. New York: The New-York Historical Society, 1868–1906.

Grant, Anne. *Memoirs of an American Lady.* 2 vols. New York: Dodd, Mead & Co., 1901.

Greene, Evarts B., and Virginia D. Harrington. *American Population Before the Federal Census of 1790.* New York: Columbia University Press, 1932.

Hanson, J. Howard, and Samuel Ludlow Frey, eds. *The Minute Book of the Committee of Safety of Tryon County.* New York: Dodd, Mead & Co., 1905.

Hart, Albert B., ed. *The [Richard] Varick Court of Inquiry to Investigate the Implication of Colonel Varick (Arnold's Private Secretary) in the Arnold Treason.* Boston: for The Bibliophile Society by H. O. Houghton & Co., Cambridge, 1907.

Heitman, Francis B. *Historical Register of Officers of the Continental Army during the War of the Revolution, April, 1775 to December, 1783*. rev. enl. ed. Washington, D.C.: The Rare Book Shop Publishing Co., 1914.

Hough, Franklin B., ed., *Proceedings of the Commissioners of Indian Affairs, Appointed by Law for the Extinguishment of Indian Titles in the State of New York [1784–1790]*. 2 vols.; Albany: Joel Munsell, 1861.

———, comp. *The New-York Civil List from 1777 to 1855*. Albany: Weed, Parsons & Co., 1855.

———, ed. *The Northern Invasion of October 1780: A Series of Papers Relating to the Expeditions from Canada under Sir John Johnson against The Frontiers of New York which were supposed to have Connection with Arnold's Treason*. New York: The Bradford Club, 1866.

Jackman, Sydney, ed. *With Burgoyne from Quebec*. Toronto: Macmillan, 1963.

Lesser, C. H., ed. *The Sinews of Independence: Monthly Strength Reports of the Continental Army*. Chicago: University of Chicago Press, 1976.

Ludlam, David M. *Early American Winters, 1604–1820*. Boston: American Meteorological Society, 1966.

Mereness, Newton D., ed. *Travels in the American Colonies*. New York: Antiquarian Press, Ltd., 1961.

Meriwether, Coyler, ed. *Publications of the Southern Historical Association*, vols. 7–8. Washington, 1903–4.

Moore, Frank, comp. *The Diary of the Revolution, 1775–1781*. Hartford: J. B. Burr Publishing Co., 1876.

Munsell, Joel, *Collections on the History of Albany from its Discovery to the Present Time*. 4 vols. Albany: J. Munsell, 1865–71.

———. *The Annals of Albany*. 10 vols. Albany: J. Munsell, 1850–59.

The Parliamentary Register; or, History of the Proceedings and Debates of the House of Commons. 17 vols. London: J. Walker, R. Lea and J. Nunn, 1802.

Peckham, Howard H., ed. *The Toll of Independence: Engagements & Battle Casualties of the American Revolution*. Chicago: University of Chicago Press, 1974.

Schuyler, Philip. Letters of 1776, 1777, 1779 in *Proceedings of the New Jersey Historical Society* 62 (April 1944).

Sparks, Jared, ed. *Correspondence of the American Revolution*. 4 vols. Boston: Little, Brown & Co., 1853.

Thatcher, James. *A Military Journal during the American Revolutionary War*. 2d ed. Boston, 1827.

Uhlendorf, Bernhard A., trans. *Revolution in America: Confidential Letters and Journals 1776–1784 of Adjutant General Major Baurmeister of the Hessian Forces*. New Brunswick, New Jersey: Rutgers University Press, 1957.

Van Zandt, Roland, comp. *Chronicles of the Hudson: Three Centuries of Travelers' Accounts*. New Brunswick, New Jersey: Rutgers University Press, 1971.

Werner, Edgar A. *Civil List and Constitutional History of the Colony and State of New York*. Albany: Weed, Parsons & Co., 1884 and 1888.

General Histories

Alden, John R. *A History of the American Revolution*. New York: Alfred A. Knopf, 1969.

Alexander, De Alva Stanwood. *A Political History of the State of New York*. 3 vols. New York: Henry Holt & Co., 1906–9.

Christie, I. R. *Crisis of Empire: Great Britain and the American Colonies, 1754–1783*. New York: W. W. Norton & Co., 1966.

Christie, Ian R., and Benjamin W. Labaree. *Empire or Independence, 1760–1776*. New York: W. W. Norton & Co., 1976.

Ellis, David M. et al., *A Short History of New York State*. Ithaca: Cornell University Press, 1957.

Flick, Alexander, ed. *History of the State of New York*. 10 vols. New York: Columbia University Press, 1933–37.

Gipson, Lawrence Henry. *The Coming of the Revolution, 1763–1775*. London: Hamish Hamilton, 1954.

Handlin, Oscar and Lilian. *A Restless People: Americans in Rebellion, 1770–1787*. Garden City, New York: Anchor Press/Doubleday, 1982.

Higginbotham, Don. *The War of American Independence: Military Attitudes, Policies and Practice, 1763–1789*. New York: The Macmillan Co., 1971.

Jensen, Merrill. *The Founding of a Nation: A History of the American Revolution, 1763–1776*. New York: Oxford University Press, 1968.

Jones, Thomas. *History of New York During the Revolutionary War*. Edited by Edward Floyd De Lancey. 2 vols. New York: Trow's Printing & Bookbinding Co., 1879.

Kammen, Michael. *People of Paradox: An Inquiry Concerning the Origins of American Civilization*. New York: Random House, 1972.

Knollenberg, Bernhard. *Origin of the American Revolution: 1759–1766*. Rev. ed. New York: The Free Press, 1960.

Lacy, Dan. *The Meaning of the American Revolution*. New York: Mentor Books, 1966.

Mackesy, Piers. *The War for America, 1775–1783*. Cambridge: Harvard University Press, 1964.

Main, Jackson Turner. *The Sovereign States, 1775–1783*. New York: New Viewpoints, A Division of Franklin Watts, Inc., 1973.

May, Henry F. *The Enlightenment in America*. New York: Oxford University Press, 1976.

McDonald, Forrest. *The Formation of the American Republic, 1776–1790*. Baltimore: Penguin Books, Inc., 1965.

Middlekauff, Robert. *The Glorious Cause: The American Revolution, 1763–1789*. New York: Oxford University Press, 1982.

Miller, John C. *Origins of the American Revolution*. Boston: Little, Brown & Co., 1943.

————. *Triumph of Freedom, 1775–1783*. Boston: Little, Brown & Co., 1948.

Mitchell, Broadus. *The Price of Independence: A Realistic View of the American Revolution*. New York: Oxford University Press, 1974.

Morris, Richard B. *The American Revolution Reconsidered*. New York: Harper & Row, 1967.

Nevins, Allan. *The American States During and After the Revolution, 1775–1789*. New York: The Macmillan Co., 1924.

Pole, J. R. *Foundations of American Independence, 1763–1815*. Indianapolis and New York: Bobbs-Merrill Co., Inc., 1972.

Robson, Eric. *The American Revolution In Its Political and Military Aspects, 1763–1784*. New York: W. W. Norton & Co., Inc. 1966.

Royster, Charles. *A Revolutionary People at War: The Continental Army and American Character, 1775–1783*. Chapel Hill: University of North Carolina Press, 1979.

Smelser, Marshall. *The Winning of Independence*. Chicago: Quadrangle Books, 1972.

Wallace, Willard M. *Appeal to Arms: A Military History of the American Revolution*. Chicago: Quadrangle Books, 1964.

Ward, Christopher. *The War of the Revolution*. Edited by John Richard Alden. 2 vols. New York: Macmillan Co., 1952.

Wood, Gordon S. *The Creation of the American Republic, 1776–1787*. Chapel Hill: University of North Carolina Press, 1969.

Wright, Esmond. *Fabric of Freedom, 1763–1800*. New York: Hill & Wang, 1961.

Biographies and Special Monographs

Abbott, Wilbur C. *New York in the American Revolution*. New York and London: Charles Scribner's Sons, 1929.

Adams, Randolph G. *Political Ideas of the American Revolution*. 3d ed. New York: Barnes & Noble, Inc., 1958.

Alexander, Edward P. *A Revolutionary Conservative: James Duane of New York*. New York: Columbia University Press, 1938.

Barck, Oscar Theodore, Jr. *New York City During the War for Independence*. New York: Columbia University Press, 1931.

Beach, Allen C. *The Centennial Celebration of the State of New York*. Albany: Weed, Parsons & Co., 1879.

Belknap, Waldron Phoenix, Jr. *American Colonial Painting*. Cambridge: Belknap Press of Harvard University Press, 1959.

Benton, R. C. *The Vermont Settlers and the New York Land Speculators*. Minneapolis: Housekeeper Press, 1894.

Billias, George Athan, ed. *George Washington's Generals*. New York: William Morrow & Co., 1964.

Bonomi, Patricia Updegraff. *A Factious People: Politics and Society in Colonial New York*. New York: Columbia University Press, 1971.

Bowler, R. Arthur. *Logistics and the Failure of the British Army in America, 1775–1783*. Princeton: Princeton University Press, 1975.

Bowman, Allen. *The Morale of the American Revolutionary Army.* Port Washington, New York; Kennikat Press, 1964.

Bradley, Arthur Granville. *Sir Guy Carleton (Lord Dorchester).* Toronto: University of Toronto Press, 1966.

Brandow, John Henry. *The Story of Old Saratoga.* 2d ed. Albany: Brandow Printing Co., 1919.

Burnett, Edmund Cody. *The Continental Congress.* New York: The Macmillan Co., 1941.

Bush, Martin H. *Revolutionary Enigma: A Re-appraisal of General Philip Schuyler of New York.* Port Washington, New York: Ira J. Friedman, Inc., 1969.

Callahan, North. *Henry Knox: General Washington's General.* New York: Rinehart & Co., Inc., 1958.

Campbell, William W. *Annals of Tryon County.* New York: Dodd, Mead & Co., 1924.

Chambers, William Nisbet. *Political Parties in a New Nation: The American Experience, 1776–1809.* New York: Oxford University Press, 1963.

Champagne, Roger J. *Alexander McDougall and the American Revolution in New York.* Schenectady, New York: Union College Press with the New York State American Revolution Bicentennial Commission, 1975.

Chester, Alden, ed. *Legal and Judicial History of New York.* 3 vols. New York: National Americana Society, 1911.

Cochran, Thomas C. *New York in the Confederation.* Philadelphia: University of Pennsylvania Press, 1932.

Collier, Christopher. *Roger Sherman's Connecticut: Yankee Politics and the American Revolution.* Middletown, Conn.: Wesleyan University Press, 1971.

Commager, Henry Steele, and Richard B. Morris, eds. *The Spirit of 'Seventy-Six.* 2 vols. Indianapolis: Bobbs-Merrill Co., Inc., 1958.

Copeman, W. S. C. *A Short History of the Gout and the Rheumatic Diseases.* Berkeley and Los Angeles: University of California Press, 1964.

Countryman, Edward. *A People in Revolution: The American Revolution and Political Society in New York, 1760–1790.* Baltimore and London: The Johns Hopkins University Press, 1981.

Cuneo, John R. *Robert Rogers of the Rangers.* New York: Oxford University Press, 1959.

Curtis, Edward Ely. *The Organization of the British Army in the American Revolution.* New Haven: Yale University Press, 1926.

Dangerfield, George. *Chancellor Robert R. Livingston of New York, 1746–1813.* New York: Harcourt, Brace & World Co., 1960.

Daniell, Jere R. *Experiment in Republicanism: New Hampshire Politics and the American Revolution, 1741–1794.* Cambridge: Harvard University Press, 1970.

Decker, Malcolm. *Benedict Arnold: Son of the Havens.* New York: Antiquarian Press, Ltd., 1961.

De Jong, Gerald F. *The Dutch in America, 1609–1974.* Boston: Twayne Publishers, 1975.

De Pauw, Linda Grant. *The Eleventh Pillar: New York State and the Federal Constitution.* Ithaca, New York: Cornell University Press, 1966.

Dillon, Dorothy Rita. *The New York Triumvirate.* New York: Columbia University Press, 1949.

Division of Archives and History, University of the State of New York, *The American Revolution in New York.* Albany: University of the State of New York, 1926.

East, Robert A. *Business Enterprise in the American Revolutionary Era.* New York: Columbia University Press, 1938.

Elting, John R. *The Battles of Saratoga.* Monmouth Beach, New Jersey: Philip Freneau Press, 1977.

Everest, Allan S. *Moses Hazen and the Canadian Refugees in the American Revolution.* Syracuse: Syracuse University Press, 1976.

Ferguson, E. James. *The Power of the Purse: A History of American Public Finance, 1776–1790.* Chapel Hill: University of North Carolina Press, 1961.

Flexner, James Thomas. *George Washington.* 4 vols. Boston: Little, Brown & Co., 1965–72.

———. *The Traitor and the Spy: Benedict Arnold and John André.* New York: Harcourt, Brace & Co., 1953.

Flick, Alexander C., ed. *The American Revolution in New York: Its Political, Social and Economic Significance.* Albany, 1926. Reprint. Port Washington, New York: Ira J. Friedman, 1967.

Fox, Dixon Ryan. *Yankees and Yorkers.* New York: New York University Press, 1940.

Freeman, Douglas Southall. *George Washington: A Biography.* 7 vols. New York: Eyre and Spottiswoode, 1948–57.

Gerlach, Don R. *Philip Schuyler and the American Revolution in New York, 1733–1777.* Lincoln: University of Nebraska Press, 1964.

———. *Twenty Years of the "Promotion of Literature": The Regents of the University of the State of New York, 1784–1804.* Albany: State University of New York Press, 1974.

Godfrey, William G. *Pursuit of Profit and Preferment in Colonial North America: John Bradstreet's Quest.* Waterloo, Ontario: Wilfred Laurier University Press, 1982.

Graymont, Barbara. *The Iroquois in the American Revolution.* Syracuse: Syracuse University Press, 1972.

Gruber, Ira D. *The Howe Brothers and the American Revolution.* New York: Atheneum, 1972.

Haiman, Miecislaus. *Kosciuszko in the American Revolution.* Boston: Gregg Press, 1972.

Halsey, Francis Whiting. *The Old New York Frontier.* Port Washington, New York: Ira J. Friedman, Inc., 1963.

Hargrove, Richard J., Jr. *General John Burgoyne.* Newark: University of Delaware Press, 1983.

Hatch, Louis C. *The Administration of the American Revolutionary Army.* New York: Longmans, Green & Co., 1904.

Hatch, Robert McConnell. *Thrust for Canada: The American Attempt on Quebec in 1775–1776.* Boston: Houghton Mifflin Co., 1979.

Hawke, David Freeman. *Benjamin Rush: Revolutionary Gadfly.* Indianapolis and New York: The Bobbs-Merrill Co., Inc., 1971.

Hay, Thomas Robson, and M. R. Werner. *The Admirable Trumpeter: A Biography of General James Wilkinson.* Garden City, New York: Doubleday, Doran & Co., Inc., 1941.

Hickcox, John H. *A History of the Bills of Credit or Paper Money Issued by New York, From 1709 to 1789.* Albany: J. H. Hickcox & Co., 1866.

Higginbotham, Don. *Daniel Morgan: Revolutionary Rifleman.* Chapel Hill: University of North Carolina Press, 1961.

Higgins, Ruth L. *Expansion in New York.* Columbus: Ohio State University Studies No. 14, 1931.

Hislop, Codman. *Albany: Dutch, English, and American.* Albany: Argus Press, 1936.

Hoffer, Peter Charles. *Revolution and Regeneration: Life Cycle and the Historical Vision of the Generation of 1776.* Athens: University of Georgia Press, 1983.

Howell, George R., and Jonathan Tenney, eds. *Bi-Centennial History of Albany: History of the County of Albany, N.Y. From 1609 to 1886.* New York: W. W. Munsell & Co., 1886.

Hudleston, F. J. *Gentleman Johnny Burgoyne.* Edinburgh: J. and J. Gray, 1928.

Humphreys, Mary Gay. *Catherine Schuyler.* New York: Charles Scribner's Sons, 1897.

Ironside, Charles Edward. *The Family in Colonial New York.* New York: Columbia University, 1942.

Jaffe, Irma B. *John Trumbull: Patriot-Artist of the American Revolution.* Boston: New York Graphic Society, 1975.

Jameson, J. Franklin. *The American Revolution Considered as a Social Movement.* Princeton: Princeton University Press, 1926.

Jay, William. *The Life of John Jay.* 2 vols. New York: J. & J. Harper, 1833.

Jellison, Charles A. *Ethan Allen, Frontier Rebel.* Syracuse: Syracuse University Press, 1969.

Jensen, Merrill. *The American Revolution Within America.* New York: New York University Press, 1974.

———. *The Articles of Confederation.* Madison: University of Wisconsin Press, 1959.

———. *The New Nation.* New York: Alfred A. Knopf, 1950.

Johnson, E. A. J. *The Foundations of American Economic Freedom: Government and Enterprise in the Age of Washington.* Minneapolis: University of Minnesota Press, 1973.

Johnson, Victor L. *The Administration of the American Commissariat during the Revolutionary War.* Philadelphia: University of Pennsylvania, 1941.

Johnston, Henry P. *The Yorktown Campaign and the Surrender of Cornwallis, 1781.* New York: Harper & Brothers, 1881.

Jones, Charles Henry. *History of the Campaign for the Conquest of Canada in 1776.* Philadelphia: Porter & Coates, 1882.

Jones, Matt Bushnell. *Vermont in the Making, 1750–1777.* New York: Archon Books, 1968.

Kelsay, Isabel Thompson. *Joseph Brant, 1743–1807: Man of Two Worlds.* Syracuse: Syracuse University Press, 1984.

Kenney, Alice P. *Albany: Crossroads of Liberty.* Albany: Michael William Printery, Ltd., 1976.

———. *The Gansevoorts of Albany: Dutch Patricians in the Upper Hudson Valley.* Syracuse: Syracuse University Press, 1969.

Kim, Sung Bok. *Landlord and Tenant in Colonial New York: Manorial Society, 1664–1775.* Chapel Hill: University of North Carolina Press, 1978.

Knollenberg, Bernard. *Washington and the Revolution.* New York: The Macmillan Co., 1940.

Kohn, Richard H. *Eagle and Sword: The Federalists and the Creation of the Military Establishment in America, 1783–1802.* New York: The Free Press, 1975.

Labaree, Leonard Woods. *Conservatism in Early American History.* Ithaca: Cornell University Press, 1959.

Lanctot, Gustave. *Canada and the American Revolution, 1774–1783.* Cambridge: Harvard University Press, 1967.

Larrabee, Harold A. *Decision at the Chesapeake.* New York: Clarkson N. Potter, Inc., Publisher, 1964.

Leonard, Lewis A. *Life of Charles Carroll of Carrollton.* New York: Moffat, Yard & Co., 1918.

Livingston, Edwin Brockholst. *The Livingstons of Livingston Manor.* New York: Knickerbocker Press, 1910.

Lomask, Milton. *Aaron Burr: The Years from Princeton to Vice President, 1756–1805.* New York: Farrar, Straus, Giroux, 1979.

Lossing, Benson J. *The Life and Times of Philip Schuyler.* 2 vols. New York: Sheldon & Co., 1872–1873; Da Capo Press edition: New York, 1973.

Lunt, James. *John Burgoyne of Saratoga.* New York and London: Harcourt Brace Jovanovich, 1975.

Luzader, John. *Decision on the Hudson: The Saratoga Campaign of 1777.* Washington: National Park Service, U.S. Department of the Interior, 1975.

Lynd, Staughton. *Anti-Federalism in Dutchess County, New York.* Chicago: Loyola University Press, 1962.

Lynn, Kenneth S. *A Divided People.* Westport, Connecticut: Greenwood Press, 1977.

MacMillan, Margaret Burnham. *The War Governors in the American Revolution.* New York: Columbia University Press, 1943.

Maier, Pauline. *From Resistance to Revolution: Colonial Radicals and the Development of American Opposition to Britain, 1765–1776.* New York: Alfred A. Knopf, 1972.

Main, Jackson Turner. *Political Parties before the Constitution*. Chapel Hill: University of North Carolina Press, 1973.

_____ . *The Antifederalists: Critics of the Constitution, 1781–1788*. Chapel Hill: University of North Carolina Press, 1961.

_____ . *The Social Structure of Revolutionary America*. Princeton: Princeton University Press, 1965.

_____ . *The Upper House in Revolutionary America, 1763–1788*. Madison: University of Wisconsin Press, 1967.

Mark, Irving, *Agrarian Conflicts in Colonial New York, 1711–1775*. New York: Columbia University Press, 1940.

Martin, James Kirby. *Men in Rebellion: Higher Governmental Leaders and the Coming of the American Revolution*. New Brunswick, New Jersey: Rutgers University Press, 1973.

Mason, Bernard. *The Road to Independence: The Revolutionary Movement in New York, 1773–1777*. Lexington, Kentucky: University of Kentucky Press, 1966.

McDonald, Forrest. *Alexander Hamilton: A Biography*. New York: W. W. Norton & Co., 1979.

McKee, Samuel, Jr. *Labor in Colonial New York, 1664–1776*. New York: Columbia University Press, 1935.

McManus, Edgar J. *A History of Negro Slavery in New York*. Syracuse: Syracuse University Press, 1966.

_____ . *Black Bondage in the North*. Syracuse: Syracuse University Press, 1973.

Miller, John C. *Alexander Hamilton: Portrait in Paradox*. New York: Harper & Brothers, 1959.

Miner, Clarence E. *The Ratification of the Federal Constitution by the State of New York*. New York: Columbia University, 1921.

Mintz, Max M. *Gouverneur Morris and the American Revolution*. Norman, Oklahoma: University of Oklahoma Press, 1970.

Mitchell, Broadus. *Alexander Hamilton*. 2 vols. New York: The Macmillan Co., 1957–62.

Mitchell, Joseph B. *Discipline and Bayonets: The Armies and Leaders in the War of the American Revolution*. New York: G. P. Putnam's Sons, 1967.

Monaghan, Frank. *John Jay Defender of Liberty*. New York and Indianapolis: The Bobbs-Merrill Co., 1935.

Morton, Doris Begor. *Philip Skene of Skenesborough*. Granville, New York: The Grastorf Press, 1959.

Nelson, Paul David. *General Horatio Gates: A Biography*. Baton Rouge: Louisiana State University Press, 1976.

Nelson, William H. *The American Tory*. Oxford: The Clarendon Press, 1961.

Neuenschwander, John A. *The Middle Colonies And The Coming Of The American Revolution*. Port Washington, New York: Kennikat Press, 1973.

Nickerson, Hoffman. *The Turning Point of the Revolution, or Burgoyne in America*. Boston and New York: Houghton Mifflin Co., 1928. Reprint. Port Washington, New York: Kennikat Press, Inc., 1967.

Palmer, Dave Richard. *The Way of the Fox: American Strategy in the War for America, 1775–1783*. Westport, Connecticut: Greenwood Press, 1975.

Pancake, John S. *1777: The Year of the Hangman*. University, Alabama: University of Alabama Press, 1977.

Parmet, Herbert S., and Marie B. Hecht. *Aaron Burr: Portrait of An Ambitious Man*. New York: The Macmillan Co., 1967.

Patterson, Samuel White. *Horatio Gates: Defender of American Liberties*. New York: Columbia University Press, 1941.

Pell, John. *Ethan Allen*. London: Constable & Co., Ltd., 1930.

Preston, John Hyde. *A Gentleman Rebel: The Exploits of Anthony Wayne*. New York: Farrar & Rinehart, Inc., 1930.

Quarles, Benjamin. *The Negro in the American Revolution*. Chapel Hill: University of North Carolina Press, 1961.

Rakove, Jack N. *The Beginnings of National Politics: An Interpretative History of the Continental Congress*. Baltimore and London: The Johns Hopkins University Press, 1982.

Ritcheson, Charles R. *British Politics and the American Revolution*. Norman: University of Oklahoma Press, 1954.

Rossie, Jonathan Gregory. *The Politics of Command in the American Revolution*. Syracuse: Syracuse University Press, 1975.

Rossman, Kenneth R. *Thomas Mifflin and the Politics of the American Revolution*. Chapel Hill: University of North Carolina Press, 1952.

Saffron, Morris H. *Surgeon to Washington: Dr. John Cochran, 1730–1807*. New York: Columbia University Press, 1977.

Sanders, Jennings B. *Evolution of Executive Departments of the Continental Congress, 1774–1789*. Durham: University of North Carolina Press, 1935.

———. *The Presidency of the Continental Congress, 1774–89: A Study in American Institutional History*. 2d printing, rev. Gloucester, Massachusetts: Peter Smith, 1971.

Schachner, Nathan. *Alexander Hamilton*. New York: D. Appleton-Century Co., Inc., 1946.

———. *The Founding Fathers*. New York: G. P. Putnam's Sons, 1954.

Scheer, George F., and Hugh F. Rankin. *Rebels and Redcoats*. New York: A Mentor Book, 1961.

Schuyler, George W. *Colonial New York: Philip Schuyler and His Family*. 2 vols. New York: Charles Scribner's Sons, 1885.

Shy, John. *Toward Lexington: The Role of the British Army in the Coming of the American Revolution*. Princeton: Princeton University Press, 1965.

Smith, Page. *John Adams*. 2 vols. New York: Doubleday & Co., Inc., 1962.

Sosin, Jack M. *The Revolutionary Frontier, 1763–1783*. New York: Holt, Rinehart & Winston, 1967.

Sparks, Jared. *The Life of Gouverneur Morris*. 3 vols. Boston: Gray & Brown, 1832.

Spaulding, E. Wilder. *His Excellency George Clinton: Critic of the Constitution*. New York: The Macmillan Co., 1938.

―――― . *New York in the Critical Period, 1783–1789*. New York: Columbia University Press, 1932.

Stanley, George F. G. *Canada Invaded, 1775–1776*. Toronto: Hakkert, 1973.

Story, D. A. *The De Lanceys*. Halifax: Thomas Nelson & Sons, Ltd., 1931.

Street, Alfred B. *The Council of Revision of the State of New York; its History, A history of the courts with which its members were connected; biographical sketches of its members; and its Vetoes*. Albany: William Gould, Publisher, 1859.

Swiggett, Howard. *War Out of Niagara: Walter Butler and the Tory Rangers*. Port Washington, New York: Ira J. Friedman, Inc., 1963.

Tharp, Louise Hall. *The Baroness and the General*. Boston: Little, Brown & Co., 1962.

Thayer, Theodore. *Nathanael Greene: Strategist of the American Revolution*. New York: Twayne, 1960.

Treacy, M. F. *Prelude to Yorktown: The Southern Campaign of Nathanael Greene, 1780–1781*. Chapel Hill: University of North Carolina Press, 1963.

Tuckerman, Bayard. *Life of General Philip Schuyler, 1733–1804*. New York: Dodd, Mead & Co., 1903.

Umbreit, Kenneth. *Founding Fathers*. New York: Harper & Brothers, 1941.

Upton, L. F. S. *The Loyal Whig: William Smith of New York and Quebec*. Toronto: University of Toronto Press, 1969.

Van Doren, Carl. *Benjamin Franklin*. London: Putnam, 1939.

―――― . *Secret History of the American Revolution*. New York: The Viking Press, 1941.

Van Schaack, Henry C. *The Life of Peter Van Schaack, LL.D.* New York: D. Appleton & Co., 1842.

Ver Steeg, Clarence L. *Robert Morris: Revolutionary Financier*. Philadelphia: University of Pennsylvania Press, 1954.

Vrooman, John J. *Forts and Firesides of the Mohawk Country New York*. Philadelphia: E. E. Brownell, 1943.

Wallace, Anthony F. C. *The Death and Rebirth of the Seneca*. New York: Alfred A. Knopf, 1970.

Wandell, Samuel H., and Meade Minnigerode. *Aaron Burr*. 2 vols. New York: G. P. Putnam's Sons, 1925.

Washington, Ida H., and Paul A. *Carleton's Raid*. Canaan, New Hampshire: Phoenix, 1977.

Weise, Arthur J. *The History of the City of Albany, New York*. Albany: E. H. Bender, 1884.

Whitridge, Arnold. *Rochambeau*. New York: The Macmillan Co., 1965.

Whittemore, Charles P. *A General of the Revolution: John Sullivan of New Hampshire*. New York and London: Columbia University Press, 1961.

Wilbur, James Benjamin. *Ira Allen: Founder of Vermont, 1751–1814*. Boston and New York: Houghton Mifflin Co., 1928.

Willcox, William B. *Portrait of a General: Sir Henry Clinton in the War of Independence*. New York: Alfred A. Knopf, 1964.

Wills, Gary. *Inventing America: Jefferson's Declaration of Independence*. Garden City, New York: Doubleday & Co., Inc., 1978.

Wister, Mrs. O. J. [Sarah B.], and Agnes Irwin, eds. *Worthy Women of Our First Century*. Philadelphia: J. B. Lippincott & Co., 1877.

Young, Alfred F. *The Democratic Republicans of New York: The Origins, 1763–1797*. Chapel Hill: University of North Carolina Press, 1967.

Articles and Essays in Periodicals, Annuals, and Publications of Learned Societies

Bail, Hamilton Vaughan. "A Letter to Lord Germain About Vermont." *Vermont History* 34 (October 1966).

Barker, Elmer Eugene. "The Story of Arbor Hill, and the Ten Broeck Mansion at Albany, New York." *New York History* 34 (October 1953).

Barrow, Thomas C. "The American Revolution as a Colonial War for Independence." *The William and Mary Quarterly*, 3d ser. 25 (July 1968).

Barrows, June. "Seth Warner and the Battle of Bennington: Solving a Historical Puzzle." *Vermont History* 34 (Spring 1971).

Beauchamp, William M. "Indian Raids in the Mohawk Valley." *Proceedings of the New York State Historical Association* 14 (1915).

Bradford, S. Sydney. "Hunger Menaces the Revolution, December 1779–January, 1780." *Maryland Historical Magazine* 61 (March 1966).

Caldwell, Lynton K. "George Clinton—Democratic Administrator." *New York History* 32 (April 1951).

Callahan, North. "Henry Knox: General Washington's General." *The New-York Historical Society Quarterly* 44 (April 1960).

Champagne, Roger. "New York Politics and Independence, 1776." *The New-York Historical Society Quarterly* 46 (July 1962).

———. "New York's Radicals and the Coming of Independence." *The Journal of American History* 51 (June 1964).

Clark, Jane. "The Responsibility for the Failure of the Burgoyne Campaign." *The American Historical Review* 35 (April 1930).

Crary, Catherine Snell. "Forfeited Loyalist Lands in the Western District of New York—Albany and Tryon Counties." *New York History* 35 (July 1954).

Cress, Lawrence Delbert. "Wither Columbia? Congressional Residence and the Politics of the New Nation, 1776 to 1787." *The William and Mary Quarterly*, 3d ser. 32 (October 1975).

Davis, David B. "Medicine in the Canadian Campaign of the Revolutionary War: The Journal of Doctor Samuel Fisk Merrick." *Bulletin of the History of Medicine* 44 (September–October 1970).

Delafield, John Ross. "An Armory of American Families of Dutch Descent." *The New York Genealogical and Biographical Record* 44 (January 1938).

Dumont, William H. "The New York-Vermont Land Dispute, 1749–1791." *The New York Genealogical and Biographical Record* 100 (April 1969).

Flick, Alexander C. "New Sources on the Sullivan-Clinton Campaign in 1779." *The Quarterly Journal of the New York State Historical Association* 10 (July and October 1929).

Flick, Hugh M. "The Council of Appointment in New York State—The First Attempt to Regulate Political Patronage, 1777–1822." *New York History* 15 (July 1934).

Friedman, Bernard. "The Shaping of the Radical Consciousness in Provincial New York." *The Journal of American History* 56 (March 1970).

Gerlach, Don R. "Philip Schuyler and 'The Road to Glory': A Question of Loyalty and Competence." *The New-York Historical Society Quarterly* 49 (October 1965).

———. "Philip Schuyler and the New York Frontier in 1781." *The New-York Historical Society Quarterly* 53 (April 1969).

———. "After Saratoga: The General, His Lady and 'Gentleman Johnny' Burgoyne." *New York History* 52 (January 1971).

———. "The Fall of Ticonderoga in 1777: Who was Responsible?" *The Bulletin of the Fort Ticonderoga Museum* 14 (Summer 1982).

———. "Trial at Quaker Hill: 'Justice to an injured Country' or 'Justice to . . . injured Gentlemen'?" *The Bulletin of the Fort Ticonderoga Museum* 14 (Fall 1983).

———. "The British Invasion of 1780 and 'A Character . . . Debased Beyond Description'." *The Bulletin of the Fort Ticonderoga Museum* 14 (Summer 1984).

Gerlach, Larry R. "Connecticut, the Continental Congress, and the Independence of Vermont, 1777–1782." *Vermont History* 34 (July 1966).

Gitterman, J. M. "The Council of Appointment in New York." *The Political Science Quarterly* 7 (March 1892).

Halsey, Francis Whiting. "General Schuyler's Part in the Burgoyne Campaign." *Proceedings of the New York State Historical Association* 12 (1913).

Heale, M. J. "Humanitarianism in the Early Republic: The Moral Reformers of New York, 1776–1825." *Journal of American Studies* 2 (October 1968).

Hendricks, Nathaniel. "A New Look at the Ratification of the Vermont Constitution of 1777." *Vermont History* 34 (April 1966).

Hull, N. E. H., Peter C. Hoffer, and Steven L. Allen. "Choosing Sides: A Quantitative Study of the Personality Determinants of Loyalist and Revolutionary Political Affiliation in New York." *The Journal of American History* 65 (September 1978).

Kenney, Alice P. "The Albany Dutch: Loyalists and Patriots." *New York History* 42 (October 1961).

Kenyon, Cecelia M. "Republicanism and Radicalism in the American Revolution: An Old-Fashioned Interpretation." *The William and Mary Quarterly.* 3d ser., 19 (April 1962).

Klein, Milton M. "New York Lawyers and the Coming of the American Revolution." *New York History* 55 (October 1974).

_____ . "Politics and Personalities in Colonial New York." *New York History* 47 (January 1966).

Kohn, Richard H. "The Inside History of the Newburgh Conspiracy: America and the Coup d'Etat." *The William and Mary Quarterly.* 3d ser., 27 (April 1970).

Koke, Richard J. "The Struggle for the Hudson: The British Naval Expedition under Captain Hyde Parker and Captain James Wallace, July 12–August 18, 1776." *The New-York Historical Society Quarterly* 40 (April 1956).

Lutz, Paul V. "An Army Wife in the Revolution." *Manuscripts* 23 (Spring 1971).

_____ . "Land Grants for Service in the Revolution." *The New-York Historical Society Quarterly* 48 (July 1964).

Lynd, Staughton. "The Mechanics in New York Politics, 1774–1788." *Labor History* 5 (Fall 1964).

_____ . "The Tenant Rising at Livingston Manor, May 1777." *The New-York Historical Society Quarterly* 48 (April 1964).

_____ . "Who Should Rule at Home? Dutchess County, New York, in the American Revolution." *The William and Mary Quarterly.* 3d ser., 18 (July 1961).

Lynd, Staughton, and Alfred Young. "After Carl Becker: The Mechanics and New York City Politics, 1774–1801." *Labor History* 5 (Fall 1964).

Main, Jackson Turner. "Government by the People: The American Revolution and the Democratization of the Legislatures." *The William and Mary Quarterly.* 3d ser. 23 (July 1966).

Manders, Eric. "Notes on Troop Units in the Northern Army, 1775–1776." *Military Collector and Historian* 23 (Winter 1971).

Maslowski, Pete. "National Policy Toward the Use of Black Troops in the Revolution." *South Carolina Historical Magazine* 73 (January 1972).

Mason, Bernard. "Entrepreneurial Activity in New York during the American Revolution." *Business History Review* 40 (Summer 1966).

_____ . "The Heritage of Carl Becker: The Historiography of the Revolution in New York." *The New-York Historical Society Quarterly* 53 (April 1969).

McAdams, Donald R. "The Sullivan Expedition: Success or Failure." *The New-York Historical Society Quarterly* 54 (January 1970).

Moomaw, W. H. "The Denouement of General Howe's Campaign of 1777." *The English Historical Review* 79 (July 1964).

Morris, Richard B. "Class Struggle and the American Revolution." *The William and Mary Quarterly.* 3d ser., 19 (January 1962).

Muller, H. N., and David A. Donath. " 'The Road Not Taken': A Reassessment of Burgoyne's Campaign." *The Bulletin of the Fort Ticonderoga Museum* 13 (1973).

Nelson, Paul David. "Horatio Gates at Newburgh, 1783: A Misunderstood Role." *The William and Mary Quarterly,* 3d ser., 29 (January 1972).

_____ . "Legacy of Controversy: Gates, Schuyler, and Arnold at Saratoga, 1777." *Military Affairs* 37 (April 1973).

_____ . "The Gates-Arnold Quarrel, September 1777." *The New-York Historical Society Quarterly* 55 (July 1971).

Nelson, William H. "The Revolutionary Character of the American Revolution." *The American Historical Review* 70 (July 1965).

Nissenson, S. G. "The Development of a Land Registration System in New York." *New York History* 20 (January and April 1939).

Northrup, A. Judd. "Slavery in New York: A Historical Sketch." *State Library Bulletin of the University of the State of New York: History No. 4,* (May 1900).

Paltsits, Victor Hugo (contributor). "The Attempt to Capture General Philip Schuyler During the American Revolution As told by an Eye Witness." *The Quarterly Journal of the New York State Historical Association* 10 (October 1929).

Pastore, Ralph T. "Congress and the Six Nations, 1775–1778." *Niagara Frontier* 20 (Winter 1973).

Reibel, Daniel B. "The British Navy on the Upper Great Lakes, 1760–1789." *Niagara Frontier* 20 (Autumn 1973).

Roche, John F. "Quebec Under Siege, 1775–1776: The 'Memorandums' of Jacob Danford." *The Canadian Historical Review* 50 (March 1969).

Rossie, Jonathan G. "The Northern Indian Department and The American Revolution." *Niagara Frontier* 20 (Autumn 1973).

Royster, Charles. " 'The Nature of Treason': Revolutionary Virtue and American Reactions to Benedict Arnold." *The William and Mary Quarterly,* 3d ser. 36 (April 1979).

Scholten, Catherine M. " 'On the Importance of the Obstetrick Art': Changing Customs of Childbirth in America, 1760 to 1825." *The William and Mary Quarterly,* 3d ser. 34 (July 1977).

Schuyler, Robert Livingston. "Philip Schuyler." *New York History* 18 (April 1937).

Scott, John Albert. "Joseph Brant at Fort Stanwix and Oriskany." *New York History* 19 (October 1938).

Scott, Kenneth. "Counterfeiting in New York during the Revolution." *The New-York Historical Society Quarterly* 42 (July 1958).

Simison, Barbara, ed. "Dr. Benjamin Waterhouse's Journey to Saratoga Springs in the Summer of 1794." *Yale University Library Gazette* 40 (July 1965).

Skeen, C. Edward. "The Newburgh Conspiracy Reconsidered," with Richard H. Kohn's Rebuttal. *The William and Mary Quarterly,* 3d ser. 31 (April 1974).

Smith, Paul H. "Sir Guy Carleton, Peace Negotiations, and the Evacuation of New York." *The Canadian Historical Review* 50 (September 1969).

Sosin, Jack M. "The Use of Indians in the War of the American Revolution: A Re-Assessment of Responsibility." *The Canadian Historical Review* 46 (June 1965).

Stevens, Frederick R. "New York in the Society of the Cincinnati." *New York History* 25 (January 1944).

Tate, Thad W. "The Social Contract in America, 1774–1787: Revolutionary Theory as a Conservative Instrument." *The William and Mary Quarterly,* 3d ser. 22 (July 1965).

Tolles, Frederick B. "The American Revolution Considered as a Social Movement: A Re-evaluation." *The American Historical Review* 60 (October 1954).

Vail, R. W. G., ed. "The Western Campaign of 1779: The Diary of Quartermaster Sergeant Moses Sproule of the Third New Jersey Regiment in the Sullivan Expedition of the Revolutionary War, May 17–October 17, 1779." *The New-York Historical Society Quarterly* 41 (January 1957).

Vivian, James F., and Jean H. "Congressional Indian Policy During the War for Independence: The Northern Department." *Maryland Historical Magazine* 63 (September 1968).

Wall, Alexander J. "The Story of the Convention Army, 1777–1783." *Collections of the New-York Historical Society* 85 (1975).

Wells, Thomas L. "An Inquiry into the Resignation of Quartermaster General Nathanael Greene in 1780." *Rhode Island History* 24 (April 1965).

Willcox, William B. "Too Many Cooks: British Planning Before Saratoga." *The Journal of British Studies* 2 (November 1962).

Williams, John A. "Mount Independence in Time of War, 1776–1783." *Vermont History* 35 (April 1967).

Yoshpe, Harry. "The De Lancey Estate: Did the Revolution Democratize Land-holding in New York?" *New York History* 17 (April 1936).

Zeichner, Oscar. "The Loyalist Problem in New York After the Revolution." *New York History* 21 (July 1940).

Zornow, William F. "New York Tariff Policies, 1775–1789." *New York History* 37 (January 1956).

Miscellaneous

Albany's Tercentenary, 1624–1924. Albany, 1924. A souvenir booklet.

Atherton, Gertrude F. H. *The Conqueror.* Philadelphia and New York: J. B. Lippincott Co., 1943.

Barker, Elmer Eugene. "The Story of the Ten Broeck Mansion." Albany County Historical Society, Albany, New York, 1953. Manuscript.

Beach, Allen C. *The Centennial Celebration of the State of New York.* Albany: Weed, Parsons & Co., 1879.

Burns, Brian. "Bloody Burgoyne and the Patriot Martyr, or, A Most Regrettable Fortune of War: British Indian Policy During the Northern Campaign of 1777." Master's thesis, University of Vermont, 1973.

Chambers, Robert W. *The Maid-At-Arms.* New York and London: Harper and Brothers, 1902.

Champagne, Roger James. "The Sons of Liberty and the Aristocracy in New York Politics, 1765–1790." Ph.D. diss., University of Wisconsin, 1960.

Comstock, Helen. "The Schuyler Mansion, Albany, New York." *The Connoisseur Year Book, 1952.* London, 1952.

Cooper, James Fenimore. *The Legends and Traditions of a Northern County.* New York and London: G. P. Putnam's Sons, 1921.

Csontos, Mildred B. "History of Legislative Apportionment in New York State, 1777–1940 with Discussion of Obstacles to Apportionment." New York State Library, 1941. Manuscript.

Cunningham, Anna K. *Schuyler Mansion a Critical Catalogue of the Furnishings & Decorations.* Albany: New York State Education Department, 1955.

De Peyster, John Watts. *Major-General Philip Schuyler and the Burgoyne Campaign in the Summer of 1777.* New York: Holt Brothers, Printers, 1877. Pamphlet, annual address to the New-York Historical Society.

Desmond, Alice Curtis. *Alexander Hamilton's Wife: A Romance of the Hudson.* New York: Dodd, Mead & Co., 1952.

Eberlein, Harold Donaldson. *The Manors and Historic Homes of the Hudson Valley.* Philadelphia and London: J. B. Lippincott Co., 1924.

French, J. L. *Gazetteer of the State of New York.* Syracuse: R. P. Smith, 1861.

Gerlach, Don R. "Philip Schuyler and the Continental Congress, 1775–1777." Master's thesis, University of Nebraska, 1956.

──────. *Philip Schuyler and the Growth of New York, 1733–1804.* Albany: University of the State of New York, State Education Department, 1968. Booklet.

──────. *Philip Schuyler's Saratoga.* Eastern National Park and Monument Association, in cooperation with Saratoga National Historical Park, 1969. Booklet.

Goebel, Julius L., Jr. "Some Legal and Political Aspects of the Manors in New York." Baltimore: Publications of the Order of Colonial Lords of Manors in America No. 18, 1928.

Gregg, C. E. "General Philip Schuyler and The Schuyler Mansion." *The Dutch Settlers Society of Albany: Yearbook, 1949–1951* 25–26 (Albany 1951).

Hamm, Margherita Arlina. *Famous Families of New York.* 2 vols. New York: G. P. Putnam's Sons, 1901.

Hannay, William Vanderpoel (comp.). "Burial Records, First Dutch Reformed Church of Albany, 1654–1862." *The Dutch Settlers Society of Albany: Yearbook, 1932–1934* 8–9 (Albany 1934).

Hatfield, Laura Adella. "The Frontier Policy of New York to 1776." Master's thesis, University of Chicago, 1916.

Holland Society. *Year Book of the Holland Society of New York, 1906 and 1907.* New York: Knickerbocker Press, 1908, 1914.

──────. *Year Book of The Holland Society of New York, 1924 and 1925.* New York: 1925.

Hough, Franklin B. *The New-York Civil List from 1777 to 1855.* Albany: Weed, Parsons & Co., 1855.

Huling, Caroline Alden. "General Philip Schuyler the Friend of George Washington." New York State Library, 1934. Manuscript.

Jenks, Major B. "George Clinton and New York State Politics, 1775 to 1801." Ph.D. diss. Cornell University, 1936.

Kaminski, John P. "Paper Politics: The Northern State Loan Offices during the Confederation, 1783–1790." Ph.D. diss. University of Wisconsin, 1972.

Kent, James. "An Anniversary Discourse Delivered Before the New-York Historical Society, December 6, 1828." New York: G. & C. Carvill, 1829.

Krout, John A. "Philip Schuyler." *Dictionary of American Biography,* ed. Allen Johnson, et al. 20 vols. New York: Charles Scribner's Sons, 1943, 16: 477–80.

Lossing, Benson J. *The Pictorial Field-Book of the Revolution.* 2 vols. New York: Harper and Brothers, 1860.

Martin, James K. "Political Elites and the Outbreak of the American Revolution: A Quantitative Profile in Continuity, Turnover, and Change, 1774–1777." Ph.D. diss. University of Wisconsin, 1969.

Mason, Bernard. "Organization of the Revolutionary Movement in New York State, 1775–1777." Ph.D. diss. Columbia University, 1958.

Mather, Frederic G., "The Schuyler House at Albany." *Magazine of American History* 12 (July-December 1884).

Munsell, Joel. "The Schuyler Family." *The New York Genealogical & Biographical Record* 5 (April 1874).

Pastore, Ralph T. "The Board of Commissioners for Indian Affairs in the Northern Department and the Iroquois Indians, 1775–1778." Ph.D. diss. University of Notre Dame, 1972.

Pearson, Jonathan. *Contributions for the Genealogies of the First Settlers of the Ancient County of Albany, from 1630 to 1800.* Albany: J. Munsell, 1872.

Proctor, L. B. "Hamilton and His Bride." *The New York Times* (1 September 1889).

_____ . "Historic Memories of the Old Schuyler Mansion," [Albany, 1888]. Pamphlet.

Quick, Michael. "A Bicentennial Gift: 'Mrs. Schuyler Burning Her Wheat Fields on the Approach of the British' by Emmanuel Leutze." *Los Angeles County Museum of Art Bulletin* 23 (1977).

Reynolds, Cuyler, ed. *Albany Chronicles: A History of the City Arranged Chronologically.* Albany: J. B. Lyon Co., 1909.

_____ . *Hudson-Mohawk Genealogical and Family Memoirs.* 4 vols. New York: Lewis Historical Publishing Co., 1911.

Robinson, Edward F. "Continental Treasury Administration, 1775–1781: A Study in the Financial History of the American Revolution." Ph.D. diss. University of Wisconsin, 1969.

Rolater, Frederick S. "The Continental Congress: A Study in the Origin of American Public Administration, 1774–1781." Ph.D. diss. University of Southern California, 1970.

Rommel, John G., Jr. "Richard Varick: New York Aristocrat." Ph.D. diss. Columbia University, 1966.

Schuyler, George L. *Correspondence and Remarks upon Bancroft's History of the Northern Campaign of 1777, and the Character of Major-General Philip Schuyler.* New York: David G. Francis, 1867.

Schuyler, Georgina. "The Schuyler Mansion at Albany: Residence of Major-General Philip Schuyler, 1762–1804." New York: DeVinne Press, 1911. Pamphlet.

Schuyler, Montgomery. "The Patroons and Lords of Manors of the Hudson." Publications of the Order of Colonial Lords of Manors in America, no. 23 (New York, 1932). Pamphlet.

_____ . "The Schuyler Family." Publications of the Order of Colonial Lords of Manors in America, no. 16 (New York, 1926). Pamphlet.

Stone, William L. *Visits to the Saratoga Battle-Grounds, 1780–1880.* 1895. Reprint. Port Washington, New York: Kennikat Press, 1970.

The Van Rensselaers of the Manor of Rensselaerwyck. Copyright 1888 by Mary King Van Rensselaer. Limited edition, 50 copies.

Van Rensselaer, Maunsell. *Annals of the Van Rensselaers in the United States.* Albany: Charles Van Benthuysen & Sons, 1888.

Williams, Sherman. *New York's Part in History.* New York: D. Appleton & Co., 1915.

Index

PROUD PATRIOT

was composed in 10-point Galliard on a Linotron 202 and leaded 2 points
by Partners Composition
printed by sheet-fed offset on 50-lb, acid-free Perkins & Squire Smooth Offset,
Smyth sewn and bound over binder's boards in Joanna Arrestox B
by Maple-Vail Book Manufacturing Group, Inc.;
with dust jackets printed in four colors
by Frank A. West Co., Inc.;
and published by

SYRACUSE UNIVERSITY PRESS
SYRACUSE, NEW YORK 13244-5160